'Exhaustive and often fascinating. As a series of snapshots it's a great way to chart the restless invention that has characterised English pop music – it even works as a potted history of the country itself. In many ways it's a more revealing portrait of Peel than his incomplete autobiography – what better way to describe the man than through the records that made him?' *Ransom Note*

by the same author

MY MAGPIE EYES ARE HUNGRY FOR THE PRIZE:
THE CREATION RECORDS STORY

GOOD NIGHT AND GOOD RIDDANCE

*How Thirty-Five Years
of John Peel
Helped to Shape Modern Life*

DAVID CAVANAGH

First published in 2015 by
Faber & Faber Ltd
Bloomsbury House
74–77 Great Russell Street
London WC1B 3DA

This paperback edition published in 2016

Typeset by Ian Bahrami
Printed in the UK by CPI Group (UK) Ltd, Croydon CR0 4YY

A CIP record for this book is available from the British Library

ISBN 978–0–571–32789–8

2 4 6 8 10 9 7 5 3 1

CONTENTS

[v]

Part Three: More of a Conversation Than a
Monologue

AUTHOR'S NOTE

Good Night and Good Riddance is a chronological history of 265 programmes presented by John Peel between 1967 and 2003. It's the story of a changing music scene, a changing radio landscape and a changing Britain. It's the story of how a shy man who played records for a living ended up having an impact as far-reaching as any rock group. The story begins with a Donovan song and ends with an event of global significance that brings Peel full circle to the Summer of Love, when his broadcasts took place against a backdrop of anti-Vietnam War protests.

A word or two about the way the book is structured. The descriptions of the 265 programmes are preceded by a list of artists whose music appears in them, as well as a news story from the day in question. These are included for a reason. For much of his career, Peel took to the air between 10 p.m. and midnight, once the day's defining dramas had been played out, and often he had the unenviable job of rounding off a turbulent or harrowing twenty-four-hour period in British life. A news bulletin during one show in December 1973 began: 'A third bomb went off in London tonight.' Another show in September 1974 was interrupted for a newsflash that Prime Minister Harold Wilson had dissolved Parliament. The rubbish was piled high in the streets when Peel played new singles by the Pretenders, the Members and the Undertones in January 1979. Were his programmes an escape route out of the darkness? Could they offer some form of illumination?

To research *Good Night and Good Riddance*, I listened to around five hundred Peel shows that survive in audio format, and also consulted the running orders of a further eight or nine hundred on microfilm and online. What were the criteria for selecting a show to put in the book? Perhaps it was a night when Peel discovered a future household name. Perhaps he played a piece of music so mind-bogglingly strange that I simply had to attempt to describe it. Or perhaps my attention was caught by something he *said*; he was a witty, thoughtful and subversive broadcaster throughout his long career.

Readers will notice that towards the end of the book the chapters cover two years instead of one. This is to give the effect of the near past coming closer into view. It should not be taken to mean that 1998 and 2002 were 'lesser' years than 1988 and 1992, or that some years blurred into others. Also, in acknowledgement of the feast of surprises that characterised Peel's best broadcasts, in which almost nothing could be foretold from a mere tracklisting, an index has been consciously omitted.

To write about Peel shows, you first need to be aware of their whereabouts and be able to hear them. The foremost Peel resource anywhere in the world is John Peel Wiki (http://peel.wikia.com/wiki/John_Peel_Wiki), where a person can easily lose several months of their life browsing endless pages of encyclopaedic facts, running orders, informative essays and mini-biographies. Look closely and you should find what you want. It's a world populated by user names and pseudonyms.

I would like to thank the following contributors to John Peel Wiki: Alan, Andrew, Andrew T, andysmith10, bbrbr57, Bill, billfromnorthwales, Bill S, Bob, bonnie43uk, Brian Hinton, brockleyal, CCM, Chris Holmes, Colin Bray, Colin Ellis, Darren, Dave, David, Decktician, deerlabsk, Doc, Dr Mango, Duff Paddy, Ed B, Eddie, Gary, gooner02UK, Gumtree Tapes, Guy Brown at U-SPACES, Hangthedj, Haze, hills1902, Isector, Jim, Jimmy, Johns corner, John Leonhard's Dad, Johnpeel3904, John Peel Papers, John Stewart, Jon Horne, Julian, K, Karl, Kat's Karavan, Ken Garner, Kevin (Kev), klacktoveedesteen, LeicesterJim, Lol, Lorcan, Mark C, max-dat, Mike Dick, ML, Monni Aldous, My Old Tapes, Patestapes, Paul, Peel Mailing List, Phil, ray_b2, RC, RF, Rich Less, Rob C, RobEmbleton, Rob F, Rocker, Rok, SB, SIG (Steve), Steve Lowman, Syrtis, thebarguest, thescourge, Tishbriz, Vegman, Wavey Davey, Weatherman22 (Stuart) and any tapers, collectors, sharers, uploaders, editors, re-editors, encoders, restorers and digitisers whose names have been lost to posterity. Thanks to Kris W. (http://theperfumedgarden.blogspot.co.uk) and the Yahoo Peel Newsgroup. Thanks also to the producers of the Peel shows – Bernie Andrews, John Walters, John Muir, Pete Ritzema, Jeff Griffin, Chris Lycett, Jonathan Ruffle, Mike Hawkes, Alison Howe, Anita Kamath and Louise Kattenhorn – and their engineers.

I'm grateful to Jeff Walden for granting me access to the BBC Written Archives at Caversham Park, where I was able to scroll through the running orders of hundreds of forgotten editions of *Top Gear*, *Friday Night Is Boogie Night*, *Sounds of the Seventies* and the *John Peel Show*. For context, I looked at programmes presented by Tony Blackburn, Noel Edmonds, Emperor Rosko, Tony Brandon, Dave Cash, Ed Stewart, Terry Wogan, Jimmy Young, David Hamilton, Johnnie Walker, Alan Freeman, Anne Nightingale, Alan Black, Mike Harding, Bob Harris, Stuart Henry, Michael Wale, Dave Eager, Gary Taylor, Dave Lee Travis, Paul Burnett, David 'Kid' Jensen, Pete Drummond, Paul Gambaccini, Tommy Vance, Mike Read, Adrian Juste, Robbie Vincent, Stuart Colman, Simon Bates, Peter Powell and Andy Peebles.

When I decided to write *Good Night and Good Riddance*, my first call was to Ken Garner, the author of the acclaimed book *In Session Tonight* (BBC, 1993), which was updated and republished as *The Peel Sessions* in 2007. Garner was immediately encouraging and went on to offer useful advice, not just once but in a number of subsequent emails. He is the world's leading authority on Peel, I would guess, and I hope he feels that *Good Night and Good Riddance* doesn't encroach too much on his own Peel writings.

My sincere thanks go to Lee Brackstone, David Watkins and Ian Bahrami at Faber and Faber, who were sensitive and patient over a longer period than any of them probably anticipated, and to my agent Matthew Hamilton at Aitken Alexander. I could not have written the book without the support and friendship of Andrew Holmes and Penelope Chong, neither of whom I can ever thank enough. Others who played key strategic roles were Steve Beeho (deep cover and surveillance), John Mulvey (laser-eyed forensics), Phil King (IPC vault-digging), Tony Sexton (stress-free removals and disco mixes), Chris Moore (cocktails and Dropboxing), Strontium Dawg (ambient trip-hop guidance), La Vache Dangereuse (additional research) and Mark Allen at Jargon Free Computers (laptop maintenance). Thanks also to my parents.

I made use of many books, newspapers, magazines and websites along the way, which are listed in the Sources and Bibliography at the back. All the remaining conclusions, assumptions, opinions, theories and mistakes in the book are mine.

David Cavanagh
Brighton, 2015

INTRODUCTION: PEEL NATION

About a mile north of Reading town centre stands Caversham Park. The grand country house, tastefully flanked by wooded pleasure grounds and set in a hundred acres of private parkland, has a Grade II listing and a history dating back to William the Conqueror. Over the centuries it has been the family seat of the Earl of Pembroke (*c.*1200), the home of a courtier to Edward VI (*c.*1580), a temporary prison for Charles I (1647) and a Georgian fortress with gardens designed by Capability Brown (*c.*1760).

In the 1830s it was a dilapidated ruin; in the 1920s a boys' boarding school. Since the Second World War it's been the headquarters of BBC Monitoring, the semi-clandestine eavesdropping wing of the British Broadcasting Corporation that tracks, translates and analyses thousands of daily news reports from around the world.

A white bungalow stands near the north-western corner of the grounds. Visitors approach it through an iron gate next to a school on Peppard Road. Anyone writing a book about a BBC broadcaster with a three-decade career will come to this bungalow sooner or later, for it houses the BBC's Written Archives. Scripts, files, memoranda, contracts and correspondence – all are archived here at Caversham.

And so are radio shows. At the conclusion of each show he presented, the Radio 1 DJ John Peel would sit down at a typewriter and fill out a Programme as Broadcast (PasB) form, an itemised list of the music he'd just played. All the song titles and names of artists. All the studio dates of sessions. Catalogue numbers of records.

Precise timings of songs. The PasB forms were sent to Written Archives, where they were preserved on microfilm.

One reason why Written Archives is important to a Peel researcher is because there's a fair-sized chunk of his career – four or five years – that might be described as an audio wasteland. As I write, not a single complete recording of any of his *Top Gear* programmes from 1971 has come to light. The same goes for 1972. While not totally barren, the first six months of 1973 yield a meagre harvest of snippets and fragments. Virtually nothing survives from 1974.

You wouldn't expect anyone to take much interest in old Radio 1 shows hosted by Paul Burnett, Simon Bates or Bruno Brookes. Nobody has ever trawled the Internet hoping to find a ninety-minute MP3 of Peter Powell (preferably with spoken links intact and unedited jingles). So why is it so frustrating that four years of Peel are unaccounted for? What was it about him that made people listen religiously to his shows during critical years of their lives? Why has a dedicated community sprung up that shares and discusses recordings of those shows online? Everyone knows Peel was influential. But do they know why? Do they know how?

The Written Archives cannot be browsed like a public library. Viewings are by appointment, granted on receipt of an emailed application. Visiting days are Wednesdays, Thursdays and Fridays. Ask to see PasB forms for *Top Gear* from 1971 to 1974 – Peel's Dark Ages, if you like – and about a dozen boxes of microfilm are brought to your table. Take out a reel from one of the boxes and mount it on the spindle of the reader machine. Carefully thread the film under a wheel and press a button so that the film advances. Soon a page of text edges into view. Adjust the lens setting.

The scanner's screen is blue, with typewritten words punched out in white. What we're looking at is sheets of photographed carbon paper stitched together chronologically, telling the story of Radio 1 in the Seventies day by day. To get to *Top Gear*, which had a Saturday afternoon slot in January 1971, we have to steer past the weekday programmes presented by Tony Blackburn, Johnnie Walker, Dave Lee Travis, Jimmy Young and Terry Wogan. Turn the speed wheel clockwise. A Monday afternoon glides by in seconds.

Top Gear is not easy to find at first. But the eyes gradually train themselves to spot a Saturday schedule in the rolling blue and white sea. Manipulating the wheel is an art in itself. A flick of the wrist slaloms us through three pages of *Junior Choice* – the Saturday morning kids' programme presented by Ed Stewart – but fail to stop the wheel in time and suddenly Radio 1 is closing down for the night. Rotate the wheel too far and fourteen days of programmes flash past in a blur. (Back we go, anticlockwise.)

Now we're at *Junior Choice* again. That's followed at 10 a.m. by a two-hour show hosted by Noel Edmonds. Time to apply some pressure on the brakes. The show immediately preceding *Top Gear* is Emperor Rosko's *Midday Spin*, a round-up of new singles and albums. Reduce speed to a crawl. Look out for telltale names. Captain Beefheart. Ivor Cutler. Vivian Stanshall.

So this is where you ended up, John. A bungalow in Berkshire, stored in little boxes of microfilm. Words hammered out on a typewriter onto carbon sheets. Here is another box. Here is another blue screen. Here is the written documentation of a post-war career in radio.

In the spring of 1960, a wealthy Liverpool cotton broker named Robert Ravenscroft sent his twenty-year-old son John on a character-building trip to America. Demobbed from National Service not long before, the young man had no obvious career path ahead of him. He had shown himself to be dismal at school, completely inept in social situations and unable to do much in a military milieu apart from clean toilets and make tea.

His first destination was Dallas, where he used his father's connections to get a job in the Texas cotton industry. When that led nowhere, he obtained a minor position at an insurance company. He then headed north to Oklahoma City. After that, west to California. Finally he returned home – but not to work in cotton or insurance. Somewhere along the way, John Ravenscroft had undergone a curious transformation. He now made his living as a disc jockey.

For it transpired that Ravenscroft, far from having no acumen whatsoever, was an authority and an expert on one particular subject: *records*. Since his early teens he'd been collecting and learning about all manner of records – from 78s to 45s to LPs; from orchestral tangos to continental pop to rock 'n' roll – and his knowledge of his vinyl dominion was staggering. In 1961 he'd approached a Dallas radio station, WRR-AM, wondering if the DJs who hosted its rhythm-and-blues programme, *Kat's Karavan*, would be interested in hearing some of his prized collection of rare blues records. They were, and invited him onto the air to talk about them. His blues spots on *Kat's Karavan* became a regular item.

Ravenscroft had caught the radio bug. Cotton and insurance were all very well, but radio offered him a line of communication to his peers, a legitimate platform, a chance to be heard and taken seriously, a means to share his passion for records, to evaluate them not as cheap artefacts but as jewels hand-picked from a treasure chest – and to try to convince others of their greatness. By 1964 Ravenscroft was a familiar voice on Dallas's premier pop station, KLIF, ensconced as their official Beatles correspondent, the man with the inside track on the Fab Four. (This entailed slightly exaggerating his Liverpool background to give the impression that he and the Beatles had grown up on the same streets. He actually hailed from a leafy village about fifteen miles away.)

By 1965, gaining in confidence, he was one half of a double act hosting a music-and-comedy programme on KOMA in Oklahoma

City. By the end of 1966 he was presenting the daily breakfast show on KMEN in San Bernardino. At weekends he would play British blues-rock groups like the Yardbirds and John Mayall's Bluesbreakers, surreptitiously smuggling them into KMEN's UK chart show. If all this peripatetic versatility makes Ravenscroft sound like a DJ in search of an identity (or at least an agent), the key thing here is that KLIF, KOMA and KMEN were Top 40 stations. Put together, it amounted to three years of experience in fast-paced, high-stakes commercial radio on the glamorous side of the Atlantic. Ravenscroft, the boy with no school qualifications, had accumulated a CV that a disc jockey in Britain would have drooled over.

Arriving back in England in February 1967, he was immediately hired by Radio London, the biggest of the pirate pop stations that had followed Radio Caroline into offshore waters in the mid-Sixties. For two weeks out of every three, Ravenscroft worked, lived and slept on Radio London's ship the MV *Galaxy*, an ex-Second World War minesweeper anchored off the coast of Essex. Fitted with two studios and a 50-kilowatt transmitter, the *Galaxy* broadcast all-day pop to the east of England, the south, the Midlands, the north, Scotland and Wales. An estimated 12 million Britons tuned in every day.

Ravenscroft found his niche presenting a late-night programme, *The Perfumed Garden*, in which he played an esoteric mix of San Francisco rock, English psychedelia, Chicago blues and socio-political folk songs – a concoction totally at odds with Radio London's Top 40-driven output. *The Perfumed Garden* coincided with the dawning of the hippie era and became a nightly hangout where young people could exchange philosophies, hear the latest Jefferson Airplane imports and listen to poems about gentle creatures living harmoniously in a violence-free paradise.

Before Radio London put Ravenscroft on the air, however, they insisted on one change. Fearing that his three-syllable surname might prove a turn-off for the listeners, they decided to rechristen him. 'What about John Peel?' suggested a secretary at the station's head office in Mayfair. *Peel*. It was catchy. It had only one syllable. It was the name he would use for the rest of his life.

When Radio London was shut down by the Marine, &c., Broadcasting (Offences) Act 1967, Ravenscroft/Peel returned to dry land and joined the new BBC pop station Radio 1. It's odd to think that his adventures in disc jockeying might have ended right there. Of the thirty DJs listed in the station's pre-launch press release, nothing about the inclusion of his name (which appeared twenty-eighth) gave any indication that he'd found a long-term home. His contract was for a mere six weeks, and even when it was renewed he remained effectively on probation. Uneasy about his hippie lexicon and perceived countercultural agenda, his superiors waited four months before letting him present a programme on his own.

Against all the odds, Peel was to stay at Radio 1 until his death in 2004, surviving every one of its periodic rebrandings and purges. His final years on Britain's foremost youth radio station may have been an implausible concept on paper – a man in his sixties playing cutting-edge music to an audience young enough to be his grandchildren – but according to BBC research, Peel had more undersixteens listening to him than any other Radio 1 DJ, including those like Chris Moyles and Sara Cox who were less than half his age. The older he got, the more credibility Peel seemed to acquire with teenagers. He was a walking confounder of focus groups.

During his thirty-seven years on British radio, thousands of musicians in hundreds of genres and subgenres passed through the gates of *The Perfumed Garden*, *Top Gear*, *Night Ride*, *Friday Night Is Boogie Night*, *Sounds of the Seventies* and the long-running *John Peel Show*. In many cases, he either gave them their first national radio airplay or provided staunch and invaluable support at a make-or-break stage in their career. Their names include David Bowie, Marc Bolan, Rod Stewart, Elton John, Pink Floyd, Black Sabbath, Free, King Crimson, Hawkwind, Thin Lizzy, Status Quo, Genesis, Roxy Music, Queen, Lou Reed, Nick Drake, Fairport Convention, Steeleye Span, the Chieftains, Bob Marley and the Wailers, Captain Beefheart, Kevin Ayers, Mike Oldfield, Loudon Wainwright III, Joan Armatrading, Ivor Cutler, the Ramones, the Sex Pistols, the Jam, the Slits, Siouxsie and the Banshees, XTC, Aswad, Misty in Roots, Elvis Costello, Gary Numan, Adam Ant, Dexys Midnight Runners, Joy Division, the Human League, the Fall, the Cure, Simple Minds, Orchestral Manoeuvres in the Dark, UB40, Altered Images, Duran Duran, Echo and the Bunnymen, Killing Joke, Scritti Politti, the Cocteau Twins, the Sisters of Mercy, Frankie Goes to Hollywood, Marc Almond, Nick Cave, Shane MacGowan, Julian Cope, Edwyn Collins, Morrissey, Billy Bragg, Björk, Chumbawamba, the Shamen, the Butthole Surfers, the Charlatans, the Farm, Happy Mondays, Napalm Death, Nirvana, Pulp, PJ Harvey, Elastica, Supergrass, Pavement, Huggy Bear, Underworld, the Orb, the Future Sound of London, Autechre, Richie Hawtin, Arab Strap, the Delgados, Kenickie, Elbow, Mogwai, the White Stripes and the Black Keys.

In 1992, to pick a year at random, Peel alerted his listeners to an up-and-coming Californian punk trio called Green Day, a psyche-delic indie band from Wigan named Verve and the young Cornish electronic musician Aphex Twin, whose debut twelve-inch, 'Digeridoo', was to be one of the groundbreaking dance tracks of the Nineties. If we travel back further – to 1984, 1979 or 1972 – Peel can be found advocating the causes, respectively, of post-punk con-frontationalists (Jesus and Mary Chain, Scraping Foetus Off the Wheel), 2 Tone ska revivalists (the Specials, Madness, Selecter) and Krautrock experimentalists (Can, Neu!, Tangerine Dream).

Usually, he was the first DJ on Radio 1 to notice a new genre.

The archives show that he championed hip hop twelve years before Radio 1 hired Tim Westwood to host its first hip hop show. And that he played African music a decade before Andy Kershaw set foot in the BBC. As for reggae, Peel promoted it so heavily that the music press in the Seventies nicknamed him Jah Peel. To paraphrase Martin Amis's *Money* on the subject of lighting up cigarettes: unless this book specifically informs you to the contrary, Peel is always playing a reggae record.

David Bowie, paying tribute in 1996 when Peel was featured on *This Is Your Life*, probably spoke for many British rock stars when he thanked him – some might say belatedly – for 'having faith in us'. Billy Bragg, giving BBC Radio 6 Music's John Peel Lecture in 2012, bore witness to the fact that Peel 'made a career in music accessible for several generations of young artists who would otherwise have struggled in the mainstream'.

It would be crass to say that David Bowie and Billy Bragg owed it all to John Peel. But it's easy to imagine both of them having very different fortunes if Peel, like George Bailey in *It's a Wonderful Life*, hadn't existed. Bragg would presumably have benefited from some useful exposure when his friend Andy Kershaw joined Radio 1 in 1985, but he would have missed out on the vital momentum created by Peel two years earlier when he got behind Bragg's 1983 mini-album, *Life's a Riot with Spy vs Spy*. By the time Kershaw entered the picture, Bragg had already had two albums in the Top 30. Part of the credit must go to Peel for introducing Bragg to his fanbase.

Bowie, for his part, had been rejected by a BBC audition panel in 1965 and was a luckless unknown with a flop single about gnomes when Peel began pushing his talents in 1967. Over the next two years, Peel ensured that the quirky, unfashionable Bowie was heard alongside the major acts of the day. Later, during a lean period that followed Bowie's 1969 hit 'Space Oddity', Peel stayed crucially loyal, a one-man support network. The journey to Ziggy Stardust, one could argue, was conceived not in a distant galaxy but on Peel's *Top Gear*, Peel's *In Concert* and Peel's *Friday Night Is Boogie Night*.

The day after Bowie's greeting to Peel on *This Is Your Life* was screened by BBC1, Peel wrote a letter to Matthew Bannister, the controller of Radio 1. 'There remains in me, I suppose, some of the old hippie and something of an evangelical fervour about the work I do,' Peel reflected. 'I think – and I hope this isn't going to read wrong – that the programmes on which I have worked ... have contributed to the enduring health of British music and the capacity of that music to reinvent itself.'

The reason for the letter was that Bannister had authorised a reduction in Peel's weekly hours to make room for a new programme, *One in the Jungle*. Radio 1 had awoken to jungle music as an urban dance phenomenon in 1995, and Bannister felt that the genre now needed its own Friday night showcase. Peel, who had a Friday 10 p.m. slot, would be the one to make way.

The precise origins of jungle have been widely debated, but nobody disputes the influence of two London acts, the Ragga Twins and Shut Up and Dance, who were there at the beginning of the ragga–techno hybrid. As it happened, there was a DJ on Radio 1's books who had tirelessly championed the Ragga Twins as far back as 1991 – and Shut Up and Dance even earlier in 1990. In doing so, he'd brought something quite new to Radio 1 and helped spread awareness throughout Britain of the music that would evolve into jungle and drum 'n' bass.

The DJ was John Peel.

But there was a lot more to Peel than being Radio 1's resident beady-eyed talent spotter. As an architect of one-hour, two-hour and three-hour music programmes, he was known for his vast frame of reference, his addiction to diversity, his empathy with outsiders, his

non-linear running orders, his sudden disappearances down musical rabbit holes and his bizarre juxtapositions.

Happy to dislocate while he educated, Peel caught the listener repeatedly off guard, revelling in surprise and innovation. A
sequence of music might go something like this: Mississippi blues
> riot grrrl > sludge metal > Berlin techno > Northumberland folk
> Toronto surf-punk > Zimbabwean chimurenga > Seattle grunge.
You don't have to be au fait with all the genres to get a palpable sense
of dizziness. The effect was like being whisked around a museum by
a caffeine-overdosed tour guide with a train to catch. Look at *this*.
Now *this*. Move *faster*. Come *on*.

Sometimes mistaken for a musical elitist or a wilful obscurist,
Peel enjoyed the work of such Neanderthals as Ted Nugent, Sham
69, the Cockney Rejects and Splodgenessabounds. He approved of
all genres with 'hardcore' in their name and he relished every pun-
ishing, remorseless sound that allowed him to unleash his inner
hooligan. Able to recall vividly the thrill of hearing Elvis Presley and
Little Richard for the first time, he was forever drawn towards music
that sounded visceral or insurrectionary. He was an early supporter
of the London acid techno scene (motto: 'It's Not Intelligent and
It's Not from Detroit, but It's Fucking Having It') and he saw clear
parallels between happy hardcore and primitive rock 'n' roll. Unlike
a music journalist, he didn't have to analyse each new genre or write
an essay explaining its provenance. And as many music journalists
will know from experience, it's difficult to analyse acid techno or
write essays about happy hardcore.

A huge number of DJs worked in radio across the British Isles
during the three and a half decades when Peel was on the air, and
more than a few overlapped with him at certain points along the
taste spectrum. Among them were Steve Barker (BBC Radio
Lancashire's *On the Wire*), Keith Skues (BBC local stations), Billy
Sloan (Radio Clyde), Dave Fanning (RTE 2), the reggae specialist

David Rodigan (Capital Radio and Kiss FM), the world music scholar Charlie Gillett (Capital and BBC Radio London) and the Radio 1 DJs Annie Nightingale, Alexis Korner, Andy Kershaw, Alan Black, Bob Harris, Pete Drummond, Mike Harding, Emperor Rosko, Tommy Vance, David 'Kid' Jensen, Janice Long, Steve Lamacq, Jeff Young, Pete Tong, Westwood, Fabio & Grooverider and Mary Anne Hobbs. All of them served. All of them had their fields of expertise.

But none of them, let's be honest, ever followed the Wedding Present with a Glaswegian pub song written by Gerry Rafferty and then veered impulsively into Steely & Clevie's dancehall cover of Carly Simon's 'Why'. And none of them ever played 'Chim Chim Cher-ee' by the tone-deaf novelty singer Mrs Miller and crowned it for horrid comedy value by pulling out 'Climb Ev'ry Mountain' by the actress Patricia Routledge. And nor did any of them ever start a show with Auchtermuchty's foot-tapping accordionist Jimmy Shand and go on to cue up eleven noisecore tracks lasting a combined total of fifteen seconds. Peel played all of these things, from the Wedding Present to the noisecore via Shand and the future Hyacinth Bucket, in a single night (26 May 1991) and still found room for the new Pixies single and a session – their fourteenth – by the Fall. At his best, and that 1991 show was Peel at something like his best, he displayed a form of erudite, neo-anarchic, abstract expressionist fearlessness that no other person on British music radio before or since could have begun to imagine how to emulate.

Juxtaposing genres and refusing to recognise boundaries were generally reckoned to be risky strategies within the Nineties music industry. Artists and record companies were wary of alienating fans by flitting from one style of music to another, while editors of magazines thought carefully about which genres to promote on their covers (and which to relegate to inside pages or ignore) with a view to targeting the highest readership. Identity politics and tribalism went hand in hand with a belief that music should be seen in terms of indie and corporate, ethical and mercenary, 'ours' and 'theirs', right and wrong, cool and crap, above reproach and beyond the pale, bands it's OK to like and bands it's shameful to mention.

For Peel, however, genre juxtaposition was a prerequisite, a *sine qua non* and a flat-out non-negotiable imperative. You like Half Man Half Biscuit? Then here's some Goa trance. You collect singles on the Sarah label? Then you're sure to love these fiddle players from Alabama. Listeners in 1978 hoping to hear an exclusive taste of the new Clash album would have to wait while Peel played a selection of Morris dances by the Albion Band. Fans of the Smiths, hunched over their tape recorders in 1986, were treated to the latest opus by Morrissey and Marr only after being force-fed Run-DMC, Benjamin Zephaniah and eight minutes of German industrial music that sounded like the council digging up a road. Still incorrigibly catholic in the 2000s, Peel made lovers of dubstep grit their teeth in frustration by interrupting the deep bass to play mood-killing ballads by the Nashville country singer Laura Cantrell.

There was nothing the listeners could do to stop him. If they wrote letters badgering him to cease playing a particular song, Peel would play the song after reading out the letters. If they dismissed a new band as moronic or worthless, that band would be guaranteed to appear in his programmes for weeks. No DJ ever credited his listeners with having such open minds; no DJ ever cared less about their complaints when their minds turned out to be narrower than he thought. Peel ruled his fiefdom like a benevolent dictatorship, whimsically for the most part but with no time for faint hearts. 'These programmes may be hateful, but they're *interesting*,' he consoled them one night in September 1982, halfway through a show that crunched through the gears with typical lack of concern for other road users. Arizona hardcore. Belgian punk-funk. Ipswich reggae. A session by Christians in Search of Filth. No compromises, no concessions.

Furthermore, while Peel was fond of sending himself up ('You're listening to the John Peel wing-ding, the programme that brings you the worst of both worlds'), his tone could just as quickly harden into admonishment if his standards weren't met. In December 1988, dismayed by the absence of black artists in the listeners' annual vote-a-thon, the Festive 50, he implicitly accused them of being racists. A warning was left hanging in the air: if you people want to continue listening to my shows, you're going to have to improve your game. It's unthinkable that any other DJ on ratings-conscious Radio 1 would have delivered a similar rebuke.

One reason why Peel had no qualms about chewing out his indie-loving listeners of the late Eighties was because the results had been spectacular when he got rid of their predecessors a decade earlier. Steering his programmes through the choppy waters of punk rock in 1976–7, Peel succeeded in shoring up his own position in the long run, but in the short term it meant riding roughshod over the seething protests of prog rock fans who loathed punk's crude sound. There were times when Peel had to be ruthless; there was even a thinly veiled back-me-or-sack-me ultimatum one night in August 1977. His entire audience didn't quite desert him overnight, as he was later to boast, but he certainly didn't implore them to have second thoughts as they streamed slowly for the exits.

Peel's endorsement of punk was immensely significant, and not just because *Top Gear* had been the main outlet for the hippie music that the punks sought to annihilate. As the DJ who'd played Pink Floyd's *The Dark Side of the Moon* for the first time on British radio, and given years of sustenance to proggy bands like Caravan and Supertramp, Peel could easily have been in the punks' firing line (like his protégé and imitator Bob Harris) if his reactions had been slower or his attitude more sceptical. Instead, in the face of genuine alarm from his Radio 1 bosses, Peel nailed his colours to the punk mast with a special programme in December 1976. Even so, it took two more years – and an explosive Festive 50 at the end of 1978 – for the *John Peel Show*'s punk metamorphosis to become complete.

Punk's iconoclastic aesthetic came just at the right time for Peel. After years of laid-back praise for Eric Clapton and Jackson Browne, he took the opportunity to make comprehensive changes as he approached forty. He cut his hair short, revised his opinion of one-time heroes and spoke in a proletarian, Midlands-inflected growl that had little to do with his original accent. Where once he had ended Sunday afternoon editions of *Top Gear* by urging his listeners to 'be gentle with one another', he now said to them gruffly: 'More of the same unpleasant and disorientating racket tomorrow. Good night . . . and good riddance.'

Punk, in short, toughened Peel up. And with bands like PiL and the Pop Group pioneering a post-punk doctrine whose premise involved devouring the carcass of punk orthodoxy like jackals, Peel's programmes by the end of the decade had a distinct atmosphere, a taste of danger, a feeling of shared intrepidness as the rhythms and voices of the new underground pulsed, throbbed, screeched and howled. The *John Peel Show*, like its presenter, had been reborn.

By 1979, his office at the BBC teemed with records and cassettes from new bands and new labels. They arrived at a frightening rate, dramatically increasing his workload. The effect of his support for this industrious generation of gung-ho newcomers was a split in the British music business. An independent infrastructure was built (with its mothership at Rough Trade Records and Distribution in west London), which blossomed by the early Eighties into a de facto alternative music society. In Peel's after-hours world, big American labels like RCA, MCA and Warner Bros, accustomed in former years to having their new releases plugged by Peel without question, now became totally irrelevant. Under Peel's gleeful auspices, the music business was demystified and made easier to penetrate than at any time before.

Here's how it worked. A new band formed. They borrowed £100 from one of their dads and recorded a single. A local independent label heard it, liked it, pressed up 1,000 copies and sent one to Peel. The fate of the other 999 copies depended on what happened next. They were lucky. Peel liked the single, played it twice and told the listeners how to order it. The label, encouraged, paid for the band to record another single. They pressed up 3,000 copies and sent one to Peel. He played it every night for a week. Now they were off: an album, tour dates, *NME* interviews, a career.

'By ensuring that up to ninety per cent of the records he played were things you wouldn't hear anywhere else on the radio, he created a non-commercial climate in which small independent labels could thrive commercially,' wrote Nick Currie, better known as the singer-songwriter Momus. 'Like some kind of greenhouse, his nightly programme protected all sorts of delicate plants from the cold winds of commerce, at least until they were big and tough enough to make it on their own.'

But Peel did more than that. In a foretaste of the Sound City festivals of the Nineties, he dragged Radio 1 out of its London-centric way of looking at British pop and showed the importance of publicising new music from Glasgow, Edinburgh, Manchester, Birmingham, Sheffield, Leeds, Liverpool, Coventry, Bristol and two cities in Northern Ireland – Belfast and Derry – where nothing had been heard for years. Long before regeneration, long before any of these cities had music industries to speak of, Peel presented them as hives of culture crackling with energy and potential.

And those were just the cities. After that he started on the towns. On Peel's programmes it was all right to be a nobody from nowhere, it was no drawback to have nothing but a demo tape in your pocket, and it was even acceptable to be on the scrounge. Listeners offered their wares for sale as though Peel were running a street market. Addresses were read out constantly. Fanzines were recommended, no matter how tiny their circulation. The shows became informal gig guides. Little networks of camaraderie and capability sprang up all over the UK. As Alan Bennett once said about the birth of Granada Television, Peel let people in the south see what was going on in the north, and a post-punk nation was introduced to each other.

In time, as Peel devolved more and more power to the regions, new influences began to seep indelibly into the philosophy of Radio 1. What Peel played tonight, David Jensen, Janice Long or Mark Goodier would play tomorrow. It might even make it onto the Simon Bates show some time next October. Suddenly Radio 1 wasn't looking at Britain and seeing a country consisting of London and a giant seaside. Britain's biggest pop station was developing an authentic national voice.

Peel and his long-time producer John Walters were dyed-in-the-wool radio men committed to upholding the values of Lord Reith, the BBC's first director-general. They would quote a passage from Reith's autobiography, *Into the Wind*, in which he recalled the BBC's early critics accusing it of 'setting out to give the public not what it wanted but what the BBC thought it should have'. Reith's response, much enjoyed by Walters, was that the public hadn't the faintest idea what it wanted.

Some fifty years after Reith's day, the well-informed Peel listeners of the Nineties and Noughties had a much better sense of what to demand from a radio station. But such was their trust in Peel that they tuned in to hear him perform that most Reithian of services: teaching them something they didn't know. 'Give us what you think we should have,' they said, and he did. There wouldn't have been much point in him playing classic hits or songs that were climbing the charts; those were ubiquitous on Radio 1 during the daytime.

But again, there was an irony there for anyone who cared to look. Thanks to years of the trickle-down Peel effect, much of the station's daily output – for example, on Jo Whiley's lunchtime show, which began in 1997 – now comprised indie guitar groups who could trace their roots back to Peel shows of the mid-Eighties. Moreover, for a man who didn't like Suede, never rated Oasis and took six years to come round to Blur, Peel had had a hell of a lot to do with the genesis of Britpop.

Peel, for all that, remained probing and inquisitive, presiding over fizzing test tubes like a white-coated boffin and hacking his way through dense undergrowth like a pith-helmeted missionary. Though he was cut from different cloth to his upwardly mobile colleagues (when the ex-Radio 1 presenter Mike Smith died in 2014, his fellow DJ Mike Read remembered him as 'a very affable guy, fantastically businesslike' – say no more), Peel nevertheless had an uncanny flair for inching forwards, snail-like, in a way that may not have been visible to the naked eye but allowed him to cover remarkable distances over time. It could be seen as appropriate that his voice changed several times over the years, adapting to new ages and new vocabularies. His chameleonic ability to blend into the cultural scenery – be it psychedelia, punk or drum 'n' bass – while simultaneously blending into the background at Radio 1, surely provides a major clue to his longevity.

But while his perspective on music was often pure subversion, in other ways Peel and his employers were made for each other. As a broadcaster he fitted perfectly – we can now see – into BBC radio's long heritage of intelligent speech, enthusiastic connoisseurs and eccentric polymaths. He was one of those eloquent souls who knew their P. G. Wodehouse and could rattle off witty sentences with impeccable grammar and daring amounts of subjunctive and parenthetical clauses. Peel, as Detective McNulty would have said in *The Wire*, was 'real BBC'.

When one of his idols, John Arlott of *Test Match Special*, died in 1991, Peel told his listeners: 'There have been some great broadcasters in my life. Wynford Vaughan-Thomas. Wolfman Jack. Humphrey Lyttelton. Alan Freeman. Russ Knight, the Weird Beard [a Texan DJ]. Peter Clayton. But John Arlott was the greatest of them all.'

It's interesting to note here how Peel recalls his life through the prism of radio, from Vaughan-Thomas's elegiac descriptions of post-war state occasions to the crazed hyperbole of American rock 'n' roll to the unhistrionic fluency of the BBC jazz presenters Lyttelton and Clayton. If we include Lyttelton's thirty years as host of Radio 4's *I'm Sorry I Haven't a Clue*, Peel's love of radio appears to encompass everything that can make him laugh, ponder, sit bolt upright, relax, daydream, sing his head off, dance around the room, feel like a citizen of his country and feel like a man of the world.

But he was much more than a composite of his radio heroes. He was wordy, but they were his words and not Arlott's or Vaughan-Thomas's. He never ranted and raved like Wolfman Jack or piled up the catchphrases like Alan Freeman. Unlike Lyttelton and Clayton, he had a fallibility that belied his easy command of the microphone. He started records at the wrong speed, blew his nose as songs were ending and flapped around looking for mislaid pieces of paper that had been there a minute ago. He once played a whole album by Robert Fripp and Brian Eno backwards without noticing. Many Peel fans found these foibles enormously endearing.

Andy Kershaw believed that some of them tuned in just to hear Peel talk. His convoluted way of saying even the most basic things could turn straightforward announcements into miniature agonies of verbosity. 'I was a little late in coming to an appreciation of this next record,' he said one night in 1982 about an Aztec Camera single, 'but having once got there, I was fully appreciative for a number of months.' Having once got there? Fully appreciative? Anyone else would have called it a grower.

He liked to quote 'the old DJ adage' that two instrumentals shouldn't be played in a row, usually just before he played two instrumentals in a row. He might then find a dedication that he should have read out the night before, and promise to play it tomorrow, when, as he fatalistically admitted, the person he was playing it for would probably not be listening. Radio 1, after years of taking him for granted and moving him around the schedules, eventually found out the hard way that he was incomparable and irreplaceable. Thereby calling to mind a different adage – the Joni Mitchell one about not knowing what you've got till it's gone.

Peel's travels in America in the Sixties had taken him to the outer circles of the California counterculture, where he'd smoked marijuana and managed a rock band. He arrived back in England in 1967 to find that people like him were the enemy. A few weeks after his return, Mick Jagger and Keith Richards were charged with offences against the Dangerous Drugs Act after a high-profile arrest in February. The guilty verdicts and prison sentences handed down to them in June appalled Peel, who threw the support of *The Perfumed Garden* behind them. He also lobbied for the release of John 'Hoppy' Hopkins, a London magazine editor and club promoter who had been imprisoned for possessing cannabis.

Jagger and Richards had their convictions reduced and overturned, respectively, in July. But Peel had been shocked by what he saw as the vindictiveness of the police, the judiciary, the newspapers and a public all too ready to condemn before the facts were known. He might not have guessed it, as he looked around him that summer, but Britain was about to go through a period of profound social change. First, in July, the Sexual Offences Act decriminalised consensual homosexual behaviour between men over the age of twenty-one in England and Wales. Then, in October, after heated debates in the Commons, Parliament legalised abortions. The death penalty, which had been suspended since 1965, was formally abolished in 1969. That same year, the Divorce Reform Act was passed, making it easier for couples to end a marriage that had irretrievably broken down.

A man like Peel would have considered all these changes essential in a civilised country. Most of them had been instigated by the Labour home secretary, Roy Jenkins, a liberal reformer who also oversaw the end of censorship in theatres and the abolition of birching in borstals. But even if Peel and Jenkins agreed on the fundamental tenets of a fairer Britain, the two men stood on opposite sides of an almighty cultural gap. Jenkins, an Oxbridge intellectual with a taste for fine wines, had nothing in common with a pot-smoking, quasi-Marxist utopian like Peel. Jenkins wore a suit. Peel wore a kaftan. Jenkins personified the rolled-up-brolly-and-horn-rimmed-glasses plutocracy that had all the power and none of the right vibes. The government that Jenkins served had showed its disdain for pirate radio stations by passing legislation to haul them off their ships. At that moment in the Sixties, Peel was a true pirate, a thief of the airwaves, a man symbolically forbidden by the laws of his own country to ply his trade on British soil.

Thirty-seven years later, he and his country were unrecognisable. Mick Jagger had a knighthood. Young people accessed music via file-sharing sites and as many digital radio stations as they could bookmark. The prime minister, Tony Blair, was a rock fan who'd named Free and Bruce Springsteen among his castaway choices on *Desert Island Discs*. Peel, the former pariah, hosted a weekly family-orientated programme, *Home Truths*, on middle-class Radio 4. In a 2002 poll to find the hundred pre-eminent figures in British history, he'd come forty-third – one place higher than John Logie Baird, the inventor of television, and two higher than Aneurin Bevan, the father of the National Health Service. Roy Jenkins was nowhere.

Peel turned sixty-five at the end of August 2004, becoming only Radio 1's second DJ of pensionable age (after Alan Freeman in 1992). In October, he took a brief leave of absence from his programmes and flew with his wife to Peru for a working holiday. A first-rate writer, he had a secondary income as a journalist; the *Daily Telegraph* had commissioned a travel article about his visits to Machu Picchu and Colca Canyon. The article was never submitted. On his ninth day in Peru, Peel died of a heart attack in the city of Cusco. He had been complaining of fatigue and erratic health for some time.

In Britain, news of his death broke during the afternoon of 25 October. It became the lead story on the BBC's rolling news channel, where it continued to run throughout the day. Rush-hour commuters in London were confronted by *Evening Standard* news boards quoting Don McLean on Buddy Holly: 'The Day the Music Died'. Expressing his personal sadness, Tony Blair hailed Peel as 'a unique voice in British broadcasting'. Over the next few days, obituaries in newspapers and magazines commended him for his 'almost religious devotion to seeking out and broadcasting unconventional rock music' (*Guardian*), his 'delight in the new, the unexpected and the good' (*The Economist*) and his 'ability to broadcast as if he were speaking to just one person' (*Daily Telegraph*).

The BBC announced plans to commemorate him by naming part of its Broadcasting House complex the John Peel Wing. The year after his death, the organisers of Glastonbury Festival named a stage for new bands after him. A more nuanced tribute, paid to him during his lifetime, was the launch of a new station – BBC 6 Music – that has often seemed to walk in his footsteps, right down to repeating sessions originally heard on his Radio 1 shows in decades gone by.

In recent years, however, there has been a much larger event – a global one, no less – over which Peel cast a conspicuous influence. His name went unmentioned on the night, but his imprint on the spectacle was inescapable. It took place in front of 80,000 people in a stadium in east London and was watched by an estimated world-wide television audience of over 900 million.

The idea for *Good Night and Good Riddance* was born on the evening of 27 July 2012, when the Olympic Stadium in Stratford hosted the opening ceremony of the London Games. The four-hour extravaganza was a vision of the United Kingdom through the eyes and cameras of director Danny Boyle, from its prehistoric settlements to its Industrial Revolution to its James Bond film franchise and its NHS. The task of overseeing the music that accompanied Boyle's choreography fell to the dance act Underworld.

What was heard in Stratford that night was nothing like the jubilee events that Britain so adores, which rely on the music of middle-of-the-road superstars like George Michael, Annie Lennox, Brian May and the Spice Girls. (As the Games' closing ceremony, sixteen days later, predictably did.) Boyle's universally acclaimed pageant showed a modern Britain that celebrated its diversity, included its outsiders and made a virtue of its bloody-minded mavericks.

One of the evening's centrepieces was Mike Oldfield's *Tubular Bells*, a landmark album that has sold multiple millions and spawned several sequels. If you wanted to use terms like 'a true British success story', you wouldn't be too wide of the mark. But when it first emerged in the spring of 1973, *Tubular Bells* had no precedent and was the work of a young musician with zero profile. Abstruse and unclassifiable, it might have sunk without trace had one man not fallen under its spell. A night-time DJ on Radio 1, he played the album's first side – all twenty-five minutes of it – and *Tubular Bells* was suddenly the talk of the rock world.

Also performing in Boyle's ceremony was the grime MC Dizzee Rascal, back on his east London home turf. Grime was a genre that the self-same Radio 1 DJ had become passionate about towards the end of his life, playing it years before Tinchy Stryder, Skepta and Wretch 32 began their takeover of the Top 40. Musical directors Underworld had their own links with the Radio 1 DJ, recording a session for his programme in 2003 and deputising as presenters when he took his fateful holiday in Peru a year later.

No doubt the drum 'n' bass producer High Contrast, who assembled the soundtrack for the athletes' parade, would have remembered the DJ playing his very first single on a small south London label in 2001. The singer-songwriter Frank Turner, who sang three songs in the ceremony's prologue, wouldn't have forgotten his early appearances on the DJ's shows in 2002 and 2003 as the vocalist in the post-hardcore band Million Dead.

The closer one listened to the music in the ceremony, the more associations became apparent. Here were Pink Floyd, practically the house band on the DJ's shows in the late Sixties. Here was the Sex Pistols' 'God Save the Queen', which he played in 1977 because he felt its message was 'a view that should be allowed to be aired' – even though it had been banned by the BBC and could have cost him his job. Here were New Order, a band he was the first to play on British radio. Here were Frankie Goes to Hollywood, the chart conquerors of 1984, whom he played in 1982 when fewer than a hundred people outside Liverpool knew of their existence.

The DJ died three years before the Bristol electronic duo Fuck Buttons put out their first record in 2007. He never had a chance to hear them. But the inclusion of two tracks from Fuck Buttons' *Tarot Sport* in the opening ceremony of a gigantic spectacular like London 2012 seemed to renounce, for one glorious moment, Britain's endemic penchant for pomp and circumstance and embrace, instead, one man's lifelong belief that the obvious should be avoided at all costs while the marginal should be highlighted at all times. It was Fuck Buttons who clinched the matter.

Prog. Punk. Indie. Drum 'n' bass. Grime. Bowie. *Tubular Bells*. It couldn't have been any plainer if the athletes had put down their flags and broken into a chorus of 'Teenage Kicks' by the Undertones. Eight years after his death, Britain was presenting itself to the world as a John Peel nation.

It's doubtful whether New Order, never mind Fuck Buttons, would have made it into Boyle's vision of Britain if Peel hadn't had such a subtle yet sweeping influence on the culture. He certainly had a sweeping influence on the lives of four young men from Salford and Macclesfield. 'If it wasn't for John Peel, there would be no Joy Division and no New Order,' guitarist Bernard Sumner said flatly on the news of his death.

Boyle himself, a former punk from the area around Manchester, has cited *24 Hour Party People* – the story of Tony Wilson, Joy Division and the Manchester independent music scene – as the one film that he would have loved to direct. Peel, of course, was the conduit in 1979 by means of whom Joy Division were able to begin their long journey into the national consciousness. He played 'Love Will Tear Us Apart' before it had sold a single copy; now it is sung as a football chant. He played *Unknown Pleasures* when it appealed primarily to Kafka-reading students; now *Unknown Pleasures* T-shirts are sold by River Island and Topman, almost rivalling the Ramones' for high-street popularity. And we don't need to be reminded who first played the Ramones.

No wonder John Walters considered Peel the fulcrum around which rock music revolved. No wonder Dan Auerbach of the Black Keys announced to the crowd during their Glastonbury appearance in 2010: 'We never had anybody like John Peel in the States.

You people are really lucky.' No wonder Jack White, whose White Stripes once performed live on the air from Peel's living room, called him 'the most important DJ of all time'.

We can see how one single decision taken by Peel in the early Seventies triggered a series of events that had ramifications for every subsequent decade. By giving a debut to a new band called Roxy Music in 1972, he kick-started a three-year whirlwind of momentum that took Roxy to sold-out shows at Wembley Empire Pool in 1975. There, during an intermission, a south-east London teenager named Steven Bailey met Susan Ballion, a girl from a neighbouring suburb. The punk band they formed the following year, Siouxsie and the Banshees, made their Peel debut in 1977. Their 1978 album *The Scream* – released on Polydor after Peel had repeatedly cajoled record labels to sign the band – was to influence the sound of early U2, the Cure, the Cocteau Twins and My Bloody Valentine. Each one of those bands has influenced at least four hundred others. The Banshees continue to inspire new artists in the twenty-first century, notably the Yeah Yeah Yeahs and Savages. And Roxy Music, to bring things back to that Peel show in 1972, left their stylistic mark on everyone from Grace Jones to Brett Anderson to Ladytron. If Peel hadn't taken a shine to Roxy when he saw them support Genesis in December 1971, how might history have been different?

Ribbons of lineage that Peel helped to weave run through the fabric of the music all around us, even if we can't always see them. Not only did he find the sounds that shaped the playlists of the future, he also had an acute and lasting influence on his listeners. Many tuned in to his programmes several nights a week for six or seven years. Think of those brains vibrating to Peel's rhythm. Think of the absorption, the osmosis, the diffusion. 'Give me a Peel listener for seven years and I will show you the man.'

For it's on those generations of listeners – teenagers, students, graduates, workers, dropouts, benefit claimants and even one or two criminals detained at Her Majesty's pleasure – that Peel's influence becomes literally incalculable. What many of them would hasten to say is that he represented something positive, a bona fide alternative to the bland confections dominating the commercial world that young people are pressurised to buy into. Aside from constantly stressing the accessibility of music and the availability of radio (*go on, you can do it, and when you do it, I'll play it*), he did more than anyone in the British media, I would argue, to get a nation of young minds interested in the idea of mistrusting the mainstream and investigating the unfamiliar. Throughout it all, he kept challenging them to listen without discrimination and tear down the walls of resistance, the better to let everything in.

The process by which Peel entered the national consciousness himself was anything but smooth. Attempts to get him to host *Top of the Pops* in the Sixties ended with him being banned by the producer for incompetence. A BBC1 talk show that he co-presented in 1968 was taken off the air after an outraged Mary Whitehouse threatened the BBC with the full fury of Middle England.

In fact, although Peel went on to present *Top of the Pops* many times in the Eighties, and made some appearances on Noel Edmonds's Saturday evening programme *The Late, Late Breakfast Show*, he never seemed terribly comfortable on prime-time television. A self-effacing man with a habit of blinking rapidly, he wasn't exactly Zoë Ball or Chris Evans material.

In 1993, Radio 1 invited him to host a week of lunchtime shows while Jakki Brambles, the regular presenter, was away. He made himself at home, playing the Fall, Huggy Bear, Sebadoh and Madder Rose, and heaping derision on songs in the Top 40. It felt as though a blow had been struck for independence – and for every skinny artist in the underground – but listening to those shows more than twenty years later is a sobering experience. Peel sounds like a fish out of water, unable to get to grips with Brambles's listeners or the job he's meant to be doing. Somewhat chastened, he returned to his night-time lair, where he was a lot surer of his surroundings.

But he got there in the end. He permeated British life until he adorned the honours lists of more than half a dozen universities (which bestowed degrees and doctorates on him) and walked the corridors of Buckingham Palace, where Prince Charles pinned an OBE on him in 1998. The cumulative result of thirty-seven years of broadcasting had taken John Ravenscroft to places an insurance salesman or cotton apprentice couldn't have dreamed of.

Good Night and Good Riddance is a book about those thirty-seven years. It looks at how Peel did his job night after night, week after week, month after month. It looks at the music he played and the music he ignored. It looks at what his words meant in context and what we might think of them now. If we want to understand how Peel helped to shape our modern culture, we'll find it revealed in the shows he presented, starting with the spellbound rhapsodies of *The Perfumed Garden* and ending with his older, wiser but no less fervent transmissions of the twenty-first century.

The era has long since ended when Peel and the weekly music papers were the only ways to find out about – and listen to – non-chart music. Today, providing your laptop or phone is switched on, it's almost impossible to avoid it. It's been said that radio was a way of killing time until Spotify was invented. Peel's old alma mater Radio 1, ordered by a BBC review in 2009 to reassess its target audience and cater for more fifteen- to twenty-nine-year-olds, now faces everyday challenges to engage with young Britons who have turned their backs on radio.

'What we need to do is to represent the zeitgeist of what it feels like to be young, to reflect and celebrate youth culture in the UK,' Ben Cooper, Radio 1's controller, said in 2014. 'If we can do that with the right presenters and content, then we can continue to be relevant.'

John Peel never gave much thought to representing zeitgeists, and it worried him that Radio 1 risked alienating young listeners by chasing their loyalty so blatantly. Without patronising them or talking down to them, his own programmes attracted Cooper's target audience with a consistency that a present-day controller would give his eye teeth for. 'Think of my programmes as your research department,' Peel wrote in his letter to Matthew Bannister, a previous controller, in 1996. 'Noisy, smelly but occasionally coming up with the formulae which you can subsequently market.'

It begs the question: if Peel were alive today, would Radio 1 dare to employ a man who was born in the 1930s? To put it another way, could it afford not to?

PART ONE

BE GENTLE WITH ONE ANOTHER

1967: THE GARDEN

'There was a feeling of unification, of people coming together of
that generation – of people questioning their supposed betters,
saying, "Why do we have to have this set of rules?" And the bands
were the glue. They were like the marching bands. They provided
the rhythm.' KEVIN AYERS

The Perfumed Garden
Radio London
12 July 1967

Peel plays: Donovan – Howlin' Wolf – The Purple Gang – Simon &
Garfunkel – Jimmy Reed – Blues Project – Jefferson Airplane – Roger
McGough – The Jimi Hendrix Experience – The Mothers of Invention

*Today's news: 3,000 workers strike in a pay dispute at Vauxhall
Motors. Barbara Castle, the minister of transport, informs the House
of Commons that the 70 mph speed limit on Britain's motorways,
introduced as a temporary measure in 1965, is to be made permanent.*

The perfumed garden is a high-walled, aromatic haven born of
Coleridgean opium dreams and Carrollian whimsy. Inside, by the
entrance to the magic wood, outsize flora and dwarfish fauna are
nodding their heads and inclining their stems to the heavy messages
of Donovan's 'Epistle to Dippy'. A Top 20 hit in America, it's an

electric boogie poem about crystal spectacles, far-out doctors and elevators in the brain. Donovan's record company won't release it in England. They don't want the messages getting out.

Deep in the perfumed garden, kaleidoscopic patterns dissolve and are recreated in colours twice as bright. Young men and women run naked through the bracken, pausing to stare transfixed at a eucalyptus tree. The phantasmagoric jukebox plays on, spinning songs with titles like 'February Sunshine' and 'Granny Takes a Trip'. This is late-night pirate radio in 1967, in the last few weeks before they make it illegal. 'Wander through in our midst,' says the presenter, a softly spoken twenty-seven-year-old named John Peel. 'Pick out a flower from the perfumed garden and plant it somewhere in your mind.'

Not for the last time in his life, Peel represents the exact opposite of what his employers stand for. Radio London might be a pirate ship, but it's a Top 40 station, American-bankrolled and tightly formatted to maximise advertising revenue. The DJs – Tony Blackburn, Ed Stewart, Dave Cash, Keith Skues and others – host fast-moving programmes with the emphasis on fun. Hi there, cats and kittens. Here's a happening sound from the Walker Brothers the Small Faces the Rolling Stones Dusty Springfield Tamla Motown. These exuberant young dandies of the sea are aural Technicolor after years of drab BBC monochrome. The time coming up to the top of the hour is another Fab 40 sound here on Wonderful Radio London.

The word 'wonderful' is mandatory on Radio London, not so much an adjective, more an ideological belief. Slick jingles zing like freshly brushed teeth. *It's smooth sailing with the highly successful sound of Wonderful Radio London. You're a pussycat and you're where it's at. Wonderful Radio London, biggest sound around, Big L.* At the end of the year, with Radio London just a memory, the Who will release an album, *The Who Sell Out*, that preserves the best of these jingles in a pop-art time capsule.

Radio London broadcasts from a 650-ton ship, the MV *Galaxy*, which lies anchored three and a half miles off the Essex coast. At night, the disc jockeys can see the lights of Frinton-on-Sea and Walton-on-the-Naze in the distance. In summer, pleasure boats come out from Frinton and the holidaymakers throw presents to the DJs. Back there on the mainland you can catch a train from Harwich into London, where young people are using terms like 'flower power' and the 'Summer of Love' to describe a youthful gathering of the tribes. Hippies and anti-Vietnam War protesters are rising up all over Europe and America. The peaceful rebellion is spreading like wildfire.

Rebellion, however, is not an option on the MV *Galaxy*. No misbehaviour of any kind is tolerated. No girls are smuggled on board. No pot is smoked. Wonderful Radio London is not a hippie love boat, it's the most professional and profitable music-orientated business in the North Sea. The Monkees the Tremeloes Wayne Fontana Sandie Shaw Cilla Black Tamla Motown.

Unless you happen to be listening to *The Perfumed Garden*.

John Peel is the midnight-to-two man. The psychedelic graveyard shift. If you want to hear four songs in a row by Frank Zappa's Mothers of Invention, or something from Jeff Beck that isn't 'Hi Ho Silver Lining', *The Perfumed Garden* is the place to be. Peel is the only Radio London DJ with carte blanche to ignore the Top 40 and play whatever he likes – not because he demanded the privilege, but because the station's managing director goes to bed before *The Perfumed Garden* starts and has never heard it. He doesn't know what he's missing.

Peel plays the sort of records that other DJs wouldn't even take out of their sleeves. *The Zodiac: Cosmic Sounds* is a mind-bending astrological concept album on the very hip Elektra label. It'll probably sell 200 copies in Britain if it's lucky, but that's of no consequence to Peel. He compiles his programmes in Jackson Pollock-style splatters of enthusiasm, juxtaposing psychedelia, blues, folk and poetry in sequences that go Jefferson Airplane > Roger McGough > Jimi Hendrix > Giant Sunflower.

McGough is one of a group of humorous, satirical poets from Liverpool. He reads a poem about the Second Coming which ends with society rejecting Christ because he looks like a hippie. The Giant Sunflower, from Los Angeles, sing a buoyant folk-rock song with harmonies like the Mamas and the Papas. 'I like [it] very much indeed,' says Peel, 'despite the fact that it neither sold in this country nor in the United States.' Now there's a credo for the next thirty-seven years.

Peel is an evangelist, but he's also an initiate. *The Perfumed Garden* can be quite cult-like. His weirdly placid voice, with its upscale Wirral Peninsula accent, sounds like it may have brainwashed itself into a trance. The word 'wonderful' has no meaning in *The Perfumed Garden*; the word 'beautiful' means everything. Peel tells us he likes walking through Hyde Park when he's not on the ship. 'You can see and meet interesting, beautiful kinds of people.' Cueing up a song by the bluesman Jimmy Reed, he goes for a make-believe wander. 'If you step across into Hyde Park from Park Lane, you go straight into all those trees that are whispering ageless, unheard-of secrets to one another and exchanging dark green words of love.'

Is this stuff preposterous to us now? Inevitably. But is he serious about it? Indubitably. Peel, in a funny way, knows his niche market. There's a place on pirate radio where a mild-mannered hippie can outpour his perorations on trees and foliage, a place where pretentious moonshine is indistinguishable from marijuana-speak, and that place is *The Perfumed Garden*. Fifteen minutes later, as if to show that the chemistry of the Summer of Love is still highly volatile, Peel plays a song that catapults the programme right to the epicentre of the counterculture.

Just released in America, Jefferson Airplane's 'White Rabbit' is a shattering combination of a bolero and a crescendo, with hallucinatory lyrics about an LSD trip taking the form of *Alice's Adventures in Wonderland*. The song promises fantastical visions and scorns the hypocrisy of those who would teach Carroll to children while warning adolescents against psychedelics. 'They are one of the most important groups in the whole world,' Peel murmurs ecstatically.

Take the drug that will reconnect you with your childlike mind, commands Grace Slick as 'White Rabbit' climaxes, and do it now. 'Feed your head!' she shrieks. In an instant, the path that runs through *The Perfumed Garden* seems to stretch all the way to the gates of the revolution.

The Perfumed Garden
Radio London
16 July 1967

The Misunderstood – The Byrds – The Rolling Stones – John's Children – Freddie King – The Lovin' Spoonful – The Doors – Simon & Garfunkel – Country Joe and the Fish – John Renbourn

Plans are under way to evacuate 1,500 Britons from Biafra, the rebel Nigerian state, where war broke out ten days ago. At home, a cross-party committee report is expected to recommend lowering the voting age to eighteen.

Peel has read a depressing statistic. A fortnight has passed since the guilty verdicts in the Stones' drug trial, and no gentle person can feel anything other than a deep sense of shock. But according to Peel's newspaper, the majority of twenty-one- to thirty-five-year-olds believe the prison sentences for Jagger (three months) and Richards (twelve) were too lenient. 'One tends to forget, I think, that not everybody has the same sort of opinions and concepts as you do,' Peel harrumphs.

By 'you', he means 'we', of course, for *The Perfumed Garden* is the most inclusive community on the midnight airwaves. The listeners are out there in Middlesex, Durham, Hertfordshire, Leeds, Norwich, Derby, Glasgow, Dublin, Merthyr Tydfil and even Utrecht and Oslo. They send him poetry and art. They're all going to start wearing badges so they can befriend each other in real life. (Peel: 'It would be nice if somebody who was very important wore one. Somebody like Paul McCartney.')

Jagger and Richards are out on bail waiting for their appeals to be heard. Last weekend, on a spot of shore leave, Peel spotted them in the King's Road. Didn't speak to them, though. He thought they might find that a bit of a drag. 'I should have gone up and said hello and, you know, thanked them for being themselves and everything.'

He went for a stroll in Hyde Park instead. 'You can walk along the edge of the Serpentine there, and a sparrow was taking a bath. And if you've never seen a sparrow take a bath, it's one of the most delightful things I've ever seen. He'd stand there on the slimy green edges of the water, and he'd look around him to make sure no one was watching. He'd dip himself very quickly in the water and get out and shake vigorously . . . I stood there for about five minutes watching him taking his bath. I felt as though I was intruding, actually, which I was. I shouldn't have been standing there watching.'

The Peel of the Eighties and Nineties will all but disown *The Perfumed Garden*, horrified by his lack of cynicism. But as they often say about the cultural phenomena of the past, you had to be there, and Peel was. Dressed in paisley threads and wearing a bell around his neck on a piece of cord, he was present at all the major happenings and be-ins. He watched Arthur Brown and Tomorrow at the UFO Club. He attended the 14 Hour Technicolor Dream at Alexandra Palace, where Syd Barrett's Pink Floyd played and

John Lennon mingled with the hippies and freaks in the audience. Wherever the story of underground rock was being shaped in London, Peel was in with the out-there crowd.

Interesting sequence tonight: Roger McGough > Ross Hannaman > Country Joe and the Fish. The McGough track is a social etiquette satire about a man being shot in the head but trying not to make a fuss in case any passers-by are offended. Hannaman, a girl singer, seems an incongruous choice for Peel since her single, 'Down Thru Summer', is very Petula Clark pop. Maybe he feels it chimes with *The Perfumed Garden*'s aura of Eden-like innocence. Maybe he has a soppy side. The song's two writers, Tim Rice and Andrew Lloyd Webber, won't be featuring in many Peel programmes in the future.

Ending the sequence, Country Joe and the Fish sing 'The Masked Marauder' from their zonked-out acid-rock LP *Electric Music for the Mind and Body*. Peel reads out the California address of their fan club, on the off chance that any listeners might be tempted to join. 'Intergalactic Fish Fan Club, Box 2233. Tell them *The Perfumed Garden* sent you.'

The Perfumed Garden
Radio London
6 August 1967

Canned Heat – The Incredible String Band – Captain Beefheart and His Magic Band – John Mayall – Moby Grape – Tim Hardin – The Mothers of Invention – Big Brother and the Holding Company

The National Coal Board meets to formulate a response to the report into last October's Aberfan colliery disaster. The report finds the NCB guilty of negligence and blames it for the deaths of 116 children and twenty-eight adults.

One night in June, Peel told his listeners a distressing story about a man in Slough who had boasted of killing 700 sparrows, claiming to be ridding the town of vermin. Peel, the champion of God's creatures, was disgusted by the slaughter. He said ominously: 'I'm a sparrow, and perhaps you are too. And just think – we may be the next ones.'

He then went on to play 'Sparrow' by Simon & Garfunkel, an allegory of a society overrun by greed. One by one, onlookers shrug their shoulders as a hungry sparrow begs for food and shelter. The oak tree puts its own priorities first. The swan is too concerned about what its friends will think. The field of wheat has no food it's prepared to share. Finally, the sparrow runs out of options and dies. Peel calls it 'our song' and plays it on *The Perfumed Garden* every night.

But if the shotgun that slays sparrows is an affront to Peel as a human being, a more urgent threat to Peel as a broadcaster – and Radio London as a station – can be traced to another shotgun. It belonged to a former Liberal Party candidate and war hero, and in June 1966 he used it to kill a business rival. The moment he pulled the trigger, the pirates' days were numbered.

Peel isn't alone on the high seas tonight. Keeping him company is a small flotilla's worth of pirate ships, including Radio 270, Radio 355, Radio Caroline North, Radio Caroline South (whose manic American disc jockey Emperor Rosko has taught his mynah bird to say 'Sounds fine, it's Caroline' between records) and Radio Scotland. All of these ships are dotted around the British coastline, from Frinton to Fife Ness. They're all in motion, and yet they're not. Radio London's MV *Galaxy* is officially en route to Holland – and has a crew of Dutch seamen to take her there – but her journey has lasted thirty-two months and she's still no nearer her destination. Her anchorage, crucially, places her outside British jurisdiction. She sails in international waters. Radio London has been playing all-day pop music to Britain's teenagers and housewives since December

1964, with neither a licence nor a government-approved frequency, and it hasn't broken a single law.

But after two years of pressure from the BBC, Harold Wilson's government has acted decisively to put an end to the pirates. Eight days from now, Radio London will cease operations. *The Perfumed Garden* is to be demolished by the bulldozers of the Marine Broadcasting Offences Act.

The first pirate pop station, Caroline, was launched in March 1964, when an Irish businessman named Ronan O'Rahilly found himself unable to secure airplay on Radio Luxembourg for any of the pop singers he managed. BBC radio was no better: its pop output was limited to *Saturday Club* on the Light Programme and Alan Freeman's chart rundown, *Pick of the Pops*, on Sundays. Hoping to circumvent what he saw as a record-company cartel and a near-total BBC disregard for pop's cultural significance, O'Rahilly bought a Danish passenger ferry, converted it into a radio ship and boned up on his maritime law. Caroline was an immediate success, attracting an audience of around 10 million pop fans.

In the summer of 1964 Caroline merged with another pirate, Radio Atlanta, to create two stations, Carolines North and South. A year after that, Caroline South planned a further merger with Radio City, a pirate that broadcast from a disused army fort in the Thames Estuary. The merger collapsed, with bad feeling on both sides. In June 1966 Radio City's owner, Reg Calvert, visited the home of a Caroline director, a retired major named Oliver Smedley, and the two men had a violent argument. In the struggle, Smedley shot Calvert dead. That month, the House of Commons held its first debate on whether pirate radio stations presented a hazard to shipping. By November 1966, the Marine Broadcasting Offences Bill was being introduced to Parliament. Many pirate DJs smelled a conspiracy, and their suspicions were not allayed when Smedley walked free from court after being acquitted by a jury.

Tonight, Peel tells the listeners emotionally, there are 'waves of stained-glass colours' crashing through *The Perfumed Garden*. They must all look forward, as he does, to the moment when they can sing at the tops of their voices and 'crack the very roof of heaven itself'.

The Perfumed Garden has been a place of safety. Now there are just eight days to go until the bailiffs move in. What's to become of them? While they wait to find out, Peel reads a poem about a sparrow by Gaius Valerius Catullus, in the original Latin.

The Perfumed Garden
Radio London
14 August 1967

The Beatles – The Attack – The Byrds – The Misunderstood – Tyrannosaurus Rex – The Velvet Underground – The Electric Prunes – Cream – Elmore James – Roy Harper – The Grateful Dead – Love

Michael Miles, the presenter of ITV's Take Your Pick, *is fined £16 at Uxbridge Magistrates' Court for being drunk and disorderly on a Heathrow shuttle bus. When apprehended, Miles abused police officers and gave his name as Hughie Green.*

This time tomorrow, it will be a criminal offence to broadcast or advertise on a pirate radio station. The Caroline South ship has promised to flout the law by continuing past the deadline, but Wonderful Radio London is shutting down and falling silent at 3 p.m. The final day begins with an unprecedented Peel marathon, a five-and-a-half-hour edition of *The Perfumed Garden* that starts at midnight and ends at dawn. By the time the sun has risen, he tells the listeners, 'all of us are just going to be part of the wind'.

In an exceptional send-off, Peel plays ninety pieces of music, reads two stories about Winnie the Pooh, moves studios twice due to equipment malfunctions and pours out his heart in a way that seems very genuine. In spite of its risqué name, which Peel unwittingly lifted from a sex manual, *The Perfumed Garden* has always been a platonic environment where people's boundaries are respected. But nobody visiting the garden tonight is likely to forget it. For hour after relentless hour, they're on the receiving end of a love avalanche.

In sheer statistical terms, it's probably the most bohemian radio show ever broadcast to mainland Britain. Peel opens with the first of nine songs by the Beatles. Three months ago Radio London was the first station in the world to play *Sgt Pepper's Lonely Hearts Club Band*, scooping America by three weeks and risking a colossal lawsuit from EMI. Peel, who was on the air with Ed Stewart that day, burst into tears as soon as *Sgt Pepper* started. Sensing that Peel was having an epiphany, Stewart kindly let him continue with the programme alone. 'I felt like the man who conducted Beethoven's Eighth for the first time,' Peel tells us. 'And people have said, "That's ridiculous, it's not that important." It *is*. It really *was*.'

Sgt Pepper has been at number 1 in the album charts for more than two months. It will stay there until the penultimate day of November. But Peel isn't playing *Pepper* because it's popular. The Beatles, to him, are superbeings whose songs are sacred texts to be pored over in awe. Their record releases are pivotal events in the second half of the twentieth century and landmarks in mankind's evolution. One night in June, as he introduced 'I'm Only Sleeping' from *Revolver*, Peel found the words he'd been grasping for. He described the Beatles as 'our leaders'.

But tonight's five-hour swansong is also about the marginal figures, the oddballs, loners and dissidents who will dominate Peel's programmes in the years ahead. Tyrannosaurus Rex are an acoustic duo with a nineteen-year-old frontman who writes Tolkienesque stories and sings them in a curious alien bleat. His name is Marc Bolan and Peel thinks he's a rare talent. ('He's bound to have all kinds of marvellous things happen for him.') Captain Beefheart is a growling blues singer from California with an amazing avant-garde brain. ('I think he must have been originally intended for another planet.') The Misunderstood are a band that Peel briefly managed during his time at KMEN in San Bernardino. Their guitar player Glenn Campbell, he feels, is up there with Hendrix and Clapton, 'searing with fiery intensity as he does, and then turning round and bubbling like mountain pebble streams very gently, very quietly'.

And then there are the Velvet Underground, who come from New York, where their eerie drones and cacophonies send most DJs running for the off-switch. This summer, Peel has been playing songs from their album, *The Velvet Underground & Nico*, that would scare the living daylights out of any flower child. 'Those are the Velvet Underground with their strange, haunting and sometimes frightening things,' he says. 'That was called "Venus in Furs". I went up during that record to have a look at the night, which incidentally is very beautiful. So if you're anywhere near a window, go out and look at it and breathe and perhaps say "I love you" into the night.'

Five years ago this man was working for an insurance company in downtown Dallas. It's been an astonishing transformation.

But whither John Ravenscroft now? He isn't the kind of DJ they employ at the BBC. He waits for eight-minute songs to end before he goes to the news. He sometimes starts reading the weather but gives up because he finds the idea of rain upsetting. He'd rather sound real and ridiculous than polished and phony. Will there be any work out there for a DJ like him?

'Perhaps,' he says, contemplating an uncertain future, 'in the perfumed garden if it expands a little bit, you'll be able to sail around from island to island in beautiful Greek boats and things like this.

There will be huge ships, you know, with great big sails and cargoes of jade and rubies and sweet wine, and it will be something very nice indeed.' As radio goes, this is abdication into desperate fantasy.

It saddens him that *Melody Maker* and *New Musical Express*, who should be allies of the pirates, haven't written more – haven't *complained* more – about Radio London's closure. Tonight's show is a valediction to the dream and the reality that have been Peel's day job and nightlife for six months. In the *NME*, it's a two-line story.

But if someone could 'feel the vibrations' of *The Perfumed Garden* and 'become aware' – and if that someone could be sufficiently moved by Tyrannosaurus Rex and Captain Beefheart to bang on his neighbour's door at 3.45 a.m. and tell him that he loves him – well, in that case Peel believes the show will have more than succeeded in its aims. We begin to see the *NME*'s predicament. This isn't someone trying to change pop radio. This is someone trying to rescue humanity. How on earth are they supposed to write about that?

About a month ago Peel played a tune by the folk guitarist John Renbourn and dedicated it to a listener named Shirley Anne. Few would have guessed that this is Peel's wife, an American whom he married two years ago when she was just fifteen. Shirley has accompanied him to London, where they live together during his weeks of shore leave. Their marriage already failing, they'll split up within a year and divorce in the early Seventies. Something of a tragic waif and faceless ghost haunting Peel's American prehistory, Shirley is to suffer a wretched life in England, going to prison for drugs and fraud offences and committing suicide in the Eighties. Peel, finding her painful to discuss, will claim he married her because her parents were dead and she didn't want to be sent to live with distant relatives. That may be true. However, her age will prove controversial when the media examines the personal lives of DJs following the Jimmy Savile scandal in 2012.

The disintegration of Peel's marriage in the summer of 1967 goes some way towards explaining why he valued the offshore asylum of the *Galaxy* and the tranquillity of *The Perfumed Garden*. It is small wonder that he yearned to prolong his time with the listeners and talked of moving the garden to somewhere they could all feel safe. It's a fair bet that he needed a sanctuary just as much, if not more, than they did.

'A man who stepped into its social atmosphere felt as if he had stepped into a written comedy,' G. K. Chesterton noted of Saffron Park, the dreamlike suburb where red-haired poets were lured into wondrous conspiracies in *The Man Who Was Thursday*. There was a whiff of Saffron Park in *The Perfumed Garden* ('More especially this attractive unreality fell upon it about nightfall'), and a little of Frances Hodgson Burnett ('And the secret garden bloomed and bloomed and every morning revealed new miracles'). Who knows, maybe even a smidgen of Alan Whicker. This floral phantasm. This anthropomorphic Arcadia.

'It simply can't just disappear,' Peel protests as time begins to run out. Then, with a puff of smoke, the garden is gone. The weather forecast at 5.30 a.m. predicts a cloudy day with occasional showers.

1968: THE LORD'S DAY

'We'd all really forgotten about the bells and beads and Hare Krishna. It was the Psychedelic Left by then.' MICK FARREN

Top Gear
Radio 1
4 February 1968

Jimmy Cliff – The Bee Gees – Tyrannosaurus Rex – The Moody Blues – Captain Beefheart and His Magic Band – H. P. Lovecraft – The Pretty Things – Albert King – Buffalo Springfield – Phil Ochs

The UK's entry into the European Economic Community is inevitable sooner or later, says Foreign Office minister Lord Chalfont. After a first application for EEC membership failed in 1963, a second was submitted last year. Both were vetoed by France.

A sleepy Sunday afternoon in Britain. The working man, exhausted after his labours during the week, enjoys a day of rest. No sport, no trading on the Sabbath, nothing to disturb God or man. Feet up, Sunday roast and back from church. *Family Favourites* on the wireless: Rosemary Clooney and Patti Page. Britain is a Christian country with a great many lessons to teach the world about how to kill time. The BBC's popular-music stations do their best to make it an event-free afternoon.

When *Family Favourites* ends at 2 p.m. and the waltzes and mambos and songs about doggies in windows subside, two stations – Radios 1 and 2 – divide and go their separate ways. Radio 2, the easy-listening successor to the Light Programme, offers *Semprini Serenade*, a selection of popular classical music played on the pianoforte. Over on Radio 1, the choice is different. A lot different.

'EEEEEEEE-LECK-TRISSI-TAAAAYY,' bellows a monstrous voice from some superelastic nether region of the throat, sounding like an indignant Dick Dastardly being shot out of a cannon. This is *Top Gear*, a two-hour review of the British and American underground-rock scenes. 'Electricity' is one of four songs this afternoon from Captain Beefheart and His Magic Band, recorded when they were over from Los Angeles a fortnight ago. *Top Gear*'s presenter John Peel, who is on friendly terms with them, reveals that they were 'incredibly jazzed' to come to England, although 'the trendies didn't receive them quite as warmly as I would have liked'.

Beefheart and his band sound like they've spent the last three years listening to Howlin' Wolf LPs while injecting psilocybin into their eyeballs. They're a blues band, but an outlandish and telepathic one, and they appear to be under the influence of forces undetectable to other humans. The imposingly otherworldly Beefheart, whose real name is Don Van Vliet, claims to write a novel a day and has been known to answer telephones before they've started ringing. It's not clear if he's a visitor from the future or a fugitive from the desert by way of a 1920s Berlin Dada exhibition. Peel has been a fan since his KMEN days and can't understand why everyone else is taking so long to catch up.

With Peel in the studio is Marc Bolan of Tyrannosaurus Rex. They too have four songs in the show: brief, ethereal, witchy incantations performed on acoustic guitar and bongos. Bolan sings like a young sheep and talks like a Beat poet amused by a private joke. Peel asks him about a character called Scenescof who crops up in some of his lyrics. 'Well,' Bolan says, 'he was a prophet cat who was very straight at one time but went through lots of hang-ups, and he just got zapped and became a sort of very bad guy now, and I use him like as just a villain in all the songs, y'know, 'cos he's real mean.' Peel doesn't even attempt to follow that.

Hang-ups are a recurring theme for Bolan. One of his songs is about 'people who are hung up with outward things'. Again Peel says nothing, letting the listeners imagine how serious a hang-up might be if outward things were involved. He introduces a song by the Pretty Things ('Talkin' About the Good Times'), which is saturated in LSD and sounds as though they managed to press the record button with seconds to spare before their sense of space and time evaporated. And he plays 'The White Ship' by H. P. Lovecraft, a baroque psychedelic group from Chicago whose music is almost as chilling as the fiction of the author who inspired it. Is anyone from the BBC listening to this? *Top Gear* is like a rogue hippie detachment planting dosed sugar cubes in enemy territory.

This time last year, the BBC's disdain for pop was seen as a key reason for the pirate ships' continued need to exist. But in September, with the pirates scuppered by government legislation, the BBC reluctantly bowed to the inevitable. It committed itself to a new pop station – Radio 1 – and employed almost the entire Wonderful Radio London workforce to help run it. Peel, Tony Blackburn, Ed Stewart, Keith Skues, Dave Cash, Pete Drummond and Tommy Vance were all handed jobs.

The pirates may be sunk, but they can look back and say they won vital battles. They revolutionised music radio in Britain. They broke up the cartel of record companies – EMI, Decca, Philips – whose tyranny over the Light Programme and Radio Luxembourg made it impossible for new groups to get heard. They lit a fire under the BBC and forced it to rethink its antiquated attitudes towards teenagers. 'The pirates were the biggest boot in the arse the BBC ever had,' former Radio London DJ Kenny Everett was quoted as saying last year. And he should know. He's been snapped up by Radio 1 too.

Five months after making the switch from the MV *Galaxy* to Broadcasting House, though, life hasn't been quite so smooth for Peel. Other ex-Radio London presenters have slipped comfortably into daytime schedules, carrying on as though nothing has happened. But the BBC, like the trendies with Captain Beefheart, is taking longer to make up its mind about Peel.

For one thing, *Top Gear* is not exclusively his show. He's one of five DJs to have co-presented it since October, including Drummond, Vance and Mike Ahern. The short-lived Radio 1 career of Ahern, a Liverpudlian who rose to stardom on the Caroline ships, has already become a cautionary tale, lasting for just one programme (*Top Gear* on 8 October) before the BBC decided it had heard enough. With limited opportunities for a DJ in the UK, Ahern has had to move to Australia to start a new life.

Peel has been luckier than Ahern, but he's yet to find many allies at the BBC. One of them, however, is an important one. Forty-four-year-old Bernie Andrews is *Top Gear*'s producer. *Top Gear*, meaning 'fab groovy', is a pet project of Andrews's and was originally the name of a pop show he produced for the Light Programme in 1964. Andrews is a workaholic, a contrarian and a forward thinker. He wears a shirt and tie, but he smokes dope and takes rock music seriously. Believing Peel to be a diamond in the rough, Andrews has been lobbying energetically on his behalf. The result is that today's *Top Gear* is Peel's 'first solo flight', as he puts it, an experiment by Andrews to see if he can handle the two hours without a co-presenter.

Peel has toned down his style since last summer. The trance-like voice has been dropped. The monologues about sparrows have gone by the wayside. He can still be twee (on politicians: 'We're going to talk to them and tickle them and feed them iced buns until they become considerably less horrid'), but at least he's stopped telling the listeners that he loves them. The word 'beautiful' has been replaced by 'nice', lending *Top Gear* a woozy, amiable, Dylan-in-*The-Magic-Roundabout* feel.

Whereas surviving tapes of *The Perfumed Garden* are a bit like stumbling on recordings of a lost civilisation, Peel on *Top Gear* sounds a lot more like a capable DJ from a world that looks quite similar to our own. His superiors evidently think so too. His lone flight safely completed, he will remain *Top Gear*'s sole presenter for the next seven and a half years.

Night Ride
Radios 1 and 2
7 March 1968

The Misunderstood – The Incredible String Band – Adrian Mitchell – Iron Butterfly – Domenico Scarlatti – Simon & Garfunkel – Fleetwood Mac – unidentified North Vietnamese musicians

Diplomatic relations between Britain and Rhodesia hit a nadir when three men are hanged for murder in Salisbury after being reprieved by the Queen. Britain's Commonwealth secretary calls the executions 'an outrage'.

For the past few months on Radios 1 and 2, long-distance lorry drivers and insomniacs have had a show they could call their own. Starting just after the midnight news on Tuesdays to Fridays, *Night Ride* keeps the conversation mellow and plays jazz from a swinging quintet with a sultry singer. The two hours are a comfort to the lonely when all outside is dark and still.

Now, however, *Night Ride*'s Thursday edition has been turned into an arts programme more suited to intellectuals and customers of radical bookshops. The idea is to combine modern verse with indigenous recordings from around the world and share them with anyone who happens to be still awake. Peel, in an unusual split, presents the first hour of the show before handing over to Radio 2's John Dunn for the second half.

'This is the first in a new series of programmes in which you may hear just about anything,' Peel promises. The old anything-can-happen cliché – how many presenters have used it over the years? But the breadth of music in Peel's *Night Ride* justifies the blurb, from a south Indian raga to a Scarlatti sonata to a North Vietnamese zither piece that he found in the BBC Sound Archive. There are some blues and rock records as well, but they seem to be the least important elements in the mix. On first listen, *Night Ride* is going far beyond any notional parameters of what *Top Gear* is trying to achieve.

Even the identity of the featured band is significant. The Incredible String Band are Scottish, but they could just as easily be nomads pitching their tents in Nepal, Morocco or the Gobi. They point their faces to the east and see a horizon without borders. A sitar isn't just an exotic instrument in their hands, it's a magic carpet that can transport them to a far corner of the globe. Future editions of Peel's *Night Ride* will include more ethnic sounds – what will later be termed 'world music' – from Azerbaijan, Ceylon and the Khyber Pass. Peel in the Sound Archive: kids and candy stores come to mind.

But *Night Ride*, or at least his hour of it, is fated to be contentious. Adrian Mitchell, a poet and campaigner for nuclear disarmament, has come to the studio to read from his new book. His first poem has an allusion to a vagina ('you've got a mouth that's whispering between your thighs') and a stanza that mentions President Lyndon B. Johnson and Adolf Hitler in consecutive lines. For Radios 1 and 2 in 1968, this is provocative stuff.

Mitchell and Peel have a discussion. Mitchell sounds like a man trying to hold his anger in. He talks about an action group that splatters buildings with red paint as a symbol of the blood being spilt in Vietnam. Peel murmurs noncommittally. He attended an anti-war rally himself in March, and on a recent *Top Gear* was heard to say that 'in some countries there's a great possibility there will be no children for the next generation'. It's been obvious to anyone listening to him since last summer where his sympathies (and politics) lie.

But not everyone has been listening to him since last summer.

Peel will write in his column for the underground newspaper *International Times* that *Night Ride* received 'a flood of angry and bewildered letters' following this edition, most of them enraged by the interview with Mitchell. Some correspondents took exception to Peel specifically. 'Many of these were of the "I-fought-the-war-for-the-likes-of-you" variety and I was variously described as "effeminate", "ignorant", "gushing" and "Communist".'

Night Ride is off to a memorable start.

Top Gear
Radio 1
30 June 1968

Fairport Convention – Eclection – Savoy Brown Blues Band – Buffy Sainte-Marie – Deep Purple – Fleetwood Mac – Traffic – Cream – Tim Rose – David Bowie – The Beach Boys – The Nice – Pink Floyd

Enoch Powell, the controversial MP who made the 'rivers of blood' speech about immigration in April, compares the Labour government to the Nazis. He accuses them of 'lawless bullying' for pledging to investigate a large pay rise awarded to the chairman of Hambros Bank.

Peel went to a free concert in Hyde Park yesterday. Thousands of people sat on the grass and listened to Tyrannosaurus Rex, Roy Harper and Jethro Tull. A peaceful atmosphere held sway and nobody got hung up on outward things. The headliners were Pink Floyd, who face uncertain times after ousting Syd Barrett, their troubled leader, in March. When they took to the stage yesterday evening, Peel had a sudden idea. He hired a boat, rowed it out to the middle of the Serpentine, lay down and listened.

'They finished their set with "A Saucerful of Secrets",' he says, referring to the long title track of their new album, 'which at the time sounded like a sort of hymn to the open air . . . I don't know what it was. It must have been the people there, the feelings that everyone was generating, because they played superbly.'

Peel must surely have approved of the whole bill. It had the look of an outdoor version of *Top Gear*. He may not have been the first DJ to play Pink Floyd – recordings of *The Perfumed Garden* don't confirm it – but he was definitely the first to play Tyrannosaurus Rex, and later this summer he'll be the first to play Jethro Tull. And we can be fairly sure that right now he's the only one playing Roy Harper.

Top Gear is unchallenged on British radio as the number-one ally and spiritual home of underground rock. And as underground rock begins to creep overground, yesterday's events suggest that people will come in their thousands to listen. Peel hopes more Hyde Park concerts will be organised. They have to be free, though. No commercial interests must be allowed to desecrate the open-air hymns.

David Bowie, a singer from Bromley, has been given the chance to sing a few songs on today's show. A Hyde Park rock festival would be the wrong venue for this young man's curious hybrid of mysticism and music hall. Next to Deep Purple and Cream, his chirpy orchestrations sound as old hat as George Formby's ukulele. But he's good at wordplay and writing melodies, and Peel sees a spark of potential in him, much as Bernie Andrews sees a spark of potential in Peel.

Tyrannosaurus Rex have completed work on their first album. It's coming out next week with a stunning title, *My People Were Fair and Had Sky in Their Hair . . . But Now They're Content to Wear Stars on Their Brows*. Three weeks ago they topped the bill at the Royal Festival Hall, a prestige night for Marc Bolan. He sat cross-legged on a rug, strumming his guitar and baa-ing away in his peculiar lamb-like voice, while his stoned-looking bandmate tapped away at a pair of bongos. Peel came out and read a couple of stories in the intermission.

Bottom of the bill was David Bowie from Bromley, performing a mime inspired by China's invasion of Tibet.

Top Gear
Radio 1
11 August 1968

Pink Floyd – The Doors – Leonard Cohen – Traffic – John Dummer Blues Band – Earth Opera – Tyrannosaurus Rex – Buffy Sainte-Marie – Cream – Duster Bennett – Jerry Lee Lewis – MC5

Britain's last steam-powered passenger train, the 1T57 'Fifteen Guinea Special', runs from Liverpool to Carlisle and back. A British Railways ban on steam trains comes into effect tomorrow.

Since its launch last September, Radio 1 has had to abide by strict regulations laid down by the Musicians' Union forbidding it from exceeding a pre-agreed number of records (singles and albums) per day. Needle time, as it's known, is an ongoing headache for producers with seven days of schedules to fill. What's a groovy pop radio station to do?

One solution is to stockpile music in advance. What this means for *Top Gear* is that the likes of Donovan, Traffic, the Moody Blues and Fairport Convention – and many more – are commissioned to go into a BBC studio and record songs in batches of four or five, which Peel plays on the air a week later. These are called sessions.

One benefit of sessions is that they often feature songs that are unavailable on record. This suits the bands, who get a chance to road-test their new material at the BBC's expense, and it also suits Peel and Andrews, who get to play exclusive music that can't be bought in the shops.

Today's session from Pink Floyd is so spontaneous that a couple of songs don't have finalised titles. One of them, which fluctuates between 'The Murderotic Woman' and 'Careful with That Axe, Eugene', will be re-recorded as a B-side in the autumn, hitting the streets some four months after *Top Gear*'s listeners first heard it. Floyd's next session, in December, will include a song – 'The Embryo' – that won't be released in an official capacity until 1970. And so on.

Thanks to Radio 1's needle-time quandary, a music-radio institution – the Peel session – has been born. And any artist who is in the country can participate. Seen in the UK recently was Leonard Cohen, a Canadian poet-turned-singer whose album of dark infatuations, *Songs of Leonard Cohen*, has been an improbable sensation since emerging earlier in the year. Peel in particular is a huge fan. Cohen recorded a session for the show while he was in London.

In keeping with what is becoming *Top Gear* protocol, Cohen sang two songs – 'Bird on the Wire' and 'You Know Who I Am' – that are destined for his next album, *Songs from a Room*, which he hasn't started making yet. Another – 'Dress Rehearsal Rag' – will be on the one after that, *Songs of Love and Hate*, which won't be available for the general public to buy for another three years. With a *Top Gear* session, you really do hear the future before anyone else.

Top Gear
Radio 1
27 October 1968

Family – Taste – The Pretty Things – David Ackles – Jeff Beck –
Brian Auger Trinity – Steve Miller Band – Muddy Waters – Jefferson
Airplane – The Scaffold – Richie Havens – Steppenwolf – Duster
Bennett – Savoy Brown – Blossom Toes

Around a thousand students have seized control of the London School
of Economics ahead of today's anti-Vietnam War rally. With the
students promising an extended sit-in, seminars are held on 'Bourgeois
Culture' and 'The Sociology of Revolution'.

Asked in 1995 to explain what caused him to write 'Street Fighting
Man' in 1968, Mick Jagger will comment that although he attended
the March '68 anti-Vietnam rally that turned violent outside the
American embassy in Grosvenor Square, he generally felt London
to be a much less febrile centre of protest than Paris. However, the
estimated 30,000 people mobilising themselves for this afternoon's
march from Charing Cross to Hyde Park may have a different perspective. Serious violence is anticipated. Tariq Ali, one of the organisers, has been fielding questions from journalists about whether he
thinks the state can be overthrown.

Ever since returning to England, Peel has been signalling his support – both implicitly and explicitly – for the peace movement and
the alternative society as a presenter of *The Perfumed Garden*, *Top
Gear* and *Night Ride*, and as a columnist for *International Times*. He
stuck up for Jagger and Richards when they were imprisoned for
drugs. He kept *The Perfumed Garden*'s listeners informed of rallies
for the legalisation of cannabis. He denounced heavy-handed police
tactics in a raid on London's Middle Earth club. He aligned himself

with students staging sit-ins at Manchester, Exeter and other universities. And he went on the March '68 rally.

Today's *Top Gear* has been pre-recorded. There are concerns that violence on the march's route may spill over and lead to central London being closed, including roads to Broadcasting House. Peel is in a funny mood as the show starts, sarcastically congratulating the Great Britain team for winning more medals than South Korea at the Mexico Olympics, which end today. Unimpressed by jingoism, Peel has been voicing anti-Olympics sentiments for the last fortnight. 'Countries like Mexico could do much more useful things with the money,' he says, 'like stopping people from starving to death.' A nice little grenade to throw into the proceedings.

Peel doesn't tell us whether he's planning to go on today's demo himself. He may have been warned not to talk about it. Recording his links before a single marcher has left Charing Cross, he worries that people 'may be getting hurt or damaged' by now. He has no way of knowing whether *Top Gear* will harmonise with events on the ground or clash horribly.

The Steve Miller Band sing ambivalently of their homeland ('Living in the USA'), muttering hippie homilies about politicians and freedom. Jefferson Airplane's 'Crown of Creation', from their new album of the same name, sounds much more like a song in sync with today's protest ('They cannot tolerate our minds ... We cannot tolerate their obstruction'). But then the Airplane always did sound like they could find their way to the barricades without difficulty.

The show is notable for its real-time news updates. 'About 500 to 1,000 people have marched through [Grosvenor] Square shouting various slogans,' reports a BBC newsreader. 'A few minutes ago thousands of supporters of a breakaway group, the Britain–Vietnam Solidarity Front, arrived at the Square to be met by a line of police on foot ...' As yet there has been no violence, but there will be. Stones and fireworks will be thrown at police as Maoist protesters attempt to storm the embassy. Some 6,000 people will be involved in three hours of clashes.

Before the last song in the programme – 'Peace Loving Man' by the psychedelic band Blossom Toes – Peel makes a short speech. 'The whole point of these [marches] is . . . completely destroyed as soon as somebody hits somebody else. Because that way you're joining their side and playing their games, which is very bad and very dangerous.' Let's hope he's not in Grosvenor Square.

Blossom Toes, given the task of encapsulating the feelings of Peel and the unpredictable nature of the day, take the pacifist line where Jagger, months ago, hungered for militancy. Blossom Toes will not be joining in the violence. Even when 'things ain't right', they emphasise, they 'don't wanna fight'. They'd rather 'go and sit in the rain'. Long live the paisley-umbrella revolution.

But 'Peace Loving Man' is not some passive hippy-dippy day-dream. A dramatically heavy rock song, it includes a war chant and an apocalyptic crescendo. At the end of this, a long scream is fol-lowed by a disembodied voice intoning a staccato message: 'Do you . . . ever have the feeling . . . that there is nothing you can do . . . to save the world . . . we do . . . we do.'

It might be preaching a policy of stoned inertia, but 'Peace Loving Man' sounds purposely designed to freak with people's heads and leave them dumbfounded. One wonders just how closely Peel lis-tened to it before choosing it, and what kind of lesson he wants his listeners to take from it. It's a powerful way to end a unique *Top Gear*.

'Be very, very careful this week,' Peel counsels. 'Be gentle with one another.' The peace-loving man hands over to Alan Freeman for *Pick of the Pops*.

Night Ride
Radios 1 and 2
12 December 1968

John Lennon and Yoko Ono – John Martyn and Harold McNair – The Deviants – Jacqui McShee and John Renbourn – Christopher Logue – Lonnie Donegan – Spike Jones and his City Slickers

Northern Ireland's prime minister sacks his minister for home affairs, William Craig, accusing him of planning a Rhodesian-style unilateral declaration of independence. Craig warns of 'greatly disturbed times ahead' for Northern Ireland, which has seen civil rights marches and fierce rioting.

In a terrific coup for *Night Ride*, Peel's studio guests tonight are one of the world's most famous couples. He's a musician and songwriter at the top of his profession. She's an artist and filmmaker on the verge of an international breakthrough. Together they are John Lennon and Yoko Ono.

But it has all the hallmarks of a very tough interview for Peel. A fortnight ago Lennon pleaded guilty to cannabis possession – the first Beatle drug bust. Early last month he divorced Cynthia, his wife of six years – the first Beatle annulment. Yoko, his Japanese girlfriend, has been demonised in the newspapers, well on her way to becoming a true hate figure for the times. Three weeks ago, under severe stress, she miscarried Lennon's baby. Yesterday the two of them spent the evening at the Rolling Stones' 'Rock and Roll Circus' in Wembley, performing in a big top alongside acrobats, tigers and fire eaters. It was a rare day of sanity in the lives of John and Yoko.

As they arrive at the BBC tonight, Lennon has the professional satisfaction – if such things still mean anything to him – of seeing the Beatles' new double album sitting at the top of the charts. But more provocatively, recent days have seen the release of *Unfinished Music No. 1: Two Virgins*, a record credited to Lennon and Ono. Slammed by music critics as an unlistenable farrago of avant-garde rubbish, it's more striking for its cover, which shows John and Yoko standing with their arms round each other, looking bravely united, marginally solemn and jaw-droppingly naked. If it were possible for them to become more notorious than they already were, they've managed it with one photo.

Peel has always been nervous around pop stars. He bears the scars of a 1966 encounter with the Byrds in San Bernardino, when, compèring one of their gigs, he approached them for a friendly chat and was superciliously rebuffed. Humiliations from favourite musicians stay with a sensitive man like Peel. He still plays the Byrds on *Top Gear*, but he'll never forgive them for that moment of rock-star hauteur. And tonight he's up against a far more caustic opponent than any Byrd.

'Our LP *Two Virgins* . . . is actually out in some hidden, underground-type, open-air shops at this moment, folks,' Lennon hucksters. 'And if they haven't got it, excuse me! Hound them!'

Peel tentatively feeds him a gimme. 'And it's been selling in unprecedented quantities?'

Lennon holes it. 'Seven hundred yesterday.'

Yoko is heard helium-sighing behind him as he adds: 'Seven hundred obscene people.'

Peel tells him he'll be playing an extract from it later.

Lennon: 'I'll be charmed if you did, John.'

Peel (laughing): 'Would you? You'd be charmed at that?'

Few DJs on British radio in 1968 credit Yoko with being an artist of any merit, let alone make the effort to address her respectfully. Peel does both without making a big deal of either. He plays a demo of a song she's brought in, 'John, My Love', which turns out to be rather sweet when you can hear her singing above the tape hiss. She makes gnomic interruptions as *Night Ride* trots along. 'If the butterflies in your stomach die,' she chirrups, 'send yellow death announcements to your friends.' Even when she's silent, she's like a presence or a perfume in the air.

Peel is holding his own with Lennon. He isn't trying to probe the Beatle about activism or politics, a national talking point since the release of 'Revolution' in August. Instead he engages Lennon's humorous side – his Liverpool side – resulting in some entertainingly agile banter. The two Merseysiders are beginning to sound relaxed in each other's company, which one of them almost certainly isn't.

Peel: 'Incidentally, the John we were talking to just now was John Lennon. We were asked to clear that up because people were phoning.'

Lennon: 'At the mouth.'

The Peel–Lennon–Ono conversational triangle is put on hold while we hear music from John Martyn and Harold McNair (a young folk singer with flautist accompaniment), the Deviants (a group of White Panthers from the Ladbroke Grove squat scene), Jacqui McShee and John Renbourn (two fifths of Pentangle) and Lonnie Donegan, whose 'Wabash Cannonball' has been plucked by Peel from a reissued 1956 LP, *The Lonnie Donegan Showcase*. That was the year that a Liverpudlian teenager named John Lennon formed a skiffle group called the Quarrymen.

'That brought back tender memories,' Lennon says after Donegan's song. 'My first Lonnie guaranteed-not-to-split guitar, which smashed in half.'

Peel plays an excerpt, as promised, from *Two Virgins*. Yoko, queerly pre-war in ambience, is heard making long shrill cries. It's *musique concrète* – and to prove it, she sounds like she's singing down a length of cement pipe. She goes for broke, giving it the full artistic psychosis, squawking hellishly to some random piano that might have been played by Lennon with his arse.

'You feel that it's unlikely that *Two Virgins* is going to get very many airplays,' Peel suggests.

Lennon: 'Yes, I can't see it being a pop favourite, like.'

Squeamish retailers are already selling it in brown paper bags. As *Night Ride* takes up the theme of censorship, Peel brings in Christopher Logue, a poet who was banned from reading a poem entitled 'He Was Very Good Looking' on national television. He reads it now, taking deep breaths. It's an intense ballad to an unnamed boy, ending with the lovers kissing 'and other things not to be mentioned on a show like this'.

Peel, sounding more spooked by Logue than he is by Yoko, says he cannot comprehend why anyone would object to such beautiful words. Finally, the four of them – Lennon, Ono, Logue and Peel – conjoin in a poem of their own, reciting the lines like a game of Consequences.

Lennon: 'Thinking is weightless.'

Ono: 'Use words only for words / things only for things.'

Logue: 'Wring your hands.'

Peel: 'The revolution is over / we are all free men.'

Next week John and Yoko are at the Albert Hall, sitting in a white sack for peace.

1969: THE HORROR COMICS

'Better not laugh too much if we want to get this on the radio.
They're likely to get us for breathing with all our holes open.'
CAPTAIN BEEFHEART

Top Gear
Radio 1
5 January 1969

The Doors – Caravan – Ten Years After – The Amboy Dukes –
Tyrannosaurus Rex – MC5 – Captain Beefheart and His Magic Band
– Blues Project – Junior's Eyes – Sam Gopal – Soft Machine

Northern Ireland's prime minister, Terence O'Neill, warns that his
government may have to call in reinforcements for the Royal Ulster
Constabulary. Yesterday the city of Londonderry exploded into violence
after a civil rights march by a radical Republican group was ambushed
by Loyalists.

On Sunday afternoons BBC1 shows a documentary and a matinee.
Today *Top Gear* is competing with *The End of the Road* – a 1957
film starring Finlay Currie as a factory worker struggling to cope
with retirement – and *The Lost Peace,* a history series about the
interwar years. This is the sensible side of the British Broadcasting
Corporation. The civilised side. The side that doesn't foment social

dissent by promoting Detroit rock bands telling people to kick out the jams, motherfuckers.

Compared to stiff-collared BBC television, *Top Gear* is the mad hippie in the attic. Wild, bearded, unkempt, drooling. But just occasionally, the mad hippie and the stiff collars overlap. Every Friday teatime between July and December last year, a youth discussion show on BBC1 called *How It Is* liked to take a breather from the social-inequality debates and pause for some music by Fairport Convention, the Moody Blues or Tyrannosaurus Rex. Two of those bands might plausibly have been the choice of Tony Palmer, the programme's producer. But only one man in Britain would have made a point of getting Tyrannosaurus Rex onto national television. Sure enough, one of the co-presenters of *How It Is* was John Peel.

Even before he hired Peel, Palmer had horned in on *Top Gear*'s turf by filming Cream, Pink Floyd, Donovan and Frank Zappa for a TV documentary about rock music, 'All My Loving', screened last November – after months of delays – as part of BBC1's *Omnibus* series. Jump-cutting between close-up concert footage and violent images of war, 'All My Loving' floated the proposition that rock was bringing about 'the most startling artistic upheaval since the Renaissance'. The words might very well have been spoken by Peel in a rapt moment on *The Perfumed Garden*.

'All My Loving' and *How It Is* had something else in common: they were both detested at the highest levels of the BBC. David Attenborough, the controller of BBC2, was so appalled by 'All My Loving' that he vowed to Palmer that it would be broadcast over his dead body. As for *How It Is*, Palmer recalled: '[The BBC] wanted to take it off after programme one because it was full of long-haired ruffians [like] Richard Neville [of *Oz* magazine] and John Peel.'

The Peel problem had risen to the surface. A year into his BBC career, the hirsute disc jockey had become a double threat to the Corporation's decency, equally offensive in sound and in vision. To the senior executives, *Top Gear* was a compost heap of abominable drug addicts, *How It Is* was even worse, and the sight of the scruffy hooligan at Broadcasting House was putting people off their soup in the canteen. All that effort to win the war and look what the cat dragged in.

There's a scene in the film *That'll Be the Day* – that homage to the early stirrings of British rock – where the petulant singer Stormy Tempest (played by Billy Fury) has a contretemps with his cocky drummer J. D. Clover (Keith Moon). Tempest loathes Clover and is looking for any excuse to sack him. 'But you can't, can you, Stormy?' Clover grins, answering his own question with a fusillade of dazzling virtuosity on his drums. Tempest has to face the fact that some people are indispensable.

For Peel, the J. D. Clover moment arrived with the results of *Melody Maker*'s 1968 poll, which saw him voted best DJ – and *Top Gear* best radio programme – by the readers of Britain's best-selling music paper. It was a major surprise to all at Radio 1 and an irrefutable endorsement of the beleaguered Peel. Founded in 1926, only four years after the BBC, *Melody Maker* had industry-wide credibility. The paper and its readers may very well have saved Peel's career.

Melody Maker assessed his win as 'a victory for all those who believe that pop music is something more than pleasant background music'. He was applauded for his 'uncompromising belief' that the 'more experimental' forms of music deserved a fair hearing. Noting that he had a 'dedicated following', the paper added: 'Probably more letters to *Melody Maker* mention Peel than any other artist or DJ.'

And that, if true, was astonishing. It was one thing to knock Radio 1's golden boy Tony Blackburn into second place in a DJ poll. It was another to dominate the correspondence in a year when the Beatles launched Apple and Bob Dylan returned from retirement. No wonder John and Yoko were so nice to him on *Night Ride*.

Top Gear
Radio 1
16 February 1969

Strawbs – Moby Grape – Bakerloo – Caravan – The Misunderstood – Locomotive – B. B. King – Judy Collins – Tyrannosaurus Rex – Procol Harum – Chicken Shack – Three Dog Night – East of Eden

A strike by 46,000 Ford car workers will begin next week, say union leaders. The proposed action comes at a bad time for Ford, which has taken £16 million worth of orders for the new Capri.

Sinister castles are the link between February's two biggest box-office hits. In *Where Eagles Dare*, the castle is a Nazi stronghold in the Alps. In *Chitty Chitty Bang Bang*, it's the home of a merciless baron and his child-hating wife. For cinemagoers who prefer damp fields and nanoseconds of nudity, the seventeenth film in the *Carry On* series, *Carry On Camping*, is due to hit local fleapits shortly. Alternatively, *Oliver!* and *Funny Girl* are still on general release months after their premieres and *Zorba the Greek* has re-entered the West End, five years after its first screening.

In the world of pop, the picture is just as stagnant. This week's chart-topping single, '(If Paradise Is) Half as Nice' by Amen Corner, is a dewy-eyed piece of schmaltz sung in an effete falsetto that soon gets on the nerves. The prolific Motown label has seven hits in the Top 40, but some are anodyne and one of them, Martha and the Vandellas' 'Dancing in the Street', is as old as *Zorba the Greek*. Aside from Cream's 'White Room', there's no rock in the Top 30. The psychedelic era is dead and the bubblegum years are upon us.

All of which makes *Top Gear* an essential listen for anyone wanting to dig deeper. *Top Gear* is where you'll hear what rock is doing this week, and what it might be doing next year. The new sound

[65]

comes from Canterbury, where the Soft Machine and Caravan are blending rock with jazz – not to show off their techniques but to come up with sophisticated chords that can turn pop songs into something much more elastic. Something better than bubblegum. The Soft Machine have toured America with Jimi Hendrix, who thinks they're out-of-sight cats. Their drummer and vocalist, Robert Wyatt, can sing Charlie Parker solos note perfect from memory. He and Peel will become good friends.

With jazz rock the prevailing trend on *Top Gear*, every second band is augmenting their line-up with a horn section. Locomotive, a Birmingham outfit, seem to mushroom in personnel the longer their song lasts. They start as a trio and end as a football team. Locomotive will never make the grade (no matter how many horn players they add), but they'll always be able to say that Peel was a fan. Whoever else might have rejected them, they had a cordial welcome on *Top Gear*. As Robert Wyatt will sing later this year in a Soft Machine song recorded especially for the show: 'To all our mates like Kevin [Ayers], Caravan and the old Pink Floyd / Allow me to recommend *Top Gear* despite its extraordinary name.'

Bakerloo, awarded the prize of a four-song session, wallow in their luxurious quarter of an hour. A blues trio led by the future Humble Pie guitarist Clem Clempson, they'll split before the year is out – leaving room for more blues bands. Blues bands are second only to jazz-rock bands on *Top Gear* this season. Blues bands hold Peel in such high esteem that one of them, Chicken Shack, have done an impersonation of him on their latest album, *O.K. Ken?* Should he be flattered? Irritated? Having told *Melody Maker* after his poll-winning exploits that he hoped his popularity wouldn't detract from the music, his choice of a B. B. King tune today – 'It's My Own Fault' – seems to have a ruefully appropriate title.

Now in great demand, Peel is currently touring the country as Tyrannosaurus Rex's support act. Bolan has written a new single,

'Pewter Suitor', a frantic piece that won't be threatening the Motown songs in the charts any time soon. Last night Tyrannosaurus Rex were at Birmingham Town Hall, where Bolan sang cross-legged on his rug and his zonked-looking bandmate tapped away at his bongos. Peel, listed as the evening's 'catalyst', narrated two stories ('which bored people rigid') and then watched from the balcony, where fans had painted stars on their brows just like the album title. Bottom of the bill was David Bowie, once again performing his mime inspired by China's invasion of Tibet.

Top Gear
Radio 1
27 April 1969

The Byrds – Canned Heat – The Bonzo Dog Doo-Dah Band – Bob Dylan – Pentangle – Creedence Clearwater Revival – Leonard Cohen – Principal Edwards Magic Theatre – The Moody Blues

Following bitter in-fighting among Ulster Unionists, Prime Minister O'Neill is expected to stand down this week. His rival, Brian Faulkner, who resigned from the Cabinet in January, is tipped to succeed him. (Faulkner will lose out to former agriculture minister James Chichester-Clark, to whom O'Neill gives his casting vote.)

'Good evening . . . he said with mounting enthusiasm.'

The reason for Peel's barbed introduction is that *Top Gear*, after eighteen months as a fixture of Sunday afternoons, has been demoted to a 7 p.m. slot. Bernie Andrews, his producer and staunch defender, has been transferred to other duties and a new man, a jazz aficionado from Derbyshire named John Walters, has been appointed with the apparent aim of reining Peel in. The changes are already making life inconvenient. This evening's programme has been pre-recorded so that Peel can go to a Pink Floyd gig. It's interesting to see where he feels his priorities lie.

In the album chart published earlier today, Leonard Cohen's new LP *Songs from a Room* has shot in from nowhere at number 3. 'Not bad for something that's dismissed by some people as purely minority music,' notes Peel. But he isn't just chuffed because it's one in the eye for the BBC's Cohen-haters. Peel actually likes the charts. For all his fondness for underdogs, he sees commercial success as nothing to be afraid of. Million-selling bands are just as eligible for *Top Gear* as cult folkies with minuscule fanbases, providing they sold a million because their music was good. Peel often asks the listeners to buy such-and-such a record to make it a hit, so that an American band might be encouraged to come over and tour, or so that a British band might enjoy some long-awaited success.

Of course, once they're in the charts, it's rare for *Top Gear* to receive any credit. 'You may have read a lot in the music papers lately about Creedence Clearwater Revival,' Peel says before playing 'Proud Mary', their single. 'They were apparently discovered a couple of months ago by Jonathan King,' he goes on, 'which will come as a surprise to regular listeners to this programme who heard them over a year ago.' Sometimes *Top Gear* is so far ahead of the curve that it's disappeared out of view.

Peel, in fact, has already found and begun promoting the four singers who will become Britain's pop superstars of the coming decade. One of them is David Bowie, now a veteran of two *Top Gear* sessions. Another is a little-known pianist, Elton John, who recorded a session for *Night Ride* last November. The third is Rod Stewart, the singer with the Jeff Beck Group, whose Bourbon-and-sandpaper voice is heard on *Top Gear* most weeks. And the fourth, of course, is Marc Bolan, so inextricably linked with *Top Gear* that some people suspect Peel of being on Tyrannosaurus Rex's payroll.

In all four cases, the talent is so callow that confident predictions cannot be made just yet. Peel just happens to like them all very much. Neither Bolan nor Elton nor Rod, in any case, will break into the big time this year. Confounding all expectations, it's the mime artist from Bromley who, by the summer, will be the dark horse to watch.

If the public needs more time to get accustomed to Bolan and Elton, one wonders what on earth it would make of Principal Edwards Magic Theatre. A self-styled arts collective from Exeter University, they have an expanding line-up that can accommodate up to fourteen members. Their session begins with an ecological elegy sung to an out-of-tune string quartet. Their second number is like a mediaeval minstrel song about a flaxen-haired damsel waiting for her intrepid knight. Their third is a Shakespeare sonnet ('My flocks feed not, my ewes breed not . . .'), which, after a prim start, metamorphoses into a derivative blues with a terrible guitar solo. Their fourth is dedicated to a hamster.

A few of Principal Edwards Magic Theatre's critics have gone so far as to call them unbearable. Peel loves them and has given them money to buy a van.

Son of Night Ride
Radio 1
7 May 1969

Leonard Cohen – Ivor Cutler – The Who – Peter Cook and Dudley Moore – Bob Cobbing – François Dufrêne – Mikis Theodorakis and Maria Farantouri – Louis Armstrong and His Hot Five

The Kray twins, sentenced to life imprisonment in March after a high-profile murder trial, are back in court. Ronnie, Reggie and elder

brother Charlie are accused of plotting the escape from Dartmoor of Frank 'Mad Axeman' Mitchell in December 1966.

A fearless adventure into alternative radio, Peel's *Night Ride* has gained a modest but loyal listenership and brought music from all over the world into homes and lorries across Britain. The show has now been moved from its after-midnight slot and dropped into an 8.15 p.m. gap between a folk programme and a jazz one. As it can no longer be called *Night Ride*, it's listed in some publications as *The World of Sound and Words*. The *Radio Times* doesn't give it a name at all. Peel calls it *Son of Night Ride*.

Son of Night Ride remains an altruistic experiment in encouraging the unencouraged. In the studio tonight is a grim-sounding Scot who sings comical songs with an air of puritanical gravity. His name is Ivor Cutler. A familiar voice on the BBC Home Service in years gone by, he had a cameo as a bus conductor in the Beatles' *Magical Mystery Tour* eighteen months ago. He accompanies himself tonight on a wheezing pump organ.

Cutler is a shambolic guest (he talks off-microphone and knocks something over) but his manner is headmasterly in its rectitude. With glacial precision he informs Peel: 'This song was inspired by Princess Berenice, a princess with a six-inch gold chain between her ankles who is to be found in Gustave Flaubert's *Salammbô*.'

The song, 'Bounce, Bounce, Bounce', is about watching a woman create a stir by the way her breasts rise and fall as she walks along the street. This is no small accomplishment, as it soon becomes clear that her movements are seriously impeded lower down: 'My woman is wearing her foot cuffs / She keeps her feet together that way.'

Peel chuckles in appreciation. It's love at first sight.

Son of Night Ride
Radio 1
28 May 1969

Jeff Beck Group – John Fahey – Pete Roche – Colosseum – Radio
Ceylon Orchestra – Krzysztof Penderecki – Phil Ochs – Shirley and
Dolly Collins – Terry Riley – unidentified Indian musicians

*Details emerge of proposed changes to the BBC's radio output. They
include a reduction in drama commissions, the disbandment of several
regional orchestras and the introduction of twenty local stations around
the country.*

This week the BBC isn't just broadcasting the news. It *is* the news.

As BBC1 prepares to follow BBC2 in going full colour, the Mansell
Report on the future of BBC radio prescribes swingeing cuts and
sweeping reforms. Radio 1 will become an all-day pop station, no
longer obliged to share jazz and light music with Radio 2. Radio 4
is to be given over to speech and magazine programmes. The moves
are not popular. Drama lovers and opera buffs feel the chill wind of
retrenchment. The Master of the Queen's Music, Sir Arthur Bliss,
who abhors pop, condemns the Corporation for throwing open its
airwaves to 'aural hashish'.

'Radio has three major functions: to inform, to entertain and to
disseminate the arts,' a listener in Essex writes to the letters page of
the *Guardian*. He could be – although he probably isn't – describing *Son of Night Ride*, which over the last ten months has informed,
entertained and disseminated the work of Louis Armstrong, Joan
Baez, Messiaen, Finnish waltz composers, a Slovakian dance troupe,
Peter Cook and Dudley Moore ('The Leaping Nuns of the Order
of St Beryl') and numerous poets. But informing, entertaining and
disseminating are not the things that tonight's edition of *Son of*

Night Ride will become famous for. Or should that be infamous.

Peel breaks the ice with some pugnacious blues rock from Jeff Beck, before running the gamut from the Sussex-based folk sisters Shirley and Dolly Collins to a Penderecki oratorio written in memory of Auschwitz victims. Pete Roche, a doleful-sounding poet on the fringes of the Liverpool scene, reads three pieces. On his loveless affairs with women: 'I give them nothing / Even my seed is collected in rubber bags.' Peel also plays a Romanian dance tune and a short burst of electronic minimalism from Terry Riley. It's a wide-ranging, open-minded hour of radio.

Two people are interviewed. One is the leader of a London drama workshop. The other is Tony Van Den Bergh, an author and broadcaster. Van Den Bergh has been looking into the subject of venereal disease, a source of considerable social stigma in Sixties Britain. His report into his findings goes out on Radio 4 next Tuesday, and Peel lets him plug it. Then comes the fateful moment.

Van Den Bergh tells Peel that real progress has been made in educating people about VD since he was a teenager in the Thirties.

'Yes, well, whilst we're being sort of frankly honest,' Peel interrupts, 'I contracted it myself at the beginning of this year, for the first time.'

Van Den Bergh asks him how it felt to undergo treatment.

'Well, I'll be quite honest with you, it was sort of . . . I wasn't embarrassed. I was really – it sounds awful – I was really quite amused.'

Peel paints a scene of quintessential English farce as the VD outpatients of Guy's Hospital stride briskly across the courtyard with businesslike manners as if they're there on innocent pretexts. Van Den Bergh can imagine it. Plugging the documentary once more, Peel wraps up the conversation with some jazz rock by Colosseum and moves on. He has just signed *Son of Night Ride*'s death warrant.

Earlier today, unbeknown to Peel, a speech was made by the

Bishop of Lichfield at a diocesan conference in Stoke-on-Trent. Calling for a 'firm stand against the permissive society', the bishop slammed the proliferation of X-rated films in cinemas, criticised the growing numbers of abortion clinics and claimed, in an unusual phrase, that sex before marriage took 'the gilt off the gingerbread'. 'For the sake of the well-being of the whole community,' the sixty-one-year-old concluded, 'we must try to reverse trends.'

Tomorrow the newspapers will give prominence to the bishop's views. They'll also report that Mick Jagger, the personification of the permissive society with every pout of his insolent lips, has been arrested for cannabis possession. It will turn out to have been a bad twenty-four hours for the kind of people that *Son of Night Ride* cares about. Tariq Ali, spokesman of the New Left, has been expelled from France. Radio stations in Australia have banned the Beatles' 'Ballad of John and Yoko' for blasphemy. And the BBC, in a shock development, is revealed to employ a DJ who openly jokes about having venereal disease on the radio.

For a few days, the story has traction and Peel finds himself under a pincer attack from bishops and clean-up-Britain campaigners. Mary Whitehouse of the Middle England pressure group the National Viewers' and Listeners' Association – the organisation that successfully lobbied BBC1 to get rid of *How It Is* – demands that Peel should be disciplined or fired. He survives, but he looks startlingly vulnerable against these implacable foes. These are not people who can be defeated with MC5 records. They don't respond to wit or irony. His card has been marked.

Reeling from the VD controversy, *Son of Night Ride* will be granted a quiet death in September and play no further part in the Mansell Report's brave new BBC. There'll be no more airtime for mournful poets. No more Penderecki and Pete and Dud. No more disseminating the arts.

Top Gear
Radio 1
6 July 1969

Fairport Convention – Third Ear Band – Crosby, Stills and Nash –
Imrat Khan and Mahapurush Mishra – David Bowie – Steamhammer
– The Mothers of Invention – Johnny Winter

*Hundreds of British holidaymakers are given polio vaccines at
Heathrow and Gatwick as a deadly outbreak hits the Costa Brava.
Five children have died. At Manchester, where no vaccine is available,
several families cancel their holidays.*

For thirty-five minutes every Sunday evening, *Top Gear* goes head
to head with *Songs of Praise*. If Peel really wants to take on the bishops, all he has to do is show up for work. Beamed into millions
of homes from Bude to Blyth, from Devizes to Arbroath, *Songs of
Praise* comes this week from a chapel on the outskirts of Swansea,
where hallelujahs are sung to the new Prince of Wales, invested at
Caernarfon Castle last Tuesday.

Top Gear has nothing to offer the prince. It has Fairport Convention larking about on a Dylan song that they've translated into
French. It has Imrat Khan and Mahapurush Mishra performing a
sitar and tabla raga. And it has the Anglo-American supergroup
Crosby, Stills and Nash singing from an album that has wowed
America with its sun-kissed harmonies and tantalising images of
canyon trails, remote mountain hideaways and stoned bodies slid-
ing from partner to partner under discreet canopies of sycamores.

Ten days from now, the BBC will begin its coverage of Apollo 11,
the mission to put a man on the moon. In a small step for *Top Gear*,
but a giant leap for a mime artist from Bromley, Peel plays a topical
song about an astronaut. 'Space Oddity' is not in the best of taste at

a time like this – the unfortunate astronaut loses contact with his base and is left to spin helplessly into infinity – but it's far and away the best song that David Bowie has put his name to. The young man is improving at a rate of knots.

'I don't see that being what we in the trade call a chartbound sound in a thousand years,' Peel scoffs as it fades. He hopes Bowie's record company will get over the disappointment of the single's certain failure and won't be discouraged from letting him make an album. Bowie must be mortified if he's listening. But Peel has underestimated the song's chances. Catching a national mood after Apollo 11's heroic landing and safe return, 'Space Oddity' will climb the charts to number 5, winning Bowie an Ivor Novello Award for originality in songwriting. Peel played it first, but it was the hit that he couldn't hear.

Last month in Hyde Park, 100,000 people saw the unveiling of Eric Clapton's new band, Blind Faith. A week ago Peel compèred a blues festival in Bath headlined by Fleetwood Mac and Led Zeppelin. More of these outdoor events are promised in London, Cheshire and Yorkshire. And yesterday was the biggest so far, the Rolling Stones giving a free concert in Hyde Park, serenading the age-old oaks with 'Midnight Rambler' and 'Sympathy for the Devil'. The occasion was a public wake for Brian Jones, their founder and former guitarist, who was sacked a month ago and found dead last Wednesday night in his swimming pool.

An immense and unstoppable lava-flow of humanity descended on the park. The Stones nation heard the call and answered in their multitudes. They came in their peacock feathers and velvet trousers, their fur coats and headbands, their CND badges and flowers, their compulsion and duty. Sam Cutler, the Stones' road manager, estimated the crowd to be 300,000 strong. It may have been closer to 500,000. They looked from a distance, wrote the man from the *Observer*, 'like a great dish of confetti'.

The *Guardian*'s reporter, Richard Gott, saw the complexion of a future Britain stretch across the park like a field of summer lilies. 'Saturday's "happening" was a great and epoch-making event in British social history,' he wrote, 'in the sense that the Caernarfon investiture was not.' Gott, a seasoned political correspondent, sized up the hippies and sensed freedom in the air; freedom that had been achieved without the help of leaders or politicians; freedom they'd just gone out there and grabbed. He summed up the day as 'an event that seemed to be taking place in a socialist society in the distant future'.

But Peel surprises us again. He didn't enjoy the Stones in the park one bit. Judging from his comments in today's show, the behaviour of some people near the front rattled him badly and wrecked his pleasant day out. He even dedicates a song to the police for getting them under control. The likelihood is that they were a posse of Hells Angels, hired by the Stones as security guards. Film of the event shows them sporting swastikas on their helmets.

Ideologically affiliated to the peace movement, but born to sing of Lucifer, the Stones inevitably sent confused signals reverberating through the park. A curious and cruel pleasure had touched them, as Graham Greene observed of Pinkie Brown, and all they had to do was let themselves easily go. Before arriving at the site, a grey-skinned Keith Richards reclined languidly on a couch and said to Granada TV's cameras: 'I hope nobody gets hurt.' He looked like a mirror-shaded Nero trying to muster up a few words about the Great Fire of Rome. Jagger, in a white smock and quoting Shelley, was the closest the Stones came to a representative of the Light. He read two stanzas of *Adonais* and butterflies filled the air. Then he put the book away and sang his songs about night prowlers and madmen.

Peel has read the Sunday papers' reviews and is unimpressed by their reporting. He suspects they've inflated the size of yesterday's crowd to alarm their readers. Peel has a term for Britain's news-papers: he calls them 'the horror comics'. As the presenter of *Son of Night Ride*, he might be expected to mistrust journalism of the sensational kind. But as a clever man of twenty-nine – older than most in Hyde Park yesterday – it's odd that he regards even the broadsheets with contempt. As yesterday's events continue to sink in, Peel will revise his opinion of the free concerts he once praised, such as Blind Faith's, calling them 'over-commercialised' and deploring the write-ups they receive in 'colour supplements and rubbish like that'.

Whatever Peel saw when the Stones held their wake in the sun, it wasn't an encouraging vision of the future.

1970: THE SEVEN CATEGORIES

'People talk about the Sixties, but really the Sixties were the Seventies. Certainly in England. The early Seventies were really the Sixties, when people actually started to "get" the whole hippy thing and the crazy anti-Establishment thing.'

GRANT SHOWBIZ, record producer

Top Gear
Radio 1
7 February 1970

Gene Vincent – Love Sculpture – Van Der Graaf Generator – Bill Oddie – Plastic Ono Band – King Crimson – Matthews Southern Comfort – Norman Greenbaum – Tyrannosaurus Rex

Enoch Powell says that citizens of the Republic of Ireland wishing to enter Britain should be required to undergo the same immigration procedures as other foreigners. His speech is condemned by the government but earns a standing ovation from Ulster Unionists.

Bill Oddie, a diminutive hairball of a comedian, has recorded a spoof version of the Yorkshire folk song 'On Ilkla Moor Baht 'at'. In the original rendition, a young man is chided for venturing out on the moor 'baht 'at' (without a hat), risking death from hypothermia. Oddie revamps it as an overwrought rock song in the style of Joe Cocker's 'With a Little Help from My Friends'. It's a good joke and it's been put out as a single by a small record label called Dandelion. Peel plays it in a sequence that goes Bill Oddie > John Lennon's Plastic Ono Band > King Crimson. A thought-provoking two degrees of separation.

Other Dandelion acts championed by Peel include Bridget St John (a young singer-songwriter from London), Mike Hart (a lesser-known Liverpool poet) and – of all people – Gene Vincent, the black leather danger boy of Fifties rock 'n' roll, whose re-emergence after a long hiatus was much trumpeted by *Top Gear* last autumn. Having got behind Vincent's comeback single, Peel is now playing tracks from his Dandelion-released album *I'm Back and I'm Proud*.

The founder and co-proprietor of Dandelion is John Peel, who is on shaky ground if one of these records should become a hit. Who gets the money? Peel has taken out advertisements in the music papers assuring people that he isn't running Dandelion for profit – his artists might theoretically get rich but he won't – but it's still a clear-cut conflict of interest since he's using *Top Gear* as the shop window for his own label's wares. Barely a week passes without a plug for a new Dandelion band such as Siren or Medicine Head. He's also signed Principal Edwards Magic Theatre, playing a track from their album last month. He even co-produced it.

But although Peel can offer bands the seductive lure of weekly *Top Gear* exposure, he's been struggling to establish himself as a serious bidder for some of Britain's hottest new talent. One band from Birmingham rebuffed Dandelion's overtures last year, signing to a label called Vertigo instead. Their name is Black Sabbath. They will go on to sell 70 million albums.

Top Gear
Radio 1
14 February 1970

The Allman Brothers Band – Arthur Crudup – Blodwyn Pig – Paul
Siebel – Juicy Lucy – Siren – Medicine Head – Kevin Ayers – Argent
– Vivian Stanshall – The Byrds – The Humblebums

*The National Union of Teachers has rejected a pay offer and its 230,000
members will refuse to supervise or mark exams from next Saturday, a
move expected to cause chaos in schools and colleges.*

Top Gear prides itself on being a broad church. No specific genre
predominates and there are no hard and fast rules of admission. On
any given afternoon (the programme moved to a Saturday 3 p.m.
slot last September and now clashes with the football rather than
Songs of Praise), Peel may play as many as twenty groups, ranging
in profile from the internationally famous (Led Zeppelin) to the
not-remotely-successful (Jody Grind) to the not-even-vaguely-
heard-of (Ian and the Zodiacs, an obscure Merseybeat combo). The
following Saturday, he may keep three of those twenty and add a
completely new seventeen.

With such a high turnover of bands, *Top Gear* could be miscon-
strued as a bit of a soft touch, a crash pad for any passing waifs and
strays with the right complement of guitars, drums, blues licks,
beards and bell-bottoms. But Peel does discriminate – even when
he appears not to – and he can be both arbitrary and doggedly consistent. Monitored over time, patterns emerge and his tastes come
into focus. More often than not, a song he plays will fall into one of
seven categories.

The first is New Country Rock and Blues Rock Releases. These
are the bread and butter of *Top Gear* and make up a large proportion

of each show. Blodwyn Pig ('Same Old Story') are a blues-rock group formed by the original guitarist in Jethro Tull. The Allman Brothers ('Every Hungry Woman') are a freewheeling American blues band. The Byrds ('Oil in My Lamp'), a once illustrious name in Sixties pop, have sheared off in a country direction and haven't had a UK hit for four years. Peel, who hates the Byrds as people, is ironically one of the few keeping the faith.

Category two: The Good Guys. The bosom friends, patron saints and hardy perennials of *Top Gear*. Vivian Stanshall, the fruity-voiced master of ceremonies in the Bonzo Dog Doo-Dah Band, is a Good Guy. He can be certain that Peel will pounce on any new music he sends him. So can Glenn Campbell, the guitarist in the Misunderstood (who, as Peel told us in *The Perfumed Garden*, 'sears with fiery intensity and bubbles like mountain streams'), now searing and bubbling in a London band called Juicy Lucy.

The handsome blond songwriter Kevin Ayers, who used to play bass in Soft Machine, is another Good Guy. So is Soft Machine's drummer, Robert Wyatt, who popped into the Radio 1 studios for a chat during *Top Gear's* Christmas show last year. And chief among the Good Guys are Tyrannosaurus Rex, who have recorded seven *Top Gear* sessions and been the subject of at least one BBC internal memo demanding to know why Peel persists in giving them valuable airtime.

Tyrannosaurus Rex, as it happens, have been having a musical rethink. After three LPs of acoustic guitars, bongos, fairies and unicorns, a lot of their time-honoured traits are being phased out. A new song from them in today's show – 'Elemental Child' – is startlingly aggressive, transforming Bolan into an anarchic guitar soloist. It's a wig-out, a total bolt from the blue. In the context of Tyrannosaurus Rex, it's as radical as Bob Dylan going electric.

Category three: Traditional Blues and Early Rock 'n' Roll. Peel's producer John Walters has booked a session from Arthur 'Big Boy'

Crudup, a Mississippi blues singer. The listeners might not know Crudup's name, but they'll be familiar with his work. Two songs he wrote in his younger days, 'That's All Right' and 'My Baby Left Me', were remade into rock 'n' roll standards by Elvis Presley. Long forgotten and now in his sixties, Crudup concludes his session with a Prohibition-era blues, 'Nobody Knows You When You're Down and Out'. The words are all too pertinent to his own life. After years of working for a pittance as a field labourer, he's been attempting unsuccessfully to claw back royalties for his old songs, which have earned hundreds of thousands of dollars for music publishers. A payment of $248,000 will eventually be made to his family – but it comes too late for Crudup, who dies in 1974 without seeing a cent of it.

Top Gear
Radio 1
21 February 1970

Juicy Lucy – Mike Hart – Mott the Hoople – Frank Zappa – Carl Perkins – East of Eden – The GTOs – John and Beverley Martyn – Billy Fury – Wild Man Fischer – Syd Barrett – Boz Scaggs – John Surman – Welfare State – Cressida – Ed Askew – Bacon Fat

The shadow home secretary, Quintin Hogg, reveals that his priorities if the Conservatives win the 1970 general election will be to 'restore respect for law' and to stamp down on drugs and pornography.

Category four: Anyone Associated with Frank Zappa. The American bandleader, humourist and conceptualist is a prolific musician and composer, and also runs two record labels, Straight and Bizarre, which oversee the activities of an exotic array of protégés. In one single *Top Gear* today, Peel plays music from three widely contrasting Zappa projects: his chamber-rock solo album, *Hot Rats*; an LP by the all-girl band the GTOs, a sorority of Hollywood groupies whom Zappa has produced and financed; and an extremely unusual release on Bizarre entitled *An Evening with Wild Man Fischer*.

The *Hot Rats* track, a knotty composition for piano and woodwind, is fairly outré by rock standards but by far the most conventional of the three selections. The GTOs' song 'Rodney' is on an altogether different plane of strangeness. It's about a friend of theirs, the obsessively starstruck Rodney Bingenheimer, and consists of the girls singing his name in operatic squeals while Bingenheimer relates extracts from his life story. He brags in a nyah-nyah-nyah voice about the stars he's met. 'I know Sonny and Cher . . . I meditated with George Harrison . . . The Hollies are my best friends.' He sounds pathetic. It could be an ingenious piece of Zappa satire, but Bingenheimer sounds much too guileless to be in on the joke. And besides, the GTOs are hardly in a position to poke fun at starfuckers.

If the groupies are trying a little too hard to sound weird, Larry (Wild Man) Fischer is the genuine article. A paranoid schizophrenic who has twice been institutionalised, he sounds like a hyperactive adolescent plonked randomly in front of a microphone. Some believe that his outbursts walk a thin line between self-validation and exploitation. Others think he's the funniest thing in years. Zappa's agenda is not clear, but Peel loves Fischer's voice – a manic yelp like a character in a Hanna-Barbera cartoon – and will play tracks from *An Evening with Wild Man Fischer* for months. When he latches onto a new record, Peel's tendency is to feed it to the listeners until (a) their resistance cracks, or (b) his passion finally starts to wane.

Top Gear
Radio 1
28 February 1970

King Crimson – The Doors – Kevin Ayers – Wild Man Fischer – Ralph
McTell – Gene Vincent – Chris Spedding – Burnin Red Ivanhoe – The
Humblebums – Al Stewart – The Dillards – Jeremy Spencer

*Bradford Park Avenue football club has been reported to the Race
Relations Board by a local resident, who argues that the club is
discriminating against white immigrants by organising a trial game for
Asian boys.*

Ralph McTell's songs about raggedy misfits are the antithesis of
Frank Zappa. The pensive McTell is much too straight for Straight
and not bizarre enough for Bizarre. But if Wild Man Fischer embod-
ies Peel's mutinous streak, the sentimentalist in Peel – the man of
conscience – is thankful for McTell's scenes from an honest-to-God
reality. Troubled kids. Lonely pensioners. Observations through a
sympathetic lens. Category five: Folk Singers.

Also heard today are the Humblebums, a duo from Scotland.
Their bittersweet Glaswegian folk tales have charmed Peel in
recent months, and he's promoted them almost as vigorously as if
they were signed to Dandelion. One of the Humblebums, Gerry
Rafferty, will write the million-selling 'Baker Street' later in the
decade. The other, a former boilermaker who has converted to
the hippie cause, chips in with whimsical rhymes ('Miss Zsa Zsa
Gabor is the world's greatest actress . . . The sex bomb of the Fifties
got her first break on a mattress'), but he'll find his true métier as
a stand-up comedian when the Humblebums separate. The people
will know him as Billy Connolly.

Meanwhile, Dandelion's in-house Joe Cocker impersonator, Bill

Oddie, is in the process of launching a comic trio with two fellow alumni of Cambridge University's Footlights Club. Their BBC2 show, *The Goodies*, will debut in November with an episode about Beefeaters in the Tower of London having their beef stolen. Clearly, anyone looking for the future household names of British comedy should have been listening to *Top Gear* this month.

Top Gear
Radio 1
4 April 1970

Crosby, Stills, Nash and Young – Manfred Mann Chapter Three – Van Morrison – Edgar Broughton Band – Quicksilver Messenger Service – Atomic Rooster – Pete Brown and Piblokto! – David Ackles

A man is shot in Belfast's Shankill Road and a series of explosions rocks the city. Sir Ian Freeland, the British Army's general officer commanding, warns that his troops will operate a shoot-to-kill policy against suspected terrorists.

Category six: Anything on Elektra. The American record label has released albums by the Doors, Love, Tim Buckley, Nico, Tom Rush and many others. Their beautiful photography and design ensure that every Elektra LP is a mouth-watering artefact even before the needle hits the vinyl. Clive Selwood, general manager of the label's London office in 1967, was quick to identify Peel as an important ally.

They first met that summer, when Selwood was trying to drum up interest in an Incredible String Band album, *The 5000 Spirits or the Layers of the Onion*. Peel, he will later write, 'was the only person on radio in the whole of Europe who was prepared to give it a listen'.

Selwood has since become Peel's manager and business partner in Dandelion. Peel continues to promote anything on Elektra that he can get his hands on: in the last few weeks he's played the Doors' *Morrison Hotel*, a Delaney and Bonnie single, a bluegrass group called the Dillards and a folk singer named Paul Siebel. Today's Elektra artist is David Ackles, a wise and thoughtful songwriter sometimes compared to Leonard Cohen. In the summer Ackles will open for one of his biggest admirers, Elton John, a *Top Gear* Good Guy, on a six-night run at the Troubadour club in West Hollywood. Elton plays the part of the gracious rookie, the Ackles fan who can't believe that his hero is his support act.

But while Elton wins rave notices from the LA critics and uses the Troubadour as his springboard to stardom, the unflamboyant Ackles is fated to remain a bit-part player in the story of the American songbook. Only on *Top Gear*, which is not quite a meritocracy and has never been a popularity contest, will the grotesque disparity in their record sales matter not a jot.

Top Gear
Radio 1
11 April 1970

Steeleye Span – James Taylor – Van Der Graaf Generator – The Humblebums – High Tide – The Doors – Andy Roberts – Argent – Kaleidoscope – Skin Alley – Wild Man Fischer – Screaming Lord Sutch – Edgar Broughton Band – The Liverpool Scene – Trader Horne

The FA Cup final between Chelsea and Leeds United ends in a 2–2 draw after extra time. It's the first time the final has failed to produce a result since its move to Wembley in 1923. The replay at Old Trafford on 29 April will end in a 2–1 victory for Chelsea.

Wherever rock has prodigally roamed, the blues has always been the understanding mother in the threadbare armchair waiting patiently to welcome it back home. But a new virtuosic form of rock, influenced by German and Russian classical music, is shaking off the blues yoke and flying the nest once and for all. Its composers take the view that they are creating new concertos and symphonies for the post-*Sgt Pepper* age. If the bluesmen are farmers in their top fields grunting with distaste at the sound of a motor car, this new generation of musicians see themselves as architects framing futuristic skylines and cityscapes. Category seven: Progressive Rock.

The pivotal band in progressive rock is King Crimson, who debuted on British radio with a *Top Gear* session last May. They've since released an album, *In the Court of the Crimson King,* which has set the bar for every other band working in the genre. Their use of mellotron, an instrument noted for its ominous sounds of cellos and choirs, adds a veil of terror to their intricate, jazzy virtuosity and their epic songs of napalm, insanity and doom. Crimson have gobsmacked everyone from Pete Townshend to Mick Jagger, who made sure to get them onto the Stones' bill at Hyde Park.

But now a band has emerged to take progressive rock into new realms of bloody history and psychic dread. Van Der Graaf Generator don't see too many girls at their concerts. Frowning existentialists and Dostoyevsky students are more their constituency. As he howls the words of 'Darkness', a gush of Raskolnikovian self-loathing with an atmosphere as malevolent as any Crimson, Van Der Graaf's twenty-one-year-old singer Peter Hammill sounds shockingly old before his years. Unlike other progressive rock lyricists, he has a knack of avoiding poetic embroidery and going straight for the pogroms and autos-da-fé. As a vocalist, his principal influence seems to be Richard III.

John Walters, who finalises *Top Gear's* running orders, follows 'Darkness' with the new single by the Humblebums, a carefree ditty about a shoeshine boy looking forward to a night of dancing with his girlfriend. It makes for a grinding gear change for the senses, and Walters has almost certainly done it on purpose. He enjoys a bit of bathos, does Walters. More of his preposterous juxtapositions will be heard as the Seventies unfold.

Top Gear
Radio 1
4 July 1970

Free – Fotheringay – Cochise – The Pretty Things – David Bowie – Country Joe McDonald – Medicine Head – Procol Harum – Wild Man Fischer – The Grateful Dead – Soft Machine

The National Union of Teachers condemns the new Conservative government's decision to allow local education authorities to convert their grammar schools into comprehensives if they so desire (as per a policy introduced under Labour). The NUT is seeking an urgent meeting with the new education secretary, Margaret Thatcher.

Festival time has come round again. Since May there have been live events at Plumpton Racecourse (headlined by Ginger Baker's Air Force), Bath City's football ground (Fleetwood Mac), a leisure centre in Port Talbot (Rory Gallagher's Taste) and a farm in Staffordshire (Traffic and the Grateful Dead). The big difference this year is that they're all charging admission.

Traffic and the Grateful Dead may have been the enticing names at the Hollywood Music Festival in Newcastle-under-Lyme, but it was an unknown skiffle group from London that stole the show. Mungo Jerry got the crowd on their feet with 'Rock Island Line' and kept them there, going down so well that they were asked to perform again the following night. Peel, who compèred, was so taken with the unpretentious newcomers that he started the next week's *Top Gear* with their new single, 'In the Summertime'.

That was in May. It's now July and 'In the Summertime' has been at number 1 for a month. Mungomania has spread like a skiffle virus. England's footballers have been knocked out of the World Cup by West Germany, but it doesn't matter because Mungo Jerry are singing about hot weather and going for a drive. There's a new prime minister in Downing Street, Edward Heath, but nobody has noticed because Mungo Jerry keep stomping their feet, blowing into their jug and reciting their artless, infectious maxim: 'Go out and see what you can find.' The song will top the charts in twenty-two countries.

Mungo Jerry aside, though, the evolution of the rock festival has panned out very much as Peel feared last July. Capitalising on the Woodstock phenomenon is the new game in town. Prices are creeping up: advance tickets for the Nottingham Festival of Blues and Progressive Music have increased from seventeen shillings and sixpence last year (in today's value about £22) to 21 shillings (about £28). In the West Country, the Bath Festival of Blues and Progressive Music has expanded fivefold, attracting a crowd of 150,000 over two days.

Peel, who was supposed to compère at Bath, was seen leaving the site early after – it is said – having his Dormobile violently rocked from side to side by Hells Angels. Not good for the image. On today's *Top Gear* he gives a shout-out to two bands from the Ladbroke Grove freak scene, Hawkwind and the Pink Fairies, who performed for free on the back of a flatbed truck for those who couldn't get into the festival. Peel, who knows Hawkwind and helped them get a management deal, is unmistakably siding with the radicals here. Next month Hawkwind and the Fairies will be part of a larger and looser conglomerate of activists, anarchists, White Panthers and

Communists attempting to gatecrash the Isle of Wight Festival and have it declared a free event. Death to breadheads. Tear down the fences. Free food for the people.

David Bowie, who has slipped back into anonymity since 'Space Oddity' was a hit seven months ago, has written a new single ('Memory of a Free Festival') about an event he organised in Beckenham in south-east London last summer. The Beckenham Free Festival may not sound very romantic on the page (after booking the recreation ground on Croydon Road, Bowie phoned round to see who was available and was turned down by Noel Redding), but Bowie the songwriter is nothing if not a mythologist. The recreation ground becomes 'God's land'. Beckenham's modest contingent of hippies are 'the children of the summer's end'. In the final verse, 'Memory of a Free Festival' heads off into sci-fi, transmitting ecstatic vibrations that cause extraterrestrial crafts to start circling the Beckenham skies. Bowie is exultant . . . but at the same time wistful. It happened. It was special. It will never happen again.

All over Britain, town councillors are hoping he's right. They've become deeply apprehensive about rock festivals, scared of drug-crazed dropouts wreaking havoc on municipal land. Shrewd promoters have moved in to fill the vacuum, hiring farms, showgrounds and sports facilities. Anyone with a ticket for a festival this summer is likely to see a name like Robert Stigwood, Freddy Bannister or Harvey Goldsmith printed at the top. Stigwood is an entrepreneur who manages Eric Clapton. Bannister will found the Knebworth Festival in the mid-Seventies. Goldsmith will make his name in the Eighties with all-star concerts at Wembley. These are the men filling muddy Britain with surrogate Woodstocks, while the children of the summer's end watch and wait for spaceships that will never land. Bowie is right to be nostalgic.

Top Gear
Radio 1
11 July 1970

Doug Kershaw – Kevin Ayers and the Whole World – East of Eden – Steeleye Span – Traffic – Fotheringay – Poco – Son House – John Simon – Jellybread – The Faces – Fairport Convention

As Protestants in Northern Ireland prepare for the annual 12 July processions, the Orange Order is banned from marching in two heavily Catholic areas. Security forces are expected to be 18,000 strong and all pubs in the province will remain closed for three days.

Peel is laughing. 'This is the programme that doesn't have the new Led Zeppelin, Eric Clapton, Eric Clapton-with-Howlin'-Wolf, George Harrison or Mothers of Invention LPs.' He's right – it doesn't. What it does have is the zaniness of Kevin Ayers and the ancient Mississippi proverbs of the blues singer Son House. Both deliver remarkable sessions.

Peel begins with a country-style knees-up in a foreign tongue, which turns out to be a Cajun two-step by the Louisiana fiddle player Doug Kershaw. Kershaw, whose career got under way in the Forties, is a million-selling artist in his own field who is finally starting to be heard by rock audiences. Peel has been a fan of Cajun music since his days at WRR and KLIF in Dallas. '[It's] from the second Doug Kershaw LP,' he explains, 'with a lady rumoured to be his mother playing triangle and doing some of the singing.'

After that rousing reveille, Kevin Ayers sings a song about horse-betting on Derby Day. 'Don't keep your hands in your pockets, my dear,' he cautions, like a queasy Noël Coward. An ungodly oompah racket strikes up behind him. This is Ayers's band, the Whole World, who have an eccentric shaven-headed saxophonist named Lol Coxhill (whom Peel discovered when he was a busker and later signed to Dandelion) and a bassist named Mike Oldfield, who is just seventeen. The Whole World sound like they all answered a *Melody Maker* advert that read: 'Musicians with nothing in common wanted for band with no commercial prospects.' More will be heard from them later.

Born in Mississippi's Coahoma County in 1902, Son House is a true progeny of the Delta. His voice and bottleneck guitar are a link with history as far back as any blues fan wants to go. He made his first recordings in 1930. A former Baptist pastor, he's also been a rail-road porter, a chef, a drinker and womaniser, a convicted murderer (he claims he shot the man in self-defence) and an acknowledged inspiration on Robert Johnson and Muddy Waters, both of whom went on to inspire everybody else.

'Son House, basically, is where it all began,' Peel says, whittling the genealogy of the blues down to eight words. The Mississippi trailblazer is currently on a tour of Europe at the age of sixty-eight.

The session begins. The first announcement out of Son House's mouth is: 'I got up this morning.' From anyone else it would sound hackneyed. From him it sounds like the opening line of a novel. His voice is a primeval moan possessed by rampant spirits. He has a habit of snorting like a bull to emphasise key points. *Pffffwwwhrrrr*. His guitar-playing is rudimentary, even clumsy, at a time when Ten Years After's Alvin Lee is bringing cinema audiences to their feet with his superfast fretwork in the *Woodstock* movie. Son House plays the guitar his own damn way and spells out the symptoms of the blues like a heroin addict going cold turkey.

'The blues ain't nothin' but a lowdown shakin' chill,' he snorts, the phlegm rattling in his throat like coins in a jar. 'If you ain't had 'em, I hope you never will.' Prior to his next song, he goes into a long spoken-word preamble, a choleric monologue about the treachery of love and how it propels the blues. He mumbles, stops, goes back.

'The blues, the B-L-U-E-S, ain't what some people think it is . . . it ain't no lot of foolishness.' It's like listening to a Delta version of *Krapp's Last Tape*.

Kevin Ayers, born in Kent but raised in Malaysia, is dry-witted and pleasantly lopsided. He sings in a plummy baritone with one eyebrow permanently arched. He and the Whole World are happy for songs to take absurd detours from wherever they're going and go off somewhere else. They improvise on a simple riff called 'We Did it Again', which Ayers wrote when he was in Soft Machine. Someone hammers out some painful free-jazz piano that goes on and on for minutes. Another band member then sings a paean to currant cake (bake it 'for old times' sake') and croons an intentionally ghastly vo-dee-oh-doe Twenties love song. With a Milliganesque squeal of brakes, the scene changes to a radio play about an aeroplane full of nervous flyers, one of whom might be a murderer. The performance seems to have lasted about half an hour. At the end of it Peel says: 'I think we'll have to have Kevin Ayers and the Whole World as resident group on the programme.' It could be nine months before they run out of material.

On this evidence, *Top Gear* can be placed high among the BBC's most audacious radio programmes. It's probably the only show on the air, now that *Son of Night Ride* has gone, that could integrate Ayers and Son House as equals without asking either of them to tone it down or conform to a formula. The only pity is that the two men never met. They recorded their sessions in different studios on different days. Otherwise it might have been nice to imagine them exchanging an inscrutable look as they passed, holding cups of dishwater coffee, in the BBC corridors.

Top Gear
Radio 1
5 September 1970

Little Richard – Family – Donovan – T. Rex – The Chieftains – James Gang – Mick Jagger – Formerly Fat Harry – Swamp Dogg – Stackwaddy – Supersister – Randy Newman – Merry Clayton

Following its appearance at the Farnborough Airshow last week, Britain's Concorde makes a supersonic test flight down 'Boom Alley', an air corridor from Scotland to Cornwall. Its maximum speed reaches Mach 1.68 (approx. 1,140 mph).

Tyrannosaurus Rex have abbreviated their name to T. Rex and recorded a catchy new single, 'Ride a White Swan'. Its production, which is spartan for 1970, uses strings and handclaps to sweeten and commercialise Bolan's *Catweazle* hocus-pocus. Peel is the obvious man to give the single its radio debut four weeks before the official release. Bolan is convinced he's got a hit. But then Bolan is always convinced he's got a hit.

Top Gear
Radio 1
12 December 1970

Derek and the Dominos – Hawkwind – Rick Nelson – The Faces – George Harrison – Yoko Ono – Keith Tippett – The Kinks – Captain Beefheart and the Magic Band – Donovan – John Philip Sousa

Christmas shop-window displays are banned as the government takes emergency measures to deal with an electricity workers' strike.

Frank Chapple, general secretary of the Electrical, Electronic, Telecommunications and Plumbing Union, has been placed under police protection.

A year of bewilderment, a year of bereavement. Jimi Hendrix died in September. Janis Joplin succumbed to a heroin overdose in October. Both were twenty-seven. In April, a music-industry open secret became public knowledge when Paul McCartney confirmed that the Beatles were no more. Reported by TV newsmen like the death of a president, it was the cue for an outbreak of international mourning. Later this month, the four Beatles will begin the formal process of suing each other.

All of them have been busy with solo projects. Peel plays two songs from George Harrison's *All Things Must Pass*, a gargantuan dam-burst of an album that stretches across six sides of vinyl. More than twenty guests appear on it, including Eric Clapton and most of his latest group, Derek and the Dominos. The Dominos have a new album too, *Layla & Other Assorted Love Songs*, a mere four sides of vinyl. Its seven-minute title track, 'Layla', is rumoured to be a love song from Clapton to Harrison's wife, Pattie. Peel isn't interested in the marriage, however, just the music, and advises the listeners to buy both albums without fail. All ten sides of them.

Also releasing a new album is Yoko Ono, the ever-controversial figure who's been blamed by the media and the fans for destroying the Beatles. Perhaps putting her in the show is Peel's way of showing solidarity; he's always had time for her. Her improvised scream-song ('Why') is harrowingly atonal and definitely worth five minutes of any experimental-music fan's time. But John Walters's mischievous decision to place two Harrison songs on either side of it can't help but give the impression that Yoko is still finding ways to come between the Beatles.

The most symbolic song today comes from a band with not a

shred of experimental music in their genes. Ex-mods and incorrigible piss-takers, the Faces are a cross between a no-frills rock 'n' roll band and a five-man private drinking club. Their first album, which came out in March, wasn't too promising – although Peel liked it anyway – but now the Faces are really hitting their stride. Their new single, 'Had Me a Real Good Time', sums up everything they're about: turning up to parties drunk, being overfriendly, being an annoyance to people of higher class and being asked to leave before the police are called.

From singer Rod Stewart to guitarist Ronnie Wood to bassist Ronnie Lane, they're the sound of uproarious laughter as a priceless Chippendale goes sailing out of an upstairs window. 'Praise God for people who aren't totally predictable,' Peel said of Kevin Ayers in July, and he might well say the same about the Faces. They could be the antidote to progressive rock and all that seriousness. Peel has found his favourite band of the Seventies.

1971: THE CHARACTER WITNESS

'Our strained relationship was a perfect metaphor for what was happening in the pop world. John was on the side of the long-haired, the dropouts, the students – all those who regarded the three-minute pop single as a blot on the face of culture. I was the happy-go-lucky dispenser of the kind of song that an audience only had to hear once before rushing out to buy it.'

TONY BLACKBURN

Top Gear
Radio 1
23 January 1971

Fleetwood Mac – The Grateful Dead – Medicine Head – T. Rex – Nico – Robert Wyatt – The Velvet Underground – King Crimson – Loudon Wainwright III

In Belfast, fresh riots break out and cars are set alight in a burning barricade across the Shankill Road. Loyalist gangs attempt to enter Catholic areas but are dispersed by troops using water cannon.

The Velvet Underground are a much changed band since Peel dropped 'Heroin' and 'Venus in Furs' like homing torpedoes into *The Perfumed Garden* at the height of the Summer of Love. He described them back then as having a 'very brutal and eerie sound' and being 'one of the few groups that can affect you with a sort of demoniac possession and/or peace at the same time' – not a bad way of getting to the heart of their dichotomy.

But a lot of water has passed under the bridge since then. These days droning violas and songs about sadomasochism are nowhere to be seen in the Velvet Underground's music. On 2 January, Peel uncorked the first *Top Gear* of 1971 with 'Sweet Jane', a pageant of New York street scenes acted out to the strutting chords of an addictive guitar riff. It's one of several radio-friendly tunes on their latest album, *Loaded*. Another is 'Rock & Roll' – today's Peel choice – which crystallises a feeling experienced by many music fans during their childhood: the fervid moment of turning on a radio and hearing a sound so thrilling that it seems to mark the proper start of their life.

The Velvet Underground, however, are hapless, broke and almost completely unknown. Some good their bold innovations did them. Last summer they lost Lou Reed, their songwriter and leader, who quit while *Loaded* was in post-production. Disillusioned and drug-damaged, Reed has turned his back on music and moved back to Long Island, where he lives with his parents and works for his father's accountancy firm. 'Never has such an outstanding rock star ... been afforded so little recognition or been confronted with such hostile rejection as Lou Reed was between 1966 and 1970,' his biographer Victor Bockris will later write.

There's no evidence that Reed and John Peel ever met. It's just possible that Reed went his whole life without knowing Peel's name. But Peel played the Velvet Underground when they needed to be played – not posthumously but during their lifetime – and he believed in Reed for years when other tastemakers and DJs pointedly cold-shouldered him. How could Peel not? He understood the importance of the life-changing song on the radio.

Top Gear
Radio 1
6 February 1971

Gene Vincent and the Houseshakers – The National Head Band –
Ralph McTell – Caravan – The Pink Fairies – Janis Joplin – J. Geils
Band – Michael Nesmith and the First National Band – David Bowie

*Belfast's streets witness the bloodiest battles yet between the British
Army and Republican militants. A soldier is shot dead by a sniper in
a block of flats, two gunmen are killed by soldiers returning fire, and a
fourth man dies when a bomb explodes as he prepares to throw it.*

In the middle of last November, 'Ride a White Swan' by T. Rex sat
at number 30 in the charts. A Top 30 hit is a Top 30 hit, but Marc
Bolan wanted much more than that. He wanted adulation, celebrity, Garboesque mystique – and bona fide chart blockbusters, not
Top 30 barrel-scrapers. 'Ride a White Swan' leapt fifteen places the
following week, then another eight. It fell in December, but January
saw it mount another climb. Number 10. Number 4. Number 2.
Only Clive Dunn's 'Grandad', that immovable obelisk of national
sentimentality, prevented it from going all the way.

Next week T. Rex will release 'Hot Love', the single that confirms Bolan as a certified British pop star. Peel, who wept tears of
joy for his friend when 'Ride a White Swan' made its surge into
the Top 20, has had his faith well and truly vindicated. All those
Tyrannosaurus Rex sessions for *Top Gear* – there were about
thirty-eight of them – had a point to them after all, a light at the
end of the tunnel. Now there'll be no more exasperated BBC
memos to John Walters wanting to know why Peel keeps playing
that awful boy that nobody likes. Bolan, as the football writers say,
has justified his selection.

David Bowie, Bolan's erstwhile support act, has a new album out. *The Man Who Sold the World* is his heaviest work to date, haunted by Boschian visions and snarling guitars. Peel picks out a more upbeat track, 'Black Country Rock', in which Bowie goes hiking with a packhorse and admires the view from a hilltop. Affectionately, in the final run-through of the refrain, he breaks into a bleating vibrato. B-a-a-a-a-a! It's a spot-on, perfectly topical parody. There really is no escaping Bolan at the moment.

Top Gear
Radio 1
24 April 1971

Jimi Hendrix – Hawkwind – Quiver – Gnidrolog – Crazy Horse – J. Geils Band – Medicine Head – Steeleye Span – Leonard Cohen – Incredible String Band – Loudon Wainwright III – Bridget St John

The Conservative backbencher Sir Gerald Nabarro demands answers from the government after his Tobacco (Health Hazards) Bill, which calls for tobacco companies to put health warnings on cigarette packets, is filibustered in the Commons.

Peel has never known what to say when a famous musician dies. He can muster a few gruff words to give the sad news to the listeners, but he's not the type for a eulogy. Mourn the music, not the man you didn't know, is his motto. It's been seven months since the death of Jimi Hendrix, seven months in which Peel has continued to treat him as a living artist, playing his music constantly and often starting shows with Hendrix songs – as he does here – as if *Top Gear* has unearthed a magnificent new talent and can't wait to let him loose on the air. Whatever it was that Hendrix did, whatever it was that he *meant*, Peel is determined it won't be consigned to the past. A slew of compilations in the Seventies will ensure that he always has some 'new' Hendrix to play.

Steeleye Span, a folk group, sing about a girl who dresses as a boy to enlist in the army. The Incredible String Band cordwangle a lilting air in their Rambling Syd Rumpo voices. Gnidrolog's jigsaw-assembly progressive rock sounds as anagrammatic as their name looks. There are obligatory Dandelion plugs for Medicine Head and Bridget St John. In session: space-boogie psychotropia from Hawkwind.

In America, where albums by Carole King (*Tapestry*) and James Taylor (*Mud Slide Slim and the Blue Horizon*) sell like coffee and sugar, singer-songwriters have become the prophets and potentates of post-Beatles pop. Everyone wants to hear a comforting voice and a new confession. Peel likes a singer-songwriter as much as the next man, but his newest American discovery sees the world through much more insubordinate eyes – and arguably more visionary ones – than heavyweights like Taylor and King.

Loudon Wainwright III is twenty-four, cynical, strident and dark. His first album has just come out in Britain, so instant comparisons would be invidious, but some hear precocity on a par with early Dylan. 'Ode to a Pittsburgh', on *Top Gear* today, is a potted history of the city that packs in fantastic amounts of detail and colour. Peel, looking like he might be dangerously smitten, is playing Wainwright almost every week. The American will record a session for him next month, the first of many. His sixteenth and final session will be broadcast – some thirty-two years, nineteen albums, two marriages and four children later – in August 2003.

Top Gear
Radio 1
22 May 1971

Slade – Loudon Wainwright III – Steeleye Span – James Taylor –
Freaks – Crosby, Stills, Nash and Young – Crazy Horse – Tonto's
Expanding Headband – Iain Matthews – Bill Fay – Little Feat

A Norwegian oil tanker collides with a motorboat off the Kent coast,
gushing oil onto the Goodwin Sands. By coincidence, a Liberian oil
tanker runs aground off Sandgate, fifteen miles away, after getting lost
in thick fog.

Pop star or not, having Marc Bolan for a friend has done little to
help boost Peel's standing with Radio 1. In the autumn, Clive
Selwood, concerned about the BBC's negative body language and
unable to get a straight answer, will approach Radio Luxembourg
to inquire about a possible transfer for Peel. There really aren't any
other options, unless he fancies following Mike Ahern to Australia
or going back to the States.

In the meantime, a cultural gulf has started to widen between
Peel and Radio 1's star DJ. Peel and Tony Blackburn never had much
to do with each other when they were shipmates on the MV *Galaxy*,
but now their mutual antagonism stands out a mile. Peel makes
niggling jokes on air about Blackburn like a schoolboy flicking his
ruler at the class swot. Blackburn, who winks and wisecracks his
way through Radio 1's morning show, is the diametric opposite of
Peel in presentation, personality, humour, disposition, sociability,
photogeneity and earning potential. Good-looking and confident,
he's as recognisable to young British women as any pop star. A soul
fan, he dismisses *Top Gear* as unmusical garbage and Peel as a cloth-
eared bore.

Blackburn's shows are governed by Radio 1 playlists, which is another reason why Peel despises him. Among the singles playlisted this week are Dawn's 'Knock Three Times', Neil Diamond's 'I Am I Said', R. Dean Taylor's 'Indiana Wants Me', Ringo Starr's 'It Don't Come Easy' and Stevie Wonder's 'We Can Work It Out'. These songs are heard on all Radio 1 daytime shows, from Blackburn at 7 a.m. to Johnnie Walker at 9 a.m. to Jimmy Young at 10 a.m. to Noel Edmonds coming live from the Civic Centre at Stourport-on-Severn at noon.

Peel naturally wants to assume the antithetical position to the playlist-regulated daytime consortium. But how does he go about it? By effectively running his own radio station within the BBC. By refusing to acknowledge that a universe exists where any play-listed songs are deemed fit for the radio. Today's *Top Gear*, like so many before, creates its own protectorate and slams the door contemptuously on the heathens outside. *Top Gear*'s universe partly resembles Laurel Canyon, where bands like Little Feat and Crosby, Stills, Nash and Young breathe pure air in country-rock mountain retreats. But it also looks a lot like rural England, where the drawing rooms of country houses are disturbed by scurrilous belches of colonial dyspepsia.

In Walters's running order, Neil Young and Neil Innes sit side by side, despite having nothing in common except a Christian name. Young's 'Don't Let It Bring You Down', a desolate pile-up of bodies and bleak symbols, follows a song by Freaks, a group of nutters from blasted Blighty put together by Innes and Viv Stanshall of the Bonzo Dog Doo-Dah Band. One of the pieces that Freaks perform is called 'Rawlinson End'.

'Rawlinson End' is a surreal upper-crust saga written by Stanshall at his most inventive. Inside its flexible text, he constructs histories within histories and families within families like a spiralling Droste effect. The Rawlinsons are faux-gentrified, disgusting, conceited, furtive, hilarious, dishonest and quite insane. The concept is perfect for years of development: Stanshall can disgorge the further adventures of the Rawlinsons from his imagination any time he likes, and like a song by Kevin Ayers and the Whole World, the story can go anywhere he wants it to. The Rawlinsons will sire a long-running series of Peel sessions, an album, a film and a book.

Tony Blackburn would find it inexplicable. Stanshall has no current single, no reason to be promoted on the playlist, no relevance to housewives and therefore – in Blackburn's mind – no right to be on Radio 1. That's where Peel comes in with his radio-station-within-a-radio-station. The housewives are overruled, the playlists are revoked and Stanshall can have the floor to expound and free-associate. The multimedia Rawlinson franchise has begun, with blimpish, brandy-stained Sir Henry shoehorned into a laid-back two hours of CSNY, Little Feat, James Taylor and Southern Comfort. The absolute bloody cheek of it.

In Concert
Radio 1
20 June 1971

David Bowie and Friends

The Campaign for the Mentally Handicapped asks regional health boards to consider phasing out institutional care for people with mental disabilities. A recent government report argued that building more hospital wards for them would be cheaper than community care.

Very few recordings of Peel survive from 1971. It seems fair to assume that the small number of listeners who had been taping *Top Gear* off their radios simply stopped at the end of 1970. Real life intervened somehow: perhaps a new job that required them to work Saturdays. Or university coursework infringing on their free time. Or they emigrated. Or a baby came along. Or they met new girlfriends who couldn't stand Captain Beefheart.

A Sunday concert by David Bowie, emceed by Peel at the Paris Theatre in Lower Regent Street, offers a rare chance to hear Peel's voice during this period. But which voice? In the space of a year it's changed substantially, deepening in pitch and shedding most of its Merseyside accent. He's a far cry from the enchanted poshboy of four years ago. He even sounds different to the genial hippie who sang the praises of Son House last summer. Geographically, his accent is now closer to Birmingham than Liverpool.

Is this some sort of insecure tic? Is it an act of social chameleonism from a middle-class public schoolboy anxious to seem more proletarian? Or – another possibility – is he subconsciously imitating the lugubrious Midlands drawl of Walters? Strangely, as if he knew that it might one day be an issue, Peel apologised for changes in his voice as far back as 1968, telling *Top Gear* listeners in October: 'You'll have to excuse me this afternoon if my accent sounds different – very contrived, anyway, at the best of times – but I've been spending the last ten days or so in the city of Birmingham, so there may be a touch of that about it.' If not, there soon will be.

David Bowie seldom plays concerts. He doesn't have a regular band, his albums don't sell and he's prone to being in a state of artistic flux. Today, apparently seeking safety in numbers, he's brought along a small horde of musicians, including three future Spiders from Mars and more backing vocalists than anyone could ever need. *In Concert* is his biggest showcase for some time.

Peel, his well-meaning mate, sets the informal tone by congratulating Bowie on an 'amazing pair of trousers'. Bowie downplays the headline billing, presenting his ensemble as more of a musical revue than a backing group. 'Queen Bitch' is tame stuff, with a vocal nowhere near as emphatic as it will be when Bowie records it for *Hunky Dory* later this summer. It's all a bit country rock. It's all very polite. He even drops out of the concert for two songs to let others sing lead vocals.

Peel tells the audience that 'Kooks' is 'a sort of personal one, so David will explain what it's all about'. Bowie (echoing, distant): 'I'd been listening to a Neil Young album and they phoned through and said that my wife had had a baby on Sunday morning. And I wrote this about the baby.'

He plays 'Kooks' alone on a twelve-string acoustic. Not all the chords are where they should be, but he's got the lines about the bullies and the cads and the homework being tossed on the fire. Peel explains that the baby's name is Zowie ('spelt, of course, Z-O-W-I-E . . . to rhyme with Bowie'). The audience titters. Bowie sounds flustered as he introduces 'Song for Bob Dylan'.

He's definitely not Ziggy; not yet.

Top Gear
Radio 1
10 July 1971

Wishbone Ash – Help Yourself – Osibisa – Rod Stewart – Loudon Wainwright III – Pearls Before Swine – Mountain – Tír na nÓg

Anthony Crosland, one of the Labour Party's most pro-Common Market MPs, announces he will vote against the government's EEC entry terms in order to 'preserve party unity'. Another key Labour figure, Denis Healey, has declared his opposition to the EEC.

As well as holding down a day job as lead singer of the Faces, Rod Stewart is also under contract to make a solo album every year. His latest, *Every Picture Tells a Story*, is a sometimes boisterous, sometimes misty-eyed collection of Rod-written and Rod-selected material. The songs are rootsy, realistic and likeable. Some of them sound autobiographical.

Peel opens the show with 'Maggie May', a song about a schoolboy trying to prise himself out of a complicated relationship with an older woman. (Stewart sometimes refers to her as a 'prostitute' when he and the Faces play live.) 'Maggie May' is five minutes long and lacks a traditional chorus, chugging along cheerfully from verse to verse on a feathery bed of mandolins and acoustic guitars. Peel is the first DJ on Radio 1 to take any notice of it – he may, in fact, be the first person to have been sent a copy of *Every Picture Tells a Story* by Stewart's record company.

Next to play 'Maggie May' will be Emperor Rosko on his round-up of new albums, *Midday Spin*, a week from now. After that, it will be chosen by the record company to be the B-side of Stewart's new single ('Reason to Believe'). Since A-sides have always taken precedence over B-sides, it looks as though 'Maggie May' will not be heard on Radio 1 again.

Top Gear
Radio 1
4 September 1971

George Harrison – Sandy Denny – Jefferson Airplane – Fanny – The Allman Brothers Band – Tim Hart and Maddy Prior – Loudon Wainwright III – Soft Machine – Jack Bruce – Bronco – Ravi Shankar

An eleven-year-old boy receives serious head injuries when a bomb explodes near a hotel in Londonderry. Eighteen other people, including a British soldier, are hospitalised but later discharged.

The Faces have been a runaway smash at rock festivals this year. Rod Stewart is being hailed by influential rock critics as the natural heir to Mick Jagger. He's flamboyant, cocksure but never narcissistic. He's a swaggering, microphone-twirling man of the people. Stewart, though, has never had much success. He's been on *Top of the Pops* once or twice with the Faces, singing a non-hit or two, but the vast majority of Radio 1 listeners wouldn't know who he was or what he looked like. They have approximately one more week to live in ignorance.

Top Gear
Radio 1
18 September 1971

Gypsy – Stone the Crows – David Parker – Dando Shaft – Yoko Ono – Curved Air – The Flying Burrito Brothers – Donovan – Jefferson Airplane – Loudon Wainwright III – Michael Hurley and Pals

It's announced that Paul McCartney's wife Linda gave birth to a daughter, Stella, in London last Monday. The baby was three weeks premature and weighed 5 lb 9 oz.

During the summer Peel had a reunion with an old acquaintance. It was Richard Neville, his former co-presenter on the BBC1 talk show *How It Is*. The venue was the Old Bailey, the occasion was Britain's highest-profile obscenity trial since *Lady Chatterley's Lover*, and the judge was as Establishment as they come.

Neville was charged alongside his fellow *Oz* magazine editors, Jim Anderson and Felix Dennis, with conspiring to debauch and corrupt the morals of young children. Last year *Oz* published a 'School Kids Issue', written and compiled by teenagers. On one page was a Robert Crumb cartoon doctored to show Rupert the Bear having sex with a comatose woman. The boy responsible for the cartoon told the court that he 'subconsciously wanted to shock your generation'. He succeeded.

Oz, while satirical, is not usually puerile. Its pool of writers includes Germaine Greer, the film director Philippe Mora and the art critic Robert Hughes. But it's been in the gunsights of the Establishment for some time, and when Jim Anderson designed a cover in 1969 that showed a white man and a black man kissing, *Oz*'s Notting Hill offices were raided and the three editors hauled off to Scotland Yard. They escaped that time with a warning. With the 'School Kids Issue', they were never going to be so lucky.

Oz is pro-drugs, pro-free speech, pro-sex, pro-feminism, pro-lesbian, pro-schoolgirl, pro-everything that's not an antiquated conformist straitjacket or an uptight bourgeois drag. And *Oz*, among other things, is pro-*Top Gear* and pro-John Peel.

Peel doesn't actually write for *Oz*. But he's a logical person to speak in support of it, which is why Neville, who is defending himself, has called him as a character witness. The sheepish, worried-looking Peel has the demeanour of a man who has seen most of his illusions comprehensively shattered. One day in court, he makes a poignant comment to Neville about the end of the counterculture dream: 'Obviously 1967 was a period of great optimism. I really thought there was going to be a lot of social change. People were beginning to think about one another rather than just acquiring property. This turned out not to be the case, unfortunately.'

The Peel of 1967 believed that a caring, unselfish society could be built from the ashes of the old. He trusted in the forward march of the flower children, convinced that love was the answer. His Eeyorish countenance in court is the punchline to that unwitting joke. It was a hoax and he fell for it. He walked right into the trap. Perhaps it's no surprise that his accent has changed, when he thinks of all the things about himself – all those hang-ups and high hopes – that he must want to leave behind.

His court attire is a pullover and jeans. He looks rather shapeless. His long hair is on the lank side. An article about hippies in the *Sunday Times* has seen his type in every town: 'Patched jeans and dirty sweaters . . . Hair seems to have run to seed, hiding ears and neck and fringing young men's faces with a fuzz of beard or whiskery overgrowth . . . They are challenging not only a particular set of conventions but all conventions alike.'

The Old Bailey judge, His Honour Michael Argyle QC, seems to react to Peel with physical repugnance. Under the prosecution's questioning, Peel confirms that he caught a venereal disease two years ago and talked about it on a radio programme. Argyle looks nauseated. When Peel steps down from the witness stand, a glass of water that he has sipped from is carefully removed by an usher. John Mortimer, defending Anderson and Dennis, later overhears the usher telling Argyle that he took the liberty of destroying the glass for hygienic reasons.

In August, the three *Oz* editors are cleared of the corruption charge but found guilty of other offences under the Obscene Publications Act. Argyle sends them to prison, where they have their shoulder-length hair sheared off by the Wormwood Scrubs barber. Two weeks later they walk free when the Appeal Court rules that Argyle misdirected the jury on no fewer than seventy-eight occasions. Peel, the character witness stigmatised as the embodiment of the unclean, plays Yoko Ono and Loudon Wainwright III like a man possessed throughout September.

Top Gear
Radio 1
6 October 1971

The Faces – Pink Floyd – New Riders of the Purple Sage – Wishbone Ash – Kingdom Come – The Allman Brothers Band – Weather Report – Leo Kottke – Flamin Groovies – Dan Hicks and His Hot Licks

Sir Keith Joseph, the social services secretary, admits that Britain has fallen behind Europe in its treatment of the elderly. Acknowledging that a third of pensioners subsist on benefits, Joseph fears Britain will be 'shown up' by other countries if it joins the EEC.

In February 1968, when Radio 1 was in its infancy, Peel was invited to host *Top of the Pops*. This, as all DJs know, is a huge honour and can lead – providing all goes well – to glittering opportunities in show business. Peel's debut was a disaster. He forgot the name of Amen Corner (who had a Top 5 hit), claimed that *Top of the Pops* was a waste of time without Captain Beefheart and was told by the furious producer that he would never be allowed on the show again. Until last Thursday, that producer was right.

But a bizarre chain of events began to unfold a month ago when Johnnie Walker, out of the blue, played Rod Stewart's five-minute B-side 'Maggie May' on his morning show on Monday 6 September. He played it again on Wednesday and again the following Monday. Stewart's record company decided to flip the single and make 'Maggie May' the A-side. Surfing a wave of daytime airplay, 'Maggie May' entered the charts at number 11 in mid-September, climbing rapidly. From then on, its momentum was unstoppable. It's currently the number 1 single in Britain and America.

Stewart, hurtling to fame, is unlikely to remember that Peel played 'Maggie May' on *Top Gear* as long ago as July, but one thing he hasn't forgotten is that Peel has been a supporter and good friend to him since his days in the Jeff Beck Group. When Peel returned to the *Top of the Pops* studio last week, he wasn't appearing as a presenter. He was an auxiliary member of Rod Stewart and the Faces, miming to 'Maggie May' with a mandolin in his hands. When it came to his solo, bassist Ronnie Lane and keyboardist Ian McLagan pointed to him theatrically as if he were the star turn of the evening. After a summer in which he faced the wrath of Justice Argyle and the worry of being sidelined by Radio 1, that moment was a cherished oasis of warm-hearted silliness. Putting Peel on *Top of the Pops* was a sweet gesture by the Faces. Marc Bolan wouldn't have thought of it.

Now that he's an international star, Rod is the new pop pin-up on the block. But as a member of the Faces, he's just one of the lads. Tonight the Faces blaze through a three-song *Top Gear* session – 'Maggie May', 'Stay with Me' and 'Miss Judy's Farm' – flaunting all the bonhomie, the gleam in the eye and the entertain-at-all-costs rowdiness that made Peel fall in love with them. Working-class authenticity is central to their charm, and much of it comes from Stewart. Down-to-earth, tartan-scarved, slightly roguish, he connects with his fans on a deep emotional level. His songs are their songs. His life could be their lives.

Next year he'll pay cash for a thirty-two-room Georgian mansion outside Windsor, buying it from a lord-in-waiting to the Queen.

1972: THE ROCK 'N' ROLLERS

'John Peel thought we'd sold out and I can see now that he was helping himself more than us . . . I haven't seen him since and he certainly never plays our records now.' MARC BOLAN in 1976

Top Gear
Radio 1
11 January 1972

Argent – Osibisa – Dion – Natural Gas – Kevin Ayers – Michael Chapman – David Bowie – The Beau Brummels – Stoneground – Faust – Electric Light Orchestra – Can – Captain Beefheart

As new measures are introduced by the Royal Ulster Constabulary to improve security for politicians in Northern Ireland, it's reported that some Stormont ministers are being armed and trained in the use of handguns.

Last October, *Top Gear* moved from Saturday afternoons to Wednesday nights. This month it moves again, to Tuesday nights. No longer a standalone programme, it's now one of five elements making up the Monday-to-Friday 10 p.m. strand *Sounds of the Seventies*, playing 'progressive pop' (as a former Radio 1 controller fogeyishly used to call it) to a clued-up, switched-on, album-buying audience of young night owls in their teens and twenties.

Peel is the big beast of this world, even if *Top Gear*'s incorpora-
tion into *Sounds of the Seventies* threatens to chip away at his authoritative identity. It's a bit like being a gorilla and having to share a
cage with the chimpanzees. But the upshot of the reshuffle is that
Peel has gained more than he's lost. *In Concert* has been taken off
him, but he's been put in charge of a new show (*Friday Night Is
Boogie Night*) and had his airtime increased to four hours a week.
This establishes him beyond doubt as the senior figure on Radio 1's
night-time airwaves, the DJ whom other *Sounds of the Seventies* presenters like Alan Black and Bob Harris look up to. The murmuring
Harris, a devotee of *The Perfumed Garden*, has a style clearly modelled on Peel's and even looks like him with his beard and high fore-
head. It all helps to create the disquieting impression that Peel, for
all his seniority, can be cloned and replaced if he steps out of line.

Tonight's *Top Gear* takes the listeners on a journey through
German rock (Can and Faust), African rock (Osibisa) and sym-
phonic rock (Electric Light Orchestra) by way of a new Argent
single ('Hold Your Head Up') and tracks from albums by David
Bowie (*Hunky Dory*), Captain Beefheart (*The Spotlight Kid*) and
Kevin Ayers (*Whatevershebringswesing*). Oddly, a lot of them are
track-one-side-ones, suggesting that Peel either didn't have time to
listen to the albums all the way through or settled for the easiest
songs to cue up. There are better ones he could have played, such
as Ayers's baleful-sounding 'Song from the Bottom of a Well' and
Can's hypno-cyclical, stone-grooving 'Oh Yeah'.

But it's when Peel goes off the beaten track that he reveals the first
hints of a dissatisfaction with modern rock that will become more
noticeable as the months go by. First he plays two versions of Dion's
'The Wanderer' – the original 1962 hit and a re-recording from
Dion's new album – and later he precedes a track by the American
band Stoneground with a 1965 US hit ('Laugh Laugh') by the Beau
Brummels, whose singer Sal Valentino is Stoneground's frontman.

More songs from the Sixties and even the Fifties will creep into Peel's shows in the spring. By the summer the trickle will become a flood.

Whatever he plays, Peel will always have a crucial edge over the other *Sounds of the Seventies* presenters in the breadth of his knowledge and the weird connections that his brain makes when his hands are pulling down records from shelves. His new Friday night show equips him with an overflow for the sounds that don't quite fit into *Top Gear*, as well as giving him more time to play rock 'n' roll and R&B 45s without fretting about falling behind with the new releases.

But *Friday Night Is Boogie Night* is not just the radio equivalent of a jukebox stuffed with oldies. It's a highly versatile programme that can flit from Anne Briggs to Gentle Giant, from Bob Dylan to the Three Degrees, and from Jerry Garcia to Sly and the Family Stone.

It can also proudly present the ultra-pioneering sounds of an indefinable new English rock band. And ten days from now, it will do precisely that.

Friday Night Is Boogie Night
Radio 1
21 January 1972

Don Nix – Roxy Music – The Byrds – Keith Tippett – David Bowie – Andy Roberts and Adrian Henri – The Attack – The Nice – Patto – Bob Dylan – Stray – Steeleye Span – The Faces – Claire Hamill

Labour MP Leo Abse criticises the price of condoms, blaming the 'sinister monopoly' of LRC International (formerly the London Rubber Company). LRC manufactures 95 per cent of the 125 million condoms used by British men each year.

Roxy Music come from fine-art courses, Cornelius Cardew lectures and Tyneside soul bands. Tipped by *Melody Maker* as a band to watch, they're making their radio debut with a session tonight. They have an unusual line-up: a heavy-rock drummer, a jazz bassist, a saxophonist who doubles on oboe, a psychedelic guitarist who used to be in the Nice, a singer who sounds like Gene Pitney channelling Edith Piaf, and a 'non-musician' who tinkers with a synthesizer – the futuristic instrument that shot to popularity with *Switched-On Bach*, Walter Carlos's 1968 album of Johann-Sebastian-meets-electronics.

Roxy Music's first song, 'Remake/Remodel', has pounding drums, wild guitars and a chorus that seems to consist of the band members chanting a car registration number. Their second, 'B.O.B. Medley', begins with the synthesizer making the sound of an air-raid siren (generating direful images of the Blitz), before moving through a series of disparate sections in which Roxy Music morph into a galumphing rock group and imitate a palm court orchestra at a tea dance.

Floating on top of the music is the gurgling croon of singer Bryan Ferry. He failed an audition for King Crimson a year or so ago, and one can see why. He adds a 'gh' to almost every word he sings: 'twenty-furrghst centuughrry schizoid maagghnn'. It wouldn't have been quite what Crimson were looking for. Peel, who saw Roxy Music play in Wimbledon last month, is much more receptive to Ferry's freakish voice. One of its most arresting qualities is an exaggerated, quasi-French vibrato – and as Marc Bolan can attest, Peel is very partial to an exaggerated vibrato.

Roxy Music's third song, 'Would You Believe', enters like a sobbing Johnnie Ray ballad before accelerating into frenzied doo-wop. It could be the cheekiest mutation they pull off all night. John Muir, *Friday Night Is Boogie Night*'s producer, has sequenced the song brilliantly to follow two Irish jigs by Steeleye Span. The effect is like Orson Welles interrupting the Ramón Raquello Orchestra to announce that Martians have landed.

Taking references from almost every decade of the century, Roxy Music could be an elaborate pastiche or a scintillating new direction for British rock. Or they could be something else entirely. On only its third outing, *Friday Night Is Boogie Night* has served up a genuine enigma. Tonight Roxy Music have neither a manager nor a record deal. The response to their extraordinary session will soon get the ball rolling.

Friday Night Is Boogie Night
Radio 1
28 January 1972

David Bowie – Jerry Garcia – If – Medicine Head – Genesis – Z. Z. Hill – Manfred Mann's Earth Band – Ry Cooder – Elvis Presley – Captain Beefheart – The Faces – The Youngbloods – Slim Harpo

The Sex Anti-Discrimination Bill is 'talked out' in the Commons after the Speaker refuses to allow a vote. Legislation to outlaw discrimination against women is now unlikely to be pushed through this year.

For over a year, Peel has been sniping at progressive-rock groups in the music papers, accusing them of being self-important, snobbish and not progressive in the slightest. He was never much of a Yes fan. Jethro Tull have started to aggravate him. And he took an instant dislike to Emerson, Lake and Palmer when he saw them at the Isle of Wight festival in 1970. The bombast. The pomposity. The insufferable cannons. Keith Emerson, as it happens, is heard on *Top Gear* every week – his previous band the Nice supplied its theme tune – but Emerson, Lake and Palmer are a new strain of progressive rock for which there is no known vaccine. Never mind the songwriting, feel the twenty-minute keyboard solos. Peel despairs.

By rights, he ought to disapprove of Genesis. They go in for all the fancy time signatures that Yes and ELP do, and they compose flowery epics inspired by Ovid's *Metamorphoses*. Peel, however, has a soft spot for these young men born into Britain's officer class, who met at Charterhouse boarding school as teenagers. Perhaps Peel, who had a miserable ten years at boarding school, feels them to be kindred spirits. And at least they keep the solos relatively short.

On their latest album, *Nursery Cryme* – and in tonight's session – Genesis indulge in a strange sort of comedy-horror-prog with songs about a man who slices off his toes ('Harold the Barrel') and a Triffid-like army of deadly weeds on the march ('The Return of the Giant Hogweed'). Peel finds the band's macabre Victoriana refreshingly original and enjoys the husky intensity of Peter Gabriel's voice. But there's another important factor that shouldn't be overlooked. Genesis don't sell as many records as ELP or Yes. They have underdog status. They're not music press darlings. For Peel, who resents being told what to like, this is a big point in their favour.

David Bowie has been recording a new album, *The Rise and Fall of Ziggy Stardust and the Spiders from Mars*, which will come out in June. He previews two songs in a session tonight ('Hang on to Yourself' and 'Ziggy Stardust') which are much more assertive – more rock 'n' roll – than the bashful Bowie at the Paris Theatre last summer. He could do with a breakthrough. *Hunky Dory* has been out for six weeks and has done nothing of note. Peel has been typically supportive, but there's no hit single, no tour, no TV presence. Tony Blackburn made 'Changes' his Record of the Week, a chink of light in the gloom, but it wasn't much help to album sales. *Hunky Dory* has been another critically acclaimed David Bowie commercial failure.

Bowie seems impatient to shed his old persona, his old skin. Last month he had his long blond tresses – which made him look like Veronica Lake in *The Blue Dahlia* – cut short and spiked. In the new *Melody Maker*, he talks outrageously in Polari and claims to be homosexual. The interview has drawn gasps: are pop singers allowed to say things like that? 'I've invented a new category of artist,' he tells the *MM* airily, 'with my chiffon and raff. They call it pantomime rock in the States.'

Friday Night Is Boogie Night has given Britain a glimpse of Ziggy Stardust while the silver-suited specifics of the character are still being fine-tuned. Suddenly in vogue, Bowie will have a second session broadcast by Bob Harris within a fortnight. Both of them feature a song by the Velvet Underground, 'I'm Waiting for the Man'. It's nice of him to think of Lou Reed at a hectic time like this, but if there's one thing Bowie isn't doing, it's waiting.

Friday Night Is Boogie Night
Radio 1
7 April 1972

Flamin' Groovies – Mahavishnu Orchestra – Stackwaddy – Argent – Audience – The Everly Brothers – The Outlaws – Captain Beefheart – The Searchers – Manassas – Todd Rundgren

Edward Heath sacks a raft of Cabinet ministers and promotes sixteen MPs to new posts. Among those moving up is Michael Heseltine, who leaves environment to become minister for aerospace.

The Flamin' Groovies are an anomaly and an anachronism. The San Franciscans have nothing to do with the Haight-Ashbury hippie subculture and prefer Little Richard to acid rock. They wear black drainpipe jeans with a thin gold thread running down them like a pinstripe, and they sing songs about reelin' and rockin' at the high-school hop. Their time-warp verisimilitude is just one component in a lifetime's dedication to the fundamental tenets of rock 'n' roll as a craft and as a calling. With Peel pining more and more for a return to purity, there are times in the Seventies when he'll play the Flamin' Groovies with all the desperation of a drowning man clutching at a sliver of broken canoe.

But as much as Peel craves simplicity, some of his inconsistencies in 1972 can boggle the mind. Straight after the Groovies' 'Gonna Rock Tonite', he plays a piece of speedy-fingered jazz fusion by John McLaughlin's Mahavishnu Orchestra, probably the most masterful virtuoso ensemble in the world. They're a solemn, spiritual bunch – much more so than Yes or ELP – which seems jarringly out of step with Peel's inclination to decry prog rockers as humourless show-offs. He'll also play music this year by several acts destined to become behemoths of mid-Seventies soft rock, including Peter Frampton, the Eagles, REO Speedwagon and Boz Scaggs. That his programmes continue to promote artists as diverse as Gong, ZZ Top, Carla Bley and Manfred Mann's Earth Band begs the questions: exactly which direction does Peel want rock music to go in, and how can it be simple and pyrotechnical at the same time?

Top Gear
Radio 1
18 April 1972

David Bowie – The High Level Ranters – Kingdom Come – Mike Hurley – Plainsong – Barclay James Harvest – Kenny Young – Tim Rose – Taj Mahal – Amon Düül II – Wishbone Ash – Elton John

Lord Chief Justice Widgery's report into Bloody Sunday, which saw thirteen civil rights marchers in Londonderry shot dead by British soldiers on 30 January, is published tomorrow. It is understood to

censure individual officers but exonerate the army from overall
responsibility.

An alien descends from outer space and gives superhuman powers to a sexually ambiguous rock singer. Ziggy plays guitar and all the children boogie. These are the final weeks of what remains of David Bowie's cult status. By the end of July, he'll be the fourth alumnus of *Top Gear*'s Class of '68 – after Marc Bolan, Elton John and Rod Stewart – to conquer the pop world. And he'll do it with 'Starman', the new single that Peel plays tonight.

An immaculately written and arranged pop song, 'Starman' is the signal for Bowie to leave the orbit of *Top Gear* and fly to other moons. Radio 1 has thrown its weight behind the Ziggy concept in recent weeks, commissioning sessions and previewing the album, and Peel will do his bit by playing 'Starman' many times. But Bowie is already slipping out of his reach. 'Starman' is the moment when the glamorous Bowie outgrows a rather unglamorous DJ who took up his cause when he had no one else to turn to. Bowie will record one further session for *Top Gear* in May, but he and Peel will never meet again.

Bolan, meanwhile, has become such a phenomenon that a new noun – T. Rexstasy – has had to be coined to describe it. It's Beatlemania with glitter. Earlier in the year T. Rex had their third number 1 hit ('Telegram Sam') and next month they'll have their fourth ('Metal Guru'). Bolan isn't just a pop star, he's a pint-sized messiah. He and his teen-screaming disciples are brightening up drizzly old Britain with a music and fashion craze called glam rock. The boutiques of Chelsea and Kensington are where the fashions are bought, but the colour television screen is where they burst into bloom. Dressed in his Biba satin and feather boa, it seems hard to believe that Bolan comes from the same species as Britain's stuffy-looking TV presenters and politicians.

'Starman' will launch phase two of glam rock, with a stunningly camp Bowie performance on *Top of the Pops* that literally changes lives. 'Next day all hell broke loose in the playground,' Marc Almond will pithily remark of that Thursday night bombshell on prime-time BBC1. And as the chart hits mount up for Bolan, Bowie, Elton John ('Rocket Man') and Rod Stewart ('You Wear It Well'), has anybody spotted that *Top Gear* is the common link between them, or is everybody having too much fun? Even old *Top Gear* retainers like Mott the Hoople ('All the Young Dudes'), Hawkwind ('Silver Machine'), Family ('Burlesque') and Lindisfarne ('Lady Eleanor') are now feeling the benefit of daytime airplay on Radio 1 and muscling their way into the charts. Peel has had more influence on the early-Seventies pop climate than he will ever be given credit for.

Late last year, Peel phoned Bolan for a chat. They'd been inseparable in former years but Peel hadn't seen much of his friend since his rise to fame. From Peel's perspective, some reservations about T. Rex had been nagging at him. He suspected them of treading water as a hit-singles machine and he'd gone a bit off-message after playing 'Get It On' last summer ('Get it on? I couldn't wait to get it off'). But he little realised what a grievous insult this amounted to in Bolan's eyes. When Peel asked to speak to Bolan on the phone, he heard him say in the background: 'Tell him I'm not in.' The call was never returned. Over the following weeks it began to dawn on Peel that he had been excommunicated.

This sea change in attitude from Bolan cut Peel to the quick and, as he later admitted, made him wary of having another close relationship with a musician. But Bolan's behaviour raises some awkward questions that cannot satisfactorily be answered. Friendship aside, did Bolan owe Peel a debt? Should he have repaid him in some way – if not financially, then perhaps by making sure that Peel was given full recognition for his early support? Or did he in fact owe Peel absolutely nothing whatsoever? Was all fair in love, war and the music business? In which case Peel, a walking reminder of

Bolan's unsuccessful past, had simply become surplus cargo in his chic new life.

But there's another question. Was Peel more involved in the fracture of the friendship than he knew? It's interesting that he pulled away from Bolan's music at the point when it began to consolidate ('Get It On') – in other words, when it stopped changing. Just as Peel had stepped back from the brink of the counterculture when it solidified into something resembling a betrayal, he would always veer away from any trend or movement once it became too concrete, too fixed and too dissimilar to what it looked like when it started. Messiah or not, even if Bolan had remained a friend, Peel would have had to consider dropping him from *Top Gear*.

Top Gear
Radio 1
4 July 1972

The Albion Country Band – Sha Na Na – The Five Satins – Caravan – The Kinks – Roxy Music – Flamin' Groovies – Van Dyke Parks – Faust – Don and Dewey – Wizz Jones – Finbar and Eddie Furey

Robin Chichester-Clark, minister of state for employment, rebuts a Labour MP's suggestion that 'millions of women are being exploited' by unfair wages. Legislation giving women the same pay as men is expected to be passed in 1975.

Six months after their dazzling debut on *Friday Night Is Boogie Night*, Roxy Music have released their first album on Island Records and will record a single ('Virginia Plain') next week. Roxy have fascinated the music press with their leopard-skin costumes and synthesizers, but a couple of them also have Fifties quiffs à la sci-fi

Teddy boys. It seems to have sent Peel harking back to the days of pompadours and finger snaps. In places tonight's *Top Gear* is like a doo-wop cavalcade.

Sha Na Na, a revivalist act whose choreographed routine in the *Woodstock* movie reawakened interest in Fifties culture across America, have been cropping up in Peel shows since 1970. They recently did a 'split' EP with the Flamin' Groovies, which Peel liked very much. Now and again they use the same saxophone sound as Roxy Music: that obstreperous 'Yakety Yak' honk. The Five Satins, also heard tonight with their 1956 doo-wop classic 'In the Still of the Night', will appear next year on the soundtrack of *American Graffiti*, a hugely influential rites-of-passage film about teenagers growing up in California's Central Valley during the rock 'n' roll years.

Peel also plays a doo-wop single from 1957 (after a track from Faust!) in the shape of Don and Dewey's 'I'm Leaving It Up to You', which will top the US charts for Donny and Marie Osmond in 1974. The Osmonds, an all-singing, all-dancing Mormon family of grinning nostalgists, take most of their cues from the Fifties – Donny's solo hits include covers of Nat King Cole, Frankie Avalon and Tab Hunter – no doubt feeling that it was the last decade of discipline and decorum before America went to hell. But even in the decadent present day, a Fifties revival is starting to build and some of its early stirrings can be found on *Top Gear* and *Friday Night Is Boogie Night*.

Friday Night Is Boogie Night
Radio 1
21 *July 1972*

Thin Lizzy – J. J. Cale – Miller Anderson – Chuck Berry – The Flying Burrito Brothers – Arthur Lee – Rod Stewart – Roxy Music – Bill Doggett – Bridget St John – Pink Floyd – The Move – Tomorrow

The IRA detonates twenty bombs across Belfast, killing eleven people.
Protestant leaders warn that Loyalists may take the law into their own
hands if the army fails to act.

Peel comes bearing samples of hard rock (Captain Beyond), blues
rock (Miller Anderson), Oklahoma rock (J. J. Cale) and Celtic
rock (Thin Lizzy) – and then, as if none of them are hitting him
where he needs to be hit, he plays five Chuck Berry songs in a row:
blam, blam, blam, blam, blam. Berry is due in London next month
for a rock 'n' roll revival concert at Wembley Stadium, where he'll
share the stage with Jerry Lee Lewis, Little Richard and Bo Diddley.
Fifties nostalgia is really catching fire. Berry was on the cover of *New
Musical Express* earlier in the year, relegating Marc Bolan to second
billing, and not many people do that in 1972.

If there's one person who links the Fifties to the Seventies, via
the Rolling Stones, the Faces and the Flamin' Groovies – and who
therefore is an honorary godfather of *Friday Night Is Boogie Night* –
that person is Chuck Berry. The five songs Peel plays are 'It Wasn't
Me' (1965), 'Oh Baby Doll' (1957), 'My Mustang Ford' (1965), 'No
Particular Place to Go' (1964) and 'Anthony Boy' (1959). A Berry
compilation must have arrived through the post and Peel decided
he couldn't pick just one track. The listeners can feel relieved he
stopped at five. He's fully capable of playing whole albums from
start to finish.

One song that Peel steers clear of, though, is Berry's new single, a version of a 1952 tune by the New Orleans bandleader Dave
Bartholomew. It will sail to number 1 on both sides of the Atlantic
in the autumn, delighting millions of fans of infantile humour with
its panoply of double entendres. Peel has a knack of being several
months ahead of the pack, but you'll have to forgive him if he draws
the line at playing 'My Ding-a-Ling'.

Top Gear
Radio 1
3 October 1972

Pete Townshend – Lindisfarne – The Chieftains – Professor Longhair
– Mel and Tim – Kevin Coyne – John Baldry – Back Door – The
Electric Prunes – Matching Mole – Rab Noakes – Roy Buchanan

*Police in Manchester carry out a series of raids on newsagents' shops,
removing pornographic magazines from shelves. A fortnight ago
the October print run of* Men Only *– about 260,000 copies – was
impounded by Scotland Yard.*

The Electric Prunes were one of hundreds, if not thousands, of
American garage bands in the Sixties. The oscillating guitars and
kaleidoscopic lyrics of their second single, 'I Had Too Much to
Dream (Last Night)', made it an exceptional record of the psych
era – as well as a US Top 20 hit in 1967. But nobody's heard anything from the Electric Prunes since a couple of off-the-wall religious albums in the late Sixties, and the rumour was they didn't
play on those anyway. Like so many other bands of the time – the
Castaways, the Remains, the Barbarians, the Shadows of Knight –
the Prunes were forgotten a long time ago.

The latest release on Elektra Records is a double album called
*Nuggets: Original Artyfacts from the First Psychedelic Era 1965–
1968.* It's a compilation of American garage bands and it starts
with the Electric Prunes' 'I Had Too Much to Dream (Last
Night)'. The twenty-seven songs on *Nuggets*, many of them one-
hit wonders, are the national anthems of garage rock, epitomising
the excitement and immediacy of the mid-Sixties and taking
contemporary listeners back to a time when the ambitions of
many bands went no further than buying a day's studio time and

recording their songs with as much teenage energy as possible.

'Look out, you rock 'n' rollers,' sang Bowie at the start of the year, 'pretty soon now you're gonna get older.' *Top Gear* has always been a corner of the radio where age doesn't really matter; you can be sixty-eight and sing the blues like Son House, or twenty-two like the members of Genesis. But as someone who has a vested interest in rock's future, Peel is growing increasingly concerned with the importance of generational renewal. 'Nowadays,' he'll tell his *Top Gear* listeners just over a year from now, 'you hear a lot of very famous bands making LPs which they don't really seem, when you listen to them, you don't feel that they really *mean* it any more.' He will speak in scathing terms of 'the hideous people' who are 'busy working on their fifth and sixth LPs', oblivious to the fact that they should have vacated the stage after their first or second.

This is why *Nuggets* is manna for Peel, who loved most of the groups the first time round and believed they captured the spirit of what music should be about. Live for your day in the studio. Give it everything you've got. And then – please, for God's sake – go away. Get in. Get heard. Get out. Better than hanging around for years and clogging up the record shops like a furred artery.

The sleevenotes for *Nuggets* were written by the New York rock critic and musician Lenny Kaye, who also compiled the tracklisting. In his notes, Kaye uses a novel term to describe the snotty, dynamic, urgent music within.

He calls it punk rock.

1973: THE CONVERSION JOB

*'It was unplayable as far as DJs were concerned ... It was
very, very fortuitous that John Peel was around.'*
TOM NEWMAN, producer of *Tubular Bells*

Top Gear
Radio 1
27 February 1973

Flash Cadillac and the Continental Kids – Pink Floyd – The Animals
– Asgard – Can – Mahavishnu Orchestra – Medicine Head – Paul
Butterfield's Better Days – Roxy Music

*As 47,000 gas workers vote to extend a two-week strike, four hundred
of London's largest gas users, including factories, offices and hotels,
are ordered to switch off appliances by 6 a.m. tomorrow to conserve
supplies for hospitals.*

One Sunday afternoon about three years ago Pink Floyd were
the guests on Radio 1's *In Concert*. Peel, who hosted it, was quite
different to his usual chatty self. He kept his announcements brief
('a Dave Gilmour composition', 'a Roger Waters composition')
and spoke in a respectful Radio 3 tone when introducing their
new twenty-six-minute suite, 'Atom Heart Mother', for which
they'd brought along a choir and a classical brass ensemble. It was

all very high culture and no coughing, please.

A year later, around the time of their *Meddle* album, Floyd appeared on *In Concert* again. This time the mood was more relaxed. There was panto-style interaction between Peel and the audience, and he used a facetious line from Roger Waters to introduce 'One of These Days', describing it as 'a poignant appraisal of the contemporary social situation'. (It was an instrumental.) But Peel kept the jokes within reason. A public cheerleader for the Floyd since his pirate radio days, he knew where the boundaries lay.

At present in 1973, Peel's programmes are the only method of engaging with Pink Floyd in any meaningful way, short of buying a plane ticket to see them on their forthcoming North American tour. One of rock's most aloof bands, they have little to do with the press, run a mile from TV cameras and keep their record company, Harvest, at the end of a long bargepole. None of them bothered to attend this evening's media launch of their new album, *The Dark Side of the Moon*, at the London Planetarium; instead, four life-size cardboard cut-outs were propped up in the foyer to greet the arriving journalists. The album appears to have some sort of concept to it, but the Floyd have made it clear to Harvest that they won't be explaining the concept to anyone. They will do no interviews. The music will have to speak for itself.

Harvest, who are hoping *The Dark Side of the Moon* will go to number 1, are relying on Peel to get it out there to the all-important students and stoners. To hear what the album sounds like, you have to listen to *Top Gear* for the next few weeks. Peel plays about a third of it tonight – 'Brain Damage', 'Eclipse' and 'Time', in that order – evidently unaware that *The Dark Side of the Moon* is supposed to have a subtle narrative thread running through it. Unceremoniously stripped of their continuity, the three songs suffer a psychotic breakdown ('Brain Damage') and find peace in a redemptive finale ('Eclipse'), before doubling back on themselves to exhibit the first discernible symptoms of rat-race ennui ('Time'). Not quite the story arc that Roger Waters had in mind.

But while listeners may puzzle over the concept, at least the lucky few will be able to get a realistic sense of the album's proportions. Last November, after five years of transmission in mono, *Top Gear* was upgraded by the BBC to FM stereo. For those with stereo receivers, progressive rock is finally coming out of the radio the way it was meant to sound. *The Dark Side of the Moon*, with its sumptuous production and layers of sound effects, has come at an opportune time for *Top Gear*'s new high-fidelity age. Those loonies on the path just don't sound the same in mono.

Sounds of the Seventies
Radio 1
22 March 1973

Queen – The Faces – John Lee Hooker – Supertramp – Steeleye Span – Mike Hart – Le Orme – John Dummer's Ooblee Dooblee Band – John Doonan – Roxy Music – Leo Kottke

As rumours intensify that the IRA is under pressure from Catholics in Belfast to declare a ceasefire, its political wing – Sinn Fein – rejects the government's White Paper on Northern Ireland, accusing it of failing to tackle the critical issue of administration from Westminster.

Following a *Sounds of the Seventies* reshuffle, *Friday Night Is Boogie Night* has been moved to Thursdays. The 10 p.m. show (which, like *Top Gear*, is broadcast in stereo) doesn't have an official name but is sometimes introduced by Peel as *You're Not Going Out Dressed Like That*. The more pedantic *Radio Times* – and Radio 1's PasB forms at Caversham Park – simply list it as *Sounds of the Seventies*.

'Two hours of progressive pop,' the magazine promises. Ah, that old chestnut again.

But if they only knew. All human life, from John Lee Hooker's homeless drifter ('No Place to Stay') to Roxy Music's glossy glamour girls ('Editions of You') to John Doonan's Irish immigrants in the shipyards on the Tyne ('The Ace and Deuce of Piping'), is contained within. Peel, in a bid to get to the heart of rock's primal urge, has been playing a lot of Jerry Lee Lewis lately, having got hold of an album called *The Session Recorded in London with Great Guest Artists*. The guest artists include members of Spooky Tooth and Heads Hands and Feet, and a slew of hotshot guitarists from Peter Frampton to Rory Gallagher. But the big headline is that *The Session* is Lewis's return to rock 'n' roll after a string of successes in the American country charts. The Killer is back! And while nobody would mistake *The Session* for the pinnacle of his career, the fact is that Chuck Berry's sales have gone stratospheric since he recorded his own London session with guest stars last year, so Lewis can hardly be blamed for wanting to see if lightning will strike twice. Peel, a long-time fan, is happy to help out his cause.

Supertramp, a lower-division prog outfit who have rebuilt their line-up after a pair of unrewarding albums and an arduous tour of Norway, perform a shop-window session of unreleased material. Their best song is 'Dreamer', a scampering Andrex puppy of a tune sung wistfully by the higher-pitched of their two vocalists. It's Supertramp's fourth session for Peel and the second time they've attempted 'Dreamer'. Persevering with it will prove a shrewd move. Re-recorded for their next album (*Crime of the Century*), it will take them out of the doldrums and into the Top 20. 'Bloody Well Right', another song they play tonight (sung acerbically by the deeper-pitched of their two vocalists), will be their passport to heavy rotation on American FM radio. This happens to Peel time and time again in the Seventies – he gives some friendly encouragement to a band who are down on their luck, and watches aghast as they become multimillion-selling rock Goliaths later in the decade.

Further back in the food chain than Supertramp are Queen, a peacockish four-piece who are aiming to manoeuvre themselves into a gap in the market between Led Zeppelin and the Spiders from Mars. They can't be criticised for lacking ambition, that's for sure. At the moment they have no record deal and a mere handful of college gigs to their name. The four songs in their session fizz with ideas – and the guitarist can play like hell – but the real validation will come in July, when Peel leads off a *Sounds of the Seventies* programme with a track from their debut album (*Queen*), which they've been shopping around for months. If Peel starts a show with a band, it's a big tick next to their name. Early next year he'll take delivery of Queen's second album (*Queen II*), which arrives with a letter from their singer, Freddie Mercury. The letter thanks Peel for his support and says that more airplay would be appreciated. Even peacocks have to eat.

Also heard tonight are four tracks from *Ooh La La*, the new album by the Faces. It's the follow-up to their splendidly wassailing *A Nod Is as Good as a Wink ... to a Blind Horse* (which had the famous 'Stay with Me'), but early indications are that *Ooh La La* is not such a rollicking good time. The album is months late – something to do with its complicated artwork, which can be manipulated to make a man's eyes and mouth open and close – and it's also surprisingly short, with a playing time of only half an hour. 'I wouldn't say we were striving for perfection,' a shame-faced Rod Stewart has admitted to *Melody Maker*. Sceptical eyebrows are being raised. So little music? And what kept you?

Top Gear
Radio 1
24 April 1973

Gerry and the Pacemakers – The Bonzo Dog Doo-Dah Band – Mike Sarne – Billy J. Kramer – Wayne Fontana – Dion – The Ronettes – Cliff Richard – Roy Orbison – The Beatles – Captain Beefheart

British trawlers fishing off the coast of Iceland come under rifle fire. Foreign secretary Sir Alec Douglas-Home is considering the government's response to this escalation of the so-called Cod War.

A fortnight ago Pablo Picasso died in France. The day before that, Cliff Richard came a disappointing third for the United Kingdom in the Eurovision Song Contest. A week from now, White House aides H. R. Haldeman and John Ehrlichman will become the latest casualties of Watergate. In both Britain and America, Dawn's 'Tie a Yellow Ribbon Round the Ole Oak Tree' is an immovable object and an unstoppable force at the top of the singles charts. If not the cruellest month, April hasn't always been the kindest one either.

David Bowie, to much anticipation, has unveiled *Aladdin Sane*, his highly stylised and Americanised sequel to *Ziggy Stardust*. The general feeling is one of faint anticlimax. Peel has played tracks from it, but it must be an odd experience for him. The Bowie he used to know had shaggy hair and boundless spirit. The Bowie of the moment, a hollow-cheeked androgynous shapeshifter in a Kansai Yamamoto kimono, is not someone he recognises. It's been eleven months since Bowie recorded his last session for *Top Gear*. It's looking as though 'last' will mean final.

'I get a lot of very nice letters,' Peel says to his studio guest tonight. 'Letters that make you think, "Well, OK, it's worth carrying on." But then you get a lot of very strange letters, too . . .'

Captain Beefheart grunts sympathetically.

'*You* must attract more strange letters than any other man in the world,' Peel suggests to him.

'I'd say Liberace attracts more,' Beefheart ponders. 'But I do run him a close second, I'm sure.'

Beefheart and the Magic Band are on a tour of Britain. Peel, who's been spending a bit of time with them, is struck by how many notebooks Beefheart seems to fill in a day. In his basso profundo Orson Welles voice, Beefheart confirms that he's written fifty-five unpublished novels. They don't take him very long: give him a notebook and he can dash off 'a book a night'. Peel asks him about a rumour that he's amassed thousands of unreleased songs. 'Oh yeah! Today I must have done at least twenty.'

Peel: 'I think a lot of people miss the point that a lot of what you write is funny?'

Beefheart: 'It's ridiculous. It's ludicrous. I write something in five minutes and the next thing it's turned into a whole essay or something. But I'm just *joking*. Mainly, humour is the whole thing that I've been doing. Everybody thinks I'm a real heavyweight.'

Peel hopes the interview will have demonstrated to the listeners that Beefheart is just a regular bloke.

In the world of football, Peel's boyhood team – Liverpool F. C. – are on the verge of clinching their first league title since 1966. By way of celebration, he has sidelined *Aladdin Sane* and *Ooh La La* for the night and put together a Sixties and Merseybeat special. There are new sessions from Gerry and the Pacemakers and Billy J. Kramer (neither of whom have been anywhere near the charts since Liverpool last won the league), and the rest of the show is made up of twenty-seven A-sides, B-sides and album tracks released between 1960 and 1969. It was a decade that began with Peel going to America to appease his father. It ended with him playing Beefheart's logic-defying, dissonant-collisionist, eco-surrealistic, avant-garde double album *Trout Mask Replica* to half a million hippies on a Saturday afternoon.

One 45 from 1961 that Peel digs out tonight is Dion's 'Runaround Sue', an American chart-topper during his Dallas insurance-selling days. Last summer, after battles with heroin and years of dwindling record sales, an older and wiser Dion got back together with his former doo-wop group the Belmonts, singing their teenager-in-love hits to 18,000 delirious baby boomers at a sold-out Madison Square Garden. America's craving for nostalgia rages unabated. And it's not just America. Opening in cinemas around Britain this month is *That'll Be the Day*, a coming-of-age film set in the late Fifties, when rock 'n' roll is filling young Englishmen's heads with intense wanderlust and Elvis dreams. Some of the period clothes worn by the actors have been made by a retro boutique in Chelsea called Let It Rock, run by a Fifties-obsessed fashion designer named Malcolm McLaren. Some might think the clientele of a shop specialising in Teddy Boy clothes would be in single figures – especially in the chichi King's Road – but they'd be surprised. In parts of London and the Midlands, the mean streets are roamed by a new Teddy Boy generation. 'I like the way they dress and I like the music,' a young Birmingham lad in crepes and drapes tells ATV's reporter Chris Tarrant. 'So I just converted, like.'

It's been a transformative ten years all right. Peel reaches for Mike Sarne's 1962 hit 'Come Outside', a song about a would-be Romeo trying to chat up a sulky girl. The girl is played by an eighteen-year-old actress, Wendy Richard. Now twenty-nine, she has landed a plum role as the dim-witted but lovely sales assistant Miss Brahms in BBC1's department-store comedy *Are You Being Served?* Six episodes in, her coronation as the nation's new sitcom sweetheart is already looking a foregone conclusion.

Sadly, last Wednesday's episode ('Diamonds Are a Man's Best Friend') was the last in the current series.

Top Gear
Radio 1
15 May 1973

John Keen – Country Gazette – Buddy Holly – Kevin Ayers – The
Wailers – Paul Simon – John Fahey – Little Feat – Paul McCartney
and Wings – Bob Dylan – Roger Daltrey – Peter Hammill

*Prime Minister Edward Heath admits to being disturbed by revelations
about the British mining company Lonrho, including large payments
to a former Conservative minister through an offshore tax haven in
the Cayman Islands. Mr Heath says Lonrho is 'an unpleasant and
unacceptable face of capitalism'.*

The Wailers, a Jamaican band, are due in London next week to
appear on Radio 1's *In Concert*. Peel, their biggest fan at Broadcasting
House, will be the compère. Fronted by the charismatic Bob Marley,
the Wailers recently made a symbolically important appearance on
The Old Grey Whistle Test – the BBC2 rock programme hosted by
Bob Harris – where they were squeezed in between the Cambridge
folk singer Pete Atkin and concert footage of Yes at the Rainbow. It
would have been many *Whistle Test* viewers' first sighting of Marley,
and for some their first taste of reggae. One almost shudders to
think what all those Yes fans made of 'Concrete Jungle'.

On the day they did *Whistle Test*, Marley and the Wailers also
recorded a session for *Top Gear*, which goes out tonight. Peel's
interest in reggae has been bubbling under the surface since the late
Sixties, though he wasn't the first British DJ to play Jamaican music,
nor even the second or third. In the week he joined Radio London
in 1967, one of the new entries in the Top 40 was Prince Buster's 'Al
Capone', a ska instrumental that helped to popularise the Jamaican
rude-boy subculture among young British mods. A few months

later, Buster's fellow Jamaican Desmond Dekker hit the Top 20 with '007 (Shanty Town)', an example of the melodic rocksteady style that had evolved from ska the previous year. Ska and rocksteady, however, were never on the radar of *The Perfumed Garden*.

Nor did Peel play much reggae when it rode a two-year commercial wave in Britain between 1969 and 1971, becoming synonymous with skinheads. The Upsetters ('Return of Django'), Harry J. All Stars ('The Liquidator'), Bob and Marcia ('Young, Gifted and Black'), the Pioneers ('Let Your Yeah Be Yeah') and Dave and Ansell Collins ('Double Barrel', 'Monkey Spanner') all chalked up Top 10 reggae hits in those years. But their popularity had nothing to do with Peel, who only really embraced one Jamaican song of that period – Andy Capp's vivacious 'Pop a Top' – which he played a number of times in 1969 and 1970. But 'Pop a Top' wasn't reggae as such; it was a ska tune that had been recorded in 1968, before ska slowed itself down to reggae's more languid tempo. Peel did notice something interesting about 'Pop a Top', though: any time he played it, he would receive venomous letters from angry listeners.

'It would be very hard to exaggerate the extent to which reggae was despised among rock fans,' Richard Williams, an Island Records A&R man in the Seventies, would tell the makers of a Bob Marley documentary many years later. 'So a job of conversion had to be done.' And that conversion job, by 1973, had to involve *Top Gear*. Peel and John Walters had shown themselves up for the challenge by commissioning two sessions in 1970 and 1971, from the British reggae band Greyhound (originally known as the Rudies).

But here's the dilemma. Reggae, to a rock fan in 1973, is music from another planet. It's a radically different way of approaching the bassline, the backbeat, the song format and the English language. To many rock fans, all reggae sounds the same. But to some reggae fans, and Chris Blackwell at Island is one of them, rock is the first frontier that needs to be crossed if reggae is to go international.

Blackwell, Island's co-founder and sagacious commander, has been recording Jamaican music since the late Fifties and probably knows more about how to market reggae than anyone else in Europe. At his insistence, the Wailers' first album for Island, *Catch a Fire*, has had extra keyboards and guitars added by white American session musicians. The hope is that audiences weaned on guitar solos and rock arrangements will find this conciliatory form of reggae agreeable to the palate. And will then dive in and go searching for the harder stuff.

But if Blackwell rejoices, and he does, when the Wailers make their historic debut on *Whistle Test*, he's under no illusions that the struggle to turn rock fans onto reggae will be an uphill one. Radio 1 refuses point blank to playlist the Wailers' new single, 'Stir It Up', even though it playlisted Johnny Nash's pop version of it last year and even though Bob Marley wrote the song in the first place. The only pair at Radio 1 who are on board with reggae are Peel and Walters, who will commission a second session from the Wailers in November. But even when Peel repeats the session in January 1974, *Catch a Fire* will still have sold only 14,000 copies.

Top Gear
Radio 1
29 May 1973

Don Nix – Amon Düül II – The Boys of the Lough – The Faces – Gong – Mott the Hoople – Tangerine Dream – Annette Funicello – Mike Oldfield – Linda Jones – Jack the Lad

It's announced that Princess Anne, the Queen's twenty-two-year-old daughter, is to marry Lieutenant Mark Phillips of the Queen's Dragoon Guards in the autumn. The couple were first linked two years ago but have always denied any romance.

The Faces were appalled when Rod Stewart gave an indiscreet exclusive to the *Melody Maker* last month, in which he dismissed the *Ooh La La* album as 'a bloody mess' and 'a disgrace'. He went on to tell the journalist how much he was looking forward to working on his next solo project. Some things just aren't done. He could have waited until *Ooh La La* had actually come out.

Now, with Stewart's damning verdict still raw, it looks like the wheels may be falling off of Peel's favourite band. Bassist Ronnie Lane, frustrated by changing dynamics within the line-up as a result of Stewart's superstardom, has handed in his resignation. But first, at a gig in Virginia this month, he decides to get something off his chest. 'Ronnie came over to me in the middle of a song,' keyboardist Ian McLagan will later recall, 'and he looked me in the eye and said: "You cunt." I got up from the piano, chased after him and kicked him off the back of the stage.' The Faces have always been a byword for camaraderie. What on earth has happened?

One reason why Lane has opted to quit is that he feels the Faces' success has driven a wedge between the group and their audience. It's a complaint that's begun to be vented in the letters pages of the music papers – that fame and money have turned Britain's biggest bands into pampered egotists. It's hard enough scraping a living in 1973 without being made to feel like a bum when a rock star screams past your pushbike in his Ferrari. Or when he finally saunters onstage with no apology after an unexplained ninety-minute delay. Have these stars completely lost touch with the real world?

Earlier in the year, Peel played a session from Bees Make Honey, one of several groups who have gone back to basics to play a good-time mix of rock 'n' roll, country and blues on the London pub circuit. Pub rock, as it's been tagged, is a grassroots reaction against prog virtuosity and glam-and-glitter superficiality. Why not see some music in a warm boozer instead of queuing for hours to sit miles from the stage in a soulless air hangar like Wembley Empire

Pool? With the emphasis on fun, beer and come-as-you-are jeans and jackets, pub rock has established a hearty rapport between the bands and the audiences (since the latter are usually standing two feet from the former at a pub rock gig). It may be the new direction that Peel has been crying out for. It hasn't taken long for him to become a pub rock fan. Chilli Willi and the Red Hot Peppers, a popular band on the circuit, recorded a session for him last month. Another lot, Ducks Deluxe, are due at the BBC studios in a couple of weeks.

Peel, however, has always put more value on a newly discovered artist – a Leonard Cohen or a Loudon Wainwright – than he puts on a new scene or movement. Tonight's *Top Gear* is a case in point. It's an opportunity to hear a piece of music that flies in the face of everything espoused by pub rock. Twenty-five minutes long, it can't even be categorised as a song, much less a back-to-basics one, and it comes from an album that nobody at the artist's record company knows how to market, promote or even describe. The album is called *Tubular Bells*.

Mike Oldfield, the taciturn young hippie who has written and recorded it, made his Peel debut on *Night Ride* when he was just fifteen, playing guitar in a duo with his sister Sally. Two years later, he was the bassist on the memorable Kevin Ayers session that aired on the same day as Son House. Now, at twenty, Oldfield has created an album that proposes an imaginary collaboration between Segovia, Sibelius, Terry Riley and the Mothers of Invention. Sent retreating into his shell by a traumatic LSD experience, Oldfield has immersed himself in *Tubular Bells* as though his very life depended on it. The composition is divided into two parts that last the full length of a side of vinyl each. Oldfield plays over a dozen instruments on side one alone.

Peel was invited to dinner last week by a twenty-two-year-old record-shop proprietor named Richard Branson, who is releasing

Tubular Bells on his new record label, Virgin. As well as shops in London, Branson owns a recording studio in Oxfordshire (the Manor) and seems keen to branch out into other areas of the music business. Over dinner he gave Peel copies of three albums – Gong's *Flying Teapot*, Oldfield's *Tubular Bells* and a multi-artist jam session entitled *Manor Live* – that are all coming out on the same day, as the first releases in Virgin's catalogue.

Now four days have passed since they had dinner and Branson is holding his breath to see which albums, if any, Peel is going to play.

He doesn't have long to wait. The sixth track in tonight's show comes from Gong's *Flying Teapot*. Not a bad start for Branson's new label. There's nothing from Oldfield or *Manor Live*, but you win some, you lose some. But then, about an hour and a half into the show, after a kooky song on a kitsch LP by the Sixties beach-movie actress Annette Funicello, Peel tells the listeners they're about to hear the first part of an album called *Tubular Bells* – one imagines Branson reaching in his pocket for a cigar – which he assures them will be 'rather remarkable'. A piano melody starts to play and repeat itself very softly.

Twenty-five minutes later, as Vivian Stanshall's roll call of musical instruments concludes and the orchestral swell of the music subsides to the gentle pluck of an acoustic guitar, Peel says these words: 'I've been introducing *Top Gear* for six years now, but I think that *that* is certainly one of the most impressive LPs I've ever had the chance to play on the radio.'

Bingo.

Tomorrow the phone at Virgin will start to ring with retailers placing orders. For Branson this is sweet revenge: all the record companies he played the album to told him it would never sell. For Oldfield the blessing of Peel comes as a psychic miracle: the uncommercial opus he wrote to save his sanity has been granted wings to fly. Within weeks, an album that might have sold 280 copies to Viv

Stanshall completists and another 360 to Kevin Ayers fanatics is on its way to becoming a word-of-mouth sensation. Its picaresque journey into the future will include a hot-ticket premiere at the Queen Elizabeth Hall, a 279-week unbroken run in the UK album charts and an eternal place in twentieth-century culture.

And it all happens because Peel understands something about radio on a fundamental level. At root, there's an irresolvable dichotomy between *Top Gear* and *Tubular Bells*. What Peel wants his programmes to offer is a lifeline for rock, just as Bees Make Honey and their compadres on the London pub circuit offer a lifeline to disenfranchised live-music fans. Rock needs to identify its essence and find its salvation or, as Ronnie Lane saw, it risks severing the connection with its audience for ever. Pub rock is people's music. It connects. It's not about blowing minds. It's an honest entertainment on which hopes can be pinned. Everything about pub rock says, 'We can do this.'

Tubular Bells, on the other hand, is a prog-rock *meisterwerk* steeped in musical virtuosity and self-absorption. The brainchild of a solitary prodigy, everything about it says, 'I can do this – but you can't.' In theory and execution, Oldfield's album is wholly unequipped for radio, but it needs radio like a plant needs water, or it will die. And there's the dichotomy. No pub-rock band will ever write a masterpiece. No masterpiece can be allowed to die. What needs to blossom and what deserves to wither? Which part of itself should rock amputate to safeguard its existence? Whose side is *Top Gear* on?

Peel lets his ears guide him through the moral maze. In an issue of life and death, they're the only parts of his body that he can absolutely trust. He reaches out a hand to catch *Tubular Bells* as it falls, falls, falls. He saves it from disintegrating into ash and dust, and Branson's benighted empire is born in that gesture.

Top Gear
Radio 1
18 December 1973

Paul McCartney and Wings – Fripp and Eno – The Faces – Jack the Lad – Queen – Bridget St John – Pink Floyd – Ian Carr's Nucleus – Ann Peebles – Thin Lizzy – Roy Buchanan

Three bombs explode in London, injuring more than sixty people. The IRA claims responsibility for the attacks and issues a statement saying there will be no Christmas ceasefire.

The energy crisis has forced the government to order the three TV channels to close down at 10.30 p.m. The population of Britain has two choices: go to bed early or turn on the radio. Peel finds it most amusing. 'It's around this time,' he says, just after a song by Tyneside folkies Jack the Lad and just before an album track by Queen, 'that we collect a whole handful of listeners that we wouldn't normally get if the television was working.'

But it's no laughing matter. The OPEC oil embargo, imposed on America in October as retaliation for its support of Israel in the Yom Kippur War, applies to Britain too. Last Thursday, reacting to the country's desperate need to conserve coal stocks, Prime Minister Heath declared the introduction of a three-day working week. It will apply to all businesses except essential shops and will begin at midnight on New Year's Eve. Britain will have to get used to prolonged blackouts, rationed electricity and truncated TV schedules until the crisis is over.

Paul McCartney, topical to a fault, was motivated to write a song called 'Power Cut' on the last Wings album. 'There's a power cut, baby,' it went, 'but I still love you.' No other songwriter has managed to encapsulate the feeling of being plunged into darkness in quite the same tender-hearted terms. A new Wings song starts *Top Gear* tonight, which is a rare state of affairs. McCartney is never going to rival Lennon as Peel's favourite Beatle, but it would be nice to think he could shrug off Wings' sluggish beginnings and have a post-Beatles career commensurate with his talent. 'Jet', full of punchy phrases and smart hooks, is the sound of McCartney starting to believe in himself again.

Robert Fripp of King Crimson has made an album with Eno, the ostentatious synthesizer player in Roxy Music, who was sacked in the summer after a personality clash with Bryan Ferry. *(No Pussyfooting)* is an experiment in sound collages, looped guitars, tape delay and dreamlike drones. Peel admires the way Fripp and Eno approach their music – semi-cerebrally, semi-mischievously – and has been a supporter of King Crimson since putting them on the radio for the first time in May 1969. How long ago it now seems since January 1972, when he did the same for Roxy.

'When I first started making music,' Eno will later say, 'it was John Peel's shows that inspired me. And then when I *did* make music, it was John Peel who played it first on the radio. So I have to thank him for my career.' Fripp, a man with a fierce intellect who is pathologically unable to keep Crimson line-ups intact for longer than a few months, seems an appropriate person for Eno to be working with.

The copy of *(No Pussyfooting)* that Fripp and Eno have sent Peel is, for some reason, in the form of reel-to-reel tape rather than vinyl. The tape has been stored 'tails out' on the take-up reel, in accordance with Fripp and Eno's standard practice, meaning that the tape must be rewound to the start in order that it can be played. At the BBC, however, storing tape 'tails out' is not standard practice. Somebody on the *Top Gear* production team misinterprets what he's looking at and reverses the reels instead.

Eno, listening to Peel at home, is the first to notice that the album's opening track, 'The Heavenly Music Corporation', is being played backwards. He hurriedly phones the BBC and demands to be put through to Peel's studio. The Broadcasting House receptionist, taking exception to Eno's tone, hangs up on him. The entire twenty-one minutes of 'The Heavenly Music Corporation' go out over the air backwards without Peel, Walters or anyone else spotting the mistake.

An hour later, after another song by Jack the Lad, Peel introduces the second track by Fripp and Eno, 'Swastika Girls', which – again – he plays backwards for its complete eighteen-minute duration. 'I'd like to see what they made of *that* on *Come Dancing*,' he chortles after it ends. Having made Radio 1 history by becoming the first DJ to play an album back to front, he wholeheartedly recommends it to the listeners ('Magnificent . . . well worth having') and compares it favourably to the recent work of Tangerine Dream.

Fripp and Eno can be impish and playful, but *(No Pussyfooting)* is not a prank. It's a bold artistic statement by two musicians who overrode the objections of their management and fought their corner to have the album released. Fripp will later recall 'getting a sheet of white paper at AIR Studios, writing "No pussyfooting" and putting it on the mixing console to remind us not to allow this music to be undermined.' In the ambient and electronic fields, *(No Pussyfooting)* is near unanimously agreed to be a groundbreaking work.

But there's no getting away from the fact that most listeners in Britain who heard *(No Pussyfooting)* in 1973 heard it backwards. And it's a testament to Peel's single-mindedness as a broadcaster that, whereas more conservative DJs like Bob Harris or Alan Black might have settled for playing a two-minute extract of it backwards, Peel had the courage to play the album backwards in full. Thus are men separated from boys. In a fitting postscript to the story that sadly came too late for Peel to appreciate it, his backward versions were included as bonus tracks when a 35th anniversary edition of *(No Pussyfooting)* was released in 2008. Both were given a twenty-four-bit digital remaster by Fripp.

1974: THE WHEELCHAIR

*'I go and see John Peel playing his favourite terrible records in
a church hall. These are things by Link Wray, Fabian, Annette
Funicello ("Jo Jo the Dog Faced Boy"), Conway Twitty, Mrs.
Mills' rendering of "A Hard Day's Night", Stark Naked and the
Car Thieves, the Cats who do "Swan Lake", Wild Man Fischer,
Bill Oddie (singing "On Ilkla Moor Baht 'at" in the manner of Joe
Cocker), "The Battle of Lieutenant Calley" by B Company, Mitch
Miller's "Peace Singalong". Later on he complains over the radio
that only eighteen people turned up.'* HERMINE DEMORIANE,
diary entry for 13 February 1974

Sounds of the Seventies
Radio 1
21 February 1974

Maggie Bell – Plastic Ono Band – Tangerine Dream – Eddie
Kendricks – Frank Zappa – Robin Dransfield – JSD Band – Duane
Eddy – Ted Nugent and the Amboy Dukes – Lynyrd Skynyrd

*The Manchester United footballer George Best, who recently
announced his retirement from the game, is remanded on £6,000 bail
on charges of theft and burglary. He's accused of stealing a passport,
chequebook and fur coat from Marjorie Wallace, the reigning Miss
World.*

The country is facing a new peril. A south London gang believed to be operating from a network of underground burrows have been making ruthless incursions overground. Not content with starring in a high-rating TV series, the well-organised Wimbledon firm are hell-bent on pop glory. Their self-aggrandising anthem, 'The Wombling Song', in which they openly boast of taking home litter that doesn't belong to them, has been unavoidable on Radio 1 for more than a month.

When Britain is in crisis, pop is escapism into Things Will Be Fine. Pop is a mantra of We've Survived Worse. Pop is about the children. Pop is Lena Zavaroni, a ten-year-old Scot who shot to fame on *Opportunity Knocks*, winning it five weeks running. Her precocity is devastating: she sounds like Ethel Merman singing through a Marshall amplifier. Radio 1 has playlisted her single, 'Ma! He's Making Eyes at Me' – yet another cover version of a song from the Fifties – because right now Britain needs a ten-year-old lass from the Isle of Bute with eyes full of confidence and hope. And it needs DJs like Tony Blackburn and Noel Edmonds far more than it needs a DJ like John Peel. A dire emergency, madam? Send for Blackburn and Edmonds. All seems lost? B & E will take your mind off it with a saucy joke and a wolf whistle. Dark skies above? These boys will greet the morning sunny side up. No electricity or water? They'll find a way to put the kettle on. It's all they can do. It's all that a listener can ask for.

Working at Radio 1 must be a bittersweet feeling for Peel nowadays. His separation from his daytime colleagues is not just a metaphor, it's a physical rupture. Every evening between Monday and Friday, Radio 1 goes off the air at 7 p.m. and Radio 2 takes over the frequency. There might be a boxing match from Wembley. They sometimes have UEFA Cup football. Failing that, something for the carpet-slippers brigade, like *Alan Dell's Big Band Sound* or *The Organist Entertains*. This evening there's a showbiz quiz with Arthur

Askey; fingers on the buzzers at home, folks. Then, like a message in Morse code coming out of the dark, Peel reopens Radio 1 at 10 p.m. with a Janis Joplin soundalike from Glasgow (Maggie Bell) and a 1969 live track by the Plastic Ono Band. He could be forgiven for wondering if there's anybody out there.

We monitor the extent of our stasis by observing changes in the lives of old friends. David Bowie, a gaunt paranoiac now shorn of his Ziggy alter ego and his Spiders from Mars, is back on the playlists with a new single, 'Rebel Rebel'. It's all dolled up and suited and booted, but it presages a dystopian concept album, *Diamond Dogs*, which apparently diagnoses incurable Orwellian doom for a planet that no Starman in his right mind would want to land on. Somewhere back in Bowie's rear-view mirror is Marc Bolan, once the haughty lord of all he surveyed, now a tiny dot fading fast. The next few years will not be kind to Bolan, who drew up the statutes of glam rock only to find himself fatally trapped by them. His lack of a Plan B will squeeze his career to death like an anaconda. For his latest trick he tries a ballad, 'Teenage Dream', but his golden touch has deserted him and this one won't even reach the Top 10.

Also on the playlist this week are Medicine Head, a down-home duo from Wolverhampton whose eccentric use of a Jew's harp makes them mumble and twang like J. J. Cale with a mouth full of rubber bands. Peel signed them to his Dandelion label at the end of the Sixties, plugging them on *Top Gear* three times a month during the early Seventies. Their new single, 'Slip and Slide', is an easygoing twelve-bar with a fair chance of charting. Given enough Radio 1 support it should capitalise on a couple of big hits they had last year. The success of Medicine Head, at least, is something for Peel to cheer about. Isn't it?

But Medicine Head have nothing to do with Dandelion any more, for Dandelion no longer exists. Worn down by the pressures of handling a roster of importunate artists in a hostile economic climate,

Peel agreed with his manager Clive Selwood that Dandelion had run its course. Medicine Head have been snapped up by Polydor, the major label that churns out all those misspelt million-sellers by Slade, and the resulting increase in promotion pushed Medicine Head's 'One and One Is One' into the Top 3 last summer. It may be some consolation to Peel that the duo are fulfilling all the potential he saw in them. But it's Polydor, not Dandelion, who have the Medicine Head gold discs on their walls.

'It never made money,' Selwood later writes of Dandelion, 'but that was never the intention. We were, in fact, naive to the point of stupidity . . . Would we do it again? Well, John probably would.'

Dandelion's artists have all drifted off to new homes. Clifford T. Ward, a writer of elegant love songs that Peel and Selwood never quite knew how to market, has signed to Charisma, the home of Genesis and Lindisfarne. Kevin Coyne, a Derby blues singer once put forward as a possible replacement for Jim Morrison in the Doors, has signed to Richard Branson's Virgin. And Bridget St John, whose lyrical, slightly erotic songs were tailor-made for attic bedsits illuminated by candles in Mateus Rosé bottles, has gone in search of a commercial crossover with Jethro Tull's label Chrysalis. There are no hard feelings. St John will continue to record Peel sessions until 1976, at which point she moves to America. The snarling voice of Coyne will be tingling spines on Peel's shows well into the Nineties and beyond.

As for the what-ifs and the might-have-beens, there was a merry band of rock 'n' roll revivalists from Wales that Peel saw playing in a London pub one night in 1970. He paid for them to go into a studio and offered them a deal for an album. However, like Black Sabbath before them, the Sunsets had last-minute second thoughts about Dandelion. The album was nixed, Peel was out of pocket and the Sunsets were away on their toes. They ended up signing to the EMI label Parlophone.

No, Peel and Selwood definitely weren't in it for the car or the holiday. But as the popular quiz show puts it, let's have a look at what they could have won. The lead singer of the Sunsets, with twenty-eight hits and a fanbase spanning all ages from toddlers to pensioners, will become Britain's biggest-selling singles artist of the Eighties. Will Peel be mentioned in dispatches? If he's lucky. But whatever happens, he'll always have the knowledge that he discovered Shakin' Stevens.

Top Gear
Radio 1
12 March 1974

Kiss – The Chieftains – Tangerine Dream – Bob Dylan – Ann Peebles – Sparks – Phillip Goodhand-Tait – Sutherland Brothers and Quiver

Harold Wilson, the leader of a minority government as a result of last month's general election, sets out his legislative programme in the Queen's Speech. It pledges to renegotiate the terms of the UK's EEC membership and create an agency to oversee the distribution of North Sea oil.

So far in 1974, Peel's shows have explored a plethora of genres including Krautrock (Tangerine Dream), space rock (Gong), prog rock (Gentle Giant), Irish rock (Horslips), southern rock (Lynyrd Skynyrd), harmonica-wailing Massachusetts bar-room rock (J. Geils Band), jazz rock (Billy Cobham), country rock (Gram Parsons), folk rock (Lindisfarne), reggae (the Wailers), gospel (the Beautiful Zion Missionary Baptist Church Choir), Sixties pop (the Kinks) and contemporary soul (Ann Peebles).

As ever, a Peel show stands for multiculturalism and scholarship, but it also lives or dies by its polar opposites. It's not enough to throw a feint instead of a jab by playing the Hollies' new single, 'The Air That I Breathe'; it's crucial to position it next to a piece of vintage nonsense by the Bonzo Dog Doo-Dah Band, or an obscure rockabilly 45 by Bobby Cisco, to divest it of its connotations of playlist blandness. Put 'The Air That I Breathe' in a Noel Edmonds show and it's a smoochy ballad about a woman. Put it in a Peel show, surround it with blues and angst, and it takes on a different mantle. The Hollies are singing about having no cigarettes, no books, no light and nothing to eat. Richard and Linda Thompson couldn't come up with a bleaker recessionary folk song.

Peel, whose taste for American rock leans towards the sleazier end, starts tonight's show with Kiss, a young band from New York who wear face paint and adopt cartoonish personas in their fire-breathing live shows. They're post-Ziggy and post-Alice Cooper, and one day they'll have such a colossal influence on America's youth that far-right religious groups will condemn them as emissaries of Satan. But these are early days for Kiss and the American Way; the Moral Majority is still only a gleam in pastor Jerry Falwell's eye. 'Nothin' to Lose', the first single from Kiss's debut album, is the point in the film where everybody comes in. It has an adequate production, and it knows one end of a bubblegum Black Sabbath riff from the other, but it reeks of borrowed arrogance. Singer Gene Simmons's sniggers and smirks are tantamount to the new boy in the mailroom handing out business cards with Managing Director printed on them. Peel rates these bozos? Seriously?

Krautrock, the progressive music of West Germany, is as far away from Kiss as mankind can travel. Mostly instrumental, frequently devotional and generally in thrall to trances and grooves, Krautrock began to infiltrate *Top Gear* about four years ago. Peel focused initially on just two bands: Amon Düül II, who lived in a commune outside Munich; and Can, whose headquarters were a

castle in North Rhine-Westphalia. Can were former free-jazz musicians and Stockhausen students. Amon Düül II had vague links to
the Baader-Meinhof Gang. It was hard to say which band was more
fascinating.

Since the end of 1971, more Krautrockers such as Neu! (a
Düsseldorf duo) and Faust (a cryptic art project run from a remote
location in Lower Saxony) have come on the scene, becoming
familiar names to Peel's night-time congregation. One *Top Gear* listener is a Staffordshire fifth-former named Julian Cope, who will
recall the intense experience of hearing Peel play a minimalist track
by Neu! in November 1972, when he was fifteen. 'Nothing ever
sounded so different to me,' Cope writes in *Krautrocksampler*, his
acclaimed mid-Nineties *kosmische musik* handbook. 'I had my attitude to ALL music changed.'

Peel, a firm believer that the West Germans have a hotline to
something unique and untamed that puts Britain's prudent prog-
gers to shame, would be glad to hear that his shows are having such a
profound effect. If Peel has a favourite Krautrock band, Neu! might
well be it. But it could also just as easily be Tangerine Dream, an
electronic trio from West Berlin whose menacingly cosmic albums
loom behind one-word titles (*Zeit*, *Atem*, *Phaedra*) and have the
vast dimensions of continents. John Walters has become adept at
embedding Tangerine Dream between two artists who are wildly
dissimilar, creating an almost paranormal disconnect. Last month
he followed 'Movements of a Visionary' (from *Phaedra*) with a
new Eddie Kendricks single on Motown. Tonight, 'Mysterious
Semblance at the Strand of Nightmares', a piece of music every bit
as ominous as its title, is preceded by a medley of Irish reels and
hornpipes from the Chieftains. You can almost hear Walters gig-
gling as he writes it down.

Four days ago the new Labour government announced the end
of the three-day week. Britain has some more light to see with, and

some more electricity to power its televisions with. BBC1 viewers tonight can watch *Film '74*'s Barry Norman presenting a special report on *The Exorcist* – the horror movie said to be causing psychological breakdowns in large numbers of American cinemagoers – which finally opens in Britain this week. One of its most effective scenes shows the mother of the possessed girl walking home along a leaf-strewn Washington street while the piano theme from Mike Oldfield's *Tubular Bells* is heard in the background. It's not even a year since Peel played those haunting notes on the radio for the first time, and now they're spreading terror throughout the world's largest superpower. See what happens when Peel has dinner with Richard Branson?

Top Gear
Radio 1
26 March 1974

Robin Trower – Maldwyn Pope – Rab Noakes – Tangerine Dream – Maceo and the Macks – The Coasters – Sparks – Meade Lux Lewis – Richard and Linda Thompson – Lynyrd Skynyrd

The new Chancellor of the Exchequer, Denis Healey, presents his first Budget to the Commons. His former membership of the Communist Party is mocked by two Conservative MPs who take their seats on the Opposition benches dressed as Mao Tse-tung.

Enough is enough. Peel fades out the side-long title track of Tangerine Dream's *Phaedra* after seven minutes. The next song is 'Soul Power 74', a horn-section funk workout by James Brown's backing group Maceo and the Macks. The song after that is a 1957 Leiber and Stoller composition for the Coasters. And the song after *that* is the best one of all: an outstanding new single by a little-known Anglo-American band called Sparks.

'This Town Ain't Big Enough for Both of Us', released on the Island label, sounds like a cross between 'Virginia Plain', some Frenchmen and a helium balloon. Indecipherable apart from a few words in the chorus, it has a nymph-like skittishness and a wide-screen cinematic splendour. Peel is the first to seize on its crazy amalgam of zoology and gun smoke, but everyone on Radio 1 will get behind it in weeks to come – Noel Edmonds, Johnnie Walker, Alan Freeman, even David Hamilton in the afternoons, who normally shuns anything weirder than the New Seekers.

Sparks will enter the Top 30 in May, making an appearance on *Top of the Pops* that nobody who sees it will ever forget. For three minutes, 15 million households will have precisely the same reaction, gawping in astonishment at the keyboard player's squint-eyed stare and Hitler moustache. Show-stopping performances on *Top of the Pops* are not easy things to accomplish after two years of glam-rock one-upmanship, but Ron Mael has the creepy eyes and even creepier moustache to flabbergast a nation. In workplaces, schools and colleges the following day, only one question is necessary: 'Did you see him?'

Top Gear
Radio 1
30 April 1974

Sir John Betjeman – The Oldham Tinkers – Richard and Linda Thompson – Dr John – Ruby Andrews – Beckett – Isotope – Robin Trower – The Turbans – Sparks – Can – Rab Noakes – Captain Beefheart – Sun Ra – Forty Fiddlers

The train robber Ronald Biggs, who escaped from Wandsworth Prison in 1965 and now lives in Rio de Janeiro, is told he is to be sent back to Britain as an undesirable alien. Biggs, however, will successfully resist the extradition and remain in Brazil until 2001.

Sir John Betjeman, the Poet Laureate, has followed in the footsteps of Genesis, Lindisfarne and Clifford T. Ward by signing to Charisma Records. Twelve of his poems have been set to music and released as an LP, *Betjeman's Banana Blush.* 'A Shropshire Lad', which he wrote about the English Channel swimmer Captain Matthew Webb, found its way into *Top Gear* last month. Tonight Peel returns to the album, playing 'Indoor Games Near Newbury', the opening poem on it, early in the show. A plaintive brass band provides a suitably Proustian backdrop for the sixty-seven-year-old Laureate to reminisce about Bussock Bottom, lemon curd and Wendy with the golden hair. The four and a half minutes move with the grace and gravitas of a stately procession. It's a heck of a contrast to kicking off the show with Kiss.

And now *Top Gear* can go anywhere. There's raffish carousing from the Oldham Tinkers, a Lancashire folk trio. Then to New Orleans, where Dr John the Night Tripper's *Gris-Gris* in 1968 was an esoteric classic of psychedelic magick and Haitian sorcery. His new album, *Desitively Bonnaroo*, eases off on the talismanic spirits but gives plenty of sly lessons in funky hokum. Sun Ra, the jazz bandleader, was born three hundred miles north-east of Dr John in Alabama, but claims to come from Saturn. Peel doesn't play much jazz – he never will – but he could play a week of Sun Ra and not even scratch the surface. Sun Ra and his thirty-piece ensemble, the Arkestra, are Egyptologists, cosmonauts and ethnological pathfinders. Peel picks out a track they recorded in 1960 ('Tiny Pyramids'), and Walters slots it next to some traditional Shetland music by the Forty Fiddlers. Even if you won't accept that Sun

Ra has ever set foot on Saturn, that's still a six-minute sequence worthy of *Night Ride*.

Recently signed by Virgin, who have been busy with their chequebook since the success of *Tubular Bells*, Captain Beefheart has a new album in the shops (*Unconditionally Guaranteed*) and is expected in Britain for a tour next month. Incredibly, Alan Freeman played his music on the early-evening programme *Youth Club Call* last week, which came live from a Presbyterian church hall in Llanelli. Beefheart cannot have been heard in many more bizarre settings than that. Not 'alf, pop pickers. But the song in question – his new Virgin single, 'Upon the My-Oh-My' – is a pale shadow of former glories, and that's being charitable. *Unconditionally Guaranteed* is a travesty, a lightweight pop abasement. Lamentable to behold, the front cover shows Beefheart clutching fistfuls of dollar bills with a greedy look in his eyes. Could he make it any more obvious?

Beefheart apparently views the album as the beginning of a lucrative new chapter in his life. Dismayed fans are worried he may have blown his cool for ever. Peel plays an awful song tonight ('Sugar Bowl'), no doubt hoping his friend will get this dross out of his system before the UK tour starts. The Magic Band are not so forgiving. They have walked out in disgust.

Sounds of the Seventies
Radio 1
4 July 1974

Eric Clapton – Supertramp – Robin Trower – Chapman Whitney Streetwalkers – Ry Cooder – Flamin' Groovies – S. F. Olowookere and His Federal Night Eagles Band – Ronnie Wood – Brinsley Schwarz – Edgar Froese – Be-Bop Deluxe

Leeds United's Don Revie is unveiled as the new manager of England. Under his predecessor Sir Alf Ramsey, who was sacked in April, England failed to qualify for this summer's World Cup in West Germany.

The music of Africa is an untapped resource where Western rock is concerned. Peel has no Internet or encyclopaedia to guide him, but there are times when he plays more African music in a month than some radio stations do in their history. Last summer, he broadcast sessions from Oseni (who are Kenyan), Fela Ransome-Kuti (Nigerian) and Bongos Ikwue and the Groovies (also Nigerian). He also played records by King Sunny Adé (Nigerian) and Getachew Kassa (Ethiopian), among others.

Peel is a fan of Osibisa, a London-based group with members from Nigeria and Ghana, who have recorded three *Top Gear* sessions since 1970. Osibisa have been able to cross over to rock audiences on the college circuit; it helps that their album sleeves are illustrated by the fantasy artist Roger Dean, a man revered by prog-loving students for his work with Yes. But aside from Osibisa, the only other African musician with a profile in Britain is Ransome-Kuti, who has worked with Ginger Baker. And although Paul McCartney was game enough to record his *Band on the Run* album in Lagos (and get mugged at knifepoint for his trouble), no audible influences from Nigeria made it into Wings' mid-Atlantic pop sound.

The music of the entire continent of Africa is distilled into a small selection of LPs in the back room of a shop selling kettles and toasters in London's Warren Street. It will be another eighteen months before Osibisa break into the charts and onto *Top of the Pops*; a further eight years before King Sunny Adé signs to Island; another year after that before the little shop in Warren Street lends its name to London's first specialist African record store (Sterns); and two years more before Paul Simon's *Graceland* controversially snubs a cultural boycott and puts Ladysmith Black Mambazo on the world stage.

Until then, Peel is a man lobbing feathers into the path of a cyclone. Tonight he plays a track by the Nigerian juju musician S. F. Olowookere and his Federal Night Eagles Band. It's conceivable that not one of his listeners has heard of Olowookere (or his Federal Night Eagles Band) or gives a damn about ever hearing them again. But if anyone thinks Peel may be wasting his time, they might take a listen to the new Eric Clapton single, 'I Shot the Sheriff', which he plays early in the show. A cover of a track by the Wailers, the single will catch a summer mood and propel Bob Marley's song all the way to the top of the American charts. Just as Chris Blackwell predicted a year ago, rock fans are opening their minds to reggae.

Top Gear
Radio 1
23 July 1974

Don Covay – Michael Chapman – The Heavy Metal Kids – John Cale – King Sunny Adé and His African Beats – Eric Clapton – Stevie Wonder – Cockney Rebel – Robert Wyatt – Otis Redding – Kiki Dee

Roy Jenkins, the home secretary, outlines his proposals for a Bill to secure equal status in British society for women. Discrimination will be made unlawful in employment, education and housing. An Equal Opportunities Commission will be given statutory powers to enforce the law.

In future decades, when Mike Oldfield, Richard Branson and *Tubular Bells* producer Tom Newman talk in glowing terms about the chivalry of Peel, they will all, oddly enough, misremember the same detail. They'll say that Peel played *Tubular Bells* from beginning to end. He didn't. He never got around to playing side two. In early June 1973, a few days before he planned to let his listeners hear the album's second half, his running orders were thrown into confusion when his friend Robert Wyatt, drunkenly larking about at a party in London, fell out of an upstairs window and broke his back.

The former Soft Machine drummer emerged from Stoke Mandeville Hospital some months later in a wheelchair, paralysed from the waist down. Pink Floyd, who'd first met Soft Machine back in the days of psychedelic light shows at the UFO Club, took time out of their *Dark Side of the Moon* touring schedule to headline two benefit concerts for Wyatt in November. With the help of Floyd's drummer Nick Mason, and a mobile studio set up in a Wiltshire field, Wyatt spent some time at a friend's farm earlier this year, recording an uncanny and unflappable solo album called *Rock Bottom*.

Rock Bottom sees Wyatt grappling humorously with some of the challenges facing him in his post-accident life. Richard Branson, clearly determined to corner the market in Peel's favourite artists, has released the album on Virgin. 'A Last Straw', served up as a taster from it tonight, is really extraordinary. The music is like underwater jazz, an aquatic caboodle of muted trumpets and tickled cymbals rolling around in a storm-tossed boat. The trumpet is actually Wyatt singing ('wa-wa-wa-wa'), his larynx almost submerged by the waves. Some unforeseen current, you might think, has dragged him away from the shore.

Drawn by his artist girlfriend Alfreda Benge, the illustration on *Rock Bottom*'s cover shows a group of children playing in a tranquil bay while a vivid world below sea level, of which they can hear nothing, teems with fantastical plant life and sudden danger. 'Who can possibly know what lies around the corner?' Benge seems to be asking. 'What are we supposed to do now?' She and Wyatt answered at least one of those questions by getting married a few days ago.

Sounds of the Seventies
Radio 1
5 September 1974

Chilli Willi and the Red Hot Peppers – Na Fili – Robert Wyatt – Betty
Davis – Peaches – Mike D'Abo – Neil Young – Peter Hammill –
Booker T. and the MG's – Sadistic Mika Band

*After a day of major political speeches on inflation, Prime Minister
Harold Wilson takes Westminster unawares by calling a general
election – the second of 1974 – for early next month.*

Beach detritus is scattered over the cover of Neil Young's new LP.
He stands with his back to the camera and his hands in his pockets, gazing out at the ocean and leaving his fans – whom he now
appears to thoroughly despise – to make sense of the symbols and
portents. A table and two chairs are buffeted by the wind. The fin
of a mustard-coloured Cadillac juts out of the sand at an angle, as
though the car fell out of the sky and is buried nine tenths deep.
Next to Young stands a pair of black shoes, waiting for their owner
to walk the earth again. A headline on a discarded newspaper reads:
'Senator Buckley Calls for Nixon to Resign'.

Consumed by Watergate, Nixon has done just that (he made his
final speech to his fellow Americans on 8 August), but that scarcely
solves the skein of riddles thrown up by *On the Beach*. The album
jacket might be inscrutable, but Young's songs show clear signs
of distress. A giant of the singer-songwriter era, whose albums
Harvest and *After the Gold Rush* are set texts of the post-Woodstock
counterculture experience, he now sounds lethally unhinged.
Haemorrhaging supportive rock critics as fast as he once accumulated them – *Rolling Stone* calls *On the Beach* 'one of the most
despairing albums of the decade' – Young pieces his new songs

together from stoned jams, catatonic fragments and eerily dis-
jointed phrases, making agitated references to the Manson Family
killings and his hatred of Laurel Canyon music celebrities.

Peel, however, doesn't hear despair or catatonia in *On the Beach*.
He hears rebirth. He's adamant that it's one of Young's finest albums,
and critical opinion will one day swing round to his point of view.
They may have sold millions with their songs of comforting melancholia, but *After the Gold Rush* and *Harvest* were just aperitifs for
Peel. *On the Beach* is a proper drink. He uses a hilariously Peelian
term ('a handsome work') to describe 'Vampire Blues', a song so
drowsy on marijuana that Young can barely open his eyelids to read
the lyrics off the music stand. The organist sounds like he's fallen
asleep with his head on the keys. When Young attempts a guitar
solo, half of his fingers are glued together. He later tells his biographer that the guiro-like percussion sound was made by the bassist
scraping a credit card on his beard. And thousands of miles away in
London, a man in a BBC studio finds it 'handsome'.

But it's that primal thing again. Even though he gave a fair bit
of airtime in the summer to Eric Clapton's *461 Ocean Boulevard*, a
vanilla post-rehab album of diluted Miami blues, Peel much prefers
his music neat and 100 proof. Peter Hammill, the paint-stripper-
voiced singer in Van Der Graaf Generator, is always likely to turn up
on a Peel show in this period, leaving scorch marks in the air with a
scowling harangue from one of his uncompromising prog-noir solo
albums. Hammill and Young are singer-songwriter soulmates in a
way: they create compulsively, refuse to second-guess themselves
and follow their muse come what may. Peel is too soft-spoken to
thump the table on this issue, but his stance is trenchant all the
same. Follow your muse. Report back from wherever it leads you.
Produce some *art*.

Sounds of the Seventies
Radio 1
10 October 1974

Ann Peebles and the Red Dog Band – Bachman-Turner Overdrive –
Van Morrison – John Sebastian – The Neutrons – James Brown – Jeff
Beck – Robert Wyatt – Ted Nugent's Amboy Dukes – Rod Stewart

*Voting day in the second general election of 1974 ends with a majority
of just three seats for Harold Wilson's Labour Party. Labour has 319
MPs, the Conservatives 277, the Liberal Party thirteen and the Scottish
National Party eleven.*

Like his friend Robert Wyatt, Peel got married this year. The wedding to his long-time girlfriend Sheila Gilhooly, a twenty-five-year-old former schoolteacher, was held in south London on the last day of August. Guests included Terry Wogan, Rod Stewart and the Faces, Ivor Cutler and Bill Nelson of Be-Bop Deluxe. John Walters was best man, which may explain why the guest list resembles a *Top Gear* running order. Thankfully for Peel, there's to be no repeat of his disastrous Sixties marriage to the American teenager Shirley. His second marriage will last the rest of his life.

Prior to his accident last year, Wyatt – another guest at the wedding – was a regular visitor to the renovated thatched cottage in the Suffolk village of Great Finborough where Peel has lived with Sheila since moving out of London three years ago. Peel will later express his sorrow that Wyatt's visits to Great Finborough have to be curtailed: there comes a point when his wheelchair is simply too wide to fit through the cottage's front door. Wheelchair access in Seventies Britain is something of a new concept for the disabled and non-disabled alike. It's only four years since legislation was passed requiring public buildings to introduce wheelchair ramps and disabled toilets.

Nor are wheelchairs seen very often on British television. Raymond Burr's paralysed detective Robert T. Ironside has got to the bottom of many a murky felony on BBC1 over the years, and will be back tomorrow night with a new episode about a mysterious case of arson. But apart from him, and the paraplegic car-crash victim Sandy Richardson in ITV's soap opera *Crossroads*, wheelchair users are seldom shown on screen. Viewers of a recent *Top of the Pops* may still be rubbing their eyes and wondering if they really did see a man singing a Monkees song in a wheelchair, or whether it was just a trick of the studio lights.

Wyatt has never been a remotely commercial artist, but his off-beat cover of 'I'm a Believer' has surprised everyone by edging into the Top 40. He takes a sideways approach to the chord structure and sings the well-known words in a high, forlorn voice, as if disappointment does indeed haunt all his dreams. The single has had rave reviews, as well as an *NME* cover story, and the ever-loyal Peel plays it tonight sandwiched between a song by the Memphis soul singer Ann Peebles and a track by the Detroit heavy-metal showboater Ted Nugent. What are friends for after all?

But an awkward problem arose a few weeks ago when Wyatt was invited to sing 'I'm a Believer' on *Top of the Pops*. Seeing him roll up in a wheelchair, the programme's dapper, bow-tied producer Robin Nash asked him if he wouldn't mind sitting in a normal chair for the cameras. Nash was heard to make a remark about *Top of the Pops* being a family show. Wyatt, offended, lost his temper and refused to budge. Nash, according to Wyatt's guitarist Fred Frith, then asked him to 'cover the wheelchair completely because [he] thought it was in bad taste or might upset the viewers'. That request was refused too.

Footage of the broadcast shows Wyatt positioned centre-stage in front of Nick Mason's drum kit, with cymbals towering above him. His eyes squeezed shut, Wyatt mimes his vocal while rocking his upper body back and forth and from side to side. It's a very 'un-pop' performance to watch, not least because Wyatt is wearing a hospital gown. His wheelchair is visible in wide shots, though Nash seems to try to obscure it several times with dolly-ins and close-ups.

It all happened forty years ago in what was undoubtedly a very different Britain, and to single out Nash for censure would be unfair. He was a long-serving BBC man much admired for his professionalism. But it's a curious thing about *Top of the Pops* in those days that a disabled singer was frowned upon and a spinal injury was taboo, but it was perfectly permissible to feign psychopathy as long as you looked like Hitler.

1975: THE UNTOUCHABLES

'There's always a pendulum swing, right? Well, we've had the high with rock. It's got to go the other way now. And that's where I see it heading, bringing about the dark era.' DAVID BOWIE

Top Gear
Radio 1
24 February 1975

Led Zeppelin – Whitehorn – Richard and Linda Thompson – Vernon Burch – Nico – Paul Raven – Mahavishnu Orchestra – The Shadows – Betty Wright – Stackridge – Mike Oldfield – Kokomo

Prime Minister Wilson faces questions in the Commons from Margaret Thatcher, the new leader of the Conservatives, about leaked documents revealing the Queen's shareholdings. The documents form the basis of an anti-monarchy story in the Communist newspaper the Morning Star.

Interviewed by the *NME* last December, Led Zeppelin's Jimmy Page explained the reason why the band hadn't released an album since the spring of 1973. It was, he said, because '1974 didn't really happen'. Now there was a sobering thought. Zeppelin, once a hard-working blues band, now dwelt in a Dionysian atmosphere so rarefied that an entire year could pass without them noticing.

The statistic-shattering Zep, whose albums account for a quarter of the annual sales of Atlantic Records, have now started a record label of their own – Swan Song – which they launched with a media party at Chislehurst Caves in October. Featuring magicians, fire eaters, inexhaustible supplies of Kahlúa and women in cages dressed as nuns, the party gave its intrigued guests a one-night-only inkling as to what it might be like to be Led Zeppelin all year round. Their new album released today, *Physical Graffiti*, is an extravagant, eighty-two-minute double that comes with intricate artwork offering a window – several, in fact – onto Zeppelin's world. It's like putting a penny in a slot and watching a peep show. One band member can be glimpsed in a window wearing lipstick and make-up. Another seems to be dressed in drag. More ballast for their mystique, *Physical Graffiti* has already blitzed its way to an instant platinum disc. Two million pre-orders ensured it was number 1 in the charts before it even made it to the shops.

Peel plays a couple of songs from it this evening. 'Kashmir' – eight minutes long and counting – is the more monumental of them, with its Middle Eastern modalities and far horizons. It's like the Nefud Desert scene in *Lawrence of Arabia* powered by titanic drums. But it's the other song, a grimy rocker called 'Sick Again', that gives real first-hand information about life in a rock band of Zeppelin's echelon. It drops the veil of mystique and shows how the apathetic eyes of untouchable gods view women in their periphery.

Countless numbers of rock songs in the mid-Seventies can be whittled down to a matter of randy young musicians whining about groupies. It's the common language of rock. It's the way of the world. 'Once Bitten, Twice Shy', a new single by ex-Mott the Hoople singer Ian Hunter, is a typical example. First Hunter scolds the groupie for her naivety and unschooled ways. Then, as she starts to play the field, he seeks to claim ownership of her. Then he rebukes her for losing her looks, and finally he ceases to care whether she lives or dies. Hunter, ironically, is regarded as one of rock's more enlightened songwriters.

But he's only one of hundreds writing songs like 'Once Bitten, Twice Shy'. Peel's beloved Kiss had a song on their last album (*Hotter than Hell*) about a girl who incurred the anger of guitarist Ace Frehley: she committed the cardinal sin of making him grow too fond of her. The song was called 'Parasite'. The latest Kiss album, *Dressed to Kill*, sees singer Paul Stanley propositioning a 'sweet sixteen' who is 'lookin' mean' – until her father turns up, looking even meaner, at which point Stanley scarpers. That was a close shave, eh, fans? Another song on the same album refers to women as 'meat'.

Time after time, on song after song, rock stars boast of their Herculean stamina and their on-the-road promiscuity, seeing no paradox in reacting with outrage when a wife or girlfriend back home is unfaithful. And on album after album, girls even younger than sweet sixteen are blamed for being sexually provocative, ridiculed for being emotionally immature and crucified for being so one-dimensional as to want to sleep with a rock star because of his fame. His multifaceted personality is simply not going to let her get away with an affront like that.

Rock stars are in no doubt: any damage that these girls suffer is brought upon themselves. 'If you listen to "Sick Again",' Led Zeppelin's Robert Plant tells a reporter in the new issue of *Rolling Stone*, 'the words show I feel a bit sorry for them.' That's sorry as in pity, not as in apology. Plant quotes from the lyrics, which describe an adolescent girl waiting in an American hotel for her rock-star sweetheart. She's fifteen and has been following Zeppelin for two years. Plant may well know her name: Jimmy Page is said to have had an underage girlfriend on the band's 1973 US tour. 'One minute she's twelve and the next minute she's thirteen and over the top,' Plant sighs to the man from *Rolling Stone*. 'Such a shame. They haven't got the style that they had in the old days . . . way back in '68.'

It doesn't make Plant's blithe comments any less distasteful to know that songwriters in many genres have always taken a keen interest in the physical development of young girls. Once again, it's the way of the world. On an old song from 1961 that Peel plays this evening, the singer is excited to see that a little girl from the neighbourhood has 'thrown away her candy bars' and started 'dressing up in her mama's clothes'. The song is called 'All Grown Up'. In the years since it was recorded, the singer, an early-Sixties rock 'n' roll also-ran called Paul Raven, has reinvented himself and rocketed to fame as Gary Glitter.

Glitter will be convicted of child sexual abuse and child pornography offences long after his pop career has ended, but in 1975 he's still a family-friendly entertainer, ripe for any TV comedian who wants to take the mickey out of his boggle eyes and exaggerated gesticulations. Last Thursday night, Ronnie Barker of *The Two Ronnies* squeezed himself into a Bacofoil suit and pranced around like Glitter in twelve-inch platform boots, to the delighted canned laughter of the audience. Millions watch *The Two Ronnies* every week; Peel may be one of them. Perhaps Barker's sketch gave him the idea of digging out some old pre-Glitter vinyl. Or perhaps he looked at the Top 20, saw the Glitter Band in there, and decided to play something to embarrass their leader, from when he was a nonentity.

Top Gear
Radio 1
17 March 1975

Be-Bop Deluxe – Tony Capstick – Jeff Beck – Lonnie Mack – Ducks Deluxe – Eric Clapton – 10cc – David Bowie – Bad Company – Slapp Happy and Henry Cow – John Martyn

Foreign Secretary James Callaghan warns it will be 'a disaster for all concerned' if the UK votes to withdraw from the EEC. A nationwide referendum is to be held in June as per a promise in last October's Labour manifesto.

It's probably been forgotten at Radio 1 (if it was even noticed in the first place) that last year Peel played Sparks' 'This Town Ain't Big Enough for Both of Us' several weeks before anyone else. He can also take credit for debuting 'I Can't Stand the Rain', Ann Peebles's minimalist soul masterpiece, in September 1973 – seven months before it made the British charts. And prior to that, in August of the same year, *Top Gear*'s listeners heard Bob Dylan's 'Knockin' on Heaven's Door' eight weeks before it appeared in the Top 40.

These are not isolated incidents. Peel can sniff out a hit like the lusty Mrs Gloria Rowe sniffing out a coffee salesman in *O Lucky Man!* His ratio at Dandelion may have erred on the low side, but 1975 is a year when his talent for hit-spotting verges on the supernatural. The Manchester quartet 10cc, renowned for their satirical songs and witty vocal arrangements, recently sent him their new album, *The Original Soundtrack*. He could have played any of the eight songs on it, but picked out a luminous, almost ambient, six-minute ballad. What made him choose 'I'm Not in Love'? Accidental prescience? A nagging feeling that the song would one day be important? If so, he may have convinced 10cc and their record company. 'I'm Not in Love' will hit number 1 in the singles chart at the end of June.

Tonight, Peel works the old magic again. David Bowie's *Young Americans* has been out for a month or so, defying his fans' expectations with its slick Philadelphia soul influences. It's a reminder of the distance Bowie has travelled since his first appearances on *Top Gear* all those aeons ago. He's had at least four personality changes since Ziggy, let alone since the Beckenham Arts Festival. *Young Americans* is the sound of him cruising through black America in a limousine, occasionally slowing down to shed a few more parts of himself by the roadside. Peel, looking for a song to play from it, goes for its funky closing track, 'Fame'. Robotic yet supple, it sounds like the Average White Band's 'Pick Up the Pieces' reconstituted as Krautrock. Bowie's record company, RCA, will issue it as a single in the summer. By the end of September, it'll be the number 1 song in America. Peel played it in Britain as early as St Patrick's Day. But would Bowie even remember Peel now?

As the DJ who premieres new works by top bands like Zep, Floyd and Quo, Peel has always been associated with albums – those foundational artefacts of modern popular culture. So it's easy to underestimate how much he values singles – those central planks of commercial radio programming. Peel has never shared the disdain of many rock fans for 45s as some sort of kid-sister format. But at the BBC, you're damned if you do and damned if you don't. Hit-spotting talents or not, Peel is blatantly wrong for a daytime show so must remain on the margins. Pigeonholed as the 'progressive pop' man, however, he's being sorely underused as each year goes by. In a fair world he might be more visible – some say he should have got the presenter's job on *The Old Grey Whistle Test* instead of Bob Harris. But there are those at the BBC who probably think he'd be too much of a liability. Loose cannon. Odd sense of humour. Bloody nuisance. Not quite right.

Rock Week
Radio 1
5 April 1975

Mick Ronson – Ian Hunter – Lynyrd Skynyrd

Fifty-five days into an IRA ceasefire, two pubs in Belfast – one
Catholic-owned, one Protestant – are bombed. Five Protestants and
two Catholics are killed. No group has yet admitted responsibility but
it's believed the second bomb was a reprisal for the first.

The lurid misogyny of Seventies rock goes on and on like a never-
ending slap to an unsuspecting face. Ian Hunter, whom Mott the
Hoople fans always looked to for wisdom and perspective, releases
his first solo album this month. On Radio 1's Saturday afternoon
programme *Rock Week*, Peel interviews Hunter's guitarist and
co-producer Mick Ronson. Ronson, an unaffected fellow with
a Hull accent, agrees with Peel that a song on the album called
'Lounge Lizard' – a contemptuous putdown of a woman who is
'pool hall poison' and 'a speakeasy sleazer of the highest degree' –
has received 'a much more subtle treatment' than it did on Mott the
Hoople's version of it last year.

Lack of subtlety detracting from a song's lyrical nuances is the
greatest fear of all rock stars. Mercifully it's not a problem that
plagues Florida rockers Lynyrd Skynyrd. Peel plays a track from
their new album, *Nuthin' Fancy*. It's a 'pretty tasty' album in Peel's
opinion, but he passes no comment on the lyrics of 'On the Hunt',
which liken women to horses ('both of them you ride') and have no
trouble understanding female psychology ('I can play your game').
Listeners who buy *Nuthin' Fancy* will hear a song called 'Cheatin'
Woman', in which Skynyrd's singer Ronnie Van Zant hits on a solution to the age-old predicament of how to deal with a wife who's

taken a lover while her husband has been partying on the road. What you do is get a pistol and shoot her dead, and then shoot all her friends.

Top Gear
Radio 1
14 April 1975

Commander Cody and His Lost Planet Airmen – Fox – John Martyn – Dr Feelgood – David Bowie – Keith Moon – MC5 – Cream – Eric Clapton – The Allman Brothers Band – Tangerine Dream

In a Commons debate on the future of the railway industry, the Conservative MP Timothy Raison claims that British Railways is 'going bankrupt' and will cost the taxpayer £770 million over the next twelve months.

Pub rock still clings to its back-to-basics credo, but only just. Several bands on the scene have been signed by record companies, and one of them, Ace, had an enormous hit in the winter with 'How Long'. Peel will air a new *Top Gear* session from Ace next month; after that they're heading off to the States, where – oh, the irony – they'll be touring with Yes. Pub rockers opening for prog rockers in American stadiums. The whole music business is swallowing its tail.

Another pub rock band are in session tonight. A high-energy quartet from Canvey Island in Essex, Dr Feelgood are a lot more combative than the country-style acts who won pub rock its early plaudits. With gangsterish singer Lee Brilleaux and paroxysmal guitarist Wilko Johnson making up an electrifying front-line double act, Dr Feelgood have already graduated from the pubs to the city halls – but, untypically for Peel, he was late waking up to them. Bob

Harris gave them their first Radio 1 session on his Monday night pro-gramme in November 1973, and had another session from them last December. The music papers may tease him for the soft-pedalling way he presents *The Old Grey Whistle Test* ('That was really, er, great in fact, yeah'), but Whispering Bob definitely stole a march on Peel with the Feelgoods.

Top Gear
Radio 1
30 June 1975

Latimore – Loudon Wainwright III – Sutherland Brothers and Quiver – Climax Blues Band – Dr Hook – Peter Frampton – Elvin Bishop – Steve Miller Band

Leeds United's three-year ban from European football competitions, imposed by UEFA after their fans rioted during last month's European Cup final, is reduced to one year on appeal. Leeds lost the final 0–2 to the West German champions Bayern Munich.

Forever at the mercy of Radio 1 controllers' whims, *Top Gear* was moved in January to an early evening slot of 5.15 p.m.–7 p.m., where it still resides, none too cosily, as if waiting for a more suitable billet to become available. As a drivetime DJ, Peel doesn't always make concessions to listeners who may be stuck in traffic on their way home. In February, they had to endure Nico, the former Velvet Underground singer, intoning her scary songs of personal anni-hilation. A few weeks later, Peel gave homeward-bound motorists a chance to hear Slapp Happy's Dagmar Krause, a woman with a see-sawing Brecht–Weillian voice that must have had them punch-ing their steering wheels in fury.

But something has changed since then. It looks as though a memo may have come down. *Top Gear*, as the summer glides by, is becoming awfully tame. Latimore, a soul singer, has had a disagreement with his lady and wants to make up with her; Peel wouldn't have countenanced starting a show with something so redolent of Barry White in the past. Dr Hook, responsible for the decade's most lachrymose hit so far with 'Sylvia's Mother', put away the tissues to sing a comical funk number that sounds like they're burlesquing Sly and the Family Stone. It might have been funnier five years ago, when Sly and the Family were still together. Elvin Bishop, Peter Frampton and the Steve Miller Band are all accessible, adult-oriented, risk-free artists who'll have extensive American success next year. To put one of them in a show is fair enough, but all three? Frampton's single, 'Show Me the Way', will next materialise on a double live album, *Frampton Comes Alive!*, which sells in the multimillions and becomes as ubiquitous as aviator sunglasses. All major rock bands will rubbish it, and all major rock bands will ask their managers how they can emulate it.

It's a rare evening this month when Peel neglects to play a track from the new Eagles album, *One of These Nights*, an illustration of how much *Top Gear* has softened in tone. The upsurge in AOR may be attributable to the earlier time slot, with Walters under instructions from above to keep Peel on a leash. We can imagine a degree of horse-trading going on: you can play Gene Vincent's 'B-I-Bickey-Bi, Bo-Bo-Go' on 26 May as long as you play something by the Sutherland Brothers and Quiver on 30 June. It does seem as though the summer is low on thrills.

Even the new ceremonies are performed with old skin. The Rolling Stones are on tour in America again, using Ronnie Wood of the Faces as a surrogate lead guitarist. Neil Young has put out an album he recorded in 1973 in honour of two dead friends, *Tonight's the Night*, which is so ragged and bereaved that he delayed its release for two years. Two of Peel's favourite German bands, Faust and Neu!, have broken up – though both of them operated so far under the radar that he may not have heard the news. 'I'm Not in Love' by 10cc is spending the first of two weeks at number 1, having dislodged 'Whispering Grass' by Windsor Davies and Don Estelle, two actors from *It Ain't Half Hot Mum*, who combine two great British passions – sitcoms and wartime love songs – in one profitable package. Oh dear. How sad. Never mind.

If 1974 didn't happen, as Jimmy Page contends, what exactly is happening in 1975?

Top Gear
Radio 1
25 September 1975

Led Zeppelin – Tyrannosaurus Rex – Joe Cocker and the Grease Band – Pink Floyd – Randy Newman – Fairport Convention – Jethro Tull – The Sutherland Brothers – Bob Marley and the Wailers

An expedition led by the British mountaineer Chris Bonington has climbed the south-east face of Mount Everest. One of mountaineering's greatest feats, the ascent took place in severe weather and follows a failed attempt by Bonington in 1972.

This is the last ever *Top Gear*. After eight years, the show has been axed.

Though most BBC radio listeners would not have been aware of a problem, there have been drastic budget cutbacks for the Corporation's music stations in 1975. Since the beginning of the year, Radio 1 has had to share three hours of airtime in the afternoons with Radio 2, on top of five hours in the evenings and at night. The

10 p.m. progressive strand *Sounds of the Seventies* was scrapped in January (hence *Top Gear*'s move to 5.15 p.m.) and five DJs – including Bob Harris and Alan Black – either lost their programmes or were made redundant. Harris has gone to Radio Luxembourg.

Peel, by a mixture of luck and judgement, has managed to ride out the storm. Next week he begins presenting a new show on Mondays to Fridays, when Radio 1 claws back an hour of its schedule (11 p.m. to midnight) from Radio 2. The man who always seems most vulnerable to Radio 1 culls has not only kept his job but is going to be heard an unprecedented five times a week. Keeping his nose clean with those Frampton and Eagles records in the summer may just have been the most politic thing he ever did.

Peel's final *Top Gear* revisits the music of bands and singers who meant a lot to him in the early years of the programme's run. Making prodigal returns are Jethro Tull (now a huge success in America) and Fairport Convention (battle-scarred folk-rockers on their eighteenth or nineteenth line-up). Much of the programme is comprised of session tracks recorded for Peel in the late Sixties and early Seventies. Diplomatically, he plays two songs by Tyrannosaurus Rex, without mentioning Marc Bolan once. Cueing up an embryonic version of 'Ride a White Swan' – the breakthrough hit that upset the equilibrium in their friendship irrevocably – he tells the listeners through gritted teeth: 'This is one of the numbers that they recorded for us around the time when they were changing from Tyrannosaurus Rex into T. Rex. Not altogether, in my view, an entirely happy move. But that's a personal prejudice and obviously it's done fairly well for them.' Fairly well if you like that sort of thing, his clipped tone implies. He later describes their other song, 'Sun Eye', from 1970, as 'the last whispers of an age of innocence'.

Bolan, who has spent the last nine months living in a luxury apartment on the palm-lined Avenue Princesse Grace in Monaco, might agree that it is indeed the end of the innocent age. Look at them all now. Look at Rod Stewart. A stagefright-afflicted singer with the Jeff Beck Group when *Top Gear* was first broadcast in 1967, he's now a tax exile mingling with movie stars. His current girlfriend, the Swedish actress Britt Ekland, is a former wife of Peter Sellers. Stewart's latest solo album, *Atlantic Crossing*, was recorded in Miami, New York, Los Angeles and Alabama. The three albums before that were all made in Willesden.

'I must have had blinkers on these last five years,' *Creem* magazine will quote Stewart as saying in November. 'I should have branched out a long time ago.' But there's no point in branching out if you can't rub it in, and this is Stewart's new forte. Famous for cackling with spontaneous delight in the middle of Faces songs – isn't this fun? aren't we all having a blast? – Stewart on *Atlantic Crossing* sounds more like a man with a bottle of champagne gloating at the beer drinkers from the VIP side of a velvet rope.

But at least Stewart has something to laugh about. Over Led Zeppelin dark clouds are gathering. Their manager Peter Grant has become accustomed to fielding death threats against the band. Blackmailers have vowed to kidnap Jimmy Page and cut his fingers off. Last month Robert Plant and his wife Maureen had a serious car crash on the island of Rhodes. Plant's right ankle has been badly broken. He'll be in a wheelchair for months and doctors have warned him he may never recover the full use of his legs. This is just the start of a nightmare that will descend on Zeppelin over the next few years.

Michael Des Barres is an English actor and singer who has been signed to Zeppelin's label Swan Song as a member of a band called Detective. A witness to Zeppelin's lawlessness, conceit and gluttony on Sunset Strip and elsewhere, he will remark many years later: 'What happens is, you get into this sort of elitist, hierarchical place in your mind where you're untouchable and immortal. All of this is fuelled by drugs, alcohol and adulation. But that's when the darkness comes in, because suddenly you don't believe it any more. You *know* it's bullshit. The myth of it all becomes so fragile, so flimsy and so absurd, that dark things start to happen. And then the fear grows . . . and that's what happened to Led Zeppelin.'

Like Rod Stewart, Zeppelin are tax exiles. David Bowie, another exile, is a cocaine wreck playing the central character in a Nicolas Roeg film, *The Man Who Fell to Earth*, which is being shot in New Mexico. Pink Floyd, whom Peel nostalgically harkens back to for a couple of tracks from their experimental 1969 period, have just released an album (*Wish You Were Here*) that reveals the great sense of nothing they all feel now that their dreams of fame, wealth and beautiful women have been achieved. 'Everything had sort of come our way,' David Gilmour will later say, 'and you had to reassess what you were in it for. It was a pretty confusing and sort of empty time for a while.'

The end of innocence will do that to a band. In practical terms, *Top Gear* has been cancelled because Radio 1 has rejigged its evening schedules. But looked at another way, it has fulfilled its mission. The moon has been landed on. America's pop charts have been conquered. There is nowhere else for rock to go. The musicians whom Peel helped to make popular have had their prayers answered by the gods. Now for the punishment.

PART TWO

GREETINGS ONCE AGAIN TO CONCERNED YOUNG PEOPLE ALL OVER NORTHERN EUROPE

1976: FAST TIMES

'*The Eagles and the Captain and Tennille ruled the airwaves,
and we were the answer to it.*' JOEY RAMONE

John Peel Show
Radio 1
15 January 1976

The Count Bishops – Ronnie Lane's Slim Chance – Ivor Cutler – I-Roy
– Emmylou Harris – Ricky Nelson – Roy Buchanan – Jerry Lee Lewis –
The Flying Burrito Brothers – Bob Dylan – The Pearls

*Asked by the Conservative MP Hugh Dykes if he will consider
introducing a one-year moratorium on immigration pending a report
into the reliability of official statistics, home secretary Roy Jenkins
replies with a single word: 'No.'*

Hillman Avenger turns into driveway. Man with briefcase. Front
door. Feet on mat. Voice in kitchen you're home early. Where the
kids? Upstairs. Radio on in bedroom. Dave Lee Travis. Programme
with stupid name. *It's D.L.T. O.K.* Probably only words he can spell.
Orang-utang with microphone. Ends 5.45 p.m. Fifteen minutes
of *Newsbeat*. Top story here are headlines Concorde prepares for
maiden flight next week. Supersonic plane with nose like Womble.
That's it from us. Radio 1 joins Radio 2. *Sports Desk*. Everton have

no injury worries for visit of Norwich City at weekend. Now 6 p.m. leave you in capable hands Pete Murray with *Pop Score*. Hello quiz fans. Thinking caps on. Connie Francis? Throw it over for bonus. Roy Orbison? Well interrupted.

Kids downstairs. Telly on. *Top of the Pops*. Dave Lee Travis. Gurning tosser. Here they are, the lovely Pan's People. Look better with sound turned down. Disco. All sounds the same. This is more like it. Caught in a landslide no escape from reality. Ninth week at number 1. *Top of the Pops* in January grey affair like unshakeable hangover from Christmas. Beelzebub Bismillah mammamia let-mego. Need drink. Radio 2 on in kitchen. Coming up at nine Wally Whyton's *Country Club*. But for now leave you in capable hands Tony Capstick with all news happening in world of folk. Aran sweaters. Fingers in ears.

And now the day is almost done. At 11 p.m., Radio 1 steals an hour back from Radio 2. New sound: a sleepy guitar blues. Dum-di-dum-di-dum-di-dum. Like the Pink Panther ambling into view with a cigarillo in his mouth and a poncho over his shoulder. 'Pickin' the Blues' by Grinderswitch (a southern rock band on the same label as the Allman Brothers) will be John Peel's signature tune for the next seventeen years. It will always be followed by something that sounds nothing like it. Tonight, pub rockers the Count Bishops get the show rolling with 'Teenage Letter' from their EP *Speedball*. Pub rock like a bat out of hell. Steam, speed and sweat. What can it portend?

Produced by John Walters, the sixty-minute *John Peel Show* has time for just one session per night. Ronnie Lane, formerly of the Faces and Small Faces, lives with his wife and a ragtag bunch of musicians and children on a remote farm near the English–Welsh border. Mangle in the kitchen, cauldron of soup on the fire. One hundred acres of sheep-grazing land. The boys in his band, Slim Chance, sleep in cara-vans dotted around the fields. Lane's music is earthy and emotional. He records his albums in his barn after getting pissed in the Drum

and Monkey in the nearby village. Microphones and amplifiers surrounded by hay bales. The local farmers have a lot of time for him.

And now he's back in the charts with a song from his past.
'Itchycoo Park', a 1967 Small Faces hit written when he was twenty-
one, has been reissued and has made the Top 10 again. The band's
ex-drummer Kenney Jones and keyboardist Ian McLagan, left at a
loose end by the disbandment of Rod Stewart and the Faces, have
hooked up with Lane and singer Steve Marriott on an informal basis.
Reunite the quintessential mod quartet. Promote the single, have a
laugh, run through some new ideas. But Lane has already stepped
away. He and Marriott had a punch-up at rehearsals. When Lane
sings the Small Faces' 'All or Nothing' in his Peel session tonight,
he does so as a refusenik, a man used to striking out on his own.
He will succeed or fail by his stubborn priorities. Yes? No? What's
success or failure when you have a communion with the land?

Four songs from a new Emmylou Harris album. A group from
Detroit variously known as the Pearls, the Five Pearls, the Fabulous
Pearls and Howie and the Sapphires sing a Fifties doo-wop song,
'The Wheel of Love'. Reggae singer I-Roy runs through the Ten
Commandments, prophesying an Apocalypse, a Second Coming
and a Day of Reckoning. Oblivious to all of them, lost in his own
fastidious time and space, is Ivor Cutler, narrating a story about a
man who stinks because a curse has been put on him.

A recent Cutler session – his sixth for Peel since his appearance
on *Son of Night Ride* back in 1969 – presented more of his impassive
lunacy, including 'Nigerians in a Tunnel' ('when a Nigerian family
entered the tunnel, an instant sympathy happened'), the deceptively violent 'Go and Sit Upon the Grass' ('while we talk I'll hit
your head with a nail to make you understand me') and the domestic childhood memoir 'Life in a Scotch Sitting Room Volume 2,
Episode 11' ('we set off in a straggly line, hugging the wall to escape
the worst of the effects of the fresh air').

'Life in a Scotch Sitting Room' is an ongoing chronicle that builds up episode by episode into a kind of Calvinist soap opera. Where Viv Stanshall has his bibulous Rawlinsons, Cutler has his abstemious father and his herring-fixated mother. New instalments of the gloomy saga will appear in Peel's programmes at roughly annual intervals until the mid-Eighties.

John Peel Show
Radio 1
3 February 1976

Supercharge – Andy Fairweather Low – Stretch – Toots and the Maytals – The Yardbirds – Jean Plum – Bux – David Bowie – Chuck Berry – Big Youth – Al Allen and Co.

The Queen has opened the National Exhibition Centre in Birmingham, the first purpose-built centre of its kind in Britain. The first event to take place is the International Spring Fair for the giftware trade.

The Yardbirds Featuring Eric Clapton is the sound of Surrey blues obsessives from Kingston, Richmond and Surbiton tearing through Howlin' Wolf and Bo Diddley numbers at the Marquee Club in 1964. It's tonight's featured album. Peel plays three tracks, the British blues boom erupts and Clapton attacks his guitar with a ferocity he would never dare attempt now. Tomorrow, warming to his theme, Peel will play some Yardbirds songs featuring Jeff Beck.

But it's the detours and vagaries, not the usual suspects, that make Peel's shows a safari into the unknown. One Friday last October, he ended the night with a 1937 song by Laurel and Hardy, 'The Trail of the Lonesome Pine'. It had just been released as a single on the United Artists label. The rock division of UA had dealt with Peel for years, sending him new records by Hawkwind, Can and the Groundhogs. But this Laurel and Hardy single came from a separate department. Alan Warner, the label manager whose idea it was, had hoped Stan and Ollie's little ditty might pick up some sentimental airplay on Radio 2. He was stunned when his promotions man told him that Britain's most influential rock DJ had played 'The Trail of the Lonesome Pine' on Radio 1. And not just once, but night after night. He'd even played the B-side.

'From then onwards,' Warner would later recall, 'the floodgates opened and it suddenly seemed that everyone in Britain was talking about and playing "The Trail of the Lonesome Pine".'

Peel didn't have the listening figures to turn the song into a Top 5 hit. But his crush on it was contagious. Paul Burnett, sitting in for Tony Blackburn on the Radio 1 morning show, played it on a Monday in November in between the Glen Campbells and David Essexes. Like a benign madness gripping the station, 'The Trail of the Lonesome Pine' was adopted as a heartwarming anthem. For two comics who'd made America laugh during the Depression, spreading a little cheer through Radio 1 after a tough ten months was a stroll in the park. A week before Christmas, Laurel and Hardy reached number 2 in the charts, behind the best-selling comedy song of the modern era, Queen's 'Bohemian Rhapsody'.

John Peel Show
Radio 1
19 February 1976

Robin Trower

Iceland breaks off diplomatic relations with Britain. Recent months have seen more clashes in this third phase of the Cod War, with Iceland claiming exclusive fishing rights to all areas within 200 nautical miles of its coast.

Peel's studio guest is Robin Trower, a blues-rock guitarist. Trower has built his reputation on finding as many ways as possible of deconstructing and recreating Jimi Hendrix's solos on 'Little Wing' and 'Third Stone from the Sun'. He leaves the singing to his bassist James Dewar, who growls and grunts like Paul Rodgers of Bad Company. Most of Trower's songs are overshadowed by the guitar solos anyway.

Peel plays his new album, *Robin Trower Live*, in full. Side one. Then some chat. Then side two. In what will prove to be an extraordinarily important year for the *John Peel Show*, it's useful to remember that conversations like this once took place without anyone batting an eyelid.

Trower: 'We haven't done a lot lately because we've been working on mixing the live album. Then we went straight in the studio and started recording the studio album.'

Peel: 'Well, we'll talk about the studio album after we've heard side one of the live album.'

Twenty minutes later.

Peel: 'You were saying about the studio album. What's that like?'

Trower: 'It's turned out well. We've gone for a much more live approach to recording it.'

Peel: 'And all the tracks are composed within the group, are they?'

Trower: 'All but one.'

Composed within the group, are they? We've gone for a more live approach with the studio album.

Come, friendly punk bombs, and fall on Peel and Trower.

John Peel Show
Radio 1
15 March 1976

Hank Mizell – Jackson Browne – Poco – U-Roy – Nell and Tim – Mel
and Tim – Keith Jarrett – The Beatles

Peter Shore, the secretary of state for trade, reveals that 452,000 cars
were imported into Britain last year, including 125,000 from Japan. He
rejects a suggestion that the figures predicate the collapse of the British
motor industry.

Hank Mizell was a rockabilly singer from Alabama who recorded
a single called 'Jungle Rock' in 1958. It had no success and Mizell
soon gave up music and joined the church. Wherever he is now,
he's in for the shock of his life. Reissued on a label called Charly, the
wonderfully primitive 'Jungle Rock' has been played by Peel almost
every night this month. It will sneak into the Top 40 at the weekend. To be fair to the other Radio 1 DJs, Peel isn't the only one who's
been playing it – but he's easily the most insatiable. He likes to start
his shows with it. A jungle drummer doing a knocked-out beat. He
could listen to it all day.

Where is the *John Peel Show* going in 1976? It's too soon to say.
The programme on 8 March – a week ago tonight – had a session
from Phil Collins's jazz-fusion group Brand X and tracks from solo
albums by Patrick Moraz and Alan White, the keyboard player and
drummer in Yes. Only Peel could loathe the music of Yes but enjoy
their individual solo albums. Tonight is another study in God knows
what. Peel's mind is terribly hard to read. Jackson Browne is an
anguished singer-songwriter who usurped James Taylor as Laurel
Canyon's pre-eminent depressive. Poco are a decent country-rock
band. Nell and Tim, a reggae duo, are followed punningly by Mel

and Tim, a soul duo. Peel does this all the time – linking songs that share the same title or artists who have similar names – but at this point in the *John Peel Show*'s evolution, it has the look of a bored man doodling absent-mindedly on an envelope. Earlier this month he played a band called the Doctors of Madness, who appeared last December on Twiggy's BBC2 variety show with blue hair and zombie eyes, singing of psychosis and urban futility. Are they the sound of something new? They certainly look like it.

Next month, though, Peel's listeners will hear every note of the new Rick Wakeman album and an interview with its caped-crusader creator. Three nights later it'll be Neil Young under the microscope: fifteen tracks from his career to date. The night after that: a preview of Led Zeppelin's *Presence*. A week after that: all forty-one minutes and twenty seconds of the new Rolling Stones album, *Black and Blue*. That's three albums in a matter of eleven days (Wakeman, Zep and the Stones) that were recorded in studios outside Britain for tax purposes. Then it's Hendrix Night. Then it's Fifties Night with Chuck Berry, Bo Diddley, Ray Charles and Jimmy Reed. Then Steely Dan Night. Peel seems to be on the brink of giving up. What's the point in searching for new bands and new music? It looks as though he's reached the conclusion that there's nothing out there any more.

And then he finds it.

John Peel Show
Radio 1
19 May 1976

Steve Miller Band – Charlie and the Pep Boys – Streetwalkers – The Who – Derek Martin – Kevin Coyne – Will Bradley and the Ray McKinley Orchestra – The Mighty Diamonds – The Ramones

*The secretary of state for Scotland grants a royal pardon to Patrick
Meehan, a Glaswegian who has been in prison since 1969 for
murdering an Ayr pensioner. Two other men were named last year as
the real killers in a book by the journalist Ludovic Kennedy.*

Nobody at Radio 1 is thinking about an overhaul of the music
industry this morning. Noel Edmonds opens up at 7 a.m. with
Andrea True Connection's 'More More More', a disco hit sung by
an American porn actress. Tony Blackburn inexplicably plays nine
songs from Elton John – who has no current single out, and it's not
his birthday – which he follows, in a Peelian curveball, with Ken
Dodd's 'Song of the Diddy Men'.

Johnnie Walker at lunchtime plumps for the blow-dried sounds
of Peter Frampton and the Bellamy Brothers. David Hamilton
entertains his housewives with the Stylistics. It's another fantabu-
lous, sensational, perfectly normal day on Radio 1.

Even Peel coasts through parts of his show, with three tracks from
the new Steve Miller Band album, *Fly Like an Eagle*, which signals
Miller's move into the AOR mainstream. An irritating sequence of
seven songs follows, all containing the word 'daddy' in their titles.
But then, with only two minutes remaining, Peel plays a song from
a new LP that has been loaned to him on approval by the staff at the
Virgin record shop in Oxford Street.

Ramones is the debut album from a New York four-piece of the
same name. They play simple, fast, unadorned, sock-in-the-jaw rock
'n' roll with an obnoxious attitude, and seem to be a reaction (much
as pub rock was a reaction) to the bloated egos and sated bellies
of those who mass-produce contemporary pop and AOR. The
Ramones' gigs at CBGBs, a seedy bar in the Bowery, are exemplars
of brevity and have been enthusiastically reported by the *NME* as
thrilling beyond words. For some time, the influential music paper
has identified New York as the place where the fightback of teenage

music is happening. The Ramones – Joey, Johnny, Dee Dee and Tommy – are leading the charge.

Peel has borrowed the LP from Virgin for none of these reasons. With a job that entails looking at thousands of record sleeves a year, he usually goes by first impressions. He likes the simplicity of the Ramones' name, written in large capitals across the top. He likes the romantic implications of Hispanic New York. And he likes the sleeve in general because it's a spartan monochrome image of four sullen boneheads in leather jackets standing against a wall.

Back at the office, he plays it. He grins. He laughs. He cannot believe his ears. What a sound. What a great album. As with *Robin Trower Live*, all but one of the tracks are composed within the group. But that, most emphatically, is where the parallels end.

'Judy Is a Punk', the last song Peel plays in tonight's show, is ninety seconds long. Its first verse compares Jackie, who is a punk, to Judy, who is a runt. The singer, Joey Ramone, has a soggy, mushy voice that's mostly unintelligible. The guitarist, Johnny, provides a constant tinny buzzsaw din that never wavers or varies. The rhythm section of Tommy and Dee Dee make Johnny Cash's rhythm section sound like Ginger Baker and Jack Bruce. The words 'oh yeah' – the key prepositions of adolescent rock 'n' roll – are uttered four times in verse one alone. Then Joey, in a strangely prissy accent, quotes from an old Herman's Hermits hit: 'Second verse, same as the first!'

They're off again. Jackie is a punk. Judy is a runt, etc. When the second verse ends, there are forty seconds of the song left. 'Third verse,' announces Joey. 'Different from the first!' Jackie is a punk. Judy is a runt. Oh yeah. Oh yeah. Oh yeah. Oh yeah. In the time it took Steve Miller to describe Billy Joe and Bobbie Sue carrying out their first robbery in 'Take the Money and Run', the Ramones have just changed the face of music.

John Peel Show
Radio 1
20 May 1976

Jess Roden Band – The Albion Country Band – The Ramones – UFO

With £1 billion worth of cuts in public spending planned for 1977, the
Conservatives accuse the government of causing severe damage to the
pound. Challenged by the Labour MP Eric Heffer, Prime Minister
James Callaghan admits that unemployment is set to rise.

Another three songs from the Ramones' album. Collectively, they
take up less time in the show than a seven-minute Morris-dance
medley performed by the Albion Country Band. 'Today Your
Love, Tomorrow the World', the third Ramones song, makes reference to Nazis and stormtroopers. The Ramones, it will become
clear, have a fairly tasteless sense of humour. Reading between
the lines, they see themselves as bored outcasts, uncouth and for-
saken, up to no good, streetwise but considered stupid by society's
standards.

John Peel Show
Radio 1
16 August 1976

Cream – Graham Bond Organisation – The Yardbirds – John Mayall
– Vivian Stanshall's Sean Head Showband – Derek and the Dominos
– Jack Bruce – Eric Clapton – Baker Gurvitz Army

Two Catholic civilians are killed and twenty-two others are wounded
when a car bomb explodes outside a pub in Keady, County Armagh.

The Ulster Volunteer Force, a Loyalist paramilitary group, is blamed for the attack.

It's been a long hot summer. In the heatwave and the drought, an obese Greek named Demis Roussos became the UK's newest pop phenomenon, singing tremulous Mediterranean ballads dressed in a billowing kaftan. Peel, averting his gaze, had a new session instead from an Australian band called AC/DC, whose guitarist dresses as a schoolboy – or possibly is a schoolboy – and his shows returned to featuring comfort-zone rock by warhorses such as Caravan and Ted Nugent. New albums by Rod Stewart (*A Night on the Town*) and Roxy Music (*Viva!*) were aired in their entirety.

Now, in August, Peel spends a fortnight cataloguing the history of British rock with a series of programmes on the Beatles, the Stones, the Who and other giants. Tonight's show is dedicated to the power trio Cream and their various offshoots. 'Time has not been very kind to a lot of Cream's music,' says Peel ruefully, playing seven examples of it anyway. When it comes to the three men's solo careers, Eric Clapton, whom Peel admires as much as any musician alive, gets the lion's share of the airtime. 'If I ever find myself in a group of people discussing Eric's greatest recorded work,' Peel says after a Yardbirds song called 'Louise', 'I usually advance *that*.' He sounds like a jazz critic in a beret talking about the birth of bebop.

Three months since he first discovered them, however, he hasn't forgotten the Ramones. Tracks from their album surfaced sporadically throughout June, and on 6 July – two days after the Ramones made their well-received London debut supporting the Flamin' Groovies at the Roundhouse – he played 'Judy Is a Punk', just like old times. 'Blitzkrieg Bop', another song from the album, suddenly emerged from nowhere to appear on the programme three nights running.

The Ramones, like reggae, polarise opinion among Peel's listeners. Their songs, to those who don't find them incredibly exciting,

seem pointlessly dumb and offensively brief. The average length
of a Ramones song is one minute and forty-five seconds. A good
prog-rock band is only getting into the second movement of the
prologue by the time Johnny Ramone hits the final chord. It really
antagonises some people that the Ramones say it all in three chords
and two minutes. A few angry listeners have even done something
about it.

'A lot of people phoned in,' Peel will recall in 1990. 'The switch-
board was jammed, which as we know isn't a difficult thing to happen to it, but people phoned in and said, "You must never do this
again." And then they wrote in afterwards and said, "You must never
play any of these records ever again." And of course I always find
that very exciting and then played a great deal more of them.'

On 4 July, the night that the Ramones played the Roundhouse, a
young band called the Sex Pistols, who'd been building a following
with some riotous live shows around London and the south-east,
played to fifty people in a Sheffield pub called the Black Swan. Their
support act was a new band: the Clash. Two nights later, another
new band – the Damned – supported the Pistols at the 100 Club in
London. A fourth band, the Stranglers, performed on the Ramones/
Flamin' Groovies bill at the Roundhouse. Those four bands – the
Stranglers, the Damned, the Clash and the Sex Pistols – are now
increasingly being linked by the music press as the spearheads of a
new type of music called punk rock.

John Peel Show
Radio 1
17 September 1976

Ted Nugent – Grand Funk Railroad – Kevin Ayers – Sutherland
Brothers and Quiver – Dr Feelgood – The Runaways – The Ramones

The Sex Pistols give an afternoon concert for inmates at HM Prison Chelmsford. The captive audience is treated to a fourteen-song set that includes 'Pretty Vacant', 'I'm a Lazy Sod' and 'Anarchy in the UK'.

Tonight, in a hugely conflicted programme, Peel presents a microcosm of the last four months in the space of sixty minutes. Kevin Ayers is the artist in session, no longer quite as witty or as novel as the plummy-voiced surrealist he used to be. The show's opening one-two comes from Ted Nugent – testosterone in a loincloth – and Grand Funk Railroad, an arena-filling Michigan hard-rock band whose new album (*Good Singin', Good Playin'*) has a title that sums up all the reasons why the Ramones felt they needed to exist. They'd be puzzled to find one of their biggest English fans giving oxygen to a hoary old cliché like Grand Funk.

But Peel ends the show a long way from where he began it. The dynamic shifts when he plays four fist-flailing tracks from the new Dr Feelgood live album, *Stupidity* – the crowning glory of pub rock and a number 1 album, to everyone's surprise, next month. Peel follows the Feelgoods with the Runaways, an all-girl group from LA who curse like sailors and rock like five Suzi Quatros. Ending the programme are the Ramones ('I Don't Wanna Walk Around with You'), dispelling all that history-of-rock stuff from August like a window being flung open to get rid of a cooking smell.

The Ramones' album has peaked at 111 in the American Top 200 and hasn't charted in Britain at all. Punk rock, for UK audiences, is confined to the live stage, where it moves like quicksilver in the hands of a new band in a different venue every night. 'It wasn't formed [yet],' Mick Jones of the Clash will later say of mid-'76 punk. 'We were just starting to find out what it could be.' This is where the *NME* and *Sounds* win out over Peel. They have breaking news to write about. He can do little but read their reports with interest.

When the Clash met the Ramones in July, they had nothing to

give them that represented their music, so they handed over a copy of 'Keys to Your Heart', a single by Joe Strummer's previous band the 101ers. But the 101ers, like Eddie and the Hot Rods and other pub rockers who pumped and sweated on Peel's shows over the past four months, have been superseded by something much more kinetic. Punk gigs, as many are finding, are life-changing events. But there needs to be a piece of vinyl at the end of it. Peel can play the Ramones any night he likes, but he can't play the Sex Pistols, the Stranglers, the Damned or the Clash until they go into a studio and make a record.

John Peel Show
Radio 1
10 December 1976

The Damned – The Seeds – Iggy and the Stooges – Eddie and the Hot Rods – Richard Hell and the Voidoids – Television – Pere Ubu – The Saints – The Sex Pistols – New York Dolls – The Ramones

Betty Williams and Mairead Corrigan, two women from Belfast who founded an organisation to campaign for an end to the Troubles in Northern Ireland, are awarded the Nobel Peace Prize.

Nine days ago, on live television, punk rock ceased to be an abstract concept. Appearing as last-minute guests on Thames TV's regional news programme *Today*, the Sex Pistols unleashed a volley of obscenities at the presenter, Bill Grundy, at a time when many families were sitting down to their evening meals. The ensuing furore went far beyond the news pages of *NME* and *Sounds*. The following day's *Daily Mirror* carried it as its banner headline: 'The Filth and the Fury!' The Sex Pistols have been fast-tracked to infamy.

The profanities of guitarist Steve Jones continue to reverberate more than a week later. Town councillors, police forces and even Pentecostal ministers have been battening down the hatches and preparing for Armageddon. What alarms them most is that the Sex Pistols are currently on a UK tour. Though the encounter with Grundy was seen only by viewers in the Greater London region, Britain's newspapers have assessed punk rock as a national scourge, and each new day sees more dates of the Pistols' tour cancelled. Caerphilly in Wales is going ahead (14 December), but a preacher and a delegation of carol singers will stand outside the venue threatening damnation for anyone who goes in. Leeds (the 6th) and Manchester (the 9th) also get the green light. The night after Manchester, John Peel clears the decks and aligns his programme with the punks.

His one-hour show will become known as the Punk Special. Coming two days after the release of the Eagles' *Hotel California*, it doesn't quite draw a line in the sand, but it certainly throws a cat among the pigeons. As a general point, Peel argues tonight that punk bands 'bring an injection of energy and crudity into a rock scene that's been painfully smug and complacent during the past few years'. He's been saying since 1973 that generational renewal is essential. Can punk mount a challenge to the tax-exile generation?

In the fallout from Grundy, the Sex Pistols have been banned by Radio 1. Controller Derek Chinnery has warned John Walters not to put any punk rock in the Peel show. 'We already have,' Walters replies uneasily. Chinnery doesn't know the half of it. Peel has been playing the Pistols' single, 'Anarchy in the UK', since mid-November – along with the Damned's 'New Rose', which preceded it by a few weeks – and Walters was asked to consider offering the Pistols a session as long ago as September. He turned them down, worried they would be too chaotic for the BBC engineers. It's a decision he'll always regret.

For Peel's few hundred thousand listeners, tonight is the first time they've heard an hour of punk rock on national radio. He plays eighteen songs: eleven from America, six from England and one from Australia. Looking past the shock-horror headlines and bondage trousers, he joins the dots between the bands of now and the bands of the past, highlighting some obvious musical influences (Iggy and the Stooges, the New York Dolls) and some credible antecedents from the Sixties (the Seeds, the Shadows of Knight).

Avoiding mention of the Grundy scandal for the first thirty-five minutes, Peel finally turns to it as he cues up 'Anarchy in the UK'. 'Their television appearance, I think, subsequently was treated with a great deal of quite remarkable hypocrisy and overreaction,' he says. 'And people don't seem to be playing their single very much, which is a great pity because it's a good stomper.'

A good stomper? Nine days in which the United Kingdom has been at war with a new enemy, and the *casus belli* is 'a good stomper'? The gig cancellations, the enraged councillors, the cat-and-mouse chases with police? That's what it's all been about? *A good stomper?* Really, there are times when Peel's introductions don't quite rise to the occasion.

But when he holds his tongue, most of the bands can speak for themselves. The Damned, who have recorded a session for the programme, are dangerously fast and exhilaratingly berserk. From New York, Richard Hell and the Voidoids ('Blank Generation') are nihilistic and sarcastic. Television ('Little Johnny Jewel') are wiry and neurotic. Pere Ubu, from Ohio, have a singer who sounds like a cage full of birds screeching at a fox, and a darkly tragicomic song ('Final Solution') depicting a teenage antihero as a maladjusted sociopathic loser. Misshapen and ugly though he may be, there's something unassailable about him. Something that deflects opprobrium.

Can Peel empathise with him? 'I'm not about to dress up as a punk or change my hairstyle,' the thirty-seven-year-old assures his listeners. 'But I'm very grateful to the bands and the people who make the music . . . for the excitement and heated debate and general bewilderment they've brought back to the rock scene.'

He fades down Grinderswitch's theme tune to read through tomorrow's Radio 1 schedule. 'Kid Jensen at 10 a.m. – he's going to be playing the very best of contemporary music, it says here. I do know that he'll be playing quite a few tracks from the new triple LP *Wings Live Over America*.'

Peel fades Grinderswitch back up. Then down again. Paul Gambaccini takes over from Jensen at noon, Peel goes on, with 'the best-selling pop and soul records from the American charts, plus a rundown of the US Top 30'. After that at 1.30 p.m. – he sounds close to losing interest in the script now – Linda Ronstadt is the guest on *My Top 12*. And then at 2.30 p.m. leave you in capable hands Alan Freeman for three hours progressive rock including side one of new Genesis album *Wind and Wuthering*.

OK. So what happens now?

1977: MIGHT TAKE A BIT OF VIOLENCE

'I had just been at Mick's flat, admiring Tony James's weekly
itinerary for Generation X neatly typed by the band's secretary,
when Mick said: "Hang on, aren't we supposed to be doing
something tonight? Oh yeah – the John Peel show."'
JOHNNY GREEN, road manager for the Clash

John Peel Show
Radio 1
3 January 1977

Thin Lizzy – The Chieftains – Bob Dylan – The Beatles – Pink Floyd
– Racing Cars – Free – The Jimi Hendrix Experience – Derek and the
Dominos – Led Zeppelin

Pat Kruse, a Torquay United defender, scores the fastest own goal in
history, heading past his goalkeeper after six seconds of a match against
Cambridge United. The game ends in a 2–2 draw.

Last November, Peel asked the listeners to write down their all-
time favourite three songs and send them to him on a postcard.
The fifty songs with the most votes would be compiled into a chart
and played over the Christmas and New Year period. Tonight the
Festive 50, as Peel calls it, concludes with numbers 10 to 1.

The votes for the Festive 50 were registered before the Punk

Special in December, but even so, considering that the listeners have been hearing the Ramones and other American punks in Peel's programmes since last May, their commitment to upholding the status quo is striking. They've voted for a pre-punk beanfeast, revealing a groundswell of support for hard-rock and prog-rock epics such as 'Child in Time' (by Deep Purple), 'Free Bird' (Lynyrd Skynyrd), 'Kashmir' (Led Zeppelin), 'Supper's Ready' (Genesis), 'And You and I' (Yes), 'Won't Get Fooled Again' (the Who) and 'Dark Star' (the Grateful Dead). Only Jonathan Richman's 'Roadrunner' at number 33 – a proto-punk stepping stone from 'Sister Ray' to 'Blitzkrieg Bop' – has any association, tangentially or otherwise, with the music Peel played on 10 December.

Ninety-six minutes of tonight's show remain when the Festive 50 countdown resumes (following some tracks from recent sessions), so one can be confident that more epics are coming down the pike. And they certainly are. Pink Floyd account for thirty-seven minutes singlehandedly with only two songs – 'Echoes' (23:35) and 'Shine on You Crazy Diamond' (13:30) – while 'Desolation Row' (11:20) is one of three Bob Dylan songs in the top ten. Derek and the Dominos' 'Layla' (7:05), at number 2, and Led Zeppelin's 'Stairway to Heaven' (8:00) take the top places.

The listeners haven't voted for these songs to spite Peel. They voted for them because they happen to like them. They voted for them because *this is their music.* This is rock's classical repertoire. These are the songs that established rock as the predominant popular-music genre of the last ten years. The punks may disparage Led Zeppelin and the Who for their hedonistic lifestyles, or for being out of touch with the common man, but let's see them try to do better. These gifted virtuosos whom the punks have the temerity to call dinosaurs are music's *crème de la crème*. From Jimmy Page to Eric Clapton to Dave Gilmour, they are the nonpareils. They are the consummate masters of rock who practised in their bedrooms and paid their dues. Their epic masterpieces, flawlessly played, are the targets the punk bands have to beat – if they can stop spitting at each other long enough to write a song, that is. Eddie and the Hot Rods? The Sex Pistols? Ricky and the Voidoids? Listen and learn.

Peel's mood is interesting tonight. Though he tells the listeners he broadly agrees with their choices, he sounds a bit distant and deflated for a DJ playing the ten greatest recordings of all time. At number 9, for instance, is the Beatles' 'A Day in the Life', the legendary final track on *Sgt Pepper*. A cataclysmic song of blown minds, English armies and 4,000 holes in Lancashire, it comes from an album that made Peel burst into tears when he first heard it, and made him feel, when he debuted it on Radio London, like the conductor of a Beethoven symphony. But there are no tears from him tonight. 'All done on four-track equipment,' he says, faintly dismissively, as the cacophonous piano chord fades. He's become a man and put away childish things.

It's early days yet, but looking at the votes cast and the reputations enhanced by the Festive 50, it's quite possible that the Punk Special achieved no purpose whatsoever. Despite the Grundy storm and the heathens at the gates, it's a case of 'ring out the new, ring in the old again' on the *John Peel Show*. And many listeners will be glad to hear it.

John Peel Show
Radio 1
16 February 1977

The Runaways – Jackson Browne – The Damned – Uriah Heep – Peter Baumann – Gentle Giant – Tom Petty and the Heartbreakers – Talking Heads

*To cries of 'Shame' and 'It's like Czechoslovakia', home secretary
Merlyn Rees tells Parliament he has issued a deportation order against
two Americans, Philip Agee and Mark Hosenball. Agee is a former
CIA agent turned whistleblower, and Hosenball is an investigative
journalist.*

Punk is both an underground buzz and a high-visibility, fast-changing narrative. It's already attracted the interest of major record companies. But controversy is everywhere you look. The Sex Pistols, signed by EMI in October, had their contract terminated three weeks ago. Yesterday they sacked their bassist Glen Matlock and replaced him with a leather-clad headcase who goes by the name of Sid Vicious. If the Pistols are serious about imposing anarchy and destroying passers-by, Vicious looks like the right appointment.

The Clash have signed to CBS – another major – for £100,000. Their fans and critics have spent the last fortnight arguing bitterly about whether this is tantamount to a sellout of their principles. 'Punk died the day the Clash signed to CBS,' the editor of the fanzine *Sniffin' Glue* has declared. But punk has done nothing of the sort. For kids living in towns in the north, it's just getting started. For those in Scotland, where no punk gigs have been booked yet, all the mayhem is still to come.

The Stranglers, shrouded in darkness and disliked by the other bands, snuck up on the blind side by signing to United Artists and releasing '(Get a) Grip (on Yourself)', the first major punk single of 1977. But it's the Damned, on the independent label Stiff, who raced ahead to record the first British punk album. *Damned Damned Damned*, housed in a sleeve showing the band in the aftermath of a food fight, comes out in two days. Peel plays five tracks from it tonight.

The Damned are viewed as dilettantes by some of the punk hierarchy – they were kicked off the Sex Pistols' December tour by their manager Malcolm McLaren without playing a note – but Peel isn't going to let his musical judgement be swayed by petty rivalries. The Damned are right up his street. Their guitarist and songwriter Brian James, a perfect synthesis of Keith Richards and Johnny Thunders, clearly knows his rock 'n' roll. The drummer is even better. His name (so many of these punks have outlandish names) is Rat Scabies. The Damned cavort onstage in a bug-eyed frenzy, with a slapstick punchline never far away. When they perform 'Neat Neat Neat' on ITV's Saturday morning pop show *Supersonic* ten days from now, Captain Sensible's bass guitar still has the price tag attached to it.

In future years Peel will tend to exaggerate (or maybe just mis-recollect) the effect the Ramones had on his listeners, making it sound as though a sweeping purge occurred in the early summer of 1976. Appearing on *Desert Island Discs* in 1990, he'll tell the presenter Sue Lawley: 'It was terrific. The whole audience changed in the space of about a month. The average age of the audience dropped by about ten years.'

His running orders of 1977 are the evidence that it simply didn't happen like that. He's keeping faith with old-guard artists like Jackson Browne long after the Ramones have burst through the dam. Tonight he plugs the ninth album by prog rockers Gentle Giant and the eleventh by boogie merchants Uriah Heep. But his enthusiastic support for bands like the Damned has undoubtedly begun to have an impact on one demographic: younger listeners living outside London.

John Peel Show
Radio 1
5 April 1977

The Clash – The Diamond Steel Band – The Table – The Jimi Hendrix Experience – Klaatu – The Jess Roden Band – King Short Shirt – The Stranglers – Iggy Pop – Max Wall

*Environment secretary Peter Shore downwardly revises his development
targets for Milton Keynes and five other new towns. He explains that
the population of England and Wales is expected to reach 51 million in
1990 – 9 million fewer than was estimated when the new towns were
designated in the late Sixties.*

The more punk records that Peel puts into his programmes, the
greater the risk of them butting heads with other genres that have
none of punk's vulgarity and rage. The second song in tonight's
two-hour show – after the Clash's debut single, 'White Riot' – is
a piece of Caribbean steel-drum music from Saint Lucia, where
Peel recently spent a two-week holiday. Neither 'White Riot' nor
'Voices of Spring' by the Diamond Steel Band is more 'important'
to an obsessive collector like Peel; he feels they both deserve to be
played on the radio and that's all there is to it. However, he'd accept
that 'White Riot' is culturally important in the sense that it's a battle
cry from the Clash to the youth of Britain. With the Sex Pistols temporarily indisposed – they signed to A&M Records in early March
but were dropped seven days later and now have no record deal –
the Clash, the most political of the punk bands, are threatening to
emerge as the movement's frontrunners.

Also in the show tonight are Jess Roden, a gravel-voiced rock
singer in the Joe Cocker vein; King Short Shirt, a calypso artist from
Antigua; Klaatu, a Canadian band of Beatle imitators whose latest
single, 'Calling Occupants of Interplanetary Craft', will be a worldwide hit for the Carpenters later in the year; and Max Wall, a veteran
actor and comedian, singing a new release on the Stiff label. Written
by a man on the fringes of punk named Ian Dury, 'England's Glory'
is a list of celebrities ('Gracie, Cilla, Maxy Miller') and inventions
('winkles, Woodbines, Walnut Whips') that made this green and
pleasant land wot it is. 'Mortimer Wheeler, Christine Keeler, the
Board of Trade.' Reasons to be cheerful – one, two, three.

At least Peel could get away with arguing that all these records are current, even if Max Wall is pushing seventy. The same cannot be said of the fifty-seven minutes of archive Jimi Hendrix that dominates the rest of the programme. Nostalgia is very much in the air at Radio 1 at present, with tenth-anniversary celebrations well under way. For every punk band Peel introduces to his listeners over the next few months (Chelsea, Generation X, the Vibrators, the Adverts, the Lurkers), there'll be a repeated *Top Gear* session from Genesis, Man, Thin Lizzy or Steeleye Span. Exactly the kind of tedious old windbags the punks are trying to eradicate.

One genre that sits well with punk is reggae. Don Letts, the DJ at the Roxy in Covent Garden, where many punk bands play, is a second-generation Jamaican who fills the intervals between bands with reggae 45s by U-Roy, Big Youth, Tapper Zukie and Culture. Johnny Rotten and one or two members of the Clash are known to be big reggae fans. If they happen to be near a radio between 10 p.m. and midnight any day between Monday and Friday, they'll hear Peel playing ever greater amounts of reggae in 1977.

But if punk and reggae sit well together, punk and folk will always be an ill-matched couple. New listeners who find their way to Peel – either by reading his weekly column in *Sounds* or by being tipped off by older friends – must surely be perplexed when he follows the Stranglers' 'London Lady', as he did one night in February, with a session of mellow accustic ballads by the seasoned folkie Ralph McTell. They might wonder what the hell Peel is playing at. The answer, of course, is that the *John Peel Show* never limits itself to one style of music at the expense of any others. Punk and folk will have to learn to coexist. Gabba gabba hey nonny nonny no.

Peel is an overweight, balding thirty-seven-year-old who never pretends to be younger than he is. He often talks about punk in ways that accentuate the age gap between him and the bands. 'Research staff at the Peel Foundation tell me that's not an enormous distance from being in the BBC charts,' he observes with Wodehousian understatement after playing 'White Riot' tonight. But punk is such a volatile cocktail of music, theatre, protest and shock tactics that Peel would be advised to watch his step. The *NME* writer Nick Kent was attacked last year with a bicycle chain by Sid Vicious for being a fan of Led Zeppelin and the Stones. Bob Harris was menaced by a group of punks at the Speakeasy Club last month. Pistols manager Malcolm McLaren and his partner Vivienne Westwood are known to be deeply suspicious of Peel. 'Never trust a hippie' is one of the key slogans of punk. If 1977 is Year Zero, why has the bearded Peel not been dispatched to the guillotines?

Peel isn't the only DJ playing punk. Tommy Vance on Capital Radio is sympathetic towards it and there are regional programmes such as *Streetsounds* on Radio Clyde in Glasgow. But Peel, who is on the air for two hours a night five nights a week, plays more punk than all of them put together. He plays new records *first* and *most often*. And his willingness to offer punk bands the use of the BBC's Maida Vale studios to record sessions – in some cases before they've been approached by record companies – works heavily in his favour.

Getting punk onto the radio is vital if the music and the message are to reach the provinces, the scattered suburbs, the rural areas, the parts of Britain where no bands play. Even the most internecine punks can agree on that much. Peel is the main conduit as things stand. His show is becoming more important all the time. It would be a real coup if he could secure a session by the Clash. 'White Riot' has been getting his shows off to a rousing start for the last three weeks, and CBS are just about to release the band's long-awaited first album. There is huge anticipation.

Peel, however, will never get a Clash session. When they finally present themselves at Maida Vale, after spurning Peel's advances for months, their road manager Johnny Green will describe the proceedings as 'a shambles from the start'. The Clash pick fights with the BBC engineers, insist on producing the session themselves and relax by smoking high-strength spliffs, much to the engineers' irritation. At last, after assessing the BBC's equipment as not good enough, they leave, having recorded no music worth broadcasting. When Peel talks about the Clash in future, he'll use the most cutting terminology he can think of. He calls the behaviour of punk's leading revolutionaries 'unbearably pretentious'.

John Peel Show
Radio 1
7 *June 1977*

Dave Edmunds – Lonnie Mack – The Faces – Slaughter and the Dogs – Van Morrison – Peter Tosh – Bob Seger – The Ramones – Dr Feelgood – Chelsea – Status Quo – Pink Floyd

Over a million people line the streets of London to watch the Queen proceed in a golden state coach to St Paul's Cathedral, where a ceremony is held to mark her Silver Jubilee. The day has been declared a public holiday.

On this felicitous day of celebration and commemoration, Radio 1 has given over six hours of its daytime schedule to a rundown of its listeners' hundred favourite singles. Running through the Noel Edmonds, Tony Blackburn and Paul Burnett shows, The Nation's All-Time Top 100 is based along Festive 50 lines. The public were asked to send in their votes during an eight-week promotion last autumn.

Peel is not involved in the Top 100, but his influence is not hard to see if one knows where to look. Roxy Music's 'Virginia Plain', the debut single they recorded six months after he brought them to national attention, is at 96. David Bowie's 'Space Oddity' is slightly higher. Hawkwind, the countercultural heroes of the early-Seventies free festivals, are represented by their hit 'Silver Machine'. Rod Stewart, a former *Top Gear* Good Guy and Peel wedding guest, has several entries in the Top 40. The highest of them, at 2, is 'Maggie May', a song given its first Radio 1 exposure by Peel before anyone in Britain had ever heard it. Does Rod ever think of Peelie now as he jets in with Britt from Cap Ferrat or Beverly Hills?

The number 1 single in the Top 100 is 10cc's 'I'm Not in Love', which topped the UK charts two summers ago and has now assumed the status of a certified pop standard. Months prior to its release as a single, Peel picked it out as an album track and let his listeners hear it for the first time anywhere. Perhaps if the Queen is still on the throne twenty-five years from now, and Radio 1 decides to mark her Golden Jubilee by updating The Nation's All-Time Top 100, the list might include some of the singles Peel plays tonight. Something like 'Right to Work' by Chelsea ('Having no future is a terrible thing'), or 'Cranked up Really High' by Slaughter and the Dogs ('Had a million thoughts to slit my wrists'), or 'Sheena Is a Punk Rocker' by the Ramones ('The kids are all hopped up and ready to go'). Stranger things have happened, haven't they?

John Peel Show
Radio 1
29 August 1977

The Sex Pistols – The Vibrators – The Stranglers – The Models – XTC – The Cortinas – Generation X – Desperate Bicycles – Buzzcocks – The Adverts – The Users – The Jam – The Rezillos

The final day of the Notting Hill Carnival is marred by street fighting for the second year running. Ninety people are taken to hospital, some with stab wounds.

The *John Peel Show* has reached the point of no return. The Sex Pistols have grown in notoriety and influence throughout the summer. Their second single, 'God Save the Queen', sold in substantial numbers despite a BBC ban, and might have been the country's number 1 single during Jubilee week if the Top 40 hadn't allegedly been adjusted to keep it at number 2. Punk's growth has been exponential. Debut albums by the Clash and the Stranglers have charted at numbers 12 and 4 respectively. The Stranglers have had two Top 10 singles – as have the Pistols – and this week's Top 40 includes new names like the Jam, the Adverts and the Boomtown Rats.

But behind the infantry sits a far larger army. Punk is speaking to the youth in terms of great urgency, and dozens of new bands form every week. Tonight Peel puts the emphasis on some of them. Much more than last December's Punk Special, this August '77 programme will be the one that establishes him as the prime champion of British punk in the media. Crucially, many of the bands in the show come from outside London.

He announces straight away that he's going to keep his comments to a minimum tonight, so that he can get through as many songs as possible. He plays thirty-eight in 120 minutes. A programme with no Hendrix and no folk singers, it instead has an abundance of fast, angry, three-chord remonstrations and gobbets of vitriol that come straight from the gullet These are the resentful, ripped-off young. They trust nobody, take pride in nothing but a modicum of self-respect and see themselves as consigned to the scrapheap in a country crippled by industrial unrest, social division, political corruption and economic catastrophe. The dole queue deadbeat in 'Ain't Bin to No Music School', a single by a Manchester band called the Nosebleeds, expresses himself in words of one syllable and states his position with the clarity of an eight-year-old in a playground brawl. 'You think you're it,' he taunts his unseen enemies, 'you think you're it, you think you're it, you think you're it, you think you're it, you think you're IT!'

The Rezillos are from Edinburgh and, like many punk bands, have released a single on their own record label. They've sent a copy of 'I Can't Stand My Baby' to Peel with bated breath and fingers crossed; if he doesn't like it – and doesn't play it – the life expectancy of the Rezillos and their label will be short. They needn't have worried. 'I Can't Stand My Baby' is his favourite single of 1977 so far (high praise indeed) and the Rezillos' manager will soon start receiving phone calls from major record companies.

The Desperate Bicycles, from London, make one or two false moves on their single 'Smokescreen', which sounds like a busker fumbling his way through 'Give Peace a Chance' while a pub pianist thumps away in the background. But 'Smokescreen' will play a significant role in punk's unfolding DIY culture. Having financed, recorded, pressed up and released five hundred copies of it (for a grand total of £150), the Desperate Bicycles will be on hand to offer a raft of punk bands written and verbal advice on how to book studios, approach pressing plants and distribute product. With their inspiring motto of 'It was easy, it was cheap, go and do it,' they'll become the de facto enablers and empowerers of punk rock.

Buzzcocks, the Manchester band who follow the Desperate Bicycles tonight, were out of the traps even earlier, in January, with their already mythical *Spiral Scratch* EP (from which Peel plays 'Boredom'). The band recorded and mixed the EP in five hours and put it out on their own label, New Hormones. But there's a vast distance between Manchester and the south in 1977, and information can take a long time to travel. Howard Devoto, Buzzcocks' insect-like singer, seems to have left them and formed another band, Magazine. According to Peel, he's 'becoming a bit of a legendary figure'. It's almost impossible to keep track of every punk band's movements, unless you read the music weeklies from cover to cover and listen to Peel every night. Even the fanzines, for all their passion and rhetoric, are out of date by the time they're printed.

Buzzcocks, the Desperate Bicycles and the Rezillos are the future of the *John Peel Show*. Nobody knows it yet, but these autonomous units of creativity and activity, which are springing up all around Britain, will result in an entirely new music business in the decade to come – a new way of thinking about music, a new way of making it and a new way of selling it – and Peel will be the axis on which this self-sufficient, subterranean world spins.

The peroxide blond singer in Generation X will have long fled by then. Billy Idol channels 1965 Roger Daltrey on his band's new single, 'Your Generation', curling his lip where Daltrey stuttered. 'Your generation don't mean a thing to me,' Idol sneers at the rule makers and law enforcers. Then, chewing on ways in which they can be overthrown, he reflects: 'Might take a bit of violence.' Disc jockeys much younger than Peel would be appalled by such a non-chalant threat. But Peel, who likes Generation X immensely and has attended several of their gigs, is happy to give Idol a national plat-form. A lot of milk has been spilt since Peel's peacenik days. He has a new image. Short hair, trimmed beard, black jacket with badges on the lapels. He walks the walk.

There follows, near the end of the show, a sort of Peel apologia. He tries to explain what he and Walters have been aiming at tonight; sadly, his words look rather flaccid written down. 'With this two-hour programme of 1977's music, we genuinely don't think we've really been trying to prove anything very much. If you like it, then you'll see this as having demonstrated how much variety there is in [punk] music. And if you don't, you'll be convinced that it's all very repetitive. You can take your choice, really, but I think it's excellent, I must admit.'

Peel turns thirty-eight tomorrow. He's the oldest DJ broad-casting on Radio 1 on this Bank Holiday Monday – older than

Ed Stewart (thirty-six), Tony Blackburn (thirty-four), Dave Lee Travis (thirty-two) and Kid Jensen (twenty-seven). But Blackburn, Stewart, Travis and Jensen are unlikely to celebrate their birthdays by going to the Vortex, the Wardour Street punk club, as Peel intends to do tonight. It will grow apparent, as the months pass and punk takes up more and more of Peel's airtime, that he was actually giving his listeners not an apology tonight, but an ultimatum. *'You can take your choice, really.'* In his mild-mannered way, Peel was telling them the time had come to decide whether to trust him or abandon him.

In a year when Radio 1 has been extra conscious of its family of listeners, gathering them to its bosom with anniversaries and lookbacks and lists, Peel is the one DJ at the station who doesn't mind seeing his listeners heading in the other direction. Even if their individual departures were to become a mass exodus, he's prepared to write it off as collateral damage. If John Peel ever told his audience to get on the bus or go to hell, he did it on the night of 29 August 1977.

John Peel Show
Radio 1
3 October 1977

The Pirates – Status Quo – Junior Delgado – The Doors – Van Morrison – Little Feat – Joni Mitchell – Kevin Coyne – Ivor Cutler – The Jays and Ranking Trevor – The Stranglers – The Sex Pistols

Funeral directors in London go on strike, claiming they deserve a 37 per cent pay increase to reflect the rising numbers of deaths in the capital. The backlog of unburied corpses is believed to exceed 800.

Radio 1's tenth anniversary celebrations roll on. Tonight a Peel listener in Wiltshire has won a competition to have seventy-five minutes of his favourite music played to the nation. He's chosen a song for every year from 1967 to 1977. Peel must be seeing his life flashing before his eyes.

What have been the major changes during his Radio 1 decade? Where would you even start? His one-time best friend Marc Bolan is dead, killed in a car crash last month, a fortnight before his thirtieth birthday. Bolan and Peel met briefly, awkwardly, a year ago at Broadcasting House, but Bolan's bear hug couldn't mend the broken fences and Peel barely recognised him anyway. The once elfin boychild had put on a lot of weight.

Elvis Presley, Peel's first rock 'n' roll hero, died at forty-two in August. Punks at the Vortex erupted in cheers at the news until one of them, *Sniffin' Glue* writer Danny Baker, leapt onstage and told them to stop being so moronic. Bowie, Elton and Bryan Ferry began the decade as nobodies and have become household names. David Ackles, Neu! and pub rock are just a memory. Captain Beefheart is off somewhere licking his wounds, deeply regretting his tilt at commercial success. Billy Connolly from the Humblebums is a stand-up comedian and a roaring success on *Parkinson*. The Rolling Stones have released a new double live album, *Love You Live*, but Keith Richards faces a life sentence in Canada for smuggling heroin into Toronto. Rolling Stones drug arrests are the only thing that 1967 and 1977 appear to have in common.

Tonight's competition winner, Stephen R. Cook, is Peel's kind of listener. From the late Sixties and early Seventies he chooses music by the Doors, Little Feat, Van Morrison and Joni Mitchell – but just as we start to form a mental picture of a moustachioed twenty-eight-year-old in a rugby shirt, he goes for a Kevin Coyne track, then a gloriously strict episode of Ivor Cutler's 'Life in a Scotch Sitting Room' (about eating herring porridge and being asked questions about it afterwards in Latin, Greek and Hebrew) and a reggae song by the Jays and Ranking Trevor.

His selection of music ends with two punk songs, 'Hanging Around' by the Stranglers and 'God Save the Queen' by the Sex Pistols. If Stephen R. Cook is at all representative, his broad-minded tastes confirm exactly what Peel has been trying since last December to get across to the listeners: that they shouldn't be frightened by punk; that it's just another form of expression like the country-rock songs and confessional ballads that they enjoyed earlier in the Seventies. (Other competition entrants, Peel complains, omitted any music released after 1973. Presumably those postcards went straight in the bin.)

However, Stephen Cook may not be typical. All over Britain, converts to punk have been junking their old record collections, fumigating their homes of Zeppelin, Floyd and Queen. Choices have been made. Sides have been taken. Even an all-inclusivist like Peel has to have some rules and terms of admission, and the likes of Ted Nugent, Kiss and Uriah Heep will no longer be welcome on his programme. He will remain loyal, however, to a smattering of rock bands that he likes for personal reasons. One of these is Status Quo, often lampooned for an inability to play more than three chords, making them perfect for Peel shows in the punk era. The Quo song he plays tonight, 'Ring of a Change' (from last year's *Blue for You* album), is as fast as anything by the Clash and would make even the Damned and the Adverts sound torpid. Francis Rossi will later admit that Quo, like many of the punk bands, got heavily into amphetamine sulphate in 1976.

John Peel Show
Radio 1
5 October 1977

Wreckless Eric – Sham 69 – Jonathan Richman and the Modern
Lovers – The Drones – Third World – Iggy Pop – Dillinger – Nick
Lowe – Roogalator – Be-Bop Deluxe – Elvis Costello

The Labour Party assembles in Brighton for its annual conference.
Much of the gossip among politicians and journalists centres on
possible conspiracy-to-murder charges against Jeremy Thorpe,
the former Liberal leader, relating to a sex scandal that forced his
resignation last year.

Punk has permeated the daytime schedules. The Stranglers' new
single, 'No More Heroes', was heard on Noel Edmonds's show this
morning, where it rather stood out alongside Leo Sayer's 'Thunder
in My Heart' and Baccara's 'Yes Sir, I Can Boogie'. Tony Blackburn,
who despises punk, continues to make a point of ignoring it (while
playing Be-Bop Deluxe, whom he probably thinks are pretty damn
edgy). Paul Burnett has judged his lunchtime listeners ready for
'Dancing the Night Away' by the Motors, a current Peel favourite from a band who used to be known as Ducks Deluxe. David
Hamilton is the real surprise, playing the Stranglers after Debbie
Reynolds's 'Tammy', a death-defying juxtaposition by his producer
Paul Williams that leads one to wonder if he's angling for John
Walters's job. If so, he fluffs his audition. Hamilton follows 'No
More Heroes' with no fewer than five Queen songs.

John Peel Show
Radio 1
27 December 1977

The Stranglers – Some Chicken – Johnny Moped – The Lurkers – The
Sex Pistols – Frankie Miller – Neil Young – Desperate Bicycles – John
Cooper Clarke – Althea and Donna – The Motors

The much-hyped Star Wars *goes on release in British cinemas. Featuring
the English actors Alec Guinness and Peter Cushing among its
American cast, the film has broken numerous box-office records in the
States.*

Peel hasn't asked the listeners to vote for a Festive 50 this year.
Perhaps, after a hectic twelve months, he's unsure of how they break
down statistically with regard to age groups, and doesn't want to be
embarrassed by a chart full of Lynyrd Skynyrd and Deep Purple.
Last week *NME* published its Readers' Poll for 1977, a startling
post-revolution ballot that took a cleaver to the Zep and Floyd generation, putting the Sex Pistols at number 1 in the list of best bands,
'God Save the Queen' at number 1 in the poll of best singles and Sid
Vicious (who isn't allowed to play on their records) at number 6 in
the best bassist category. The best DJ was John Peel.

Instead of a Festive 50 Peel has chosen his sixty favourite songs
of 1977, which are played in reverse order over several nights this
month. His so-called 'Festive 60' includes Devo's 'Jocko Homo',
Elvis Costello's 'Watching the Detectives' and Wreckless Eric's
'Whole Wide World' – all released on the enterprising, go-getting
Stiff label – and there are also high placings for DIY singles by the
Desperate Bicycles (at number 6) and the Rezillos (at 4).

Some of Peel's choices are more idiosyncratic. Gracing his top
ten are 'Like a Hurricane' by Neil Young (a dramatic guitar blowout

from the mercurial Canadian), 'Right Track' by Marlene Webber (a reggae B-side with a long dub outro) and 'Suspended Sentence' by John Cooper Clarke (an abrasive piece of social commentary from a nasal-voiced poet attached to the Manchester punk scene). At number 2 in Peel's chart is Althea and Donna's 'Uptown Top Ranking', a reggae song by two Jamaican teenagers that he's been playing for about a month. It's just entered the lower reaches of the Top 40 and will climb to number 1 in February, toppling the hated 'Mull of Kintyre'. Peel remarks that Paul Burnett, who has started playing 'Uptown Top Ranking' for the lunchtime crowd, will probably get the credit for making it a hit. Like most good jokes, it's funny because it's true.

The two other songs in Peel's top three both come from the same band. The Motors are seen by some critics as uninvited guests at the 1977 party, more of a souped-up new-wave band than a true punk one. New wave is the 'in' phrase of the moment. There are new-wave labels. There are new-wave singles released on new-wave coloured vinyl. Peel is without doubt the biggest Motors fan on national radio, but that will change next year when they have a new-wave hit with 'Airport'. The song is so cheesy that Peel will pray they give the credit for its success to Paul Burnett.

Putting the Motors at numbers 1 and 3 is a defiantly right-of-centre alternative to the musically leftist orthodoxy of the *NME*. 'Dancing the Night Away', Peel's Festive 60 chart-topper, didn't even graze the *NME* writers' end-of-year top thirty. And his love of Neil Young's marathon guitar solos hardly tallies, either, with the didactic tirades that fill the pages of punk fanzines. Peel is largely unaffected by any concerns of hipness, though he's usually conscious of the latest trends. He's heard from reggae experts that Ranking Trevor (whose song 'Truly' with the vocal group the Jays, is at number 13 in his chart) is considered by hardcore dreads to be a bit of a lightweight. Peel isn't bothered; he's not after brownie points. Nor does he think twice about lauding the Lurkers – Uxbridge punks at number 12 with 'Shadow' – who are dismissed as provincial by punk tastemakers at the Wardour Street epicentre.

Peel's programmes have been going through a user-friendly phase for the past few months. He starts each one with a helpful (and lengthy) list of the bands he'll be playing. If a new punk single is released and rave-reviewed by one of the music papers, Peel can be guaranteed to play it straight away. No punk album, meanwhile, escapes his notice. On 24 October, three days before its official release, he played all thirty-eight minutes and twenty-two seconds of the momentous new Sex Pistols LP, *Never Mind the Bollocks . . . Here's the Sex Pistols*, a marvellous taping opportunity for any listeners too impecunious to buy it. It was one of the most public-spirited things the *John Peel Show* did all year.

Have you heard that geezer John Peel? He's old enough to be your dad and he's got a beard and a bald spot. And when he talks about his missus he calls her 'the Pig' – something to do with the way she laughs, but it's still weird. And he goes on about stuff like 'such-and-such a song is by no means disgraceful' and 'I find it to be easily the most rewarding of the works they've released so far'. But that doesn't matter. He cares about music. He gives young bands a fair shake. He supports new initiatives. He reads out your letter and writes back wishing you all the best with your next endeavour. He puts ideas in your head. If he stopped playing all the fucking folk songs, he could be one of us.

1978: ATOM SPLITTING

'I can tell immediately by their expressions that the studio
engineer and producer are not happy to be doing this session.
They keep telling us we can't do this and we can't do that. The
same obstructive attitude and closed-mindedness we encounter
wherever we go.' VIV ALBERTINE of the Slits on their
first Peel session

John Peel Show
Radio 1
22 May 1978

Mink DeVille – Jah Lloyd – The Rolling Stones – British Lions –
Dave Gilmour – The Slits – Radio Birdman – Essential Logic – The
Residents – The Stranglers – Link Wray

The minister of overseas development, Judith Hart, allocates £770,000
for the construction of a road between Stanley and Darwin in the
Falkland Islands. The islands, which lie in the South Atlantic, have
been under British administration since 1833.

The first five months of 1978 have borne witness to punk's commercial miracle. The new music has changed the look of *Top of the Pops,*
the sound of the Top 40 and the physiognomy of the British record
industry. Every second band now wears skinny ties and has 'The' at

the beginning of their name. There are more independent record labels than at any time in the UK's history. The music business is no longer a closed shop, and never will be again. The new wave has rolled in, inundating the blasé Canutes who stood on the shore and watched.

Since January there have been hit singles for the Stranglers, the Jam, the Rich Kids, the Tom Robinson Band, Blondie, Nick Lowe, Elvis Costello and the Attractions, the Boomtown Rats, Squeeze, the Patti Smith Group, Ian Dury and the Blockheads, and X-Ray Spex. And not just one-hit wonders. The Stranglers, the Jam and the TRB are all now major bands touring the Odeons and Apollos.

Punk, the music that Peel took a chance on by playing a ninety-two-second album track by the Ramones just over two years ago, has spread throughout the country, creating the delirious feeling of constitutional overthrow. It will become fashionable, years from now, for rock groups like Queen and Pink Floyd to say that punk never troubled them in the slightest. Others like Led Zeppelin will be a bit more honest. And still others – including some who were eight or nine years into their careers – will admit they were wiped completely off the map. Bands like Caravan, Curved Air and Budgie: gone.

Throughout 1977, punk was an attack on the music business (and the people who ran it); but now, in 1978, punk has found a place in the market where it can appeal to younger teenagers who relate to the excitement of a new parade of bands rattling out fast, melodic singles. Sixteen months ago Buzzcocks were borderline sinister. Now they're a pop group. Peel, who brought punk to Radio 1 despite Derek Chinnery's warnings not to play it, now sees it pervading the station's daytime schedules, leaving indelible imprints on the Top 40 that Radio 1 holds so dear. Dave Lee Travis plays punk. Paul Burnett plays it. Kid Jensen plays it. Tony Blackburn still hates it, but has to lump it. Peel's job is to let them all get on with

their programmes and keep a vigilant eye out for the bands they'll
be playing in the autumn and winter (whether they know it or not).
In the meantime, one of the issues – or iniquities – to which he
devotes his energies in 1978 is his belief that some of the best punk
bands in Britain are being squeezed out of the equation because no
record company will sign them. Peel's Radio 1 colleagues couldn't
care less which punk bands have record contracts and which ones
don't. He sees it as a cause worth fighting for.

Last December he played a session by the unsigned Siouxsie and
the Banshees (led by the fearsome Siouxsie Sioux, who was part
of the Pistols' entourage at the Grundy debacle) and urged any listening A&R men to snap them up at once. This was not a straightforward matter; the Banshees were at the darkest end of punk's
spectrum and had made a lot of demands about artistic control.
But Peel repeated the same session, and the same exhortation, a
month later. And he did the same a month after that. Siouxsie and
the Banshees are now poised to sign to Polydor, who have acceded
to their demands, and thanks to the *John Peel Show* there'll be a
forewarned and forearmed army of listeners waiting to go out and
buy anything they release. In a few months, the Banshees will be in
the Top 10 with their debut single, 'Hong Kong Garden', and Tony
Blackburn will be introducing them on *Top of the Pops*. It shows
what can happen when Peel fights a band's corner. Four young
people can have their prospects utterly transformed. They could be
the next Stranglers or Buzzcocks. They could come off the dole and
earn money. They could have a future.

Another band for whom Peel has been valiantly canvassing is the
Slits, a group of energetic girls who – as well as having one of the
most provocative names in punk – braved a barrage of chauvinis-
tic catcalls when they performed around the country on the Clash's
high-profile 'White Riot' package tour last year. Criticism of the
Slits' primitive musicianship is common, even from boys who can

scarcely play any better. If the Slits are sometimes wayward about staying in tune, their animated stage presence and lop-sided humour hide a multitude of sins. As writers, they bring something organic, giddy and new. Peel is premiering their second session tonight.

Peel doesn't normally watch sessions being recorded. He feels a studio is a place of work, not a tourist site. Inveterately tongue-tied around musicians, he's rarely seen at Maida Vale from one year to the next. But he made an exception for the Slits' first visit last September, turning up with Walters to offer moral support (which the girls appreciated) in their wrangles with the institutionally sexist BBC engineers. Tonight's session, like their debut, includes songs that will appear on their album *Cut*, which they'll release on Island in the autumn of next year. For the moment, though, the Slits are still unsigned. The only way to hear them is to listen to Peel. The only way to hear the Crabs, the Smirks, Adam and the Ants and all the other unsigned punk bands is to listen to Peel.

Once again tonight, he voices his disappointment that no label will take a punt on the Slits, urging them to reconsider. The number of women in bands has increased as a result of punk's anyone-can-do-it policy, and Peel will play music from hundreds of them over the next few years. Women writing and recording music of their own makes a refreshing change from women being used to decorate albums recorded by men. Two years ago feminist groups protested at posters advertising the Rolling Stones' *Black and Blue*, which showed a woman bruised and bound by ropes, with her legs splayed open. The Stones are back this summer with a new album and a new controversy (a song called 'Some Girls' contains the line 'Black girls just wanna get fucked all night'), but their current single, 'Miss You', suggests they may at least have awoken from a self-induced coma and taken notice of a changed world. Influenced by New York clubs and discos, the song is fresh and danceable, and restores some of the credibility the Stones lost before the punk explosion. The sleeve, moreover, shows how carefully they've been monitoring what's been happening back home. Slouched against a wall in PVC and leather, they look more like the Clash than the Clash do.

Peel plays 'Miss You', but he's in no mood to welcome the Stones back with open arms. Taking a leaf from the hardline punk manual, he suggests it would have been better if they'd disbanded after recording '(I Can't Get No) Satisfaction'. That was thirteen years ago. Not even *Sniffin' Glue* at its most vituperative ever went so far as to say the Stones should have called it a day *that* early.

John Peel Show
Radio 1
7 July 1978

The Dickies – The Pirates – Punishment of Luxury – Magazine – The Leyton Buzzards – Frankie Miller – The Shirts – X-Ray Spex – La Düsseldorf – Sham 69 – Alternative TV – Talking Heads – Dire Straits

Investigations are ongoing into a fire on a train at Taunton in Somerset in the early hours of yesterday morning, which claimed the lives of eleven passengers. The fire broke out in a sleeping car when bags of dirty linen were stacked against an electric heater.

If Peel were a punk writer for the *NME* or a fanzine, his programmes would be very different. He might be contemptuous, for a start, of a singer like Frankie Miller, a raucous Glaswegian who holds true to the old virtues of boozy bar-room blues that punk was supposed to have done away with. Miller has his fourth Peel session going out tonight, alongside one by the Pirates, a veteran cauliflower-eared trio who used to slug away behind Johnny Kidd ('Shakin' All Over') in the Mesozoic Era of British rock 'n' roll. Shivers down me backbone! There's plenty of falling off bar stools and draining the amber liquid on the *John Peel Show* tonight.

But even more unpalatable to a certain kind of punk purist would be Peel's affection for the cheap-and-cheerful, boot-boy end of punk personified by Sham 69, a band from Hersham in Surrey with a football-terrace fanbase. Their loutish new single, 'If the Kids are United', has found a big supporter in Walters, who thinks – wrongly – that it's a cert to reach number 1, and Peel is not far behind in his enthusiasm. Sophisticated art-school graduates Sham 69 are not, but they speak for the downtrodden punk proletariat in ways that the Banshees and Buzzcocks cannot, and Peel's listeners will just have to put up with the fact that he loves them. When they get round to releasing an album, *That's Life*, in October, he'll play the whole thing in a single night.

More cerebral are Howard Devoto's Magazine, whose first album for the much-changed, fast-reacting Virgin label came out a fortnight ago. Icily aloof and unafraid of its intellect, *Real Life* is one of the first examples of a new strand of music that will become known as post-punk. But then again, Peel is just as fond of the Dickies, a novelty punk band from California, who play speeded-up parodies of famous hits like Black Sabbath's 'Paranoid'. The Dickies are a joke that even small children will one day tire of, but they'll still be getting belly laughs out of Peel for some years to come. He may be an Ivor Cutler and Viv Stanshall fan, but he also delights in a good custard-pie gag.

One of the most tangible changes from the album-dominated Peel shows of the early Seventies is that about a hundred new singles now arrive at his office at Broadcasting House every week. The seven-inch single is the ideal medium of punk, partly due to the directness of the message, and partly due to the fact that the majority of small labels are unable to finance albums. If a band cannot afford to make a single, a popular way of approaching the *John Peel*

Show is to send in a demo tape and hope to be invited to record a session. Later this month Peel will apologise to any bands that are waiting to hear back from him. His office is now receiving thirty tapes a week – on top of the one hundred singles – and a serious backlog has developed.

John Peel Show
Radio 1
31 July 1978

Magazine – XTC – Patrik Fitzgerald – Steel Pulse – Van Der Graaf – Buzzcocks – The Cars – The Carpettes – Snakefinger – Bunny Wailer – The Dead Boys – The Human League – The Zones

The under-secretary of state for the environment, Kenneth Marks, considers options to tackle the problem of annual solstice festivals at Stonehenge, which have seen illegal camping and trespassing in recent years. He rejects the idea of mounting a massive police presence to deter festival-goers in future.

Peel has been described as 'monomanic' in the pages of *Black Music & Jazz Review* magazine. He's not sure what it means, but he doesn't like the sound of it. Peel is a keen reader of all manner of music publications and is one of the few Radio 1 DJs to mention punk fanzines on air. He's got hold of one called *Live Wire*, written by Alan Anger, which has a column listing all the bands that Anger hates. They include the Drones, the Yachts, the Models, XTC, Pere Ubu, the Residents and Eater. All of them have been played by Peel.

Walters has looked up 'monomanic' in a dictionary. *Madness confined to one subject or an unreasonable interest in one thing.* Peel becomes defensive. He points out that his shows encompass folk, blues, reggae, punk and rock. 'That doesn't seem to be particularly monomanic to me, but there you are. Who cares?'

He obviously does.

John Peel Show
Radio 1
2 August 1978

Tuff Darts – Siouxsie and the Banshees – Penetration – Jellybean – The Shangri-Las – Reggae Regular – The Lurkers – Lone Star – Godfrey Daniel – The Dickies – Suicide – Stiff Little Fingers

Jeremy Thorpe, the former Liberal Party leader, takes part in a Commons debate about the future of Rhodesia. It's his last act as a parliamentarian before being arrested and charged with conspiring to murder Norman Scott, a male model, in 1975.

Nine years into the Troubles, Northern Ireland is a country where few bands venture. It's not just the insurance problems inherent in booking gigs there, or the fear of getting caught up in a security alert; it's also the worry that an overnight stay in central Belfast can be a gamble with the unknown: the city's main hotel, the Europa, has been bombed more than twenty times. So while the young people of Northern Ireland, arguably, have more reason to feel alienated and disillusioned than any punks on mainland Britain, the live-music scene in Belfast lags at least eighteen months behind cities like Manchester and Liverpool.

Stiff Little Fingers, one of a small handful of Northern Irish punk bands, came to Peel's attention earlier this year with a superb single, 'Suspect Device', in which they railed against the state of their homeland after almost a decade of killings. Peel digs out the song again tonight; it's become a real favourite. Stiff Little Fingers have since recorded a second single, 'Alternative Ulster', which offers some flickers of hope where 'Suspect Device' screamed with impotent rage. 'Alternative Ulster' is being distributed by Rough Trade, the west London record shop and independent label, but Peel thinks Stiff Little Fingers can do better than that. 'I must confess I'm still amazed that none of the major record companies have signed the band,' he'll say, back on his familiar theme, when he plays 'Alternative Ulster' later this month. 'I don't know if it's stupidity, cowardice or possibly because Belfast isn't much of a place to go on an expense account.'

If any other punk bands in Northern Ireland should make a record, they'll know who to send it to.

John Peel Show
Radio 1
15 August 1978

The Lurkers – The Who – The Fall – Tyla Gang – Inner Circle – Devo – Poet and the Roots – Ultravox – Stiff Little Fingers – Nick Lowe – Half Japanese – Aswad – Siouxsie and the Banshees

Sid Vicious, shortly to leave England for New York, performs a farewell concert at the Electric Ballroom in London. His set list includes the unreleased Sex Pistols song 'Belsen Was a Gas', and ends with a version of Frank Sinatra's 'My Way'.

One of the many labels to have sprung up during 1977 was Step Forward, launched in the summer to release singles by Chelsea and the Cortinas. Its founder is an American, Miles Copeland, who used to manage the prog-rock group Caravan until he realised the road to the palace of wisdom led to the Vortex, not to the land of grey and pink. Copeland's current clients are the Police, a punk-reggae trio for whom his brother Stewart plays drums. Yesterday the Police released their second single for the major label A&M, 'Can't Stand Losing You'. It's onwards and upwards for the Copeland brothers.

On the still operational Step Forward, meanwhile, the latest release is an EP by a Manchester five-piece called the Fall. Musically unrefined and proud of it, the three songs on *Bingo-Master's Break-Out!* are notable for some original lyrics, including one about a depressed bingo caller who cracks up under the strain of his humdrum job. The Fall's singer, Mark E. Smith, delivers the thought-provoking text in an unmelodic yowl that sounds like he's heckling his own song. Behind his sharp poetry, guitars and drums make tense, awkward thrusts. Peel and Walters brought the Fall down to Maida Vale in May to record a session, which went well. Tonight Peel applauds 'Bingo-Master' for being 'full of the kind of guitar-playing which we smart alecks who aren't sure whether it's very clever or just out-of-tune call "angular"'.

The angular Fall will record a second session in November, followed by twenty-two more over the next twenty-five years.

John Peel Show
Radio 1
25 August 1978

Status Quo – The White Cats – Tanz Der Youth – King – Bob Dylan – Culture – Siouxsie and the Banshees – The Jam – Hot Water – Godley and Creme – Talking Heads – The Helmettes

The New Statesman *magazine warns that 2 million Britons may have their names listed on a new Special Branch computer by 1985. The*

*computer will collate intelligence on crime, drugs, immigration, fraud
and national security, and will be based at a police centre in Putney.*

One thing Peel always enjoys doing is reading out the line-ups of
punk bands. The Helmettes are Dutch.

'The lead singer is called Half Two. The guitarist and vocalist, or
assistant vocalist, is called Pi Pi, which is written in Greek charac-
ters. The guitar player – another guitar player – is Frankenstein. The
bass player is Frankie, and the drummer, I'm afraid, is called Ronnie
Tampon.'

John Peel Show
Radio 1
29 August 1978

The Real Kids – The Zones – Prag VEC – The Rich Kids – The
Pop Group – Paul Revere and the Raiders – Jay Boy Adams – The
Upsetters – Dave Edmunds – George Thorogood and the Destroyers

*Willie Gallagher, a twenty-year-old Republican serving twelve years
in Long Kesh Prison for bombing a British Legion hall, ends his
forty-eight-day hunger strike. Gallagher, who claims his confession
was forced by police beatings, has had his case taken up by two US
congressmen.*

Early in tonight's show, Peel makes reference to a group of girls
who were hanging around outside Broadcasting House this afternoon. He says he walked past them several times in the hope that
they would recognise him ('that fatherly but still fiendishly attractive John Peel'), but they were obviously waiting for someone
more famous. It's not uncommon for Peel to talk about his age

and physical appearance in ironic terms. It's one of his primary self-defence mechanisms. In a programme in mid-October, he will describe himself poetically as a 'raven-tressed tempter'. He turns thirty-nine tomorrow.

There's a session from Prag VEC, a band from London who sent in a demo tape. They're fronted by Sue Gogan, the latest female punk singer to be added by Peel to the ranks of Ari Up (the Slits), Pauline Murray (Penetration), Poly Styrene (X-Ray Spex) and Siouxsie Sioux. So new and unestablished are Prag VEC that they haven't got any gigs lined up. Peel asks promoters to get in touch. They probably will, too. You never know who might be listening. Repeating a session by the Pop Group – a feverish, discordant Bristol quintet who are anything but a pop group – Peel notes that it was first broadcast in August, when Patti Smith happened to be in the country. Hearing them on the radio, she immediately booked the Pop Group to be the support band on her upcoming British tour.

John Peel Show
Radio 1
12 September 1978

The B-52's – Tyla Gang – The Prefects – Dave Edmunds – The Undertones – The Pleasers – Marquis de Sade – Ashley Hutchings – Sham 69 – Ras Michael and the Sons of Negus – Brian Eno

Mystery surrounds the case of Bulgarian writer and dissident Georgi Markov, who died in a London hospital yesterday after being attacked near Waterloo Bridge. Markov, a defector to the West nine years ago, was apparently stabbed by an unknown assailant with a poison-tipped umbrella.

Opportunity knocks for a young band from Derry in Northern Ireland. The Undertones' 'Teenage Kicks' – played tonight for the first time on British radio – has none of the anger of Stiff Little Fingers from Belfast. It's not about the Troubles or religion. It's a schoolboy *cri de coeur* about an unattainable girl, shot through with a lovesick ache. The singer, Feargal Sharkey, wet-dreams his way through the song in a sobbing gurgle, articulating the frustration of a hundred thousand agonised adolescents in lonely bedrooms. His heart bursts and the listener feels the explosion. Over the next few days Peel, who is nineteen years older than Sharkey, will have an intense emotional reaction to 'Teenage Kicks'. It brings tears to his eyes and he can't stop playing it.

John Peel Show
Radio 1
25 September 1978

Radio Stars – The Europeans – The Skids – David Bowie – Devo – Motörhead – Penetration – Tubeway Army – John Cooper Clarke – The Saints – Black Sabbath – Wire – The Cravats – The Undertones

Ford car workers in Dagenham vote to strike for more pay. This follows walkouts by thousands of workers in Southampton and on Merseyside, and leads to the temporary closure of all Ford plants across Britain.

'That is a mighty, mighty record, you know.'

Peel has just played 'Teenage Kicks' twice in a row – something he hasn't done with a song for years. He's fallen head over heels in love with it. 'Come the end of the year,' he tells the listeners, 'that will be battling with "Suspect Device" and [Magazine's] "Shot by Both Sides" as my record of the year.'

Why has 'Teenage Kicks' hit him so hard? The Undertones aren't quite sure; they don't even think it's the best song on their EP. But perhaps Peel isn't hearing what the Undertones hear in it, or feeling what they feel. Unlike the young Derry lads, for whom 'Teenage Kicks' has real-life relevance in their quest for girlfriends, Peel doesn't live the song in real time when Sharkey sings it. He's thrown back to the Fifties and memories of his teenage isolation at an all-boys public school, where he immersed himself in dreams of girls and love affairs. When a painful memory is two decades old, the pang of recalling it can be exquisitely bittersweet, and that's what's happened to Peel. He has romanticised 'Teenage Kicks' for all he's worth, mourning the loves he missed and the girls who eluded him all through his youth. The reason the song resonates so deeply with him isn't because it reminds him of his teenage kicks. It's because it reminds him, overwhelmingly, that he had no teenage kicks at all.

John Peel Show
Radio 1
3 October 1978

The Bishops – Matumbi – Wire – Van Morrison – Chelsea – M – Buzzcocks – The Physicals – Penetration – Protex – The Undertones – The Beatles – Siouxsie and the Banshees

The second series of the American soap opera Dallas, *featuring the exploits of the villainous oil tycoon J. R. Ewing, begins on BBC1. The show will gradually gain in popularity throughout 1979, peaking in 1980, when J.R. is shot.*

When Peel played 'Teenage Kicks' three weeks ago and explained that the Undertones had no record deal, their lives changed in an instant. Seymour Stein, president of the American label Sire, whose roster includes Talking Heads and the Ramones, was in England listening to Peel on a car radio. Stein knew all about Peel and the Ramones, but who were these new kids? 'Pull over!' he shouted to his driver. 'Pull over! I've got to sign them!' The Undertones hadn't even got halfway through the song.

Today contracts with Sire were signed. Peel celebrates by – what else? – playing 'Teenage Kicks' again. He also debuts a single by another Northern Ireland band, Protex, from Belfast. Like London's Rough Trade, Belfast now has its own independent record label, Good Vibrations, run from a shop of the same name. More bands from the province – Rudi, the Outcasts, the Tearjerkers – will follow Stiff Little Fingers, the Undertones and Protex onto the *John Peel Show* in the next few months. This is the atom-splitting process that has been energising cities around Britain since Peel's programmes announced 'open sesame' to punk. He plays a band from a particular area and suddenly six others from the same area send him demo tapes. Three months ago that area looked like a wasteland; now it's a musical nerve centre. He can spark an entire regional scene merely by playing one song.

And tonight brings the first clear hint that he believes he now has a much younger audience than he had two years ago. Siouxsie and the Banshees' first album, *The Scream*, is released next month and Peel has an advance copy. BASF and TDK cassettes at the ready, Banshees fans: this is a unique scoop. 'The only track on it that isn't a group composition is "Helter Skelter",' Peel tells them. 'It occurred to me that you might not have heard the original from 1968, from the Beatles' White Album.'

They might not have heard the Beatles? How old does he think they are? And what might a Festive 50 look like if these young music fans were to vote for it? After giving them a flavour of what the Fab Four sounded like back in the day, he plays *The Scream* from beginning to end, with no interruptions. 'That's the one, boys and girls,' he says when it's over. 'That's the one.'

John Peel Show
Radio 1
25 October 1978

The Velvettes – Hawkwind – The Fabulous Poodles – The Flying Lizards – Metal Urbain – XTC – Misty in Roots – Wreckless Eric – Japan – UK Subs – Prince Far I – Temple City Kazoo Orchestra

Fifty Vietnamese refugees, who were rescued from their sinking boat in the South China Sea by cadets on a British training ship, have arrived in England. The government has offered them sanctuary, and many of them hope to settle in the Kent countryside.

Peel plays a song called 'Convent Girls' by the new-wave band the Fabulous Poodles. He says it could have been written with him in mind. The lyrics are about a schoolgirl-obsessed motorist who tails a girl in 'short white socks' until a panda car appears. It's a dismayingly grubby-sounding Peel who follows it by saying: 'Would you like a lolly, my dear?' Preserved for posterity on tape, it makes the heart sink.

An unsavoury moment of poor judgement from a married father of two? Or just a contextually run-of-the-mill Seventies attitude that now sounds horribly improper? Peel certainly seems to fit a British type in that decade: the uptight man getting hot under his collar about a girl young enough to be his daughter. Comedy films and television sitcoms have been full of these men in the Seventies, all of them convulsed by fantasies of pneumatic teenagers and pouting dolly birds. If *Carry On*'s Sid James and Kenneth Connor, with their combined age of over a hundred, say 'phwoar' once, they must say it a thousand times. When Stan the bus driver goes looking for a young poppet in a bikini to tempt back to his chalet in *Holiday on the Buses* (1973), nobody stops the film to protest that the actor playing Stan is fifty-seven. In sexually askew Seventies Britain, Peel's comment about convent girls – while skin-crawlingly inappropriate to future historians – constitutes no more of a threat, a transgression or a professional faux pas than Basil Fawlty peeking at the cleavage of the Australian tourist as she signs the register.

Peel will make other remarks about schoolgirls in other programmes, and they'll all have the same soft chuckle of hopeless middle-aged desperation. But again, some context is necessary; he hasn't just plucked the subject out of thin air. The Boomtown Rats' 'Mary of the Fourth Form' – a Top 20 single in December 1977 – was about a schoolgirl of fourteen or fifteen 'hitching up her short skirt', moving 'her hips aside' and dropping a pencil in the classroom and bending over in front of the teacher. A culture of fantasising about girls with pigtails and hockey sticks is one tradition that didn't die out when punk set about rewriting the vocabulary of rock. The Police ('Don't Stand So Close to Me'), the Regents ('7 Teen') and even cuddly ABBA ('Does Your Mother Know') will all write songs in 1979–80 about girls who are, as the Regents put it, 'not yet a woman'. None of them will cause a stir. The Police's *Lolita*-inspired hit will win a Grammy.

Peel, then, is not on some predatory crusade. He isn't even unusual. And if a letter he read out during a show in August 1977 is any guideline, his listeners are happy to be complicit in whatever pipedream he thinks he's weaving. 'Darling John,' it began, 'two nubile young nymphets who always listen to your programme whilst naked in the bath would be willing to show our appreciation at your convenience.' Nudity in the bath is a Peel in-joke: the sleeve of a 1972 Dandelion sampler album, *There Is Some Fun Going*

Forward, showed him sitting naked in a bath with a model. But just as it's not strictly fair to take an in-joke out of context and call it to account, it's a step too far to envisage the thirty-nine-year-old Peel having a real-life tryst with the girls who wrote the letter. If he were serious about sharing baths with his female listeners, one imagines his wife Sheila would have either divorced him or slapped some sense into him.

A Radio 1 DJ reading out a letter containing the phrase 'nubile young nymphets' in 2015 would be likely to be sacked after a Twitterstorm and a media outcry. But as obediently as the modern cynic laughs on cue at the tired cliché 'the Seventies were different times', it mustn't be forgotten that the Seventies were different times. Searching for the values of twenty-first-century Britain on Radio 1 tapes from 1978 is a fool's errand. They will not be found there. Women, in that foreign country, were buxom housewives slaving over a hot double entendre while hubby was at the office, or flirtatious airheads who liked having their bum pinched as long as it was a bit of fun.

Peel, in fact, showed more evidence of respecting women as creative artists than any other male DJ in the eleven-year history of the station. His joke about offering lollies to schoolgirls was dismal, but it was in keeping with the comedy of the times, and much of the comedy of the times was even worse. It might be best to trust the women on this. In the final analysis, if Peel had been a predator or a lecherous pest, it is very likely that Siouxsie Sioux would have been as sickened by him as she was by Bill Grundy, and would have said so. And a group of highly intelligent young women like the Slits, in all seriousness, wouldn't have allowed Peel to go anywhere near them, no matter how many times he repeated their sessions.

John Peel Show
Radio 1
26 December 1978

The Who – The Doors – The Rolling Stones – Poco – Free – Derek
and the Dominos – Led Zeppelin – Siouxsie and the Banshees – Neil
Young – The Flying Lizards – The Sex Pistols – The Jam

*At a Boxing Day festival at the Kelvin Hall exhibition centre in
Glasgow, a carriage on the Concorde Flyer fairground ride snaps from
its mountings and overturns. A thirty-seven-year-old man and his two-
year-old daughter are killed.*

Tonight we find out how much Peel's audience has changed since
the Punk Specials of December 1976 and August 1977. As a warm-up
to the Festive 50, he plays an hour of selections from the previous
chart in 1976. Hearing him dole out 'Layla', 'All Right Now', 'Riders
on the Storm' and 'Stairway to Heaven' so early in proceedings, one
is bound to wonder if any of them have made the list this time.

The Festive 50, it will become plain over the next four nights, is
full of change. Radical, extraordinary change. 'I really do think you're
going to find it most intriguing,' Peel says, like Houdini pointing at a
tank full of water. 'I've been looking forward to this programme for
many weeks.' The number of listeners voting is more than 400 per
cent higher than in 1976.

And so farewell then. It's the end of the road for a lot of what Peel
calls 'elderly' music, and a thorough vindication of his decision to
focus more and more on punk over the past two years. Where once
were songs by Yes (at number 50), Roy Harper (47), the Grateful
Dead (40) and Jefferson Airplane (24) are now songs by Siouxsie
and the Banshees, the Flying Lizards, the Stranglers and the Jam.
Dylan's 'Desolation Row' has plummeted from 3 to 46. 'Layla' has

plunged from 2 to 31. They're two of only seven songs from the previous Festive 50 to make the transition.

The listeners – who were voting for their all-time favourite pieces of music, remember – have spoken almost in unison, and the key years by some distance are 1977 and 1978. Catapulted into the top twenty are the Rezillos, the Only Ones, the Clash, the Damned, Stiff Little Fingers, the Undertones, Magazine and the Sex Pistols. 'Teenage Kicks' (at 10), 'Suspect Device' (4), 'God Save the Queen' (3), 'Complete Control' (2) and 'Anarchy in the UK' (1) are the new classics of Peel's modern generation, rendering 'Free Bird' (at 19) and 'Stairway to Heaven' (14) as ludicrously antiquated as a pair of penny farthings at a Superbike event. If the Festive 50 isn't an unqualified rejection of the past (a track from Van Morrison's *Astral Weeks* lands just outside the top twenty), it's certainly a ringing endorsement of the present. Peel sounds thrilled by it.

Most symbolic of the changes to Peel's show and Peel's audience are the seven placings achieved by Siouxsie and the Banshees – over half of their recorded output – which is absolutely remarkable given that he first began enthusing about them just a year ago. The Banshees, who have gone from having no record label to peppering the Festive 50 with tracks from a one-month-old debut album, are the new stars of the *John Peel Show*.

Peel will pursue his new music policy throughout next year. Music has changed, and he has done more than any individual in Britain to change it. He's the one who played the new bands night after night, week after week. *NME*, *Melody Maker* and *Sounds*, publishing every seven days, simply cannot provide, for all their interviews and reviews, the sort of immediate access that Peel can. His show is the hotline to the new music.

There's only one small cloud on the horizon. With twelve songs left in the 50, Peel says to the listeners: 'From here on to the top, things get pretty hard-nosed. In fact, you've probably figured out what quite a few of the records are. It's just a question of the order that they're in.'

Oh? Some predictable choices, in other words? A top ten with few surprises? Surely, as he closes the door on 1978, Peel isn't going to find that his new audience will be just as conservative in its thinking as the old one?

1979: NOW IS THE WINTER

'The anguished singer had achieved total physical self-expression
by the climax of "She's Lost Control", and, evidently having lost
control, he was helped offstage at the conclusion of a set which,
for practical reasons, could not be extended.' Review of Joy
Division in Leeds, *Sounds* magazine

John Peel Show
Radio 1
10 January 1979

Jerry Lee Lewis – The Mahotella Queens – Elvis Costello and the
Attractions – The Parrots – The Cure – The Shirkers – Throbbing
Gristle – Kleenex – The Residents – Winston Edwards – O Level

*Returning from an economic conference in the Caribbean, James
Callaghan is asked by journalists to comment on the 'mounting chaos'
facing Britain. His dismissive reply inspires a headline on the front page
of the* Sun: *'Crisis? What Crisis?'*

On 23 November last year, amid a deluge of trailers and jingles,
Radio 1 changed its wavelength from 247 metres – which had been
its home on the medium-wave band since 1967 – to a new frequency
of 275/285. The DJs made personal appearances all over the country, explaining to the people of Britain which of the two frequencies

(275 or 285) their area fell in. Peel was not invited to accompany them. Instead, in the first phase of a major Radio 1 reshuffle, he had his Friday night slot taken off him and is now down to four shows a week.

Peel is bitterly unhappy about the situation (and will bitch about it for months), particularly as the slot has been given to Tommy Vance to present a new programme, *The Friday Rock Show*, that makes a big fuss about the sort of leather-trousered cock-rock posturing that Peel's shows have pointedly left behind. It can't be denied that hard rock had a strong year in '78 – with albums like Thin Lizzy's *Live and Dangerous*, AC/DC's *Powerage* and an impressive debut by Van Halen – but Peel has been infuriated to learn that one of *The Friday Rock Show*'s selling points is the repeat of classic radio sessions from the past – sessions originally broadcast on *Top Gear* by the very man whose two-hour slot Vance has taken.

John Peel Show
Radio 1
29 January 1979

The Rolling Stones – The Ruts – James Carr – Generation X – The Members – Fatman Riddim Section – Steve Hillage – The Monochrome Set – The Lurkers – Pierre Moerlen's Gong – I-Roy

After a month of industrial action by ambulance drivers, gravediggers, refuse collectors and other public-sector workers, lorry drivers vote to accept a 20 per cent pay rise and end their three-week strike. The scale of the increase sets a template for other unions' demands.

Stay tuned, Peel counsels, for a blinder of a session; do *not* go to the pub. The Ruts are a London punk band with reggae leanings, and their debut single, 'In a Rut', is a brooding, prowling inner-city paranoia attack with a glorious chorus. For some months the band's name has been cropping up in fanzines – Peel once again stresses the importance of fanzines – and he wishes he had paid more attention.

The Ruts have a serrated edge, but are tightly controlled by a powerful drummer. As much as as he exerts discipline, however, they're blown wide apart by their singer, a Joe Strummer sound-alike named Malcolm Owen. A man of odd pronunciations ('hate' is sung as 'hoit'), he brings a visceral anger to the *John Peel Show*, but also a thinking brain, and he's a big improvement on the bovver-boy bands like Sham 69. The Ruts' session includes 'Babylon's Burning', which will put them in the charts in the summer.

Peel reads out a list of the Ruts' forthcoming gigs. One of them – with Misty in Roots, a reggae band – is a benefit concert for Rock Against Racism. This organisation was founded in 1976, when a hero of Peel's, Eric Clapton, launched into a racist speech onstage at the Birmingham Odeon. 'Get the foreigners out,' he said. 'Get the wogs out. Get the coons out. Keep Britain white.' Peel, who either wasn't following events too closely or was quick to forgive, presented a one-hour Clapton special eleven nights later.

But he wouldn't do that now. As RAR and other anti-racist groups grow in popularity, a demonstration by the Anti-Nazi League will take place in April in the heavily Punjabi west London area of Southall, aiming to neutralise a meeting of the National Front at the town hall. In the resultant fighting, the manager of Misty in Roots, Clarence Baker, will sustain head injuries from a police truncheon that put him in a coma.

Politically and racially, 1979 has an even more combustible atmosphere than 1976, as if the running battles at the Notting Hill Carnival which inspired 'White Riot' were merely the prelude to a longer war. In this context, Generation X, the other band in session tonight, are proof that old mannerisms no longer cut it in these high-anxiety times. Billy Idol sings of leading a youth uprising ('I'm still the seeker for your English dreams'), but he sounds like a bluffer where Malcolm Owen sounds like a desperado. This third Peel session looks a step too far for a jaded Generation X. 'They're not the band that had me tapping my toe arthritically down at the Roxy all those years ago,' Peel laments.

All those years ago? More like two.

John Peel Show
Radio 1
3 April 1979

The Angelic Upstarts – Essential Logic – The Sex Pistols – The Members – Urban Disturbance – Big in Japan – Nicky and the Dots – Shock – Bram Tchaikovsky – Nina Hagen Band – Linton Kwesi Johnson – Graham Parker and the Rumour – The Molesters – Kevin Coyne

Margaret Thatcher declines to appear in a TV debate with James Callaghan in the run-up to May's general election. With the Conservatives well ahead in the polls, she tells London Weekend Television that presidential-style debates are 'alien to this country'.

Poor Sid Vicious. The nihilistic poster boy for wanton self-destruction was arrested in New York last October and charged with stabbing his twenty-year-old American girlfriend, Nancy Spungen, to death. As the horror sank in, Peel was surprisingly compassionate. Announcing a benefit gig by the Doomed (the Damned under a new name) to raise money for Vicious's defence fund, Peel took a parental tone: 'Those journalists who, over the past year or so, presented Sid's drug problems as a modern romance might well like to contribute to that [fund].'

A stricken Vicious slashed his wrists with a broken light bulb the day before Peel's programme aired. As it turned out, there was no point in a defence fund for him anyway. Allowed out on bail, Vicious died two months ago from an overdose of heroin given to him by his own mother.

The Sex Pistols are a defunct band, for obvious reasons, but they're also, like a headless chicken, incapable of completely expiring. 'Silly Thing', a new single played by Peel tonight, will be the second of three Top 10 hits for them this year. It bears scant resemblance to the terrifying band of old. A pale commercial Xerox of how the Pistols sounded with Johnny Rotten, it's little more than a bunk-bed revolution for the twelve-year-old younger brothers of the original eighteen-year-old punks. This is a story with a tragic ending whichever way you look at it.

But just like the Pistols, the show goes on. Essential Logic have a female saxophonist and are inventively arty. The Fall have put an album out (*Live at the Witch Trials*), and Peel plays its opening track, 'Frightened'. 'I don't want to dance,' yowls Mark E. Smith in an eerie precognition of a future Mancunian gladioli brandisher, 'I want to go home.' The Jamaican-born poet and reggae artist Linton Kwesi Johnson (who must be new to Peel; he mispronounces 'Kwesi') worries about apolitical tendencies among bored young blacks ('It Noh Funny'). There's a discombobulating four minutes in the company of the Nina Hagen Band, from Berlin, whose song '*Naturträne*' is like a stadium-rock ballad that keeps being interrupted by an opera singer doing vocal exercises.

Geoff Travis, the quiet man with Afro hair who runs the Rough Trade label, has been in touch with the programme. He's promoting a gig at the Acklam Hall in Ladbroke Grove and wants the band Swell Maps to play. The trouble is he doesn't know their phone numbers. Peel, the information exchange for all things punk, asks the band to give Geoff a ring.

John Peel Show
Radio 1
30 April 1979

Dr Feelgood – Shake – Lene Lovich – Neon Hearts – Jonnie and the Lubes – The Undertones – The Fall – Sperma – Kleenex – Dillinger – The Human League – The Piranhas – The Cure – Crisis

Prince Charles opens the London Underground's new Jubilee line. The result of seven years of tunnelling work, it comprises the old Stanmore branch of the Bakerloo line and a new route from Baker Street to Charing Cross.

'These are Jonnie and the Lubes, and "I Got Rabies".'

The Brighton-based Lubes, who like all good punk bands have a female saxophonist, play in a rudimentary but strangely hypnotic way, sounding – though they might resent the comparison – like early Hawkwind. Lead singer Jonnie Condom grabs the microphone and sings in the geezerish voice of a window cleaner: 'We-got-rabies, we-got-rabies, we're-gonna-give-everybody-rabies.'

The Lubes will split up at the end of the year, having played twenty-five gigs.

John Peel Show
Radio 1
19 July 1979

UK Subs – Little Feat – Russians – Angelic Upstarts – Burning Spear – Dead Kennedys – 48 Chairs – Joy Division – The B-52's – PiL – Kevin Coyne – The Inmates – The Specials – Prince Buster

For the first time since 1975, MPs debate the reintroduction of capital punishment. The vote is 243 in favour of restoring the death penalty and 362 against. The 119 majority is much larger than expected.

John Walters has gone to a health farm. The strain of wading through the huge piles of records and demo tapes in the office must be getting too much for him.

Peel has received letters from listeners who have been to America. Young people over there are bored senseless by Kiss and Styx, apparently, and are checking out the new wave. Peel is encouraged to hear it. In all the excitement about punk in Britain, maybe he shouldn't give up on the States just yet? He plays two of their new bands. The B-52's, from Athens in Georgia, are the musical equivalent of a game of beach volleyball. Much more serious are the Dead Kennedys from San Francisco, whose single 'California Über Alles' is a scathing attack on the state's Democrat governor Jerry Brown. As is customary, Peel embraces the music and leaves the listeners to figure out the politics.

In a piece he writes this month about Siouxsie and the Banshees, Peel uses the term 'post-punk'. The definition of post-punk is flexible, and it's hard to know exactly when and how it started, but the term implies a slower, darker, more experimental music than the frantic one–two–three–four approach of 1977. So far this year Peel has played several bands – Gang of Four, Cabaret Voltaire, the Cure, PiL, Throbbing Gristle – who will be synonymous with post-punk, but perhaps the most important (especially to listeners of the *John Peel Show*) are Joy Division, a band from Salford and Macclesfield, who began appearing on his programmes in January.

If post-punk is characterised by darkness and atmosphere, Joy Division have clear advantages over their peers. On their debut album, *Unknown Pleasures*, from which Peel is playing songs every night this week, they've been framed by their producer Martin

Hannett in a paradoxically spacious and claustrophobic sound-world. There are weird extremes of bass and treble, and the musical instruments move about like Caligari silhouettes. The songs, which are pessimistic to the point of clinical depression, are sung in a deep sonorous moan by a twenty-three-year-old named Ian Curtis. Until tonight, Magazine's 'Shot by Both Sides' was the best song of the last two years about a Kafkaesque cipher in the thick of an unfathomable plot. That was until Peel played Joy Division's 'Shadowplay', a white-knuckle tale of assassins and hostages, and now Curtis is edging out in front. Is it too early to call this the music of the future?

If Joy Division are all about the self, the Specials – a multiracial ska revivalist band from Coventry – are all about the community. Positive messages, education through music, reggae against racism, we can effect change. 'Gangsters', a single the Specials have released on their own 2 Tone label, is certainly no stranger to paranoia (its first line is 'Why must you record my phone calls?'), but the ska beat is exceptionally danceable and the song looks likely to enter the Top 40 any day now. Kid Jensen has made it his record of the week on the late-afternoon show. Peel, who first played it two months ago, has noticed it's the most frequently requested song when he DJs in public.

For anyone wishing to catch the country's hottest new sensation while they can, the Specials are playing a gig in London at the weekend with another young ska band, Madness. For those who can't wait for live entertainment, there's always the Radio 1 Roadshow, which comes tomorrow from Beaumaris on the Isle of Anglesey, a half-hour drive from the Royal Artillery camp at Ty Croes, where a young John Ravenscroft was stationed during his National Service.

John Peel Show
Radio 1
24 July 1979

Dead Kennedys – Jackson Browne – The Monitors – Scritti Politti
– Sham 69 – Augustus Pablo – Adam and the Ants – The Specials –
Fatal Microbes – Poison Girls – Secret Affair – Dennis Brown

*Lynda Chalker, the under-secretary of state for health and social
security in Margaret Thatcher's new Conservative government, is asked
to comment on research suggesting that half a million elderly people
will be at risk from hypothermia this coming winter. Chalker denies
there is any such risk.*

One of the most disturbing songs Peel plays this year is 'Violence
Grows' by the Fatal Microbes. They're a band of school-age punks
with a fifteen-year-old singer, Donna Boylan, who uses the stage
name Honey Bane. 'Violence Grows' begins with a line of stunning
verve ('While you're getting kicked to death in a London pedestrian subway . . .'), and never have eleven words set a more explicit
scene. What follows is blurred and harrowing, with phased guitar
and a tentative bassline prodding away behind Bane's whining,
taunting voice. It's a physically oppressive song to listen to, and in
places almost an unbearable one. Bane's overlapping vocals in the
final nightmarish thirty seconds are like waking up under anaesthe-
sia in mid-operation and staring into the eyes of a horrified doctor.

The psychological problems alluded to in 'Violence Grows' are
very real. Peel tells the listeners that Bane is 'currently on the run
again' and has been replaced in the Fatal Microbes' line-up. She'll
subsequently spend time in a juvenile detention facility. To follow
'Violence Grows' – and it's not an easy challenge – Peel plays a
song from the first B-52's album, which is a bit like seeing Elvis

Presley's *Blue Hawaii* on a double bill with Alan Clarke's *Scum*.

The Fatal Microbes have close links with another band, the Poison Girls, whose forty-four-year-old singer Frances Sansom (alias Vi Subversa) is the mother of the Microbes' guitarist and drummer. The Poison Girls' song 'Crisis', from a new EP called *Hex*, is just as traumatic as the single by her children. In a cracked voice, Subversa recounts the ghastly details of a housewife having a mental collapse after several bouts of domestic violence. The song ends with the sound of an ambulance siren. Peel admits there are parts of *Hex* that he cannot take, but recommends that everyone hears the songs at least once. It's a protean show tonight, from Augustus Pablo's dub melodica to the mod revival soapboxing of Secret Affair, but next to 'Crisis' and 'Violence Grows', most of them sound terribly trivial.

John Peel Show
Radio 1
9 August 1979

XTC – The Cravats – Clive Pig and the Hopeful Chinamen – Penetration – The Freeze – Rudi – Prince Pampado – The Quads – Swell Maps – The Tearjerkers – Lori and the Chameleons – Madness

Brighton is to become the first British seaside resort to allow nude bathing. A designated beach for nudists gets the go-ahead from the council, despite concerns from critics that it will attract 'perverts and voyeurs'.

There's now a backlog of around 1,500 demo tapes in Peel's office. New ones arrive at the rate of fifteen to twenty a day. He and Walters promise to listen to every one of them – eventually – and return the ones they don't like. In a poem Peel reads out tonight, a band called the Winners, from Birmingham, speak for hundreds of unsigned musicians around the country who are desperately waiting for a phone call:

> You're a DJ, influential and kind
> We are a group going out of our minds
> No money, no jobs, our lives at stake
> In this cruel world of showbiz, not one lucky break
> But one spin on your show might just do the trick
> So come on, our John, and don't be a . . .

'Nuisance,' Peel finishes diplomatically. The Winners have clearly had a long wait for Peel to pull out their tape. Since recording it, they've changed their name to the Quads, obtained a deal with a local record label and released an excellent single, 'There Must Be Thousands', which runs rings round all the new mod anthems that bands like Secret Affair have been trying to write. Tonight Peel plays both sides of the single, declaring it 'terrific' and adding that he's been dying to play it all day. He then decides on the spur of the moment to play the beginning of the A-side again, and promises to repeat the whole song on Monday. He ends the show with an extract of the B-side instead of his signature tune. The Quads must be in dreamland.

But of course one result of this heartening story is that it serves as a blatant invitation to every other new band in Britain. As efforts to send demo tapes to Peel are redoubled, the backlog in his office will soon exceed 2,000.

John Peel Show
Radio 1
30 August 1979

The Undertones – Gene Vincent – Siouxsie and the Banshees –
Lonnie Donegan – Medicine Head – Mike Hart – Freda Payne – The
Silicon Teens – Little Richard – Duane Eddy – The Quads

Two suspected IRA men are arrested over the murder of Lord
Mountbatten, the former First Sea Lord and Chief of the Defence Staff.
Mountbatten and three others were killed earlier this week when a
bomb exploded on their fishing boat off the coast of Ireland.

Today is Peel's fortieth birthday. 'Gangsters' by the Specials is at
number 6 in the charts. The Flying Lizards, whom he discovered
almost a year ago, are at 8. Sham 69, whose boot-stomping mani-
festos he can't stop promulgating, are at 12. Gary Numan, whose
band Tubeway Army he debuted eighteen months ago, is at 20. The
Angelic Upstarts, another of those football-terrace punk bands that
Peel swears by, are just inside the Top 30.

Nowadays the other Radio 1 DJs play these bands as though
it's the most natural thing in the world. Kid Jensen, Paul Burnett,
Andy Peebles, Mike Read – at times their programmes are like
Peel shows decaffeinated. Peel, the man whom nobody at Radio 1
wants to take to meet local shoppers or host a Roadshow, has surreptitiously been setting his colleagues' agendas all year. To hear
how pervasive his influence on the station is, just listen to Mike
Read's two-hour new-wave programme on Mondays to Fridays at
8 p.m. No more *Folkweave* or *Sing Something Simple* filling the gap
between 7 p.m. and 10 p.m. No more leave you in capable hands
Radio 2. Read fills his shows with the Undertones, Banshees,
Buzzcocks, Members and Ruts.

All the same, Peel remains a conspicuously uncompromising voice in punk and post-punk radio. Last night he played *Join Hands*, the new Siouxsie and the Banshees album, in its entirety – and it's not an LP that goes out of its way to make friends. 'The Lord's Prayer', a fourteen-minute heathen jeremiad that lasts for most of side two, is a racket that Yoko Ono would have been pleased to put her name to.

Even tonight's programme, a selection of some of the records that Peel has enjoyed most in his four decades, has its moments of bleakness and turmoil. He refers to an unhappy love affair and recalls a very unpleasant-sounding incident in Oklahoma. 'I was driving back from a gig on an Indian reservation with a local band called Damn Yankee and the Carpetbaggers, and I'd just been severely beaten up by a couple of lads whom I'd appointed bouncers at the gig. The John Peel Roadshow was as popular in those days as it is now.' Finally, he bids his puzzled young listeners adieu with a song by the Bonzo Dog Band that ends in a locked groove with the sound of a man maniacally laughing his head off.

Peel in 1979: there's something of the night about him.

John Peel Show
Radio 1
12 September 1979

Gary Numan – The Merton Parkas – Flowers – Earl Zero and Soul Syndicate – The Au Pairs – The Selecter – The Accused – 021 – The Undertakers – Comsat Angels – Static Routines – The Outcasts

Having failed to qualify for the World Cup in 1974 and 1978, England look certain to book their place in the 1980 European Championship after beating Denmark 1–0 at Wembley tonight. The goal was scored by Kevin Keegan.

After playing a single by a Sheffield band called Vice Versa last week, Peel made the point that music is 'devolving out of London' and 'devolving also away from large record companies'. Devolution has been in the air for some time, and Peel has been its key catalyst. To paraphrase a song that the Clash will release in December, the *John Peel Show* has been calling to the faraway towns for a good two years. Now the response is coming back, revealing just how far into the marrow of Britain punk has penetrated.

London independent labels like Rough Trade, Cherry Red and Small Wonder have been joined by Factory in Manchester, Zoo in Liverpool, 021 in Birmingham and Fast Product in Edinburgh. But those are major cities and you'd expect that. What's more telling is that the young bands played by Peel this month come from Northampton (Bauhaus), Harlow (the Newtown Neurotics), Luton (the Jets), Blackburn (IQ Zero), Swansea (Y Trwynau Coch), Stowmarket (Film Cast), Solihull (the Cracked Actors) and Redditch (the Cravats).

The music is becoming regionalised. 'You can notice it all over the country; a Bristol sound and so on,' Peel says. And his shows are helping enormously. He hasn't put an end to playing bands who are signed to major labels but wealthy corporations like EMI and CBS need no leg-up from him. He demonstrates, instead, a clear bias towards a self-financed, have-a-go culture – the sort of bands who may release only one single in their lifetime, or be represented by a two-minute track on a various artists compilation of unsigned bands from Brighton, Bristol or Cardiff.

Most of these bands he will never meet or exchange a word with. Many of the records will be shambolic in their execution, and often he'll be the first to say so. But his gut feeling is that the independent (or 'indie') sector is where the most interesting ideas – the most playful, the most serious, the most truthful, the most indescribable – are being shaped. As the music business prepares to split along indie-versus-major lines, Peel is confident that he bats for the right team. The importance of his judgement from now on cannot be overstated. He effectively decides where indie music goes from here.

John Peel Show
Radio 1
16 October 1979

The Jam – The Vapors – The Specials – Joy Division – Talking Heads – Don Drummond – Spherical Objects – The Ruts – Psykik Volts – Stiff Little Fingers – Fad Gadget – Swell Maps – Zebra

A new satirical comedy show begins on BBC2. Starring Rowan Atkinson, Mel Smith, Pamela Stephenson and Chris Langham, Not the Nine O'Clock News *will run for four series and spawn several albums and books.*

Peel plays a single by a Dublin reggae band – surely there can't be too many of those – called Zebra, who have a connection with Belfast's Good Vibrations label. But one Dublin band's joy is another's heartbreak. An EP that Peel intended to play tonight has developed a technical problem. 'I was given two copies of this earlier in the week, but if anybody from U2 is listening, both copies were far too warped for me to ever possibly play on the radio.'

Thus are showbiz dreams shattered.

John Peel Show
Radio 1
23 October 1979

The First Steps – The Jam – Spizzenergi – The Gladiators – The Art Attacks – Contact – The Moondogs – The Expelaires – The Fall – The Mekons – Gloria Mundi – The Wall – Hardware – 4" Be 2"

Labour MP Gwilym Roberts condemns government plans to give education authorities the choice of whether to continue providing free school meals. He says the proposals will lead to meals becoming prohibitively expensive for working-class families.

Absurd Records in Manchester specialise in releasing records by local experimental bands who are hated by the music papers. The latest local experimental release on Absurd is 'Does It Matter Irene?' by the Mothmen, which the music papers, sure enough, hate. 'I'm tempted to nominate Absurd Records as the label of the year so far,' Peel says.

Bored in the studio, he reads an article in the *Daily Mail* about social class. There's a guide to help readers work out which class they belong to. Peel wonders which class disc jockeys would be in. The 'partly skilled', he thinks, along with brewers and postmen.

John Peel Show
Radio 1
18 December 1979

Spizzenergi – Madness – Holly and the Italians – Elti Fits – Split Enz – The Dodgems – Misty in Roots – The Beat – Basczax – Tanya Hyde – Gregory Isaacs – The Regents – The Cockney Rejects – The Clash

*Britain's next nuclear power station, which the government has ordered
to be built in 1982, will have the same model of American-designed
reactor that broke down at Three Mile Island in Pennsylvania earlier
this year, causing a nuclear meltdown. David Howell, the secretary of
state for energy, calls the government's plans 'prudent, realistic and
indispensable'.*

And so ends a decade that began with Peel playing Tyrannosaurus
Rex and Kevin Ayers and asking his listeners to be gentle with each
other. His programmes are unrecognisable now; the music has
changed and so has he. His political idealism has long faded (or is
better concealed) and the cosy communal woolliness of *Top Gear* has
been supplanted by tough love and acidic wit. 'Good night,' he says
these days, sounding like a grumpy Brummie, 'and good riddance.'

The regeneration that he called for in November 1973, with his
'hideous people' comment about rock groups going through the
motions, came to pass – breathtakingly – and transformed not
only his taste in music but the way he did his job and the people
who tuned in to listen to him doing it. A session tonight from
Manchester post-punks Elti Fits is full of sounds and attitudes –
the aggressive girl singer with the atonal voice; the spidery guitar
figures; the pathological need to unbalance – that had no place on
Radio 1 before Peel put them there. It's wonderfully ironic, too, that
the most boneheaded band in tonight's show are testament to just
how far Peel has travelled in a decade. The Cockney Rejects, a junior Sham 69, sound almost comically enraged; and it's those voices
of rage, those instruments of inarticulate fury, that have been heard
on Peel's programmes virtually every night since the autumn of
1977. Compositional expertise, laid-back guitar solos, lush harmonies – the musical values of four and five years ago – have become
redundant on Radio 1 on Mondays to Thursdays between 10 p.m.
and midnight.

The Festive 50 this year is again won by 'Anarchy in the UK' – now established as the punk generation's 'Stairway to Heaven' – with the familiar sounds of 'New Rose', 'Teenage Kicks', 'Complete Control' and 'Alternative Ulster' as good as pre-inked into the top ten. The Ruts do well, and the Specials do even better, but they're not voting in any great numbers for the Cure and they haven't voted at all for Joy Division, the Quads or Fatal Microbes.

The listeners, it seems, aren't always pulling in the same direction as Peel. There are unlikely to be many votes next year for Basczax, a band from Redcar whose song tonight ('Madison Fallout') comes from the we-are-all-alienated-shadows school of northern art punk; nor, for that matter, Tanya Hyde ('Herr Wunderbar'), who gives a flavour of the Eurodisco and synth pop that lie ahead; nor for Scritti Politti, whose abstract structures, cryptic basslines and reggae-influenced drums sometimes make them seem like a post-punk negative of the Police.

One of the music papers has asked Peel for his hopes and predictions for the Eighties. Excommunicated by Bolan and Bowie in the past, he recoils slightly from the idea. 'They want you to name the stars of the future, and I really rather hope that there aren't going to be any. At least not very big stars. Small stars perhaps, if you like. Fourth-division stars.'

Little does he know he's played five of the biggest bands of the coming decade in the last eight days alone. It's worth mentioning all five of them – Adam and the Ants, Madness, Simple Minds, U2 and Dexys Midnight Runners – because they won't be appearing much on Peel's programmes after 1980. A sixth band, a reggae outfit from Birmingham called UB40, have recorded a debut session for him this month, which he'll be playing in the New Year. So much potential waiting to be tapped. So many fourth-division stars heading for the top flight. Peel won't make the mistake of befriending any of them.

'It's very easy, you know, when you're a Radio 1 DJ, to start imagining from time to time that you're actually quite an important and significant person,' he reflects tonight. 'Whenever I feel this creeping over me, I always remind myself that in aeons of droning away on Radio 1, I've created precisely nothing.'

Having got that modest digression out of his system, he snaps out of his reverie and plays a new twelve-inch by Misty in Roots.

1980: KITCHEN APPLIANCES

'The new wave sold out a sight quicker than any other fucking wave.' MARK E. SMITH

John Peel Show
Radio 1
14 February 1980

Planxty – The Buttocks – The Stiffs – Magazine – The Visitors – X-O-Dus – The Chords – Sad Among Strangers – Anorexia – Orchestral Manoeuvres in the Dark – The Fabulous Thunderbirds

Questions are asked in the Commons about the propriety of a recent visit by five Soviet scientists to Dounreay nuclear power station in Scotland. The government insists no rules were infringed.

Record Business, a music-industry trade magazine, has begun publishing a weekly Top 30 of Britain's best-selling independent singles. To qualify, a single must be released and distributed by companies that have no connection with any of the major labels. The first single to top the indie charts – it will stay at number 1 for seven weeks – is 'Where's Captain Kirk?' by Spizzenergi, an exuberant Devo-in-space number that Peel has been playing on and off since November. Running alongside the singles chart is a Top 15 albums chart, headed in its first week by Adam and the Ants' *Dirk Wears White Sox.*

The independent charts (which include records from America as long as they have some form of UK distribution) are the brainchild of Iain McNay, the founder of the Cherry Red label. McNay has signed the Dead Kennedys, one of the most eye-catching bands to emerge last year, and borrowed $10,000 to help them record an album. *Fresh Fruit for Rotting Vegetables* will spend seventy-three weeks on the indie chart when McNay puts it out in September. It won't hang around long in the official UK album chart (which is compiled using different data), but that won't worry McNay, because Cherry Red, like Rough Trade, Factory, Crass, 4AD and all the other labels that enjoy success in the independent charts, can function perfectly adequately without the average HMV or Woolworths shopper being aware of their product.

When it comes to the crunch, however, most independents are dependent on one thing: the support of Peel. The Crass label, with its street-level tactics and swarm intelligence, can get away with little to no Peel airplay, but that's not true of a label like 4AD or Factory. The only band on 4AD with a profile is Bauhaus, a postpunk quartet from Northampton, and that profile would be much lower if Peel hadn't played their first single ('Bela Lugosi's Dead') last September and broadcast a session from them a month ago. As for Factory, if Peel hadn't so comprehensively got behind its leading band Joy Division when he did, the vast majority of *NME* readers, for all the glittering reviews of *Unknown Pleasures*, would probably still be wondering what it sounded like.

Of course, not every band wants to go the independent route. Orchestral Manoeuvres in the Dark, a synthesizer duo from Merseyside, have signed to Dindisc, a label owned by Virgin, which disqualifies them from the *Record Business* charts as Virgin is distributed by CBS. But Orchestral Manoeuvres in the Dark are just as eager as Bauhaus or Joy Division to get their records played by Peel, since his listenership is their potential audience. After half a dozen spins by Peel, they might be able to start dreaming of Mike Read or Kid Jensen. But they can't go straight to Jensen without passing Peel, and it's Peel's support that gives them the buzz that attracts Read.

The Visitors, from Edinburgh, have all of this to look forward to. With one limited edition indie single to their name, will they accept the investment (and the compromise) of a deal with a major, or opt to go their own way and take their chances? Their stern, minimalist music suggests there'll be some late-night bouts of existential self-martyrdom before they come to a decision. Their session tonight is quintessential late-1979 Peel post-punk . . . but they need to be careful, because it's 1980 now.

Other bands, to be blunt, have no hope of getting anywhere near the Read or Jensen shows. 'Bonanza', from an EP by the Buttocks, is the sound of angry young Hamburg – there's another embryonic scene for Peel to keep an eye on, as if he didn't have enough on his plate – but the evolution of punk in Britain, unless you're the Cockney Rejects, has moved on apace since this sort of ill-tempered din was de rigueur. The Stiffs, from Blackburn, have an irascible streak themselves (Peel describes one of their songs as tantamount to 'civil disorder'), but they also have ambitions in the satire business. Another track from their session is a disco spoof that makes an amusing feature of a randomly blown referee's whistle. The indie sector is not above a bit of well-aimed lampoonery at times, and the Stiffs may be having a joke at the expense of the Factory band A Certain Ratio, whose music has been going in a funk direction.

A flattering start to the new decade for Peel, meanwhile: he was voted number 1 in the *NME* readers' Most Wonderful Human Being category, just ahead of the Ayatollah Khomeini.

John Peel Show
Radio 1
27 February 1980

The Cockney Rejects – The Beat – The Edgar Broughton Band – The
Radiators – Stiff Little Fingers – Ebba Grön – Another Pretty Face –
Killing Joke – Crass – The Mekons – Andy Partridge – Blackbeard

*The minister for sport, Hector Monro, clashes with Labour MPs on the
issue of Great Britain's participation in the Moscow Olympic Games
this summer. The government is strongly opposed to a GB team taking
part while the USSR continues its occupation of Afghanistan, which
it invaded in December. But Monro is accused of hypocrisy as the
government admits it has no plans to cease trading with the Brezhnev
administration.*

It will be a year of multitudinous namechecks and dedications
for Peel's listeners. The show is a real community of the air now.
He's constantly being stopped in the street, approached at gigs and
buttonholed outside Broadcasting House and given tapes to listen
to or lists of names to read out. His new audience is not as passive
as the old one, nor as backwards in coming forwards. These people
want to be heard. They want to get involved. They want to network
and trade and self-start. They work as trainee nurses, they attend
schools or universities, and they even write on the headed note-
paper of chartered accountancy firms. And a surprising number of
the congregation take a hands-on interest in the nightly sermon of
the vicar.

Realising he's dealing with smart people, Peel has been brushing
up his introductions at the top of the programme. 'All hail, twerps,'
he greeted them on 27 September last year. 'Good evening, my
beauties,' he saluted them on 24 October. 'Evening, pals of mine,' he

winked on 3 December. 'Greetings once again to concerned young people all over northern Europe,' he quipped on 7 February.

Tonight he's suffering from a cold, so it's: 'Good evening and welcome to another disease-ridden programme.'

John Peel Show
Radio 1
6 March 1980

The Cockney Rejects – Any Trouble – The Scars – The Bodysnatchers – Deutsch Amerikanische Freundschaft – Ebba Grön – Liket Liver – Honey Bane – The Psychedelic Furs – Delta 5

The Conservative MP Michael Spicer calls on the government to monitor the movements of what he calls 'Irish tinkers'. There are believed to be several thousand gypsy families in Britain and he would like to see an agreement between the British and Irish governments to limit future numbers.

Peel has mentioned in the past that major record companies have a habit of descending on a city en masse (recently it's been Coventry), expecting all the bands there to be touched with the same magic as, for example, the Specials. In February he played a single called 'Falling and Laughing' by a young Glasgow band, Orange Juice, after two young men – their singer Edwyn Collins and their manager Alan Horne – turned up unannounced at Broadcasting House. Peel was rather taken aback by them; they weren't especially friendly. 'Why do you play all that Manchester shit?' Horne scoffed at him. But 'Falling and Laughing' was worth the aggravation; Collins's arch, cultivated love song was like the Undertones with a thesaurus. By the spring of next year Orange Juice – and Horne's label Postcard

– will have taken off as the trailblazing post-punk sound, and the record companies currently descending on Coventry will be booking their plane tickets to Glasgow.

Honey Bane, the disturbed teenager who used to sing with the Fatal Microbes, has resurfaced after a period of detention in a home for juvenile offenders. She has a new EP out on the Crass label, with Crass themselves as her backing group. Peel plays the opening song from it, 'Girl on the Run', which one assumes is part autobiographical. The story is as chilling as anything Peel has ever played on the radio. The girl on the run is homeless, hungry, kicked out by her mum. Drifting about in London, she is attacked and raped. She falls pregnant. When she returns home, her mother is disgusted and kicks her out again. Back on the run, the girl goes into labour and collapses and dies in the street, with the child inside her. It's like Simon & Garfunkel's 'Sparrow', with real human beings instead of metaphors. Bane's delivery of the lyrics is not so much a vocal, more a psychotic episode. She and Peel occasionally talk on the phone. Heaven knows what they say to each other.

John Peel Show
Radio 1
27 March 1980

Sham 69 – Stranger Cole – The Cure – The Diagram Brothers – Q-Tips – The Teardrop Explodes – The Pop Group – John Foxx – Vice Versa – Percy Sledge – Echo Valley Boys – Hollywood Brats – Ludus

An RAF Nimrod reconnaissance aeroplane joins the search for missing North Sea oil-rig workers who were thrown overboard when a floating drill platform capsized in heavy weather. More than 120 members of the Norwegian, British and American crew are feared to have drowned.

March is the glummest month. The Cure, a band from Sussex whose off-kilter new-wave songs Peel has been playing for about a year, have a new single called 'A Forest'. Grimly enigmatic, it has a hairs-on-the-back-of-the-neck bassline and a frightened-boy vocal, and it's smothered in irresistible reverb. Visions of dire misfortunes in Gothic forests are conjured up and suddenly the Cure are a force to be reckoned with. 'A Forest' graduates with honours. Peel > Read > Jensen. It'll be on *Top of the Pops* by this time next month.

In one bound the Cure have leapfrogged Joy Division, who, while accumulating comparisons to some of the greatest bands in history, are still a long way off the Top 40. That seems to be the way they want to play it; an egoless bunch, they work hard on their shadowy exclusivity. This month Peel has been playing both sides of their new single, 'Licht und Blincheit', released only in France in a print run of just over 1,500. It's quickly acquiring the reputation of a collector's item. The two songs on it – 'Dead Souls' and 'Atmosphere' – show some fascinating progress since *Unknown Pleasures*.

From time to time Peel gets sent records from Australia. He's become a fan of a Melbourne band who can't decide whether they're called the Boys Next Door or the Birthday Party. Whatever their name is, they're going for the flagrant gesture, the theatre of the absurd. They sound positively determined to be the shriek of mirth that laughs last and lasts longest. But just like Tod Browning's circus acts, no band is so misbegotten that it can't find acceptance on the *John Peel Show*. In the song he likes most, the Birthday Party sing of a young boy receiving presents on his birthday – a bicycle, a samurai sword, a ninja suit – but none delights him as much as the 'dog chair' that can 'count right up to ten' and go 'rampaging . . . round and round the house'. Their singer, Nick Cave, sounds hysterically excited and upset, as if the boy is he and the party is today and he hasn't enough air left to blow out his candles.

John Peel Show
Radio 1
3 April 1980

Whirlwind – The Revillos – The Bodies – The Tea Set – Young Marble
Giants – The Coasters – Papa Levi – I'm So Hollow – Wah! Heat –
Stranger Than Fiction – The Versatile Newts – Robert Wyatt

The BBC2 current-affairs programme Man Alive *examines the
controversy surrounding dyslexia. Though the condition has been
identified by the medical profession for eighty years, the Department
of Education has yet to acknowledge its existence. The situation will
change with the Education Act 1981, which recognises dyslexia as a
disability.*

For the past few nights, Peel has been working his way through
Hicks from the Sticks, a compilation album of post-punk bands from
the north of England. An *NME* journalist named Kevin Fitzgerald
has given it a panning in his review, calling it 'the most desperately
self-conscious, apologetic sample of northern provincial music
that could possibly have been conceived and compiled'. Peel plays
another four tracks from it.

Fitzgerald's review, though, has him worried. If Peel thinks an
album is so important that it's worth playing every track from it
over the course of several nights, and if an *NME* journalist vehemently believes otherwise, to the extent of rubbishing the album
and wondering why it was even made, then which of them is right
and which of them is wrong? Fitzgerald makes the point – which
Peel finds hard to refute – that bands on independent labels tend
to be over-praised and viewed as high-principled merely by virtue
of having cobbled a hundred quid together and whiled away three
hours in a cheap recording studio. Why shouldn't they be judged by

the same criteria as bands on EMI? Why shouldn't their music be called a half-arsed, derivative bore if that's what it is? This is a swipe at Peel, and he knows it. For good measure, Fitzgerald has a dig at Dandelion in his review.

Throughout the show, Peel returns again and again to Fitzgerald. The ties between Peel and the *NME* are long established and virtually sacrosanct. There are times when the job Peel does is effectively to be the broadcasting arm of the *NME*. Fitzgerald's review is like the *NME* turning on one of its own. And when the *NME* doesn't like something, it doesn't hesitate to put the boot in.

'I think my problem is,' Peel tries to explain, 'or my weakness . . . one of them . . . is that it's very difficult for me to be *objective* about records. To back away from them far enough to assess them in any kind of logical way. I either, when it comes right down to it, like them or don't like them. And I think they're either good or bad – which is a bit feeble, I know. It's mainly, I suppose, a physical reaction rather than a mental one.' This is a long soliloquy for Peel and it leads to more and more soul-searching as the show proceeds. He admits to being concerned that a negative or rude response to a new record might demoralise the young band who made it, or – just as bad – might be hurtful to any of their parents who happen to be listening that night.

With the programme now threatening to become a two-hour crisis of confidence, it becomes all too clear that Peel's instant verdict – that a record is 'either good or bad' – can make or break a band and elevate or ruin a label. This is an intolerable state of affairs for the head of Shanghai Records, a small indie in the Midlands, who has written an angry letter because Peel didn't play a single that he sent him last month. In sending it again, he's minded to give Peel a dose of hard reality.

'You can't imagine what it's like,' he writes, 'listening from ten till twelve, Monday to Thursday, hoping that your latest release will be played. The first record I put out on Shanghai was Felt. It was ignored by you. It took time and hard-earned money to release it – only five hundred copies – and to still have three hundred left a year later is no pleasing reminder. Felt received good reviews from the press, but without a spin on your show I was unable to sell them.'

The author of the letter (and founder, chairman and one-man workforce of Shanghai Records) is Lawrence Hayward, the eighteen-year-old leader of Felt. Peel can only hold his hands up. He understands exactly why Lawrence is frustrated. 'It is a problem, I know that,' Peel says. 'I feel terrible. But somebody has to make a decision, and at the moment it seems to be me and Walters who make it. It's not a good position to be in at all, because it means a lot of records don't get played.'

The least he can do is give some airtime to the single that Lawrence has sent him. Confused, however, by the lack of label copy on 'Newtrition' by the Versatile Newts, Peel unwittingly plays its B-side ('Blimp') by mistake. For two minutes a nation listens. The song, which sounds like it was recorded in an upturned bucket, consists of a scratch-and-scrape guitar, a muddy thump of drums and a maddeningly erratic two-note keyboard part. There are no verses or choruses: despite their name, versatility is not the strong point of the Versatile Newts. 'Blimp' might not be the worst song ever recorded, but one hopes for Lawrence's sake that he didn't send a copy to Kevin Fitzgerald of the *NME*.

John Peel Show
Radio 1
19 May 1980

The Stranglers – Joy Division – The Monochrome Set – UB40 – The Chords – The Jam – The Shadows – The Clash – Desmond Dekker and the Aces – X – PiL – The Drifters – Girls at Our Best

As the issues raised by last month's controversial ITV drama-documentary Death of a Princess *continue to make the news, MPs discuss the importance of having clearly understood policies towards Islamic countries. The ITV programme, which has infuriated the Saudi government, reconstructed the public execution of a princess and her lover in a country referred to as 'Arabia'.*

It's a rare Peel show in 1980 that doesn't feature Joy Division. They've become part of the fabric of his programmes. Six weeks ago they finished recording a new album, which Factory is planning to release in the summer. The four band members have spent the last few days preparing to fly to America to play their first ever dates there. But the tour has now been cancelled.

Yesterday Ian Curtis hanged himself in the house he shared with his wife Deborah and their one-year-old daughter. 'There are few things . . . in fact, *nothing* I dislike more than being the bringer of bad news for you,' Peel tells the listeners, 'but I heard during the day that Ian Curtis of Joy Division has died. And beyond this I don't know any details about it at all. But obviously our sympathies are due to the other members of the band, and most particularly to Ian's family and friends.'

He plays 'New Dawn Fades', the slow song that ends side one of *Unknown Pleasures*. Curtis's voice comes out of the radio, sounding more wounded than ever, singing of 'no regrets', too many tears and a loaded gun that won't set you free. Peel sometimes gives the impression of not listening very closely to lyrics, but his choice of 'New Dawn Fades' must surely be deliberate. The references to suicide are so overt that Curtis seems to be singing from beyond the grave.

Two of the music papers, *NME* and *Melody Maker*, are currently off the shelves due to industrial action, so for those who miss Peel's show tonight, the shocking news of Curtis's death may take some time to percolate through. The other three members of Joy Division, distraught at the calamity that has befallen them, must face the fact that their band is now over. But the importance of their music to the *John Peel Show* will only grow and grow from here, taking on a life of its own. The far-reaching emotional effects of the songs that Curtis left behind will be an abiding epitaph.

After passing on his sympathies to the family once again, Peel gets on with the show. The sombre mood soon evaporates. There are no black armbands, no funeral music in Curtis's honour. Anyone tuning in during the second hour would have no idea that a death had been announced at the start. There's a session from the Monochrome Set, a Dindisc band of waspish wits and Warholians led by a dashingly handsome Indian. There's the *Batman* theme re-recorded by the Jam, which Peel follows twangily with the Shadows' 'Shindig' from 1963. There's a competition to win an out-of-date Radio 1 calendar: fun, fun, fun. And there's a letter from Scritti Politti. 'Love the show,' they write. 'Keep up the good work. P.S. . . . more Priest, Purple and Zep.'

It's an excellent joke.

John Peel Show
Radio 1
27 May 1980

The Almost Brothers – Anti Establishment – Athletico Spizz 80 – The Bongos – Charge – Cheeky – Collective Horizontal – The Cramps – Crash Course in Science – The Crawdaddys – Cult Figures

An inquest into the death of London teacher Blair Peach, who was killed during an Anti-Nazi League demonstration against the National Front in Southall last year, returns a verdict of misadventure. Peach's girlfriend protests that the police officer allegedly responsible for the assault has got off 'scot-free'.

Tonight's show is in alphabetical order. The songs – all thirty-five of them – are taken from a pile of singles, released on indie labels, that Peel believes have 'some merit' and therefore have earned their right to have their moment in the sun. His crisis of confidence in early April evidently didn't last long.

He begins at A (for the Almost Brothers, Anti Establishment and Athletico Spizz 80) and has no concept in mind beyond seeing how far he gets in the alphabet. Some letters (B, H and K) are represented by only one band. Others (G, J and L) don't get any. The Cramps ('Garbageman') are ghoulish and magnificent and are being written about in the music press, but most of these bands will be new names to the listeners. The quality fluctuates, passing through various degrees of interesting on its way to mildly annoying, and the musical styles encompass earnest rhythm and blues, nerdish industrial tomfoolery, punk *ordinaire* impervious to the changing times, and robotic adventures in bedroom synthesizing. At one point the whine of kitchen appliances is impersonated by the members of a Philadelphia band named Crash Course in Science. But this turns

[271]

out to be the whine of actual kitchen appliances, which goes to show you never can tell.

Peel runs out of time at M (the MonDellos and the Mystere V's), whereupon this strange, almost obsessive alphabet of indie music is truncated by the midnight news. Still, it feels like a public service has been performed somehow.

John Peel Show
Radio 1
26 August 1980

Dead Kennedys – The Selecter – Roky Erickson and the Aliens –
Young Marble Giants – The Cravats – A Certain Ratio – Big in Japan
– Modern English – Augustus Pablo – The Soft Boys – Simple Minds

England cricket captain Ian Botham has been told to shed a stone in
weight or risk losing his place on the winter tour to the West Indies.
Selectors fear he may aggravate a back injury and are considering
appointing Brian Rose, Botham's county captain at Somerset, to
replace him.

Debate has been raging about a recent session by Furious Pig, a band from Totnes in Devon, who avoid instruments and perform using only their voices and whatever percussion comes to hand. Some people find them too challenging. Others are more in favour. But are Furious Pig already passé? A listener from Glasgow, Gordon McNicol, writes to advise Peel to be on the lookout for a new Scottish band who have hit on, he says, 'a revolutionary new concept in musical structure'.

The letter explains: 'The band in question come from the northern part of Scotland and have been in existence for some years now.

And while they've been ignored totally by the reactionary music papers, they have drawn the occasional mention in the national dailies, with the result that they have now a fairly sizeable following, which travels from gig to gig with them. Like Furious Pig they forsake instrumentation totally, and so onstage the band members – freed from the tedious chores of having to play bass, drums, etcetera – are at liberty to wander at random about the performance area.

'The line-up is fairly fluid, changing from performance to performance, and the songs themselves, which consist entirely of short, sharp vocal inflections, are largely made up on the spot, often under the influence of the group leader, who is stationed at the back of the arena, or their manager, who normally lurks just out of sight at the side. The name of this band who have made such leaps forward in the name of musical progress? Brechin City Football Club.'

John Peel Show
Radio 1
23 October 1980

Killing Joke – Smack – The Who – Robert Wyatt – The Petticoats – The Fall – Israel Vibration – Rockpile – Fashion – The Passions – U2 – Gene La Marr and His Blue Flames – The Teardrop Explodes

The last MGB Roadster sports car rolls off the production line at the Abingdon plant in Oxfordshire. The factory closes its doors tomorrow as part of a British Leyland rationalisation plan, ending fifty-one years of production.

Since recording their second session for Peel in November 1978, the Fall have been through some personnel changes. Mark E. Smith is now the only surviving member from the original line-up.

Corrosively intelligent, Smith moves the Fall from label to label – they're currently on Rough Trade – and from single to single ('Fiery Jack', 'How I Wrote Elastic Man', 'Totally Wired') with a restlessness that is part work ethic and part contempt for what passes for the competition. 'How I Wrote Elastic Man', which came out in July, is Peel's favourite song of the year and he grows more and more curious about the Fall's prolific, impenetrable, splenetic music from week to week.

Tonight is a second chance to hear their third session, recorded at Maida Vale last month. Confirming them as one of the most intriguing groups to have come out of the Manchester punk scene, it includes two standout tracks for which Smith has delved deep into his imagination. 'New Puritan', a song that stretches to seven minutes, is a denunciation of huge swathes of modern life, from the menace of renovated pubs to the smug back-scratching of the post-punk music industry. 'Why don't you ask your local record dealer how many bribes he took today?' Smith cries at one point, invoking the uncomfortable spectre of indie-sector payola. It's not the sort of comment that would go down well at Rough Trade, a company run on Marxist principles, equal opportunities and brown rice.

Just as impressive is 'New Face in Hell', which has the Fall playing a riff like the Velvet Underground's 'What Goes On' while Smith recites a story about a radio ham who gets sucked into a Cold War murder conspiracy. Smith's stroke of genius is to narrate the events in telegraphese ('aghast, goes next door to his neighbour secretly excited as aforementioned was a hunter whom wireless enthusiast wanted friendship and favour of . . .'), thereby proving that any fool can tap into Cold War paranoia but only an expert can do it with writing that elicits laughter, admiration and rapt attention. At twenty-three, Smith is the most original lyricist to emerge on either side of the Atlantic since the punk explosion, and people have already started to imitate him.

John Peel Show
Radio 1
30 December 1980

Echo and the Bunnymen – The Cure – Bow Wow Wow – The Ruts
– Misty in Roots – Joy Division – Stiff Little Fingers – The Damned –
The Undertones – Dead Kennedys – The Jam – The Sex Pistols

*The BBC broadcaster Robin Day receives a knighthood in the New
Year Honours List. Comedian Arthur Askey and England football
manager Ron Greenwood are made CBEs. There are no awards for
any of the athletes who competed in the Moscow Olympics against the
wishes of Margaret Thatcher.*

Years are remembered for those who were born and those who are
gone. Earlier this month John Lennon was murdered outside his
apartment block in Manhattan, an act of inexplicable annihilation
that has devastated the baby-boomer generation. Lennon's music
has re-entered the world's charts (he currently has three hits in the
UK Top 10) as people turn to his voice for comfort and for answers
to impossible questions. Peel was immensely saddened, it goes
without saying; but 1980 was a year when death seemed all around.

One of the losses that hit him hardest – coming in July, two
months after the suicide of Ian Curtis – was the death from a heroin overdose of the Ruts' singer Malcolm Owen, who was twenty-
six. Owen was always conscious of the dangers of heroin, and
wrote about them openly, so the manner of his death was both
terribly foreseeable and terribly depressing. Peel repeats a session
tonight that the Ruts recorded when Owen was somewhere near
full strength, which includes 'Staring at the Rude Boys' (a Top 30
hit that he lived long enough to see) and 'In a Rut', the 1978 debut
that announced him as the most electrifying punk vocalist since

Strummer. 'In a Rut' appears at 19 in the Festive 50 of 1980, which culminates with numbers 1 to 10 tonight.

There are major changes in the listeners' choices this year. Notable surprises so far have included steep declines for 'White Riot', 'God Save the Queen' and 'Suspect Device', while Siouxsie and the Banshees have no song placed higher than 37. Buzzcocks and Magazine have completely dropped off the radar. Newcomers include Killing Joke and the Teardrop Explodes. The Fall, who had one song in the 50 last year, increase their tally to four.

But the indisputable stars of the Festive 50 – and plainly the most important music-makers in the lives of Peel's listeners right now – are a band that ceased to exist in May, when their singer decided to switch off his television and end his own life. Unplaced in last year's Festive 50, Joy Division have no fewer than seven songs in this year's chart: 'Twenty Four Hours' (41), 'She's Lost Control' (22), 'New Dawn Fades' (20), 'Decades' (14), 'Transmission' (10), 'Love Will Tear Us Apart' (3) and 'Atmosphere' (2). A couple of them are taken from the band's second album, *Closer*, which topped the independent charts for two months in the summer. A third, the valedictory single 'Love Will Tear Us Apart', made the national Top 20 in July. Joy Division, like the Cure, have been introduced to a Mike Read and Kid Jensen audience – too late.

But why do they have so many songs in the Festive 50? Is it some sort of mark of respect? Grief? Fond memories of a band that commingled beauty and despair like no other songwriters of their age? Surely not some misplaced notion that a suicide in the band must mean they should now be taken seriously. Is that it? Is it because Curtis's lyrics were looking over the precipice all along, or because his suicide proves the depression wasn't an act? How do you calculate the emotional mathematics of a listenership voting for seven Joy Division songs, when the weights and measures of the songs have undergone such internal changes since May?

'I always think of them in a rather romantic way as being intro-spective and rather Russian,' Peel will remark of Joy Division years from now. 'I read somewhere that that kind of introspection was classed as Russian . . . Obviously, the death of Ian Curtis sort of mythologised them to a degree, which I think the surviving mem-bers of the band must have found very difficult to cope with.' But not even Peel will sound too sure what it was about those songs – the melancholia? the memories of his own teenage isolation and gloom? – that pulled him in. He's fortunate, he really is, if the only decision he has to make about music is whether it's good or bad.

The Festive 50 has been won by the Sex Pistols' 'Anarchy in the UK' as usual, but it's the high preponderance of Joy Division – and particularly, one imagines, the sudden arrival of 'Atmosphere' in the top three – that gives Peel pause as he winds down the chart for another year. All those young listeners. All those unknown souls lis-tening in the darkness to 'Atmosphere', a fragile song of unspeakable distress that could be about a failing marriage or a failing life.

'Happy New Year to all of you,' he says, and fades up the signa-ture tune. Then he thinks of something else and fades it down again. 'Obvious thing to say . . . but I do mean it.'

He'd better.

1981: THINK OF NOTHING

'Looking back, it does seem to be a very slack period. It seemed to be a million and one bands called Dance something. Punk had become an historic thing. It was a trough after a peak.' JOHN WALTERS

John Peel Show
Radio 1
4 February 1981

The Teardrop Explodes – The Fall – The Room – Roots Radics – Brian Copsey and the Commotions – The Heptones – The Klingons – Fay Ray – New Age Steppers – Ruts DC – B-Movie – I'm So Hollow

Following the fifty-three-day hunger strike last autumn by IRA and INLA prisoners in Northern Ireland's Maze prison, a statement is issued saying that a second hunger strike is set to begin. The British government has refused to meet the prisoners' demands for increased rights, which include the restoration of the Special Category Status withdrawn from them in 1976.

Julian Cope, the teenage Krautrock fan from Staffordshire who discovered Neu! and Faust on Peel's shows in the early Seventies, went to Liverpool in 1976 to study at a teacher training college. There he became immersed in the city's burgeoning punk scene, and by

1978 he was singing and playing bass in a band called the Teardrop Explodes. His life was about to come full circle. In October 1979 Peel invited the Teardrop Explodes to record a session for his programme, prompting Cope to write a song about his newfound fame. 'Bless my cotton socks . . . I'm in the news!' The song, 'Reward', is the band's current single and has just entered the Top 75.

The Teardrop Explodes are one of several Liverpool bands – others are Echo and the Bunnymen, Wah! Heat, Orchestral Manoeuvres in the Dark, Big in Japan, Pink Military, Nightmares in Wax and the Room – to have been flagged up by Peel over the last eighteen months. He would dearly love Liverpool to overtake Manchester as the unequivocal birthplace of the best new northern music – which is deeply ironic, as Manchester owes much of its credibility to Peel. For a while, the two cities ran neck and neck, and record companies targeted Liverpool's neo-psychedelic scene as the next important wave. The Teardrop Explodes and Echo and the Bunnymen were both signed by major labels. But behind the psychedelic turquoise veneer, the Liverpool scene is riddled with jealousies and rivalries. Cope, Ian McCulloch (Echo and the Bunnymen) and Pete Wylie (Wah! Heat) make up a loquacious triumvirate that is seldom out of the music papers. The three are either great friends or can't stand the sight of each other, depending whose interview you read. Post-punk is a cut-throat field and no one is prepared to give an inch.

Although Echo and the Bunnymen released an acclaimed album last July (*Crocodiles*), and though Orchestral Manoeuvres in the Dark had a Top 20 single in June ('Messages'), it's the Teardrop Explodes who now look like making the biggest pop crossover. The jubilant 'Reward', which kicks off tonight's Peel programme in a rush of radio-friendly conceit, will leave the other Liverpool bands for dust as it gleefully ascends the charts between now and the end of March. Cope, the Peel listener who became a Peel favoured son, is headed for the highest heights of the hit parade.

John Peel Show
Radio 1
16 February 1981

Ruts DC – The Rezillos – The Barracudas – The Human League –
New Order – The Slits – Musical Youth – Brian Eno and David Byrne
– Reverend C. L. Franklin – The Lines – Pylon – The Melodians

The proposed sale of The Times *and* Sunday Times *to the Australian
media mogul Rupert Murdoch will not be referred to the Monopolies
and Mergers Commission, reveals John Biffen, the secretary of state for
trade. A number of MPs are sceptical about Murdoch's assurances that
he will not interfere in the newspapers' editorial policy.*

Last July, on a Wednesday night in a small club round the back of
the Arndale Centre in Manchester, the three surviving members of
Joy Division took their first faltering steps on the road to a post-Ian
Curtis future. They weren't billed, had no name and the guitarists'
flight cases still had 'Joy Division' stencilled on them. In October,
with half a dozen gigs now under their belt, they invited Gillian
Gilbert, the girlfriend of their drummer Steve Morris, to join the
line-up as a keyboard player. The fledgling band – New Order –
made their London debut a week ago. Like Joy Division, they will
record for Factory. But first they've decided to test the waters with
a Peel session.

All these months after Curtis's death, the music press is still giving New Order time and space, respectfully keeping a distance and
wishing them well on what cannot be an easy journey. But tonight
all the compassion and the kind words will be stripped away and
the music of New Order, whatever it should sound like, will stand
naked. Peel waits for almost twenty minutes before playing the
first of their four songs. It's a session, he tells the listeners, that he

thinks they're 'going to appreciate a great deal'. For some of them, it wouldn't be going too far to call it the most momentous Peel session of their lives.

At last, after songs by Ruts DC (another trio making a poignant return following the death of their singer), the Blitz Boys (a catchy pop-punk band from Gloucestershire), the Rezillos (a repeat of a well-liked session from 1977), the Barracudas (an Anglo-Canadian band with a Ramones-go-surf sound), the Standells (a Sixties garage-rock group from LA) and the Human League (a mixed-gender electronic project from Sheffield), Peel is ready to let New Order be heard for the first time.

They sound even more fragile than Joy Division. They may be a quartet, but it feels as though there's a crucial fourth member missing. Their sound is instantly familiar, especially the bass of Peter Hook and the attacking guitar of Bernard Albrecht. There are phrases here and there that seem to allude to the events of last May ('No reason ever was given', 'no looking back now, we're pushing through'), but what really comes across is a sense of frailty. Hook and Albrecht have no confidence as singers, trapping themselves in repetitive up-and-down patterns that they don't have the experience to unlock. They sound so shy, so hesitant. This Peel session is a brave start, but in the cold light of day, when the listeners press rewind and play tonight's tape again, what they will hear are four songs that sound like they're still being written.

'We've been trying to get New Order in to do a session for several months now,' Peel says, 'but they – showing a greater wisdom than us perhaps – decided to wait until they felt they'd got it absolutely right.'

His loyalty is admirable, but it's an odd thing to say about something so transparently unfinished.

John Peel Show
Radio 1
25 March 1981

UK Decay – Aztec Camera – Orange Juice – Positive Noise – New
Order – PiL – The Marching Girls – The Visitors – The Fall – The
Associates – Scientist – British Electric Foundation – The Exploited

Four former Labour Cabinet ministers prepare to launch a new centrist
political party. Roy Jenkins, David Owen, Bill Rodgers and Shirley
Williams – dubbed the 'Gang of Four' by the media – will unveil
the Social Democratic Party (SDP) at a press conference tomorrow.
Among the names they considered but rejected are the Radical Party
and New Labour.

Alan Horne, the truculent young Glaswegian who confronted Peel
at the BBC early last year, is the unlikely toast of the London music
press. His Postcard label, which releases its tenth single this month
('Just Like Gold' by Aztec Camera), has become ridiculously fashionable, receiving lavish praise from all quarters for Orange Juice's
charming indie-pop and Josef K's more neurotic post-punk-in-a-
Prague-discothèque. Interest has snowballed in what Orange Juice's
Edwyn Collins – in an interview with Peel tonight – drily calls 'the
new Scottish beat boom'. A&R executives from major record companies are now flying to Glasgow and Edinburgh to check out bands
they wouldn't have deigned to go down and meet in reception six
months ago.

Peel has been spending the week in Edinburgh, presenting his
programmes from Broadcasting House in Queen Street and talking
to some of the bands on their home turf. One of them, the Visitors,
made their first appearance on his show almost two years ago, so it's
a chance to put faces to names. He also plays music throughout the

week from Edinburgh bands Boots for Dancing, the Fire Engines and the Scars, and from Glasgow's Altered Images, Cuban Heels and Positive Noise. The two cities are currently white-hot.

But that may be a distorted perception. Fifty miles to the west of Edinburgh in Glasgow, a new venue has opened – the Roseland Ballroom – catering for some of the new indie bands. Next month it will play host to Orange Juice, who are doing a short tour. The dates are announced by Edwyn Collins in person, a sharp-witted twenty-one-year-old who wears a Davy Crockett hat onstage and has lately been rivalling Julian Cope and Ian McCulloch for column inches in the *NME*. Peel is up-to-speed enough with the travails of Glaswegian music fans to know that a new venue is 'something which they very much need'. Collins concurs. Orange Juice managed to play only four gigs in Glasgow last year. Some beat-boom revival!

Collins and Alan Horne (who, mercifully for Peel, appears to have a prior engagement tonight) face all kinds of dilemmas, and finding suitable venues in their home city is only one of them. No matter how much Orange Juice are loved by music journalists, their use of inexpensive local recording studios – and the resulting plucky-but-imperfect production – won't help them in their quest to be heard by a wider audience. 'Simply Thrilled Honey' and 'Poor Old Soul', their two most recent singles, may sound delectable to fans of punk's DIY spirit and influential Londoners at Postcard's distributors Rough Trade; but Collins indicates to Peel that he and Horne are looking much farther afield as they plan ahead for Orange Juice's debut album. Peel doesn't often get to interview the bands he plays, so it's an interesting insight for him into their thought processes.

'Hopefully with this single ["Poor Old Soul"] we've already penetrated to about 100 in the national charts,' says Collins. 'I know that sounds probably ludicrous to somebody like EMI that's listening in, but it's a big achievement for us. But hopefully from that amount of sales, we can afford a decent enough producer.'

Peel: 'Have you got anybody in mind as a producer?'

Collins: 'Erm . . .'

Peel: 'Or can't you say?'

Collins: 'I don't know. I think the ideal thing would be to get the Chic Organization to produce it, or perhaps John Fogerty.'

Peel (laughing): 'There are very few connecting points between the Chic Organization and John Fogerty. That's *very* eclectic.'

Collins: 'Well. You don't know what kind of underpants they wear.'

To which Peel has no answer. For a moment there's an awkward silence as if Collins has lost interest in the conversation. It's obvious that he and Peel are at cross purposes here, even if neither of them knows why. Peel can't fathom why Orange Juice would want to change their sound and go commercial. Collins can't comprehend how Peel can fail to hear the similarities between Orange Juice, Chic and Creedence Clearwater Revival. It's a useful lesson for Peel, if he thinks about it. Don't spend eight hours a week playing eclectic music if you don't want your teenage listeners growing up with eclectic tastes.

But there's a deeper importance to tonight's programme than merely sending Peel north to interface with the Postcard crowd. He isn't the only Radio 1 DJ to have relocated to Scotland for the week. They all have. The pop station that usually ventures no further than Cleethorpes or Porthcawl (or wherever the Radio 1 Roadshow happens to roll into town in the summer) has opened itself up to the first glimmers of devolution. As a result, Simon Bates presented his programme on Monday from the window of a Topman branch in Edinburgh, while Andy Peebles hosted the mid-morning show from a radio car being driven around the Dundee area. Bates and Peebles (and Mike Read, Paul Burnett and Dave Lee Travis, who also travelled to Scotland) might guffaw at any suggestion that Peel had something to do with them being there – although the *John Peel Show*, they would surely agree, is far and away the most devolved programme on Radio 1 – but the presence of these DJs in Edinburgh is a foretaste, as it happens, of what their station will begin to look like during the next decade. DJs, like A&R men, are going to start descending on cities of interest. And if anyone is still denying Peel's influence by then, they really will be deluding themselves.

John Peel Show
Radio 1
21 April 1981

Siouxsie and the Banshees – The Diagram Brothers – Stiff Little Fingers – A Certain Ratio – Bona Dish – The Fall – Martian Dance – The Cramps – Classie Ballou – Modern English – Tony Blackburn

On day fifty-two of the Maze hunger strike, Margaret Thatcher refuses requests for urgent talks by members of the Irish parliament. She tells a press conference: 'We are not prepared to consider Special Category Status for certain groups of people serving sentences for crime. Crime is crime is crime. It is not political.'

One DJ who wasn't involved in the Edinburgh week was Tony Blackburn. The former golden boy of the breakfast and mid-morning shows is now heard on Radio 1 at weekends, presenting the Top 40 countdown and *Junior Choice*. His years as the station's happy public face now seem a long time in the past. Gradually, he'll make the transition to BBC Radio London (no relation to the old pirate station), where he already hosts an afternoon programme. His morning show in the mid-Eighties will be legendary for its steamy soul ballads and risqué double entendres. He certainly can't whip out his big twelve-inch too often on *Junior Choice*.

Peel outlasting Blackburn is a concept that would simply not have seemed possible when Radio 1 was launched. For much of the Seventies they clashed like spiteful children. But time moves on and a lot of the old faces have gone now. Alan Freeman went to Capital a couple of years ago. David Hamilton moved across to Radio 2, and so did Ed Stewart. Johnnie Walker fell out with the top brass and went to America. When Blackburn goes, only Peel will survive from the original intake of twenty-two DJs who sat on the steps of All Souls Church in Langham Place, opposite Broadcasting House, and had their photograph taken in September 1967. There sits Peel at the far right on the bottom row, clutching a rolled-up magazine. There stands Blackburn at the far left – literally as far away from Peel as he can get – looking ever so punk in his black jacket, skinny tie and badges.

Peel will one day make peace with his grinning nemesis, the man he regarded for years as a living Antichrist. But not yet. Tonight, for the hell of it, he plays a track from *Tony Blackburn Sings*, a 1968 album recorded when Blackburn had aspirations to become a young Matt Monro. 'There! I've Said It Again', a song written in the Forties, was taken to number 1 in America by Bobby Vinton (of 'Blue Velvet' fame) in 1964, the same year Blackburn started out as a pirate DJ on Radio Caroline. 'I tried to drum up . . . a phrase that would sum up . . . all that I feel for you,' Blackburn croons devotedly, like Robert Wagner gazing into the eyes of Joanne Woodward in *A Kiss Before Dying*. Peel follows it with the new single by Vice Squad, a punk band from Bristol fronted by a singer named Beki Bondage.

John Peel Show
Radio 1
27 April 1981

Out on Blue Six – Killing Joke – Roy Richards – Dead Man Fish – The
Meteors – Pauline Murray – Israel Vibration – The Undertones –
Mutabaruka – The Blue Orchids – Was (Not Was) – Discharge

*John Moore, the secretary of state for energy, tells MPs his department
is conducting long-term research into renewable energy sources such as
wind and solar power. Predicting that the government will spend £13
million on research in the next twelve months, he agrees with fellow
MPs that these energy sources will become more relevant to people in
the twenty-first century.*

There's a session tonight from the post-punk band Killing Joke.
Reckoned by some on the front line to be even more hardcore than
Crass, they're a menacing, woad-daubed presentiment of apocalyptic war and man's return to savagery. Their songs are war cries;
their instruments are stone-tipped spears. They build their music
from the drums up, and the drums in Killing Joke are tribal, formi-
dable, like four John Bonhams on the rampage. One song is called
'Butcher'. The grind of machines. The stampeding of terrified animals. The song seems to be one long sharpened knife. These are
songs that are certain they know more about the realities of the
world than we gullible sheep ever will. Killing Joke don't preach
anarchy like Crass, because putting a name to their politics would
be juvenescent semantics. They make New Order sound like a
bunch of maudlin undergraduates.

John Peel Show
Radio 1
14 May 1981

The Psychedelic Furs – Modern Eon – New Order – Misty in Roots
– Splodgenessabounds – Pigbag – Killing Joke – UB40 – The Cure –
Magazine – Talisman – Deutsch Amerikanische Freundschaft

Nine days into the Old Bailey trial of the suspected serial killer
Peter Sutcliffe – the so-called Yorkshire Ripper – Dr Hugo Milne,
a consultant psychiatrist, tells the court he believes the defendant
is suffering from paranoid schizophrenia. Sutcliffe is accused of
murdering thirteen women and attempting to kill seven others
between 1975 and 1980.

Peel tells the listeners that Modern Eon, a band who had a song
called 'Choreography' on the ill-fated *Hicks from the Sticks* compilation last April, are searching for a new drummer. The bass-playing
on their new single, 'Child's Play', is a shamelessly undisguised imi-
tation of Joy Division. Perhaps they should search for a new bassist.
Peel also has suspicions about their singer, who reminds him of Jon
Anderson of Yes. It's not looking good for Modern Eon.

A new band called Splodgenessabounds have formed in Peckham
– watch out, world – and their version of the *Hawaii Five-O* theme
contains some well-timed laughs. The first part is played on surf-
punk guitars before an inept brass section takes over, pushing the
performance into Portsmouth Sinfonia territory. The track ends
after forty-six seconds, its point made. Splodgenessabounds: raising and lowering the bar for new punk comedy.

A more professional brass section dominates the music of
Pigbag, a Cheltenham band. Their entire line-up, in fact, appears to
be one large brass section, parping away on an instrumental track

entitled 'Papa's Got a Brand New Pigbag'. They're reported to have an ex-member of the Pop Group in their ranks, but nobody would know it from this funky, cock-a-hoop debut single. With Peel behind it, it could really take off in the independent charts.

UB40 also have a new single, a double A-side of 'Don't Let It Pass You By' and 'Don't Slow Down'. That's a lot of don'ts from a band who are starting to spread themselves thin. 'Don't Slow Down', a disappointing trudge of a song, looks like being the beginning of the end for them and Peel. Not that UB40 will mind. They'll achieve colossal success later in the decade but by then they'll stand for the complete opposite – affluence, capitalism, Malibu suntans – of what they stood for last year. Peel often loses interest in a band on their second album (as UB40 are now), sensing that there's nothing to be gained by pretending to still like them. Will he soon be saying goodbye to the Cure, now on their third album (*Faith*) and sounding desperately arid? Or to Magazine, now on their fourth (*Magic, Murder and the Weather*)? Or even, God forbid, to the Undertones, whose third album (*Positive Touch*) came out a fortnight ago?

Peel has been reading an article in the *Sun* about shy women. Lady Di – the media's nickname for Lady Diana Spencer, the nineteen-year-old nursery assistant who got engaged to Prince Charles in February – is mentioned as a perfect example of how shyness can have a powerful effect on men. Peel finds the article hilarious, cracking up at the line '. . . when she peeps out coyly from under those long lashes'. The *John Peel Show* is in good fettle at the moment, even if some difficult choices lie ahead. Coming out of 'Alles Ist Gut', a stark slab of German synthesizer music that includes the words '*bitte denk an nichts*' in the lyrics, Peel says: '"Think of nothing," advise Deutsch Amerikanische Freundschaft. Don't worry, *meine Herren*. We're trained for that.'

John Peel Show
Radio 1
27 July 1981

Concrete – Hugh Mundell – Drinking Electricity – The Bush Tetras –
The Birthday Party – Josef K – Boots for Dancing – Calling Hearts –
Crown of Thorns – Delta 5 – The Remipeds – Lui Lepki

Spectators and guests from around the world flock to London for the
wedding in two days' time of Prince Charles and Lady Diana Spencer.
Newspapers report that America's First Lady, Nancy Reagan, who is
her country's official representative at the wedding, refused to curtsey to
the Queen at a private meeting yesterday.

'RAAAOWR! BITE!'

The Birthday Party, the Australian band whose demented play-
pen music Peel started promoting last year, are based in London
and living in abject poverty. They hate all the English bands except
for the Pop Group, but it's typical of the Birthday Party's luck that
they arrived in England virtually on the exact day that the Pop
Group split up. Peel has been playing songs from the Australians'
acclaimed new album, *Prayers on Fire*, which they recorded back in
Melbourne over Christmas, but judging from their session tonight,
they've since become much more hostile. When they perform live,
singer Nick Cave lashes out angrily with his boot at anyone unwise
enough to stand too near the stage.

Three of their four songs are entertaining in a bloodcurdling sort
of way, but the best track by far is 'Release the Bats', which will have
an extraordinary effect on the British post-punk scene. Suddenly
the Birthday Party come into focus: a five-headed organism that
looks like a godforsaken monstrosity but strikes with the speed of
a black mamba. From his upwardly sprouting tufts of backcombed

hair to his berserk Gothic argot ('she says damn that horror bat sex vampire cool machine'), Cave is the uttermost exponent of pure-instinct stagecraft that anyone has seen since Iggy Pop poured candle wax over his chest. Two months ago they were calling the Birthday Party 'avant-garde Beefheartian art-punk'. Now they don't know what to call them.

John Peel Show
Radio 1
18 November 1981

The Fall – Talisman – Rip Rig + Panic – The Chefs – Pigbag – A Flock of Seagulls – DNA – Red Rockers – The Outcasts – Linton Kwesi Johnson – It's Immaterial – The Gun Club – Crisis – Artery

Labour's education spokesman Neil Kinnock moves a motion condemning the government's planned cuts in higher education. After Kinnock's forty-three-minute opening speech, the motion is defeated by 284 to 240. The number of eighteen-year-old school leavers in Britain is due to reach an all-time high in 1983.

The New Order session from February has been repeated three times. The Killing Joke session from April has been repeated twice. The Birthday Party session will have had three repeats by the end of the year. These sessions have built up a strong word-of-mouth reputation and many fans appreciate another opportunity to tape them. But there's also a practical reason for repeating sessions. Following changes at the BBC that Peel seems unwilling to disclose (other than telling the listeners last year that 'things are going to get worse before they get better'), only two Peel sessions a week are now recorded. This means a lot of impatient and disgruntled bands drumming their heels in an increasingly long queue. Walters can't help; he has his own arts review show, *Walters' Weekly*, and was replaced as Peel's producer earlier in the year. The new man is Chris Lycett, a former locum producer for Tony Blackburn, Paul Burnett, Simon Bates and Peter Powell.

Even so, it's still worth sending a demo tape to Peel because you never know when your number might come up. But a better option is to give the tape to him in person, especially if you encounter him at a gig in the north, because there's every chance he might play it in the car on the way home. This is what happened to the seventeen-year-old singer in a young band from Sheffield who saw Peel DJing at the local polytechnic. In recent months Peel has been stepping up his appearances at polys and universities, treating the students to what he calls the 'John Peel Roadshow' – a bit of Undertones and a load of reggae they don't want to hear. He always comes away with pocketfuls of tapes.

The tape from Sheffield proved to his liking and the band were thrilled to receive a phone call inviting them to London a week later. Their session goes out tonight. They're still at school, learning their way around their instruments, changing direction every time they write a new song. 'Turkey Mambo Momma' has Tarzan shrieks, Pigbag brass and bing-bong glockenspiel. 'Wishful Thinking' is a love song, callow enough to make even Orange Juice blush. But 'Refuse to Be Blind' is more ambitious and could be the way for them to go. Not unlike Roxy Music used to sound in their Eno days, its synthetic European textures are just about held together by the fifteen-year-old drummer.

As he reads out the band's line-up, Peel wonders if their singer might be related to Joe Cocker. 'Don't know . . . suppose he could be. They come from the same town.'

But no. Jarvis Cocker of Pulp, tonight's young Sheffield band, is no relation to Joe.

John Peel Show
Radio 1
30 December 1981

Altered Images – The Higsons – The Twinkle Brothers – The Fire
Engines – The Clash – Dead Kennedys – The Cure – Joy Division –
The Undertones – New Order – The Sex Pistols

*The Penlee lifeboat disaster fund stands at £1,200,000, making it the
largest comparable fund since the Aberfan colliery disaster of 1966.
The Penlee fund was launched earlier this month after eight lifeboat
volunteers from Cornwall drowned in heavy seas when they went to the
aid of a ship whose engines had failed.*

The Festive 50 hasn't always been the most reliable index of the
listeners' personalities and daily lives. But Peel's facetious show-
opener of 7 February last year ('Greetings once again to concerned
young people all over northern Europe') has begun to look distress-
ingly prescient. There has been an unusual amount of votes in this
year's Festive 50 for Joy Division's 'New Dawn Fades' – the song of
abandoned hope which Peel played after announcing Ian Curtis's
death – and some of the votes come from Poland, a country currently under martial law.

He calls this 'a horrible irony', because the votes for 'New Dawn
Fades' were posted at least a fortnight before General Jaruzelski
sent in his army to crush Lech Wałęsa's independent trade union.
'Our homeland is at the edge of an abyss,' Jaruzelski said on Polish
television on 13 December. 'People have reached the limit of their
psychological tolerance. Many people are struck by despair.' If they
weren't before, they are now. Michael Foot, the Labour Party leader,
has spoken of the 'black shadow that Poland casts across the whole
of this Christmas'.

When he puts it like that, which other band could anyone vote for? Joy Division and New Order account for four songs in the Festive 50's top five. 'Atmosphere' has usurped the number 1 slot from 'Anarchy in the UK', a symbolic moment that seems to slam a door on any hope of political change that the 1977 generation may still have harboured. Dread stalks wintry lands. For every band like Pigbag determined to party till the bomb drops, there are three more like Killing Joke reaching for the Book of Revelation and preparing for the breakdown of human order.

Even the Undertones, who appear in the top ten with 'Teenage Kicks' as ever, have sung songs this year about the hunger strike in the Maze prison, after years of criticising Stiff Little Fingers for sensationalising the Troubles. 'It wasn't until the third record, *Positive Touch*, that I finally felt confident to start writing about the war at home and how it affected me and my friends,' the Undertones' songwriter John O'Neill will admit to an American journalist many years later. 'During the early Eighties I certainly became a lot more political . . . By that stage I was happy to support Irish Republicanism, not necessarily the armed struggle, but certainly do what I could to make people aware of the injustices [that] British and Unionist rule was causing in the north of Ireland.'

With ten hunger strikers dead and an intractable prime minister in Downing Street, whom Republicans now accuse of being a cold-blooded murderer, the Troubles have no hope of ending next year or the year after – or possibly even this decade. In Poland, Lech Wałęsa has been arrested and hundreds of opposition activists interned without charge. Jaruzelski's soldiers patrol the streets in tanks; national borders have been sealed; airports have been closed; and telephone lines have been disconnected. In the Commons, appalled MPs have discussed the possibility of making food donations via the Red Cross in Geneva.

Two months ago a quarter of a million people marched through

London to protest against American nuclear missile sites in Britain. The Labour MP Tony Benn said it was time to tell President Reagan to take his missile bases elsewhere. 'This is our continent and we will shape it for ourselves,' he said. The Campaign for Nuclear Disarmament (CND) has reported a significant rise in membership this year. A post-punk band called the Sound – one of many who seem to fear something eerie in the wind – have a song in their set list that goes: 'Who the hell makes those missiles . . . and who the hell *lets* them?' Speaking to the CND marchers in October, Michael Foot announced: 'In this autumn of 1981, we stand at the most dangerous moment of all.'

Peel is his usual discursive self as he counts down the top five ('the B-side of ["Ceremony"] was number 54, my old locker number at school'), but it's sobering to think that some listeners, as they stand at the most dangerous moment of all, tune in to Peel at 10 p.m. to hear songs of loneliness and apocalypse, because they find that these two hours of the day make more sense to them than anything in the previous twenty-two.

1982: ECLIPSED AGAIN

'In case you're thinking to yourselves, "Who is that twerp?"
I'm the bloke who comes on your radio late at night and plays
you records by lots of sulky Belgians.' JOHN PEEL hosting
Top of the Pops

John Peel Show
Radio 1
18 January 1982

The Revillos – Mary Monday and the Bitches – A Certain Ratio –
Timmy Thomas – Pink Industry – Danse Macabre – The Method
Actors – Yellowman – Captain Beefheart – Mickey and the
Milkshakes

An episode of the BBC1 documentary series Police, *which follows
Thames Valley Constabulary over a nine-month period, causes
controversy when three male officers are seen aggressively questioning
a woman who claims to have been raped. After viewing the episode,
Thames Valley says it is considering special units staffed by women to
deal with rape complaints.*

Last Friday was Captain Beefheart's birthday. He and Peel no longer
meet and chew the fat, but Peel plays three songs from Beefheart's
career as a tribute, recalling his reaction to seeing the Captain and

his Magic Band at the Whisky a Go Go in 1966. ('I will never see anything finer, or indeed stranger, than that.') Beefheart, embarrassed by his attempts in the Seventies to pander to the mainstream, has rediscovered his singular muse on the albums *Shiny Beast (Bat Chain Puller)* and *Doc at the Radar Station*. He's something of a hero to the more perspicacious punks and is as hip as any artist you could name. 'Still several laps ahead of the field,' as Peel puts it tonight. But 1982 will be the year, though no one knows it yet, when Beefheart makes his final musical statement (*Ice Cream for Crow*) and disappears from public life.

As the Captain prepares to exit stage left, new faces enter stage right. Mickey and the Milkshakes, from Kent, hint at the first green shoots of a south of England garage-rock subculture on their album *Talking 'Bout Milkshakes*. Their guitarist, Billy Childish, has been pestering Peel to play a track from it for weeks. Yellowman, a Jamaican dancehall DJ whose albinism made him an outcast as a child, has released three albums in Britain this year – not bad going in eighteen days. *Them a Mad Over Me*, like his other two albums, swaggers with massive self-confidence, boasts and innuendos. Reggae hasn't wasted time in finding a new direction since the death from cancer of Bob Marley last May; one love and redemption songs are yesterday's morals. Dancehall is getting down and dirty. Yellowman has been inspired by the Old Testament to write 'Adam and Eve', but he's not talking about original sin. Adam has noticed what Eve has between her legs. 'Entirely wonderful,' Peel says. He could, of course, be referring to the bassline.

The show takes a soul detour. Peel plays Jimmy Thomas's 'Hang Right on in There' – a popular floor-shaker at the last few remaining Northern Soul clubs after last year's closure of the Wigan Casino – and Peel can't resist following Jimmy Thomas with Timmy Thomas. But 'Why Can't We Live Together', that best-selling single in the era of 'Move on Up' and 'Love Train', now sounds like an anaemic hymn in a derelict church, a prayer aimed at stopping a warhead. 'Of course the problem then, as it is now,' says Peel, 'is that everybody *didn't want* to live together.' He has a friend in Poland who hosts a radio show over there. He hasn't heard from him since martial law was imposed.

Top of the Pops
BBC1
4 February 1982

Theatre of Hate – Orchestral Manoeuvres in the Dark – The Jets – Soft Cell – Gillan – Shakatak – AC/DC – XTC – George Benson – Christopher Cross – Kraftwerk – Meat Loaf

Attempts to save the budget airline Laker Airways are in jeopardy after negotiations falter between the Bank of England and Freddie Laker's merchant bankers, Samuel Montagu & Co. The airline will collapse after a four-hour board meeting at Gatwick tomorrow morning, owing £270 million and leaving 6,000 passengers stranded.

One of the most amusing – and no doubt surprising – events to happen in Peel's life last year was being invited to co-present the Christmas edition of *Top of the Pops*. 'The last time I had a speaking part on *Top of the Pops* was in the spring of 1968,' he told his Radio 1 listeners as midnight on Christmas Eve approached. Many of them would have been shocked to hear he'd ever appeared on the programme at all. If they tuned in to watch on Christmas Day, they'd have seen him back announcing 'The Kids in America' by Kim Wilde ('nice head of hair, nice pair of boots') and introducing the Human League – after a bit of preamble about the time he forgot the name of Amen Corner – as the 'Human Leagues'. The joke, which he admits was pitiful, sailed over many viewers' heads. Stiff letters drifted in telling him it was 'League' not 'Leagues'.

This evening Peel is on *Top of the Pops* again, hosting the whole show alone. 'This is my first *Top of the Pops* in fourteen years,' he says into the camera, looking spiffy in a black suit jacket and red and yellow scarf, 'but it's consistency that counts.' A girl with crimped hair wearing something electric blue made out of spandex stands behind him, clapping her hands. She's probably cursing her luck that she got this boring old man instead of Peter Powell.

The charts are awash in synthesizers – Kraftwerk, Soft Cell, Orchestral Manoeuvres in the Dark – and Peel could, if he wanted, regale the viewers about how he used to play OMD when they used a phone box on the Wirral as their business office. Keep it tight, John. Don't overdo the Wodehousian cladding. He cues up 'Say Hello, Wave Goodbye': 'Now Soft Cell. The last time I saw them was a rather squalid gig in Leeds.'

By debunking the show's traditional positivity ('"Love Makes the World Go Round" . . . an interesting philosophy'), he manages to hang onto a few shreds of dignity as the girl in spandex waves to her friends at home. The viewers may or may not like him, but *Top of the Pops* has a revolving cast of presenters and pop is nothing if not a revolving industry. It's coming up to 8 p.m. and they'll have forgotten Peel's name by ten past. Next week it's Tommy Vance. 'I'll be back in 1996,' Peel promises.

No he won't.

John Peel Show
Radio 1
22 February 1982

The Nightingales – TV21 – Action Pact – The Lone Ranger – The Fun Boy Three with Bananarama – The Cure – Van Morrison – The Higsons – Oliver Mtukudzi and the Black Spirits – Ranking Toyan

The future of The Times *and* Sunday Times *is in doubt after ten hours of talks break down. Their proprietor, Rupert Murdoch, who has demanded redundancies, has warned that 210 clerical staff will be given their notice tomorrow, but he stops short of announcing the newspapers' closure.*

After remarking that it's rare to find an old hero from the Seventies making commendable records in the Eighties, Peel plays a Van Morrison song, 'Dweller on the Threshold', from his new album *Beautiful Vision*. It has a fleet-footed Celtic skip to it, but long-time Morrison listeners might point out that the new album doesn't do much that Van didn't do on the previous six. Peel seldom goes near old mainstays like Morrison and Jackson Browne any more. Even Loudon Wainwright III, who has recorded seven sessions for him, hasn't been asked back since 1979.

It's at around this point in his career that Peel starts to become the acknowledged champion of *all* new music, as opposed to just post-punk and reggae. His programmes in this part of the decade have an urgent wanderlust, jetting off from Britain (which has been his primary focus for the last four years) to different parts of America, to Africa, to Australia and New Zealand, to West Germany, Belgium and Holland. Peel is no longer a post-punk DJ, unless you accept that 'post-punk' is a temporal term, not a musical one, and includes anything new happening in any part of the globe. The proliferation of unknown bands and unknown record labels between 1977 and 1981 has blown the doors of the *John Peel Show* wide open. Now literally anyone can walk in.

Looking for clues to where Peel will go next is never easy, since he's notorious for his mini-discoveries and micro-epiphanies. But 1982 will see rap start to play a greater role – he dipped a toe in the water with a track by Grandmaster Flash and the Furious Five last September – and there'll be more Yellowman and more dancehall. Supple, joyful African guitars will be heard almost every week, played not only by Africans but by young British bands soaking up the influence of King Sunny Adé and others.

Peel was given thirteen demo tapes at a gig in Edinburgh on Saturday night. He's always struggling to catch up, to make a dent in the overspill pile. Today he estimates he had forty-five albums and twenty-one twelve-inch singles to listen to before leaving home in Suffolk to drive to work. 'An impossible task,' he shrugs helplessly. Unlike some other Radio 1 DJs, he doesn't believe work should stop when he walks out of Broadcasting House.

It's starting to get to him. He has migraines, he tells the listeners, and has been put on tablets. There are times when he feels 'very tense, neurotic and stressful'. The situation seems to be under control for the moment, but he was upset to leave Edinburgh University on Saturday to find that someone had spat over the back window of his car. Between the migraines and the demo pile, it's another enemy he doesn't need.

John Peel Show
Radio 1
26 April 1982

Zanti Misfitz – The Cure – The Teen Idles – Kan Kan – China Crisis – New Order – The Defects – The Clash – Modern English – Jodie Foster's Army – Artificial Peace – Cabaret Voltaire – Endgames

British troops recapture the island of South Georgia in the Falklands. The island was invaded by Argentine forces on 3 April and has flown the Argentine flag since a civilian occupation on 19 March. The Falklands War, as it has become known, is now in its fourth week.

'Just like a flower when winter begins. And just like a fire in icy winds. Just like a doll that is wanted no more. That's how I sometimes feel.' Peel pauses. 'This achingly lovely verse is a translation from the winning German entry in the Eurovision Song Contest.'

At a time when countries are at war, 'A Little Peace' – sung by the seventeen-year-old high-school student Nicole Hohloch – brings to mind horses and stable doors. But one man's trite shibboleth is another man's poem of hope. Having romped to a sixty-one-point victory over Israel two nights ago at the Harrogate International Centre, 'A Little Peace' has been added to the Radio 1 playlists and will rocket into the charts at number 8 next week, leaping to number 1 the next. 'I picture a light at the end of the road,' Nicole sings, strumming a white guitar, 'and closing my eyes I can see through the dark.' People all over Europe are buying it in their millions.

For those who can picture no light at the end of the road, *Flex Your Head* is a compilation of American hardcore punk bands released on the Washington DC label Dischord. It finds its way onto Peel's turntable twice tonight, first with the Teen Idles'

'Commie Song' – similar to the Ramones' 'Judy Is a Punk', but at almost twice the speed – and later with Artificial Peace's 'Outside Looking In', which is not just viciously fast but uses violent triplet accents like early Black Sabbath. Between them, 'Outside Looking In' and 'Commie Song' have lasted a second under two minutes. The British second-wave punk bands that make it onto Peel's shows (Action Pact, Vice Squad, the Exploited) are long-winded solipsists compared to this stuff.

Even more abrupt are Jodie Foster's Army, a hardcore band from Arizona who record for the Placebo label. Peel likes the fact they 'seem to treasure brevity for its own sake'. The three tracks he plays from their EP *Blatant Localism* last, respectively, a minute and fifteen seconds, seventeen seconds and three seconds. In the third song, all that can be heard is frantic screaming and a few quick bashes of a drum kit. Not even the Dead Kennedys, America's foremost hardcore punks of the last four years, have thought of recording a three-second song. They must be kicking themselves.

Peel will return to *Flex Your Head* tomorrow night – and two nights after that – to play tracks by Minor Threat, whose singer Ian MacKaye is one of the co-founders of the Dischord label. At this early point in Dischord's story, with only half a dozen releases in its catalogue, Peel is of course responding to *Flex Your Head* viscerally rather than culturally. Minor Threat will become a band of huge influence and importance, but Peel doesn't know that, and can only keep going back to *Flex Your Head* because its short sharp shocks of hardcore punk sound so strange and extreme to him.

John Peel Show
Radio 1
3 May 1982

The Clash – The Passage – Andy Kirk and His Twelve Clouds of Joy
– The Associates – Altered Images – Richard and Linda Thompson –
Scritti Politti – Miles Davis and Charlie Parker – Dennis Brown – Fear

The General Belgrano, *an Argentine Navy cruiser, is presumed sunk
in the South Atlantic after being hit by torpedoes from the submarine*
Conqueror *while sailing outside the British-declared exclusion zone.
There is no word yet on the 1,000 seamen believed to have been on board.*

Peel has lent his talents as a backing vocalist to the new Altered
Images album. The Glasgow band, who recorded their first session
for him in 1980, have changed during the interim eighteen months
from a Banshees-type post-punk band into a bouncy pop group
fronted by the gamine Clare Grogan. Peel is in love with Grogan, in
a sort of ruefully middle-aged way, and plays Altered Images inces-
santly. *Pinky Blue*, which will reach number 12, has been criticised
by some reviewers for excessive tweeness. Nothing on it is quite as
twee as Grogan singing Neil Diamond's 'Song Sung Blue' – with all
the artlessness of a teenager singing into a hairbrush – while a chorus of men, Peel among them, bellow along behind her.

Listening to himself on *Pinky Blue*, which is something he does
several times a day, leaves Peel feeling emotional. Wisdom dawns
on him in a flash; 'Song Sung Blue' is his Archimedes moment. At
last he can truly understand 'why it is that people make their own
records. Even if they only make five hundred of them and only sell
half of those, it's still a wonderful thing to have done.' Eureka!

Another two tracks from *Pinky Blue* tonight. Peel's unrequited
crush on Grogan shows no signs of abating.

John Peel Show
Radio 1
4 May 1982

The Cure – The Marine Girls – Michael Smith – Killing Joke – Blue
Poland – Hunters and Collectors – Skat – Sam and Bill – Nelson –
The Paragons – Duane Eddy – Gang of Four – Altered Images

*The Ministry of Defence reveals that the British destroyer HMS
Sheffield has been hit by an Argentine Exocet missile. Casualties are
feared. The Sun's one-word headline today about the sinking of the
Belgrano – 'Gotcha' – draws much comment.*

'I must say,' Peel winces after the newsreader at 10 p.m. has given
out an information hotline for families who may have sons on HMS
Sheffield, 'it does seem in the worst possible taste to do a jolly radio
programme after a news [bulletin] like that.'

There's little jolliness to be had tonight. The mood of the show
modulates from the moribund to the merely broken-hearted as the
Marine Girls, singing about a girl who can't get over her ex-boyfriend,
follow the Cure ('I look in the mirror for the first time in a year'),
trapped in a personal hell on their bleak new album, *Pornography*.
The Cure seem to get more depressing with each passing year, or
maybe it's just that each passing year gets more depressing.

A Peel show in this frame of mind is never too far from a Killing
Joke song, and it arrives fifteen minutes in. 'Dregs' – what a title
– sarcastically taunts those who failed to see the warning signs of
an imminent nuclear bloodbath, with gruesome hacking noises
that sound like singer Jaz Coleman coughing up blood. We'll all be
doing the same when the presidents press the big red button, and
Coleman will have four minutes to enjoy the kudos of being post-
punk's last trendsetter.

Michael Smith, a session guest tonight, is a Jamaican poet with a post-Brixton riots repertoire. His material, like his delivery, is in heavy patois. 'Long time we no have no fun,' he intones in a doleful voice, a line that sums up the last three Cure albums beautifully. Another of his poems, 'It a Come', is a long political admonition that foresees assassination attempts for any leader – he mentions Thatcher – who thinks the subject of apartheid can be brushed under the carpet. One verse mentions a 'little fella' whose name will be spoken more and more by British musicians over the next few years: Nelson Mandela.

Pulling the programme taut with foreboding, Peel wonders aloud if the listeners will still be alive to vote in a Festive 50 in December. Whatever is out there, it a come. He plays a doo-wop song from the Fifties, 'Florence', by the Paragons, which shares its name with the baby daughter he and his wife brought into the world just four days ago. She's their fourth child. As the Paragons fade, the show is interrupted for a statement by John Nott, the defence secretary. The number of dead on HMS *Sheffield* may stand at thirty. Britain has now been at war with Argentina for over a month. Peel follows the newsflash – was he intending to play this anyway? – with a spectral version of 'Blueberry Hill' by Duane Eddy. Behind his twanging guitar notes, three or four girl singers coo wordlessly like a choir of angels.

John Peel Show
Radio 1
13 July 1982

Echo and the Bunnymen – The Crabs – Wire – Dolly Mixture – Pulsallama – Charlie Parker – Joy and Trevor – Slim and Slam – Rockers Revenge – The Birthday Party – Thirteen at Midnight

A security investigation is under way after a thirty-three-year-old
man broke into Buckingham Palace and made his way to the Queen's
bedchamber. Michael Fagan, who scaled a perimeter wall and entered
the palace via an unlocked window, was escorted out of the bedroom by
a footman after police failed to respond to the alarm.

Attitudes have changed so much in the last five years that Peel
wouldn't dream nowadays of going along to Maida Vale to protect
a female band from the misogynistic BBC engineers, as he did with
the Slits in 1977. But attitudes are changing at different speeds across
different age groups. And in some sections of society they're hardly
changing at all.

Television comedy, for so long the province of Benny Hill, Les
Dawson and a million mother-in-law jokes, will be infiltrated later
this year by a new wave of alternative writers and performers who
have cut their teeth at the Comedy Store in London. *The Young
Ones* will debut on BBC2 in November, becoming an instant hit
with teenagers. Channel 4, Britain's long-awaited fourth TV station, will launch the same month with a spot-on satire of Enid
Blyton (*Five Go Mad in Dorset*) that gives viewers their first sight of
Dawn French and Jennifer Saunders. But no symbolic baton will be
handed over from the Jimmy Tarbucks to the Rik Mayalls. Comedy
is generational, and neither generation finds the other one funny.

The new comedians are race-conscious, gender-conscious and
cliché-conscious. They break new ground every time they open
their mouths, but they observe far more taboos, when you add
them up, than Tarbuck, Tom O'Connor or Ted Rogers ever have.
So how does a young person with limited experience of comedy go
about framing a joke now? What exactly is out of bounds?

The Crabs are from Norwich. No relation to the Crabs from
Great Yarmouth who recorded a punk session for Peel in 1978,
these Crabs comprise three girls and a male bassist and drummer

borrowed from another band. The boys hold down a disco beat – very 1982, very ironic – while the girls sing in uninflected unison like a slightly posher Bananarama. Three quarters of their session tonight is utterly unremarkable. The fourth song, 'Rape Rap', is jaw-dropping.

To hear three girls joking about going to a party and being raped subverts all the known laws of logic, as well as most of the unknown ones, but the song doesn't sound like subversion was its aim. 'Rape Rap' has a buoyant beat and an excited soundtrack of party noises and laughter. It jokes about dancing with boys and getting raped, and that's what's so troubling about it. The whoops of delight following lines like 'raping rap's the best in town' are every bit as contradictory as the lines themselves. How is a listener of the future supposed to react to a song like this – apart from with their mouth open in disbelief?

Peel shows no concern, not even hesitating as he announces the title. Nor does it seem to bother the listeners. The session is a repeat, going out two months after Peel first played it in May. There can't have been many complaints. Did anyone find themselves laughing? Perhaps the Crabs, in a forward-looking year for British humour, believed they'd come up with some innovative comedy about sexual manners. But as to what 'Rape Rap' finds so funny, only three girls in Norwich in 1982 will ever know.

Thirty years later, when the BBC's Keeping It Peel website digitises all his sessions into an exhaustive online chronology, the title of 'Rape Rap' will be changed by an unseen hand to 'Rap Rap'. Someone obviously takes it to be a ghastly typo. After all, Peel would never have played a rap about rape.

John Peel Show
Radio 1
22 September 1982

Serious Drinking – The Daintees – Jah Woosh – Animal Magic – OK
Jive – Cocteau Twins – Laurel and Hardy – Anne Clark – Wham! –
Tears for Fears – Undivided Roots – The Better Beatles – Pere Ubu

*The TUC holds a day of action in support of a pay campaign by health
workers. Marches are held throughout the country; major disruptions
affect ambulance services, buses and schools. Rodney Bickerstaffe,
leader of the National Union of Public Employees (NUPE), warns of
further action.*

The Better Beatles, a quartet from Omaha, perform Flying Lizards-
style versions of Beatles songs and 'their ambition is to split up'.
Their take on 'Penny Lane' has a frigid monotone vocal and an electronic keyboard that makes a noise like a fruit machine about to pay
out. According to the letter they've sent Peel, only thirty copies of
the record have been pressed.

As more and more newly forming post-punk bands take influences from jazz or African music (or shortcut their education by
listening to Pigbag and the Bristol free jazzers Rip Rig + Panic),
everybody wants to be an auxiliary percussionist or blow a whistle. Horn players are as busy as they've been since the heyday of
the Average White Band. Animal Magic, in session, have Africa on
the brain ('Bus to Bulawayo') and a belief that music should reach
out rather than in, but their rubbery basslines and skronking saxes
sound like they stood in the front row at every Pop Group gig, taking meticulous notes. Their bus never quite gets there.

The battle between hedonism and didacticism rages in the *NME*,
often between its own writers in tit-for-tat squabbles. Peel could

fill his programmes with horn sections and white boys playing African guitars, and plenty of *NME* freelancers would applaud him for putting an end to all that dreary indie suicide music. But the dark bands are still forming, still gigging, still making records. And they're still dependent on Peel introducing them to the rest of the country. The Cocteau Twins, a trio from the petrochemical town of Grangemouth in Scotland, are the next reductive stage after the Banshees have been reduced to the Altered Images. Reduce them still further to a female voice, a drum machine and so much guitar reverb that the songs appear to float in mid-air. What's she singing? Or does it not matter?

Laurel and Hardy, a reggae duo from Battersea, have released a ten-inch single called 'You're Nicked'. The humorous title is deceptive. It's a withering attack on institutional racism in the police force, and it's exactly the kind of thing that some of the more political *NME* writers – the ones who don't think Peel should play frivolous party music but also don't think he should play let's-commit-suicide music – think Peel should play. 'You're Nicked' is an indictment of a police force that has been under the microscope since the Brixton and Toxteth riots, and to hear it on Radio 1, even at night, is quite something. Most of his listeners will know that Peel rarely makes direct statements about politics, but he makes a hell of a lot of indirect ones. And as a Merseysider, some of the policies of the Thatcher government quite clearly revolt him.

Peel the citizen, however, is not the same as Peel the disc jockey. His programmes welcome songs of national politics, songs of angry politics, songs of conciliatory politics, songs of personal politics and songs of no politics. Tonight he plays the new single by a young Hertfordshire duo whose debut flopped in the summer. It's not quite make-or-break time for them yet, but some support from Radio 1 would be appreciated. The song, which is due for release in three weeks, is a modern soul tune, partly rapped, and offers friendly advice from a promiscuous lad-about-town to his best buddy, who's about to threaten their friendship by settling down with a girl. Peel seems to anticipate that the listeners will hate it. 'The first person to write in and say, "You shouldn't have played that, you should have played the UK Subs instead," will be turned into a toad.'

The song – 'Young Guns (Go for It)' by Wham! – will peak at number 3 in the charts in November, and no one will ever believe that Peel played it two months before it came out.

John Peel Show
Radio 1
23 September 1982

Musical Youth – The Meditations – Christians in Search of Filth – Shriekback – Dance Fault – Jah Warriors – Killing Joke – The Farmer's Boys – Robert Wyatt – Stiff Little Fingers – Meat Puppets

The TUC Health Committee lobbies for sixteen days of action
by health workers, one for each region of the NHS. Labour's
deputy leader, Denis Healey, attacks a government think tank's
recommendation that the NHS should be privatised, contending that
this would bring 'a return to the morality of the Dickensian poorhouse'.

Already acclaimed in the music papers as the outstanding single of the year, Robert Wyatt's 'Shipbuilding', with lyrics written by Elvis Costello, recalls all the dread, bunting, accusation and counter-accusation of the Falklands War. Reflecting a current obsession with jazz, the song swings gently like a torch song at the end of the night. But Wyatt, in his disconsolate voice, is pointing out bitter ironies: the shipyards saved from closure by the war are obliged to construct ships to send their young men off to die. And anyone who points out the paradox risks getting his head kicked in by tabloid-incited patriots. An immediate Peel favourite, 'Shipbuilding' captures the imagination of the listeners too, who will place it second behind New Order's 'Temptation' in this year's Festive 50.

Only a day after playing 'Penny Lane', Peel has mislaid his Better Beatles single. He wonders if he could have one of the other twenty-nine copies, if anyone who knows the band happens to be listening.

John Peel Show
Radio 1
12 October 1982

The Nightingales – The Sisters of Mercy – Icicle Works – Black Uhuru and Prince Jammy – Blancmange – You've Got Foetus on Your Breath – The Gymslips – Killing Joke – Brilliant

An estimated 300,000 people line the streets of London for a Falklands victory parade. In a speech at the Guildhall, Margaret Thatcher congratulates the Task Force for 'one of the most brilliant achievements of modern times'.

Earlier this year Jaz Coleman of Killing Joke, having liberally dosed himself in the occult, flew to Iceland to await the day of reckoning for the human race. To him had fallen the task of surviving the apocalypse and fathering a new civilisation from the ashes of the old. When the apocalypse didn't come, arguments within Killing Joke about Coleman's mental state led their bassist Youth (Martin Glover) to hand in his resignation. Youth has started a new project, Brilliant, and recorded an acrimonious single ('That's What Good

Friends Are For') vilifying his former comrades. Trust Killing Joke not to split up amicably.

Peel plays 'That's What Good Friends Are For' back to back with 'Birds of a Feather', the new single by Killing Joke – a juxtaposition unlikely to please either party – so that the two bands can duke it out on air. The fight is won by Brilliant. Killing Joke have commercialised their sound, going for an Adam and the Ants drumbeat and a chorus that sounds like a football chant echoing around a stadium. Brilliant, who have inherited the other band's guttural nastiness and cabalistic power, are shaping up to be the superior Killing Joke.

A letter has arrived from a Scottish punk fan in London who is starting a new club. The Communication Club will put on gigs by new bands in Camden Town and details of the inaugural night are enclosed. Peel pauses. The sender has forgotten to include the date. How can Peel publicise a gig when there's no date? For Alan McGee, the man who will one day sign Oasis, it's not an auspicious start to his entrepreneurial career.

John Peel Show
Radio 1
28 October 1982

The Higsons – Wah! – Sister Nancy – The Wake – The Heptones – Simple Minds – V-Effect – James Blood Ulmer – Kraut – Savage Republic – The Virgin Prunes – Bunny Wailer – Life in General

Rolls-Royce announces it is making 750 redundancies at its Crewe plant. Gwyneth Dunwoody, the local MP, blames Margaret Thatcher's economic policies. Meanwhile, workers at BL – the company formerly known as British Leyland – have backed their union's call for a series of one-day strikes.

Early in June, Peel played a second session by New Order. Beginning with a cover of a 1975 reggae track by Keith Hudson and ending with the sound of jazz piano and rimshots, it was a study of a band in transition as they set about exploring a more minimalist, rhythm-based sound. Peel got the radio exclusive, of course.

But earlier, in April, he had complained on air that David Jensen (as the former 'Kid' is now known at Radio 1), whose show preceded his at 8 p.m., had been sent early promo copies of new singles by New Order and the Cure, and was now pre-empting Peel by playing Peel-type music two hours before Peel came on and played it himself.

The complaint was good-natured – Jensen, whom Peel likes very much, was sitting next to him in the studio when he said it – but the serious point was that the notional dividing line between Radio 1's 8 p.m. and 10 p.m. programmes has now, after four years of Jensen and Mike Read, become so blurred that Peel no longer has first call on a lot of the music that he personally discovered. He even learned to his chagrin that Jensen had been trying his hand at some Peelian couplings: one night in August, after following a single by the Bankrobbers with the Clash's single 'Bankrobber', Peel was told that Jensen had done exactly the same thing a week earlier. 'What can I say?' said Peel in mock exasperation. 'Eclipsed again.'

But it's not just that Jensen has been doing a Peel. Peel, just as often, has been doing a Jensen. Greater quantities of pop have been introduced into his shows during the year, no doubt inspired by his appearances on *Top of the Pops*. Tears for Fears, Wham!, the Associates, Musical Youth and Culture Club have all had their new singles played by Peel. Musical Youth's chart-topping 'Pass the Dutchie' may be a new sound to most of the country, but Peel had a session from them eighteen months ago.

If some of his listeners bristle at the idea of chart pop, they might remember that a large percentage of the artists now featured on *Top of the Pops* every week made their debuts on Peel shows when they were considered anything but commercial. Out of eighteen acts on last year's Christmas Day *Top of the Pops*, eight had been played on Radio 1 by Peel before anyone else, including Adam Ant, Altered Images, Depeche Mode, the Human League and the Teardrop Explodes. It's an undeniable fact that Peel has always played pop records, even if the record wasn't classified as pop when he first played it a year and a half ago.

After making further appearances presenting *Top of the Pops* in April, May, July and August, Peel now has the look of a man who is finally being brought in from the cold after fourteen years of being left to freeze on the doorstep. Last month he began a new chapter in his TV career as a weekly guest on *The Late, Late Breakfast Show*, a new Saturday evening light-entertainment programme hosted by his old Radio 1 colleague Noel Edmonds. The job didn't go too well – after reading his autocue like a deer in the headlights of a Land Rover, he was 'rested' after three shows – but there's nothing to say he couldn't pursue TV as a legitimate avenue if he learned to relax a bit more.

Where this leaves the *John Peel Show*, however, is a moot point. Tonight finds him water-treading for the first forty-five minutes. There's a repeat of the Michael Smith session and a surfeit of irony in every link. Judging from Peel's inability to shut up about Jensen, it's another one of those nights when Jensen has stolen his thunder. It doesn't help that the other session comes from the Higsons, a group of students from Norwich. Peel, who tends to give preferential treatment to bands from Norfolk and Suffolk, is going through a phase of enjoying wacky, play-that-funky-music-student-boy bands from the east of England at the moment, and the Higsons fit all his criteria. Oh great. More irony.

An American enters the studio. Bob George, co-author of a book called *International Discography of the New Wave*, has brought a pile of records from New York for Peel to play. Over the next twenty minutes, Peel is reduced to a spectator as George takes over the decks. Not all the records he spins are fantastic, but they don't shout 'get down!' as they play their funky student beats, which is more than can be said for some of Peel's choices tonight. James Blood Ulmer, a jazz guitarist from South Carolina, is probably the closest a Peel show has ever come to playing music that comes from the same universe as Captain Beefheart's *Trout Mask Replica*. But Peel, in thrall to pop and undergraduate humour, hears too much virtuosity in Ulmer's playing and not enough zany fun. 'There seem to me to be a lot of references in that music to the mid-1970s,' he tells George, 'which was a period that was fairly dull.' Revisionism and rebirth have kept Peel at the forefront of music radio, so the comment is fair enough, but it's a stupid thing to say about a piece of modern jazz.

When George pulls out a Bunny Wailer twelve-inch direct from the Kingston production line, it's clear that it's a bad night for Peel to be plugging Simple Minds B-sides and album tracks by the Wake (a New Order copycat band from Glasgow). Wailer's reggae-funk crossover groove has been setting the New York clubs alight, but Peel can't understand what George sees in it. 'I have to confess that I'm not in a frenzy about that,' he says as it ends. 'I prefer Bunny Wailer doing what he normally does. I suppose the rootsier things. You say that this sort of thing is now very voguish in New York?'

In a more reciprocal exchange, George reminds Peel that earlier in the year he was the first DJ in Britain to play Grandmaster Flash's 'The Message' (even if it was George's copy that he was playing), which gives him his self-respect back after he seemed to be getting out of his depth. But Peel is at a disadvantage tonight, not knowing what to say about the hippest music in New York, and too content to play the most superficial music in Britain.

A letter with a Watford postmark landed on his desk today. 'You are the largest pile of masculine excrement I've ever come across,' writes a listener named Sue Bailey, 'and I don't live in Manchester. We are everywhere. My hearing of you tonight is not of my own choosing and brings me no pleasure.'

'What on earth has engendered *that*?' says a stunned Peel into the silence.

What indeed? It's possible that Sue Bailey thought she was being funny and, like the Crabs, miscalculated the dosage of her humour. Or she could be a genuine adversary, or a green-ink nutter having a bad day. As Noel Edmonds could have told Peel during their brief time working together last month, people who put their heads above the parapet and lark about on prime-time television can expect to be shot at by invisible enemies. Maybe this is the first bullet. Welcome to celebrity, Mr Peel.

1983: THE CORPORATIONS ARE BIGGER
THAN ANY NATIONS

'When I accidentally meet John Peel over the years (two times,
and both in motorway service stations), he shyly has nothing to
say on both occasions.' MORRISSEY

John Peel Show
Radio 1
9 March 1983

Shockabilly – Robert Görl – The Three Johns – Julie London – Screen
3 – Lone Ranger – XTC – Bobby Ellis and the Revolutionaries – Gods
Gift – Pregnant Insomnia – Jah Jesco and Juicey Bravo

Twenty-one women are ordered by the High Court to leave the peace
camp at RAF Greenham Common in Berkshire, where ninety-six
American cruise missiles are sited. The peace camp made the news
last December when 30,000 women joined hands around the six-mile
perimeter fence in an event called 'Embrace the Base'.

The Undertones are back with a Motown-influenced new album,
The Sin of Pride, from which Peel plays three tracks tonight. But
these are worrying times for the band. Their last single, 'The Love
Parade', tanked – it got to number 97, which is another way of getting
nowhere at all – and their new one, 'Got to Have You Back', is about

to bite the dust at 82. These are terrible chart positions for the makers of 'Jimmy Jimmy' and 'My Perfect Cousin'. Morale and energy levels in the line-up are low. How will the Undertones break it to Peel that they've fallen out of love with the band he loves so much?

The Peel sessions this year are telling a striking story. Rubella Ballet (8 February), Julian Cope (10 February) and the Three Johns (tonight) have all emerged from bands that Peel played in 1978 and 1979 – the Fatal Microbes, the Teardrop Explodes and the Mekons – when they were new to the music business. One-time punks such as Howard Devoto, Marc Riley and Stuart Adamson (of Big Country) will go on to record Peel sessions this year, just as they did with their old bands Magazine, the Fall and the Skids. It's strange to think that the young musicians who were galvanised by the Sex Pistols and the Clash to get up onstage and do it themselves are now into the second phases of their careers. And that the seven-inch singles Peel championed as spirited one-offs four years ago were actually the first entries in long discographies.

Other bands have been much too busy to set aside time for Peel. Orange Juice, who recorded two sessions for him in October 1980 and August 1981, move in different circles now, basking in pop stardom with their Top 10 hit 'Rip It Up'. Tears for Fears, who did a session last autumn, have been in the Top 5 twice since then (with 'Mad World' and 'Change') and won't be needing Peel's help again. Echo and the Bunnymen, whose first session was back in 1979, still value Peel's patronage but won't have a chance to hit Maida Vale until June, once they've finished touring their gold-selling album *Porcupine* around Europe. And as for Pete Wylie and Wah!, their fourth session – Peel will play it next month – was recorded in the middle of February, when they could spare a few hours between all the TV appearances, radio spots, magazine interviews and photo sessions that made up the promotional duties for their breakthrough single, 'The Story of the Blues (Part 1)'.

The kids have grown up and left home, in other words, and a few of them look like being able to fend for themselves for some years to come. But it would be wrong to think that the *John Peel Show* has now found its milieu as a talent-spotting agency. Commercial success can be an eventual by-product of Peel's early support, as these bands have shown, but he wouldn't want his programmes to become a conveyor belt that young Scots and Scousers could clamber onto and be whisked magically off to fame. That's not the reason why he prioritises new music. While other Radio 1 DJs are locked into the Top 75, delivering year-on-year consolidation for the industry, Peel is the only presenter at the station who has no idea in March what his programmes will sound like in December. And he'd like to keep it that way.

John Peel Show
Radio 1
23 March 1983

The Fruit Pastilles – The Fall – Don Carlos – Ivor Cutler – Cook da Books – 1919 – The Upsetters – Colourbox – Gabi Delgado – The Undertones – The Wailing Souls – Orchestra Super Mazembe

The pound has fallen to a record low on the foreign exchanges. Hit by a rising dollar and fears of an imminent oil price war, it's also been undermined by currency market apprehension about the next set of trade figures. At one stage today it fell to $1.45.

Nobody has done more Peel sessions than Ivor Cutler. The songs and stories of the sixty-year-old Scot inhabit a dreamlike realm reminiscent at times of Flann O'Brien, but there's a pragmatic reason as well as an artistic one for inviting Cutler back to Maida Vale so often. He's London-based, easy to book, prompt, cheap and reliable. He's also happy to step into the breach if there's a last-minute cancellation.

Tonight's session is his twelfth. The herring-reared siblings in 'Life in a Scotch Sitting Room' have been raiding their mother's purse for pennies to buy school rulers. ('All the children were busy looking guilty. It was our custom.') A transvestite boy in a white dress dances despite the contempt of his father. A pedestrian is felled by a blow from a woman's shopping bag. And a henpecked man worships an unusual god: a lump of sandstone measuring nine by six by four. ('"Why that one?" asked his common-law wife with asperity, sitting on the shore giving suck to their darling.') Cutler's pinched voice, as ever, smacks of porridge and abstinence.

Anyone who saw the Fall play at the Venue in London this week would have been struck by the powerful aura of Mark E. Smith. His back half-turned to the audience, he prowled the stage with an authoritative arrogance, directing his musicians with terse nods as they hunched over their instruments. A left-handed guitarist picked out dissonant arpeggios, a bassist and two drummers elaborated them into structures and Smith declaimed over the syncopated onslaught like a profane Brutus. 'They seem to have stripped away all non-essentials,' Peel suggests during tonight's session – their sixth.

A Fall song ends when Smith runs out of words, and that can take time. 'Garden', at ten minutes, lasts almost as long as their first session did in 1978. It's longevity with a purpose to it, though, because the guitarist's non-chords start to sound like ingenious riffs once he's played them twenty-five times; it's just a question of relearning how to hear. Peel isn't sure that he absolutely gets it, and he wishes that 'Smile' and 'Hexen Definitive – Strife Knot' had stronger tunes, but his ears prick up at the rambunctious 'Eat Y'self Fitter' and his fond way of referring to the band as 'the mighty Fall' will stick. He's been their most vocal fan in the media for the last few years, an ally and a friend. Yet he's never met them and wouldn't dare to go backstage at a gig to say hello. Remembering Bolan, he stays in the crowd.

The two sessions tonight have done what some people believe the *John Peel Show* does best: provide a platform for eccentric talent that has no designs on the mainstream, and allow imaginative writers to perform new material while it's still fresh from the muse and the typewriter. The Fall recorded their session only forty-eight hours ago, a fast turnaround by any standards, and two tracks were so new that they'd never been played live before. A Peel show is pretty close to being music in the present tense.

A little disgracefully, as Cutler's 'Life in a Scotch Sitting Room Volume 2, Episode 17' dies away in wheezes of dolorous harmonium, Peel fades in a breathy softcore porn song by Gabi Delgado, the singer in Deutsch Amerikanische Freundschaft. The smell of Cutler's ascetic language is still musty in the room as Delgado's crotch-fondling electro-funk prances in, expunging all trace of chastity with a scandalous lack of ceremony. No offence to the herring-fed siblings, but Peel would point out that Delgado's album is new, so must be heard without a moment to lose. Like Mark E. Smith, Peel prowls back and forth in his self-constructed enclosure, listening for new nuances and dynamics to get his blood going. Good as they were, the Cutler and Fall sessions are already in the past tense.

Top of the Pops
BBC1
28 April 1983

Galaxy featuring Phil Fearon – Sweet Dreams – China Doll – The Creatures – Cook da Books – Nena – David Bowie – Tears for Fears – Kissing the Pink – Spandau Ballet – The Kids from Fame

The Conservative Party is divided on whether Margaret Thatcher should call a general election for June or wait until October. The party

has a 15 per cent lead over Labour in the opinion polls, but some Tories feel the prime minister should wait for the economy to show clear signs of recovery before announcing a date.

In a voice dry enough to desiccate coconut, Peel is counting down the official, Gallup-compiled Top 10: 'The multi-talented Tracey Ullman . . . the multi-talented Cliff Richard . . . the multi-talented David Bowie . . . the multi-talented F. R. David.' It's been another great week of pop. At number 1 are the multi-talented Spandau Ballet, listening to the multi-talented Marvin Gaye all night long.

Peel has become a familiar sight on *Top of the Pops*, co-presenting it once a month with David Jensen. Peel plays the case-hardened, seen-it-all inspector to Jensen's idealistic, up-and-at-'em sergeant. Peel has a way of honing the irony so that his cynical putdowns sound like amiable wisecracks even when they're deadly serious. He and Jensen pause to trail next week's show, the gala 1,000th edition since *Top of the Pops* began in Merseybeat monochrome in 1964.

'It's a specially extended programme,' Peel explains, 'and it's going to be carried in stereo on Radio 1.'

Jensen: 'And there'll be all sorts of exciting personalities.'

Peel: 'And the Radio 1 DJs have promised to come along as well.'

Meant, of course, with no due respect.

Bowie is at number 6 with 'Let's Dance', a booming ghetto-blaster hit that has topped charts in nine countries, boosting his brand recognition to near Michael Jackson levels. Three dates at the Milton Keynes Bowl have been added to Bowie's tour so that another 180,000 people can get a look at his bleach-blond hair and royal-casual pastel suits. Last month he granted Radio 1 an exclusive audience to discuss his amazing comeback face to face. Did he give the interview to his old chum Peel?

Did he hell. Jensen got it.

John Peel Show
Radio 1
31 May 1983

1919 – Fast Forward – Canal Terror – Offspring – Christiana –
Belfegore – Brent Dowe – Andy Giorbino – Toxoplasma – Sugar
Minott – Test Dept – Lavell Hardy – Die Ich's – Misty in Roots

Sixty people are arrested on the first day of a blockade of the US Air
Force base at Upper Heyford in Oxfordshire. More than five hundred
people join the CND-organised sit-down protest outside the gates of the
NATO base, which houses about seventy F-111 nuclear bombers.

Fast Forward is a one-man art-and-sound project based in New
York. His records are not the sort of things that DJs in England are
sent in the post. It's more a case of stumbling on one at a later date
and picking it up on impulse. 'Bye Bye Love', which Peel bought in
a shop in Düsseldorf on a whistle-stop visit to West Germany last
week, is Fast Forward's 1981 cover of a 1957 Everly Brothers tune. No
one would know it was an Everly Brothers tune from listening to it,
though. Sharing Cabaret Voltaire's passion for short-wave radio and
metallically treated voices, it sounds like a test transmission from
a ghost radio station somewhere on the Siberian border. 'A most
curious version,' says Peel.

Fast Forward belongs to an international network of artists who
repudiate all notions that music should be played on musical instruments. In West Berlin, Einstürzende Neubauten (whose name
translates as Collapsing New Buildings) create music by hammering on scrap metal and drilling through pipes. Their counterparts
in London are Test Dept, who have similar ideas about productiv-
ity by means of pulverisation, and SPK – originally from Sydney
– who supported the Birthday Party at the Electric Ballroom in

Camden Town last month and nearly demolished the stage. Test Dept's 'Shockwork', which Peel plays tonight, sounds like the lifers on Death Row banging their plastic cups on the bars of their cells. SPK will do a terrifying session in August.

With a running order dictated by the records Peel bought on his spree in Düsseldorf, tonight is a proper two hours of anxiety and menace. Christiana is a twenty-one-year-old singer whose confessions of a heroin addict, *Wir Kinder vom Bahnhof Zoo*, were dramatised in the film *Christiane F.* two years ago. Her music has an icy electro glare like Grace Jones held captive in a room full of mechanical handclaps. She has links with Einstürzende Neubauten, whose importance seems to be spreading. The Birthday Party have recently been recording with their co-founder and leader, Blixa Bargeld, in Berlin. This may be significant, because everyone knows that the Birthday Party make a point of going where other bands fear to tread.

More Germans, more unease. 'Tod durch die Blume' ('Death from the Flower') by the Düsseldorf band Belfegore is splintery, slithery and not safe to be alone with. The screams of their singer leave horrible question marks hanging in the air. Peel is really getting into the swing now. 'Werkzeugmacher' ('Toolmakers') by Andy Giorbino, from Hamburg, patents a wild splatter-paint hybrid of industrial post-punk, Hawaiian sunrises and sea shanties, smashing the occasional bottle to keep the listener's attention from wandering. Die Ich's ('Draussen im Wald' – 'Outside in the Forest') sound like the Cure would sound if they had a trombone player and couldn't find the off switch on their echo pedals. Canal Terror and Toxoplasma are hardcore bands. Lost Gringos play smoochy tangos with French accordions and Stéphane Grappelli violins. The whole show has been a disorientating experience, but it's Lost Gringos, finally, who tip the balance into blank incomprehension. If the maracas aren't incongruous enough, the slap bass certainly is.

David Jensen is alongside Peel in the studio – they're going for a curry later – and it would be interesting to know his thoughts. Does he sense that Peel has given up trying to compete with him? Can he see the rationale in that? Peel's antennae are much more tuned to the far extremes than his are, and that may be where Peel intends to steer his course from now on. Head for the turbulence? Either that or crash the plane.

John Peel Show
Radio 1
6 June 1983

The Smiths – Little Richard – Zerra 1 – Mona Mur – Mood of Defiance – T. Rex – High Five – The Cure – Die Hausfrauen – Buzzcocks – Clock DVA

Labour's shadow secretary of state for education, Neil Kinnock, is criticised for comments he made on television last night about Margaret Thatcher's handling of the Falklands War. Appearing on ITV's regional programme The South Decides, *Kinnock responded to a shout from the audience – 'At least Mrs Thatcher has got guts' – by replying: 'And it's a pity that people had to leave theirs on the ground at Goose Green in order to prove it.'*

After two years of ploughing his own furrow as a radio personality, John Walters returned as producer of the *John Peel Show* in April. A week after being reinstated, he followed up a tip-off from a publicist at Rough Trade and made sure to be standing in the sparse audience at the University of London Union to watch a young support band from Manchester take the stage. For the next thirty minutes, Walters heard a sound that intrigued him. It wasn't quite punk and it wasn't quite folk and it wasn't quite rockabilly. The singer was tall, bequiffed and charismatic, making expansive gestures with his gangly arms as he sang to the meagre crowd. The songs seemed to matter desperately to him, and Walters had the feeling they might matter to others too. Acting unilaterally for Peel, he spoke to his Rough Trade contact and offered the Smiths a session on the spot.

The four songs they recorded at Maida Vale two weeks later – 'What Difference Does It Make?', 'Reel Around the Fountain', 'Handsome Devil' and 'Miserable Lie' – were broadcast five nights ago. Peel agrees with Walters that the Smiths have something distinctive about them, but like Walters he's not altogether sure what. It's more a case of what they *don't* sound like. 'When I first heard a demo tape from the Smiths,' Peel will later recall, 'it was immediately obvious that here was something rather unusual. A band with no obvious influences whatsoever.'

But Peel, in fact, has almost certainly not heard a Smiths demo tape. They recorded one last month, it's true, but they gave it to their producer, Troy Tate, for reference purposes only. It's unlikely that Peel heard their earlier demo, which they recorded last December, because he would surely have offered them a session in January and not waited five months. Like his reaction to their music, his memory of how he came to discover the Smiths is ardent but vague. But whenever or however he discovered them, he definitely heard something special. Their session is superb and will be repeated twice by the end of the summer.

Tonight he plays 'Hand in Glove', their first single for Rough Trade. A carillon of jangling guitars and lyrics that sound like self-empowerment slogans for the terminally sensitive, 'Hand in Glove' is one of those exhilarating debuts that seem to sense that they stand at the crossroads of history. 'The sun shines out of our behinds,' the singer yodels, and he could be applying the words to his own band as much as to his fictional lovers. With only ten gigs to their name, the Smiths are already starting to decide which of their music-industry suitors to flirt with and which to haughtily rebuff.

John Peel Show
Radio 1
13 June 1983

The Fall – Altered Images – The Natural Ites – Slapp Happy – Brigandage – Lightnin' Slim – Mark Stewart and the Maffia – Icicle Works – Jane – Jah Wobble – Set the Tone – Blitz – Sonic Youth

J. Sainsbury has become the first supermarket chain to put cash dispensing machines in its stores. Three machines went into operation at the Crystal Palace branch in south London today. Sainsbury's believes that using cash may be quicker than paying for groceries by cheque.

Mark Stewart, a singer from Bristol with a voice like a political prisoner being given electric-shock torture by the CIA, knows a thing or two about post-punk paranoia. With his previous band the Pop Group he wrote the book on it. Stewart's new album, *Learning to Cope with Cowardice*, is a spine-chilling labyrinth of coded notebooks, tapped phones and wire intercepts. Listening to his song 'None Dare Call It Conspiracy' is like watching Gene Hackman tear his flat apart in the final scene of *The Conversation*. Stewart's spooked wail darts across the mix from right to left, and from left to right, ducking out of the crosshairs of snipers. 'The corporations are bigger than any nations,' he warns as the footsteps behind him grow louder. 'I think I know who you're speaking about,' says Peel, the Corporation man. Oh, how recklessly he tempts fate.

At the other end of the post-punk rainbow, unicorns still frolic.

Bite, the new Altered Images album, has arrived in the office this week, which ought to be good news for Peel and the massed ranks of besotted Clare Grogan fans. But the three songs he plays from it tonight have a pop-soul glibness that sacrifices all the best traits of Grogan's girl-next-door personality, and she sounds unhappily swamped by the gadgetry of glamour and sophistication. Orange Juice and Aztec Camera have shown that the hits are out there for any indie-style bands who take a bit of care over their production, but Grogan's voice is much too Pixie and Dixie to carry off an album of adult-orientated pop. She sounds like Little Orphan Annie trying to be Dionne Warwick.

Poor Peel. There never was a love like Clare. But he lost her to *Smash Hits* and *Saturday Superstore* a long time ago. And like the frozen Traitors in Dante's ninth circle, she won't be coming back from that hellhole any time soon. 'You're just a face in the crowd to me, dear, I'm afraid,' he sighs, as one of her facelessly glossy new songs floats by. Tomorrow night he will play all four tracks from Altered Images' first session in October 1980, just to prove that he's completely over her in every way.

John Peel Show
Radio 1
14 June 1983

Killing Joke – The Chameleons – Catastrophe Bizarre – Red London – The Sisters of Mercy – Delroy Wilson – The Birthday Party – Bibi Den's Tshibayi – George Nooks – Altered Images – Winona Carr

The Amalgamated Engineering and Electrical Union (AEEU)
announces it will support Roy Hattersley in the contest to replace
Michael Foot as Labour Party leader. The union's president, Terry

*Duffy, says it decided not to back Neil Kinnock, the other main
candidate, because he advocates unilateral nuclear disarmament.*

Four months ago the *NME* published an article about a new British
subculture called 'positive punk'. Fashion-conscious and incen-
tivised, positive punks liked to congregate at clubs such as the
Batcave in London, where they posed at the bar or watched bands
like Rubella Ballet, Specimen, Brigandage and Sex Gang Children.
They steered clear of drugs – according to the *NME*, anyway –
and favoured a Lily Munster look in their hairstyles, clothes and
make-up. Peel, who'd been playing Rubella Ballet and Sex Gang
Children since last November without really thinking about the
implications, had become the unsuspecting patron of a new wave
of gothic rock.

The *NME* has since jettisoned the term 'positive punk', Peel notes,
and the ubiquitous new word for most of these bands is 'goth'. The
southern branch of goth seems reasonably jovial, but in the north
they wallow in darkness and *Weltschmerz*. In goth's West Yorkshire
heartland, the key band is the Sisters of Mercy, whose doom-laden
sound is manna for their black-haired, black-clad, black-nailed,
black-lipped followers. Having come along three years too late for
Joy Division, these lads and lasses have found in the Sisters of Mercy
a true gothic band that they can call their own. Peel has been playing their music for almost a year, and has promoted other Yorkshire
groups in recent months, such as the March Violets (from Leeds),
Southern Death Cult (Bradford), Danse Society (Barnsley) and
Skeletal Family (Keighley).

And since it was the records of Bauhaus, the Cure, Siouxsie and
the Banshees and Killing Joke that motivated most of these goths
to form bands and explore their dark side, Peel's influence on the
movement could be described as gigantic. Goth is attracting new
disciples by the week and has reached as far as Hamburg, where

the band Xmal Deutschland have streaked ahead as the pace-
setters of the German new wave. Their Peel session last November
included a song called 'Incubus Succubus', which, when translated
into English, read like a goth manifesto. 'Sun and moon / cold and
hot / black and red / mind and body / love and chaos.' Till death
us do part.

The big news tonight is that the Sisters of Mercy have recorded
a new EP (*The Reptile House*). They've sent it to Peel with a warning that it 'may be too dirge-ridden' even for him. His imagination
pricked, he selects its opening track, a long, slow, lugubrious instrumental called 'Kiss the Carpet'. At least it has all the hallmarks of an
instrumental, until the listeners are jolted out of their trance by the
sudden appearance after four minutes of singer Andrew Eldritch's
hollow baritone. This is the sound of the gothic north all right.
Twilight zombies roam through windswept graveyards at lethar-
gic speed on a one-way hell ride to a post-Bauhaus underworld.
Eldritch's voice is so sepulchral it could be coming from inside a
coffin. (Perhaps it is. These goths have to sleep somewhere.) But
how disquieting that Peel's shows in the Thatcher–Reagan era keep
coming back to these anthems for doomed youth.

John Peel Show
Radio 1
13 September 1983

3D – Dub Syndicate – Modern English – The Popticians – Tools
You Can Trust – Serious Drinking – Dyke and the Blazers – The
Undertones – Alton Ellis – This Mortal Coil – Xmal Deutschland – PiL

Sir Kenneth Newman, Commissioner of the Metropolitan Police,
warns that Britain faces a growing heroin problem. Increased

*quantities of the drug have almost halved its street price in the past
year, while its purity has risen dramatically. Research by the DHSS
suggests that Britain may have as many as 30,000 addicts.*

There were times when Peel played the Undertones so often that
other bands must have wondered if Feargal Sharkey was his bio-
logical son. From 1979 to 1981, it would almost be quicker to list the
nights that Peel *didn't* play an Undertones song. But their Motown-
influenced album *The Sin of Pride* was yet another example of a Peel
band seeking sophistication by pursuing a soul direction – and it
was asking a lot of John O'Neill, for all his nous as a songwriter, to
be Holland–Dozier–Holland.

The Undertones split up in the summer, sadly, with O'Neill and
Sharkey no longer on speaking terms. Peel, who by the simple act
of reaching across his desk for their *Teenage Kicks* EP in 1978 had
opened the door to the rest of their lives, would be hugely saddened to know that two members of his favourite band will barely
exchange a word in the next thirty years. He plays a song tonight
from a more innocent time. 'Girls That Don't Talk' was the penultimate track on their second album, *Hypnotised*, when they were so
wide-eyed that a lobster apron in a seafood restaurant represented
the height of decadence. What will the Undertones do now that the
teenage kicks are over?

Sharkey has announced his intention to start a solo career. The
plans of the others are unknown. Will any of them look back with
regrets? Will they think of the day they sent Peel their EP? Their
future had a rosy glow, but it was also a binding contract. He may
seem to be offering the world when he bestows his blessing on a
debut single or a demo tape, but once Peel opens that box, it can
never be closed again.

John Peel Show

Radio 1

28 November 1983

The Lucy Show – Aswad – Dead Can Dance – Billy Bragg –
Nocturnal Emissions – Shiny Two Shiny – Grand Mixer D. ST – The
Birthday Party – The Smiths – The Sisters of Mercy – Einstürzende
Neubauten – Fear Amongst Friends – The Twinset – Designer

*Three tonnes of gold bullion stolen from the Brink's-MAT warehouse at
Heathrow two days ago has probably been melted down and smuggled
out of the country, detectives believe. The 6,800 ingots, worth £25
million, were individually marked, but Scotland Yard admit they have
no clues to the whereabouts of the raiders.*

Peel has always had a flair for making wildly inappropriate comments
when introducing or back-announcing a solemn piece of music.
When the first New Order session was repeated in May 1981, he said
chirpily after one song: 'New Order and "Truth". Average serving:
854 calories.' Whatever gossamery web 'Truth' had painstakingly
woven, Peel had just put his fist through it.

Then there was the night in December 1982 when he introduced
Killing Joke's 'Psyche' like this: 'Hark! I hear the plaintive call of
the meadow pipit!' The more that a song sounds befitting of a
remembrance service (lately, a shivering, sorrowful cover of Tim
Buckley's 'Song to the Siren' by This Mortal Coil has been a case in
point), the more likely that Peel is to make a comment about fruit
and vegetables after it.

Tonight he applies his tactlessness to a duo named Dead Can
Dance, who have recorded a session for him. Dead Can Dance
are on the same label as the Cocteau Twins and This Mortal Coil,
but are even more pale and ethereal. Peel compares their singer's

voice to Buffy Sainte-Marie. Then, after a wraithlike elegy entitled 'Ocean', he enthuses: 'Well, that one gets the thumbs-up from our man on the terraces with the runny nose and the bottle of Beaujolais Nouveau.' The song is about a girl drowning.

The Birthday Party have fallen apart somewhere between Berlin, London and Melbourne. Nick Cave is the latest singer from a leading post-punk band to have to face the reality of starting again as a solo artist. Before disintegrating, he and the Birthday Party recorded an EP called *Mutiny*, from which Peel plays 'Swampland', a song written from the point of view of an escaped convict slowly sinking up to his chin in quicksand. A graphic black comedy, it's a reminder of just what a powerful band Peel and his listeners will be missing. Some of the neophytes that the Birthday Party have influenced – the Inca Babies, Bone Orchard, Turkey Bones and the Wild Dogs – will have Peel's support in the coming year, but none will be much of a replacement.

John Peel Show
Radio 1
8 December 1983

The Smiths – Irma Thomas – The Violent Femmes – Cocteau Twins – Red Lorry Yellow Lorry – The Call – Maxi Priest – The Higsons – Dislocation Dance – The Membranes – Papa Levi – Sonny Stitt

The House of Lords votes to allow TV cameras to broadcast some of its proceedings on an experimental basis. The Conservative peer Lord Soames, moving the motion, describes television as 'the most important and influential medium of communication' in Eighties Britain. MPs voted to reject a similar experiment in the Commons in 1975.

A second session by the Smiths was broadcast on 21 September. Word of mouth was instant. Realising that they'd found a band for the ages, Peel and Walters repeated the session on 10 October and 9 November. Tonight Peel plays it for a fourth time. There can't be a Smiths fan in the country who doesn't have it recorded on a C90, and it's looking as though this Manchester quartet with the prosaic name may already have overtaken New Order and the Cure as many listeners' favourite band.

Their second single, 'This Charming Man', which Peel began playing in October, is currently in the fourth week of a sixty-six-week run in the independent charts. It also made the national Top 30 and put the Smiths on *Top of the Pops*. Waving a bouquet of gladioli and wearing enough beads to rival a Marrakech bazaar, the singer gangled and jangled his way into the living rooms of Britain looking like an emotionally delicate botany student. His name is Morrissey. Just Morrissey.

There's a lot to assimilate every time Peel plays a Smiths song – and he's now playing them all the time. Morrissey's words are witty and touching, creating images of such richness in 'Back to the Old House' and 'This Night Has Opened My Eyes' that one can either listen to them as songs or watch them as little films. The music seems to pour out of their guitarist, Johnny Marr, and although no debut album has been released yet by Rough Trade, the eight songs on the two Peel sessions – and six others recorded for David Jensen – have given the Smiths so much momentum that an album is almost superfluous.

There's no question that the momentum began with Peel. The Smiths' universe is at odds with almost everything happening on a cultural or commercial level in Britain's Eighties, and Peel is the arbiter of taste in the alternative society. The Smiths are a rejection of pop culture in 1983, and you don't reject something by signing your name on its contract. That's why Morrissey and Marr didn't take up an offer from a major label, judging them all to have terrible reputations and dismal understandings of Morrissey's cultural references. And that's why Rough Trade didn't bypass Peel and go straight to the larger listenership of David Jensen. Jensen may be a fine DJ, but he has no reputation as a discoverer of bands that change lives. Peel, who does, simply had to be the one to play them first.

Whether he heard their demo tape or not is no longer of any concern. Peel has become inseparable from the narrative of the Smiths. He and Walters have found one of the most important bands in their show's history, and because Morrissey makes no bones about despising the mainstream pop machine, Peel has re-established his impeccable credentials as the indie sector's supreme standard bearer. For the listeners, the Smiths will forever be a 'Peel band', irrespective of any success that they have next year and beyond. The proof, as always, is in the Festive 50. The Smiths will appear in it four times this month, including three entries in the top ten at 9, 6 and 2. The song at 6, 'Reel Around the Fountain', comes from their first Peel session in June.

By this time next year, demand for the Peel sessions will have become so intense that Rough Trade release a compilation album (*Hatful of Hollow*), with the principal objective of putting as many of the songs in the public domain as possible. In years to come, Johnny Marr will freely acknowledge that the first session established a permanent link between Peel and the Smiths in the public's mind. 'There was a phenomenal reaction to the session,' Marr will say in 2010. 'John Peel personally was bigging us up massively. It became like our sort of bulletin to our audience.'

1984: FEELING DIZZY AND UNWELL

*'One of the basic tenets that underlies my maxim for Self-
Immolation is the idea of positive negativism.'*
JIM THIRLWELL of Scraping Foetus Off the Wheel

John Peel Show
Radio 1
2 *January 1984*

Sudden Sway – International Rescue – Hagar the Womb – Frankie
Goes to Hollywood – 10,000 Maniacs – The Leather Nun – New
Model Army – Furious Apples – Toxic Reasons – Zoviet-France

*The Queen asks Fleet Street editors to tell photographers to stop
harassing the royal family on their New Year holiday at Sandringham.
Pictures were published in four newspapers over the weekend showing
Peter Phillips, the Queen's six-year-old grandson, shooting pheasant
with his father.*

One night in December 1982, Peel notified his listeners that he
had an upcoming Roadshow gig at North Cheshire College in
Warrington, supported by a band from Liverpool called Frankie
Goes to Hollywood. The unsigned five-piece, whose name had
been inspired by a painting of Frank Sinatra by the Belgian artist
Guy Peellaert, were fronted by a pair of flamboyant and overtly gay

singers, Holly Johnson and Paul Rutherford. Accompanying the band onstage were two dancing girls in studded leather outfits with whips and chains. Johnson and Rutherford wore skimpy G-strings and bondage gear. Peel, dressed more soberly, loved them.

Frankie Goes to Hollywood recorded a Peel session towards the end of 1982, which contained a prototype of their future number 1 hit 'Two Tribes'. Peel repeated the session the following March and then, in late autumn, began playing the band's debut single, 'Relax', released by ZTT, a label launched by their producer, Trevor Horn. 'Relax' synthesised all of Johnson's and Rutherford's outrageous stage moves and actualised them in a slamming, sweating four-minute disco song about gay men having oral sex. Sales were disappointing. 'Relax' was not the hit that ZTT had hoped for. 'Still not in the charts, I'm aggrieved to see,' Peel said after playing it again on 1 December.

Now, after two months, 'Relax' has finally appeared in the Top 40 at 35. It's not exactly kicking the door down, but at least it's there. So Peel plays it again, in its promo seven-inch version, the 'warp mix'. This coming Thursday, three nights from now, the band will perform it – in dinner jackets – on *Top of the Pops*, watched by Peel and co-presenter David Jensen. The following Sunday, 'Relax' will leap twenty-nine places to number 6 and Frankie Goes to Hollywood will never have to support the John Peel Roadshow again.

Three days after that, on the morning of 11 January, Radio 1's breakfast-show host, Mike Read, will announce on air that he's had enough of Frankie Goes to Hollywood and is banning 'Relax' because he finds it immoral and offensive. Two days later, on 13 January, Radio 1 will defend Read and confirm that the ban on 'Relax' is station-wide. Peel will ignore it completely. He'll play a second session from Frankie Goes to Hollywood on 17 January, and will continue to play 'Relax' for as long as it's in the charts. And since 'Relax' is now bearing down on Paul McCartney's chart-topping 'Pipes of Peace' at a rate of knots, that could be for some time to come.

By the end of January, 'Relax' will be at number 1. When Peel and Jensen next co-present *Top of the Pops* on 2 February, they won't be allowed to play it, or show the video for it, or do anything much except shrug their shoulders in apology, even though it's the best-selling song in the country. Peel will then repeat the second Frankie Goes to Hollywood session on 13 February.

A firm believer in free speech even when it runs counter to BBC policy, Peel pays no attention to the prudishness of his colleagues or the diktats of his superiors. There's no more chance of him banning 'Relax' than there was of him banning the Sex Pistols' 'God Save the Queen'. Which is why it will come as a shock, in context, when he bans another debut single later this year, and accuses the band who made it of having 'no redeeming qualities whatsoever'. And irony of ironies, the song is about homosexuality.

John Peel Show
Radio 1
30 January 1984

The Dickies – James Brown – Yip Yip Coyote – The Interns – The Meteors – 3 Mustaphas 3 – Bernthøler – The Cravats – Girls of the Golden West – The Fall – Lord Kitchener

Four women from the Greenham Common peace camp are jailed, and twelve fined, at Newbury Magistrates Court after being found guilty of criminal damage during a demonstration at the base on 29 October. It's revealed in court that several of the women have lived at the camp for more than two years, and are now on the electoral register as official residents.

The John Peel Roadshow has been out and about again. It rolled up in Guildford last weekend, where Peel manned the wheels of steel in front of a particularly unresponsive audience of local students. 'I'm not sure why they came, a lot of them,' he complains tonight. 'There were about thirty or forty people who were dancing quite a bit, and I was grateful to see them.' The venue was invaded at one point by a large group of skinheads looking to cause trouble. Peel was later told they liked to gatecrash the events to engage in 'student-bashing'. He goes on: 'I must confess that by the end of the evening I was in some sympathy with them. Give me an iron bar and I'd have joined them, I think.'

Peel has been shopping for country-and-western records. He picked up an album on the wonderfully named Old Timey label called *Classic Country Duets*. 'When I saw that there was an ensemble on there called Girls of the Golden West, I fell upon it pretty darn hungrily, as you might imagine.' The sleevenotes on the back provide some detail about the Girls, revealing that Mildred Good (b. 1913) and her sister Dorothy (b. 1915) were born and raised in Muleshoe, Texas – a town where Peel claims he once tried to sell insurance – and 'grew up with cowboy songs'. Peel plays their charming 'Will There Be Any Yodelling in Heaven?' and warns the listeners that *Classic Country Duets* also features the Buchanan Brothers' '(You Got to Pray to the Lord) When You See Those Flying Saucers' and a duo called Johnny and Jack singing 'Hank Williams Will Live Forever'.

'And if you think you're not going to hear those on the programme during the week, then you misjudge me by a mile.'

Yip Yip Coyote are a band from the south of England. Peel has given them a session. Their style of music is known as 'cow-punk' and sounds like Bow Wow Wow with Stetsons. The fun never stops. Peel has lately become much more smitten with comedy songs than he was during the Fatal Microbes and Poison Girls era, and a Fringe Festival element has entered his running orders, to their detriment.

His other session tonight comes from 3 Mustaphas 3, a faux-Egyptian, faux-Turkish, faux-Russian send-up act featuring ex-members of Magazine and the Damned. Their stuff can be pretty wearing even for those with a sense of humour. God knows what the goths think of it.

Other comical outfits have become staples of the show in the last nine months or so, such as John Hegley and the Popticians, who sing songs about wearing glasses and being in love with brown paper bags. There's also Serious Drinking, a soccer-fixated group of students from the inevitable University of East Anglia. Perhaps that was what went wrong for Peel with the audience in Guildford last weekend. As Ken Dodd said, you can tell a joke in East Anglia but they won't laugh in Guildford.

'Why's that, Ken?'

'They can't hear you.'

John Peel Show
Radio 1
29 February 1984

The Chameleons – Tools You Can Trust – Girls of the Golden West – Dead Can Dance – Misty in Roots – 23 Skidoo – The Fire Engines – D.O.A. – Felt – Minutemen – Two Sisters – Dirty Rotten Imbeciles

After a four-hour emergency session, the TUC pledges industrial action if any of the 4,000 civil servants from the Government Communications Headquarters (GCHQ) in Cheltenham are sacked for retaining their union membership. A GCHQ ban on unions comes into effect tomorrow. TUC general secretary Len Murray calls the ban 'abominable'.

When he wrote his disgruntled letter to Peel in April 1980, protesting at the lack of airplay for the Versatile Newts, Lawrence Hayward of Shanghai Records in the Midlands might as well have added a forlorn postscript: 'And something tells me you're not planning to play my other band, Felt, very often during the next four years or so either.'

Tonight is a rare chance to hear Felt's music on the radio. 'Mexican Bandits', one of four instrumentals that they've put on their album *The Splendour of Fear*, sounds like a mid-tempo Smiths song waiting for Morrissey to write lyrics for it. It's perhaps not the finest example of Felt's work, but in fact Peel's half-heartedness, all joking aside, will be a serious blow to their career. The next recorded instance of him playing one of their songs ('Primitive Painters') will be in December 1985 – and that's only because the listeners have voted it into the Festive 50. 'The reason Felt didn't make it,' Hayward will lament in the 2011 documentary film *Lawrence of Belgravia*, 'is because John Peel didn't like us.' There's some truth in that.

The Smiths are heard yet again on a Peel show with 'Suffer Little Children', the closing song on the debut album they released nine days ago. It's gone to number 2 in the charts – a tremendous feat – and will spend over a year in the independent Top 20. Why Peel dislikes Felt and likes the Smiths is as random as a lottery, but the latter are certainly fortunate that their music appealed at once to this extraordinarily influential disc jockey's capricious taste.

John Peel Show
Radio 1
16 May 1984

The Mob – The Smiths – Home T-4 – Simple Minds – Pogue Mahone – The Inca Babies – The Valentinos – King Sunny Adé – DYS – Starchild and Disco Bee – Under Two Flags – Working Week – De Dannan – Velvet Tongues – The Great Unwashed – Misty in Roots

Anne Scargill, the wife of the National Union of Mineworkers'
president, is arrested and charged with obstruction at Silverhill colliery
in Nottinghamshire. Miners have been on strike since March, after the
government announced plans to close twenty coal mines with the loss of
20,000 jobs.

On a cold night in November 1978, Peel became the first DJ to break
the important news that the London punk band the Nipple Erectors
had shortened their name to the Nips. To mark the occasion, he
played a single they'd sent him ('All the Time in the World'), a song
of sexual angst in which their singer urged a girl to 'lie on your back
and think of England'. The singer has since spent the intervening
years thinking of Ireland, forming a new band that plays a frenetic,
punked-up variety of Celtic folk. His name is Shane MacGowan.
The band is called Pogue Mahone, which is Irish for 'kiss my arse'.

Pogue Mahone's first Peel session is just one diversion in a multi-
faceted show tonight. He plays Northern Soul (the Valentinos),
Boston hardcore (DYS), New York electro (Starchild and Disco
Bee), Nigerian pop (King Sunny Adé), London goth (Under Two
Flags) and Brian Auger-style jazz (Working Week). He even makes
time for oldies by Ray Charles and Gene Vincent, a 1978 single by
Siouxsie and the Banshees sung in German, and a 1972 album track
from the now-retired Captain Beefheart.

It's the new single by the Smiths, however, that a lot of listeners will have come to hear. Released by Rough Trade next week,
'Heaven Knows I'm Miserable Now' receives a preview tonight as
the second song in the show, sandwiched between an anarcho-punk
band from Yeovil and some digitally programmed reggae from Sly
and Robbie. In a fortnight, Peel will again repeat the two Smiths
sessions from last year. It's the fifth time the second session has been
broadcast. A week after that, 'Heaven Knows I'm Miserable Now'
will be the first Smiths single to break the Top 10. Songs predicated

on feelings of solitude and outsiderdom have found a national audience that now stretches into six figures. The cinema of Sixties social realism and the poetry of Oscar Wilde have been put forward as the new iconography of the indie-rock generation. 'For quite a long time we've had all this candyfloss,' Morrissey orated in an interview with *TV-am*'s Paul Gambaccini and Henry Kelly a couple of months ago. 'Modern groups seem to be hiding behind lots of props and pantomime. The Smiths don't. It's just very real people saying very real things.'

The new buzzword is 'alternative'. Whatever Eighties pop is built on (artifice? videos? cocaine?), the Smiths are the alternative to it.

John Peel Show
Radio 1
2 July 1984

Frankie Goes to Hollywood – Albert Ammons – Actives – Laibach – Guana Batz – East Bay Ray – The X-Men – Party Day

Questioned in the Commons about the effects of the miners' strike, secretary of state for energy Peter Walker says that striking Coal Board employees have lost a total of £350 million in wages since March. He claims that more than 20,000 miners 'have expressed an interest in the generous early retirement and voluntary redundancy schemes'.

While the Smiths look to increase their fanbase and graduate from playing polytechnics to headlining hippodromes, Frankie Goes to Hollywood are contemplating the possibility of being crowned Britain's biggest band of 1984 with only six months of the year gone. 'Relax' spent five weeks at number 1. Their current single, 'Two Tribes', will spend nine.

Peel repeats the two sessions they recorded for him, including the early version of 'Two Tribes' in 1982, which sounds like Orange Juice compared to the juddering Sensurround battering ram of their Trevor Horn-produced chart-topper. In this season of vindication for Peel, he could probably get away with playing the Smiths sessions one more time if he felt like it, but he and Walters will instead commission a new one – for broadcast next month – in which the band will unveil a new single ('William, It Was Really Nothing'), a dramatic six-minute epic ('How Soon Is Now?') and two songs from the studio album (*Meat Is Murder*) that they want to begin recording in the winter once they've toured Britain (twice), Ireland (twice) and Europe.

Alan McGee, the young Scot who forgot to enclose the date of his club's opening night in his letter to Peel in 1982, has started a label called Creation. His sixth single is an *Addams Family*-style piece of ghoulish rockabilly by the X-Men called 'Do the Ghost'. No one else is convinced by it, but Peel thinks CRE 006 is Creation's best single yet. However, it will be CRE 012 – the Jesus and Mary Chain's 'Upside Down', which McGee releases in November – that really puts Creation on the map.

John Peel Show
Radio 1
10 September 1984

Chinese Gangster Element – The Cramps – The Smiths – The Fall – Bring Philip – The Higsons – Float Up CP – Black Uhuru – Life – Earl Bostic – The Mighty Wah! – The Go-Betweens

Roy Jenkins, former leader of the SDP, tells their conference that the party should be prepared to form a permanent alliance with the

Liberals. But David Owen, who succeeded Jenkins as leader after the 1983 general election, remains strongly opposed to a merger.

The Fall have welcomed a new American member into their line-up, the guitarist and backing singer Brix Smith. Twenty-one years old, she married Mark E. Smith last year and began appearing on stage with the Fall in the autumn. Her effect on the band has been to push them into more melodic areas on their recent singles 'Oh! Brother' and 'C.R.E.E.P.' Peel, alas, wouldn't have thanked her for her efforts. Previewing three songs from next month's album, *The Wonderful and Frightening World of the Fall*, he pays the Brix-augmented Fall a backhanded compliment:

'There have been aspects of the Fall's recent work that have had me staring into the night skies and poring over the entrails of goats. But I think they're going to be all right based on the evidence of the three tracks we've heard. I look forward to hearing the rest of the LP.'

What a relief.

John Peel Show
Radio 1
20 September 1984

Cabaret Voltaire – Jerry Lee Lewis – Dead Can Dance – Alien Sex Fiend – The Special AKA – Grand Mixer D. ST – Tonto Irie – The Wild Indians – Billy Bragg

With the miners' strike now into its sixth month, the Transport and General Workers' Union offers the National Union of Mineworkers an interest-free loan of £500,000 and pledges to issue guidelines to its members on restricting the movement of coal. Power cuts are predicted by early November.

A fortnight ago Peel hosted *Top of the Pops* for the ninth time this year. His co-presenter was Janice Long, a bubbly Liverpudlian who took over Radio 1's evening show from David Jensen in the summer. Jensen, seeking a new challenge, has gone to Capital Radio. Peel misses him terribly. Long is enthusiastic about indie bands and does her best during the handovers, but Peel deserves a much higher level of wit and needs someone he can insult, belittle and exasperate. Jensen going to Capital is like the Smiths making a Godley and Creme video. It's just not right.

'The charts at the moment could cause you to question whether there's life before death,' Peel comments tonight. Stevie Wonder is at number 1 with 'I Just Called to Say I Love You', a schmaltzy ballad from a feelgood movie (*The Woman in Red*) that will take $25 million at the box office and still only be a fraction as lucrative as nine-figure blockbusters like *Ghostbusters* and *Beverly Hills Cop*. The Eighties are slipping away from Peel. They're too garish. He's too morose. The Eighties want to meet up and do lunch. He wants to sit on his own in a curry house.

Having found the Smiths and Frankie Goes to Hollywood – the two most important groups of the year – the best thing Peel can do is scour the indie sector, keep watching the skies for new hip hop and hardcore, buy up old copies of Girls of the Golden West LPs and dismiss the Top 40 as a foppish, feather-brained waste of time.

In the meantime, he and *Top of the Pops* have a two-month trial separation.

John Peel Show
Radio 1
25 September 1984

Red Guitars – Chakk – Culture – Coleman Hawkins – The Screaming
Tribesmen – Slim Gaillard – The Impossible Dreamers – Demob –
Jimmy Ross and M. T. Foundation – Gene Loves Jezebel – The Loft

Picketing miners ambush a convoy of 140 lorries carrying coal and
iron ore on the M4. Several vehicles are damaged by missiles as they
pass under bridges. The convoy reaches its destination of the Llanwern
steelworks at Newport with no serious injuries.

Peel likes playing electro records from the East and West Coasts,
like Grand Mixer D. ST's 'Megamix: Why Is It Fresh?' and Daniel
Sofer and the Unknown DJ's 'Rhythm Rock Rap' (an early outing
for Dr Dre). He's a bit late on the scene. Electro is on a steep decline
as a creative force when Peel attends a party thrown by *City Limits*
magazine next month and hears people saying it's the best music
on the radio. In March, New York's Run-DMC released a self-titled
album that took hip hop in a wild new direction and slammed the
final nail in electro's coffin. But Peel, to be fair, is only playing music
that he likes – not music that he wants to be congratulated for being
the first white English radio presenter to promote. He would never
claim to be in the electro vanguard; certainly not at a time when
Morgan Khan's *Street Sounds* compilations are up to volume four.

Gene Loves Jezebel are a goth band. Last year they released a single with the unbeatable goth title of 'Screaming for Emmalene', an
indie Top 20 hit. Peel dedicates it to a listener who is in prison, presumably to remind him that there's always someone worse off than
yourself. He can have a time-travelling two hours in his cell tonight,
listening to boogie woogie from the Forties (Slim Gaillard), jazz

from the Fifties (Coleman Hawkins), bossa nova from the Sixties (Astrud Gilberto) and country music from the Seventies (Jerry Lee Lewis).

Peel claims there are so many demo tapes in the back of his car that he's had to have special springing fitted. He also complains, more worryingly, of feeling dizzy and unwell. These health bull-etins will be a feature of his programmes in years to come. There are some nights when it appears to be a bit of a struggle for him.

John Peel Show
Radio 1
26 September 1984

Portion Control – Terry and Gerry – Died Pretty – Michael Palmer – Sacred Cowboys – Float Up CP – Ike and Tina Turner – The Nightingales – Nadjma – George Darko – Look Back in Anger

The terms of the Sino-British Joint Declaration, an agreement to transfer sovereignty of Hong Kong from the United Kingdom to the People's Republic of China, are finalised in Peking. The handover, scheduled for 1 July 1997, signals the end of the British Empire.

'As Walters and I took breakfast this morning at our favourite café, a moon-faced youth sauntered over to tell me that he didn't listen to the programmes any more and to wish me good luck with anything I undertook in the future. This programme is for him, for getting my day off to such a punchy start.'

A six-day festival of indie music is being held next month at the ICA in London. Rock Week is curated by Peel, who has selected the bands and will be broadcasting some of their performances on his programmes. The bands include Yip Yip Coyote, Marc Riley and the Creepers, Yeah Yeah Noh, the Very Things and Helen and the Horns. Peel has gone for a down-to-earth, up-for-a-laugh consensus. These bands tend to be unassuming, self-deprecating, pleasant if approached and happy with their lot. They've all recorded sessions for Peel in the last year. They're the sort of bands he wouldn't mind going for a biryani with. The sort of bands who, if he suggested them to the producer of *Top of the Pops*, would result in a long quizzical stare. The sort of bands who won't be following Morrissey onto the sofa at *TV-am*. Are they really the zenith of indie music in 1984?

One indie band who have received glowing reviews for their debut single this month are conspicuous on ICA Rock Week's bill by their absence. The Shockheaded Peters, whose swishing, shuffling 'I Bloodbrother Be' resembles a post-punk version of the Stray Cats' 'Stray Cat Strut', have become the first group that anybody can remember to be banned from the *John Peel Show*. The ban is not easy to explain, but it's absolutely emphatic. When the band's publicist rings Peel to ask if anything can be done, Peel swears at him down the phone.

The song is a wry celebration of homosexuality, a subject that normally wouldn't bother Peel at all. The lyrics revel in the sort of dark humour that he would have accepted from the Birthday Party without a second thought. But one of the Shockheaded Peters, Karl Blake, has some history with Peel. Blake claims to the *NME* that the ban on 'I Bloodbrother Be' has nothing to do with the lyrics but relates to a curious encounter a few years ago between Peel, Blake and the singer Danielle Dax, with whom Blake performed in the avant-garde band the Lemon Kittens.

Dax and Blake, it appears, paid a surprise visit to Peel one day to ask why he never played the Lemon Kittens' music. Their behaviour was so intense that Peel was freaked out by them. Whatever they did to disturb him – Blake suggests that Dax started tickling his feet, which Peel misinterpreted as a sexual come-on and led him to throw them out – the inescapable truth is that Peel, like Mike Read, has the power to ban a record when his limits are reached. It's just that he and Read have different limits.

John Peel Show
Radio 1
17 October 1984

Billy Barrix – Terry and Gerry – Everything But the Girl – Dennis Brown – The Three Johns – Die Kreuzen – Grandmaster Melle Mel and the Furious Five – Scraping Foetus Off the Wheel – The Seize

Lord Denning, the Master of the Rolls, suggests that last week's Brighton bombers could be hanged for high treason. The IRA explosion at the Grand Hotel during the Conservative Party conference killed five people and injured thirty-one. The bombers 'are just as guilty as Guy Fawkes was 380 years ago', Denning says.

Peel is under stress. He's booked himself a long weekend in the Lake District to calm his nerves. Today he found out that his hotel is five miles from Sellafield nuclear power station, where a notorious incident last year resulted in highly radioactive discharges being accidentally emitted into the Irish Sea. A ten-mile stretch of beaches was closed and the public were warned not to go swimming for their own safety. Peel sets off tomorrow morning.

If he doesn't return, tonight's fidgety running order will be a fitting farewell. Billy Barrix's 'Cool Off Baby', from an old Chess Records rockabilly compilation, is like Elvis Presley doing an impression of a man with a terrible stutter. The new Cabaret Voltaire single which follows starts with a fit of the giggles, as though they've been clustered around the radio listening to Billy Barrix.

Everything But the Girl, a duo with a jazzy sound that would work well on Radio 2, are not obvious contenders for a Peel session, but they've been given one anyway and they certainly know how to reach out to his demographic. 'Never Could Have Been Worse', their first song, will placate anyone who's spent the last thirteen months endlessly listening to 'This Night Has Opened My Eyes' from the second Smiths session. It's even got a title that Morrissey might have thought of.

Scraping Foetus Off the Wheel, a one-man Throbbing Gristle from Melbourne who lives with Lydia Lunch, is a big favourite with Peel. Foetus's music, which he releases under a slightly amended brand name each time (Foetus Art Terrorism, You've Got Foetus on Your Breath), can be hostile, bestial and overwhelming – at least when he's doing it properly. 'Water Torture', from his latest album *Hole*, is an imagined colloquium of the Birthday Party, Rip Rig + Panic, King Kurt and Fats Domino, a sound akin to being head-butted in a Thirties jazz bar. But Peel says an interesting thing about *Hole* when the song finishes:

'One of those LPs which is timeless, I think. It will still sound pretty good in ten years' time. Whereas a lot of the records that I was playing on the radio ten years ago, by and large, they sound awful to me.'

So what was Peel playing ten years ago that he now finds so unpalatable? If we go back to 15 October 1974 – it was a Tuesday edition of *Top Gear* – he had new sessions from Lol Coxhill (ex-Kevin Ayers), Duane Eddy and Can. He opened the show with the Detroit rocker Ted Nugent and went on to play the Isley Brothers, John Mayall's Bluesbreakers, Alemayehu Eshete (a singer from Ethiopia), Bob Dylan, Rod Stewart, Little Richard, Ace (the famous 'How Long', still a month away from charting), Richard and Linda Thompson, Ry Cooder, the Lafayette Afro Rock Band (an American funk combo who'd moved to France) and Rufus with

Chaka Khan. It's about as diverse a two-hour selection of records as one could ask for.

'I can't believe I ever thought they were any good at all,' Peel shudders. 'I hope that's always the case.'

1985: GOD MADE THEM HIGH AND LOWLY

'My guitar is totally out of tune, because my guitar is for kicking. But William's guitar is completely in tune. Not that you would notice any difference.' JIM REID of the Jesus and Mary Chain

John Peel Show
Radio 1
2 January 1985

The Nomads – Nero and the Gladiators – Sorry – Onward International – Body of People – Buzzcocks – Katie Love and the Four Shades of Black – Dr Calculus – Sam Dees – The Primevals – Nitzer Ebb – The Scars – Michael Palmer – The Three Johns

The National Union of Mineworkers is said to be delighted with figures showing that only three to four hundred striking miners returned to their pits after Christmas. A major propaganda campaign by the National Coal Board had been launched to tempt thousands of miners back to work.

There was a time in the Seventies when Peel was on Radio 1 every night from Monday to Friday. That changed in November 1978, when he lost his fifth slot of the week to Tommy Vance's *Friday Rock Show*. And last October the *John Peel Show* was cut again – to three programmes a week – as Vance was handed Thursday nights for a new programme, *Into the Music*. Dedicated to melodic rock and described by the *Radio Times* as 'putting the music back in your ears', the arrival of *Into the Music* may well explain why Peel felt a sudden desire to de-stress with a long weekend by the lakes.

Ken Garner, the author of *The Peel Sessions*, has written that Peel's 1978 and 1984 demotions were merely two of the more visible manoeuvres in a long-running Radio 1 campaign to oust him completely from the schedules. This could have a lot of validity; frankly, there was little need for *Into the Music* to exist, since it covered much of the same ground as Andy Peebles's Friday evening show, Vance's *Friday Rock Show* and Richard Skinner's *Saturday Live*. Nor could Vance, at forty-four, be explained away as a younger and groovier replacement for an ageing Peel. It makes more sense to evaluate *Into the Music* as a move on Radio 1's part to ease Peel out (without alerting the music press or his highly partisan listenership) and turn the 10 p.m. slot into something more consistent with Radio 1's daytime output. Peel, for his part, felt deeply slighted by the loss of 25 per cent of his airtime to a programme that hardly anyone could see the point of.

So: just Mondays to Wednesdays from now on.

Peel's favourite record at the moment is 'Programme 7', a hypnotic twelve-inch single by the mysterious Dr Calculus, which amalgamates electro, Pigbag, New Order's 'Blue Monday' and a host of sampled voices to create a giddy joyride. It sounds like a science project that was so much fun someone decided to release it. Peel and Walters both love the song, and after playing it again next week they'll approach Calculus – who may be one person, two, or simply a very intelligent robot – to record a session for the show. It will air at the end of the month. Ken Garner's book, which lists all the producers, engineers, studios, musicians and instruments for every band that ever did a Peel session, has five Us in the entry for Dr Calculus. Each one stands for Unknown. Oo-ee-oo.

John Peel Show
Radio 1
7 January 1985

City Limits Crew – Stark Raving Mad – Hoodoo Gurus – Al Campbell
– Little Richard – Skeletal Family – Comsat Angels – The Membranes
– The Inca Babies – Dr Calculus – The Kick – The Kingsmen

*Terry Waite, the Archbishop of Canterbury's envoy, has arrived in
Libya to negotiate the release of four Britons being detained there.
They've been held hostage since last May and one of them, Alan
Russell, has just been sentenced to three years in prison for allegedly
passing state secrets to BBC journalists.*

Spending its fifth week at number 1 in the charts is Band Aid's 'Do
They Know It's Christmas?', an all-star famine-aid single written
by Bob Geldof and Midge Ure. The two men can't be blamed in
the slightest for wanting to help the dying in Ethiopia, but one
unforeseen consequence of their efforts is that it reveals the massive musical and political dichotomy that now exists in Britain's
music industry. One-time Peel favourites like Status Quo, Queen
and Paul Weller are involved in Band Aid, but no calls went out to
New Order, the Smiths or other bands in Peel's night-time world.

Geldof and Ure would argue that their aim was to raise millions
for starving children, not to get Single of the Week in the *NME*;
but it's ironic that a song about hunger has flagged up a divide in
British music between the major labels and the independents; the
wealthy and the insolvent; the bourgeoisie and the proletariat; the
haves and the have-nots.

On Geldof's and Ure's side of the industry, a Peel show in 1985 is
less than irrelevant. Why does he play music that doesn't sell? Why
does he promote artists who refuse to be commercial? Surely he's

just being perverse. Why can't he accept that hits are the currency of radio, and that videos are the magic ingredient of hits, and that the Brit Awards are the icing on the cake? If he can't see that Annie Lennox, George Michael and Phil Collins are the most talented individuals in British music, then – market forces being what they are, old boy – maybe Radio 1 is right to start phasing you out. If only you could discover a great band like Frankie Goes to Hollywood instead of all that dreadful student rubbish like the Smiths.

On the other side of the barrier, the perspective is turned on its head. The Top 40 is derided. Videos are cheesy embarrassments. The Brit Awards don't even register as an event worth caring about. The blandness of modern pop alienates a generation of ears attuned to punk, while the grinning, winking camaraderie of the stars in the Band Aid video nauseates their peers in the indie sector who wonder what the hell there is to smile about. 'I'm not afraid to say that I think Band Aid was diabolical,' Morrissey will comment. 'One can have great concern for the people of Ethiopia, but it's another thing to inflict daily torture on the people of England . . . It was the most self-righteous platform in the history of popular music.'

Morrissey isn't just criticising a song. He's criticising an aesthetic, an orthodoxy, a pop elite, an economic system and (in his mind) an egregious pyramid of vacuous pomposity – all of which, to an indie fan or musician in 1985, the omnipotent trinity of Lennox, Michael and Collins appears to epitomise. The Eighties have split into two. Indie is no longer just an abbreviation for 'independent'. It's not just a style of music or a preference for Rickenbacker guitars over programmed drums. For many, it's a political choice and a way of life. The Smiths and other bands embody it. The music weeklies write about it. Peel's shows are the place you go to hear it. It would be hard to overestimate, now, the contempt with which Peel's listeners view the stars of mainstream pop, or the complete indifference with which the stars of mainstream pop view them.

John Peel Show
Radio 1
5 February 1985

The Smiths – The Marabar Caves – Big Flame – Play Dead – Minimal
Compact – Oscar McLollie and His Honey Jumpers – The New
Christs – Pam Hall – The Jesus and Mary Chain – Guadalcanal Diary

*In a midnight security operation, 1,500 Royal Engineers take over a
disused RAF station at Molesworth in Cambridgeshire to reclaim the
land from nuclear protesters. Two camps of demonstrators awake to
find a six-foot-high wire fence erected around the seven-mile perimeter.
RAF Molesworth is due to become a cruise-missile base within the next
three years.*

When Alan McGee watched the Jesus and Mary Chain soundcheck
in the afternoon before making their live debut at his Living Room
club (upstairs at the Roebuck pub in Tottenham Court Road), their
guitars were squealing with so much feedback that most people
witnessing the din would have instinctively put their hands over
their ears. Not McGee. He walked up to the band and asked them if
they'd like to sign to Creation Records.

That was last June. In November he released their first single,
'Upside Down', a genuine bombshell of a record that put the East
Kilbride band's guitar feedback in the foreground of the mix – virtually as a lead instrument – so that the song itself, a scuzzy punk
update of early Elvis attitude with a few bizarre undercurrents of
the theme to *Scooby Doo, Where Are You!*, came through more as a
vague outline than an audio reproduction. It was music as visual-
ised by the crucified man on the Turin Shroud.

'The band that everybody's talking about,' said Peel in an exag-
geratedly hype-y voice when he played 'Upside Down' in December

– but he added, in his own voice, that he thought the single was excellent. Making a modest showing in the Festive 50 at number 37 (the Smiths' 'How Soon Is Now?' was the clear winner), 'Upside Down' became more of a talking point when the Jesus and Mary Chain played a bad-tempered, opinion-dividing gig at the ICA later that month. Those who liked them were now starting to talk of them as the new Sex Pistols. To everyone else, they were a mystifying racket. How could they base a career on a sound like *that*? 'They were using feedback to the point of excruciating pain,' their music publisher would later recall. But he paid McGee £40,000 to own the rights to it.

'Upside Down' finally climbed to number 1 in the indie charts last week, just as the Jesus and Mary Chain's first UK tour began attracting a tabloid controversy rather similar to the Pistols' 'Anarchy' tour in 1976. Last-minute nerves caused venue owners to cancel gigs in Sheffield and Birmingham. At those that have gone ahead, the Mary Chain have tended to play extremely short, fifteen-minute sets that leave the audience experiencing conflicted feelings of anger at the shambolic performance and resentment at the poor value for money. One of the first things the singer, Jim Reid, does when he gets onstage is berate the audience that has turned up to watch. 'Listen,' he hissed at a London crowd in November, 'we don't want to fucking know you. We fucking hate you. We despise you.' It ramps up the animosity. It raises the stakes.

Peel wouldn't subscribe to any of Reid's behaviour, never having had any time for Malcolm McLaren's whipped-up media storms and shock-horror strategies, which Alan McGee, the Jesus and Mary Chain's manager, is deliberately imitating. But as a fan of the band's debut single, Peel is useful to them in a wider context because he essentially boils everything down to a simple question: do you or do you not think that 'Upside Down' is a great record? The idea of making great records, funnily enough, is very close to the Mary Chain's hearts. Secretly, they entertain dreams of becoming top pop songwriters, and are much more interested in hit singles and *Top of the Pops* appearances than they are in zigzagging around Britain playing to drunk goths and incredulous Echo and the Bunnymen fans. Their second single, 'Never Understand', which Peel previews in the show tonight, is a more than worthy follow-up to 'Upside Down', and will creep into the Top 50 next month. At the end of the year, everyone will see precisely what an effect the Jesus and Mary Chain have had on Peel's listeners. Their chaotic gigs may be powder kegs out there in the physical world – and will soon descend into full-blown riots – but here on the *John Peel Show*, believe it or not, it's all about the music.

John Peel Show
Radio 1
13 May 1985

Gregory Isaacs – The Sedgemorons – Xmal Deutschland – The Boothill Foot Tappers – The Three Johns – Hard Corps – The Nip Drivers – The Meteors – New Order – The Simonics – Hüsker Dü

A judicial inquiry is to be held into the deaths of fifty-three people in a fire at Bradford City's football stadium two days ago. All Third and Fourth Division clubs will be required to improve safety. It emerges that Bradford had received two council warnings that their antiquated wooden stand constituted a fire hazard.

The Three Johns are a trio of Johns – Langford, Hyatt and Brennan – and come from Leeds, although strictly speaking Langford is a Jon and Brennan's first name is Phillip. They play a jagged, akimbo, guitar-driven and heavily political music that is sometimes likened to Captain Beefheart if he'd had a Militant Band rather than a Magic one. Peel is a big Three Johns fan and has broadcast four of their sessions. They're also popular with the anti-Thatcher *NME*, invariably being the second name added to the bill of any left-leaning benefit concert. Last month they took part in a tour called 'Jobs for Youth', sponsored by Neil Kinnock's Labour Party, in which politicians mingled and chatted to fans in between bursts of music and poetry.

The 'Jobs for Youth' tour was headlined by the twenty-seven-year-old singer-songwriter Billy Bragg, the first name to be added to the bill of any left-leaning benefit concert. Bragg has become a mainstay of miners' strike fundraisers and other activist endeavours designed to keep the pits open, save the coal industry, kick the Tories out and get Labour in. Bragg, a Peel regular, created a good impression early on by enterprisingly delivering an Indian takeaway to him at Broadcasting House a couple of years ago on condition that he played a track from Bragg's mini-album, *Life's a Riot with Spy vs Spy*. Peel, having one of his nights, played it at the wrong speed.

Peel himself is pro-miners, like Bragg, and is an admirer of the four bands – Orange Juice, Aztec Camera, Everything But the Girl and the Woodentops – who played a miners' benefit at Brixton Academy in January. He also plays lesser-known outfits like the Membranes (who are based in Blackpool) and the Redskins (in York), who have been organising gigs for the miners on the club circuit. On 22 January Peel dedicated a song by the Fire Engines, a defunct Edinburgh band, 'to the lost boys of Bilston Glen colliery' just outside the city, which had seen months of bitter clashes between flying pickets and strike-breakers.

Then, in March, the strike ended. In an anticlimactic defeat for the trade union movement, the National Union of Mineworkers delegates voted by a small majority to return to work without having won any concessions on pit closures from the National Coal Board. The strike had lasted just under a year.

The end of the road, however, does not mean the end of protest, or of Billy Bragg, or of the bonds that now unite some of Peel's favourite bands and the labour movement.

John Peel Show
Radio 1
3 June 1985

John Lee Hooker – Nick Cave and the Bad Seeds – Cookie Crew – The Fall – 10,000 Maniacs – Roy Orbison – Western Promise – New Order – Freddie King – Clan of Xymox – Deadline – Negazione

Margaret Thatcher tells the Commons that radical changes are needed if football is to survive as a spectator sport. Following the deaths of thirty-nine supporters at last week's European Cup final in Brussels between Liverpool and Juventus, she announces a ban on alcohol at all British football grounds and pledges to give police greater powers to control crowds.

On 22 May, a Wednesday night, Peel opened his show by telling the listeners: 'One week from tonight, dear friends, I'll be in the whatever-it's-called stadium in Brussels, hopefully in an advanced state of delirium.' The plan was that he would combine work and pleasure by compèring the annual Pinkpop Festival in Holland on 27 May (featuring the Stranglers, Steel Pulse and China Crisis) and then driving to Brussels with Sheila to watch his team Liverpool in the European Cup final two nights later.

The 'whatever-it's-called stadium' was Heysel, and thirty-nine people – most of them Juventus fans – never left it alive. Liverpool supporters went on the attack before kick-off, crushing trapped Italians against a wall, which collapsed under their weight. A horrified Peel, seeing bodies carried out, ushered Sheila away from the stadium, where incensed Juventus fans were looking for revenge, and warned her not to speak English until they were safely in the car. Once inside with the doors locked, they burst into tears and held each other. Peel's Zelig-like knack of being in attendance at news-making events – the *Oz* trial in 1971; the world-exclusive first unveiling of *Sgt Pepper* in 1967; the press conference in Dallas before the shooting of Lee Harvey Oswald in 1963 – had led him to the site of a major disaster that would be described as European football's darkest hour.

'The events in Brussels have already been seized upon by a wide range of interests to prove points that they wanted to make,' Peel says tonight on his first show since arriving back at work. 'Witness the discussion on Janice's programme about the licensing laws, earlier on tonight. I'll just say that, as a boy, I never understood why my dad wouldn't tell us about his experiences in North Africa and Italy during the war . . . and now I do.'

John Peel Show
Radio 1
12 August 1985

The Smiths – Dignitary Stylish – Loudon Wainwright III – The Folk Devils – The Cure – Sanny-X and P-Rez – Winston Jarrett – The Pogues – The Very Things – Wild Jimmy Spruill – T La Rock

The Commission for Racial Equality calls for urgent action after a spate of arson attacks on Asian homes and businesses in London. Last year the Metropolitan Police recorded 1,289 racial incidents in the

capital, but this may be a considerable underestimate. Some of the most
serious attacks resulted in families being burned to death.

The Very Things, a band from Redditch who recorded four sessions for Peel in their previous incarnation as the Cravats, were the
architects of one of last year's screwiest singles. 'The Bushes Scream
While My Daddy Prunes' was a glorious gallimaufry of deranged
guitar twanging, primitive drumming and surreal horror in a subur-
ban garden, which their singer, The Shend, intoned in a Boris Karloff
voice à la 'Monster Mash' (and with almost as many quotable lines).
'The Bushes Scream . . .' spent fourteen weeks in the independent
chart and was voted by Peel's listeners into twenty-seventh place
in the Festive 50. That may not sound much, but it was higher than
the Special AKA's 'Free Nelson Mandela', Robert Wyatt's 'Biko' and
three songs by the Cocteau Twins.

The Very Things have recorded another in this ongoing series of
Gothic penny dreadfuls, and the news is that their standards have
not slipped. In the latest one, 'Mummy, You're a Wreck', a woman
lies on the floor unconscious, probably inebriated, while her house
falls to rack and ruin. A bell tolls. Her concerned son, a fastidious
Quasimodo of a youth, is prevailed upon to help ('Perhaps I will flick
round with the duster'), but every appliance in the house is eating up
electricity and his mother has parked the Chevrolet halfway through
the garage wall. The boy is appalled by her slovenliness ('I think I
ought to speak my mind'), humming to himself ominously as the
bell begins tolling again. Given some more Peel airplay, 'Mummy,
You're a Wreck' will appear in the indie chart later this month, but it's
a shame the Very Things aren't on a label ambitious enough to take it
further. The tolling bell would sound great over the public speakers at
the Radio 1 Roadshow (coming today from the West Promenade in
Bournemouth) or on Gary Davies's *Bit in the Middle* or – who knows
– as the song that ruptured a marriage on Simon Bates's 'Our Tune'.

The Pogues, who used to be Pogue Mahone, have made it to a second album, *Rum, Sodomy & the Lash*. Featuring re-recordings of two songs they performed on a Peel session last December, it's getting fabulous reviews. The Cure have been thriving, too, scaling the southern face of the Top 20 with a new single, 'In Between Days', and shortly to release their most successful album to date (*The Head on the Door*). Purely to be contrary, or perhaps because he finds 'In Between Days' too vivacious for his liking, Peel plays the second track on the B-side of the twelve-inch ('A Few Hours After This'), which is shrouded in woe and brings back memories of Joy Division's 'Atmosphere'. That's more like it. That's the Cure of 1982. The Cure of desolate bedsits with cobwebbed mirrors.

Neither the Pogues nor the Cure will need Peel's help in the remainder of their careers – though the Cure have been considerate enough to record one last session for him before flying, bat-like, into the great black yonder. The Cocteau Twins, the Sisters of Mercy and Nick Cave have all recorded their final sessions too; there are no official announcements to that effect, but the ninety-odd sessions commissioned this year (the lowest number since 1976) tend to come from bands more likely to be grateful to be asked. The Sensible Jerseys: jangly pop with a Sixties slant. The Housemartins: librarians and social workers from Hull. The Noseflutes: capers and japers from Birmingham. Pink Peg Slax: rockabilly from Leeds. The Folk Devils: wild rustic passion meets the Smiths' 'Handsome Devil'. Terry and Gerry: retro skiffle.

It's fallen to 3 Mustaphas 3 to thank Peel for his continued support of the misfits and the malcontents. They tell *Folk Roots* magazine this month that they've named a mountain after him.

John Peel Show
Radio 1
2 September 1985

Sugar Minott – Billy Bragg – The Janitors – Hassan and 7-11 –
Sydney Lipton and His Grosvenor House Dance Orchestra – The
Shop Assistants – Dignitary Stylish – Mission Impossible – Momus

*Margaret Thatcher's Cabinet reshuffle has been more extensive than
expected. Douglas Hurd, the Northern Ireland minister, becomes home
secretary, replacing Leon Brittan, who moves to trade and industry.
Norman Tebbit is appointed Conservative Party chairman. John
Selwyn Gummer, his predecessor, goes to agriculture.*

Peel remarked in a programme last month that he'd recently managed to find a fanzine that didn't have an interview with Billy Bragg
in it. The listeners would have enjoyed the joke. A fanzine without a
Billy Bragg interview? In 1985? There must be some mistake. Bragg
is everywhere. In the past twelve months he's networked with everyone from Jimmy Somerville to Ken Livingstone, headlining dozens
of benefit gigs, getting arrested at an anti-apartheid demonstration
and even having tea with Neil Kinnock to discuss how Labour's policies might appeal to more young people.

Bragg's fourth session for Peel goes out tonight, after which he
and others will begin assembling the cast of musicians for Red
Wedge, a collective launched to the press in November. The goal
of Red Wedge is political: to focus the voices and personalities
of Bragg, Somerville and Paul Weller on the job of convincing as
many young Britons as possible to vote Labour at the next general
election. Weller isn't much of a public speaker, as it happens, but
Bragg is. Bragg, who can think on his feet and use straight-shooting
rhetoric that MPs like Robin Cook and Roy Hattersley cannot, has

made himself increasingly visible, voluble and indispensable.

One of the most reductive performers on the circuit, Bragg sings the way he talks – in Estuary English with no fake emoting – while chopping away at an electric guitar like a busker in a tube station. His new session is a handy primer on the various elements that make up his work. He's wistful (on a cover of a Smiths B-side, 'Jeane'), romantic but hard-headed ('The Marriage'), indignantly anti-Thatcher ('Days Like These', his next single) and good at finding an historical analogy for a contemporary plight ('There Is Power in a Union', a pre-First World War folk song). Like the Pogues last December and the Smiths last August, Bragg has let Peel debut two songs that won't appear on an album for many months (*Talking with the Taxman about Poetry*). But unlike so many artists who drift away from Peel once other distractions come calling, Bragg will never forget the man who first let him sing to the nation.

It's a show of peaks and troughs tonight, rather than goofy juxtapositions and enigmatic arcs. Peel is oddly stilted, as if reading from a hastily revised script, and he fumbles several introductions. He sounds a bit under the weather. He's happiest when he cues up a dancehall seven-inch from Jamaica, 'Pon de Attack', by a DJ known as Dignitary Stylish. One of the listeners has written in to request it after hearing Peel play it last month. This pleases Peel very much: a request for more dancehall! Of course, had the listener written in to implore Peel never to play it again, the result would have been exactly the same.

John Peel Show
Radio 1
22 October 1985

Screaming Blue Messiahs – The Woodentops – Half Man Half
Biscuit – Ted Hawkins – Terry and Gerry – 1,000 Violins – Sophia
George – Giant Sand – Yeah Yeah Noh – Mike Hart – Einstürzende
Neubauten – Babla and Kanchan – Corrosion of Conformity

*The government is to consider banning coaches from the fast lanes
of motorways after yesterday's multiple pile-up on the M6 that left
thirteen people dead. The coach driver said to have been responsible
for the crash – the worst ever seen on Britain's motorways – remains in
intensive care.*

A Tyneside secret went national this year. The editor of a scabrous
underground comic called *Viz*, based on the *Beano*, *Dandy* and
Whizzer and Chips comics that a generation of British children
grew up reading in the Seventies, agreed a distribution deal with
Virgin, putting *Viz* into W. H. Smith, John Menzies and other shops
and chains up and down the land. The comic, which abounds with
swear words, football gags and gratuitous references to minor celebrities of years gone by, is attracting a few hundred more evangelical
followers with each issue.

The coalescence of Seventies nostalgia, music and football
(which comes, unfortunately, at the worst possible time for the
game) has given rise to a band of dole-queue wits from Merseyside,
Half Man Half Biscuit, whose debut album, *Back in the DHSS*,
has found its way to Peel. Their songs touch on a variety of topics,
including Jim Reeves, snooker referees, retired cricketers ('Fuckin'
'Ell It's Fred Titmus'), poker-faced Benny Hill sidekicks ('99% of
Gargoyles Look Like Bob Todd') and – in 'God Gave Us Life', a

modern-day 'All Things Bright and Beautiful' – a parade of TV light-entertainment figures, from Wendy Craig to Lionel Blair, whose existence on earth leads Half Man Half Biscuit to wonder if God is some kind of sadist.

The listeners are hearing Half Man Half Biscuit for the first time. 'God Gave Us Life' is the start of a close relationship between the band and the *John Peel Show*. Their first session, which they'll record in November, will feature the soon-to-be-famous 'All I Want for Christmas Is a Dukla Prague Away Kit' and 'The Trumpton Riots'. Peel has found a band that would infuriate Billy Bragg: a band that regards sitting in front of a TV all day as the most honourable pursuit for a fully sentient adult. 'It's the little things that drive me up the wall,' singer-lyricist Nigel Blackwell will confide to the *NME* in December. 'Margaret Thatcher means nothing to me. I neither hate or love her.' His dream is to own a Breville toaster.

Will the name of Tommy Vance appear in a future Half Man Half Biscuit song? At this stage we can only speculate. *Into the Music*, Vance's programme that aimed to put the music back in your ears on a Thursday night, didn't last a year. Three weeks ago it yielded its Thursday slot to a new show hosted by Andy Kershaw, a twenty-five-year-old from Rochdale who co-presents BBC2's *Whistle Test*. Kershaw, a sometime roadie for Billy Bragg, performed well under difficult circumstances on the BBC's all-day coverage of Live Aid in July (which Peel took no part in) and has a boyish, irrepressible manner on radio that complements Peel's dry sarcasm. If Peel is Eeyore, Kershaw is Dill the dog from *The Herbs*. Kershaw is excited by what might lie around the corner. Peel has seen his house blown down too many times to expect anything but misfortune. Peel is always losing his tail. Kershaw chases his around the garden.

Peel and Kershaw have some taste overlap, but they're nothing like interchangeable. They're both fans of a Mississippi blues singer named Ted Hawkins, who has spent his life in and out of prison and only got round to releasing his first album in 1982, at the age of forty-five. But they disagree about the Paisley Underground, a Kershaw-endorsed wave of American guitar bands that Peel finds tedious. This is one of the reasons why examining the composition of a mid-Eighties Peel show can be a frustrating business. He has myriad inconsistencies. He can be indulgent towards the fluffiest, frothiest British indie groups imaginable, while deploring the effeteness of their American cousins. He can have a blind spot with R.E.M., reject a listener request for the Long Ryders (in June) and snipe at 10,000 Maniacs for turning into Katrina and the Waves, but a twee band of over-influenced Morrissey fans from Sheffield called One Thousand Violins meet with his unconditional approval. 'My life is a barrel of laughs,' their song goes, 'but an empty one.' And then they go home and they cry and they want to die.

Whatever genres may have flickered into being in the summer, Peel has been at his most Peelian this year when he's played records that few other DJs would have a copy of – or even know about – and they haven't necessarily been new releases. 'Reckless Night on Board an Ocean Liner', a 1938 recording by Sydney Lipton and His Grosvenor House Dance Orchestra of a tune immortalised in several *Looney Tunes* cartoons, was a lovely thing to drop into a show in September ('because of the apparent discovery of the *Titanic* last week', Peel explained, quoting a news item about a Franco-American seabed expedition); and the same night saw him unearth a strange, muddily recorded track by a Swedish band, Mission Impossible, which included dialogue from a 1982 German Bundestag debate involving Chancellor Helmut Schmidt and his successor Helmut Kohl.

Nevertheless, Peel's most far-reaching decision this year has been to give his backing to a new breed of indie pop that takes as its template the Postcard sound of the early Eighties. A few of the bands sound good, particularly the tougher ones like the Shop Assistants, from Edinburgh, whose records try to recapture the rawness of the first Ramones album. But other bands just sound pathetic. They've either left their ideas in the pockets of their anoraks or they've reduced Orange Juice to a flavourless gloop.

These are the early stirrings of C86, a movement that will lead to feuds at the *NME*, an implausible ideological battle between indie and hip hop, and never-ending arguments about white music fans and involuntary racism. It will ultimately lead Peel to chastise his own listeners for voting indie songs into the Festive 50, when all they've done is express a preference for a style of music that he himself has championed to the hilt. And at least, unlike Peel, the listeners will be able to claim that they exercised some quality control in their judgements – whereas he appeared to have no filter, no discernment and no satiation point.

The road to 30 December 1986 has begun.

1986: RUCTIONS AT THE TUFTY CLUB

*'The dawn of independent music has meant anyone can
make a record. And that's a bad thing. There have been
more crap records in the last eight years than ever before.'*
BOBBY GILLESPIE of Primal Scream, 1989

John Peel Show
Radio 1
27 January 1986

Yeah Yeah Noh – Hya Nya – Half Man Half Biscuit – Microdisney
– The Chicago Bears Shufflin' Crew – The Chills – Mighty Ballistics
Hi-Power – Traddodiad Ofnus – White Flag – Frankie Paul

*The dispute at News International's Wapping printing plant,
where 6,000 workers have been dismissed for going on strike, takes
a surprising turn when members of the Electrical, Electronic,
Telecommunications and Plumbing Union (EETPU) are brought in
to replace the sacked workforce. Three and a half million copies of the
Sun are produced overnight, about 75 per cent of its normal print run.*

Last March, after more than seventeen years in Broadcasting House,
Radio 1 moved to new premises in nearby Langham Street. Egton
House is an unsightly glass and concrete building that looks like
the main block of a large Midlands comprehensive. In an earlier

life, before its Sixties facelift, it was the BBC's emergency HQ after Broadcasting House was bombed by the Luftwaffe. Now, in a small office numbered 318, it houses John Peel, John Walters, Andy Kershaw, two chairs, piles and piles of vinyl, a random clutter of record-company promotional gifts and an upturned stainless-steel wastepaper bin for Kershaw to sit on.

Peel, like Egton in the Blitz, soldiers on, making the necessary readjustments. And so do his listeners. Their Festive 50 at Christmas (for which only songs released during the calendar year were eligible, a rule introduced by Peel in 1982) delivered an emphatic validation for the Jesus and Mary Chain, the much-maligned feedback terrorists, who placed first and second with their singles 'Never Understand' and 'Just Like Honey'. A festive one–two; not even Joy Division ever pulled off a feat like that. The scourge of the music business last March after a gig at a London polytechnic ended in a riot, the Mary Chain crowned December with a mandate from a Peel listenership that views them more as classicists than iconoclasts.

'I should have played that [song] more, you know,' Peel sighed one night in late October as the final chord of 'Just Like Honey' died away. It was a ballad that might have been written for the Ronettes. The opening track on the band's debut album, *Psychocandy*, it offered a kiss instead of a fist, just as their cultural pathfinders had lulled hippies into sweet deception with 'Sunday Morning' on *The Velvet Underground and Nico*. But after 'Just Like Honey' came 'The Living End': a million dentist drills tuned to C.

John Peel Show
Radio 1
26 February 1986

New Order – Duane Eddy – The Wedding Present – Blitzkrieg Zone
– African Melody – Siouxsie and the Banshees – The Psylons – James
– Addis Rockers – Menticide – Honolulu Mountain Daffodils

Following a three-month inquiry into Militant, Labour's National
Executive Committee votes to start expulsion proceedings against
members of the Trotskyist 'party within the party'. Those targeted
include Derek Hatton, the deputy leader of Liverpool City Council.
Left-wing Labour MP Tony Benn condemns the inquiry as an
'inquisition'.

'On last night's programme,' says Peel, cueing up a compilation
album released on a label called Rock 'n' Dole, 'I was talking about
the "Heroes" concert at the Albert Hall in London on Sunday night.
Six fifteen kick-off, incidentally. And I've discovered more about it
since last night. Paul Weller, Tom Robinson, Ralph McTell, Ewan
MacColl and Peggy Seeger, Lindisfarne, the Flying Pickets and
Hank Wangford are amongst the contestants there. And here's a
track from the *Heroes* LP.'

A voice sings a cappella. 'Easington Explosion' is a folk song by
the poet and former Durham coal miner Jock Purdon, lamenting
the deaths of eighty-one miners in a Fifties colliery accident. 'There's
no medals made for miners,' he sings, 'but they are heroes all.' The
songs on *Heroes* – and the concert on Sunday – are raising money
for a miners' support group in Durham and Northumberland,
where the families of striking miners have relied on food parcels
for almost two years. Bruce Springsteen wrote a $20,000 cheque to
the fund when he played a concert in Newcastle last June. Peel gave

quite a bit of exposure to *Heroes* when it first came out in October. In the main, his support for the miners has been unspoken and understood.

One of the speakers at the Albert Hall will be Tony Benn, the Labour MP, who tried unsuccessfully to introduce a bill in the Commons last year that would have granted an amnesty to all miners imprisoned for offences during the strike. Benn's bill was never going to gain much traction. Not when two miners in Wales are serving eight-year sentences for manslaughter after dropping a concrete block from a footbridge to frighten a strike-breaker en route to the Merthyr Vale colliery. The concrete block landed on his taxi, killing the driver.

Almost a year after the strike collapsed, the wounds are still terribly raw. But *Heroes* is not the only record in tonight's show to hint at a society riven with divisions. 'Somewhere in the dim unknown,' sing the UK reggae band Addis Rockers, 'stands a God taking care of His own.' The title of their song, 'Broadwater Farm Affairs', refers to the housing estate in Tottenham where a day of police arrests and race riots last October led to the death from heart failure of a forty-nine-year-old black woman and the murder (and attempted decapitation) of a white police constable.

Three songs later, Peel reaches for the 1972 album *America Eats Its Young* by George Clinton's politically charged Funkadelic. Track two on side one is a piece of sardonic social commentary that warns of rude awakenings for human ostriches with their heads in the sand. Or perhaps it's a warning that demos and benefit gigs are just a drop in the ocean, and that the time for waving placards is over. 'You picket this and protest that and eat yourself fat,' Funkadelic chant sceptically. 'Ain't you deep in your semi-first-class seat?' The song is called 'If You Don't Like the Effects, Don't Produce the Cause'.

'A title that was never more appropriate than now,' says Peel, hedging his bets somewhat. But what an interesting time to play it.

John Peel Show
Radio 1
5 March 1986

The Shop Assistants – Bogshed – The Primevals – Twang – The
Wolfhounds – The Len Bright Combo – Eton Crop – In the Nursery
– We've Got a Fuzzbox and We're Gonna Use It – The Soup Dragons

*Bob Geldof's Band Aid charity announces plans for Sport Aid, a
week of fundraising ending with a global marathon in May. Countries
already confirmed as taking part in the 'race against time' include
Japan, Korea, Australia, the United States, the Philippines and most of
Europe.*

Although the Smiths would protest that they don't get nearly
enough airplay on Radio 1, they're the next best thing to pop stars
in the minds of most Peel listeners. They tour 5,000-seat arenas,
they've sold out the Albert Hall and the Hollywood Palladium, and
their last album (*Meat Is Murder*) charted at number 1. New Order,
too, have come a long way since their first Peel session, headlining the WOMAD festival last year and enjoying Top 20 hits with
a machine-driven dance music that gleams with digital precision.
Even the Jesus and Mary Chain, once the sort of band you could
read about in a fanzine, are an upwardly mobile touring attraction,
signed to a subsidiary (Blanco y Negro) of the major label WEA.
Indie in 1986 is serious commerce. Not everyone feels a part of it.

The tour dates of a Leeds indie band called the Wedding Present,
which Peel read out on the air last week, are much more intimate
and accessible. They can be watched at venues like the 200-capacity
1 in 12 Club in Bradford (founded by a local anarchist collective),
the Old White Horse pub in Brixton (which alternates between
indie nights and cabaret acts) and the Plough Inn in Perth (where

the carpets stick to the punters' feet and the toilets would fail even a cursory hygiene inspection). These are unpretentious venues for unpretentious gigs, where the band dress just like the audience and the audience can hop backstage to interview the band for their fanzines. Small and manageable, the scene is an indie version of pub rock. Back to basics. Back to the original spirit of things. Back to fun.

The Wedding Present are part of a subterranean movement of indie bands – others include the Pastels, the Shop Assistants, the June Brides, the Flatmates, the Soup Dragons and the Razorcuts – who yearn to forge something as exciting as punk, but would rather sing about boys and girls than hate and war. They've been operating deep underground as little of pockets of resistance to the mainstream, putting on gigs, publishing fanzines, starting up indie labels, stapling their own record sleeves, doing-it-themselves in emulation of their 1977 punk antecedents. Some of the new names to conjure with are the Pink Label in London, the Subway Organization in Bristol, Vindaloo in Birmingham, Ron Johnson in Long Eaton (near Nottingham) and 53rd & 3rd in Scotland. Certain labels specialise in jangly guitar pop, or ramalama Buzzcocks homages, but Vindaloo has one or two dark horses, and Ron Johnson is showing signs of being a law unto itself. There's no uniform sound. It's the DIY ethics that are homogeneous.

A new indie age is dawning. Andy Kershaw and Janice Long are following it with interest (Kershaw had a Wedding Present session on his show before Peel did), but Peel has the bit between his teeth and has become the movement's leading evangelist. Tonight he plays no fewer than six bands who will appear on a cassette compiled by the *NME* in May – the Shop Assistants, the Soup Dragons, the Wolfhounds, Bogshed, Half Man Half Biscuit and We've Got a Fuzzbox and We're Gonna Use It. They don't all adhere to the same musical codes of practice, and there's a world of difference between the Shop Assistants' sha-la-la melodies and Half Man Half Biscuit's curdled thoughts on Nerys Hughes, but the title of the *NME* cassette will do more than lend a cachet of modernity to the movement. It will also give it a name: *C86*.

John Peel Show
Radio 1
18 March 1986

It's Immaterial – Half Man Half Biscuit – The Art of Noise featuring Duane Eddy – The Television Personalities – Rodney O – Tynal Tywyll – Raymonde – Tetrack – Biff Bang Pow! – LL Cool J

Budget Day. Chancellor Nigel Lawson delights the Stock Exchange with the introduction of his Personal Equity Plan (PEP), allowing savers a tax-free way to invest up to £2,400 a year in British shares. Smokers face an eleven-pence rise on a pack of twenty cigarettes, bringing them up to £1.46.

Another night of tireless Peel promotion for the new wave of British indie. The Soup Dragons, recording their first session for him, combine the campness of Pete Shelley with the wayward tuning of the Fire Engines. Many C86 bands look to the Buzzcocks as gurus, but Scottish indie pioneers like the Fire Engines, who found a national night-time audience through Peel in the early Eighties, cast an equally potent influence. Orange Juice recently had a song covered on a Peel session by the Wedding Present. They may have split up last year, but it would be no hyperbole to say that Orange Juice are held by some C86-ers in awe. Or that Postcard Records, which put out its last single almost five years ago, is revered *in absentia* as the absolute pinnacle for new indie labels to aspire to. Does Peel ever think back to the time he interviewed Edwyn Collins and carried a torch for Scottish pop? He should. What went around is now coming around.

Orange Juice, however, are far from flattered by C86, seeing it as a debasement of their lofty ideals. It's often forgotten that they loved Philadelphia soul and disco as much as the Velvet Underground. The new class of Scottish indie bands such as Primal Scream and the Pastels, both of whom Peel likes very much, sing songs of such enervated sheepishness that Orange Juice are repulsed to think they might have been an influence on them. 'If you'd told us in 1980 or 1981 that there was going to be this thing called C86,' Orange Juice's drummer Steven Daly will later remark, 'we would have just laughed. Or killed ourselves.' Remember Edwyn Collins telling Peel that they wanted their album to be produced by Chic? How many of these C86 bands would even have a Chic record in the house?

The Soup Dragons take their name from a character in the Seventies children's series *Clangers*. The Pastels' singer dresses like an eleven-year-old and wears a Tufty Club badge in honour of the yellow-trousered squirrel who taught British children how to cross the road safely. At its most extreme, C86 is a throwback to primary school, jelly babies, elasticated mittens and a credulous incorruption. And in a hilarious non sequitur tonight, Peel exposes every one of its qualities and its flaws.

'Love's Going Out of Fashion' by Biff Bang Pow! – an indie band fronted by Creation's Alan McGee – is a down-in-the-dumps break-up song so apathetic and defeatist that it practically assumes the foetal position. Peel follows it with 'Rock the Bells' by the eighteen-year-old rapper LL Cool J. Both songs are the respective artists' third singles, so you could say they should be marking out their territory by now. On 'Rock the Bells', sure enough, LL Cool J is cocky and brash, boasting of his growing wealth and world fame. Meanwhile, on 'Love's Going Out of Fashion', Biff Bang Pow! wonder whether it's worth getting up in the morning. LL Cool J brags that he's got the listener's girlfriend on his lap. Biff Bang Pow! are miserable because their girlfriends are fluttering their eyelashes at other men. LL Cool J is straight in your face. Biff Bang Pow! are sorry to bother you. The two songs might honestly come from different planets.

But LL Cool J doesn't automatically win the showdown. A lot of Peel listeners will shut their ears to 'Rock the Bells', either turned off by the machismo or allergic to rappers in general. They find LL Cool J's world an alien one, with no pertinence to their own. Give them an indie band, a heartbreak song and a jangling guitar. Something they can relate to. Something they can feel a part of. As much as it may drive Peel to distraction – and future Festive 50s will become a serious test of his patience – there's a large percentage of his audience that wishes he would just forget about rap (and dancehall and electro) and concentrate on playing songs like 'Love's Going Out of Fashion'.

'Some suckers don't like me, but I'm not concerned,' LL Cool J grandstands. 'Six Gs for twenty minutes is the pay I earn.'

These lyrics say nothing to C86-ers about their lives. But they would have to admit, six Gs is a lot higher than the going rate at the Plough Inn in Perth and the 1 in 12 Club in Bradford.

John Peel Show
Radio 1
4 June 1986

Run-DMC – Aaron Neville – The Razorcuts – African Head Charge – Nick Toczek's Britanarchists – Misty in Roots – Anthony Adverse – The Close Lobsters – That Petrol Emotion – Stump

Scotland lose their opening World Cup match 0–1 to Denmark in the Mexican city of Ciudad Neza. England lost to Portugal by the same

score yesterday in Monterrey, while Northern Ireland drew 1–1 with
Algeria in Guadalajara. Wales and the Republic of Ireland failed to
qualify.

The *NME*'s cassette *C86* is now available for readers to buy. Send
a cheque or postal order, allow fourteen days for delivery. A week
of gigs at the ICA, featuring most of the twenty-two bands on the
tape, is planned for next month. Naturally the *NME* intends to write
about them. Keeping the *C86* cycle going, Peel is playing tracks
from the tape as though it's an exciting new album, rather than a
round-up of songs by bands he's been promoting for a year.

The *NME*'s staff and writers are divided on the wisdom of *C86*,
with some arguing that the bands are mediocre, amateurish and a
poor advert for the paper. In an ideological reverse of the rap-haters
among Peel's listeners, there are some at the *NME* who feel it's time
to take a step back from indie and devote more energy to reporting
on black music. But what can a Peel listener (or an *NME* reader) do
if they simply don't like hip hop, electro or dancehall? Pretend that
they do?

As the man who has done more than anyone else to popularise the C86 movement, Peel seems to view it, in his catholic way,
as one of many disparate musical ingredients that should make up
a young person's overall diet. As he'll find out, though, there are
some listeners who see C86 as the only food worth consuming.
If any of them should have their fingers perched over their tape
recorders tonight, there'll be plenty of pausing and skipping. Peel
starts the show with 'You Be Illin'' by Run-DMC – from a new
album, *Raising Hell*, that hasn't been released in the UK yet – and
then alternates between black and white artists for the first half
hour. Aaron Neville, the New Orleans soul singer, follows Marc
Riley and the Creepers. African Head Charge, a psychedelic dub
ensemble, follow the Razorcuts. Misty in Roots, who recorded

Peel's favourite reggae album (*Live at the Counter Eurovision*) in 1979, follow the Smiths.

But the *C86* cassette (which ought to come with a sticker saying 'As heard on John Peel') starts to make its presence felt in the programme's second half. Peel plays three tracks from it, almost willing its critics to hear the variety. But if so, he's chosen the wrong tracks. Close Lobsters, from Paisley, are another of those jangling sons-of-Postcard bands, exactly the kind of lukewarm indie backsliders that the naysayers on the *NME* object to. The Shop Assistants are better, but their tender ballad, 'It's Up to You', could have been written by the Jesus and Mary Chain on the same day they wrote 'Just Like Honey'. Only the manic Stump, from Cork, who disprove the theory that *C86* and *Trout Mask Replica* have no point of convergence, go to the trouble of putting together some words and music that people haven't heard before.

Of the other nineteen tracks on the cassette, Peel might have played 'Console Me' by We've Got a Fuzzbox and We're Gonna Use It, an all-girl band from Birmingham whose Crazy Color hair and weird sunglasses give them a cartoonish persona like the Banana Splits. Their fizzy, fuzzy noise fits onto *C86* in ways that nobody can quite explain, except that the girls are on Vindaloo and Vindaloo is a C86 label.

Or Peel might have played 'From Now On, This Will Be Your God' by Age of Chance, a Leeds band who deconstruct punk and spit it back out like a mutant industrial band. Or 'Bullfighter's Bones' by the Shrubs, who approach their guitars from the most Pythagorean of angles and sound like they've listened carefully to American intellectuals like Pere Ubu. Or he could have played 'Run to the Temple' by Bogshed, four astute village idiots with a low boredom threshold who have removed all the conventional melodies from Jilted John's *True Love Stories*, leaving only babbling incoherence.

But don't worry. He'll get around to playing those another night.

John Peel Show
Radio 1
1 September 1986

Terry and Gerry – Divine Sounds – The Bhundu Boys – The Natural
Ites – Freiwillige Selbstkontrolle – Deep Wound – Bing Crosby – Ina
Kamoze – The Nixons – Charlie Chase – Gang Green – James

*There are angry scenes on the first day of the TUC conference in
Brighton, where EETPU leaders are jeered by demonstrators as they
arrive at the hall. TUC general secretary Norman Willis is criticised
for not disciplining the EETPU, whose members are keeping Rupert
Murdoch's newspaper plant at Wapping in production.*

Peel and Andy Kershaw may not see eye to eye on R.E.M., but
they're united in their love of the Bhundu Boys. The Zimbabwean
group, whose glittering, interweaving electric guitars sound like
Johnny Marr overdubbing in heaven, have recorded their first session for Peel, which he'll repeat twice. Later in the year, after making
a decision to base themselves in Scotland for an extended period,
they'll record another. Peel's appreciation of African music dates
back to the early Seventies, but this is the year when he's graduated
from a well-meaning dilettante to a fully fledged apostle.

When it comes to the Bhundu Boys, Peel and Kershaw are not
so much radio presenters as unpaid publicists working on a pro
bono basis. In tandem, night after night, they preach the gospel of
those interweaving guitars, trying to keep the excitement in their
voices down to the steady level of mere obsession. Which isn't
easy for Peel, who wept like a baby when the Bhundus made their
London debut in May.

'If you missed them LAST time, go and see them THIS
time,' he'll urge the listeners in capital letters when the Bhundus

return in November. 'You will NOT be DISAPPOINTED. I can GUARANTEE it.'

If he keeps this up in 1987, Ivor Cutler's record of fifteen sessions won't be looking so unassailable.

John Peel Show
Radio 1
26 November 1986

The Untold Fables – The Freeze – 14 Iced Bears – The Passmore Sisters – Emanon – The Da Vincis – Throwing Muses – Taxman – Roy Orbison – Kaptain Jam and the Mighty Finesse – Talulah Gosh

An inquest into the death of a haemophiliac hears that pathologists at St Mary's Hospital in Paddington refused to carry out a postmortem for fear they might catch Aids. Recent statistics show deaths from Aids to be on the increase in Britain, with 102 people dying of the disease between January and August this year compared to ninety-one in 1985.

The search for ever-janglier indie bands to feature on his programmes has led Peel to Brighton, the home of 14 Iced Bears. Having been overlooked by the compilers of the *C86* cassette, 14 Iced Bears are making up for lost time by writing some of the shyest, floppiest-fringed songs that any C86 fan has ever heard. 'Excellent, very good indeed,' says Peel after the first song in their session, apparently not sated by that south-coast jangle just yet.

Later, he casually throws 14 Iced Bears under a bus by playing their third song ('Shy Like You') after Screamin' Jay Hawkins's demented hoodoo classic 'I Put a Spell on You'. How on earth does he think that an unsigned indie band could possibly live up to that?

It's like tossing a puppy into a pit of ravenous alligators. 'I like those Iced Bears, every 14 of them,' Peel beams, trying to drown out the chomping noises.

The other band in session, the Passmore Sisters, come from Bradford and served their C86 apprenticeship by playing the 1 in 12 Club as early as 1983 (and then again in 1984 and 1985). In a year when the Smiths have branched into music hall on *The Queen Is Dead*, the Passmore Sisters sound like a Smiths that have zeroed in on 'Up the Junction' by Squeeze. 'Sally had two things in life,' one of their jaunty songs goes. 'Nothing to do and nowhere to go.' Sally makes the mistake of getting married too young. Domestic doldrums result. But then the song takes a dark turn. Her husband is violent and abusive. Sally gets beaten up. 'The problem with Sally,' we hear her husband complain, 'is when she's punched in the face, the bitch cuts so easy.' The Passmore Sisters have turned 'Up the Junction' into Lou Reed's *Berlin*.

'I should like to hear that sort of thing on the radio a lot more,' applauds Peel, who must have popped out for a coffee after the first verse. 'There's nothing strange or difficult about it . . . nothing alienating . . .'

Peel is unusually chipper tonight – he's heard the Bhundu Boys are back in the country – but the levity falters when he reveals that a band in Bristol have been trying to fix the Festive 50. This is believed to have happened on a previous occasion, in 1984, when the Blackpool band the Membranes, who aren't known for having thousands of fans, unexpectedly leapt into the 50 at number 6, with a single that hadn't even made the Top 10 of the independent charts. Peel had his suspicions, but nothing was ever proved.

This time, however, there can be no doubts. The Bristol band have sent in hundreds of postcards, all in the same handwriting, with the same songs listed in the same order on every one. Peel, entirely unamused, wants them to know that their votes have been disqualified. 'I shan't tell you who they are, but I think I shall always hate them after this.'

Eyes turn expectantly towards 1987 to see which Bristol band mysteriously disappears from Peel's running orders. The Flatmates? The Blue Aeroplanes? The Brilliant Corners? Mark Stewart and the Maffia?

John Peel Show
Radio 1
2 December 1986

Age of Chance – K-Rob – Ronnie Dawson – D.R.Y. Project – D and V – Earl Gaines – Mantronix – Pigbros – Abstürzende Brieftauben – The Beastie Boys – My Bloody Valentine – Extreme Noise Terror

In the light of new evidence from a former West Midlands police officer, MPs from all sides call for the home secretary to reopen the case of the Birmingham Six. The Northern Irish prisoners, who are serving life sentences for the Birmingham pub bombings of 1974, maintain that false confessions were beaten out of them by police.

To look at the make-up of tonight's programme, no one would ever think that 1986 had erupted in indie-versus-hip-hop name-calling earlier in the year. The Beastie Boys, a New York trio whose debut album (*Licensed to Ill*) came out two weeks ago, have blueprinted an audacious kind of rap-rock that lends new context to a lot of Seventies music previously considered repugnant. 'No Sleep Till Brooklyn', the track that Peel pulls out tonight, could – at least until Ad-Rock starts rapping on it – be a head-banging song by AC/DC. Among the other uncool rock giants that *Licensed to Ill* samples are Led Zeppelin and Black Sabbath. Heavy metal is abhorred by the indie generation, but the Beastie Boys have reclaimed its riffs without embarrassment. 'Open your mind to whatever sounds good,' they seem to be saying, 'and don't stress about categorising it.' Peel wouldn't go near an AC/DC or Led Zep album these days, but he can't resist *Licensed to Ill*.

Even a band on the *C86* cassette, Age of Chance, see a future in a mix-it-up culture, having engaged head-on with a piece of black funk from way outside their indie domain. Prince's 'Kiss' was an American number 1 single in April, and only a fool or a brave man would attempt a cover version of it. Age of Chance give it the boldest of makeovers, knowing they risk humiliation if they fail. They replace Prince's soft, spongey rhythm beds with a belligerent bass guitar and swap his kittenish falsetto for an agitated post-punk holler. They make a great big dirty row and leave messy footprints all over Prince's spotless cashmere rug. He'd resent the ugliness of it, but thousands of Peel listeners, who may very well find Prince's rampant libido as much of a turn-off as LL Cool J's, will vote it to number 2 in the Festive 50.

But the cacophony made by Age of Chance is as nothing compared to the sonic warfare produced by Extreme Noise Terror. A hardcore band from Ipswich, they begin cautiously, as if they need a moment to agree on a tempo for 'No Threat' (from an album entitled *Radioactive Earslaughter* that features them on one side and a band called Chaos UK on the other), before, after twenty seconds, simply putting their heads down and playing as fast as humanly possible. Their singer, more demon than man, spews out abrupt spasms of unintelligible vengeance in a voice midway between a roar and a vomit. It's an unbelievable minute and a half of music, justifying every one of the words in the band's name. Extreme Noise Terror will have a major impact on Peel's ever-changing tastes next year, as will a band of fellow travellers in the Midlands with another hard-to-live-up-to handle: Napalm Death.

Tomorrow night Peel has dancehall from Papa Biggy and Admiral Tibet; New York electro from Mantronix; a pinch-yourself Sonic Youth cover of Madonna's 'Into the Groove'; and Scandinavian folk music from Spælimenninir, a group who live and work in the Faroe Islands. It's another month of fearless mutation on the *John Peel Show*, and the flowers and fringes of C86 belong to a fleeting summer that now calls itself the past.

Don't they?

John Peel Show
Radio 1
30 December 1986

The Wedding Present – Big Flame – Billy Bragg – The Soup Dragons – Stump – The Weather Prophets – The Jesus and Mary Chain – The Shop Assistants – The Smiths – Primal Scream – Age of Chance

Harold Macmillan, the former Conservative prime minister (1957–63), has died at the age of ninety-two. He accepted a peerage in 1984, famously criticising Margaret Thatcher's handling of the miners' strike in his maiden speech in the House of Lords.

Sushil Dade is not a household name. A Scots Asian born in Glasgow to a family that migrated from a Punjabi village in India, Dade plays bass in the Soup Dragons. The odd half-page in the *NME* aside, they're not a band that have much in the way of a media profile. But Dade is worth mentioning, because for the past two nights he's been the only non-white musician on the *John Peel Show*.

There were times in the Seventies when Peel hosted all-white programmes. The Punk Specials in December 1976 and August 1977 were – as one might expect – bereft of black bands, and certain featured-artist shows, for example a Fairport Convention omnibus in the summer of 1976, were understandably low on black faces. Peel had promoted so much reggae and funk by then, and had enthused about black American blues records since first setting foot in a radio studio in Dallas as a twenty-one-year-old, that the occasional white-only programme here and there needed no comment.

But the two hours last night, and the two hours tonight, which have focused on the top twenty of the Festive 50 and hand-picked songs from Peel's favourite sessions of the year, have been to all intents and purposes an indie carve-up. The C86 bands have been rolled out for one more curtain call – back come the 14 Iced Bears, the Wedding Present and the Soup Dragons, along with Stump, Big Flame and the Weather Prophets – while the listeners have placed six songs by the Smiths, two by the Wedding Present and one each by the Shop Assistants and Primal Scream in the upper regions of their Festive 50.

As Peel, Walters and Kershaw sat in their cramped room in Egton House earlier this week, did neither of the other two think to comment on the stereotypical look of these two running orders? When Peel says tonight that he's heard a band from Finland who have recorded one of the best records he's heard in years, one longs for him to interrupt the Soup Dragons in mid-flow and put it on. The sessions he's repeating tonight, moreover, include four songs that have already featured in the Festive 50 lower down. It all makes for an atmosphere of rather annoying self-congratulation. Not to mention a two-hour show that grossly misrepresents Peel's programmes as a whole in 1986.

He can hardly blame the listeners for this, since three quarters of the show has been his own choice of music. But blame the listeners he will, almost two years from now to the day. He will tut-tut about their 'ultra-conservative' tastes, take them to task for ignoring black artists and reproach them with the remark that there's more to life – and much more to music – than indie bands strumming guitars.

If they were listening to his show on the night of 30 December 1986, they'd be well within their rights to retort that he has a very short memory.

1987: ONCE AGAIN WE WRONG-FOOT QUALITY CONTROL

> 'What do your children think of the music they hear you
> playing? Do they ever express an opinion?'
> 'Yes. It's unfavourable in almost every instance.'
> JOHN WALTERS interviewing Peel for the Radio 1
> series *Peeling Back the Years*

John Peel Show
Radio 1
27 May 1987

The Beastie Boys – LL Cool J – The Stupids – Jackdaw with Crowbar
– Ausgang A-Go-Go – Jimmy Reed – The Fall – C.I.A. – Sackgasse –
Sonic Youth – Admiral Tibet – Muslimgauze – The Sea Urchins

*The death of a twenty-eight-year-old mother-of-three from London
brings the number of fatalities in the* Herald of Free Enterprise
*disaster to 188. The woman had been in hospital with a broken neck
since being rescued from the stricken ferry, which capsized on 6 March
after leaving Zeebrugge harbour with her bow door open.*

The first five months of 1987 have seen some new names in the Top
40, including the Fall with an unlikely resurrection of a Northern
Soul classic ('There's a Ghost in My House'); Steve 'Silk' Hurley,

spearheading a new genre of dance music from Chicago called house ('Jack Your Body'); and Iggy Pop, first played by Peel on *Top Gear* in 1969 when he was in the Stooges, now making his UK chart debut at the grand old age of thirty-nine ('Real Wild Child').

Then there's a band that *Just Seventeen*, a teenage girls' magazine, predicted in December would make it big this year. Peel paternally disagreed, chuckling at the article on air. He should have had more faith. The band was the Beastie Boys, and their abrasive rap–metal single '(You Gotta) Fight for Your Right (to Party!)' reached number 11 in March. (*Just Seventeen* also predicted that leather trousers and 'not wearing any underpants' would be popular this year. 'I don't think I'm going to subscribe to that,' Peel grimaced.)

The Beastie Boys have since toured Europe with Run-DMC, generating exponential levels of notoriety that would leave the Jesus and Mary Chain gasping. The *Sun* and *Daily Mirror* have quoted Conservative MPs condemning the Beasties as 'diabolical creatures' and demanding they be refused work permits to tour the UK. Following allegations of drunken loutishness, the rappers have been banned by an airline and a hotel chain in America and accused of mocking terminally ill children in Switzerland (a claim they strongly deny). As hostility towards them intensifies, their two concerts at the Brixton Academy at the weekend were notable for the large numbers of police on horseback in the surrounding area.

This evening the three rappers have been guests on Janice Long's show, where they behaved surprisingly well. 'Extraordinary scenes,' Peel reports. 'There's our Janice talking to the Beastie Boys. Nothing destroyed, no one terrorised, none of *those* words. What can it all mean? Here's another reminder of how they started out.'

He plays 'Holy Snappers' from their 1982 EP *Polly Wog Stew*, recorded when they were a hardcore punk band. It's taken some chameleonic chutzpah on the Beasties' part to move from a white music style into a black one (while adding the guitar riffs of another white one), and it's a measure of their confidence as rappers that they haven't had flak from all sides. Peel, no doubt, would agree with the journalist Jack Barron, who wrote in the *Guardian* on Saturday: 'Since Live Aid, modern music has suffered from a tyranny of social conscience to the point where a musician's ability to spout quasi-political rhetoric is deemed more important than any sheer hell-for-leather enjoyment the music can invoke . . . And it's [their] dovetailing of styles, the crush collision between the black New York street beatbox rhythms of hip hop and white heavy metal guitar, that has made the Beasties' music irresistible to many.' Irresistible is certainly the word. *Licensed to Ill* has so far sold 4 million.

Peel plays hip hop almost every night now. He likes the debut album by Public Enemy, *Yo! Bum Rush the Show*, and one of his favourite songs this month is the new single by Eric B. and Rakim ('I Know You Got Soul'). Tonight he plays a darkly atmospheric twelve-inch by Witchdoctor and the Dominating Three MCs ('Kickin' It Live') and a track entitled 'My Posse' from an EP by the Los Angeles trio C.I.A., produced by a twenty-one-year-old Dr Dre and written by a seventeen-year-old Ice Cube. Peel is doing a lot more than simply regurgitating the same four or five names. But he's no match for a DJ like Dave Pearce, the host of BBC Radio London's Monday night hip-hop show, *A Fresh Start to the Week*. Pearce has emceed some of the biggest hip-hop events in London and will be heard whipping up the crowd on Public Enemy's next album, *It Takes a Nation of Millions to Hold Us Back*. It would be ridiculous to imagine Peel doing something like that.

As it happens, a new track tonight by LL Cool J – whose records he's been playing for about eighteen months – leads Peel to make a curious statement about hip hop. His words arrive with no hint of warning and seem to be a clumsy attempt to make a citizen's arrest for a crime that hasn't been committed yet. The consensus on LL

Cool J's new album, *Bigger and Deffer*, is that it's disappointingly tepid and not as hard-hitting as his debut LP, *Radio*. Some critics have been crestfallen to find a 'rap ballad' on the album ('I Need Love'), interpreting it as a blatant bid to appeal to mainstream soul fans. Peel has a different view of *Bigger and Deffer*, and it has nothing to do with its commercial production.

'Now that, I think, is awe-inspiring,' he says after playing a track from it called 'Go Cut Creator Go'. Then he adds: 'But there's a real problem with this LP and I don't know how I shall resolve it. Because most of the rest of the LP contains some of the most misogynist stuff I've ever heard in my life. Some of it really quite sickening, I think.'

Apart from a track with some unpleasant lyrics about a prostitute, *Bigger and Deffer*, some would argue, is no guiltier of misogyny than *Licensed to Ill*, which Peel thought was wonderful. And the Beastie Boys' album, to trace it back to its sources, was no more misogynistic, surely, than the AC/DC and Led Zeppelin records that it sampled. Peel himself played hundreds of disparaging songs about women in the Seventies without feeling the need to comment on them afterwards.

However, the Eighties are not a continuation of the Seventies but a decade with a separate identity, and Peel is not the same person that he was in 1975. The parameters of what he considers acceptable in song lyrics have contracted with age, experience and parenthood, and as the father of daughters aged nine and five, he's more sensitive to the ways in which men portray women than he once was. If there's one thing that ten years of punk, post-punk, indie and C86 have told him, it's that lyrics don't need to perpetuate hateful clichés.

It won't be LL Cool J, however, who has to defend himself in the media against accusations of misogyny. It will be the Beastie Boys who spend years living down their early raps, their frat-boy sexism, their go-go dancers in cages and their twenty-one-foot motorised inflatable onstage penis. None of these ever seem to matter to Peel. Is it because the Beastie Boys have paid their dues on the hardcore punk circuit?

Both the Beasties and LL Cool J will release their next albums in 1989. Once again Peel will take a firm stand. The Beastie Boys' *Paul's Boutique* – containing lines like 'I threw the lasso around the tallest one and dragged her to the crib' and 'With that big round butt of yours, I'd like to butter your muffin, I'm not bluffin'' – will meet every one of Peel's stringent requirements, receiving enthusiastic airplay for over a month. LL Cool J's *Walking with a Panther*, on the other hand, will be dismissed by Peel as 'a load of sexist codswallop' and get no airplay at all.

How fickle the judgement of the middle-aged hip-hop DJ. Itchy trigger finger but a stable turntable, as someone might say.

John Peel Show
Radio 1
9 June 1987

The Noseflutes – The Fat Boys – The Clash – Section 25 – SS-20 – Frankfurter – Phuture – Billy Bragg – Kool G Rap and DJ Polo – Pop Will Eat Itself – T-Coy – Unity Station – Davy D – Shirati Jazz

With two days to go before the general election, and an estimated 8,000 voters said to be undecided, Margaret Thatcher addresses a campaign rally in Harrogate, while Neil Kinnock is in Leeds. The latest opinion poll has the Conservatives twelve points ahead of Labour.

The Bristol band who tried to fix last year's Festive 50 have their identity revealed. They're called Unity Station and they sound like the Clash circa *Combat Rock*. Military fatigues and Strummer rasp. Paranoia in the Eastern Bloc. 'Our Man in Washington', taken from their new EP, rumbles with a fervour that almost brings on a Proustian rush. Unity Station would have stuck out like a sore thumb among the C86 quorum in the Festive 50; they should have tried fixing the one in 1982 instead. Peel can't keep holding a grudge, however, and he'll play 'Our Man in Washington' again in August to show there are no hard feelings. Who knows? Maybe someone will vote for it.

Steve 'Silk' Hurley's 'Jack Your Body' climbed to number 1 in January, where it stayed for two weeks, giving British schoolchildren, motorists, housewives, factory workers and office staff a taste of a sound they'd never heard on their radios before. Farley 'Jackmaster' Funk's 'Love Can't Turn Around' had been the first house record to make the UK charts four months earlier, but it came from the more soulful, discofied side of Chicago house. The other side is the stripped-back, machine-like sound, which is arguably more revolutionary. Peel didn't make either of those two records a hit, but the machine side of house seems to appeal to him as he goes searching for sounds that don't have precedents.

One such record is 'Acid Tracks' by Phuture, a Chicago group, which takes house (itself a partial descendant of electro) to the next stage in its evolution: acid house. At twelve minutes, 'Acid Tracks' is not remotely radio-friendly. As with house in general, most radio DJs would find it impossible to justify asking their listeners to sit through a metronomic, unchanging, endlessly looping piece of music of that length, assuming the DJ even liked it in the first place. Gone are the days when Peel would programme an entire side of a Tangerine Dream LP into a sixty-minute show.

Tonight he plays one of the two shorter pieces on the B-side of 'Acid Tracks', 'Phuture Jacks', sequencing it to follow a cover of Pink Floyd's 'Arnold Layne' that's been released on a tribute album to Syd Barrett. It's ironic that the Barrett song is comprehensively un-psychedelic (the band who perform it, SS-20, are regulation boy–girl indie) while 'Phuture Jacks' sounds dark, experimental and deeply avant-garde. And another track Peel plays tonight, 'Cariño' by the mysterious T-Coy, seems to suggest that DJs and musicians in Britain – the song comes from Manchester and features an ex-member of A Certain Ratio – are getting on board with Chicago house and applying its techniques to their own dancefloors.

Neither Phuture nor T-Coy will follow Steve 'Silk' Hurley into the charts. Peel is essentially playing club music on the radio tonight. The question is, does it make his listeners wish they'd gone to a club, or does it make them wish he'd play something else?

John Peel Show
Radio 1
15 June 1987

The Thieves – Ivor Cutler – The Marxist Brothers – The Mekons – The Stone Roses – Ripcord – L8 Connexion – Happy Mondays – Eric B. and Rakim – Beautiful Pea Green Boat – Aaron Allen

After its defeat in the election, Labour prepares for a return to the opposition benches when Parliament reconvenes. Margaret Thatcher is the first prime minister this century to lead a party to three successive election victories. Her majority is 102, down from 144.

The success of Frankie Goes to Hollywood ushered in something of a golden age for Liverpudlian pop. Following a bonanza of hits in 1984 for virtually every band the city could produce, the years 1985 to 1987 have brought commercial success for Dead or Alive, It's Immaterial, the Christians and Black. Some of their records would be a bit bland for Peel's tastes, but the proud Merseysider in him would tip his hat to their achievements none the less. He's always waved the flag for Liverpool as a music city.

All of which seems to leave Manchester, traditionally Liverpool's greatest rival, as a busted flush. The Smiths, New Order and Peel's long-time favourites the Fall are more popular than ever, but none of them are exactly young and thrilling. Morrissey is twenty-eight. Mark E. Smith is thirty. Bernard Sumner and Peter Hook of New Order are thirty-one. No significant band from Manchester has emerged via Peel's shows since he played debut sessions by James (a folky quartet) and Tools You Can Trust (an industrial post-punk duo) in the second half of 1983. James have since signed to Sire and lost their way. Tools You Can Trust last recorded a Peel session at the end of 1984.

So Peel is in no sense thinking of a Manchester renaissance when he features two of the city's newer bands tonight. On a track called ''Enery', Happy Mondays lay down a rainswept Britfunk groove with mad interjections at irregular intervals from their singer, who appears to be some kind of tone-deaf urchin. The track comes from an album with the extraordinary title of *Squirrel and G-Man Twenty Four Hour Party People Plastic Face Carnt Smile (White Out)*. Happy Mondays' label, Factory, isn't promoting them aggressively; its co-owner Tony Wilson doesn't even like them much. He's more interested in organising retrospective celebrations like last year's 'Festival of the Tenth Summer', when Manchester cast its mind back to the Sex Pistols gig in 1976 that kick-started the city's punk scene. All those years ago.

But Factory will wake up to the importance of Happy Mondays. A few months from now, some of the band's friends will return from holidays in Valencia and Ibiza. In their luggage will be tablets of a drug called Ecstasy. Happy Mondays will find that it fits perfectly with the Chicago house records played by DJs Graeme Park and Mike Pickering at Manchester's Haçienda nightclub. Ecstasy makes people lose their inhibitions, causing them to dance unstoppably. Manchester is going to come out of Liverpool's shadow and it will never look back mistily to 1976 again. But first the rest of Britain needs to catch up with the Haçienda, which will take at least a year.

In a different part of Manchester are the Stone Roses a band of C86 fans who have released one single ('So Young') in the four years they've been together. 'Sally Cinnamon', their follow-up, jangles and chimes like a more musically proficient Primal Scream. It's full of oranges, lemons, sugar and spice and rainbows. The Stone Roses missed the C86 bus and it's not clear whether the movement is alive or dead. Major labels in London snapped up some of the bands on the *NME*'s cassette, but the charts are so full of Whitney Houston and Johnny Hates Jazz that guitar bands need to sound like U2 on *The Joshua Tree* to stand any chance of breaking into the Top 75. And it helps if they can sing like Bono, which the Stone Roses cannot. Their paisley-patterned music sounds lost in a time warp.

Peel quite enjoys 'Sally Cinnamon', but says after it fades: 'Rather unpromising title. I was initially rather wary of something called "Sally Cinnamon". I mean, it seems to sum up the worst of that kind of late-Sixties whimsy. But a fine record, I think, in the event.'

Late-Sixties whimsy? Yes, it's doubtful that Peel would be in favour of a revival of that. Warning: may contain hang-ups, bad scenes and sparrows.

John Peel Show
Radio 1
29 July 1987

Loop – AC Temple – The Bhundu Boys – The Great Leap Forward – The Lemonheads – Benny Profane – Mahendra Kapoor – Miracle Legion – Gore – Bert Howell and His Show Band – The Smiths

*The Liberal Party and the Social Democratic Party (SDP) look set
to merge. David Steel, the leader of the Liberals, says the two parties
should unite and prepare for the post-Thatcher era. However, the
SDP's chief whip, John Cartwright, warns that his colleagues won't be
railroaded into a 'shotgun wedding'.*

'Once again we wrong-foot quality control to bring you the John
Peel wing-ding from the nation's number one.' Peel, who sounds
merry, has been for a drink with Andy Kershaw and Biggie Tembo
of the Bhundu Boys. He came away with an advance copy of the
Bhundus' new single, 'Jit Jive', their first since signing to the major
label WEA. But all is not well.

Listen to what happens when a band of subtle Zimbabwean tap-
estries and textures goes up in the world: a slick Eighties production comes in and crushes all the magical qualities that made them
special. The Bhundus have been saddled with a Go West drum
sound and a brass section from a Wham! record. Peel sizes 'Jit Jive'
up with vague incredulity, like a boy who asked for Mouse Trap and
got a mouse trap. 'As you know,' he says, 'I'm a great admirer of the
Bhundu Boys. But this doesn't sound much like them.'

It could be said that 'Jit Jive' is merely the latest unfortunate totem
of the dollar-chasing vulgarity of the music business. Buy indigenous art and turn it into an Athena poster. Isn't that why Peel has for
so long been pushing independent music, left-field music, different
music, *better* music? Isn't the whole point of Peel to promote a valid
alternative to the values and agendas of the major labels? We might
be surprised by his answer.

Kershaw has recently been to Amsterdam, where he bought Peel a
Chinese record as a gift. There's nothing Peel can tell us about the art-
ist or title, but it sounds like a Chinese Cilla Black singing a Chinese
'Love of the Loved' produced by a Chinese George Martin in the
Chinese Year of the Rabbit. All we need is a Chinese Morrissey to

tell us that the Chinese Cilla's early singles are woefully undervalued. Kershaw, the international traveller, is now mentioned in Peel's programmes as often as David Jensen was in 1982. 'I heard Andy play this.' Would this be to Andy's liking? Would this appear in one of Andy's shows? Is this the sort of thing that might interest Andy?

Kershaw would probably duplicate a good 40 per cent of tonight's show, which may or may not be a good thing. He'd certainly share Peel's fondness for 'Little Old Country Church House' by the bluegrass brothers Carter and Ralph Stanley, which Peel takes from a compilation called *The Stanley Brothers of Virginia Vol. 1*. Kershaw would also be interested in Peel's copy of *Sue Instrumentals 1959–67*, from which he plays an Ike Turner track. But quite apart from the music, Kershaw would surely envy the nonchalant, surreal dialogue that Peel is able to have with his listeners after so many years together. 'The mystery voice was Joe Bugner,' a listener in Epsom writes in to suggest. 'Pretty close, Phil,' says Peel with a laugh. 'Pretty close.'

Then there are the silly records that Peel takes a sudden shine to; the novelty records that Kershaw would see the humour in, but which Peel somehow seems to hold so much dearer. 'I would like to pretend,' he notes, 'that tens of thousands of people are writing in to say, "Hmm, John, *really* liking those tracks you're playing from that double LP of Australian records, *Antipodean Atrocities*." So far nobody's mentioned it at all . . . but I live in hope. This time it's Bert Howell and His Show Band. "The Aussies and the Yanks Are Here".'

Howell and his band, by now all presumably scattered to the wind, launch into a fanfare of pre-war clarinets and trombones as though preparing to meet Douglas Jardine's England cricket team off the boat at Sydney. Some of the other songs on *Antipodean Atrocities: 40 Terrifically Tacky Tracks 1930–1977* – to give it its full title – are sepia-tinged encomiums for Don Bradman, Captain Cook and the Queensland aviation pioneer Charles Kingsford Smith. These are songs that not even the drunkest or most desperate listener would have tuned in to hear. But Peel is like a dog with a bone when he gets hold of one of these compilations, and more atrocities from the Antipodes are bound to be forthcoming in the nights ahead.

'Free Africa', a single by Women in Music, is the second track Peel has played this week that has connections with a community group called the Islington Music Workshop. Their leaflet, which Peel reads out, states that female musicians are given a raw deal in every department of the industry. 'They're underrated, under-encouraged, under-recorded and under-promoted.' Women in Music aim to provide support, tuition and rehearsal space. Though Peel is the obvious DJ at Radio 1 for them to approach, he's also the one man they didn't need to send that leaflet to. One reason why the band he plays next, the Sheffield quintet AC Temple, have two female members is because the *John Peel Show* made it clear throughout the punk years that music belonged to women as much as men. It may, in a career full of quiet achievements, be the area in which Peel has effected the most change.

Ten minutes of the show remain when Peel turns his attention to today's announcement by Rough Trade that Johnny Marr has left the Smiths. It follows rumours in the music papers that he and Morrissey have had a falling out. Marr's departure surely means the end of the Smiths, so crucial is he as a guitarist and songwriter, but nobody seems to be officially admitting as much. As far as the public body language is concerned, it's a blow, but not an irrecoverable one. Johnny has his reasons. Life will go on. Peel, who sounds as though the news has taken him completely unawares, says: 'How this is going to work out, frankly I can't imagine. I prefer not to try and imagine it, I must confess.'

Although Peel is the DJ who brought the Smiths to Radio 1, he and Marr have never actually met. Furthermore, thanks to the hours he works and the schedules of the Smiths' UK tours, he's never had an opportunity to see them live. Maybe he hoped to catch them on their next tour. But he's enough of a fan to know that he's now missed his chance for ever. This isn't a blow. It's a bereavement. The Smiths, who reached out to so many and meant so much, are over.

'One of these situations when quite clearly they came together for the right reasons,' Peel concludes, 'and are almost certainly going in their separate directions for the wrong ones. And I'm sad to see it happen.'

John Peel Show
Radio 1
3 August 1987

Laugh – Criminal Element Orchestra – Heresy – Dog Faced Hermans – The Fall – Coldcut featuring Floormaster Squeeze – The Gap Band – George Trevare and His Dance Orchestra

Two doctors in a Cleveland child-sex abuse case have been given the backing of the Northern Regional Health Authority. Six children were returned to their parents after a High Court hearing last week, but the NRHA says it has no plans to suspend the doctors, who have been accused of misconduct and incompetence.

A listener from London is going on holiday to Wales. He promises to bring Peel back a Harry Secombe album. 'That's the kind of friendship that really counts with me,' says Peel warmly. 'When I get it, I shall file it next to this Australian double LP.'

Tonight's selection from *Antipodean Atrocities* is 'a grand paean of praise to our noble ally Josef Stalin', Peel reads aloud from the sleevenotes. Composed for a 1944 solidarity rally in Sydney, and performed by George Trevare and His Dance Orchestra with featured vocalist Joan Blake, it's a tune that exhorts Stalin to 'curl the mo' (curl his moustache with pride) because his Reds have 'helped to keep the red in the red, white and blue'. As an example of diplomacy, 'Curl the Mo, Uncle Joe' may once have made sense. As propaganda, it pushes its luck. Stripped of context four decades later, it defies rational analysis. It's possible that Peel hears something winsome in Blake's voice, or is tickled by the guileless way that the song ('one from what must be a limited catalogue in praise of Stalin,' he thinks) finds jolliness in the facial hair of a terrifying dictator, but whatever made Peel include it in the show, it hasn't scratched his itch. He'll still be finding tracks from *Antipodean Atrocities* to play in September.

Heresy are a grindcore band from Nottingham. The word 'grindcore' implies stealth, but the speed of the music is supersonic. The first song in Heresy's session, 'Flowers in Concrete', is like Billy Bragg fronting the world's fastest heavy-metal band. Peel was moved to comment on Heresy's 'squalid musicianship' in a recent live review for the *Observer* – and he wasn't being insulting, he was just stating a fact. The BBC producer Dale Griffin and his Maida Vale engineers deserve credit for getting this session down on tape, because Heresy's exceptionally tempestuous music can't be easy to record. Their guitars sound horrendous and the drums sound like massively amplified centipedes doing a clog dance, which only goes to show what a conscientious job Griffin and his technicians did.

Heresy's lead singer, John March, is more intelligible than most vocalists working in the grindcore genre. The lyrics of one song ('Sick of Stupidity') end with him blurting out the words 'squalid musicianship' – which makes Peel laugh in recognition – and in other songs the words 'shoes', 'disbelief', 'Alison', 'in your salad' and 'Bruno Bruno Bruno' are all distinctly audible. Heresy, indeed, seem to operate at the friendlier end of the grindcore spectrum. They recorded five tracks for this session, whereas Napalm Death – the definitive grindcore band, some would contend – will squeeze an incredible twelve tracks into their first Peel session next month. One of them, 'You Suffer', will last for just one second.

Peeling Back the Years
Radio 1
17 October 1987

John Peel in conversation with John Walters; music from Eddie and the Hot Rods – The Ramones – The Vibrators – The Damned – The Sex Pistols – Generation X – The Slits – Adam and the Ants

The clean-up continues after the severe storm that hit England in the early hours of yesterday morning. Hurricane-force winds caused substantial damage in several counties, uprooting millions of trees and leaving thousands of homes without power.

Peel, now forty-eight, has been at Radio 1 for twenty years. He's the only survivor from the pool of DJs who launched the station in 1967. As well as his weekly column for the *Observer*, he contributes articles to the *Radio Times*, that bastion of Beebness that is read in 11 million households. After a good run on *Top of the Pops*, he was dropped from the panel of presenters earlier this year (which doesn't seem to have disappointed him), but there's no immediate threat to his Radio 1 employment and he retains a programme on the World Service, given to him some years ago, in which he presents a half-hour digest of new music for BBC radio listeners around the world. Nobody would have believed it, but Peel is growing into the role of a senior statesman.

Confirming the fact that he's no longer a marginalised figure, Radio 1 has awarded him the accolade of a six-part series, *Peeling Back the Years*, that celebrates his two decades as a BBC broadcaster.

Interviewing him is John Walters, who guides him through the processes of sometimes hesitant steps and forgotten intentions that led him from Shrewsbury School to downtown Dallas; from *Kat's Karavan* to the Nation's Favourite; from Johnnie Ray to the Butthole Surfers.

Today's episode, the fourth in the series, looks at punk and Peel's reaction to it. Walters, fascinated by Peel's evasive replies and his lack of self-validation from one dimly recalled anecdote to the next, wants to pin him down to a watertight methodology that would explain why he hears music so differently to the common man. Peel resists Walters by either not following his premise or disagreeing with his conclusion. It's an entertaining *pas de deux*. The closest that Walters gets to teasing a mission statement out of Peel comes during a discussion about the Ramones.

Walters: 'What you said attracted you to the Ramones was really a kind of minimalist approach, getting it down to the basics . . . Is it really just the very basic, simple things in rock 'n' roll that you're about? The more sophisticated things become, the less you like it? Is that right?'

Peel: 'Yes, that is true. To a certain degree, that is true. Even things like the Pink Floyd's more complex numbers were still at the same time actually rather simple. You know, they were basically just the same tune played over and over again over the whole side of an LP, in essence. So the simplicity was the rule there as well.'

But the most telling comment from Peel in the series – and the one that seems to suggest that he's recently re-evaluated the nature of his job at Radio 1 – comes in episode two, when he tells a sceptical Walters: 'I think it's fair to say that I have, by and large, seen what I play on the radio as being . . . not so much an *alternative* to, but an *addition*.'

Waters must look at him askance.

'People always talk about [the *John Peel Show*] as an alternative programme,' Peel continues, 'and they talk about independent records and so on, as if there were something inherently *desirable* about being independent. As though this meant that the music was going to be *better*.'

'Are you really saying,' Walters challenges him, 'that right through those twenty years, you have *not* been trying to say, "Here's *my* sort of music, which is *instead* of the mainstream" . . .?'

Peel: 'Not at all.'

Walters doesn't sound convinced. And nor should he be. It's pure revisionism from Peel. Unquestionably, there have been periods when he's devoted airtime (for months and years on end, sometimes) to musicians who are anti-careerist, anti-commerce, anti-corporate and anti-mainstream; plenty of listeners will say that Peel still offers precisely the same service in 1987. He promotes music that sees itself not as an 'addition', but as an alternative and an antidote to the corporate Eighties. Music that regards its independence as 'inherently desirable', because independence is all that it has. If the Smiths weren't an alternative, then what the hell were they? And why was Peel so sad to see them split up?

Among the BBC personalities who have been marking the twentieth anniversary of Radio 1 is the chat-show presenter Terry Wogan – himself a former Radio 1 DJ – who recently invited the once unthinkable duo of Peel and Tony Blackburn onto his BBC1 couch to share a few one-liners and reminisce about old times. Peel and Blackburn, the sworn enemies of Radio 1 in the Seventies, are on cordial terms these days, all differences forgotten. 'He used to . . . out on the [pirate] ships, he used to have all those joss sticks going on,' Blackburn says, jerking a thumb at Peel. 'Yes, I did,' Peel says gravely, 'and that's not all, listeners, I'm afraid.' Drug references on *Wogan*? But their easygoing smiles defuse the danger. Two men who once loathed each other could now be described, at a push, as friends.

Wogan, turning to Peel, alludes to the famous photo of the DJs on the church steps in 1967. 'Look at that picture. You're the only one who's still on Radio 1. But if one was taking bets, one would have said that you were possibly one of the first to go.'

'This is true,' Peel agrees. 'If you had to pick somebody off that picture and say, "Which of these brutes isn't going to last five minutes?", you'd have said, "I'll have that one on the end."'

But who would discard him now? Relaxed, suntanned, one leg lazily draped over the other, Peel is the perfect chat-show guest. He's articulate, convivial, quick with his repartee. He's a totally dependable BBC pro, getting a big laugh from the audience when he protests to Wogan: 'I'm missing *The Archers* for this!' Not just a funny line, but a plug for Radio 4 too. You'd have this man on *Pebble Mill at One*, *Call My Bluff*, *Blankety Blank* and any radio quiz show you could name. You wouldn't stick him out in some midnight ghetto.

After all, Peel has never been an alternative to. He's more of an addition to.

PART THREE

MORE OF A CONVERSATION
THAN A MONOLOGUE

1988: GOODBYE TO ALL THAT

'I tend to analyse the way letters are written. Often the incidental
details are very revealing. Someone might write in and say,
"Hello, Bruno, just thought I'd drop you a line whilst I was doing
my homework." Already, that sentence has told you so much.'

BRUNO BROOKES

John Peel Show
Radio 1
18 January 1988

Bomb the Bass – The Woodentops – DJ Lebowitz – Bob – The
Wedding Present – Big Daddy Kane – Mighty Mighty – Stella
Chiweshe – Stitched-Back Foot Airman – Sugarcubes – Spoonie
Gee – The Rumbles – Blind Willie McTell – The Pogues

Prince Edward, the Queen's youngest son, is to begin work as a
production assistant for Andrew Lloyd Webber's Really Useful Theatre
Company. The prince, who dropped out of a Royal Marines training
course a year ago, conceived and organised the BBC TV programme
It's a Royal Knockout *last June, which was savaged by critics.*

In one of those Radio 1 directives that come down periodically from
on high and must be obeyed at all times without question, today has
been declared 'More Music Monday'. This means that all of the DJs

on the air today – Adrian John at 5.30 a.m., Nicky Campbell at 7 a.m., Simon Bates at 9.30 a.m., Gary Davies at 12.45 p.m., Steve Wright at 3 p.m., Bruno Brookes at 5.45 p.m. and Simon Mayo preceding Peel at 7.30 p.m. – have had to rein in their usual patter and cram as many records into their shows as possible. None of them is happy about it. Bates, who likes to spin out his daily 'Our Tune' feature to the length of a Boris Pasternak novel, would not have taken to reticence well.

'I understand there's been some sulking about "More Music Monday",' Peel begins brightly, 'so I've put together a good rockin' programme to cheer the guys up a bit.'

Nice idea, but he knows they won't be listening. They'll be off to bed, or holding court in Stringfellows, complaining to anyone who'll listen that Radio 1's management, policy unit and audience-research team should be sacked on the spot and a DJ put in charge. Look, they'll say, it isn't hard to see the flaw in 'More Music Monday': Bates, Davies, Wright and Brookes, who together form the spine of Radio 1's daily output, can all justifiably claim that it's their personalities, rather than the music, that make the listeners tune in every day in their millions. It's those chummy voices, daft quizzes, slushy dedications and crazy afternoon boys that make the British public cherish Radio 1 as a big, friendly, mirthful, jelly-shaped house of fun. Even Peel, the most music-focused DJ of all of them, tends to be at his best on the nights when he has most to say. 'Twice as Much Talking Tuesday' might be a better directive next time.

The Wedding Present, who Peel seems to believe might fill the void left by the Smiths if he plays them often enough, have a guitarist whose father was born in Ukraine. Normally the Leeds quartet play fast, wrist-cracking indie music, scrubbing at their guitars while their tall, beetle-browed leader David Gedge sings his agony-aunt stories of guilt and suspicion. For their fourth Peel session, however, the Wedding Present have stepped behind the Iron Curtain, drafting in two auxiliary members – a Russian-language speaker and a Ukrainian friend – and recording a set of traditional Ukrainian songs on accordions, balalaikas and mandolins.

It's an idea that could have backfired on them like 'More Music Monday'. But what's impressive is that they've found a way to perform the songs idiomatically (and with great gusto) while still sounding like the Wedding Present, even in a foreign language. The Ukrainian session goes over so well that they'll record another one in March. A year from now, they'll have a Top 30 album (*Ukraïnski Vistupi v Ivana Peela*) and a record company begging them to release 'Davni Chasy' ('Those Were the Days') as a single. Gedge, who refuses to hear of anything so opportunistic, might be wondering by then if he'll ever get that Ukrainian genie back in the bottle.

John Peel Show
Radio 1
2 February 1988

Twang – The Disappointments – Bing Crosby – Fantasy Club featuring J.R. – Cookie Crew – 27 Devils Joking – Bastard Kestrel – UT – Crucial Youth – Sugarcubes – Cud – The Primitives – STD – Doom – Sir Drew and Rapski – The Chesterfields – A. C. Marias

A group of gay-rights activists abseil into the House of Lords to protest at the passing of Clause 28 of the Local Government Bill. The controversial clause, which forbids local councils from promoting homosexuality in schools and libraries, was voted through the Lords earlier today by a majority of eighty.

'Presumably, when Clause 28 of the Local Government Bill comes into effect,' says Peel eight minutes into the show, 'I won't be able to play you this . . .'

The cosy bass-baritone of Bing Crosby floats atop a dinner-jacketed orchestra. Under twinkling stars and a silvery moon, the dejected singer finds himself alone. His thoughts turn to his beloved ('the happy spell of you now holds me tight'), for his beloved's gay love is the kind of gay love that Crosby adores. 'Gay Love' comes from an age when 'gay' had a quite different meaning. But can the BBC take that chance? Peel may think he's being satirical, but as the government reacts to tabloid panic about Aids, and as dark claims are made in the *Daily Mail* about Labour-controlled education authorities putting homosexual literature on the primary-school syllabus, perhaps the crooners of the Twenties will have to join Frankie Goes to Hollywood's 'Relax' in the BBC's *verboten* pile. And if 'Gay Love' contravenes Clause 28, then what about the scene in *Hollywood Victory Caravan* where Crosby shares a bed with Bob Hope? Where will it end?

In an episode of *Peeling Back the Years* last October, Peel remarked to Walters that he received 'a lot of letters' from listeners who'd written to him in 1985 and 1986 asking him to stop playing hip hop, but who were now writing to him again to tell him they'd become hip-hop converts. Tonight's show is a chance for those listeners to compare their feelings about hip hop then and now. Peel is repeating a 1985 session by the Cookie Crew, recorded when the two eighteen-year-old Clapham girls were Britain's callow answer to New York's sassy Salt-N-Pepa. They were unsigned and unknown. This week, their hip-house collaboration with the Beatmasters, 'Rok da House', stands at number 5 in the charts. From Peel session to pop stars – and before Salt-N-Pepa have had their first UK hit, too.

Back in 1985 the Cookie Crew's raps might have irritated a fair few indie fans who hadn't got to grips with the technicalities of content and flow yet, and who simply heard a lot of teenage boasting. It was a brave session to broadcast, but it didn't get the girls a record contract. It was at Maida Vale, funnily enough, where tracks like 'It's

Gotta Be Fresh' created the strongest impression. 'What a professional and pleasant duo,' Dale Griffin scribbled in his production notes on 28 April 1985. Peel reads that comment out tonight, knowing full well that Griffin, the former drummer in Mott the Hoople, isn't renowned for his compliments. If Peel has made a hip hop convert out of Griffin, the sky really is the limit.

The Cookie Crew – still unsigned – recorded another session for Peel in September 1985. They finally signed to the dance label Rhythm King in 1987, and are now so popular that they turned down Peel and Walters when they contacted them about the possibility of doing a third session. Everyone may be converting to hip hop, but clearly the girls don't see their target audience as being Wedding Present fans any more.

John Peel Show
Radio 1
30 May 1988

The Primitives – Colorblind James Experience – The Heptones –
Extreme Noise Terror – EPMD – Napalm Death – Earl Mallard and
His Web Feet of Rhythm – House of Love – Morrissey – Joe Smooth

ITV's twenty-seven-hour broadcast Telethon 88, *hosted by Michael Aspel, raises £21 million for charity. It's reported that a £1 million donation from the Department of Health and Social Security may have been an administrative error, and that the DHSS intended to pledge £10,000 instead.*

Even with a live review to write for the *Observer* each week, Peel doesn't get to as many concerts as he'd like. But last week he saw two on successive nights. Shirley Bassey at the Albert Hall was an emotional triumph for the iconic diva (and for Morrissey, whom Peel noticed in the audience), while Extreme Noise Terror at the Caribbean Centre in Ipswich was notable for the war zone of flailing fists that constituted the mosh pit at the front of the stage. Peel must surely have been the only person who attended both gigs. And certainly the only one at Extreme Noise Terror to have his wife and twelve-year-old son with him.

'They were like some previously unknown force of nature,' Peel marvels. 'People who had not seen them before – who were unfamiliar, like my wife – stood there open-mouthed.' Extreme Noise Terror's session from last November, which he's repeated twice, is now available to buy on an EP. He plays a track from it called 'False Profit', which is fifty seconds long, insanely angry, bewilderingly violent and full of the vomiting sounds that in grindcore pass for lead vocals. To go from 'Diamonds Are Forever' to this in the space of twenty-four hours must have shifted even the imperturbable Peel's paradigm on its head.

Napalm Death, who sometimes play in Ipswich on the same bill as Extreme Noise Terror, have three songs in tonight's show from their own Peel sessions EP. These EPs have come out on a label called Strange Fruit, owned by Peel's friend and manager Clive Selwood. Many listeners assume that Peel owns the rights to his sessions (and can even make money out of them), but as he has to keep explaining, the BBC owns the copyright and it's the bands who get paid, not him. It took Selwood six months to thrash out a commercial agreement with BBC Enterprises to take Strange Fruit this far. The Cure and New Order have allowed their old sessions to be released – 'anything for John', the Mancunians told Selwood – but other bands have been more elusive. Some are now so successful that getting them to agree to a modest deal with Strange Fruit would be impossible. Some just don't want to be reminded. Every musician on a session has to give written consent before it can come out.

The House of Love have been booked to record their first session next month. A guitar band on the Creation label, they have a trippy, kaleidoscopic sound that appeals to a certain kind of indie fan who longs for a band as meaningful as the Smiths and resents reading about rave culture in the *NME*. As clubs like Shoom and Future in London become mini-Ibizas, playing acid house and Balearic beats to euphoric crowds on Ecstasy, the ubiquitous smiley face seems to taunt the indie hold-outs for being in the wrong place at the wrong time. Why wear black jeans and listen to minor-key guitars, you intransigent reactionaries, when the new Utopia is on your doorstep? But there's an almighty gulf between the House of Love and the house of Chicago, and Peel is one of the few people who seem equally enamoured of both.

Only one thing bothers Peel about the House of Love. Their album has been sent to him on a new format that's become popular with a number of record labels. It's round and silver and it entails Peel, with Luddite trepidation, holding his breath and operating 'the compact disc machine'. New inventions in consumer audio are something that technophobic middle-aged DJs really don't need. Just as the indie diehards will be hoping that acid house soon blows over, Peel will want to see the back of these newfangled CDs as quickly as possible.

John Peel Show
Radio 1
27 July 1988

Botswana Defence Force Dance Band – House of Love – Ripcord – Tuff Crew – Carcass – The James Dean Driving Experience – The Wild Swans – Public Enemy – Amayenge – Thee Hypnotics – Dub Sex

Howard Marks, a Welshman arrested in Majorca on suspicion of masterminding a billion-dollar hashish-smuggling operation, speaks from Palma prison to protest his innocence. The forty-two-year-old admits to trafficking eight hundred kilos of hashish in 1973, but says he's had no involvement with drugs since then.

'Here's an inspiring letter from John Whitmore, who writes to me from Colkirk near Fakenham in Norfolk, saying in part: "When I was driving in my dad's car the other day, I got him to put on your show on the pretext that you sometimes play jazz records if somebody notable has died. Anyway, you then played some Extreme Noise Terror, and after a sort of stunned silence my mum goes: "It's a lot like Little Richard, isn't it?"'

Just in case Mrs Whitmore is listening tonight, Peel follows her son's letter by playing 'Vomited Anal Tract' by the Liverpool grindcore band Carcass, from their new album on Earache Records, *Reek of Putrefaction*.

John Peel Show
Radio 1
19 September 1988

Big Lady K – Shalawambe – Billy Bragg – Frankie Paul – The Waltones – Electro Hippies – Sugar Bear – Kool Moe Dee – The Railway Children – The Searchers – Nick Cave and the Bad Seeds – Baby Ford

At the inquest into the deaths of three IRA members in Gibraltar last March, a police witness claims the SAS marksmen who fired at them 'had no alternative'. In a TV documentary screened earlier this year, Death on the Rock, other witnesses suggested that the IRA members were unarmed and were shot while attempting to surrender.

Big Lady K's 'Don't Get Me Started' is a hip-hop twelve-inch from Riverside in California. Once, many lifetimes ago, Peel managed a psychedelic rock band, the Misunderstood, in the same city. There are no other similarities between the Misunderstood and Big Lady K. 'Don't Get Me Started' is so full of attitude and hubris that it comes with a warning to Peel that it may destroy his bass speakers. Big Lady K is fifteen.

The sessions tonight come from Billy Bragg – his sixth – and a band from Manchester called the Waltones. They're a beat group in a Sixties haze, with a melodic bassist who does most of the heavy lifting while the singer mopes around feeling sorry for himself. If they were twenty years older and less susceptible to despondency, they might be the Searchers, whose 1964 tune 'Saturday Night Out' is played later in the programme. The B-side of the immortal proto-Byrdsian chart-topper 'Needles and Pins', 'Saturday Night Out' could, until recently, be found on the jukebox that stood proudly in the Peel family home in Suffolk. They've now had to sell the jukebox, Peel explains, as they've been short of money. 'Children needed shoes,' he says.

Peel is suffering from kidney stones. He sounds wobbly tonight. Never shy about sharing details of health problems, he talks about the urine samples he's collected prior to going into hospital for his operation. After eleven years of starting his programmes at 10 p.m., he'll be moving to a new time slot of 8.30 p.m. next month, when Radio 1 changes transmitters and rebrands itself as 1FM. Peel has mixed feelings about the switch (some listeners might experience poor reception, depending on where they live), but what he won't miss are the late finishes. There are nights when he can't face the long drive back to Suffolk and spends the night at his mother's flat in Notting Hill. He tires badly in the last twenty minutes of some programmes, he admits, no doubt dreading the two hours on the M11 that await him.

Kidney stones? Cash-strapped? Gruelling motorway journeys? Shoeless kids? The picture that Peel paints of his life at the moment is a melancholy one indeed.

John Peel Show
Radio 1
28 September 1988

The Darling Buds – James – The Siddeleys – M. D. Shirinda and Family – Big Drill Car – The -Ists – Cerebral Fix – Dinosaur Jr – Three Times Dope – Plaid Retina – Mighty Sam – Unseen Terror

The British sprinter Linford Christie finishes fourth in the Men's 200 metres final at the Olympics in Seoul, South Korea. Christie, who won bronze in the 100 metres final four days ago, has since been promoted to silver medallist after the winner, Ben Johnson of Canada, failed a post-race drug test.

'To meet some of these audiences, like you do on the Roadshow, 25,000 people at a time, is quite incredible,' says Bruno Brookes in a new documentary, *One on One: 21 Years of Radio 1*. 'I really enjoy it. Because so many people turn up and they really are *with* you. Every single one of those people down there are fans of Radio 1. They like what we do. They like everything about it, and they go bananas.'

But now those fans must prepare for change. Peel's final 10 p.m. show begins with an announcement: 'If you're listening to Radio 1 on FM stereo between ten and midnight on the Radio 2 frequency, then from this Friday you'll only find Radio 1 between 98 and 99 megahertz. So make sure you're ready for the change this Friday, when Radio 1 starts its autumn schedule and Radio 1 FM will be between 98 and 99 . . .'

The eyes glaze over. The Nation's Favourite has never been good at making change sound exciting.

And sadly, one man's change is another man's terminus. Tonight is the end of an era for Peel listener Alan Proudfoot of Newcastle, who won't be able to pick up 1FM in stereo at 8.30 p.m. where he lives. He'd rather not hear Peel at all than hear him in mono. Another listener – in Swindon – writes to tell Peel that as 8.30 p.m. clashes with the football, he'll regrettably be saying goodbye too. None of Peel's listeners, unlike those of Bruno Brookes, 'Woo' Gary Davies and 'Stark Raving Mad' Steve Wright, had much enthusiasm for Radio 1 the way it was. But the last thing they wanted was for it to be any different.

Clive Selwood has released a double album on Strange Fruit called *21 Years of Alternative Radio 1*. It includes Jimi Hendrix, Procol Harum, Elton John, Jethro Tull, Lindisfarne and Queen – names that, as Peel rightly points out, don't seem terribly alternative now – before it then moves into the Eighties with New Order, the Smiths, the Pogues, the Wedding Present and the Jesus and Mary Chain. Looking down the tracklisting of the two discs is a bit like speed-reading the story of Peel's radio career since 1967. But although he plays a track by Echo and the Bunnymen tonight, *21 Years of Alternative Radio 1* is not an album that Peel seems to want to dwell on. The past is a foreign country and all that. Some artists on the first disc, once regarded as not commercial enough for Radio 1, have since become fixtures on Radio 2. It's no surprise that Peel would hesitate before endorsing their work. Can Napalm Death and Extreme Noise Terror expect, in that case, to be played by Jimmy Young and Gloria Hunniford twenty years from now?

No, but New Order, the Smiths and the Pogues will all be played on Jeremy Vine's Radio 2 lunchtime show. And it won't take twenty years.

John Peel Show
Radio 1
10 October 1988

Pixies – The Bizzie Boyz – 808 State – The Da Vincis – The Jairos Jiri
Band – The Butthole Surfers – Grand Groove – Soul Two – Big Drill
Car – Rob Base and DJ E-Z Rock – The Stupids – Cool House

*The Conservative Party holds its first conference in Brighton since being
bombed by the IRA at the Grand Hotel four years ago. The Special
Boat Squadron, the marine equivalent of the SAS, has been patrolling
the shoreline as part of a security operation that will cost an estimated
£1.4 million in extra policing.*

Peel began the year by playing 'Beat Dis' by Bomb the Bass, a
collage-style dance track created from twenty-five samples, including James Brown's 'Funky Drummer', songs by Kurtis Blow and
Afrika Bambaataa, and at least half a dozen TV and movie themes.
By the time Peel played it again in February, 'Beat Dis' was picking
up airplay on Radio 1's Saturday evening soul show. A few weeks
later it crashed into the charts at number 5, putting DJ culture front
and centre on daytime radio – and on the cover of the *NME*.

Like 'Rok da House' by the Beatmasters and the Cookie Crew,
'Beat Dis' was released on Rhythm King, a label that cemented
its reputation as Britain's fastest-growing dance imprint when
S-Express's 'Theme from S-Express' reached number 1 in April.
Rhythm King has since kept Peel furnished with all its releases
(such as Baby Ford's 'Oochy Koochy' in September), but he's also
explored a few avenues of his own. A couple of house compilations
in the summer, *Jackmaster Acid Trax* and *Jackmaster 3*, made him a
fan of the Chicago producers Joe Smooth and Fast Eddie, while a
track he played in September, 'Acid Off a Way', was a real find: an

underground British acid house record made by the Bristol-based production duo Smith and Mighty.

Peel puts two acid house tracks in tonight's show, and a third is also worth mentioning. First, from Chicago, comes 'Rock This Party Right' by Cool House, which was made at Underground Studios, where Joe Smooth and Fast Eddie record. The squelchy bassline that comes in after a minute is one of the signature sounds of acid house. If the arrival of the bassline is a sit-up-and-take-notice moment, Peel makes it doubly so by sequencing 'Rock This Party Right' after the frazzled punk-rock guitars of the Massachusetts trio Dinosaur Jr. Here's what's happening on one plane, as it were; and here's what happening on the other. What's the expression? You pays your money and you takes your choice.

The second acid house track tonight is 'E Talk' by the Manchester trio 808 State. Their name is a reference to the Roland TR-808 drum machine that's essential to acid house (as is the Roland TB-303, which makes the squiggly sounds and the basslines), and 'E Talk', with its busy polyrhythmic feel, is a good enough house track to have emanated from Chicago or Detroit. It comes from 808 State's debut album, *Newbuild*, which Peel started receiving requests, inquiries and phone calls about before it was even released. That could have been the band hyping it, of course, or it could be that something bigger is happening in Manchester than anyone in London realises.

Tomorrow night Peel will start playing a single released by a member of 808 State under his own name: A Guy Called Gerald. 'Voodoo Ray', conceived and produced with the Ecstasy-euphoric dancefloor of the Haçienda in mind, feels instantly new. Fluffier and sexier than anything on *Newbuild*, it picks up on the Latin influence of T-Coy's 'Cariño' but takes it in a more tribal direction. 'Voodoo Ray' is mysterious, spectral, dubby and has a unique musical fingerprint. Peel is playing one of the first classic British house tracks. And typically of him, he plays the B-side first – 'Rhapsody in Acid' – just to be bloody-minded.

The explosion in popularity of acid house will now dominate the remainder of the year. The Second Summer of Love first confuses and then enrages the attack dogs of the *Sun*, who this month are offering their readers smiley T-shirts and next month will be vowing retribution against Roland TB-303s and Ecstasy dealers ('Ban Acid Cult That Killed Our Girl', 'Shoot These Evil Acid Barons'). But the *Sun* will have to be fleet-footed to keep up, because acid house is about to evolve into rave, which has faster BPMs, more intense basslines and a more hardcore aesthetic.

This development is sure to prick the interest of Peel, who loves hardcore in all its manifestations. A father-of-four pushing fifty, he makes a highly unlikely rave fan: he's never taken Ecstasy, never been to Shoom and has no experience of illegal raves or warehouse parties. He's been playing acid house for the one purpose that none of its creators foresaw: to be heard in darkened student bedrooms between songs by Billy Bragg and records by Zimbabweans. But whoever Peel thinks he's playing acid house for, he's playing it. And as much as he presents no threat to Graeme Park or Mike Pickering at the Haçienda (who were spinning Detroit techno by Derrick May and Inner City while Peel lagged behind with his Rhythm King promos), there'll always be an intrinsic open-mindedness in Peel, a curiosity, that makes him want to stay abreast of acid, rave, techno and each new dance genre that comes along – even if he can't be an acolyte or a participant himself. It's the same impulse that made him take his wife to the Extreme Noise Terror gig in May. He may not have been in the mosh pit, but at least he was on the premises.

1989: THIS PARTY IS FAR FROM EXTINCT

'In New York it's just starting to get cool to spit on the bands. So Sonic Youth really appreciate getting spit on. It's like, you know . . . it's not cool in Seattle where we're from, but Sonic Youth, they know you like them if you're spitting on them.'

MARK ARM of Mudhoney to the audience at Manchester University, opening for Sonic Youth, 20 March 1989

John Peel Show
Radio 1
2 January 1989

Suicide – Skinny Boys – The House of Love – Carcass – The Verlaines – Soundgarden – Sandoz – Captain Beefheart and the Magic Band – Nirvana – Pépé Kallé and Nyboma – Culture – Mudhoney

The Pan Am flight from Frankfurt that exploded in mid-air two weeks ago may have been carrying mail sacks that had not been checked by airport security staff, it's reported. Authorities have yet to uncover a motive for the bomb, which killed all 259 passengers and crew on board. Eleven people in the Scottish town of Lockerbie died when parts of the aircraft crashed to the ground.

Five days have passed since the Great Reprimand of 28 December. Five days since Peel broke off from counting down the Festive 50 to put the listeners well and truly in their place. He didn't raise his voice. He didn't lose his temper. But he made it crystal clear – in his measured, headmasterly way – that they'd fallen well below the standards he expected of them. They were 'ultra-conservative', he said. They were either consciously or subconsciously racist, he implied. They'd failed to absorb the hip hop, techno, Soweto pop and dancehall that he'd been feeding them during the year, and had let him down by voting for one white indie band after another. 'Young lads strumming guitars,' he sniffed. Not good enough.

Five days later, he's still not over it. 'It was just so predictable,' he moans. 'I knew what was going to win even before I started doing it.' But whose fault is that? The listeners could just as easily counter that it was Peel, not they, who perpetuated the idea of 1988 as an outstanding year for guitar groups. Perched at numbers 2, 4, 8, 15 and 49 in the Festive 50 were the Wedding Present, a band whose music he'd promoted relentlessly throughout the year. At numbers 1, 9 and 18 were the House of Love, whose debut album he'd played religiously for most of the summer. And at 5, 7, 19, 29, 30, 39 and 45 were the American bands Dinosaur Jr, Sonic Youth and Pixies, whose respective LPs – *Bug, Daydream Nation* and *Surfer Rosa* – Peel had deemed epochal enough to be featured over the course of several weeks like long-awaited masterpieces. From Dinosaur Jr to My Bloody Valentine, the sound of the guitar was a core pillar of Peel's curriculum in 1988.

If these bands have now become a problem for Peel – not to mention his concern about the listeners' conscious or subconscious racism – he can always shift the balance of his programmes more towards 'black genres' and Roland drum machines in 1989. But in fact, just the opposite will happen. Tonight, a mere forty-four hours into the new year, he turns the spotlight on three American guitar bands, all from the north-western state of Washington, who will take US rock into its next phase and have a huge impact on the British music industry in the Nineties. Their names are Nirvana, Mudhoney and Soundgarden. And they don't own a Kool Moe Dee or Joe Smooth twelve-inch between them.

Mudhoney's debut single last summer, 'Touch Me I'm Sick', was a wild two-and-a-half-minute tantrum of sludgy guitars and unspecified social diseases. Peel liked it and played it, but he may not have realised that Mudhoney had a lot more up their sleeve. It will become apparent when they tour the UK in March what kind of values they stand for. Values like raw power, visceral excitement, maximum amp distortion, a true affinity with audiences and a deep attachment to a fuzzed-up, garage-punk heaviosity that makes people grin their heads off and lose their inhibitions. One could imagine somewhere like the Caribbean Club in Ipswich being more than moderately keen to book a Mudhoney gig at their earliest convenience.

The Mudhoney track that Peel plays tonight ('Need') comes from their import EP *Superfuzz Bigmuff*. It gives an intriguing clue as to what qualities Peel may hear in them. Slower than the average American punk song, and not as brutishly over-the-top as 'Touch Me I'm Sick', 'Need' has a humane, heart-tugging integrity that isn't a million miles from the Undertones' 'Teenage Kicks'. Mudhoney aren't ostensibly trying to start any revolutions on *Superfuzz Bigmuff*, but beneath their dishevelled everyman veneer they're pretty much the sound of American rock at a crossroads. To the left is post-hardcore. To the right is the college rock of R.E.M. and the Smithereens. To the rear are Bon Jovi, Mötley Crüe and a host of LA bands with poodle hair and sucked-in cheeks. And up ahead is a mountain over which nobody can yet see.

Soundgarden – who like Mudhoney come from Seattle – have a punk grounding too, but they've allowed themselves to be influenced by the monsters of rock. There are parts of their album *Ultramega OK* that could be Black Sabbath or Aerosmith.

Soundgarden recorded it for the California punk label SST, but they previously put out two EPs on a small Seattle label – Sub Pop – for which Mudhoney are the flagship band. Sub Pop is a name that Peel's listeners are going to get used to hearing. And Sub Pop, even 4,700 miles away, is well aware of the importance of Peel.

'And here's another new band from Sub Pop Records,' he announces two thirds of the way into tonight's show. This record has the heaviness of Soundgarden, the scruffy fallibility of Mudhoney and something else besides: a vulnerable crack in the singer's voice that sits oddly with the muscular guitars, bass and drums. This is 'Big Cheese' by Nirvana, the B-side of a debut single ('Love Buzz') that Sub Pop released in the States last November. Nirvana, unlike Mudhoney and Soundgarden, don't come from Seattle – but that's not going to stop people from saying and writing that they do. So much will be said and written about Nirvana, indeed, that their origins will take on almost folkloric proportions.

'Chris [Novoselic, bass] and me are from Aberdeen, which is a really dead logging town on the shores of the Pacific Ocean,' their singer Kurdt Kobain (sic) will explain to Sounds magazine later in the year. 'The nearest town was Olympia about fifty miles away, which is where we've moved to.' Nirvana are the baby band on Sub Pop. The Sounds article will describe them as 'the natural descendants of Mudhoney and Dinosaur Jr'. It will also serve notice of 'the beautiful yet horrifying voice' of the twenty-two-year-old Kobain.

Peel first encountered Sub Pop two years ago, when it put out a sampler album called Sub Pop 100. He didn't play much from it, and it had already been out in America for some months by the time it reached his turntable, but even one or two belated mentions would have sounded sweet to the ears of Sub Pop's founders Bruce Pavitt and Jonathan Poneman. And the best is yet to come. Now that Peel has a clearer idea of who Mudhoney are – and has heard Nirvana – he sits down at his trusty Olivetti and starts to type.

'Right around Christmas of '88,' Pavitt will later recall, 'we released a three-record box set with this gorgeous booklet called *Sub Pop 200*. It sold out immediately. We did 5,000 pressings, but the real payoff was John Peel writing a review in the London *Observer* in February of '89, in which he stated that Sub Pop "had the most distinctive regional sounds since Tamla Motown". That is a statement. That is a huge endorsement by possibly the most influential person in alternative music on the planet.'

By the middle of February, Sub Pop is getting more airplay on the *John Peel Show* than any other record label in the world.

John Peel Show
Radio 1
27 February 1989

The Wonder Stuff – Happy Mondays – S.O.B. – Outo – Lip Cream – Eric B. and Rakim – Happy Flowers – Bad Dream Fancy Dress – The Justice League of America – Shonen Knife – The Terminators – Thule

A delegation of British Muslims meets the Home Office minister John Patten to urge for the banning of Salman Rushdie's novel The Satanic Verses, *which has been the subject of worldwide protests and book burnings. A fortnight ago the Ayatollah Khomeini pronounced a fatwa on Rushdie, who is now in hiding.*

Meanwhile, in Manchester, the party rages underground. Reports from local journalists have fuelled rumours in London that the northern city's music scene is about to break nationally. Factory Records are at the helm of it, and the Haçienda's acid-house nights have changed the complexion of grey Manchester from a pallor to a flushed fluorescent pink. The connection between Factory, the

Haçienda, acid house and the city's riot of colour is a six-piece band that recorded its first Peel session three years ago.

Happy Mondays, in April 1986, would have been nobody's idea of messiahs pointing the way towards a new rainbow-hued reality. They were more like a gang of hooligans who'd hijacked a car, hightailed it to London, jemmied their way into Maida Vale and recorded four songs for Peel before the police got there. But their second album, *Bummed*, which Factory released last November, won them a lot of critical respect with its swirling, leering grooves and its dark, dingy aura. Happy Mondays are a shopping-precinct funk band with an intimidating face, and the songs on *Bummed*, which reference gangster movies and Hogarthian women, are as sensory as a headbutt and as hallucinatory as a sleep disorder. Peel liked it very much, the way someone would like a well-taken photograph of a bull terrier with blood on its jaws.

As everyone in Manchester knows, Happy Mondays are swimming in drugs, especially Ecstasy, which helps one of them – the maraca-shaking dancer Mark 'Bez' Berry – to keep moving even when the music stops. Shaun Ryder, the hunchbacked, hook-nosed singer, and his flinty-eyed brother Paul, the bassist, are two of the other principals to look out for onstage, but it's not unknown for the band to have assorted guests clambering up to join them, which can make distinguishing the musicians from the stage invaders difficult. One frequent intruder, a middle-aged man with a grey ponytail, is the Ryders' father, a former semi-professional comedian and joke writer for *The Two Ronnies*. You couldn't make it up.

Peel got his first look at Happy Mondays when they played the London Astoria in early December. He mentioned them the following night on a weekly show that he records for the British Forces Broadcasting Service (BFBS), which goes out to troops stationed in Germany. 'Very good they were, too,' he said of Happy Mondays. 'Of course, there were some very dangerous-looking lads who hang around with them, and sort of tend to rather dominate the stage later in the evening. The band disappear and these people carry on without them. Disconcerting-looking boys, I must say.' The soldiers in Germany must have been nonplussed. What on earth is happening back in England?

Tonight is Peel's first airing of a new Happy Mondays session, which features re-recordings of two songs on *Bummed* ('Mad Cyril' and 'Do It Better') as well as a new version of a 1987 single ('Tart Tart'). The session was recorded with Dale Griffin only six days ago, so Peel has clearly been impatient to put it on the air; there'd normally be a wait of two to three weeks. But there are reasons for wanting to hurry, because 'Wrote for Luck,' the band's recent single, got to number 7 in the independent charts – their biggest seller to date – and in December they supported New Order at the 12,000 capacity G-Mex Centre in Manchester, a concert awash in London media. Perhaps Peel felt a familiar sensation when he saw them at the Astoria – a sense of things spiralling out of control? – that made him want to put some music down on tape while he could. If Manchester is poised to break, as the media are saying, he might not get another chance.

'I wouldn't say we were ahead of our time,' Shaun Ryder suggested to a *Melody Maker* journalist in November, in a two-page article that Peel will certainly have read. 'I can't say there's no one quite like us, when I know whose music we rip off. We rip off everybody! No exceptions! I can't tell you who, though. Paul Daniels doesn't give his secrets away, does he?'

There are more questions than answers with Happy Mondays at the moment. Is their music the sound of what Manchester hears on Ecstasy? Did Bez dance to the songs with his maracas when Dale Griffin recorded the session? Was the studio invaded by dangerous-looking associates? What's that threshing-machine noise on 'Tart Tart'? Whatever the secrets that Ryder won't reveal, Peel will repeat the session three times as Happy Mondays' name spreads between now and December.

John Peel Show
Radio 1
22 June 1989

Pixies – Doctor and the Crippens – Cocoa Tea – Fish Karma – Can – The Pastels – The Fall – Norman Cook – Thriller U – Tar – Nirvana – Mega City Four – Concrete Sox

The press officer of the Football Association, Glen Kirton, gives evidence before Lord Justice Taylor at the Hillsborough Stadium Disaster Inquiry. Ninety-six people died and hundreds were injured at the FA Cup semi-final between Liverpool and Nottingham Forest on 15 April. The inquiry also hears from Dr Wilfred Eastwood, an engineer whose company carried out construction work on the stadium in 1986.

Peel has been sent the first album by Nirvana, just released in America. It's called *Bleach*. 'This is an LP you're going to come to know and love, I think,' he said last night, playing 'Love Buzz', the fifth track on side one. Tonight it's the turn of the morbid song that follows it, 'Paper Cuts', an interior monologue of a boy who has either been kidnapped or has barricaded himself into his bedroom and severed contact with humanity. On Tuesday it will be the sullen, teacher-hating 'School'. On Wednesday Kurdt Kobain will point a sociopathic finger at ultra-masculine authority figures ('Mr Moustache'). Nirvana's debut album takes teenage angst into whole new realms.

Peel will play tracks from *Bleach* for about a month. It only cost $600 to record, but the band had to endure a frustrating delay while

Sub Pop scrabbled together the money to press it up and release it. When a label works within the narrow margins that Sub Pop does, Peel's consistent promotion of Nirvana in the UK is beyond price. And he plays *Bleach* every week on his BFBS show, too, so that the troops in Germany can get acclimatised to that beautiful yet horrifying Kobain voice. There are nights when a soldier listening to *John Peel's Music* on BFBS is as well-informed about the Seattle sound as any reader of the weekly music papers.

'I do hope they come over here,' Peel says of Nirvana tonight. 'I'll make sure I don't miss them. Mind you, I said that about Mudhoney.'

Well, yes. Contriving to miss Mudhoney in March was unfortunate. On most of their dates they opened for Sonic Youth, taking the stage at around 8.30 p.m., just as Peel was starting his programmes at Egton House. But he could have seen them headline a Friday night at the Fulham Greyhound if he'd wanted to; and he could have driven to any one of three shows in London, Portsmouth or Leeds when they returned to Britain in May. He would have been an honoured guest. Mudhoney would have shown their appreciation by showering beer over him in the dressing room, and they don't do that to just anybody.

And when Mudhoney arrived in London off the ferry from Holland, what was the first thing they did? They recorded a Peel session, of course. Peel prioritises the Sub Pop bands, and the Sub Pop bands prioritise Peel.

John Peel Show
Radio 1
8 August 1989

The Ramones – Victim's Family – Elle – MC 900 Ft Jesus with DJ Zero – Dub Syndicate – Loop – Pixies – Intense Degree – Daisy Hill

Two England cricketers contracted to play on the rebel tour of South Africa have withdrawn from the squad. Phillip DeFreitas of Lancashire and Roland Butcher of Middlesex, who are both black, had received strong criticism from black sportsmen and women in Britain. Their withdrawal is welcomed by anti-apartheid organisations.

Besides Mudhoney, Peel has played new sessions this year from Sonic Youth (in March), Dinosaur Jr (May), Soundgarden (June) and the Pixies – the Boston band whose *Doolittle* album, released by 4AD in April, stunned the indie sector by reaching number 8 in the national charts. The Pixies' session was their third. Their second, broadcast last October, was a sort of mini-demo of *Doolittle*, recorded at the Golders Green Hippodrome a few days before they flew home to Massachusetts to start making the album. When *Doolittle* was finished, Peel was allowed by 4AD to play most of the album's fifteen tracks in a two-week period prior to the 18 April release date. His listeners have grown accustomed to being spoiled with Pixies exclusives. In March, a couple of fans phoned the studio after Peel played the new single, 'Monkey Gone to Heaven', and asked him to play the B-side as well. No doubt so that they could have the songs next to each other on a tape.

Tonight, as Peel plays their cover of Neil Young's 'Winterlong' from a new compilation album (*The Bridge: A Tribute to Neil Young*), the Pixies are in Cleveland, four dates into the American leg of an exhausting eight-month tour. They may no longer be speaking to each other backstage, but career-wise they're riding high on critical acclaim in Europe and college-radio support in the States. Peel is just one of many cogs in that machine, but it shows how much the Pixies value him that the session they recorded in April (which they didn't need to do by any commercial measure) was, like Mudhoney's in May, virtually the first activity they undertook on setting foot in England, before meeting the press, before playing a gig.

John Peel Show
Radio 1
14 August 1989

Doctor and the Crippens – The Only Ones – Schoolly D – The
Vivians – Ian McCulloch – The Orchids – The Together Brothers – Big
Black – Lieutenant Stitchie – Happy Flowers – Inspiral Carpets

*The chief constable of West Midlands Police disbands his entire Serious
Crime Squad after repeated allegations of incompetence, corruption
and fabrication of evidence. Almost fifty officers are transferred or
suspended. A number of prosecutions brought by the Serious Crime
Squad since the Seventies, including some that led to prison terms, will
now be reviewed.*

The narrative of Peel and US alternative rock goes back several
years; it certainly didn't start with the Pixies. He's been championing Sonic Youth since their 1983 debut album *Confusion Is Sex*,
when they were sticking screwdrivers down their fretboards to get
the unearthliest guitar sounds imaginable, and he was mesmerised
in the mid-Eighties by Big Black, a piledriving Chicago trio with
a drum machine whose taboo-flouting 1987 album *Songs About
Fucking* Peel always had to take special care when announcing. (He
called it 'Songs About You-Know-What'.)

Big Black's singer-guitarist Steve Albini is a fast-emerging Jimmy
Page, producing the Pixies' *Surfer Rosa* last year with a grasp of room
ambience and bass-drum dynamics not heard since *Led Zeppelin
II*. Albini disbanded Big Black two years ago, but Peel has never
officially stopped playing them. Tonight he goes back to their first
album, *Atomizer*, for the tense, gripping 'Kerosene', a song about
a man so bored by life in a provincial town that he decides to set
himself on fire. The prolific Albini will work on literally hundreds

of albums over the next fifteen years as a musician, producer and engineer. Peel can't promise to like all of them, but he'll do his best to publicise as many as he can – and he'll always listen to them. It's a deal that most prolific artists would be happy to shake on.

'He listened religiously to every single record he received in the mail, devoting hours every day to the task,' Albini will tell a Melbourne music conference in 2014, ten years after Peel's death. 'I sent him a copy of the first album I ever made and not only did he play the record on air, he sent me back a postcard with a personal remembrance of Chicago, of visiting a matron aunt as a child in Evanston, the suburb where my post-office box was kept. I treasured that note as the first indication that John Peel was a great man.'

Asked by *GQ* magazine in 2010 if anybody could ever fill Peel's shoes, Albini will begin his 231-word answer with the word 'No'.

John Peel Show
Radio 1
29 August 1989

New Order – The Rainkings – Wrecks-N-Effect – The Telescopes – Home T., Cocoa Tea and Shabba Ranks – The Sundays – Abdul Tee-Jay's Rokoto – My Bloody Valentine – Cud – Das Damen – 808 State

Inquests into the deaths of six victims of the Marchioness *disaster are opened and adjourned. It's now nine days since fifty-one people were drowned in the Thames when the* Marchioness *riverboat, which was hosting a birthday party, collided with a dredger near Southwark Bridge.*

John Walters turned fifty in July. This morning Peel did the same. An aggregate of a hundred years of life experiences and obsessive record-collecting between them. Two men born before the war (only just in Peel's case) and still this droll pair of idealistic cynics with beards and gloomy dispositions continue to set the musical agenda for a listenership less than half their age.

Next week Peel will be on the cover of the *NME*, a man as old as their father saluting the readers with a bottle of beer in his hand. Yesterday Radio 1 marked his final day as a forty-nine-year-old by bumping him off the air in favour of a Bank Holiday special hosted by the reggae presenter Ranking Miss P. The station now has a reggae presenter. Peel and Walters could probably share a wry smile about that.

'Unlike most of his colleagues, he does not gallivant around in a whirl of inane self-publicity and lucrative supermarket openings,' the monthly music magazine *Q* wrote of Peel in 1986. 'Last year he earned about £40,000. Mike Read makes that much from about ten gigs.' It went on: 'He speaks of his awards, not as an accolade to himself, but as a "terrible indictment" of the other DJs.'

And now he is fifty. This evening's programme has been pre-recorded, it will later emerge, because Walters needs to get Peel away from Egton House and whisk him off in a taxi to west London. The listeners, unaware of Walters's ruse, simply hear a fast-paced August programme that moves from New Order to new jack swing, and from Jamaican dancehall to the street music of Sierra Leone. The dancehall track – 'Stop Spreading Rumours' – features the gravelly scowl of a twenty-three-year-old newcomer named Shabba Ranks. A lot more will be heard of him.

It's a brisk show with few digressions from Peel. In April, Radio 1 cut his programmes back from two hours to ninety minutes, and he's tended to keep his introductions short ever since. To make the loss of the half-hour more palatable, he was given Thursdays back after losing them in 1984 to Tommy Vance's *Into the Music*. Vance, who will be fifty next year himself, remains the presenter of *The Friday*

Rock Show, the programme that ended Peel's run as a five-nights-a-week broadcaster in 1978. Peel will never scale those heights again. With four children, he probably wouldn't want to.

As a result of their reduction to ninety minutes, the shows have had their sessions halved from two per night to one, a serious blow to young bands around the country. One trio from Leeds called the Pale Saints recently circumvented this problem by getting a friend – who happened to be David Gedge of the Wedding Present – to phone Peel in the middle of a programme and urge him to pencil in a Pale Saints session without delay. It's nice to have influential friends, but it must have been galling for bands on lower rungs of the ladder, who simply don't have those kinds of connections to fall back on.

As this programme goes out, Walters shepherds Peel under false pretences to Subterania, a venue under the Westway flyover in Ladbroke Grove, where an audience has gathered and a surprise birthday concert is about to start. Peel enters to cheers and backslaps. The Fall have come down from Manchester to play for him, and the Wedding Present, who appeared at the Reading Festival three days ago, are also on the bill. The special guests were supposed to be the Undertones, reconstituted for one night only to send Peel sobbing off into the night with the sound of 'Teenage Kicks' ringing in his ears. But they've had to cancel due to a death in the O'Neill family, and what might have been an awkward reconciliation between the O'Neill brothers and Feargal Sharkey will now not be taking place. The House of Love have stepped in as replacements. They're a band on the up, but 'Destroy the Heart' and 'Christine' hardly pack the same emotional punch as a teenage dream so hard to beat. Peel is too polite to show disappointment and the House of Love are too polite to ask him why he had a problem with them winning the Festive 50.

'This party is far from extinct,' announces The Shend from the Very Things, emceeing for the night, in his finest Karloffian voice. 'Throw a few shapes. Cut a rug. Please welcome the Fall.' Peel is probably having too good a time to notice all the white boys strumming guitars. The House of Love and the Wedding Present, thanks to his crucial support over the past two years, are currently recording their first albums for major labels. They may be guitar bands, but they're technically no longer indie ones. The blessing of Peel secured their upgrade. Now the rest is up to them – not forgetting their producers, their A&R men, their radio pluggers and the marketing departments of Phonogram and RCA.

John Peel Show
Radio 1
31 August 1989

Ultramagnetic MCs – Nat Couty and the Braves – The Butthole Surfers – Where's the Beach – Sofa Head – The Aggrovators – Happy Mondays – A Witness – Happy Flowers – SNFU – Tuff Crew

The sixteen-year marriage of Princess Anne and Captain Mark Phillips is over. A terse statement from Buckingham Palace notes that the couple have decided to lead separate lives. The princess will remain in residence at the family home of Gatcombe Park in Gloucestershire.

Peel has developed a passion for the work of a bizarre duo from Charlottesville, Virginia, called Happy Flowers. They have a similar name to Happy Mondays (who also appear in tonight's show), but a radically different concept and approach. Happy Flowers are the architects of a new genre best described as infantilist post-hardcore. One of them, the guitarist and singer, calls himself Mr Anus. The other, who plays drums, is Mr Horribly Charred Infant. Their songs are twisted stories of freak accidents around the home, often involving pets and usually containing lots of screaming.

[439]

A couple of weeks ago Peel played 'Just Wait Till I'm Bigger Than You', from the duo's compilation *Too Many Bunnies (Not Enough Mittens)*, which sounded like a boy with a penny whistle being beaten senseless by a boy with an enormous bass drum. 'Some sort of anthem for our children there, I think,' Peel said ruefully, possibly meaning his own. Tonight he goes for the feedback-drenched 'Bobby Made Me Eat a Frog', the hysterical panic attack of a toddler who has had a live amphibian forced down his throat and is terrified that surgeons will have to cut his stomach open.

Other tracks on the compilation include 'I Want My Tooth Back', 'The Vacuum Ate Timmy', 'Why Didn't You Tell Me You Were Bringing Home a Baby?' (sung from the point of view of a boy who thought his parents were going out to buy a puppy) and 'I Don't Need Another Enema'. When Happy Flowers are around, the traumas of the nursery become the lifelong grudges of adulthood. If their songs should suddenly take off with the listeners, December could see the most childish Festive 50 in history.

John Peel Show
Radio 1
20 November 1989

The Jactars – The MD Connection – Happy Mondays – Majority of One – Arabian Prince – Toumani Diabaté – Kevin Seisay – The Adventures of Stevie V – I, Ludicrous – Gary Clail and the On-U Sound System – Elvis Hitler – Fire Party – Twin Hype

The Court of Appeal hears from journalists seeking to overturn a government ban on interviews with political and paramilitary groups in Northern Ireland. Members of Sinn Fein, the IRA, the Ulster Volunteer Force (UVF), the Ulster Defence Association (UDA) and

seven other organisations are currently prevented from speaking on
British television and radio, a rule condemned as 'an unprecedented
interference with free speech in this country in peacetime'.

This week Manchester's music scene exploded nationally. There were
first-time Top 30 entries for the Stone Roses ('Fools Gold'/'What
the World Is Waiting For') and Happy Mondays (*Madchester Rave
On* EP), both of which will climb several places next week. Three
days from now, the two bands – henceforth forever conjoined in
the public's mind – will appear on *Top of the Pops* in a Mancunian
double whammy that will take on a symbolic meaning as more and
more magazines and newspapers write about it.

Peel has lost Happy Mondays to a baleful new world of Madchester fashion spreads, speak-like-Shaun-Ryder glossaries and tabloid gossip-column stitch-ups. Ryder and his cohort Bez are drilling
their way into the culture as figureheads of a hedonistic, apolitical,
non-stop-partying, ducking and diving, live-today-for-tomorrow-
we-die lifestyle that will see one of them end up with gangrene,
the other one end up a crack addict and both of them end up as
contestants on reality TV shows. Peel will keep playing their new
releases right up to 1991, until eventually he, like almost everyone
else around them, gives up in exasperation.

The Stone Roses released their debut album in April. Widely
agreed by critics to be the runaway album of the year, it left Peel
cold – too melodic? too bombastic? – and he pointedly declined
to play any songs from it while other DJs and tastemakers spent the
summer singing its praises. Whatever fleeting interest Peel had in
the Stone Roses in 1987 has now completely evaporated. They've
become another of his blind spots, like R.E.M., Depeche Mode and
Patti Smith. This is the man who preferred Donovan to Bob Dylan,
and he prefers the Inspiral Carpets – a band from Oldham who
dress in Manchester's ubiquitous rainbow uniform of flared jeans

and baggy tops – to the much more exalted Roses, whose popularity he finds mystifying.

The listeners will have their revenge on Peel, however, when they vote five Stone Roses songs into the Festive 50 next month, including two in the top ten. He grudgingly admits that one of them ('Made of Stone' at 17) has 'agreeable singalong potential', which for Peel is like conceding that Dylan's *Blood on the Tracks* is quite well written, but otherwise he's no more impressed by the listeners' choices this year than he was twelve months ago. Young lads strumming Jackson Pollock splatter-painted guitars are still young lads strumming guitars. In a chart dominated by Manchester anthems and American alternative rock, there's scant recognition of a life beyond sliced-up eyeballs and Joe Bloggs sweatshirts. And with Mudhoney only showing once in the chart and Nirvana not featuring at all, the tastes of Peel and his listeners appear oddly dislocated after Seattle looked like it might unite them in the spring.

Nirvana finally made it to Britain in October, playing seven gigs in an eight-day spree that took them to Newcastle, Manchester, Leeds, London, Portsmouth, Birmingham and Norwich. Peel missed every one of them.

1990: LION ROCK IN LYON TRAFFIC

*'I didn't come up out of trying to be cool and all that. We came
out of the streets, the struggle. There is a lot of pain, struggle,
death, tears and blood in our music, and real people recognise
real.'* GAWTTI of the Boo-Yaa T.R.I.B.E.

John Peel Show
Radio 1
18 January 1990

The Would Be's – Code 3 – Moving Targets – Abana Ba Nasery –
Galaxie 500 – The Orb – Bastro – Anthony Malvo and Collin Roach
– Jellyfish Kiss – Frankie Bones – Zulu Warriors – Friction

*The Community Charge – the so-called Poll Tax – will come into force
in England and Wales on 1 April after a vote in the Commons narrowly
goes the government's way. The controversial tax, which replaces the
current rating system with a fixed charge per adult resident, has been in
force in Scotland since last April.*

Peel ended the Eighties just as he began them. Alerted by a listener
in Bristol (who evidently keeps some sort of elaborate filing system), he wrapped up his final show of the decade on 28 December
by playing the same song that had started his programme on 1
January 1980. 'Life in the 1980s' by the Martian Schoolgirls was one

of those self-financed singles on short-lived independent labels that a band would send to Peel with a little note attached listing their next three gigs (if they had any). From Wimborne in Dorset, the Martian Schoolgirls had a new-wave sound once described by that circumspect local boy Robert Fripp as 'effective'. But after their Ballardian premonition of the Eighties ('Deadbeat, nothing to eat in the Depression Zone'), the band went their separate ways in 1981.

A new decade and Peel is flitting from Kenya (Abana Ba Nasery) to the emerging New York rave scene (Frankie Bones) and then to Northern Ireland for an album of archive sessions by Stiff Little Fingers on Strange Fruit. Peel plays just one track from it, recorded in the autumn of 1979. 'At the Edge' is the sound of four young men trying to find metaphors for the oppression of the Seventies at a time when nobody but the Martian Schoolgirls has a clue how the Eighties are going to pan out. The song is about a generation gap in a family, but as with everything that Stiff Little Fingers ever wrote, there's a temptation to apply it to life in Northern Ireland. Their hopes of an alternative Ulster would have been delusional ten years ago. But ten years ago was ten years ago. In a speech last March, Sinn Fein president Gerry Adams declared that he was seeking a 'non-armed political movement to work for self-determination' in the province. Twenty years into the Troubles, his words were gingerly dissected and everyone held their breath.

As is now customary, there's only one Peel session tonight – and curiously, there's only one song in it. Dale Griffin's production notes indicate that the band consists of two people, one of them charged with DJing and sampling, the other with mixing and engineering. But these job descriptions scarcely hint at the joys and surprises to come. The Orb's 'Loving You' begins with the sound of a cock crowing and for the next twenty minutes it ebbs and flows on a lapping tide of sensual textures and exquisite sounds. The voice of Minnie Riperton, an American soul singer who died young, enters six minutes in, trilling the 1975 hit that gives the piece its title. The Orb place her in one channel, and an echo of her in the other, so that the ghost of her memory follows the outline of her apparition. Above her and all around her is the oscillating sound of helicopter blades. Later, these blades will return but the landscape will have changed to a prehistoric forest where a hidden river runs and squawking pterodactyls glare down from skeletal trees. Tribesmen chant. The helicopter hovers. The cock crows. It's peaceful but ever so eventful. The canopy of musical detail covers the earth in light – and cloaks it in shadow – like Philip Glass scoring *Koyaanisqatsi*.

'Loving You' belongs to a genre called ambient house. Because Peel never sets foot in nightclubs, he may not know about the upstairs chill-out room at Heaven, the gay club near Charing Cross station, where the Orb's Alex Paterson and Jimmy Cauty have been giving Ecstasy-gorged clubbers a pillowy landing in a non-threatening VIP space, using record decks and an Akai mixer to create blissfully oceanic soundscapes and soothing aural bubble baths. Peel might think it deeply odd that Paterson was once a roadie for Killing Joke, while his collaborator Cauty was a member of the Killing Joke spin-off project Brilliant. Just about the two least soothing bands Peel played in the Eighties.

The Orb are making, in a sense, the first three-generational Peel music. Both Paterson (b. 1959) and Cauty (b. 1956) are old enough to have been *Top Gear* listeners in the early Seventies. In the years that followed, they got a foothold in the music business thanks to the post-punk perestroika that reigned on the *John Peel Show* from around 1978 onwards. In 1981 Cauty recorded a long-forgotten session as a guitarist in a band called Angels 1-5. He now creates ambient house with Paterson that sounds purpose-built for an Ecstasy nation. 'It was the beginning of a new era, a new society,' Paterson will reflect in 1997. 'It was a new drug [that] everyone enjoyed as opposed to everyone suddenly dying from it.'

Praise for the Orb is not universal. Andy Kershaw, highly sceptical, notes the resemblance of 'Loving You' to prog epics like Pink
Floyd's 'Echoes', and phones the duty office to complain about it the
first time it goes out. Paterson and Cauty will later tell Ken Garner
in *The Peel Sessions* that they had trouble explaining their methods
to Dale Griffin, who couldn't appreciate the rapid-fire sampling and
real-time mixing that underpin their work. Peel himself is into what
the Orb are doing, but more as an attentive onlooker than a vocif-
erous fan. It's a sort of dance music, er, isn't it? He tactlessly kills
the mood tonight, after playing 'Loving You' for the second time in
four weeks, by revealing that in the Seventies, when twenty-minute
songs were the norm, he and Sheila once had sex in the studio during a Soft Machine track. Oh thanks.

'Loving You' has since been retitled 'A Huge Ever Growing
Pulsating Brain That Rules from the Centre of the Ultraworld' and
is now available as a nineteen-minute single with several remixes
on it. It will chart just outside the Top 75 in the summer. The Peel
session, though, will generally be agreed to be the definitive performance. As listeners rush to re-request it, somebody tips off Fleet
Street about Peel's Soft Machine incident. Absurdly, a story will run
in one of the tabloids next week, under the headline 'Veteran DJ
John in Saucy Sex Romp', which briefly makes Peel the subject of
prurient gossip in his Suffolk village.

John Peel Show
Radio 1
19 March 1990

Robert Lloyd – Equation – Dawson – The Would Be's – Nile Kings –
The Walking Seeds – Los Muñequitos de Matanzas – Rig – MC 900
Ft Jesus with DJ Zero – Rapeman – Boo-Yaa T.R.I.B.E.

*The Institute of Trading Standards Administration calls for
government action on bovine spongiform encephalopathy (BSE),
commonly known as mad cow disease. New cases of the disease are
being reported at a rate of 150 to 160 per week and a former government
scientist has warned the Ministry of Agriculture that the open-air
burning of animal carcasses is a potential threat to public health.*

When Big Black split up in 1987, Steve Albini's next band was called
Rapeman. Peel hated the name at once (which Albini took from
a Japanese comic book) and was always faintly squeamish about
playing their records on his programmes. One night in September
1988 he read out the details of a forthcoming gig at a student union
in Leeds featuring Dinosaur Jr, Band of Susans and the 'miserably named Rapeman', as he dubbed them. 'I do wish they weren't
called that,' he went on, 'but they are and there's nothing I can do
about it.' Six years after 'Rape Rap' by the Crabs had passed by on
his show without comment, the mere word had become too toxic
to touch.

Albini stood his ground, even when staff at Rough Trade Distribution refused to handle Rapeman's album (*Two Nuns and a Pack
Mule*) that autumn. The student union in Leeds faced calls to ban
Rapeman from the premises. The gig went ahead, but Albini told an
audience at London's Mean Fiddler in October: 'Due to the feminist complaints about our name, we've decided to change it. From
now on we will be called Rapeperson.' Peel would have sighed sadly
at the laugh it got.

Rapeman appear to have broken up now, which may explain why
Peel judges the coast to be a bit clearer tonight. He plays their val-
edictory single, 'Inki's Butt Crack' – a title he declines to announce
– in response to a listener request. There's nothing offensive about
'Inki's Butt Crack' (there are no words in it for a start), but the way
Peel hesitates before reading out Rapeman's name suggests that he

still has an involuntary flinch when he sees it. But note the demarcation. 'Rapeman' he can say. 'Butt crack' he cannot.

The record that he plays next, 'Pickin' Up Metal' by the Boo-Yaa T.R.I.B.E., is a lot more provocative than any Rapeman song. The products of an infamous Los Angeles battleground of Bloods and Crips, the Boo-Yaa T.R.I.B.E. – five Samoan brothers – boast of carrying guns and shooting members of rival gangs who step out of line. ('That's how we settle our problems in the ghetto . . . Anyone who stands in the way will get smoked.') This is a quandary for a liberal like Peel, who has no truck with misogynistic rappers but no wish to censor or gloss over the realities of bad things happening in bad places. He won't be the first or the last liberal to feel simultaneously thrilled and appalled by gangsta rappers unapologetically glorifying violence.

'Judging from newspaper articles that I've read, it seems to be a cruel world that they inhabit,' he says of the Boo-Yaas when the cavalier death threats of 'Pickin' Up Metal' subside. 'Cruel' is an interesting adjective. Does he mean that cruelty has been done to them (in which case perhaps he can just about convince himself that they're justified in fighting back using whatever weapons they have) or is he saying that the cruelty lies in their own behaviour (in which case why doesn't he put every one of the misogynistic rappers back in the show and let the listeners decide whose lyrics, if anyone's, are beyond the pale)?

The dictionary of the *John Peel Show* will have to be rewritten in the light of gangsta rap, as Peel tries to juggle these double standards, to be paternal without being hypocritical, while all the time pushing the limits of radio. But for the moment, Rapeman can't say 'butt crack' and the Boo-Yaas can say whatever they like.

John Peel Show
Radio 1
4 April 1990

Happy Mondays – Apna Sangeet – Half Man Half Biscuit – A Guy
Called Gerald – The Tinklers – Poor Righteous Teachers – Cath
Carroll and Steve Albini – Fugazi – The Orb – Sofa Head – Big Chief
– Patrick Mkwamba and the Four Brothers – The Shamen

Four days after an estimated 100,000 people marched through London
to protest against the Poll Tax, the Labour MP John Hughes presents
a bill to repeal it. Calling the tax 'an immoral government measure',
he claims it will make the rich richer and the poor poorer. Saturday's
march ended in widely reported scenes of rioting, with 113 injuries and
339 arrests.

Madchester raves epidemically on. Happy Mondays start a spring-
time Peel show with a new anthem of the north ('Step On'), which
goes on sale next week. Their singles used to chart in the lower
60s; this one will end up in the Top 5. A Guy Called Gerald, whose
'Voodoo Ray' encapsulated every tactile sensation of the Haçienda,
is still around, now on his second album (*Automanikk*). Manchester
sneezes and a town south of Derby or north of Blackpool catches
cold. Primal Scream, doyens of C86, are in this week's Top 20 with
a sample-heavy dance track ('Loaded'). The Soup Dragons, un-
believably, will be next.

Other bands had their Damascene conversion early. Four
Aberdonian psychedelians called the Shamen (or 'the Shammen', as
Peel prefers to pronounce it) recorded a session for him in 1986, but
were among the first to ditch their guitars after hearing acid house.
That '86 session had Granny Takes a Trip song titles like 'Strange
Day's Dream' and 'Through My Window'. The new material, all

electronic, speaks the lexicon of Ecstasy and Shoom: 'Pro-Gen', 'Omega Amigo', 'Human NRG'. The Shamen and Happy Mondays are the show's apostolic bookends, dancing in saucer-eyed exaltation with their hands carving helices in the air. A new session from Half Man Half Biscuit is the sound of ale-quaffing gatecrashers blowing a derisive raspberry.

John Peel Show
Radio 1
8 May 1990

Buffalo Tom – Compton's Most Wanted – The Orchids – Leatherface – Crane – What? Noise – Soho – Hipno featuring Rootee – Barkmarket – Bim Sherman – Sonic Youth – MC Shan – L7 – Bamn

Construction work on the Channel Tunnel is halted after the accidental death of a member of the British team. William Cartman, a grouter, is the sixth Briton to die since work began near Dover in December 1987. The 31.4-mile-long tunnel is expected to be completed in 1993.

The baggy fashions of the Stone Roses and Inspiral Carpets have subjugated the high streets of cities previously thought impregnable to the return of the flared trouser. Post-Madchester, life is much changed. In recording studios, drummers spend weeks reading magazines at the back of the control room while producers assemble rhythm tracks from samples and loops. Bobby Gillespie, the singer of Primal Scream, barely appears on their records now. Remixer DJs – Andy Weatherall, Paul Oakenfold, Danny Rampling – are the new George Martins, Brian Wilsons and Phil Spectors. The word 'irrelevant' is brandished at rectilinear guitar bands like the House of Love who baulk at loose fits and hip-hop beats.

This is where Peel becomes important, because not everyone in Britain is a rave fan or an outgoing lunatic on MDMA. There are plenty of wallflowers and hold-outs. Those who shun the dance-floor need a radio outlet that clings to the virtues of the old world as well as celebrating the vicissitudes of the new. Step forward John Peel, who never tires of hearing sensitive boys and girls sing bitter-sweet songs of Morrissey-esque dolour on low-selling seven-inches. Come strum your guitars, ye floppy-fringed bands of Oxford and the Home Counties. There's no such concept as irrelevance to a musical omnivore like Peel.

The Orchids, tonight's session band, record for the Bristol label Sarah, which has chronicled the melancholy thoughts of many an indie crew – the Sea Urchins, the Field Mice, 14 Iced Bears – on a series of unassuming singles since 1987. This sort of fanzine-and-flexidisc culture is the last bastion of pure indie: the clocks at Sarah never did tick past midnight and greet the dawn of Andy Weatherall and A Guy Called Gerald. Are you dancing? Are you asking? No, I'm revising. Introverted and studious, Sarah will endure some ter-rible abuse in the press. But like the last bungalow in a terrace that developers urgently want to demolish to build a motorway, it will hold out for as long as it can. Peel will be a staunch supporter.

Only on a Peel show is it possible to hear the cherubic jingle-jangle of the Orchids in such close proximity to the calculated ultra-violence of Compton's Most Wanted. The gangsta rappers' single, 'One Time Gaffled 'Em Up', has undergone some pretty severe censorship before reaching Egton House. Every alternate line has a bleeped-out swearword or a dip in the vocal. At least the Orchids, with their songs of rainy days and hurt feelings, will never have to suffer the indignity of submitting a cleaned-up radio edit.

John Peel Show
Radio 1
20 August 1990

The Pocket FishRmen – Mega Sonic Boom Blast – Mav Cacharel
– Pixies – The Heart Throbs – Jaz – That Petrol Emotion – Happy
Flowers – Culture – The Farm – Woody Guthrie – K-Klass

*More than 120 Britons have been rounded up by Iraqi invaders in
Kuwait, who say they will use them as human shields to deter an
American air attack. Despite calls from Conservative MPs, there are
no plans to recall Parliament to discuss the invasion, which took place
eighteen days ago.*

Peel's subtle influence can be detected on one person close to
home: his elder boy William, now fourteen. Those Extreme Noise
Terror gigs that Peel took him to at the Caribbean Club when he
was younger seem to have rubbed off. The first single in tonight's
show, by a Texan punk band called the Pocket FishRmen, is a
William Ravenscroft favourite. Piercingly berserk, it would polarise opinion in many families but proved a popular choice with the
Ravenscrofts as they drove *en famille* through France on a recent
holiday. Another band whose music was a hit on the car stereo was
Culture, the veteran reggae outfit, and indeed there they all were,
Peel reports, singing along lustily to 'Lion Rock' (from the 1982
album of the same name) while stuck in traffic in Lyon. 'Lion Rock'
is about ridding Jamaica of British colonial influences and strength-
ening her long-standing cultural ties with Ethiopia. What a progressive family they are.

Messrs Anus and Horribly Charred Infant of Happy Flowers
have recorded a new album of nappy-filling exploits, *Lasterday I
Was Been Bad*. Peel plays two tracks from it, 'I Don't Want to Share'

and 'Rock Bottom'. The first describes the distress felt by a child at having to let a friend or sibling play with his toys. The second is a weirdly faithful cover of an old song by Seventies rockers U.F.O., complete with 'shredding' guitar solo. Peel lets slip – and this will come as a surprise to those who have heard Happy Flowers' music before – that he played a tape of 'some of their earlier material' in the car as the Ravenscrofts cruised towards their destination of Provence. 'They were interested in it, and sort of quite liked it,' he hedges, 'but I did note that they didn't ask me to play it again as the holiday unfurled before us.'

U.F.O., for their part, recorded a Peel session in 1977, during a peculiar wrinkle in time when punk rock, folk rock and spandex rock all coexisted and jockeyed for position on his programmes. It would be the huntsmen's horns and Morris dances of the Albion Country Band one night, and the pogo-dancing amphetamine din of the Vibrators the next. The night after that it would be the Steve Gibbons Band with pints of Double Diamond and Chuck Berry twelve-bars. A strange transition period to be sure. Then again, you could argue that every period is a strange transition period on the *John Peel Show*.

John Peel Show
Radio 1
21 August 1990

Pixies – Wildski – The Prudes – Cutty Ranks – The Fall – Napalm Death – Link and Chain – Dwarves – Troop – The Ex – The KLF – Th' Faith Healers – CPO – Gregory Isaacs – The Bridewell Taxis

At Heathrow, Britons flying home from Kuwait recount their escape through the desert in a thirteen-car convoy, disguised as Bedouin

*women. In Paris, Mrs Thatcher joins with France, Spain, Italy, the
Netherlands and Belgium in agreeing to enforce sanctions against Iraq,
but again resists calls to recall Parliament.*

The growing demand for compact discs has encouraged many
bands to release their back catalogues on CD. Sometimes, if a
batch of them comes out at once – last summer, for example,
the Mute label sent Peel eight CDs by the German band Can –
it can be a good way for him to rediscover music that he hasn't
heard for years. But the rise of the CD is not without controversy.
They cost twice as much as an LP and a CD player is at least £100.
Complicating matters for a lot of groups, their record companies
now require them to record separate, additional B-sides for the CD
format of their singles. Marketing wisdom dictates that a single has
a better chance of reaching the Top 40 if it's multi-formatted – i.e.
made available on vinyl, cassette and two or three individually sold
CDs with their release dates staggered a week apart – since fans
will want to buy all the formats to hear all the songs. Thus will the
band's chart position be artificially boosted. Peel is disappointed
to see that the Fall, the ultimate refuseniks of the post-punk age,
have joined the ranks of the multi-formatters with their new single
for Phonogram.

'The chances are that you're pretty confused about the release of
"White Lightning" by the Fall in the various formats that are available,' Peel says, sounding like the presenter of a consumer phone-in.
'I've got a piece of paper here which explains it all. There's the
seven-inch, of course, with "White Lightning" and [the B-side]
"Blood Outta Stone". Then there's the compact disc single, which
has "White Lightning", "Blood Outta Stone", "Zagreb" and "Life
Just Bounces". Then there's going to be the twelve-inch limited
edition with poster – the *Dredger* EP, only 5,000 of them available
and only for one week – and that's going to be "White Lightning",

"Blood Outta Stone", "Zagreb (Movements I, II and III)" and "Life Just Bounces". Then there's the twelve-inch – the more generally available one – which is "White Lightning", "Zagreb", "Blood Outta Stone" and "The Funeral Mix". And then there's *this*, which sounds to me like some sort of a remix, or am I hallucinating?'

He cues up an oddly muddy-sounding Fall track that may indeed be a remix of 'White Lightning', and then plays a snippet of the B-side, which sounds like a different band performing the intro of what could be a version of the Bangles' 'Manic Monday'. As it's a white label, there's no helpful information anywhere to be found. 'Obviously something of a collector's item,' Peel muses. 'I just want you to know that I've got it, and you probably haven't.'

If the 'Remix with Unrelated B-Side' is yet another cunning format to nudge the Fall one place nearer the Top 40, the tactic fails. 'White Lightning' will climb no higher than 56. It's back to the drawing board.

John Peel Show
Radio 1
14 October 1990

Fluke – Cheba – The Family Cat – Bleach – The Shamen – Barkmarket – Jimmy Rogers – The Wedding Present – Celelalte Cuvinte – Florian din Transilvania – Rebel MC – Metal Duck – Aural Corpse – Zero Zero – Inspiral Carpets – Ballou Canta – James

There are angry denials from foreign secretary Douglas Hurd about the purpose of a proposed visit to Baghdad by former prime minister Ted Heath. A number of British hostages are being held in Iraq, but Hurd rejects Heath's claim that the visit, during which he planned to appeal to Saddam Hussein for their release, was the Foreign Office's idea.

It's been a year of New Kids on the Block, *Twin Peaks*, Madonna getting poor reviews for *Dick Tracy*, Sofia Coppola getting even worse ones for *The Godfather Part III* and New Order teaming up with the unlikely rapper John Barnes on England's World Cup song. There's been a backlash against the Pixies (with a lukewarm critical reception to their latest album, *Bossanova*), but there have been stirring signs on Peel's programmes of a new wave of female-fronted American punk (Babes in Toyland, L7, Dickless, Hole). However, 1990 has seen guitar bands slide lower and lower down the Top 75, until the genre of indie rock has effectively ceased to have any commercial traction. One reason for the multi-formatting craze.

Peel has been troubled this year. In January he confided to the listeners that sleeping at his mother's flat had become a serious problem owing to late-night engineering work at nearby Notting Hill tube station. The fatigue he'd mentioned in the past was becoming more of a predicament. By May he felt so tired that he asked Radio 1's controller Johnny Beerling for some time off. He also requested a move to a weekend time slot to let him see more of his family.

Last month Peel got his wish, but the new changes don't look great from the outside. He now presents two shows a week, on Saturday and Sunday, both of which start at 11 p.m. and end at 2 a.m. With three hours at his disposal, he has reinstated the second session that he lost in April 1989, and has been able to introduce competitions, phone interviews, studio guests and other entertaining time-fillers. In a packed programme tonight, he focuses on the music of Romania, a country that has been in and out of the newspapers since its revolution and the executions of the Ceaușescus last December. A general election in May – the country's first free ballot since the Thirties – saw Ion Iliescu's National Salvation Front (FSN) win a landslide victory. Opposition to the FSN since the election, though, has been ruthlessly suppressed, in ways all too worryingly reminiscent of the previous regime. The summer saw bitter fighting between anti-Communist protesters and thousands of pro-government coal miners summoned by Iliescu to restore order in Bucharest. The demonstrations in the city's University Square continued into August. But the fact remains that the Socialist Republic of Romania, as the world once knew it, is no more.

For about twelve months (in other words, while Nicolae and Elena Ceauşescu were still alive), Peel has been playing examples of Romanian folk music on his programmes, which are sent to him by Electrecord, a Bucharest-based record company. He has occasionally wondered aloud what Romanian pop groups might sound like, or even if Romanian pop exists.

His guest tonight, Ionel Dumitrascu, is from Moldavia, eastern Romania, which will become part of the Republic of Moldova next year when the Soviet Union collapses. Dumitrascu, who has brought several records with him, explains that the music he's about to play isn't popular in Romania by any stretch of the imagination. Very few bands there have access to anything that might be called a recording industry. Electrecord, founded in 1932, has for some forty years been Romania's only record label.

'Heavy metal's quite popular over there, though, isn't it?' Peel asks.

'We have a few groups, but not too many,' Dumitrascu says. 'Most of them don't have any recorded music.'

Even playing live is a problem, he goes on. There are a handful of venues putting on concerts, but 'certain limits' are in place, as he puts it, as to what bands can and cannot do. In his part of Moldavia, close to the Soviet border, live music is mostly confined to the spring and winter.

Peel plays three of Dumitrascu's records. The first is a prog-rock song in multiple time signatures with virtuoso drumming and a Curved Air-style female singer. Had Celelalte Cuvinte (which translates as Other Words) been British, Peel would have wrenched this song off the turntable, taken it upstairs and thrown it under the nearest taxi driving past in Langham Street. (Although, had he heard them in 1971, he might just as easily have snapped them up for a *Top Gear* session and tried to sign them to Dandelion.) Since they're Romanians, he merely blinks a couple of times and asks Dumitrascu if he's brought any punk.

Dumitrascu mentions a band called Iris, who were around some years ago, playing a heavy sort of music.

Peel: 'Was that quite dangerous?'

'Yes, they had lots of problems with the society. The people that, you know . . .'

'That ran the place?'

'Yes, exactly so.'

The second record is by Alexandru Andrieş, a blues singer in his mid-thirties. Peel immediately picks up on a slight similarity to an old Kevin Coyne song. Andrieş sings in English accompanied by jazz piano, saxophone and harmonica.

The third of Dumitrascu's selections is the most commercial, and probably the closest to what Peel means by Romanian pop. Florian din Transilvania's 'Fiul Zburatorului Cu Farfuria', a song about a flying saucer, is modern enough to feature a drum machine and, if it was British, one might expect it to date from the late Seventies, possibly made by a band trying to capitalise on the success of M's 1979 hit, 'Pop Muzik'. It actually comes from 1986, chosen by Dumitrascu from an album (*Tainicul Vârtej*) that means 'Mysterious Swirl' in English.

'Are there more bands waiting to record?' Peel asks him. 'Can we look forward to a flood of excellent records from Romania?'

Dumitrascu tells him that some foreign bands have now had records released on Electrecord, which might make things interesting in the future. And the *NME* is now on sale in Romania, which would have been unimaginable a year ago.

The conversation ends. Peel plays the West Coast rapper Too Short. Approaching 12.30 a.m. on a Monday morning, the DJ suddenly finds himself back in *Perfumed Garden* territory. Here he is again, manning the graveyard shift while the greater population sleeps. People have jobs tomorrow. Or school. Or revolutions to fight. Is anyone out there listening to him? Was the move to a later slot too much of a gamble?

'The building is by and large deserted most of the time,' he says of Egton House in the hour of the wolf. He feels a chill. He suspects Radio 1 of turning off the radiators after midnight. He reads out a list of football fanzines that have come in. Port Vale. Wolverhampton Wanderers. Gillingham. Cliftonville in Northern Ireland. Keenly supported clubs all, but not a top-flight team between them. Peel reads out their titles anyway. *The Memoirs of Seth Bottomley. A Load of Bull. Brian Moore's Head. The Wee Red.* His programmes have never been about winners. They're more about struggling to stay solvent in the third tier.

In five hours, Simon Mayo will wake Britain up with the breakfast show. Monday morning will yawn and pad in its slippers to the bathroom. Rise and shine. Kettle and toaster. The *Sun* and the *Mirror*. MC Hammer and the Beautiful South. All the radiators in the building will miraculously come back on again, purring with warmth.

Peel will stay in touch with Ionel Dumitrascu. In March 2000 Dumitrascu will return to the UK and apply for asylum. The authorities place him in Campsfield House, an immigration detention centre in Kidlington, near Oxford. Peel acts as his guarantor, making several appearances in court on his behalf, until Dumitrascu wins his appeal in 2002. British nationality is granted to him in 2005, though Peel, sadly, doesn't live to see it.

1991: BITS AND PIECES

'I don't see Nirvana getting as big as Metallica or Guns N' Roses.
There's just no way those people would like us.' KURT COBAIN,
June 1991, three months before the release of _Nevermind_

John Peel Show
Radio 1
12 January 1991

Prince Far I – Heavenly – The Scientist – Ween – LFO – Ride –
Nyboma and Madilu – Frankie Paul and Stinger Man – Dinosaur Jr –
My Bloody Valentine – The Art of the Legendary Tishvaisings – Die Art

John Major, who succeeded Margaret Thatcher as prime minister in
November, tells steel workers in Lanarkshire that he will take measures
to safeguard the region's economic structure, following British Steel's
announcement that it is temporarily closing the Ravenscraig blast
furnace due to the recession. Labour's shadow industry secretary,
Gordon Brown, warns of the steel industry's 'closure by stealth'.

Having put together a three-hour show that roams from Pennsylvania to Leipzig via Zaire, and having typed out a running order
that time-travels back to 1934 for Jessie Matthews's high-spirited
'Tinkle, Tinkle, Tinkle' from the musical _Evergreen_ (and then to
1948 for Roy Milton and his Solid Senders' upbeat post-war blues

'Keep a Dollar in Your Pocket'), Peel begins not with a song of gre-
gariousness or optimism, but with the ominous growl of Prince Far
I, a reggae DJ, echoing into dub infinity with a sermon about war.

On a single originally released in 1978, Far I's voice rumbles and
thunders like a Jamaican Vivian Stanshall poking into the musty
crannies of Rawlinson End. 'So you are the one who came here to
mash up the place, eh? . . . Why, man, the Bible no write himself . . .
You know is a man write the Bible, eh? . . . When you see a champion, you don't kill him. You race him.'

There has been heavy fighting. The destruction to the earth was
ferocious. But now? 'No more war . . . war is over,' rejoices Far I,
sounding as close as he'll ever get to invigorated. 'Well, there's a
barrel-load of ironies for you,' says Peel, who has chosen 'No More
War' as the show opener for a reason.

Earlier today, the US Congress passed a resolution approving
the use of military force to drive Saddam Hussein out of Kuwait.
Operation Desert Storm is five days away. British Army regiments,
RAF squadrons and Royal Navy ships wait to be mobilised in the
Persian Gulf. As with the Falklands War in 1982, the BBC will be
interrupting its radio broadcasts for frequent news bulletins. Sixty-
seven songs with inappropriate titles have been banned by Radio 1
for the duration of the conflict, including 'Midnight at the Oasis',
'Walk Like an Egyptian', 'Fools Rush In', 'Stop the Cavalry' and
'Everybody Wants to Rule the World'.

'No More War' by Prince Far I is not on that list, but then Peel
wouldn't be expected to observe a station-wide censorship policy,
or indeed play any of the sixty-seven offending songs anyway, so
the memo, as usual, doesn't apply to him. When you're known for
filling your programmes with bands that have names like Carcass,
Napalm Death, Rancid Hell Spawn and Coffin Break, working off a
list of proscribed song titles would be the very definition of point-
less. And so, now that the danger to the globe has been invoked in

the opening minutes, Peel quickly glances at the running order and moves on.

On the Sarah label, Amelia Fletcher, the singer in the post-C86 band Heavenly, pines for her dream boy ('he looks real cool in his shades') and wishes he would notice her. It's a very Sarah feeling. Over on Creation, a label that had a full-scale personality change last year after discovering acid house, Ride, a quartet from Oxford, get things back on an even keel with a cargo of Rickenbacker guitars and tremolo pedals. LFO, an electronic duo on the Sheffield-based label Warp, have the unique honour of being praised by the incomparably influential Kraftwerk while being decried by Radio 1's Steve Wright, who called their debut single 'LFO' the worst record he'd ever heard. Wright is not mad on the Sheffield bleep scene. Or for that matter the Oxford tremolo scene or the Sarah post-C86 scene.

Peel, who must have been asked to include this next bit in the script, reads out tomorrow's Radio 1 schedule in a listless, distracted manner. There are times this year when he sounds more dissociated than ever from the rest of the station. They should all be pulling together in times of war, shouldn't they? Well, shouldn't they? 'Nine thirty. Dave Lee Travis. Including "Give Us a Break" and the "Think Link", plus Dave's featured group, Wilson Pickett. I've never really thought of Wilson Pickett as a group, but perhaps he's been putting on a lot of weight recently. Two thirty. *Going Live* with Phillip Schofield, who's joined by live guest Phil, er, Paul Young rather. Phil Young – he couldn't make it, alas. And he also finds out what Rick Astley's been up to for the last couple of years, which I'm sure has been troubling you as much as it's been troubling me.'

Dinosaur Jr's singer-guitarist J. Mascis is in a similarly languid mood, emerging sleepily from behind a curtain of hair to strum an acoustic version of David Bowie's 'Quicksand'. He starts off by changing a word in the lyrics here and there, then a few more, then a whole verse, then virtually the entire song, and then begins changing the chords to ones that he prefers. It's available on an EP called *The Wagon*, which Dinosaur Jr dedicate to a car that they used to own (and apparently crashed).

The final hour of the show includes records from Leipzig in the former East Germany, now part of a reunified nation after the fall of the Berlin Wall. The Art of the Legendary Tishvaisings are a competent death-metal band – clearly, Napalm Death have no problems getting their records distributed in Leipzig – while Die Art are a sort of East German Wedding Present, with strangulated Gedge-like vocals that sound like they're getting deep into the nitty-gritty of domestic relationships. The members of Die Art would have grown up listening to Peel on the World Service, as Ionel Dumitrascu in Romania did.

But not all of Die Art's songs are about domestic dramas. 'Wide Wide World', another track on their album (*Fear*), was written in 1989 after they'd circulated some underground cassettes. The lyrics of 'Wide Wide World' mention London, America, Paris, Italy and Australia. This cost Die Art the chance of a record contract with the state-owned pop label, Amiga, in the period shortly before reunification. It was felt that the song was a subliminal appeal to the group's fans to attempt to escape from the former East Germany.

John Peel Show
Radio 1
26 January 1991

Half Japanese – Manic Street Preachers – Orbital – Definition of Sound – Galaxie 500 – Fluke – Virginia's Scrapings – Gang Starr – Nardo Ranks – Black Cuban Opera – Boss Hog – Flaming Lips

As the Gulf War enters its tenth day, the BBC and ITV decide to scale back their rolling coverage. Data from the Broadcasters' Audience

Research Board (BARB) suggests that extended news programmes have been popular with viewers, but the BBC admits to receiving over 2,000 complaints about 'saturation coverage'.

Manic Street Preachers are a young band from a bygone coal-mining community in South Wales. They write songs that look beyond localised angst into deeper areas of existential despair and generational helplessness. Somehow they seem perfect for an international war situation. Their latest single, 'Motown Junk', contains a line that Peel would glower at ('I laughed when Lennon got shot') if he was concentrating more on the lyrics. Although twenty-four years have passed since he described the Beatles as 'our leaders', he doesn't joke about the murder of Lennon. But he might broadly welcome the meat of the song's argument, which denounces everything from 'underclass betrayal' to the mindlessness of chart pop music. 'Motown Junk' is punky but melodic, recalling Stiff Little Fingers, the Rich Kids, the Boys and many other bands that Peel liked in 1978. However, it will become apparent, once Manic Street Preachers start doing interviews to promote it, that they're not counting on Peel for help. Their ambition is to be a stadium-rock band with number 1 singles all over the world. His interest in the young Welshmen will proceed no further.

John Peel Show
Radio 1
10 February 1991

Milk – Super Cat and Nicodemus – The Melvins – The Wake – Planet Cook – Yank Rachel and Dan Smith – The Charlatans – Shut Up and Dance – Yen – Damnable Excite Zombies! – Orange Baboons

John Taylor, a thirty-eight-year-old black barrister, is selected by the Conservative Party as its prospective candidate for Cheltenham. The son of Jamaican immigrants, Taylor is vehemently opposed by a group of local Conservatives, one of whom is expelled from the party for referring to him as 'a bloody nigger'. The Tories have held Cheltenham since 1950.

The Radio 1 newsroom provides half-hourly updates on events in the Gulf. There are five in every Peel show. Today, the allied forces confirm that they have lost twenty-five aircraft since the war began on 17 January. A US Harrier is the latest, shot down over Kuwait. Meanwhile, Iraq has rejected a peace plan proposed by Iran. Saddam Hussein has made a speech on Iraqi radio, claiming that his people are more determined than ever to win. The speech has been condemned by President Bush. At home, five peace protesters are arrested at RAF Fairford in Gloucestershire, the British base for USAF B-52 bombers.

Peel has a session tonight from the Charlatans, a band from the West Midlands who are so brazenly influenced by the Stone Roses that everyone assumes they hail from Manchester. They've been filling a gap in the market with Roses-style hit singles (including last summer's omnipresent 'The Only One I Know'), while the Roses themselves retreat into a long silence pending the outcome of a legal battle with their record company. The Charlatans are arguably on course to become the bigger of the two bands. Having breezed to number 1 with their debut album (*Some Friendly*) in October, they're currently on tour in America.

'They're in Houston, Texas, tonight,' Peel says, 'and tomorrow night in Dallas – my old stomping ground – and then they move on to California. Just in case you feel like flying out there to see any of the gigs, there's plenty of seats on the planes at the moment, I understand.'

Jokes about the Gulf War? Goodness gracious.

John Peel Show
Radio 1
26 May 1991

Jimmy Shand – Pixies – Backwards Sam Firk – 70 Gwen Party – The
Humblebums – Steely and Clevie featuring Suzanne Couch – Patricia
Routledge – Transglobal Underground – Seven Minutes of Nausea

The IRA explodes a 300 lb bomb in a Protestant housing estate in
Cookstown, County Tyrone, injuring thirteen people and damaging
120 houses. The attack comes a day after a Sinn Fein councillor was
shot dead by the Loyalist Ulster Freedom Fighters (UFF) in County
Donegal.

Some Peel shows have a wonderfully unfettered sense of fun. There
are nights when he seems to revel in indiscipline and be open to
the possibility of playing absolutely anything. Football songs.
Memphis jug-band music from the Twenties. Hardcore punk from
Japan. Eccentric swamp rock from Austria (this is a band named
the Orange Baboons, who have won Peel's respect by re-recording
a 1968 album by Lee Hazlewood in its entirety). Idiot savant cave
paintings by the Shaggs. Sentimental oldies by Manfred Mann.
Prodigious amounts of ragga. The massed saxophones of the
Orquesta Sensación del Mantaro from Peru. A session from the folk
singer June Tabor. Brutal grindcore from a band called Anal Cunt.

Peel has been having a clear-out of records at home, trying to
thin the collection down to something approaching acceptable levels before the floorboards give way. As he takes them down from
shelves and puts them in boxes, he inevitably finds forgotten odd-
ities, rarities, curios and collectibles that simply have to be shoehorned into his next show. Which is how he comes to be playing a
record tonight by Patricia Routledge, a Wirral-born actress who was

the redoubtable spinster Kitty in *Victoria Wood as Seen on TV*. Last autumn she had top billing in a new six-part BBC sitcom, *Keeping Up Appearances*. But Routledge has a lesser-known talent as a singer of songs from Broadway musicals – lesser known by everyone except Peel, that is. Tonight, from a 1967 budget-label recording of *The Sound of Music*, he plays Routledge's eye-watering, loin-girding version of 'Climb Ev'ry Mountain'. It's a voice that sounds like it ought to be singing 'Rule Britannia' on a ship's deck as the last viceroy sails out of India and the sun sets on the British Empire. 'She has a fairly hearty pair of lungs,' Peel applauds. 'It's all right, I'm not going to play all of it.'

Routledge appears fifty-two minutes into a quite mad three hours that begins with Jimmy Shand, the kilt-wearing accordionist from Fife, squeezing away on his 1955 signature tune, 'The Bluebell Polka'. Peel claims to be able to whistle 'The Bluebell Polka' from memory; those ten years at boarding school must have been harsher than anyone thought. Then, after a series of violent left turns, the listeners find themselves, some eight or nine minutes later, in a nightmarish, knife-slashing Brian De Palma world of telekinetic teens, bloodstained prom dresses and decapitated dolls. These are Babes in Toyland, an all-female trio from Minneapolis, with a track from their not-for-the-squeamish EP, *To Mother*. And four minutes after that, the scenery changes again to the blue hills of an earlier America, where the Country Gentlemen sing of 'Little Bessie' clinging to her mother's bosom with frail fingers as the poor sick girl falls asleep for the last time and joins the angels. No one writes a nineteenth-century child-starvation song quite like the Baptists.

Later, after a track from a new Wedding Present album, we drop in on the late-Sixties Glasgow folk scene. Peel has found (while sifting through his boxes of records at home) an old LP by the Humblebums, who used to prop up the bar of *Top Gear* in 1969–70 but haven't been seen on a Peel show in almost twenty years. And why would they be? The two Humblebums are far from Glasgow's folk circuit now. Gerry Rafferty lives behind electric gates on a sixteenth-century farm in Sussex, reportedly earning fortunes in royalties from his 1978 hit 'Baker Street'. The other Humblebum, Billy Connolly, is Britain's funniest stand-up comedian and was launched into millions of American homes last year with a bravura performance in a Whoopi Goldberg TV special. Of all the people Peel has set on the road to fame in the last twenty-five years, Connolly's may well be the most astonishing success story.

A new addition to the *John Peel Show* this year has been the 'Uproar Break' in the middle of a programme. An 'Uproar Break' is an excuse for Peel to rattle through a lot of grindcore and death metal in a short space of time. The Radio 1 Roadshow did something like it in the Seventies and Eighties with the 'Bits and Pieces' feature, one of many competitions and quizzes that were played by the hyped-up townsfolk of Tenby, Great Yarmouth, Clacton-on-Sea, Walton-on-the-Naze, Dunoon, Saltcoats and Bowness-on-Windermere when the Roadshow rolled its way around Britain. Named after a 1964 hit by the Dave Clark Five, 'Bits and Pieces' was a test-your-reactions musical quiz that compressed brief clips of ten songs into thirty seconds, which the contestants wrote down as fast as they could identify them.

Tonight's 'Uproar Break' knocks even the most quickfire 'Bits and Pieces' into a cocked hat. Stunningly, Peel plays eleven songs in fifteen seconds – complete songs, not excerpts – recorded by an Australian band called Seven Minutes of Nausea. The eleven songs appear on an EP with the onomatopoeic title *Bllleeeeaaauuurrrrgghhh!*, released by the San Francisco-based Slap-a-Ham label. The EP is available on seven-inch vinyl and has a staggering twenty-eight songs by twenty different bands on the A-side, and an almost inconceivable thirty-six songs by twenty-one bands (including Impetigo, Mouthfart, Meat Shits and

Splatterreah) on the B-side. Knowing Peel, he will have listened to all sixty-four songs before selecting the ones by Seven Minutes of Nausea as the EP's eleven highlights.

'I'll give you the titles of the tracks before I play them,' he says. '"SDI Theory", "Rights Inherent", "Destruction Is On" . . . er . . . "Rude Word [i.e. Fuck] to No Justify", "Carcass Pulp", "Grind Infect", "Heavy Satan", "Lorro Morte", "Blood on the World", "What I Feel" and "Stoked". See what you make of this.'

Pencils at the ready and off we go. See how many we can spot. "SDI Theory", first off, sounds like someone attacking a bass guitar by cutting its strings with pliers and bouncing the fretboard off a wall, at which point two people shout the word 'exacerbation' roughly simultaneously. And that's it. The eleven songs are over. Somewhere in there were 'Rights Inherent', 'Destruction Is On', 'Fuck to No Justify', 'Carcass Pulp', 'Grind Infect', 'Heavy Satan', 'Lorro Morte', 'Blood on the World', 'What I Feel' and 'Stoked'. Eleven songs, as promised, in fifteen seconds. It took Peel longer to read out their titles than it took Seven Minutes of Nausea to play them.

The next record, needless to say, comes from the Democratic Republic of Congo.

John Peel Show
Radio 1
27 July 1991

Babes in Toyland – Therapy? – Stretchheads – Gunshot – Burro Banton – Morbid Angel – Gumball – The Farm – Mudhoney – The Ukrainians – Black Radical Mk II – Robert Johnson – Swervedriver

Fourteen years after being banned by the BBC, the television play
Scum *is finally shown on BBC2. The drama about life in a borstal*

was written as a Play for Today *in 1977, but was suppressed by the then controller of BBC1, Bill Cotton. It was remade as a feature film in 1979 with the same director (Alan Clarke) and leading actor (Ray Winstone).*

The first hour of the *John Peel Show* can be picked up on medium wave in many European countries. Peel knows this because listeners in Finland, Austria and Bulgaria write to him. He's a truly international broadcaster – although, as he wryly pointed out one night in April, his employers are quickly catching up with the New Europe after a slow start. Playing a trailer for a series of European-themed Radio 1 specials which included Steve Wright presenting the afternoon show live from Brussels, Peel muttered: 'For years I asked if I could do programmes from Europe – and they told me not to be so stupid.'

Returning from a recent visit to Bulgaria, Peel found his job at home becoming more arduous by the day. The piles of new releases had grown to their most mountainous heights yet. To give the listeners a sense of what his office currently looks like, Peel has got out his measuring tape and calculated that the pile of new CDs stands at six feet five inches. 'The CDs come last, of course,' he says, still bitching constantly about the new format. 'Singles come first, then the LPs.'

But as Peel knows, vinyl has been a victim of the CD revolution, and some shops no longer stock LPs because they want to free up more floor space for CD racks. It's a trend that Peel deplores. 'I really like seven-inch singles as objects. And when you have to concentrate your mind on making some sort of impact in three minutes and twenty-five seconds, you work harder at it somehow.' It's a point that many listeners would have heard him make in the late Seventies and early Eighties, when seven-inch singles on independent labels were, for his money, the gold standard. He's now planning to put together a three-hour show dedicated entirely to the seven-inch single 'as a continuing and viable form'. But it's a bit like King Canute trying to push back the sea. The new Mudhoney album on Sub Pop, *Every Good Boy Deserves Fudge*, has been sent to Peel in the CD format. It's the way the music industry is going, whether vinyl addicts like it or not.

John Peel Show
Radio 1
8 September 1991

Kasambwe Brothers Band – P.M. Dawn – Anhrefn – Stereolab – Killbrains – Ivor Cutler – Robert Wyatt – Leatherface – Pornography – West Coast Pop Art Experimental Band – Dirtsman

The assistant chief constable of Essex Police says he is close to finalising his report into the conviction of Winston Silcott, one of three men serving life imprisonment for the murder of PC Keith Blakelock in the 1985 Broadwater Farm riots. Silcott's supporters accuse the police of fabricating evidence against him.

Peel begins with a song from Malawi called 'Check Your Step . . . AIDS About'. Recorded by the Kasambwe Brothers Band, it's sung in English but aimed at the population in their own country, where the ninety-four-year-old president, Hastings Banda, forbids contraception and outlaws public discussion of sexually transmitted diseases. 'I mean you, boy,' the Kasambwe Brothers urge. 'I mean you, girl. Check your step. AIDS is a killer.'

'An appropriate title,' says Peel, 'on a day in which I read in the *Observer* that Uganda has banned the advertising of condoms. Really smart move. This is as a result of pressure from the churches, so a ripple for them, and tens of thousands of people condemned to hateful deaths as a consequence no doubt.'

Peel is on the side of the powerless and the vexed tonight. The new Top 40 has come out. Bryan Adams's '(Everything I Do) I Do It for You', from the $300 million-grossing Kevin Costner movie *Robin Hood: Prince of Thieves*, has been at number 1 for ten weeks. That's one week longer than Queen's 'Bohemian Rhapsody', John Travolta and Olivia Newton-John's 'You're the One That I Want' and Frankie Goes to Hollywood's 'Two Tribes'. It's a feat that was judged worthy of a special Radio 1 news report this morning. Everyone with an interest in music is pessimistically resigning themselves to Bryan Adams being at number 1 for the rest of their lives.

'The only record that's been at number 1 longer was "Rose Marie" by Slim Whitman,' says Peel, who is old enough to remember. 'The other day I heard Simon Mayo, in what I'm sure is called something like *The Morning Posse*, rather taking the mickey out of "Rose Marie" by Slim Whitman. Which wounded me. I tried to find a copy of it to play to you, without interrupting it with clever remarks.'

But surrounded as he was by cardboard boxes and teetering shelves full of LPs and singles, he couldn't lay his hands on Whitman's 1955 country ballad. He's going to have to play something else instead. He opts for a white label of a techno track, 'LMG', which has been recorded at Sheffield's FON Studios by a member of 808 State and a few friends. Their band is called Pornography, FON stands for 'fuck off, Nazis' and 'LMG' is short for 'lick my gash'. It's a decent track, but perhaps not the most felicitous tribute that Peel could have paid to Slim Whitman's legacy.

John Peel Show
Radio 1
28 September 1991

PJ Harvey – A Tribe Called Quest – Nirvana – Thousand Yard
Stare – Surgery – Messiah – Moe Tucker – Captain Condoms – Rum
and Black – Bass Kruncher – Moondog – Some Have Fins – Primal
Scream

A three-hour ferry journey from Fishguard in Wales to Rosslare
in Ireland turns into a thirty-seven-hour ordeal for five hundred
passengers when severe gales make their crossing impossible. With
wind speeds reaching 40 knots, those travellers who aren't overcome by
seasickness pass the time by dancing to the ship's band and drinking the
contents of the duty-free bars.

When Peel previewed Mudhoney's new album in the summer,
there was no indication that Seattle would soon become the obsession of the world's media. The album, in fact, made no dent in the
American charts and achieved its highest sales per capita in Britain,
where it briefly appeared in the Top 40. Number 1 albums in the
States this year for Van Halen (*For Unlawful Carnal Knowledge*),
Metallica (*Metallica*) and Skid Row (*Slave to the Grind*) show heavy
metal to be in no danger of a commercial decline, while two albums
released by Guns N' Roses this month (*Use Your Illusion I* and *Use
Your Illusion II*) will debut at 1 and 2 on the US charts, selling 1.5
million copies between them in the first week.

Four days ago Mudhoney's friends Nirvana – who last year left
Sub Pop to sign with a major label, DGC, because they wanted to
see their records get a bit more promotion – released a new album
of their own, *Nevermind*. It has an arrestingly self-mocking cover
photo (a baby swimming towards a dollar bill on a hook) and was

recorded at a studio in Los Angeles where platinum-selling albums were made in the Seventies by Fleetwood Mac, Foreigner and Tom Petty and the Heartbreakers. But nobody, least of all the executives at DGC and its parent company Geffen, are expecting overnight miracles with *Nevermind*. Guns N' Roses, Van Halen and Metallica didn't get to be behemoths of the US entertainment industry by being the sort of bands that could be easily overthrown. They'd probably regard Nirvana as up-and-coming young pups, not as a threat. And for the time being, they'd be right.

Nirvana recorded their third and most recent Peel session earlier this month at Maida Vale, but it won't be aired until November. By then, Nirvana will be back in Britain for three concerts and a live appearance on Channel 4's youth-orientated Friday night TV programme, *The Word*. That performance will catapult them into the public consciousness. Just before they explode into 'Smells Like Teen Spirit', Kurt Cobain – as he now (correctly) spells his name – will say to the studio audience: 'I'd like all you people in this room to know that Courtney Love, the lead singer in the sensational pop group Hole, is the best fuck in the world.' Peel wouldn't know anything about that, but when the chaotic performance ends, many people in that studio – and many of the million or so viewers watching at home – will suddenly be feeling that 'Smells Like Teen Spirit', a single that Peel first played back in August, is a record they urgently need to add to their collections. Less than three weeks later, Nirvana will be back in England singing it on *Top of the Pops*.

At this juncture in late September, though, Nirvana are on the promotional trail in New York (a Tower Records in-store, of all things) and 'Smells Like Teen Spirit' is just another single tussling for attention on a Saturday night Peel show. Whatever sales records it may go on to annihilate, *Nevermind* is at the moment such a mint-new release that nobody knows where, or even if, it's going to chart in Britain or America next week. Peel plays 'Smells Like Teen Spirit' once again, for no other reason than he likes it and wishes the lads well, and he also plays 'Drain You', a song on side two for those who are still buying albums on vinyl. For those who aren't, it's track eight.

It's funny how things look in hindsight. Without giving a moment's thought to musical influences and bloodlines, Peel follows Nirvana tonight with the Pixies. As history will go on to prove, the laws of symbolism dictate that it should have been the other way round.

1992: THIS ENERGY OF WHICH YOU SPEAK

'It's touching some nerve somewhere. I like the rawness of it,
and I think maybe that is what people are looking for now.
They want a bit of rough around the edges.'
PJ HARVEY talking about her debut album, *Dry*

John Peel Show
Radio 1
4 January 1992

The Wedding Present – Red Hour – Unsane – Leatherface – Sultans of Ping FC – The KLF vs Extreme Noise Terror – Bang Bang Machine – The Phantom Surfers – Piss – Professor Nuts – Grotus – D-Nice

The Muslim Parliament, a 155-member body claiming to represent Britain's 1.5 million Muslims, opens in London. Its founder, Dr Kalim Siddiqui, accuses Britain of directing 'a lava of hatred' against Islam, but his parliament has failed to win support from many Muslim academics and community leaders, who describe his views as 'divisive', 'provocative' and 'marginalising'.

One day about four weeks ago Bill Drummond – the shorter-haired, Scottish half of the KLF – was doing what he'd done many times before: he was listening to the *John Peel Show* in the bath. As a linch-pin of the post-punk scene in Liverpool in 1978–81, Drummond had been the co-manager and co-producer of the Teardrop Explodes and Echo and the Bunnymen. In the mid-Eighties he'd been an A&R man at WEA, working with the band Brilliant, whose guitarist Jimmy Cauty would become his confederate and partner-in-crime in the KLF. And even though the KLF have spent the last eighteen months brainstorming and conceptualising their way to becoming Britain's biggest-selling pop-dance act, Drummond still likes to stay *au courant* with the latest advances in underground music by running a bath and listening to Peel.

It might have been 7 December, when Peel played 'Knee Deep in Shit' from the new EP (*Phonophobia*) by Extreme Noise Terror. Or it might have been the following night, when he played 'Lame Brain' from the same EP. If it was 7 December, Drummond heard a ninety-four-second blizzard of malign guitar riffs and satanic vomit-vocals. If it was the night after, the riffs were faster and downright evil, and the vomit-vocals were accompanied by lacerating screams. Either way, the effect on Drummond was Archimedean. He got out of the bath and reached for the phone.

'He had the idea of getting them to work with him and the KLF,' Peel picks up the story tonight, 'to re-record [their number 1 hit] "3 a.m. Eternal" for the Christmas *Top of the Pops*. Now, if you watched the Christmas *Top of the Pops*, you'll know that it actually never got shown.'

Peel goes on to explain that he has been sent an acetate of the two bands' highly implausible collaboration – a union that horrified the producer of *Top of the Pops* so much that he vetoed its broadcast, since it was due to be screened a matter of minutes before the Queen's traditional Christmas Day speech. But the acetate has got lost somewhere in the Christmas rush and Peel has given up hope of finding it. Now the story takes a surprising turn. This afternoon, at Portman Road football stadium in Ipswich, Extreme Noise Terror's local team Ipswich Town played an FA Cup third round match against Hartlepool United, a match that Peel happened to attend. Outside the ground he bumped into a member of Extreme Noise Terror, who gave him a cassette.

'And so here it is.'

The listeners now hear, for the next two minutes and forty-eight seconds, the world premiere of '3 a.m. Eternal' by the KLF vs Extreme Noise Terror. The Suffolk grindcorists – or crust punks, the term they seem to prefer – make their presence felt in the song even before the music starts, with a roar of 'KLF!' inserted into the introduction after the gunfire and the Radio Freedom call sign. From then on, it's evil guitars and triple-speed drums all the way. At first, a certain amount of hilarity is unavoidable. But with crust punk, the laugh soon dies on the lips. The implications of the KLF's 3 a.m. eternity are subverted horribly in the new reading of the song. Beatific feelings of being at one with mankind in an outdoor communal dance ritual are exterminated and replaced by feelings of waking up on the floor of a foul-smelling crypt and seeing nails embedded in the walls.

A lot of people don't care for the KLF. Too many concepts, they say. Too many pranks. When Extreme Noise Terror heard the message from Drummond on their answer machine, they were dubious rather than flattered. But the KLF need ENT for just one more prank, which takes place at the Hammersmith Odeon on 12 February. It will be Drummond's act of revenge on the corporate music world.

Peel, who indirectly brought the two bands together, is too peripheral a figure in the mainstream music industry – even now – to be invited to the annual Brit Awards. So he isn't there to see the KLF and ENT perform '3 a.m. Eternal' to a seated audience of CEOs, A&R heads, PR gurus and sales executives in dinner jackets and cocktail dresses. At the climax of the song, Drummond burns all his bridges in the space of five seconds by pulling out a sub-machine gun and firing it at the audience's heads. A voice over the PA can just be made out: 'Ladies and gentlemen, the KLF have left the music business.' For good measure, the KLF deposit a dead sheep outside the venue of the post-awards party, just to show that they had a flair for the gratuitous gesture as well as the grand one.

It's a hell of a way to retire. And it's just as well that Peel, a strict vegetarian since his youth, wasn't there for the denouement. But he was there, without knowing it, for the inception. It began on a night in December, when Drummond climbed into his bath, turned on the radio and listened to one of the few presenters still capable of triggering mutinies in the music business.

John Peel Show
Radio 1
22 February 1992

Revolver – The Fall – Dennis Alcapone – Curve – Aphex Twin – Loudspeaker – Bunny General – Babes in Toyland – Kar – Smith and Mighty – Mantis – The Boo Radleys – Daniel Johnston – Ninjaman

A hunt for the killer of eleven-year-old Lesley Molseed in 1975 has been relaunched by West Yorkshire Police after Stefan Kiszko, the man who has served sixteen years for her murder, was cleared last week by the Appeal Court. It's emerged that scientific evidence exonerating Kiszko, who signed a false confession after three days of police interrogation, was available at the time of his trial.

Peel is not a raver. Nor is he a clubber. Ecstasy is a closed-off avenue to him. Weekenders take place without his presence or participation. Not for him the midnight phone call at the M25 service station. The Ministry of Sound, open since last September, is somewhere he's yet to venture. Quite often, introducing a techno or rave track, he'll come across as every bit the well-meaning, middle-aged parent that he is. 'A bit of a toe-tapper' is how he'll describe a white label hot off the presses from Detroit or Berlin. 'Goes like the clappers, doesn't it?' He's akin to a football commentator unsure how to pronounce the name of a Polish substitute. So instead he says it would make a good hand at Scrabble.

'I'm not much of a dancing man,' reiterates Peel tonight as he cues up an EP by a twenty-two-year-old from Cornwall, 'particularly since the webbing slipped. But I think you'd be hard pushed to dance to this.' He's read in the dance pages of the music papers that the EP will 'transform the whole of the nature of dance music and so forth'. Are they serious? Could they be right?

Digeridoo by Aphex Twin is not quite a debut EP. He released two others last year under the name of AFX, and one of them, *Analog Bubblebath Vol 2*, led with 'Digeridoo (Aboriginal Mix)', which has now been re-released as the title track of an EP credited to Aphex Twin. This is what Peel plays tonight. Seven minutes long, it twists and bends the sound of a didgeridoo and combines it with the heart-in-mouth sensation of a journey in a bumpy jeep through the Australian bush. 'Digeridoo' points the way out of a cul-de-sac for dance music: suddenly a road is illuminated ahead, leading to a new world that exists somewhere between the ambient movement and the saucer-eyed rave aesthetic. Peel is playing one of the most influential tracks in years.

He only gets one thing wrong. 'Digeridoo' is not especially hard to dance to. Aphex Twin has used it to end his sets in Cornwall and it's been played by DJs in fields around Greater London as 4 a.m. approaches and bodies jerk uncontrollably. But it's also a piece of music to *listen* to. It's intelligent, not utilitarian. Peel calls it 'a great record', and for once there's nothing questionable about his terminology.

Aphex Twin? Smith and Mighty? The Boo Radleys? Note how Peel's shows in early 1992 anticipate the musical landscape of 1996. Some of his running orders read like the soundtrack to an imaginary Danny Boyle film.

John Peel Show
Radio 1
1 March 1992

Nirvana – Digital Excitation – Butterfly Child – Scrawl – Abana Ba Nasery – The Frank and Walters – Green Day – Jacob's Mouse – Happy Flowers – The Werefrogs – Jad Fair – Whirling Pig Dervish

Fifty protesters occupy Twyford Down, an area of chalk downland near Winchester in Hampshire, on the day that bulldozers arrive to begin work on the M3 motorway extension. Environmental groups have lobbied for the extension to be built in a tunnel under the Down, rather than cutting a trench through the landscape. It's thought the new route will save motorists several minutes on the journey from London to Southampton.

Early last month, *Nevermind* by Nirvana sold its three millionth copy in America. Five days ago Kurt Cobain married Courtney Love in Hawaii. 'Smells Like Teen Spirit', which fell out of the UK Top 75 in January after reaching a scarcely imaginable number 7 in its second week, has done for guitar rock what 'Digeridoo' is doing for dance music. It has pointed the way to the future.

All the major labels in America are now signing grunge bands – as this dressed-down, amped-up strain of north-western rock has been dubbed – and all the tabloids in Britain are running cut-out-and-keep guides to flannel shirts and ripped jeans, just as they did with smiley T-shirts and bandanas in 1988. The little trio from Aberdeen in Washington whom Peel played when they were Sub Pop's baby band are now impacting on the music industry at gut level, setting the British and American A&R agendas for the next two years and scaring the living daylights out of every rock group beneath the level of AC/DC.

Tomorrow Nirvana's record company, DGC, will release a second single from *Nevermind*, 'Come as You Are'. Peel plays one of the tracks on the CD format, a live version of 'School', early in this show. With 'Smells Like Teen Spirit' having been such a socio-musical phenomenon – a record that appealed to metal heads and indie fans alike – there's no way that Radio 1 can leave Nirvana out of its daytime schedules. 'Come as You Are' has made it onto the playlist. But that doesn't mean that Britain will be waking up to Nirvana on the breakfast show, or even hearing them in the afternoon. 'It's one of those curious categories where it's on the playlist but doesn't get played,' Peel muses. 'It's quite a Zen-like thing.' But on the playlist it is, which means Nirvana are regarded by the Nation's Favourite as a pop group as well as a rock one. Pop? Grunge? Indie–metal crossover? When a band sell as many records as Nirvana do, the first thing they forfeit is the right to define their own music.

The three members of Nirvana, already separating dangerously from each other under the influence of Courtney Love, have been on tour since January. Following first-time visits to Australia and Japan, they were due to go to Ireland next, but the dates have been postponed. There are rumours that Cobain and Love are addicted to heroin.

John Peel Show
Radio 1
14 March 1992

The Gories – Sipho Bhengu – Cybersonik – Crane – Cutty Ranks – PJ
Harvey – Spiritualized – Suckdog – Nirvana – Spawn – Ambassadors
of Swing – Loveblobs – Pavement – Verve – Sebadoh – Ministry

*The first MORI poll of the 1992 election campaign shows Labour three
points ahead of the Conservatives, leading some analysts to predict a
hung parliament on 9 April. A proposal by ITN and the BBC for a live
presidential-style debate is welcomed by Labour's Neil Kinnock and the
Liberal Democrats' Paddy Ashdown, but is rejected by Prime Minister
John Major.*

PJ Harvey are a trio from Dorset and Somerset. Their leader is Polly
Jean Harvey, a slightly built, severe-looking young woman who
plays a huge red Gretsch guitar onstage and has her hair tied back in
a bun. Her band's first two singles, 'Dress' and 'Sheela-Na-Gig', have
drawn comparisons with Patti Smith for their take-me-or-leave-me
aggressiveness and their strong female voice. Peel was never a fan of
Smith (although he liked everyone she influenced, from Prag VEC
to a late-Eighties indie band called the Heart Throbs), but Harvey
has a way of opening herself up in a song – getting to the heart of a
painful neurosis with a complete lack of fear – that impressed Peel
straight away.

'John was the first person ever to take notice of what I was doing,'
and he was the first person to place my music on the radio,' Harvey
will later say, looking back at their long mutual admiration. 'He
became my friend early on. I remember sending him my demo
tapes before anyone had heard what I was doing.'

Tonight Peel plays three songs from *Dry*, PJ Harvey's debut album, which comes out in two weeks. The images in Harvey's lyrics are like pages torn from the Old Testament: the washing of feet, the use of leaves to hide genitalia, the body of the sinner being cut down from the hanging tree. There's such an elemental force at work in her music that when she starts doing TV interviews to promote *Dry*, she seems so incongruously polite as to be timid. Her lyrics are like slashes from a dagger, but her manners are impeccable. 'As she enters the big time, will Polly Harvey be the person to put Yeovil on the map?' wonders Richard Jobson, the presenter of Thames TV's *01-For London*. Faced with her disarmingly level gaze, it's the least stupid question anyone can think to ask.

One of the last songs Peel plays tonight is 'Married, 2 Kids', from a new album by the Fall (*Code: Selfish*) that sounds like Mark E. Smith immersed in techno. Machines fill the spaces in their music that guitars once occupied, and guitars patrol the perimeter, performing the roles of machines. The character in 'Married, 2 Kids' is on his second pint of lager in a featureless pub, lost in self-loathing, unable to feel fulfilled at work or at home. Smith's writing now has the bleakness of the weary alcoholic.

Peel's own tiredness has become a matter of regular discussion. 'This energy of which you speak,' he said after a Dutch techno track called 'Here It = N.R.G.' a few weeks ago. 'Describe it to me.' He recently confided to the listeners that he pre-records some of his shows, so that he can have more time to relax at weekends. John Walters has already taken early retirement from the BBC, leaving last June after twenty-two years as Peel's producer. Peel can't go on for ever. Alan Freeman, back at the Beeb and reinstalled as presenter of the *Saturday Rock Show* at sixty-four, is twelve years his senior – but Freeman's programme ends at 9 p.m. and he hasn't far to go. Peel's show ends at 2 a.m. and it's a long drive home.

John Peel Show
Radio 1
1 May 1992

Fudge Tunnel – Arrested Development – The Fall – Monkey 101 –
Chapterhouse – Seaweed – Lee Perry – Mosquito – Mighty Force –
Storms – Lagowski – Llwybr Llaethog – PJ Harvey – Morrissey

*Following Neil Kinnock's resignation on 13 April after Labour's
election defeat, the shadow transport secretary, John Prescott, gives a
TV interview in which he appears to back Bryan Gould, the shadow
environment secretary, as the party's next leader. Gould's rival, shadow
chancellor John Smith, is the clear favourite to win the ballot.*

When Peel began hosting his new three-hour shows in 1990, the
initial plan was to have interviews and studio guests as part of the
line-up. These guests wouldn't be anyone famous, but perhaps
someone like David Gedge or a member of an American hardcore
band who were touring the country. The interview idea was soon
discontinued. Peel is too placid to demand that record companies
give him access to their artists. Were he more assertive, the kind of
favours he might call in – Nirvana, New Order, Happy Mondays,
Nick Cave – would be tantalising indeed.

Tonight he promises a mystery guest, his first in a while, which
is a good way to keep the listeners glued to their radios when BBC1
has *The Mummy* with Peter Cushing as its midnight movie. Peel's
first hour takes in sludge metal from Nottingham (Fudge Tunnel),
hip hop from Atlanta (Arrested Development) and an indie band
from Reading whose motionless stage performances and dreamily
psychedelic guitar sounds have seen them labelled by music journalists as 'shoegazers'. Now that the last Madchester-influenced
latecomers have left the party, shoegazing bands like Chapterhouse,

Slowdive and Spiritualized are the UK alternative scene's main contenders in the fight against the grunge invasion. So far it hasn't been
much of a contest.

There's new music from Mudhoney, who are probably wondering what madness they helped to create when they asked Nirvana
to be their support band in 1989, and the Wedding Present, whose
clever idea (or marketing gimmick) has been to release a new single every month this year. Peel has been faithfully plugging them
all, and the one they're putting out this month, 'Come Play with
Me', will make the Top 10. Peel may not be quite so enthusiastic,
of course, if all twelve singles end up hogging the top spots in
the Festive 50. But then again, there may not be a Festive 50. Peel
aborted the voting last year after fewer than a hundred postcards
came in. Grunge fans are supposed to be apathetic, but not quite
that apathetic.

The mystery guest arrives. It's Polly Harvey. She sets up her
equipment – a microphone, an amplifier and an electric guitar –
and throws herself into a rendition of Bob Dylan's 'Highway 61
Revisited' that sounds like it's coming from a black, oily, bottomless
well of anguish. When she giggles afterwards about the sound problems (she couldn't hear herself sing), her little voice doesn't seem to
correlate to her music at all. Peel asks her if she wants to keep going
or wait until the technical problem has been ironed out. Another
giggle. She'd rather wait.

We come back to her five minutes later for 'Rid of Me', a new song
that she hasn't recorded with her band yet. And into the bottomless well we go. 'You're not rid of me,' she warns some poor wretch,
snarling not so much like Patti Smith as like Glenn Close in *Fatal
Attraction*. 'I'll make you lick my injuries. I'm going to twist your
head off, see.'

It must be daunting for Peel to be in the same room as such
untrammelled fury. 'PJ Harvey, of course,' he murmurs into his

microphone as she finally stops screaming. 'Is that enough? You've done two now?'

It's enough.

John Peel Show
Radio 1
12 June 1992

Helmet – Drive Like Jehu – Datblygu – Geater Davis – Sonic Youth – Voov – Chumbawamba – The Orb – Superconductor – Tranceformer – Big Stick – Maarten van der Vleuten – Poison Chang – Crayon

The composer Andrew Lloyd Webber is knighted and the novelist Jeffrey Archer is made a life peer in the Queen's birthday honours list. Other public figures receiving honours include actor Michael Caine and turkey-farming tycoon Bernard Matthews, who are awarded CBEs, and cricketers Ian Botham and David Gower, who are made OBEs.

No studio guest tonight, but a member of Datblygu (pron. 'Dat-bluggy'), a band from Cardigan in Mid Wales, says a few words of introduction before each of the songs in their session, as though they recorded them in one continuous chunk with no cigarette breaks or visits to the cafeteria. Datblygu's music has lots of interior juxtapositions going on. One song is sleepy techno with birdsong. Another has a rattling sound as if there's a snake trapped inside the guitar. Their fourth ('This is an anti-bullfighting song in Spanish') explores jazz and funk, eventually slipping into a lengthy, proggy coda. 'A national treasure if ever there was one,' surmises Peel.

The national treasure could be Datblygu collectively, one of several Welsh bands who appear in his shows on a regular basis. Or Peel might specifically mean David Edwards, their singer, the man who does the introductions. There's an endearing hint of repressed anarchy in the way Edwards appears to give a piece of equipment a kick before each song, like John Shuttleworth taking a few moments to adjust the bossa nova setting on his organ. Edwards sings in Welsh, Spanish and what may be German, except for a passage in one song in which names suddenly fly out of the fray like disturbed birds. 'Florence Nightingale! Laurie Anderson! Paul McCartney crap!'

John Peel Show
Radio 1
14 August 1992

Nirvana – Crackerbash – The Hallucination Generation – Small Factory – Future Sound of London – Blue Boy – Arcwelder – Messiah featuring Precious Wilson – Hula Hoop – The Orb – Zion Train

An Old Bailey jury has spent a fifth night in a London hotel after failing to reach verdicts on five people accused of laundering £14 million from the 1983 Brink's-MAT gold bullion robbery. The jury will continue its deliberations today. Detectives believe that gold worth £10 million is still missing.

Earlier this month the anarcho-punk band Chumbawamba recorded their first Peel session. The band have been active for at least a decade, picking up Peel airplay for their 1985 single 'Revolution', their 1986 album *Pictures of Starving Children Sell Records* and, two months ago, their new album *Shhh*. That evidently doesn't constitute enough support in Chumbawamba's eyes, because the four songs they've presented as their debut session could hardly drip with more condescension: 'Agadoo', 'Knock Three Times', 'The Birdie Song' and 'Y Viva España'. When Peel plays them next week, some listeners will write to complain, feeling that Chumbawamba have picked the wrong Radio 1 DJ to attack. Peel will defend the band, even repeating the session, which he would have had every right to reject.

It's odd, then, that his reaction tonight to a session by the Orb – their third – is one long disgruntled sulk. The duo's double album *U.F.Orb*, released last month, has been immensely successful, knocking Lionel Richie off number 1, and in June the Orb appeared on *Top of the Pops*, playing chess in space suits to promote their forty-minute single, 'Blue Room'. Ambient house is (to borrow the title of a genre-leading album by the Irresistible Force) flying high. Persuading the Orb to make time in their schedule for a day at Maida Vale was some coup.

Peel doesn't see it that way, though. His deadpan comments about the two tracks they've submitted tell their own story. The first is a cover of the Stooges' 'No Fun', recorded almost exactly the way the Sex Pistols did it in 1977 on the B-side of 'Pretty Vacant'. A four-minute punk song with a sneering vocal from Alex Paterson, it goes a bit ambient for a few seconds in the middle, but is otherwise a straight facsimile. 'Probably seemed like a good idea at the time,' Peel harrumphs.

The other track, 'Oobe', is much longer and quintessentially Orbian. There are deliciously calm scenes of grazing animals. There are gentle swooshes and swishes of synthesizers. A young American boy speaks. Pan pipes beckon us forward. The music reaches a clearing, or perhaps looks down on a picnic near a hanging rock. Oh, is this where the spaceship will land? A pulse starts to throb. Things begin to feel more urgent. Something vast passes slowly overhead, searching in vain for a runway. Tranquillity returns.

'Crazy name, crazy guys,' Peel mutters. He can see the funny side of 'Agadoo' by Chumbawamba, but burlesquing ambient house is apparently not something to joke about.

John Peel Show
Radio 1
4 September 1992

Cop Shoot Cop – One Dove – Therapy? – Smashing Pumpkins –
Public Enemy – Stereolab – Unrest – The Fabions – Holographic –
Shonen Knife – The Melvins – N-Trance – Dump – Fun-Da-Mental

*Buckingham Palace issues a statement denying reports that Diana,
Princess of Wales, has been having secret assignations with a friend,
thirty-three-year-old James Gilbey. Two weeks ago the* Sun *revealed it
was in possession of a tape recording of a conversation between Diana
and Gilbey, in which Gilbey addressed the princess as 'darling' and
'squidgy'.*

Last year at the Reading Festival, Nirvana performed early on the
first day, appearing before Chapterhouse. This year, on a day of
apocalyptic rain and mud, they headlined the whole event. Tonight
Peel gives the listeners his report on the festival, which seems to
have turned into a family holiday for the Ravenscrofts. As grisly
Chinese whispers swept the backstage area about Kurt Cobain
dying in London from a heroin overdose the night before, Peel was
negotiating to get his younger son Thomas and his elder daughter
Alexandra onto the side of the stage to watch Nirvana's set. 'They
could see everything that was going on,' he says.

Cobain was brought on in a wheelchair, his skinny body enfolded
in a white hospital gown. It was a comment on his life as dark as
any rumour ever spread about him. Days earlier, he really had
been in a hospital gown, detoxing at Cedars-Sinai Medical Center
in Los Angeles while Courtney Love gave birth to their daughter.
The baby at once attracted the attention of the local social services.
In a devastating profile of Love, the latest issue of the American

magazine *Vanity Fair* alleges that she took heroin for the duration of her pregnancy.

'And then when the band went off,' Peel says in the tones of a proud parent, 'to kind of regroup or do anything at all, they had to come and stand by where [Thomas and Alexandra] were sitting. Obviously, they were very pleased to be in that position.'

Cobain and Love now despise the media and have sworn vengeance on the *Vanity Fair* reporter. More pressingly, they're terrified of losing access to their child. In LA, Love waits for news. Cobain gets the crowd to give her a pick-me-up. 'This song is dedicated to my twelve-day-old daughter and my wife,' says Cobain, the hospital gown falling below his knees. 'There's been some pretty extreme things written about us, especially my wife. She thinks everybody hates her now. So, um . . . this is being recorded, so I want you to give her a message.' He gives 60,000 people a count of three. They respond on cue. 'Courtney, we love you.' The film footage doesn't show whether bassist Krist Novoselic or drummer Dave Grohl joined in.

'Afterwards I was hoping they were going to say, "Kurt turned round and said something really interesting,"' Peel continues, talking about Thomas and Alexandra, 'or pass on some bit of gossip.'

In the weeks and months ahead, when two biographers start asking unwelcome questions for a semi-official book they're writing about Nirvana, Cobain and Love leave almost an hour's worth of death threats on their answer machines. 'Smells Like Teen Spirit' wins two MTV awards. At the ceremony, Axl Rose of Guns N' Roses threatens to have Cobain beaten up.

'But in fact, what they were saying was, "Oh, he winked at me" or "He trod on my foot,"' Peel goes on. "So they were more impressed by the status of the artistes than anything else.'

Nevermind has now sold an estimated 10 million copies. Nirvana will make South America their next target market.

'The ninety-minute set sounded pretty good to me. Kurt didn't look particularly fit, but then at the same time, what had been written about them in the papers and the tabloids didn't seem to be evidence of it anyway.'

Peel and his children have just watched Nirvana's last British show.

1993: THE PRIME EXHIBIT IN THE ZOO

'Please play some real music before we go mental.' A listener's fax
read out by Peel on 8 April 1993, during a week when he sat in
for Jakki Brambles on Radio 1's lunchtime show

John Peel Show
Radio 1
26 February 1993

Therapy? – Noel Ellis – Codeine – Pixies – The Dambuilders – Blood
Sausage – God Is My Co-Pilot – Ecstasy of Saint Theresa – 81
Mulberry – Solid State – Even as We Speak – Seefeel – Sidi Bou Said

John Major's government is rocked by a MORI poll in The Times
*showing that 80 per cent of voters are dissatisfied with the way the
country is run. The poll comes two days after Labour leader John Smith
proposed dramatic reductions in the power of trade unions to influence
the selection of Labour parliamentary candidates.*

Peel is now as closely associated with dance music as he is with
grunge and hardcore punk. At one of his recent Roadshow events,
he was castigated by a punter in Scunthorpe for not playing more
dance tracks. His listeners frequently hear him refer to (and in some
cases defer to) Pete Tong, the presenter of Radio 1's flagship dance
show *Essential Selection*, with whom he shares a producer. The

well-connected Tong tends to get the exclusives – like New Order's new single, 'Regret' – that used to be mailed straight to Peel.

'Old loyalties,' he chuckles, sounding more amused than offended. 'They count for nothing, do they really, in these competitive times?' Mind you, there's a chance he might be more offended than amused.

A multitasking businessman, dance-label founder (FFRR) and in-demand club DJ, the thirty-two-year-old Tong is too prosperous, in any case, to merit Peel's professional jealousy. Tong probably spends more on hair products than Peel spends on shoes. Tong wears sharp suits. Peel wears the T-shirts of indie bands who split up in 1991. Both DJs are highly respected tastemakers who excel at what they do, but Tong will consider it a bad year if his taxable income doesn't exceed Peel's five times over.

While Tong is broadly seen as a man who can make or break a dance record, Peel has always been someone whose enthusiasm can kick-start the career of a young guitar band. Lately he's been playing Radiohead, an Oxford quintet whose moody single 'Creep' got some attention last autumn; Pulp, a Sheffield band who did a session for him in 1981 and are finally picking up momentum in the music press; Cornershop, a British Asian lo-fi group with an EP released on curry-coloured vinyl; and Therapy?, a Northern Ireland trio walking a punk–metal knife edge with songs obsessed by American serial killers.

Therapy? start tonight's programme. Peel discarded his long-running theme tune some months ago (after years of threatening to) and his programmes now roar out of the gate instead of loping slowly into view like a bow-legged cowboy. Peel will be conscious that DJs at Radio 1 are getting younger, and that the older he gets, the more he needs to adapt to a louder, faster, more energetic station. Tommy Vance will soon be out the door, replaced as host of the *Friday Rock Show* by a twenty-six-year-old, Claire Sturgess. The daily lunchtime programme has a younger presenter still. Indeed, when Jakki Brambles was born in March 1967, Peel was catching the tender boat out from Harwich to the MV *Galaxy* to do his first few broadcasts for Wonderful Radio London.

One thing Peel will never change, however, no matter who comes and goes on Radio 1, is his much-admired microphone style: that warm, discursive, absent-minded, trustworthy, self-deprecating delivery that matures like a Châteauneuf-du-Pape in a Rhône Valley cellar as the years go by. The self-deprecation is as important as the trust, and both come as a result of the warmth. In an age of jargon-spouting cyborgs, he's a wonderfully malfunctioning *Homo sapiens*. Has any other disc jockey in the history of radio been so experienced yet made so many basic errors? Have any of them begun a show by apologising for leaving their glasses on the Manchester to London train (as Peel does tonight)? Do any of them struggle, as Peel struggles tonight, to differentiate A-sides from B-sides? Do they play, as Peel repeatedly does, the wrong techno singles at 33 rpm and the right noisecore albums at 45 rpm? His rueful digressions are as entertaining as some of the records.

'I find myself increasingly having to phone up record companies and say to them, somewhat shamefacedly, "Can you tell me what *speed* the record that you sent me the other day is supposed to be played at?" This very day, I phoned somebody up to ask them this – and they didn't know themselves. No names, no pack drill, but there should be one or two lunches in it for me. And this is one of the records that I had to phone up and ask about last week.'

We hear the shimmering chords of 'Come Alive' by the shoe-gazing band Seefeel. They sound a bit slow.

'I can't remember what the answer was,' Peel admits.

John Peel Show
Radio 1
12 March 1993

Small – Sonic Youth – X-103 – PJ Harvey – Bikini Kill – L'Orchestre
Empire Bakuba – Militia – The Wedding Present – Nectarine No. 9 –
Peyote – Pulp – Diblo Dibala – Tindersticks – Guided by Voices

The BBC has cancelled its Costa del Sol soap opera, Eldorado, *after
less than a year. Scorned by critics for its poor acting and erratic scripts,
the show has managed to capture only a quarter of the audience of
ITV's* Coronation Street. *BBC1 controller Alan Yentob, who wielded
the axe, called it 'a brave venture'.*

Iron-fisted and implacable, 'Curse of the Gods' by X-103 is as hypnotic a piece of techno as Peel has ever played on the radio. You'll
find it on a Berlin label, Tresor, which has evolved out of a club of
the same name. Tresor has formed an axis with the second wave
of Detroit techno producers, two of whom – Jeff Mills and Robert
Hood – are the brains behind X-103. 'Curse of the Gods' is on their
EP *Thera*, inspired by a volcanic eruption on a Greek island in the
second millennium BC. (These Detroit producers love their Atlantis
mythology.) As minimal as you like, 'Curse of the Gods' seals the
fate of Thera with a distorted kick drum and an ominous gathering
storm. Mills and Hood are laying the blueprint for the next two decades of techno.

But as pioneering as they are, X-103 don't have the field to themselves. Peel, who back in January told his listeners that he believed
1993 was going to be a great year for music, played a track that
month by a German duo named Hardfloor. 'Acperience 1' might
have been hard trance, or it might have been acid techno. It came
at a time when the techno scene had splintered and virtually every

new record had its own genre. 'Acperience' seemed to unite two or three in one: a Roland TB-303 burbled along, and then a more aggressive second acid line faded in, followed two minutes later by a gurning third. The breakdown at the five-minute mark sounded like acid techno having summit talks with Pink Floyd's 'Shine on You Crazy Diamond'. The track was dark, Wagnerian and beyond epic. If Andy Kershaw had been listening, he would have had the duty office on speed dial.

That January show also featured Polygon Window (an Aphex Twin pseudonym), Taste Experience (a UK trance trio) and Sulphuric (alias the DJ and journalist Kris Needs, whose trance project Secret Knowledge recorded the 1992–3 club hit 'Sugar Daddy'). Then, in another flurry of twelve-inches and white labels last month, Peel's listeners heard progressive house from a duo called Tenth Chapter – on the producer William Orbit's label, Guerilla – and something quite different from Church of Extacy, one of many pseudonyms of the prolific husband-and-wife duo Michael Wells and Lee Newman. Church of Extacy's 'Modulator' was overdriven and drooling, a bug-eyed track that almost fell into the hardcore subgenre of gabba, much enjoyed by skinheads in Rotterdam. Which of these dance genres will dominate the rest of the year? Will any? Which will fall by the wayside?

There's plenty for Peel to get his head round, week by week, as he opens his new packages from Berlin, Detroit and London. If he's finding it a challenge to keep up, he's not the only one.

Jakki Brambles Show
Radio 1
5 April 1993

The Fall – Snow – Annie Lennox – PJ Harvey – The Undertones
– Madonna – Underground Resistance – Chris Isaak – Camille
Howard – Sunscreem – Sybil – Anthony Malvo – L-Dopa – Sub Sub –
Madder Rose – Altered Images – Go West – Suede – The Faces

*An inquiry is to be launched into the starting procedures at the Grand
National, after Saturday's race was abandoned and declared void. It's
estimated that bookmakers will have to refund around £70 million
in bets over the fiasco, which occurred when thirty horses kept racing
despite being called back for a false start.*

Jakki Brambles began her radio career on a local station in Ayr,
where she was raised from the age of four. She speaks in a middle-
class Home Counties accent that bears no audible trace of her life
story. Her microphone manner is ambitious head of sales meets
eager-to-please Butlins Redcoat, and her rise on Radio 1 has been
swift. On her daily show between 12.45 p.m. and 3 p.m. she plays the
latest hits, pokes fun at the uselessness of men (but you gotta love
'em) and shakes her head in amazement at the absolutely bonkers
world going on out there in the office blocks of Britain, where her
listeners slave away at desks and talk to her by fax. 'Jakki Brambles,'
one of her jingles goes. 'Not bad for a girl.'

In the week leading up to Easter, Brambles has taken a holiday. Sitting in her chair for the next five days is John Peel, a man
just over twice her age. He likes the Fall, Cornershop, the Berlin-
based Tresor label, African *soukous* music, football songs and any
record that involves Steve Albini or yodelling. Unlike Brambles, he
broadcasts while sitting in a chair, rather than standing up at the

microphone to get the adrenalin flowing. He doesn't address his listeners as 'guys', 'you lot' or 'your good selves'. He leaves his glasses on the Manchester to London train.

There are suggestions at Radio 1 that asking Peel to deputise for Brambles may have been the result of two people at management level having a *Trading Places*-style bet. It's as good a theory as any. Peel has confessed to pre-match nerves. 'I'm hoping that I shall be able to get one or two rather decent records onto the radio,' he told his regular listeners on Saturday night, immediately demonstrating why he was so unsuited to the job, 'and that you'll listen to it. I need to feel that I've got one or two allies out there.' Fingers crossed. It could be a long week.

The number 1 single in the UK Top 40, exclusively counted down by Bruno Brookes yesterday afternoon, is 'Young at Heart' by the Bluebells, a nine-year-old hit revived by a Volkswagen car advert. All the best songs are sooner or later revived by Volkswagen car adverts, aren't they? At numbers 2, 3 and 4 – and this will not have escaped the notice of the dancehall- and ragga-loving Peel – Shaggy ('Oh Carolina'), Snow ('Informer') and Shabba Ranks ('Mr Loverman') make up a triumvirate of reggae fusion artists. Meanwhile, in the album chart, which Brambles reads out every Monday after the 2 p.m. news, stadium-filling names prevail: Eric Clapton, Annie Lennox, Sting, Paul McCartney. These are some of the records that Peel will be expected to play this week, not only by Brambles's producer, but by her millions of fans, who may have forgotten that she told them last Friday that she was going on holiday.

It's 12.45 p.m. on Monday 5 April. *Newsbeat*'s Richard Evans hands over to Peel at the end of a fifteen-minute bulletin, putting the moment in historical context: 'For the first time in twenty years – it says here – it's John Peel in the daylight.' Peel thinks it might be twenty-three. Someone shouts, 'Whoopee! Yeah!' reminding us that, yes, bloody hell, this is Radio 1 in the daytime. Peel has made it to the bear's den. He's about to host a week of lunchtime shows. It's a remarkable state of affairs.

'Hello, fans, it's gorgeous, pouting John Peel here,' he says in a confident start, 'bringing you two and a quarter hours of top tunes for all the family.'

He opens the show with the new single by the Fall, a contextually shocking thing to do on Radio 1 in the early Nineties. 'Why Are People Grudgeful?' is their cover of a 1968 reggae song by Joe Gibbs, which, being Peel, he plays as the next record in the programme. While undeniably bold, these are not necessarily alienating choices. They may even make sense, in an odd sort of way, in the digital reggae climate of Shaggy, Snow and Shabba. Peel may, after all, have thought of a way of getting his favourite music onto the lunchtime show while keeping Brambles's listeners on-side.

But they might already be feeling uneasy fifteen minutes later when they make the acquaintance of PJ Harvey for the first time. Those listeners closest to their radios will hear her spell out the word 'fuck' on her sexually ambiguous new single '50ft Queenie', from an imminent, Steve Albini-produced album, *Rid of Me*. And if they're beginning to get a bad feeling off Peel, they might well take exception to the blithe way he dismisses the artists they go to Brambles to hear. Guaranteeing 'no Simply Red' is harmless enough, not even a topical insult any more. But Peel's album chart countdown ('At number 5, *Unplugged*, Eric Clapton – if only') risks riling people who *don't* see Clapton as a villain, and his comment about throwing a Chris Isaak CD across the studio ('That's what happens when you get a computer to write your songs') will simply bewilder pop fans who don't understand why a man they don't know is getting so wound up about music.

He does some things they'd recognise. He talks over the end of songs. He says his name. He says Brambles's name. He says 'chartbound sound' and '1FM, where the hits keep happening' – although this makes him sound like David Hamilton circa 1974. He reads out the weather. He reads out the traffic. He reads out the fax number, though soon he'll wish he hadn't. He interacts with the Man Ezeke, Brambles's hyperactive outside reporter, who is billeted in Dumfries today. ('Are you hearing me, Man Ezeke?' 'John, your show is cool. Keep the vibes going. One love!') He plays a recorded message from his children. He reads the traffic again. He does everything except explain what the hell he's doing sitting in for twenty-six-year-old Jakki Brambles on Radio 1's lunchtime show.

In latent terms, the contribution of Peel to Radio 1 in 1993 is enormous and can be seen on the posters and gold discs on the corridor walls all around him. New Order's 'Regret', the first single in three years from a band who probably owe their existence to him, is such a major event at Radio 1 this month that a special New Order Day is being trailed. The station's week-long coverage of the Sound City festival in Sheffield – featuring performances by Pulp, Aphex Twin and the Fall – is nothing less than the first sign of the overground manifestation of Peel's underground. It was Peel who took Sheffield seriously enough as a city to play independent singles from its punk and post-punk bands in the late Seventies, beginning a process that led to chart success in the Eighties for the Human League, Heaven 17 and ABC. Had Peel not shone his light on Sheffield, Radio 1's interest in the city would have gone no further than Tommy Vance playing Def Leppard on the *Friday Rock Show*. Be under no illusions: Peel made Sheffield Sound City happen.

He's too modest to mention any of this to Brambles's listeners, which is a shame because a bit of background information about his importance and his achievements might not go amiss. It might help them understand why he plays the Undertones today. Or the Faces. Or the Jesus and Mary Chain. But he hides his light under a bushel, and so the ice between him and Brambles's audience remains – disastrously – unbroken.

At the end of the show, after playing a track by the Congolese guitarist Diblo Dibala that has almost certainly never been heard by such a large radio audience before, Peel hands over to Gary Davies, who is sitting in for Steve Wright.

'It's been hard work, but I've thoroughly enjoyed myself, I must admit,' Peel gasps. 'It's over to you, Gary.'

'That's it?' says Davies.

Peel is taken aback. 'That's it, yes. Am I supposed to do something else?'

'That's it?' Davies repeats.

'That's it, yeah.' Peel sounds nervous.

'"And it's over to you Gary?"' Davies is incredulous.

'That's right.'

'Fine.'

Was it the terseness of the handover that made Davies so crabby? Had he prepared an eight-page script of Undertones and Faces jokes? Or was Davies, the ultimate Radio 1 medallion man and a former lunchtime presenter himself, merely letting Peel know – as coldly as his smile would permit – that he'd get no help this week from the daytime boys? It was a rather sour note to end on.

Jakki Brambles Show
Radio 1
6 April 1993

Apache Indian – X-103 – R.E.M. – Michael Jackson – Pooh Sticks – Shaggy – Boom Operators – Hole – The Cure – Whitney Houston – Betty Boo – New Order – Mambo Taxi – The Smiths – Car and Driver

Families of six of the ninety-six victims of the Hillsborough disaster win their application to appeal the original inquest verdicts of accidental

death. The South Yorkshire coroner's decision not to examine any events after 3.15 p.m. on the day of the disaster has been widely criticised.

Day two of Peel's Brambles stint, and the results are in. He's even more unpopular with the listeners than he is with Davies. Today and tomorrow, their faxes will start to twist the knife.

Peel has never been frightened by the idea of people thinking he has freakish music taste. It's been the story of his life. But what he does fear is being disliked. Sincere anxiety could be heard in his voice last month as he presented the first in a series of shows syndicated to two hundred American stations, *Peel Out in the States*. He came across as insecure and obsequious, with his talk of 'your country' and 'my country'. Whether it was a bet or not, what Radio 1 has done to Peel this week is take an intelligent, resourceful but unostentatious marsupial out of its natural habitat and make it the prime exhibit in the zoo. Some members of the public are decent enough to show curiosity. The rest want the lions and gorillas back.

'Play some good music,' one fax to him reads. 'Where's Jakki?' another asks. 'John Peel, please stop.' Tomorrow they'll start making bets that he won't last the week. This is dog-eat-dog radio, and the listeners can smell fear. Today he begins to lose patience with these idiotic people who seem to value continuity over adventure; these people who, as he testily points out after reading one hostile fax, don't even know how Brambles spells her Christian name.

It must have become obvious to him that he's failing at the job. It was a shot in the dark, but now he's just playing for pride, as the World Cup pundits say. What would go through the mind of a Radio 1 executive switching on at 1.50 p.m. and hearing the oompah strains of a Barcelona football song – with parts sung in Dutch in honour of their manager Johan Cruyff – in a pre-news slot where an Annie Lennox single should be? Peel, in fact, fades the Barcelona song out, making us wonder if the fax machine has disgorged an

angry memo from a hastily convened Radio 1 meeting upstairs. Peel
tells the listeners they don't 'deserve' to hear the song in full. And
the odds on him lasting the week lengthen.

It's been thrilling for fans of alternative music to hear the Fall,
Sonic Youth, PJ Harvey and Huggy Bear played on Radio 1 during daylight hours, and it's been a fascinating experience – for some
people, at any rate – to listen to a conversation between Peel and the
Man Ezeke and genuinely have no idea whether the next song on
the Nation's Favourite will be punk, blues, *soukous*, boogie woogie,
acid techno or riot grrrl.

But this is not a Peel who is ready yet for the mainstream, nor a
mainstream that is ready yet for Peel. Over the course of five increasingly heart-sinking days, he goes a long way towards confirming
that his rarefied nocturnal dominion is a world apart from 1FM's
exuberant daytime hubbub of titillation and trivia. The handovers
to Gary Davies never get any friendlier, and by Wednesday Davies
has stopped bothering to congratulate him on 'a great show'.

John Peel Show
Radio 1
11 June 1993

Reverend Horton Heat – Peach – Sex Clark Five – Senser – Polvo
– Ecstasy of Saint Theresa – Moonshake – Brian Sewell – Simba
Wanyika – Alluring Strange – Camille Howard – Fly Ashtray

*The Transport and General Workers Union is to cast its block vote
against John Smith's proposed reforms for the Labour Party. Bill
Morris, the TGWU's general secretary, says he will oppose moves at the
party's conference in September to exclude unions from parliamentary
selection meetings and leadership contests.*

Back on terra firma, Peel is like a character in a Russian short story who foolishly allowed himself to be over-promoted to the post of senior bureaucrat and is now relieved to be demoted to the position of impoverished clerk again. He can play what he likes without fearing the screech of angry fax machines.

Camille Howard was a boogie-woogie pianist from Texas who died earlier this year aged almost eighty. Brambles's listeners didn't appreciate Peel's attempts to pay tribute to her with a boogie-woogie song a day, but he knows he can lever her barnstorming 'Fireball Boogie' into an 11 p.m. show on a Friday night and nobody will turn a hair. A more eccentric selection, maybe, is 'Her Majesty' by Brian Sewell, a refined art critic reading the throwaway lyrics of a song on *Abbey Road* in a cut-glass voice that delights Peel, who found it on a new album of Beatles exotica.

Some listeners have been asking why Peel hasn't had a session from the Velvet Underground. The avant-garde New Yorkers, whose low-selling albums in the Sixties became the primary influence on literally thousands of bands in the following decades, have been talked into a surprise reunion tour, beginning their twenty-two-date European leg in Edinburgh at the start of the month. Not the least bizarre sight has been Lou Reed leading the Velvets, who once could have counted their British fans in the dozens, onto the stage of a sold-out Wembley Arena. Fourteen days from now, they're due to play to 40,000 people in the open air at Glastonbury Festival. After that, they go on tour with U2.

'We made every conceivable effort,' Peel says. 'We sent messages along the lines of . . . that I was the first person to play their stuff on the radio. Played it extensively when the first LP came out in 1967, all that kind of stuff. And in their warm-hearted way, they've completely ignored all our requests, haven't replied to phone calls or letters or anything else.'

He repeats instead a session by Ecstasy of Saint Theresa, a

shoegazing band from the Czech Republic, whom he booked near the end of last year when their country was still called Czechoslovakia. The Velvet Underground's tour will be taking them to the Palace of Culture in Prague, the Czech Republic's capital, on Sunday. It's not known if the members of Ecstasy of Saint Theresa have tickets, but President Václav Havel will be in attendance.

John Peel Show
Radio 1
11 December 1993

Man or Astro-man? – Prolapse – Bounty Killer – Eric's Trip – Meat Puppets – Infinity Project – Elastica – Julian Cope – Labradford – Teenage Filmstars – Ian McCulloch – Crunt – 8 Storey Window

Princess Diana is criticised for apparently reneging on a commitment to attend a royal premiere of the film Mrs Doubtfire. *The event was expected to raise £150,000 for several charities, including the National Society for the Prevention of Cruelty to Children. The princess recently announced her retirement from public life.*

Ian McCulloch is speaking down a phone line. The former Echo and the Bunnymen singer, now five years into a solo career, shares Peel's love of Liverpool FC and, like the DJ, has been dismayed by their current run of poor form. It's a good job McCulloch, an acidic thirty-four-year-old with a world-weary voice, is on hand to do the team's decline justice. 'It was a game of no halves,' he tells Peel about today's 2–2 draw against Swindon Town. 'Can I say "crap" on the air?'

McCulloch and Peel are talking because Peel's Saturday programme was moved in October to 4.30 p.m. Football reporting is part of his remit these days. He reads out the full-time results as they flutter across the teleprinter on BBC1's *Grandstand*, peering over his glasses at the TV monitor positioned at an inconvenient angle to his desk. He's like Desmond Lynam if Desmond Lynam played obscure surf-punk records. It's not a very hi-tech set up. 'Cheapskate BBC,' groans McCulloch when Peel tells him that Radio 1 won't be paying for the phone call.

Peel's other programme is now on Friday nights at 10 p.m. He finishes at 1 a.m., which is better than finishing at 2 a.m. but it's still 1 a.m. Rather than drive home to Suffolk and have to drive back in again the following morning, Peel spends Friday nights at a small hotel in Paddington. He used to make use of his mother's flat when she was alive, but she died last year.

'It's perfectly acceptable,' Peel will insist of the arrangement. 'Rather a nice hotel, as a matter of fact. I enjoy going there, up to a point. But you always feel as though you ought to go somewhere where there are amusing people, you can sip a glass of red wine and talk a load of nonsense far into the night. You get depressed about it. I think the number-three man in the *Melody Maker* poll ought to be doing something more interesting than just trekking off to a hotel.'

Just as they've had to be ruthless with Ian McCulloch's phone bill, Radio 1 have made it clear to Peel that they aren't prepared to cover his overnight expenses. He pays the £80 hotel bill each Friday out of his own pocket. It's getting hard not to see the BBC's treatment of him as unduly petty.

But in some respects Peel is lucky. A new Radio 1 controller was appointed in October. Matthew Bannister has come from Greater London Radio (GLR) with brash ideas of revolutionising the Nation's Favourite and overseeing an exodus of star names. His policies have already rubbed some well-known Radio 1 DJs up the wrong way. 'I told him,' Gary Davies, now in a Sunday 10 p.m. slot, revealed to the *Independent* last month shortly after handing in his resignation, 'that mine is the most popular night-time show you have on radio. He told me "yes, it is". But then he said he preferred "shows that lead". I'm afraid I've no idea what that means.'

Peel, however, is staying. Bannister approves of what he does and what he brings to the station. The former GLR man favours a mix of thought-provoking music and irreverent chat, and Peel, it seems, presents shows that lead. Next year Bannister, in a high-risk and deeply controversial move, will let Jakki Brambles fly off to a new career in America and place Emma Freud, the privately educated daughter of the politician and broadcaster Sir Clement, in charge of a new Radio 1 lunchtime show that seeks to be intelligent, witty and diverse while challenging listeners to look beyond the Top 40 format.

Bearing in mind what happened in April when he tried to do the same, Peel could be forgiven for stifling a hollow laugh as he nods goodnight to the Egton House doorman at 1 a.m. and heads for his £80-a-night Paddington hotel.

1994: THE SUN COME OUT AND STOLE
MY FEAR AND GONE

---

*'There was resentment that someone was deliberately trendifying
and Soho-izing Radio 1 rather than actually making it the
people's station.'* MATTHEW WRIGHT, showbiz reporter

John Peel Show
Radio 1
8 April 1994

Autechre – Supersuckers – Ivor Cutler – Mudhoney – AC Acoustics –
Neuropolitique – Pulp – Ultrahigh – Credit to the Nation – Underdog
v. Sabres – Mazey Fade – Loop Guru – Gorky's Zygotic Mynci

*A record compensation payment of £300,000 is made to a former
army major who was forced to resign when she became pregnant.
The industrial tribunal describes Helen Homewood, forty-four, as an
exceptional officer who suffered discrimination before her dismissal in
1981. The Ministry of Defence is expected to appeal.*

This afternoon, a Friday, Peel met his children off the school bus. He
told them that Kurt Cobain was dead. Something terrible had happened in Seattle. '[He] broke the news to them in much the same
manner,' Sheila Ravenscroft will write in *Margrave of the Marshes*,
'as if it had been a close family member who had died.' US news

channels are saying Cobain committed suicide with a shotgun, possibly the day before yesterday. They can't agree whether he was twenty-seven or twenty-eight.

Peel has the difficult job, as his show starts at 10 p.m., of curbing the party atmosphere he inherits from Pete Tong's *Essential Mix*, which has come live from a club in Glasgow, and offering some thoughts on a young man who has shot himself. 'What a night it's been, as you've probably heard by now,' Peel says. 'Kurt Cobain is dead, apparently by his own hand.' He reads through a prepared list of musicians gone too soon. Buddy Holly. Eddie Cochran. Jim Morrison. Jimi Hendrix. John Lennon. Brian Jones. Sid Vicious. Marvin Gaye. Sam Cooke. Otis Redding. Only on reflection does it seem strange that he left out Ian Curtis.

The BBC reporter Tom Feilden has joined him in the studio. The time in Seattle is just after 2 p.m. 'It has actually been officially confirmed now by Seattle police that the body found at the house is that of Kurt Cobain,' Feilden tells him. 'They say that they were called to the house earlier today when an electrician doing some maintenance work discovered a body of a man thought to be in his twenties.'

The police have confirmed the cause of death. 'He died of a shotgun wound to the head and a note was found near by. They're not releasing the contents of that at the moment.'

Thirty Nirvana songs race through the mind at once. No joy, just pain and sorrow. The sound of that scream. But surely not so painful that he had to blow his head off.

Cobain's mother, contacted by reporters at her home in Aberdeen, is putting her son's death in a similar context to Peel, mentioning some of the same names in his list. 'I told him not to join that stupid club.' The words sound odd from a mother. They should be more . . . *bereaved*, shouldn't they? Feilden and Peel leave it there for the moment. Two months ago Peel held a competition to win

Nirvana tickets for April. They were supposed to be coming to Britain.

There are no Nirvana songs in tonight's programme. It wouldn't have been hard to send someone out to HMV to buy a CD, so the omission must be deliberate. Does Peel think it would be too upsetting for the listeners to hear Cobain screaming? As his thoughts turn to Courtney Love and the twenty-month-old daughter that Kurt left behind, he slowly moves the show through the gears. An Ivor Cutler session. A band from Suffolk called Jacob's Mouse. And then – in what appears to be a pure coincidence – Peel plays the most appropriate piece of music that could possibly be played tonight in the circumstances.

It's a 1989 song by Mudhoney – Clive Selwood has just reissued it on a Strange Fruit album – which they recorded in their first Peel session. 'By Her Own Hand' is about a girl who has decided to kill herself. Mudhoney are trying to talk her out of it, but they don't know what to say. She's in so much pain that nothing can get through to her. 'She's looking for any way out / I can't stand what she's thinking about.' They want to tell her that everything will be fine, but they can't – because they know it won't be.

It's sometimes a moot point whether Peel listens closely to lyrics. He doesn't pass any comment on 'By Her Own Hand' when it ends, or even mention Mudhoney's link to Nirvana. But what an extraordinary song to put in the show for no reason. Almost as if something registered in his subconscious when he first heard it, and then lay there for years, waiting for the thought to crystallise and the moment – the optimal, calamitous moment – to be right to play it.

'People are always looking for some sort of significance,' Peel will say later this year, when an American magazine asks him if Cobain's death represents the end of an era. 'It doesn't mark any beginning or end. It only demonstrates the destructive nature of fame. But it's just incredibly sad. You feel that you could have done something to help. "Come and stay with us for a couple of weeks." But that's not the case.'

The story of Sub Pop's baby band is over.

John Peel Show
Radio 1
13 May 1994

Jeff Mills – Further – Chumbawamba – Don Van Vliet – Pure Morning – Pulp – Neuro Project – Lazy Lester – Heavy Vegetable – Polvo – Country Joe and the Fish – King Tubby – Mothers of Invention

Shadow home secretary Tony Blair has been installed as favourite to succeed John Smith, the Labour leader, who died of a heart attack yesterday at his London home. John Prescott, the shadow employment secretary, is expected to be Blair's deputy. But shadow chancellor Gordon Brown has indicated that he may also stand for leader.

On twenty-eight nights between September and December last year, Peel played *Trout Mask Replica*, the astounding 1969 double album by Captain Beefheart and His Magic Band, to a new generation of listeners one track at a time. It was an album that he'd first been sent from Los Angeles in June 1969 – months before its official UK release – and little phrases from it, such as 'fast and bulbous!' and 'a squid eating dough in a polyethylene bag', had peppered Sunday evening and Saturday afternoon editions of *Top Gear* until his listeners knew them as well as any Beatles lyrics.

As he revisited it last autumn, it was clear that *Trout Mask Replica* still enchanted, bamboozled and stupefied Peel all these years later. He doesn't scatter the word 'genius' around liberally; in fact, he hardly uses it at all. But Beefheart, Peel is certain, was a genius. And since his retirement in 1982, the music world just hasn't been the same somehow.

Beefheart, under his earthly name of Don Van Vliet, is having an exhibition of his paintings at Brighton Museum and Art Gallery in September. This is exciting news for a fan like Peel, though it's unlikely that Van Vliet will be flying in to attend. Now fifty-three years old and highly reclusive, he is rumoured to have a serious illness. 'Last time I spoke to him,' says Peel, 'which was a couple of years ago on the phone, he sounded very old and very ill. It was quite distressing.'

The Van Vliet exhibition, which has already shown in Germany and Denmark, is called 'Stand Up to Be Discontinued'. Peel has obtained a copy of the German catalogue. 'A very handsome volume it is, too. I thought that I'd looked all the way through it.' But he hadn't. And slotted into the back cover is a CD.

This CD contains half a dozen readings by Van Vliet of his lyrics and poems. One of them, which he reads in a frail voice, is 'Fallin' Ditch' from *Trout Mask Replica*. It's a near-death-but-full-of-defiance piece of writing which Beefheart's biographer Mike Barnes will compare to Dylan Thomas's 'Do Not Go Gentle into That Good Night'. Frail, yes, but looking death in the face and thumbing his nose at the grave. 'When I feel like dying,' Van Vliet reads, 'the sun come out and stole my fear and gone.'

He wrote the words when he was twenty-eight, bellowing them fearlessly from his elastic throat as the Magic Band flew at each other like Christians and Saracens. He led the charge while they did the fighting, clanking their swords at insane angles.

Where do they go, these former heroes of *Top Gear*? Frank Zappa, Van Vliet's high-school buddy and later adversary, died in December of prostate cancer. His schizophrenic protégé Wild Man Fischer is probably now in his fifties, if he's still alive. Whatever happened to David Ackles? Country Joe McDonald? Medicine Head?

Bridget St John? Does Kevin Ayers still make records? Or does he recline in a hammock under a shady parasol in an Andalusian garden and drink bottle after bottle of wine?

Van Vliet is a bigger enigma than they are, partly because he always was and partly because nobody knows what's wrong with him. Might his illness be incurable? Further poems and lyrics on the CD that Peel found in the art catalogue will appear in his programmes on Radio 1, BFBS and the World Service throughout the month. He treats it with the awe and respect of a new Beefheart album. Perhaps Van Vliet, with his sphinx-like antenna tuned to the east, senses the vibrations.

'More recently,' Sheila will write in a perfectly matter-of-fact passage in *Margrave of the Marshes*, 'Beefheart would call to discuss matters of livestock, since both he and John kept chickens.'

John Peel Show
Radio 1
24 June 1994

Team Dresch – Cuckooland – Beenie Man – Madder Rose – Bandulu – Ben Waters – Terminal Cheesecake – Pussycat Trash – Dreadzone – Luciano and General Pecos – Neil Young – Orbital

Liverpool City Council votes unanimously to press for a fresh inquiry into the Hillsborough disaster. Three weeks ago the ITV current affairs programme The Cook Report *exposed procedural flaws in the 1989 inquest and cast doubt on the coroner's premise that all ninety-six victims were dead by 3.15 p.m.*

The Glastonbury Festival begins today. Peel is broadcasting live from the site. Radio 1 is out in force, getting ready for a seven-hour transmission tomorrow, with Johnnie Walker at the helm. The station has started taking Glastonbury seriously now that it's overtaken Reading as the UK's foremost music festival. Radio 1's coverage began last night with a preview of the three-day event by Mark Radcliffe, a former Peel session producer who has joined the station as a presenter. BBC television, however, isn't interested in Glastonbury; not with Wimbledon, European Cup athletics, the Irish Derby and the 1994 FIFA World Cup going on. MTV is covering it instead.

Peel, snug and warm in a BBC van while 80,000 festival-goers get soaked by the rain, is playing extracts from today's live sets by Madder Rose (a New York band who came second in last year's Festive 50) and Dreadzone, a British reggae-fusion band who recorded a session for him last November. More prominent Glastonbury names this year include Nick Cave, Paul Weller, Elvis Costello, Björk, James, Ride, Radiohead, Blur, Oasis and Pulp – any one of whom might have been a more enticing prospect than Madder Rose or Dreadzone. But if you broadcast live from a festival on a Friday night, you do leave yourself at the mercy of stage times. Most of the major artists are playing tomorrow or on Sunday. So effectively Peel has been fobbed off with the support bands so that Johnnie Walker can have the headline acts.

John Peel Show
Radio 1
23 July 1994

Pentatonik – Harvey's Rabbit – Oasis – The Beatles – Terry Edwards – Rodan – Simon Joyner – Sun City Girls – Armagideon – Bender – Total Eclipse – Government Alpha – Sonny Terry – Velocity Girl

Tony Blair has opened up a thirty-eight-point lead over John Major just two days after being appointed Labour Party leader, a poll reveals. Hitting back at Conservatives who accuse him of lacking substance, Blair tells workers in his County Durham constituency of Sedgefield that the Tories are now 'in a state of total confusion'.

Peel visualises his listeners lounging by their swimming pools on this sunny Saturday afternoon. When a phone call immediately comes in from a listener who doesn't have a swimming pool, Peel feigns amazement. 'Hard to believe in this day and age,' he says. 'Tony Blair will take care of it all, though, I'm certain of that.'

Is that a tinge of sarcasm in the old socialist's voice? 'But Tony,' Peel goes on, 'Guns N' Roses?! Come on, do me a favour.' Blair, the first British political leader to have been the singer in a rock band, has listed *Appetite for Destruction* among the albums he keeps by his CD player. He likes to tell people he modelled his vocal style on Paul Rodgers of Free. Behind the scenes, his people are reaching out to the *NME* and the hipper bands in the UK music industry.

Peel watched Oasis, a hotly tipped five-piece from Manchester, when they played at Glastonbury, enjoying them so much that he made a point of thanking them afterwards. He particularly liked their version of the Beatles' 'I Am the Walrus', an acetate of which has since found its way into his hands. He's not sure if Creation – Oasis's label – intends to release it. The band have a new single, 'Live Forever', scheduled for next month.

'In the meantime, I suppose it's EXCLUSIVE,' Peel says of the acetate, breaking into an insincere mid-Atlantic gurgle, 'to this programme.'

Oasis will then release their first album, *Definitely Maybe*. All this is on the back of two previous singles ('Supersonic' and 'Shakermaker'), both of which received lavish acclaim, and a raft of hilariously argumentative interviews and carefully finessed media storms. Liam and Noel Gallagher have an exaggerated swagger noticeably lacking in the art-school gait of their southern counterparts, Blur. It's salutary to note that the two spearhead bands in the nascent Britpop movement have had minimal airplay – and in Blur's case, none – from Peel, who traditionally sets the guitar-music agenda for the next three years. Peel, in fact, watched Blur at a festival a few years ago, after being advised that they had more depth than their singles suggested, but he found them irritating and has never heard anything to sway his low opinion of them. He prefers Pulp to Blur and Oasis in any case.

'EXCLUSIVE,' he repeats in his mid-Atlantic voice. 'You're supposed to say that a lot these days,' he adds. It must be another Radio 1 memo that's been sent round. Peel doesn't sound happy about it. Is the Bannister regime starting to aggravate him? A postcard arrives from two listeners on holiday in Knossos who wish that Peel was DJing at their hotel. He tells them he may be taking them up on their offer sooner than they expect. He says this in the same voice he used earlier when he was expressing confidence that Tony Blair would put a swimming pool in every garden. The layers of irony today are getting positively onion-esque.

Brighton Museum and Art Gallery has sent out a press release publicising the Don Van Vliet exhibition. It describes him as 'one of the most influential and challenging contributors to the post-war artistic spirit' and 'a landmark figure in alternative rock music'.

'*The* landmark figure,' Peel corrects curtly, not joking this time. The listeners on their poolside sun loungers will note the distinction.

John Peel Show
Radio 1
5 August 1994

Mike Ink and Burger Industries – Magnapop – Luscious Jackson
– Salt Tank – Stereolab – Pressure of Speech – The Klezmatics –
Prozac Memory – Ren and Stimpy – Ornette Coleman – The Source

*The so-called 'tuna wars' between Britain and Spain take an
unexpected turn when a Royal Navy patrol vessel seizes nets belonging
to a British trawler. EU regulations state that nets should have a
maximum length of 2.5 km (1.5 miles), but some UK fishermen use 6
km nets (3.3 miles), which they claim are being deliberately wrecked by
Spanish boats.*

From Guildford in Surrey, Salt Tank are an electronic trio who have
released two EPs, *ST1* and *ST2*. They've also put out a mini-album,
ST3. Another mini-album is planned for next month ('See if you
can guess what it's going to be called,' says Peel) and Salt Tank have
recorded a session for the show tonight. Trance-like with ambient
leanings, they'll end up falling between two stools: not quite hippyish enough for the ambient-dub crowd, but too hippyish for the
superclub hordes at Ministry of Sound and Cream. Salt Tank will
later release the Peel session as an EP called – what else? – *ST5*.
  Peel's final record tonight comes from the Source, an alias for MC
Jay-J of SL2, the rave act that had a hit two years ago with 'On a Ragga
Tip'. Before playing the Source's track, 'High Powered', Peel says:
'Have you noticed how everything all of a sudden is "jungle"? How
long before the Barbra Streisand jungle remixes? Not long, I think.'
  'Jungle' is the word on everyone's lips all right, but there are
two ways of looking at the music. You could call it the break-
through dance genre of 1994, or you could say it owes its origins to

pre-existing genres like breakbeat hardcore. Peel has had a part to play in its evolution, championing the Ragga Twins and Shut Up and Dance (the two acts credited with introducing breakbeats to rave) in the early Nineties. But if 'everything all of a sudden is jungle', that doesn't mean Peel is bored of it. In fact, he's just getting to the point of recognising its potential to be the next big force in music. And this has a lot to do with another evolutionary change. Earlier today, a compilation was released on the Romford-based Breakdown Records, featuring tracks by DJs such as Roni Size, Alex Reece, DJ Hype and Danny Breaks, who recorded proto-jungle tunes under the name Sonz of a Loop Da Loop Era. And while this compilation is certainly full of jungle, these DJs will go on to forge a more 'produced' sound that puts less emphasis on breaks.

The title of the compilation is *Drum 'n' Bass Selection 2*. Peel has already been photographed deep in the bowels of his record collection with a copy of its predecessor, *Drum 'n' Bass Selection 1*, jutting out from a shelf. He could have chosen any one of 25,000 records to pose with, but he chose that one. Maybe it's because he sensed that, before he knew it, everything all of a sudden was going to be drum 'n' bass.

John Peel Show
Radio 1
3 September 1994

Guitar Wolf – Shellac – Zion Train – Sleeper – Stereolab – Palace Brothers – Proyecto Uno – Dumb – The Mountain Goats – Full Moon Scientist – Tuff-to-the-Bone – Finnish Shouting Choir – Baboon

The former England football captain Billy Wright, who won 105 caps and was never booked during a twenty-year playing career, has died of

pancreatic cancer, aged seventy. Awarded a CBE in 1999, he is survived
by his wife, Joy, a member of the Beverley Sisters vocal trio.

In Simon Garfield's 1998 book *The Nation's Favourite: The True*
Adventures of Radio 1, which lifts the lid on Matthew Bannister's
divisive tenure as controller, Peel will observe wryly: 'Matthew has
always been very kind to me, and said that as long as he's controller
there will be a John Peel programme to delight the nation's youth.
Unfortunately, he said the same thing to Johnnie Walker, and he
departed Radio 1 only a few months afterwards.'

Simon Bates has left. Gary Davies has left. Jakki Brambles has left.
Dave Lee Travis has left. And so, more problematically, have four
and a half million listeners since Bannister took over and rearranged
the schedule. Bates, with mighty *Schadenfreude*, called last month for
Bannister and Liz Forgan, the BBC radio executive who employed
him, to resign over the catastrophic ratings. Bates announced his
own resignation days before the reshuffle – some would call it a
purge – that spelled the end of his morning show. He used to have
9 million listeners. Oh, how Radio 1 could do with some of them
now. Peel's comment in July about looking for a job as a hotel DJ in
Knossos was a clear dig at a mistimed and misjudged jackboot. In
essence, Bannister has gone stomping into the offices of the *News*
of the World and tried to turn it into the *Observer*. If Radio 1 keeps
haemorrhaging listeners at the rate of a million a month, which presenters, one wonders, will survive the inevitable *next* purge?

Peel ploughs on, as he always does, keeping his head down, going
out to forage for food when the larger animals have had their fill
and withdrawn. He talks a lot this afternoon, rather more than
usual. He feels nicely rested, refreshed even. The show moves from
Britpop (Sleeper) to Anglo-French drone pop (Stereolab) to Latin
house (Proyecto Uno). The funniest track comes from the Finnish
Shouting Choir, who do exactly as their name suggests, making the

sound of forty angry squaddies trying to shout their way out of a locked gymnasium. Peel explains he had a comfortable sleep at the hotel in Paddington earlier. Liverpool have made a great start to the season. Nine points out of nine. Life could be worse.

Just then some travel news lands on his desk. Heavy flooding has caused dangerous driving conditions and road closures in many parts of Britain, especially the Midlands and the south. Back to the hotel for the night, it seems. The rain come out and stole the sun and gone.

1995: THE HALL OF FAME

*'It was the first demo tape we'd ever done and you said you'd listen
to it in the car on the way home. I thought: "Hmm, I wonder
about that . . ."'* JARVIS COCKER to Peel on 30 September
1995, recalling their first meeting in 1981

John Peel Show
Radio 1
17 March 1995

Wire – The Bluetones – Universal Spirit Warrior – Th' Faith Healers
– Pond – Beatnik Filmstars – DJ Hell – Hooton 3 Car – Menswear –
Buddy Max – Quickspace Supersport – Panash – Hole – Joyrider

*Ronnie Kray, the former gangland boss, has died at the age of sixty-
one. He was serving a life sentence for the 1967 murder of Jack McVitie,
a criminal associate. Kray's twin brother Reggie, who was convicted
at the same trial of murdering gang rival George Cornell in 1966, is
currently detained at HM Prison Maidstone.*

Courtney Love didn't make it to the 1992 Reading Festival to see
Nirvana's headline set, but she did play there last year with her band
Hole, attracting a rubbernecking crowd to the main stage just four
months after her husband's suicide. If they'd come to witness a car
crash, she didn't disappoint.

'Courtney's first appearance backstage certainly caught the attention,' wrote Peel in the *Guardian*. 'Swaying wildly and with lipstick smeared on her face, hands and, I think, her back, as well as on the collar of her dress, the singer would have drawn whistles of astonishment in Bedlam. After a brief word with supporters at the foot of the stage, she reeled away, knocking over a waste bin, and disappeared.'

But Peel is a true rock 'n' roll fan, and this is what he wrote next: 'Minutes later she was onstage giving a performance which verged on the heroic . . . Love steered her band through a set which dared you to pity either her recent history or that of the band . . . [They] teetered on the edge of chaos, generating a tension which I cannot remember having felt before from any stage.'

Hole, by common consent, are one of the few grunge bands left standing who can recapture the glory days of 1992. In Britain, it's become awfully unfashionable to look to Seattle. As Peel might say, have you noticed that everything all of a sudden is Britpop? He's been playing many bands linked to the movement: Pulp, Supergrass, Sleeper, Elastica, the Boo Radleys and, tonight, Menswear and the Bluetones. Boycotting Blur on principle, he's also snubbed Oasis since his brief interest in their Glastonbury performance. But who needs Oasis when Pulp, Elastica and Supergrass, bands once known only to Peel listeners and *NME* readers, are well on the way to becoming pop stars? This time next year, could Pulp or Elastica emulate the achievement of Blur at the 1995 Brit Awards by winning four categories out of four?

Radio 1 hasn't yet declared itself the official Britpop station, but it's rebranding itself fast all the same. The slogan you hear a lot these days is: 'The UK's new music . . . first.' If there'd been any room for a second sentence in that slogan, it might have gone: 'You know, like John Peel has been playing every week for the past twenty-eight years – only now we're all doing it.' But Peel, as ever, is casually and carelessly undermined by Radio 1 colleagues who should know better. It didn't occur to Steve Wright, when he urged listeners last October to switch off their radios and watch his new Saturday evening programme on BBC1, that it clashed directly with Peel. But old Peelie won't mind a bit of professional discourtesy between friends, will he? And no one listens to him anyway, do they?

But tactless co-workers are not Peel's only problem. Two of the three bands heard in Radio 1's 'new music first' trailer are Ash and Sleeper, who have crept into the daytime schedules after a year of Peel support. In times past, he would have discovered them on their first single or demo tape, and then watched as they rose up the schedule, from evening to late afternoon to Steve Wright to Simon Bates, becoming Radio 1 mainstays. But now the situation is a lot more complicated. Peel, in fact, no longer has much to do with nurturing future stars and putting bands on the road to success. They're more likely to receive their crucial early momentum from airplay on the *Evening Session*.

Appointed by Matthew Bannister soon after his arrival in 1993, the *Evening Session*'s co-presenters are Steve Lamacq, a music journalist, and Jo Whiley, a former researcher for Channel 4's *The Word*. Lamacq, in particular, is a real asset. Not only does he attend gigs like a man possessed, seeing new bands every night of the week, but a record label that he co-founded in 1992 – Deceptive – is the label that signed Elastica, one of Britpop's hottest prospects. Released four days ago, Elastica's self-titled debut album is expected to burst into the charts at number 1 this weekend. And whereas Peel used to play fast and loose with Radio 1 and Dandelion, Lamacq has agreed to step down from Deceptive to avoid any accusations of favouritism. The stakes are a lot higher in the mid-Nineties than they were when Peel was Lamacq's age in the late Sixties.

While Lamacq goes looking for the young bands that will justify Radio 1's claims to be a 'new music' station, Peel finds himself stuck out on Friday nights between Pete Tong's *Essential Mix* and Tim Westwood's *1FM Rap Show*, and marooned on Saturday afternoons in a two-hour slot before Danny Rampling's *Lovegroove Dance Party*. Never mind Britpop, Radio 1 is more like the UK's official trance, progressive house and hip-hop station, with a fifty-five-year-old man stranded in the middle.

Peel would make more sense in a Monday to Friday slot immediately following Lamacq and Whiley at 9 p.m. This would at least provide a modicum of thematic continuity. But Peel doesn't crave a return to that kind of working week, and in any event Radio 1 has filled the post-*Evening Session* hour with talk shows and comedy. Peel might as well stay where he is, broadcasting to the football fans, the Friday night after-the-pub crowd and impatient ravers waiting for the lovegroove party to start.

John Peel Show
Radio 1
31 March 1995

Dick Dale – Tommy McLain – Peepshow – La Machoire – Thee Shatners – Faust – Hole – Yummy Fur – Buddy Max – Sabres of Paradise – Babes in Toyland – Lung Leg – Holy Ghost – Archers of Loaf

An appeal court judge has overturned the two-week prison sentence of Manchester United's Eric Cantona, who attacked a Crystal Palace fan during a match in January. He is instead sentenced to 120 hours of community service. The FA has banned him for eight months.

Earlier this month Peel told his listeners about Buddy Max, a man who calls himself 'America's Singing Flea Market Cowboy' and stands at a junction on Highway 44 in Lecanto, Florida, singing country songs. Peel had played several tracks from Max's album *I Love Miss America*, and advised anyone interested in hearing more to send away to an address in Brighton for a free copy. 'Response to this has been, I have to say, poor,' he noted a couple of weeks ago. Only two people had come forward.

Tonight, Peel is excited to report that thirteen listeners have now taken the plunge, putting their names down for a copy of Max's album, which includes 'Pretty Girls on TV', the plaintive 'And I Hung Up My Old Cowboy Hat' and the provocatively titled 'Desert Storm'. Andy Kershaw has recently been to Florida, and was asked by Peel to visit the junction on Highway 44 where Max stands. Kershaw, who presumably had more important things to do, failed to carry out the request. When not even Kershaw is interested in a cowboy, that cowboy may consider his career to be at a low ebb.

Peel recovered quickly, shaking the hand of an ever bigger icon – Dick Dale, the king of the surf guitar – at a concert two nights ago in London. Dale has experienced a renaissance as a result of his 1962 single 'Misirlou' being featured in the opening credits of Quentin Tarantino's *Pulp Fiction*. Peel informed Dale, in what was surely a charged moment, that he used to work at KMEN in San Bernardino in the Sixties, which he believes was the first station to play Dale's records in America. Dale seems to have been impressed. Yesterday he took his guitar to Maida Vale and recorded his first Peel session at the age of fifty-seven.

Buddy Max, who made his first record in 1949 and is almost a decade older than Dale, is on even more plaintive form than usual tonight. 'They Call Me a Cowboy', from *I Love Miss America*, amounts to a fatalistic admission of the dwindling opportunities for flea-market cowboys who stand at interstate junctions in Florida. 'Cowboy's for youngsters, not a man of my age,' Max sings. 'They call me a cowboy, but I'm a cowman.'

'I'd never really thought of it like that,' Peel admits.

John Peel Show
Radio 1
7 *April 1995*

Sonic Subjunkies – Teengenerate – Black Star Liner – Mug – Harry
Pussy – Dread Bass – Uncle Wiggly – Arsedestroyer – Anal Cunt –
Van Basten – Distorted Waves of Ohm – Snuff – Supergrass – Pulp

The jury at the inquest into the 1989 Marchioness *disaster returns a*
verdict of unlawful killing. More than fifty people drowned when the
riverboat, which was hosting a party, collided with a dredger on the
Thames. Prosecutions are expected to follow.

Lapsed Peel listeners who remember him playing grindcore tracks
in the mid-to-late Eighties with titles like 'Carbonized Eyesockets'
and 'Regurgitation of Giblets' – ah, Carcass, what sonnets flowed
from their poetic nibs – probably wouldn't think it possible that his
programmes in the Nineties could be any more violent. They might
take a different view if they heard the three hours of pulverising
music that he puts his listeners through tonight.

Sonic Subjunkies are a German digital-hardcore act whose track
'Central Industrial II: The Lockdown' is based around an American
news report of a high-security prison in the aftermath of a riot. The
warders are panicky, claustrophobic and fearful of more confronta-
tions, or maybe the warders are perfectly sanguine and the listener
is merely feeling a weirdly synthetic empathy. Peel's second record,
by Tokyo garage punks Teengenerate, is a frenzied reworking of
'Shake, Rattle and Roll' that takes the famous Bill Haley hit and
feeds it to a wolfpack. But even from there, things accelerate.

Of the two bands in session, Mug are discordantly Bogshed-
like and Black Star Liner create a sort of Asian techno with volatile undercurrents of Killing Joke. Black Star Liner will be signed

to a label co-owned by Feargal Sharkey after he hears Peel's show tonight, which is a thought that needs quite a bit of processing, while Mug are almost too febrile for a label to touch; the kind of band who drink eight cans of super-strength cider and foam at the mouth as they plug their guitars in. One song sounds like it might be about lepers, but there's always a chance, of course, that it might be about leopards.

Peel is always very calm when he plays music that pummels the head and batters the kidneys. Rarely, indeed, throughout his decades on Radio 1, has he ever so much as warned the listeners that they may be in for a shock or a dislocating experience. Harry Pussy, a Miami band on a small Bristol label, have a lawlessness to match Mug, a policy of seizing the nearest instrument in the room and wringing as extreme a noise as possible from it. Peel follows them with six minutes of woofer-punishing jungle from the Birmingham duo Dread Bass, completing possibly the most uncompromising opening thirty minutes of any show in recent memory. It's strange to think that just two years ago, Radio 1 thought he'd be the ideal man to sit in for Jakki Brambles at lunchtime.

But the first half hour is just an aperitif, it turns out, for the sonic brutalisation that characterises the rest of the programme. The Swedish hardcore band Arsedestroyer (a name that Peel can just about get away with saying on air) grunt, scream and vomit their way through a song so evil that a cloven-hoofed goat creature would quail. The studiously offensive Massachusetts grindcore band Anal Cunt (whose name Peel obviously can't say – he calls them 'A.C.') slaughter and child-sacrifice their way through a version of Elton John's 'I'm Still Standing'. Talk about an inapt night for Peel to debut the new Pulp single, 'Common People'. At the end of this three-hour assault, which he concludes with seven more minutes of intense jungle, you can almost hear him say 'follow that' as he hands over to Tim Westwood.

John Peel Show
Radio 1
21 July 1995

Dave Clarke – Kenickie – Dadomo – Yummy Fur – Green Nuns of the
Revolution – Urusei Yatsura – Gorky's Zygotic Mynci – June of 44 –
Dub Narcotic Sound System – Vulva – Goober Patrol – Movietone

*The UN Human Rights Committee has criticised the government for
releasing Lee Clegg, a soldier serving a life term for the 1990 murder
of a Belfast teenager. Karen Reilly died when Clegg fired at the car
in which she was travelling as it drove through an army checkpoint.
The decision to free him has sparked rioting in nationalist areas of
Northern Ireland.*

Britpop will at some stage need a second wave of bands, and one of
them might be Kenickie, a quartet of three young women and one
young man from Sunderland. The girls have names like drag queens
– Lauren Laverne, Marie du Santiago – but their punky songs
are full of pep and personality. Three years ago their record sales
would have been negligible. Ten years ago they would have been
the Shop Assistants. But now bands like Kenickie can take heart
from the success of girl-fronted Britpop success stories like Sleeper
and Elastica; two or three songs in their Peel session tonight could
be chart hits one day on the all-new, Britpop-loving 1FM. Peel was
probably the first DJ to play Kenickie, on a north-east compilation
album in January, but Lamacq and Whiley are waiting in the wings,
ready to steal them from under his nose. The new slogan of the
Evening Session is 'music with attitude'. And no, they're not joking.

Peel has received a letter from the Rock 'n' roll Hall of Fame, an
organisation in Ohio that inducts four or five legends of Fifties and
Sixties music into its ever-growing membership ranks each year. An

actual hall has now been built in Cleveland, and the founders are planning a 'DJ exhibit' that will have room for 'a few' names from England. Peel reads out the letter sardonically, savouring every word.

The Rock 'n' roll Hall of Fame needs him to send back, as early as he can, a 'bio' that itemises his 'radio history', so that it can judge whether or not he'd be suitable as one of the English names in the 'DJ exhibit'. He reads: 'This can also include any special phrases or routines that you're famous for' – he suggests: 'Oh no, I'm playing this at the wrong speed' – 'and any of your accomplishments in the music world.'

All things considered, he doubts he'll be replying.

John Peel Show
Radio 1
8 September 1995

Flying Saucer Attack – The Bomb Bassets – Murmur – Baby Bird – DJ Poppy – Sportsguitar – Heron – Mouse on Mars – Prolapse – Solid Jackson – Space Bike – Friends of Dean Martinez – Panel Donor

After yesterday's discovery of a 500,000-year-old hominid tooth at an archaeological site in Boxgrove, West Sussex, the remains of four 250,000-year-old Neanderthals are found in a cave at Pontnewydd, near St Asaph in north-east Wales. One of them is believed to be a child of eight.

About forty-five minutes into the show, Peel plays a sweet, meditative reggae song by an Englishman named G. T. Moore. Peel remembers Moore from the early Seventies as a member of a folk band called Heron. At the Reading Festival a couple of weeks ago (which resembled a 1992 Peel show with its post-grunge and proto-grunge line-up of Smashing Pumpkins, Green Day, Hole, Teenage Fanclub,

Pavement and Mudhoney), Peel was talking to some friends back-stage when a tall figure approached, appearing to expect Peel to recognise him. It was an ex-member of Heron, he knew that much, but there were people around so he gave him short shrift and has spent the last two weeks feeling guilty about it. He's decided to bal-ance the karma by playing a track from a Heron LP called *Twice as Nice and Half the Price* – a double album that sold for £2.30 in 1971. The song sounds warm and full of Guinness. They were a bit like Lindisfarne. G. T. Moore – was that you at Reading?

The big hit on the Carlsberg Stage, Peel has heard, were Prolapse, a combative bunch from Leicester who played on the Friday. Their set was recorded by Radio 1 and Peel plays eighteen minutes of it. You can see why they made an impression. They have two singers, one of them a choleric Scot like Ivor Cutler moonlighting in a punk band. As he fumes away, a female singer shouts completely different lyrics to a separate rhythm. It's barmy but it works. Perhaps Peel will be approached at a Reading Festival twenty years hence, and the apologetic interrupter will be a member of Prolapse. 'Hi, John, remember us?' He'll probably tell them to piss off because he's talk-ing to G. T. Moore.

John Peel Show
Radio 1
30 September 1995

Steve Stoll – Eggplant – Tapper Zukie – Pulp – Pablo Lubadika – Link Wray and His Ray Men – Cat Power – DJ Scoobie – Billy Williams – Crime – Dave Clarke – Cheater Slicks – Loop Guru

The British boxer Prince Naseem Hamed wins his first world title, becoming WBO featherweight champion with a victory over Steve

Robinson at Cardiff Arms Park. Robinson, the defender and home favourite, was knocked down by a Hamed left hook in the eighth round, leading the referee to stop the fight.

When Peel first played Pulp's 'Common People' in April, its release was still some six weeks away. It came out in the fourth week of May, flying into the charts at number 2 on a wave of 1FM airplay and national goodwill. It then perched behind Robson and Jerome's 'Unchained Melody' for a fortnight before dropping to 3. Britpop has become such a commercial force that music-industry analysts are genuinely surprised if a single doesn't go to number 1, particularly if it's a single as good as 'Common People'.

As Jarvis Cocker and his band prepare to release a new album, *Different Class*, next month, they find their path crossing once again with Peel's. Cocker doesn't need Peel's support any more, and could easily give *Different Class* to Lamacq and Whiley to preview on the *Evening Session*, but he doesn't think along those lines – or rather he's worldly enough to think along two lines at once. This morning he and Pulp mimed to their new single, 'Mis-Shapes' (the more child-friendly half of a double A-side with 'Sorted for E's and Wizz'), on BBC1's *Live & Kicking*. This afternoon Cocker and the band's drummer, Nick Banks, are driving up from London to be interviewed by Peel in his Suffolk home. It's a journey that takes Cocker back almost fourteen years. When he and Peel first met, he was a sixth-former at the City School in Sheffield. He's now Britain's most iconic spectacle wearer since Michael Caine in *The Ipcress File*. That's what a Top 2 single can do.

The exclusive tracks from *Different Class* that Peel has been given to play today have gone to the right DJ, one can't help feeling. The *Evening Session* may offer 'music with attitude', but Peel spotted Pulp's potential when Radio 1's evening show was still presented by David Jensen. And he did so by carrying out a simple promise made to Cocker at a northern polytechnic gig. 'I'll play your tape in the car on the way home,' he assured him. Cocker had met the one DJ on Radio 1 who not only made promises like that, but kept them.

While Cocker and Banks make their way up from London, Peel repeats the 1981 Pulp session that led from that first meeting. Parts of it sound truly peculiar in the context of 'Common People' – though of course Pulp had a different line-up back then – and many bands would object to Radio 1 reminding them of their juvenilia when they have a new album to promote. On arriving at Peel Acres, however, Cocker is happy to let his mind drift back.

'We didn't know how to finish the song,' he says of 'Refuse to Be Blind', a track that ends in electronic voices. 'We were looking at all the bits of exciting machinery in the [Maida Vale] studio that we'd never seen before. The bloke started turning this knob and the voice started sounding like a Dalek, and we thought that was really good. We went back up to Sheffield in the van thinking it was fantastic.' Their drummer was fifteen. The *Sheffield Star* learned of the session and gave them a front-page mention. 'They wanted to take pictures of us in school uniform and stage gear – "before" and "after" – but we refused to do that.'

Taking a tour of Peel's house, Cocker notices that he gives pride of place to his trophies and awards. 'Top Disc Jockey British. John Peel. *Melody Maker*. 1968. Very nice!' They move on before Peel can tell him that those *Melody Maker* readers saved his career. The studio is so tiny that in order to have a face-to-face conversation, Cocker and Banks have to walk round the house and stand outside the window, leaning in. A jovial foil to Cocker's dry wit, Banks joined Pulp in the late Eighties after 'the third incarnation collapsed in acrimony'. A dicey moment comes when Peel forgets the title of their new album – and then, less forgivably, Cocker's name – but the visit is so amicable that nobody cares. 'You get so used to these pop stars filling the house,' Peel improvises. And off they go, back to London and fame.

1996–7: THE THOUGHT OF IT
ALL GOING WRONG

---

*'What with one thing and another, life became a little gothic
for us.'* PEEL *on his BFBS show, 8 January 1998*

John Peel Show
Radio 1
22 March 1996

Lucky Monkeys – Spare Snare – Guided by Voices – Panasonic – Low
Rocks – Cows – Sleater-Kinney – Modest Mouse – The Fugees –
Lizard Music – Virtual Zenith – Coping Saw – Melt-Banana – Spatula

*Princess Diana has been involved in a car crash. She was driving home
to Kensington Palace when a Fiat struck her car in heavy traffic near
Earls Court. Neither driver sustained any injuries.*

Peel's appearance on *This Is Your Life* in January looked like a pleasant evening, if not exactly a star-studded one in the studio, but
just before it aired he got the bad news that Radio 1's soon-to-be-
launched jungle and drum 'n' bass show, *One in the Jungle*, was ear-
marked for his Friday night slot. Politely but firmly, he protested by
letter to Matthew Bannister, putting the case (since they couldn't
speak for themselves) for the minority genres and subgenres that
were going to be losing out.

'There are several things going on now which may or may not evolve into something substantial,' Peel wrote. 'It would be disappointing, in the event of one or other of these being really popular, to lose yet another hour so that you could schedule time for programmes devoted to it.' Touché! A record company wouldn't penalise the head of A&R for signing 80 per cent of its successful roster. A football club wouldn't demote the chief scout for finding half the team that had just won the Premier League. 'Think of my programmes as your research department,' Peel urged Bannister. 'Noisy, smelly but occasionally coming up with the formulae which you can subsequently market.'

It was an eloquent plea, but it fell on deaf ears. From next month, 'Radio 1's bearded Svengali' (as the *Radio Times* calls him) will lose Friday nights and move to 8 p.m. on Sundays, between Andy Kershaw and the weekly documentary. Add his two hours on Saturday afternoons and Peel now has only four hours of airtime per week. Jo Whiley has ten and a half.

Tonight – one of his last Friday shows before the Sunday switch – proves the truth of Peel's letter to Bannister. He has a session from the Fugees, a hip-hop trio with a huge buzz around them and a new album (*The Score*) top-heavy with future million-sellers: 'Ready or Not', 'Killing Me Softly', 'No Woman, No Cry'. Two of them will be UK number 1 hits this year. Peel, though, was playing the Fugees a long time before anyone at their record company could have predicted a sensational hip hop/R&B crossover. He had a Fugees session back in 1994, indeed, after their first album, *Blunted on Reality*, had charted in the low hundreds. And sweetly, they seem to remember it. If Bannister is listening tonight, he'll hear the Fugees mention Peel by name twice, and one of them, Wyclef Jean, will go so far as to call him 'my man John Peel'.

Of course Peel, being Peel, finds *The Score* and its host of chartbound hits to be 'slicked up a little bit too much for my barbaric tastes'. But he enjoys tonight's session and, to be fair to them, the Fugees seem to give him something raw, spur-of-the-moment and out of the ordinary. Two of the tracks, 'Freestyle' (a reworking of 'How Many Mics' from *The Score*) and 'Blame It on the Sun' (a Stevie Wonder song), are exclusive and won't emerge in an official capacity until August, when they'll make up the numbers on a CD format of 'Ready or Not'. The third song in the session, 'Haitian in England' – a complaint, by the sound of it, about the Fugees' treatment by immigration officers at Heathrow – will never be released anywhere. His exclusive is small comfort, though. The *John Peel Show* is now officially under siege.

John Peel Show
Radio 1
1 June 1996

Time Stretch Armstrong – Stereolab – Stock, Hausen and Walkman – The Candyskins – The Fall – Palace – Eilert Pilarm – Swandive – Mad Professor and Jah Shaka – EKO – Nicos Jaritz – Chicane

The BBC TV programme Watchdog Healthcheck *claims to have evidence from neuroscientists in Europe and America that people who use mobile phones are at risk from cancer, asthma and Alzheimer's disease. Britain has an estimated 5 million mobile-phone users, and the number is rising year on year.*

These are disconsolate times for the Fall. A new album, *The Light User Syndrome*, sees the depleted band struggling to claw back a few of the thousands of listeners who have abandoned them since the early Nineties. Mark E. Smith, a thirty-nine-year-old missing most of his teeth, is in the grip of a debilitating alcohol problem that can no longer be ignored or denied. The Fall's 1996 line-up includes two women, one of whom may be Smith's current girlfriend; the other is certainly one of his ex-wives. Brix Smith has returned to help her ex-husband through his dark night of the soul.

It's not that the Fall are a spent force. *The Light User Syndrome*, from which Peel plays two tracks, doesn't lack inspiration. They still *create*. It's just that they appear from the outside to be in an irreversible tailspin. The Peel session they'll record later this month – their twentieth, incredibly – will be Brix's last. Her emphatic departure, for the second and final time, comes in the middle of a tour (after a fight with Mark E. Smith) and leaves the Fall lurching from crisis to crisis. At this point, most journalists give up on them. But one DJ keeps the faith. One man has belief. One disciple is hopeful that Smith can turn things round. A Fall fan for eighteen years, it's too late for Peel to think of backing out of the relationship now.

John Peel Show
Radio 1
2 November 1996

Rok/Jonzon – The Ghouls – Apex – Gorky's Zygotic Mynci – Hardfloor – Alastair Galbraith – Dumb – Silver Jews – Neurotek – Low – Pimp Daddy Nash – Deutschmark Bob and the Deficits – Agathocles

Prime Minister John Major has accused Tony Blair of being 'untrustworthy' after the Labour leader appeared to break an agreement that neither party would refer to the Dunblane massacre during the conference season. Forty-three-year-old Thomas Hamilton murdered sixteen children and a teacher at a Scottish primary school in March, prompting a speech on handgun control at Labour's conference last month.

Gorky's Zygotic Mynci are a band from Carmarthen in Wales. Their name looks as though it ought to mean Gorky's Psychotic Monkey, but apparently this is wide of the mark. They don't really know what it means. Nor are they sure what kind of music they write. Psychedelic Celtic folk would be in the ballpark. Their songs have buttery electric keyboards and sticky-sweet choruses like apple and cinnamon muffins. Peel insists on a session from them every year.

There's the vague threat of disaster tonight. New studios have been installed at 1FM, and we all know who has difficulties adjusting to new technology. Peel admits he hasn't completely mastered the desk. The show is troubled, as we knew it would be, by mechanical breakdowns, glitches and inexplicable silences. Computer failure. Human error. Why distinguish? A listener writes to tell Peel that a customer at the shop where he works warned him recently there might be a problem with the fridges. They were making a funny clicking sound. 'It's the radio,' the boy explained. 'I'm listening to John Peel.'

And with the thought of it all going wrong adding extra frissons to already tautened senses, we press on. A techno track by Hardfloor makes a feature of Beavis's idiosyncratic sneezing laugh in *Beavis and Butthead*. Alastair Galbraith, a New Zealander, gets his guitar to serrate and squeal like Big Black and Sonic Youth. A version of Merle Haggard's 'Okie from Muskogee' is sung by some Texans who make records for the local expat Bohemian and Moravian community. (Who knew?) And as another machine starts acting up, Peel stops announcing what the songs are called and decides to just press the button and see what happens.

Deutschmark Bob and the Deficits are from Louisiana, but have emigrated to Germany. They use a slide guitar made from a metal plate stolen from a Turkish restaurant in Hamburg, Peel reads in some ludicrous press release. Their single, 'Mexicano Americano', is regrettably short on slide guitar (unless the restaurant demanded

the plate back) but a slide guitar *in excelsis* adorns the DIY production of Twenty Miles, a Mississippi duo, who wang, dang and
doodle like a pair of loonies on mezcal rocking back and forth on a
dilapidated porch. It goes without saying that Peel bought most of
these records on spec.

Agathocles, who are Belgian, have left the grindcore scene and
now describe their music as 'mincecore'. (Peel laughs.) The difference between grindcore and mincecore is one for the audiophiles.
The satanic vocals have a cylindrical timbre, as though being sung
through a trombone, while the drums are shrill and trebly like knit-
ting needles on Formica surfaces. In another deviation, the singer
in Agathocles actually appears to vomit in mid-song, instead of
just sounding like he's going to. 'Top Belgian entertainers,' Peel
enthuses. Years later, they'll release an album entitled *Keep Mincing*.

John Peel Show
Radio 1
22 December 1996

Infinity Project – Servotron – Billy Bragg – Back 2 Basics – Paul Kelly
– The Prodigy – DJ Shadow – Broadcast – Zion Train – White Town –
Force and Styles – Aphex Twin – Belle and Sebastian

*On a day when Catholic and Protestant schoolchildren unite for a
peace rally in Belfast, a bomb explodes in a mainly Catholic area of the
city, stoking fears that the two-year-old Loyalist ceasefire may be over.
David Ervine of the Progressive Unionists warns that his party will not
represent any Loyalists who 'return to war'.*

There's the oddly comforting presence of Billy Bragg in the studio
this evening, performing his ninth Peel session live on the air rather

than recording it at Maida Vale. The session features a couple of his greatest hits ('A New England', 'Levi Stubbs' Tears') and concludes in a spirit of Yuletide camaraderie with Bragg, Peel and an unruly choir of onlookers and accordionists singing 'Deck the Halls with Boughs of Holly'. Bragg sounds softer than the abrasive Essex lad of yore, neither badgering nor hectoring. He tells Peel that since becoming a father he's found that his singing voice isn't really suited to lullabies – certainly not to their traditional purpose of getting a child off to sleep, anyway – and so he has 'subsequently developed a gentler tone'.

John Peel Show
Radio 1
16 February 1997

Topper – Underworld – Blur – Potential Bad Boy featuring Melissa Bell – Headbutt – Dimension 5 – Northpole – Joe Williams' Washboard Blues Singers – Clinic – Scratchy Muffin – Pavement

The Attorney General is to consider whether the Daily Mail *committed contempt of court this week when it named five south London men as the killers of the black teenager Stephen Lawrence. Photographs of the suspects were published on the newspaper's front page under the headline 'Murderers'. Lawrence was stabbed to death in a racially motivated attack in 1993.*

Underworld, a British techno and progressive-house trio, have been recording in one guise or another since 1983. Last year they exploded overground when their track 'Born Slippy' (a remix of a 1995 song of the same name) rose to number 2 in the charts after appearing in the film *Trainspotting*. Since last summer, no compilation of Britpop, electronica or Top 40 hits has been complete without Underworld.

Peel has a new compilation called *Foundations: Coming Up from the Streets* – twenty tracks of jungle, techno, trip hop and more – and sure enough, Underworld appear on it with a 1993 single, 'Spikee'. Peel fades it out early, apologising, having apparently meant to play one of the tracks either side of it. This is no slight on Underworld, whose music he likes; it's just that 'Spikee' is twelve minutes long (as he's just spotted on the CD display) and there's a meticulously timed list of records typed out on a sheet of paper in front of him. When you've been reduced to four hours a week, precious minutes are of the essence.

Underworld's 'Born Slippy' remix was voted to number 5 by Peel's listeners in their Festive 50 at Christmas. The chart also included Orbital, Aphex Twin, Dave Clarke (the DJ whom Peel calls 'the baron of techno'), the trip-hop act White Town and the happy-hardcore duo Force and Styles. The last-named pair, whose track 'Fireworks' appeared at number 30, were an intriguing inclusion. They seemed to confirm that a few listeners out there – like Peel himself – enjoy happy hardcore for musical reasons, dare one say even aesthetic ones, and not just because its manic BPMs are perfect to go apeshit to. Peel started putting happy hardcore in his shows about two years ago, seeing something wonderfully primitive in the zany repetition of those BPMs even as frowning dance journos dismissed it as council-estate drug-nutter music.

Peel, in fact, is probably the only DJ at Radio 1 at the moment who takes happy hardcore seriously. Danny Rampling wouldn't be caught dead playing it, and Pete Tong probably refuses to admit that it even exists. But the really weird thing about Peel and happy hardcore is that no happy hardcore addicts will ever hear him play it: that community is wholly oblivious to Peel. He's championing one of the most formulaic, un-eclectic types of music ever invented, but doing so to the wrong audience on the wrong radio station in a highly eclectic, non-formulaic way. (By juxtaposing it between Pavement and Half Man Half Biscuit, for one thing.)

With happy hardcore, Peel is both an evangelist and a dilettante. While true lovers of hard dance will be getting their fix from pirate stations and DJ tapes, Peel continues to play it as a sort of benevolent genre tourist, tapping his foot nineteen to the dozen while not being remotely aware of the minor fluctuations in style that make up the hard dance sub-subgenres. That said, and this is crucial, he has a distinct advantage when it comes to hard dance genres, because he only ever needs to play one track from them at a time. He doesn't run the risk of alienating the hardcore haters with a whole hour of it. It's precisely because Peel has never specialised in hard dance that he's able to put hard dance in every show.

Hence the dilettantism. At least with reggae and African music he had a fighting chance of getting his listeners to convert. But even Peel must realise sooner or later that hard dance may be a holy headfuck to experience for the first time – for the duration of exactly one song – but is a case of rapidly diminishing returns thereafter. No wonder the likes of Rampling never go near it.

John Peel Show
Radio 1
10 April 1997

Servotron – Mouse on Mars – Can – I-Roy – Run On – Gorky's Zygotic Mynci – Meth O.D. – Alliance – Piano Magic

The latest opinion polls point to a Labour landslide in the general election on 1 May, with the party now establishing a fifteen-point lead over the Conservatives. Voters have identified education, health care and crime as the key issues in the campaign.

The *John Peel Show* has had the removal men in again. Two months ago its stoical fifty-seven-year-old host bid farewell to his weekend slots and took up residence on Tuesday, Wednesday and Thursday evenings at 8.30 p.m., where he follows Steve Lamacq's *Evening Session*. With three two-hour shows, Peel has seen his airtime increased by 50 per cent (or, looked at more phlegmatically, restored to what it was before *One in the Jungle* interfered with it). Either way, it's now clear that Matthew Bannister is not Peel's enemy. Peel hopes Bannister will in time allow him to start broadcasting his shows from home, which may help to assuage his fatigue.

Lamacq, who has presented the *Evening Session* alone since Jo Whiley's promotion to a daytime show at the beginning of the year, is a long way from being the hidebound indie fan he's sometimes unfairly portrayed as, but his taste in music is still a lot narrower than Peel's. An *Evening Session* listener expecting some sort of seamless transition between the two shows as 8.29 p.m. ticks into 8.30 p.m. would soon be disabused of his error. The impulse purchases, cock-eyed juxtapositions and singular running orders of Fat Jack Peel, as he now calls himself, ensure that there's a jarring, psychologically different atmosphere between his programme and any programme that precedes it, with no logic sometimes to the selections of music other than the self-evident fact that all of them seem to be popular with Peel himself, who offers neither explanation nor justification for his reasons. Is this what the BBC call watercooler radio?

He's always been an old-fashioned DJ in the classic application of his craft. Whether 1FM is trying to reach out to Oxbridge-educated mums or going hell-for-leather for the Spice Girls fans, Peel never dumbs down and never gussies up. He talks to the listener one-on-one as opposed to posse-to-posse (the reason he failed in the Jakki Brambles slot, it could be argued, was because he couldn't mentally visualise his listener), and while other DJs witter and blather about what an awesome single this is and what a wicked tune that was,

Peel makes his links in the least demonstrative way, announcing the artist, the song title, the name of the record label and nothing else. All he says tonight about 'Angel Pie/Magic Tree' – a track by an English trio called Piano Magic – is that it's 'the last record I have for you this week'. No breathless hype. No 'it's a little bit "hello?", so get your heads round this one'. No waffle, no drivel.

What this means is that a song is able to tell its story undisturbed and unadulterated. Peel, to change the punctuation slightly on a 1995 1FM slogan, is putting 'the UK's new music first'. First as in before him. First as in more important. Piano Magic's 'Angel Pie/ Magic Tree' might have wilted like a daisy if he'd said something facile about it. Instead its effect is spellbinding. A tinkling, chiming instrument is shadowed by the drone of a cello. A young girl reads a story, pulling alternate words out of a children's book and an American Civil War history. 'Confederate general from Big Sur sat on my lap like a happy cat,' she says like the little girl in the Fairy Liquid advert. 'I can sleep and read at the same time, and day and night are just words.' Her voice bobs ever so slightly up and down, as if she's telling a story to her dolls.

The cello and the chiming instrument fade out and are replaced by a guitar and a monophonic synthesizer that plays random notes. The notes first nag, then annoy and then become an enigmatic study in disorientation. The girl is absent from this second half of the song, but her fingers seem to be operating the synthesizer, so her quizzical illogic is still in the room. Every random note she hits curls round the conundrum of her story like the tail of a question mark. What a piece of music for Peel to finish the week with. 'Angel Pie/Magic Tree' could haunt a listener from Thursday to Tuesday. Perhaps he should take a leaf out of the book of a fellow BBC presenter, who likes to end his *Crimewatch* programmes with the words: 'Don't have nightmares, do sleep well.'

Blur at Peel Acres
Radio 1
5 May 1997

Blur – Orbital – Billy Bragg – The Charlatans – Supergrass – Shed Seven – Propellerheads – Gene – Comsat Angels – Silver Apples – The Fall – Kenickie – Dreadzone – Wire – Melanie – Suckle

Tony Blair, the new prime minister, moves into Downing Street today with his wife Cherie, a barrister, and their three children. Four days ago the largest election victory in the Labour Party's history gave Blair a majority of 179. Conservative leader John Major is expected to resign.

A few months ago, in between hammering six-inch nails into the listeners' cerebella with his latest consignments of happy hardcore and drum 'n' bass, Peel said an interesting thing. He'd just played a song called 'M.O.R.' by Blur – yes, Blur – from a new album (called *Blur*) that sounded like a conscious attempt to rip up the Britpop handbook and reinvent the band. The song was noisy and uncommercial (though their large fanbase will send it to number 15 in the charts when it comes out as a single in September), and it seemed to relish its newfound liberation, its messy delinquency, its lack of any obligation to clean its teeth and comb its hair.

'You see,' said Peel with a chuckle of satisfaction, 'I knew these buggers would come good in the end.'

That comment appears to have caused some influential wheels to start revolving behind the scenes. Today's programme, which comes pre-recorded from Peel's home, is a Blur special. But Peel is going to be doing more than just playing tracks from the new album. Whereas Pulp's Jarvis Cocker and Nick Banks merely visited Peel Acres for an interview, Blur are going to perform a concert in his back garden.

The two-hour programme works on three temporal levels. Some of it is live (Blur's seven-song set); most of it was recorded on 22 April (the day they came and played); and Peel's top-and-tail links were edited in at a later date. Radio 1 had to pre-record the bulk of the show in a brief hiatus in Blur's European tour. As their performance at Peel Acres goes out this evening, the band will be somewhere between Lyon and Nice.

'A few days ago,' Peel begins, sounding his usual gruff self, 'Blur came to our house, played football, had a look around the house, drank tea, played some tunes, had some food, then went home. It was an astonishing day. Let me tell you all about it.'

After a blast of 'Bank Holiday' from *Parklife* to focus the mind, we cut to a more relaxed, beatific-sounding Peel – recorded on 22 April – speaking to us in his Suffolk countryside habitat. 'It's 8.30 in the morning. You can probably hear birdsong in the background. This is not the Sound Effects Library. It's real birds. Well, session birds anyway.'

Minutes ago, as Peel walked his dogs, a van pulled up at the house and Blur's drum technician got out. Sheila is giving him breakfast. More music is dropped in. The theme from *Mission: Impossible*.

It's now forty-five minutes later. 'Our garden is starting to look like a van-hire lot.' Peel introduces some of the personnel. Blur's audience will comprise the Ravenscrofts, their friends and their combined children. Teenage daughters, unless they're Oasis fans, don't pass up opportunities to meet Damon Albarn. Sheila is out of view and off microphone, but many of Peel's listeners will know that the past eighteen months have been an anxious time for the family. Sheila suffered a brain haemorrhage last year and was fortunate to survive. Peel has talked about it often. How they appreciated people's support. How Dick Dale asked an audience at one of his gigs to pray for Sheila's recovery. *Blur at Peel Acres* is partly about the Ravenscrofts as a family. When Cocker and Banks were here, Peel sounded like a disc jockey. Today he sounds like a dad.

It's 10 a.m. A cloud pauses on its way overhead. Flight cases concealing instruments stretch the length of the lawn. No sign of Blur as yet. Peel: 'The Radio 1 live-music team have arrived, of course, nursing hangovers, which is their natural state.' His choice of music is Britpop: Supergrass, Shed Seven, Gene. It's the music that Blur have gone out of their way on the new album to leave behind. Unless, of course, Peel didn't choose the records. *Blur at Peel Acres* is a Bank Holiday special and is not in one of his usual slots.

Blur arrive. They wander through the house and browse through Peel's record collection. Albarn asks if he has any albums by the Sixties electronic duo Silver Apples. He's in luck. 'They're very hard to find,' Albarn says. 'I knew you'd have one.' Peel has heard that Silver Apples are back together again. Albarn's interest in them will grow, culminating in a collaboration with them at the Royal Festival Hall next year. With Blur, a whim can quickly become an enterprise.

Blur aren't as easy for Peel to engage as Cocker and Banks. There are four of them for a start, three of whom are pretty quiet, and after all Peel did spend six years stating publicly that their music was rubbish. They don't sound overjoyed to be at his house. 'I've got a Robert Wyatt record,' Albarn tells him, eyeing him suspiciously. 'It's a Virgin compilation. It's got the top DJs and all their top records. And your choice for 1971. I think there's a Genesis record in there.'

'Surely not,' Peel protests mildly.

Graham Coxon, the guitarist, is pulling albums down from shelves. '*Two Sides of Keith Moon*,' he wows.

'Oh no, come on,' Peel protests more loudly.

Coxon: 'My word! That's good to see. Peter Hammill. Van Der Graaf Generator.'

Steve Lamacq is here. He and Peel talk about the best way to file demo tapes. It's a good job neither of them will ever have to fill eight hours when it rains on *Test Match Special*. 'Like this,' Peel suggests. 'In polythene bags on the floor.'

'It's good to see them,' Albarn chips in, 'because they were always a mystical thing, as a teenager, for me. Your demos.'

'Did you ever send me one?' Peel asks.

'I think we did, yeah, as Seymour.'

'It'll probably turn up one of these days. You'll get a patronising letter saying, "I quite liked the third tune."'

Radio 1 must have hoped for something more dramatic than this when they cleared their Bank Holiday schedules. Blur sound on edge. There's an audible gap of about three generations between Albarn and his host. When Peel leans across a desk to reach for something, time seems to stand still for several minutes. He can't find what he's looking for. More minutes pass. Can't someone volunteer to help him? He opens and closes a drawer, then another, then another. It sounds like he and the desk are wrestling. If this couldn't be edited out, it doesn't say much for the bits that were.

Just over thirty minutes of the programme have elapsed, but several hours of 22 April have been conflated and accelerated. Blur are almost ready to start. The audience has gathered. Peel sets the scene. 'They're playing, it should be pointed out, outside our kitchen. There's a kind of paved area and the band are having to squeeze into that, with a temporary tarpaulin over them should it rain.' Anxious dogs bark at the sudden noise. Coxon's feet touch his pedals. The dogs are drowned out. A pause. A ringing telephone.

Blur play six songs from their new album – including the two most violent ('Song 2', 'Chinese Bombs'), Peel will be pleased to note – and they also slip in a 1992 single, 'Popscene', that suits their current uncouth sound. Not·many tracks on their last album, *The Great Escape*, would have belonged on a Peel show. But these songs are atonal and just right. Some of the sounds emanating from Coxon's guitar would have Steve Albini or Thurston Moore peering at his fingers to see how he produces them. The Ravenscrofts and friends greet the end of each song with polite applause.

Now it's becoming an enjoyable radio programme. In an easy-going conversation in the study afterwards, Peel takes the anecdotal chair, telling a story from his *Top Gear* days about the folk singer Melanie visiting him when he was bedridden with jaundice. Before he could stop her, she started singing songs to him from the end of the bed because her manager thought it might help her record sales. There's another story about a man from *Record Collector* who came round to value Peel's collection. 'Obviously a lot of them have never been played,' he explains, on form now. 'All those early Blur LPs.'

The most valuable records in the collection, the man from *Record Collector* told him, were the ones that he and Sheila had just put in boxes to take to the car-boot sale. He pulled out one of them and immediately valued it at £400. Another album was so rare that many collectors argued it didn't exist. Blur crack up at this. Peel holds court like Sir Henry regaling the dinner guests at Rawlinson End. Couldn't we have had twenty minutes of these stories and skipped the preliminary hoo-ha about drum techs and flight cases?

'So obviously we put them all back on the shelves,' Peel finishes in triumph. 'That's my pension scheme you see on the walls.'

1998–9: THE ORDER OF THE INSTITUTE OF NATIONAL TREASURES

---

*'Popular music guru John Peel turns sixty this week, yet he is
still in-the-know when it comes to what artists, musicians,
singles and albums will make or break in the cut-throat world
of the music industry.'* DAILY RECORD

John Peel Show
Radio 1
5 February 1998

Impossible Music Force – Cristian Vogel – Hellnation – Bardo Pond
– Add N to (X) – Gringo – Coldcut and Hexstatic – Liquid Wheel –
Aerial M – Dawn of the Replicants – Totemplow – The Delgados

*On a visit to Washington, Tony Blair promises Britain's full backing
for any American military strikes against Iraq. The country's president,
Saddam Hussein, stands accused of failing to comply with sixteen UN
Security Council resolutions. Blair also offers his personal support to
President Clinton, who has been rocked by a sex scandal involving the
former White House intern Monica Lewinsky.*

As a marketing term and as a Nineties music trend, Britpop lost the
final vestiges of its brand power some time between 21 August and
21 September last year. On the first of those dates, Oasis's *Be Here*

Now became the fastest-selling album in UK history, with 350,000 copies bagged up and sold between the hours of 9 a.m. and 6 p.m. An ensuing backlash of titanic proportions, however, saw *Be Here Now* just as abundantly discarded, as the racks of Britain's used-record shops buckled under the weight of unwanted Oasis albums. Within a month, Britpop was dead.

Since that Pyrrhic pinnacle last August, music sales have fallen off a cliff. Even the most successful albums (Catatonia's *International Velvet*, for example, released this week) sell fewer than 35,000 to go in at number 1. A culture of self-preservation is setting in across the music business, coupled with a strong desire on the part of major labels to reinstate boy-band pop as the nation's official music. This year will see Blur and Oasis toppled by Steps and S Club 7. The Midas-like supremo of the Eighties, Pete Waterman, has returned from exile to rule the charts a second time.

In a practical sense, none of this makes much difference to the *John Peel Show*. Aside from Pulp and latterly Blur, Britpop was never Peel's scene and the major labels don't generally impact on the way he does his job. But a massive slump in indie sales (and 'indie', of course, means any band on the front of *Melody Maker* or the *NME*, whether they're on Geffen, Parlophone or Wiiija) has life-or-death implications for many people on Peel's side of the industry, who, to be blunt, are going to need him more than ever. It's looking possible that the indie sector may be facing a long period in the wilderness. Creation Records, the money-spinning market leader of the last three years, now struggles to get a single in the Top 75.

Indie music came out of the underground, and that's where Peel has always looked for talent. One could add up the record sales of two indie labels in Glasgow – Creeping Bent and Chemikal Underground – and they might appear, in economic terms, to be failing businesses. Peel, though, would argue that Creeping Bent and Chemikal Underground are currently two of the most important labels anywhere in the world, each with a roster to salivate over. He regards every one of their releases as a cause for celebration, which is enough to give them the impetus to release more. The focus of the *John Peel Show* has turned, as it did in 1981 and 1986, to Glasgow – the city where British indie music as we know it was born, and the city where it has been resurrected.

Both Creeping Bent and Chemikal Underground owe a spiritual debt to Postcard, but neither of them looks likely to peak too early or run out of steam the way Postcard did. Creeping Bent's roster includes Nectarine No. 9 and Adventures in Stereo, bands led by ex-members of the Fire Engines and Primal Scream, so the label has essentially grown up with Peel over a two-decade period. Chemikal Underground, which like Creeping Bent was set up in 1994, has the critically acclaimed groups Mogwai and Arab Strap, but is best known for an EP in 1996 (*The Secret Vampire Soundtrack*) by Bis, which became a Top 30 hit when the producer of *Top of the Pops*, Ric Blaxill, surprisingly invited Bis onto the show to perform a track from it ('Kandy Pop') as part of a 1FM-style 'new bands' campaign. Peel, who'd been playing Bis for around six months by then, was modestly embarrassed when they recorded a song called 'We Love John Peel' in their next session for him. But the thing about that title was, bands like Bis really do.

Chemikal Underground is owned by the Delgados, a quartet from Motherwell who impressed Peel with their very first single, 'Monica Webster', in January 1995. A post-Pixies, post-Pavement guitar band, the Delgados sing in charmingly natural voices and write haiku-like, harmonically crooked songs that have grown in stature – and in musical ambition – over the course of three Peel sessions. The song he plays from them tonight, 'Pull the Wires from the Wall', features a string quartet and shares some of the autumnal mood and drowsy melancholy of Nico's *Chelsea Girl*. Peel deems it 'almost unbearably pretty' and so, too, will the listeners, who'll vote it to number 1 in their Festive 50 at the end of the year. Mogwai, with the eleven-minute instrumental 'Xmas Steps', will be second in the chart, securing a Chemikal Underground one–two. And to complete a Scottish top three, in third place will be Belle and Sebastian – a band whose hypersensitive lyrics and spiralling reputation recall nothing so much as the first eighteen months of the Smiths – with the title track of their album *The Boy with the Arab Strap*, which references a *fourth* Scottish band, and another one signed to Chemikal Underground.

Confused? Not if you've been listening to Peel's programmes all year you won't be. To anyone following the renaissance of Scottish indie music, it all makes perfect sense.

John Peel Show
Radio 1
3 March 1998

Urusei Yatsura – Brass Wolf – Uilab – The Fall – Ultravibe – Lee Perry – Le Mans – Fauna Flash – Aphasic – Ruins – Soft Machine – Bionaut – Skimmer – William Reid – Solex – Sizzla

It's reported that Diana, Princess of Wales, left nearly £13 million in her will to her two sons, William (fifteen) and Harry (thirteen). The princess, who was killed in a car crash in Paris last August, also bequeathed £50,000 to her butler, Paul Burrell, and various mementos to her seventeen godchildren.

The footage shot by a hand-held camera is dark and grainy, but clearly shows the drummer jumping out from behind his kit to grab the singer and land a blow on him. The Roland keyboard nearly goes flying as the two men fight, at which point the bassist stops playing. The fight is broken up and the music restarts, but then collapses again as the audience hoots and heckles. 'A Scottish man,' says the singer in a slurred Salford accent, pointing to each band member in turn, 'a fucking animal on drums, and a fucking idiot. I've been assaulted in public.' Twenty years after Peel first played their debut EP *Bingo-Master's Break-Out!*, Mark E. Smith and the Fall look to have finally self-destructed live onstage at a dingy club in New York's East Village.

Peel's favourite band used to take pride in rising above the undignified antics of rival outfits. The morning after the gig at Brownies, Smith is arrested by New York police and charged with a third-degree assault on the Fall's keyboard player, Julia Nagle. He soon sobers up in Rikers Island correctional facility. But when he and Nagle fly home days later to England, they find they're the only two members of the Fall who haven't resigned. Borrowing a drummer, they play Camden Dingwalls as a three-piece. 'Where's the band?' the crowd taunt Smith. Once, people stood riveted to the spot when he prowled a stage. Now they either sneer or cringe.

Smith and Peel have rarely spoken over the years – maybe three times, maybe four – so on a personal level Smith's decline is none of Peel's affair. But it can't be easy to watch all this sorry turmoil from the sidelines. The Fall's latest session, which he plays tonight, must surely be their last. It sounds stripped to the bone and divested of strength. But of course, the future is a dream that the present, still awake, has not imagined yet. No listener would possibly believe that one of the Fall's four songs tonight, 'Touch Sensitive', will advertise Vauxhall Corsas in a prime-time TV campaign in 2002. But advertise them it will, while Smith will remarry, rediscover his muse, rebuild the Fall and wrench himself back from the brink. To give an idea of how supportive Peel is prepared to remain, not only is tonight's Fall session not the last he commissions from them, it isn't even the last he commissions from them this year.

John Peel Show
Radio 1
2 April 1998

Evelyn – Yummy Fur – Michael Rose – Terry and the Tyrants –
Caroline Martin – Boards of Canada – Plastic Hip – Six by Seven
– 60ft Dolls – Mogwai – The Splash Four – Bargecharge – The
Delgados – Aerial M – Tram – Sizzla – Pnu Riff

*Police in Ireland have intercepted a 1,000 lb bomb in a car believed to
be on its way to Aintree racecourse, where the Grand National is being
run tomorrow. The car was about to board a ferry at Dún Laoghaire,
south of Dublin, to cross to Holyhead in Wales. Last year's Grand
National was postponed for forty-eight hours after an IRA bomb hoax.*

Peel is still playing a lot of techno. The Chilean-born, Brighton-
based abstract techno artist Cristian Vogel recorded a session for
him in January; Dave Clarke and Jeff Mills have made frequent
appearances; and Liquid Wheel, from Ireland, hit hard with their
'Bloodclot' twelve-inch earlier in the year. Peel and techno are as
inseparable as Peel and reggae. Furthermore, any listeners who
managed to sit through the five head-kicking minutes of Johnny Go
Fruity Mental's 'Killer' in February – a track released on the self-
explanatory Bonkers label – will know that Peel is still quite the fan
of happy hardcore.

At the more commercial end of the dance-music scale, where
Peel doesn't much venture, sit genres like trip hop (Massive Attack,
Portishead), big beat (Fatboy Slim, the Prodigy) and the trance
that they play in the superclubs. But at the more experimental end,
where Peel is happy to wander around and buy on impulse, are genres like minimal (spearheaded by Richie Hawtin aka Plastikman,
whose first Peel session in 1994 now seems highly prescient) and

IDM, an ambient, cerebral form of electronic music synonymous with Warp label acts such as Boards of Canada; Peel has been playing their debut album, *Music Has the Right to Children*, all week. Other points along the dance spectrum where Peel can be found bopping away include glitch, a German-pioneered form of digital defacing that makes customers in shops ask the staff if their fridges are broken; and London acid techno, a hard-dance squat party subgenre whose leaders, the Liberator DJs, recorded a Peel session a year ago. On all of those, he's on the case.

Not that he actually says the words 'minimal', 'acid techno', 'IDM' or 'glitch' when he's introducing a track by Plastikman, the Liberators, Boards of Canada or Pole. He's never been the sort of DJ to flag up the disorientating leaps in his running orders by saying 'and now for something completely different' or 'that's enough post-rock, time for some mincecore'. In an interview with the *Independent on Sunday* this month, Peel admits: 'I get baffled by the sheer number of categories. Mary Anne Hobbs will come steaming into my studio before she goes on and say: "What was that great speed garage record you played?" and I won't have known it was speed garage.'

A dance DJ who can't tell the difference between genres? They certainly won't be booking Peel in the clubs of Ayia Napa this summer. Imagine the riots if he dropped an eight-minute glitch track on the mad Brits at Emporium one night. But Hobbs, whose 10.30 p.m. programme has been following Peel's for over a year, should know by now that he divides music into just two genres: the stuff that he likes and the stuff that he doesn't. He sees more similarity between happy hardcore and rockabilly than a rockabilly fan sees between rockabilly and blues. It's the wiring in Peel's brain that makes him receptive to certain kinds of dance music, not the community or clique that he wishes to belong to. But he does leave himself open, with his veneer of gung-ho unenlightenment, to criticism from those who think he's incapable of discriminating; that he just dips a toe in whichever pool of water happens to be under his foot at the time.

Glastonbury 98
BBC2
26 June 1998

Finley Quaye – The Lightning Seeds – James – Portishead – Embrace – Catatonia – Taj Mahal – Eric Bibb – Rolf Harris – Jools Holland

About five hundred English football fans have been arrested after skirmishes in Lens, northern France, in the hours ahead of England's World Cup game against Colombia. England's 2–0 victory, with goals from Darren Anderton and David Beckham, means they qualify in second place from their group and will face Argentina in the next round.

It's getting on for twelve years since Peel was part of the regular presenters' team on *Top of the Pops*. The odds are that he'll never host it again. He's fifty-eight; the presenter this week, Zoë Ball, is twenty-seven. In recent years producers of BBC television programmes have either removed Peel's name from their Rolodex or have judged him unsuitable for their quiz shows, arts shows, chat shows and panel shows. Is it his slight stammer? Is it the way he blinks nervously and avoids looking people in the eye? Or is it the elaborate way he frames his sentences, slowly deleting them in mid-flow and replacing them with more circuitous ones? ('You may have been listening last night when I played this next track, although there's no reason why you should have been, but if you happened to be doing so, which as I say is not a foregone conclusion, but if so . . .')

He might have made a good contestant on a 1974 episode of *Call My Bluff*, but he wouldn't be much use on an obstreperous free-for-all like *Never Mind the Buzzcocks*.

Peel and BBC TV, however, have not quite finished with each other. On BBC2 last weekend he co-hosted seven hours of Glastonbury coverage with Jo Whiley. It wasn't Peel's charisma, or his ability to flam his way through a ninety-second link, that got him the job; he was there to provide history, context and depth. There was a Peel connection to around 40 per cent of the 170 acts playing on Glastonbury's various stages. Blur. Pulp. Sonic Youth. Plastikman. Kenickie. Gorky's Zygotic Mynci. Cornershop (last year's Festive 50 winners). The festival also featured Dr John, whom Peel first played in 1968, Julian Cope and the Jesus and Mary Chain. Even that pop singles machine the Lightning Seeds are led by Ian Broudie, who recorded a Peel session with Liverpool post-punks Big in Japan when he was just out of his teens. Finlay Quaye? His jazzy reggae may be the antithesis of Peel, but his half-brother Caleb Quaye was heard all the time on *Top Gear* in 1970, playing guitar for Elton John. And don't get Peel started on Roni Size/Reprazent: as he civilly pointed out in his letter to Matthew Bannister, he woke up to drum 'n' bass three years before the rest of Radio 1. Peel was at the first Glastonbury in 1970, when it was a hippie picnic for a select few. If any BBC man has a right to blink into a camera and talk about what Glastonbury meant and what it has become, it's this grey-bearded, gnomic figure in shorts with his black T-shirt straining over his belly and his habit of starting sentences with adverbs.

John Peel's Meltdown
Radio 1
1 July 1998

The Delgados – Marlene Webber – Woodbine – Mudhoney – Mogwai – Al Ferrier – Hystrix – Sonic Youth – D.O.S.E. – Mac Meda – Culture – Pole – White Hassle – Stomp and Weaver – Twp – Psyche Out – Sound Tank – Spiritualized

David Beckham has publicly apologised for his red card in the World Cup game against Argentina last night, which England lost on penalties. Beckham was dismissed early in the second half for kicking the Argentine midfielder Diego Simeone, who had fouled him. The England squad flew home from France today.

Meltdown is an annual music and arts festival held on London's South Bank. The chosen director (a different person every year) makes a list of his or her favourite performers from around the world, who are then assembled into a personal 'dream festival'. Elvis Costello and Laurie Anderson are among those who have curated Meltdown in the past. This year the organisers asked Peel.

Peel's Meltdown comprises a dozen or so concerts spread over two weeks, which span the full range, or something like it, of his music tastes, from Warp Records to Ivor Cutler. His love of Scottish indie bands accounts for one of the nights, and another is dedicated to reggae. Yet another sees him unite Silver Apples with Damon Albarn and Graham Coxon – on the same bill as Half Man Half Biscuit, if you please – which is an idea that may have been born on the day Blur visited Peel Acres fourteen months ago.

Tonight's main event is a concert at the Royal Festival Hall with Sonic Youth, Spiritualized and the Delgados. *John Peel's Meltdown* – a 110-minute radio show – moves back and forth from the stage to a studio somewhere in the building, where Peel is playing records by Mudhoney, Mogwai, the reggae chanteuse Marlene Webber and the Louisiana country singer Al Ferrier. 'We're going to have Sonic Youth with you [in] . . . I don't know, something like ten, twelve minutes' time, perhaps even less than that,' Peel says. You can see him in your mind's eye peering through slits in a concrete bunker at the back of the labyrinthine complex, watching Sonic Youth's roadies tighten hi-hats and untangle guitar leads.

When Peel hands over to the New Yorkers – though not literally; his Meltdown has a curiously impartial detachment, and he doesn't emcee the events in person – Sonic Youth play a set of tunes from their latest album, *A Thousand Leaves*, which Peel previewed back in April. Peel goes unmentioned in their song introductions; the band could be doing a gig in Hull or Heidelberg. But Sonic Youth are not this evening's only attraction. Elsewhere in the complex, an orchestra plays while Laurel and Hardy's silent films are shown on a screen, and Ardal O'Hanlon from *Father Ted* gives a stand-up performance at the Queen Elizabeth Hall. In case anyone doesn't realise that these events, too, are part of Peel's multimedia Meltdown, his choice of art may help. 'There was a small but rather pleasant exhibition of traditional early 1960s oil paintings,' one reviewer will write, 'which mainly featured views around Ipswich.'

John Peel Show
Radio 1
3 December 1998

Ratio – Sizzla – Cinerama – Shortfall – The Wisdom of Harry – Decoder – Cul de Sac – Fugu – Cato – Playhouse – Couch – Brockie and Ed Solo – Mus – Jullander – 10,000 Maniacs – Castigate

*Only twenty-four hours after Tony Blair negotiated a breakthrough in
the deadlocked Northern Ireland peace process, it's emerged that the
deal has unravelled. The Ulster Unionists, who had agreed that Sinn
Fein would have two seats in the new Northern Ireland Assembly, now
say that this cannot happen until the IRA decommissions its weapons.*

Peel opens his microphone at 10.10 p.m. – his new time slot since
a Radio 1 reshuffle in October – and says: 'I could do with some
decent nose-hair clippers as well.' The unusual phrase is not the
only non sequitur phosphorescing in the winter air tonight. Peel,
who brought Britain the sounds of Wild Man Fischer, the Finnish
Shouting Choir, Johnny Go Fruity Mental and Carcass's 'Crepitating
Bowel Erosion', went to Buckingham Palace last week to receive an
award from Prince Charles for 'services to radio broadcasting and to
popular music'. He is now John Peel OBE.

'It's an interesting experience,' Peel said after the ceremony. 'It's
a bit like going to a church service in a church to which you don't
belong. The band plays continually and not especially well. I don't
want to be unkind.' Peel wore a suit and a red tie. Charles walked
along the line of recipients, talking to each one for forty-five seconds.
Have you come far? Is this your first visit to the Palace? Is happy
hardcore a subgenre of acid techno? And with a handshake and a
turn to the right, John Robert Parker Ravenscroft, the former pirate
and pariah, was appointed to the Order of the British Empire. 'Jolly
interesting event,' he summed it up, his real thoughts unreadable.

After years of setbacks and snubs in the corridors of the BBC,
it's as if Peel began 1998 by retaining the services of a top public
relations firm. In April he began presenting a new show on Radio
4, *Home Truths*, which has done wonders for his public image.
Some old friends – John Walters being one of them – are appalled
by this hour's worth of domestic homilies every Saturday morning.
But Peel has been sharing details about his family with his listeners

for years, and now he has a cosy little programme in which other people share details about theirs. *Home Truths* is striking a nerve with middle-class Britain, and whatever the cynical Walters may think – and he has apparently begged Peel to stop presenting it – the programme is here to stay.

Tonight, Peel fulfils a long-held ambition by broadcasting the *John Peel Show* live from his own house. Halfway through a single by the ragga artist Sizzla, a glass of red wine is brought to Peel by one of his daughters. 'At midnight,' he says, 'I shall be able to walk the dogs and go to bed, instead of having a two-hour drive through the night.' Have you come far? In a sense, not at all. In another sense, further than words can say.

Sounds of the Suburbs
Channel 4
13 March 1999

The 60ft Dolls – Lucy Chivers – Reviver Gene – Richard Thomas

Stephen Hawking, the physicist and author of A Brief History of Time, *has predicted that genetically redesigned human beings will emerge at some point in the next thousand years. Speaking at a lecture in Cambridge, he said he also expects computers to develop brains as complex as humans'.*

For this late-night Channel 4 series, Peel is on a round Britain trip in his car. He stops in Cornwall or Humberside or Oxford and meets local musicians, learning about the economic and social conditions in their area. In Oxford the indie bands live with their parents. In East Kilbride they die of boredom. Some areas are desolate with unemployment, scarred by the death of their former industries. It's funny how the countryside looks unspoilt to one songwriter and bleak as hell to another. Music is getting by on a shoestring.

'There aren't that many industries,' said Peel in the first episode, which looked at Lanarkshire, 'that Britain is still world-famous for. But music is one of them. In fact, youth culture in all its forms is an industry worth billions of pounds a year, but it's developed by and large unaided by corporate sponsorship and government funding. Unless you count the Jobseekers' Allowance, of course.'

In episode one, Peel surveyed the now deserted site of the former Ravenscraig steel works in Motherwell. Tonight he visits the towns and valleys of industrial South Wales. In Newport, a live gig scene grew out of the miners' strike in the mid-Eighties and still shakes the walls at T.J.'s nightclub. T.J.'s is one of those indie venues that Peel has mentioned in his on-air gig guides for years. He's never been inside it before, but it's acquired an almost mythical significance for him.

The 60ft Dolls, Peel favourites and T.J.'s regulars, met in the dole queue. 'Maggie Thatcher never let you down. You knew she was going to screw you,' says their guitarist Richard Parfitt, a tense young man in a high-collared black coat. He and Peel agree it was a shame that Neil Kinnock never got in. 'Too working-class. The people of Middle England are not going to vote for a red-haired Welsh yobbo,' Parfitt decides. No, they're not. Otherwise there would have been no need for Tony Blair. 'Whatever the politics,' Peel's voiceover cuts in, 'bands like the 60ft Dolls exist in spite of them.'

In Cwmaman, where the old mines have been razed to the ground, Jason Knott sings in a band called either Kerb or Reviver Gene. (Voiceover: 'There seems to be some indecision over the name.') Knott is twenty-two. He and Peel sit high on a hill behind the town, looking down at the streets of houses. Knott has a girlfriend and a baby son. 'That all of that energy should have come to this,' sighs Peel, a sentence that only he could say to a twenty-two-year-old

Cwmaman factory worker. 'On the other hand, you wouldn't want to go down a mine, would you?'

'I don't think I would have fancied it,' Knott admits, hands buried deep in jacket pockets. 'I'd rather be a rock 'n' roll star, I think.'

John Peel Show
Radio 1
26 May 1999

High Fidelity – The Problematics – Belle and Sebastian – Winnie Melville – Robert Fear – Isabel Jay – George Baker with Orchestra and Male Quartet – The Hellacopters – Melys – The Delgados

Buckingham Palace has lodged a complaint against the Sun *newspaper after it published a topless photograph of Sophie Rhys-Jones, the fiancée of Prince Edward. The photo, which is several years old, shows Rhys-Jones in a clinch with the radio and TV personality Chris Tarrant. The Palace calls its publication 'premeditated cruelty'.*

Peel is coming live from the Glasgow School of Art, where the Delgados are playing a gig in the Assembly Room tonight. When Peel started taking an interest in Scottish punk rock in 1977, gigs in Glasgow were monitored carefully by the city fathers. 'Saints and Sinners' by Johnny and the Self Abusers – the band that later became Simple Minds – was written about a rare punk gig that slipped through the council's net; but the Saints and Sinners, a pub in St Vincent Street, was smashed up by overexcited teenagers and the Glasgow punk ban was reinforced. In 1993, after the venue had reopened as King Tut's Wah Wah Hut, Alan McGee first saw Oasis there.

When Peel looked around for Glasgow bands to put in his Second Punk Special in August 1977, there was no music industry in the city to speak of, let alone an indie sector. One play on the *John Peel Show* was considered as priceless as water in a desert. A session was a fountain. Twenty-two years later, the Nordoff Robbins charity hosts an annual Scottish Music Awards and nobody ever needs to get on a train to London again. The Delgados, feted far and wide, are bound to be winning an SMA soon. As are Belle and Sebastian, whose 1996 debut album *Tigermilk* – just released on CD – now changes hands on the Internet, Peel hears, for £1,000 in its original vinyl pressing. There's your Glasgow indie sector.

Live or not, however, tonight's show is sluggish in places. Peel spends an age cueing up a gaggle of crackly records from 1905, which are going out as part of a century-of-music series called the Peelenium. They don't do much to banish the suspicion that most of the programme is killing time. But there are frantic moments too. The Delgados' support band, the *Screamadelica*-influenced High Fidelity, have flown in a classical violinist from Bombay to join them on their final song. It sounds like a tall story, but Peel makes it sound as though the plane literally just landed at the airport. Before the song begins, High Fidelity's singer Sean Dickson – whom Peel has known since his days fronting the Soup Dragons – proposes to his girlfriend from the stage. He gets the answer he wants, but what on earth would have happened if she'd said no? More hastily programmed records from 1905?

'That was a genuine proposal,' says Peel in a breathless link, probably feeling as much relief as surprise. 'They've been going together, Sean tells me, for fourteen years and he was waiting for a really special occasion. I've invited myself to the wedding.'

Tonight's venue, the Glasgow School of Art, is where Orange Juice, the band that started it all, played their first gig in 1979. They were so fey and effeminate that the punks in the audience threw pints of beer and shouted threats at them. Now Glasgow revels in a new indie resurgence, never to be rid of the ghosts that haunt each generation's clubs and venues. And Peel, who connects all the generations together, comes to the School of Art to celebrate a renaissance and ends up buying a hat.

John Peel Show
Radio 1
1 September 1999

Dick Dale – Autechre – Nectarine No. 9 – Lexxus – Bonnie 'Prince' Billy – El Escandalo – Can Can Heads – Billy Bragg – Tampa Red – Charlie Barnet – Bing Crosby and the Andrews Sisters – Panacea

The secretary of state for Northern Ireland, Mo Mowlam, warns the Ulster Unionists and Sinn Fein that neither side should think of boycotting next week's review of the Good Friday Agreement. The review, headed by former US senator George Mitchell, is widely seen as a last-ditch attempt to save the peace process.

Peel turned sixty at the weekend. BBC2's *John Peel Night* on Sunday was not without controversy. Several minutes of tonight's show are taken up with an apology to his elder son, William, for the unflattering way he described him in *Father and Son*, a *Home Truths*-style rumination on family life that turned into rather an unpleasant soliloquy. William has been receiving mentions in Peel's radio shows from practically the day he was born: the listeners were present during his childhood as he learned the saxophone, attended a gig by Swedish rockers Europe (of 'Final Countdown' fame) and visited a dentist because he was growing two rows of teeth. But William is twenty-three now and few men of that age enjoy having their personal hygiene picked apart by their fathers on BBC2. Peel's contrition is self-flagellatory, though he implies his comments were deviously edited.

In Radio 1's current schedule, the *John Peel Show* stays where it is at 10.10 p.m. and other programmes move around it. Lamacq and Hobbs still bookend him on certain nights, but tonight Peel sits between a film review round-up and a two-hour show hosted by the DJ, record-label owner and godfather of acid jazz, Gilles Peterson. Peel remains Peel. It's like what the jazz writers in America used to say about Miles Davis when they were trying to find a way into *Live-Evil* or *On the Corner*: 'Miles is still playing Miles.' Hard bop. Modal. Electric. Fusion. Whoever happens to be in the backing band, Peel is still playing Peel.

John Peel Show
Radio 1
30 November 1999

Melt-Banana – Klute – Echoboy – Swearing at Motorists – Robert Görl – Khaya – Big Block 454 – The Cuban Boys – Frankie Machine – Speedball Baby – The Undertones – Cephalic Carnage

Tony and Cherie Blair appear on the cover of the celebrity magazine Hello!, *with a seven-page interview inside. Earlier this month it was announced that Cherie, who is forty-five, is pregnant with their fourth child.*

The Peelenium caught up with its host in August. He was now playing songs from the early Forties that had been released during his lifetime. It made for some lively shifts in tone: one night Low and the Ragga Twins were followed by Bing Crosby and the Andrews Sisters. In the early stages of the Peelenium, most of the songs were pulled out of the archives not by Peel but by his production assistant Lynn, but now that the year has reached 1978 it's unmistakably

Peel's hand on the tiller. Just think if Lynn had presented him with four songs from that year and none of them had been 'Teenage Kicks'. It's a thought too dire to contemplate.

Whom will he play when the Peelenium reaches 1999? The blistering Tokyo punks Melt-Banana? The UK drum 'n' bass producer Klute? Perhaps Echoboy, a Nottinghamshire four-piece whose session traces a psychedelic journey though time, beginning at the dawn of Duane Eddy's 'Peter Gunn' and ending in the apocalypse of the Doors' 'When the Music's Over'. Or perhaps Robert Görl, formerly the synth player in Deutsch Amerikanische Freundschaft, who has completed his last album before leaving for Thailand to start a new life as a Buddhist monk. ('On Disko B Records,' Peel says with lovely economy when the song ends, 'that's Robert Görl, now a monk in Thailand.')

With the exception of Annie Nightingale, still going strong at fifty-nine with her 4 a.m. weekend chillout show, Peel's Radio 1 peers have all vacated the stage. Matthew Bannister, the purger-in-chief, relinquished the controller's job last year, having tried hard to cancel out the chaos he caused on his arrival. His intelligent-speech experiment failed, and his Mark-and-Lard breakfast show was an idea whose time had not come, but Radio 1 undeniably feels younger and less flabby thanks to Bannister. So how does Peel survive on a youth station? And why, now, is he allowed to broadcast from his own home, while his daughter mans a computer and reads the listeners' emails? What has Peel done to earn the inconceivable privilege of being left alone?

It's possible that some BBC guilt has set in; that the Corporation realises it underused Peel in the past and didn't always play fair by him. Or it could be that everyone now sees clearly what was so hard to see in 1967. That Peel, with his hippie beads and bells, wasn't the beginning of a pernicious new breed of anti-BBC iconoclast. That he was, instead, the last of an old breed that they would have recognised if they'd looked past his kaftan and long hair. Peel was pure BBC to his bootstraps. He was as BBC as Richard Dimbleby, Robin Day, Alvar Lidell, John Arlott, Robert Robinson, Michael Parkinson, Dan Maskell and David Coleman. Peel was friend, not foe. He was the kind of broadcaster a nation grows up to treasure.

2000–1: THE LONG JOURNEY HOME

*'I was talking to some friends from New York the other day,
and they were saying Detroit is a ghost town. But Iggy Pop
said in Detroit you're one in a hundred; in New York or LA,
you're one in a million.'* JACK WHITE

John Peel Show
Radio 1
5 January 2000

Persil – Brian and Tony Gold – Screamfeeder – Breakestra – Justin
Berkovi – Pulseprogramming – The Go – Murry the Hump – Chalice –
Lali Puna – Cats Against the Bomb – Muslimgauze – Nick Drake

*Investigations are being held into the problems that dogged London's
Millennium Eve celebrations last week. Three thousand guests at
the Millennium Dome in Greenwich were left ticketless, while others
had to endure queues of several hours. The Millennium Wheel on the
South Bank was declared unsafe for passengers due to a faulty clutch
mechanism.*

'There's a worldwide recession in the music industry,' Creation boss
Alan McGee fulminated in an article in the *NME* eighteen months
ago. 'They might be all smiley-smiley at the Brits, but it's an industry
in absolute crisis.' Among the items on the agenda at the industry's

EGM are consumer apathy, moribund quarter-on-quarter record sales and the power of the Internet to make even the strongest infrastructure wobble. Everyone from CEOs to record-shop counter staff is wondering what the future may hold.

One inspired idea to emerge from the indie sector is to pack a suitcase and head for the beach. Last April the Bowlie Weekender, a three-day festival of British and American indie pop organised by Belle and Sebastian, played host to twenty-five bands and several thousand music fans, all of whom descended en masse on Pontins holiday camp in Camber Sands. The fans stayed in chalets, the bands dined with the fans and the event had a refreshingly non-corporate feel. This year the same holiday camp is hosting a new festival, All Tomorrow's Parties, curated by Mogwai. Peel hopes to book a chalet and do a spot of DJing.

Once the holiday is over, though, the future has to be confronted. The Internet is changing the rules of engagement so comprehensively that the ever quotable McGee, in that same *NME* piece, gave the British music business ten more years – at the most – to survive. Search engines can now connect a reasonably computer-literate person to new music without the need to leave the house, and downloading is *le dernier cri*. One Internet label owner in America, explaining to the *Guardian* how his costs have been cut by 70 per cent now that he is able to circumvent the usual distribution channels, is proselytising about 'an incredibly exploded music industry' in the near future. 'It's akin to the punk movement,' he adds.

If the atom is poised to split once again, as it did in 1977, the importance of someone like Peel, whose taste and judgement are widely respected, could be quite pronounced. He could perform the function of a guide (or filter), sifting out the rubbish and isolating the good stuff – and some would say he'd be the perfect candidate, having fulfilled that very role on British radio since 1967. That's providing, of course, that Peel is able to manoeuvre his way round the Internet himself. So far the signs are looking good. The BBC recently started broadcasting his programmes online, and the technophobic sixty-year-old has become a convert.

'I think this whole Internet thing is just fantastic,' he says tonight, after hearing from his daughter that an email has arrived from California. 'I love doing these programmes more than I've ever enjoyed doing them before. The Internet has made the crucial difference. The fact that Cathy can listen to these programmes in San Francisco and react to what's going on is just amazing.'

The idea of listeners commenting on Peel shows while they're going out is, of course, nothing new. Who could forget Jakki Brambles's listeners and their indignant faxes? But here Peel sits in his Suffolk home, miles from a main road, sipping a decent glass of red and playing two hours of obscure records late at night, and a woman in San Francisco is listening to his show in mid-afternoon. He can't get over it. No more phone calls to the duty office. No more pockets stuffed with requests and dedications, which he'll lose and read out two days too late once he's found them again. This is instant feedback from a friendly, supportive, musically curious audience that stretches the length and breadth of the globe. How could it not make a disc jockey feel optimistic about his job?

'For the first time ever,' Peel will say, sounding rather emotional at the thought, 'the programmes have become a conversation instead of a monologue.'

Two months later, he receives an email from Antarctica.

John Peel Show
Radio 1
21 March 2000

Lolita Storm – Furious – Little Roy – Gilded Lil – Hammer Damage – Sirconical – The Festival of Dead Deer – Elephant Man – The Relict – Elektrotwist – Pariah – The Pussycats – Ovuca – The White Stripes

In his Budget, Chancellor Gordon Brown pledges an extra £2 billion for the NHS, including the recruitment and training of 10,000 nurses. He also promises an extra £1 billion on education and raises tax allowances and winter fuel payments for pensioners.

Two bands from Detroit appear in tonight's show, one of them defunct, the other one very much active. SRC, which stood for the Scot Richard Case, were peers of the MC5 in the Sixties and often played at Detroit's Grande Ballroom, where *Kick Out the Jams* was recorded over two steamy nights in 1968. SRC never made it to the MC5's level, but they had a keen supporter across the Atlantic in *Top Gear*'s John Peel. Their 1968 single 'Black Sheep', a piece of organ-heavy psychedelic angst, was one of several songs from their self-titled album that Sunday afternoon listeners to Radio 1 would have heard that year. Why Peel has suddenly thought of them again thirty-two years later is unclear (as is his reason for starting 'Black Sheep' at the wrong speed), but maybe something has put him in a Detroit frame of mind, and maybe that something is the White Stripes.

An intense-looking duo with jet-black hair and fixed gazes, the White Stripes wear distinctive red and white clothes and claim to be brother and sister. Their latest release is a split single with another Detroit band, the Dirtbombs, who have a retro garage-punk sound. The Dirtbombs' 'Cedar Point '76', a fuzzy stomper like the Monkees meets the Electric Prunes, is not the easiest of songs to upstage, but that's until you hear 'Hand Springs' by the White Stripes. A young man with a fast voice has an argument with his girlfriend and makes amends by taking her to the bowling alley. Then a monolithic guitar enters and plays a louche, back-to-front riff at three times the volume that the boy has just been talking. The riff stops and the boy tells us about a butterfingers moment when he dropped the girl's glass of Coke. Uh-oh. The riff slams back in again, then waits. Our fast-talking hero is having a dispute with a guy at the pinball machine. Back to the riff while we wait for more information.

A couple of months ago Peel was in Holland, where he goes to a music festival at Groningen every year, and found an album by the White Stripes in a record shop. In their red and white outfits the boy and girl slouched against a wall, just as the Ramones did on their first album cover in 1976, and Peel picked it up to have a closer look. And then he knew. 'I just liked the look of it,' he later told an interviewer. 'I looked at the titles. You develop an instinct, do you know what I mean?' He took it home to England and was very impressed. It had the primeval howl of early Led Zeppelin but sounded as fresh as any contemporary punk. The singer sang in a high-pitched whine like Black Francis, but the White Stripes were far advanced from the myriad Pixies copycats of the Nineties. They covered two major-league blues songs – and a track off Bob Dylan's *Desire* – and rather than come unstuck, they precociously sailed through all three of them.

It hasn't yet got to the stage where Peel is telling his Groningen record-shop story on a regular basis. That will come later, when White Stripes mania sweeps Jack and Meg onto the front pages of magazines and to the top of festival bills. But he'll certainly be playing 'Hand Springs' again, and next time it will start the show. Peel has already declared it a contender for single of the year.

John Peel Show
Radio 1
28 March 2000

Hefner – The Mighty Wah! – Calexico – The Berzerker – Foehn – Jah Cure – Dirty Three – Fireballs of Freedom – Atomic Soul Experiences – The Get Up Kids – Timo Maas – Lazycame – Decoder

Following a criminal investigation costing almost £2 million, the head of the Jill Dando murder squad has concluded that her killer is a psychotic loner. Ms Dando, the co-presenter of BBC1's Crimewatch, was shot dead on her doorstep in west London last April. The media has speculated that it may have been a contract killing ordered by a Serbian warlord.

Now approaching its tenth anniversary, Radio 1's Sound City festival rolled into Liverpool last October, the latest destination on a long, slow tour of Britain that has taken in Norwich, Sheffield, Glasgow, Bristol, Leeds, Oxford and Newcastle. It's exactly the philosophy that the *John Peel Show* has been proposing since the late Seventies: for a music radio station to be truly national, it must explore and promote the music of the whole nation.

The map of Peel's Britain this month extends from Torquay in the south-west, where the synth-pop group the Cuban Boys are based, to Stowmarket in the east, where a computer whiz-kid named Cowcube has made it onto Peel's show by passing a demo tape to his son William in a pub. Vertically, the map goes from Brighton on the south coast, where Lolita Storm shout and sloganise in the electronic-punk genre known as digital hardcore, to Galashiels in the Scottish Borders, the home town of the duo Pluto Monkey, an offshoot of the indie band Dawn of the Replicants. Left to his own devices, Peel could probably organise a Sound City in any one of these places.

Hefner, who played at Sound City in Liverpool five months ago, come from east London and Essex. A vehicle for the songs of singer-guitarist Darren Hayman, they took second and third places in last year's Festive 50 with 'Hymn for the Cigarettes' and 'Hymn for the Alcohol', two examples of Hayman's trademark brand of open-heart-surgery indie pop, which tends to linger longer on the minutiae of relationship break-ups than even the most self-recriminatory C86 bands. The twist with Hayman is that some of his songs have deceptively perky melodies. One could almost convince oneself that this bespectacled geek and his bandmates were the reincarnation of John Hegley and the Popticians, if Hegley had been a bit less preoccupied with losing his glasses and a bit more consumed by sexual jealousy.

Tonight's Peel session is Hefner's fifth. Now that their feet are under the table, so to speak, they have some fun with a cover of a David Soul ballad from the Seventies ('Don't Give Up on Us') – the sort of MOR hit that will become known as a 'guilty pleasure' a few years from now – before tackling some new songs. 'Kate Cleaver's House', the first of them, is uncharacteristically proactive for Hayman: he plans to pluck up the courage to knock on the door of the girl who dumped him, asking her to take him back. But the next song, 'Milkmaids', is the sort of fantasy that causes alarm bells to ring. It's as well Hayman doesn't name the girl whose teeth he wants to brush while she sleeps, and whose wet towel he longs to bury his face in after she's stepped out of the bath. Near the end of the show, when he should be playing the fourth song in the session, Peel repeats 'Milkmaids' by accident. Here we go again, burying the face in the towel and cleaning the sleeping girl's teeth. And there goes Hayman, stuck in a fantasy he can't get out of. Kate Cleaver, whoever she is, may very well feel she's dodged a bullet.

John Peel Show
Radio 1
18 July 2000

Sender Berlin – Nasum – The Busy Signals – Junior Kelly – Fuselage –
Aden – Murphy's Oil Soap Boys – Blonde Redhead – Mukka – Watts
– Pacou – 90° South – Luciano – Winner – Yr Hwntws – DJ TeeBee

*Forensic tests have confirmed that the body found yesterday in a field
near Pulborough, West Sussex, is that of the missing eight-year-old
Sarah Payne. She disappeared seventeen days ago at Kingston Gorse,
about fifteen miles away, while out with her family. Sussex Police have
started a murder investigation.*

Peel has been to New York. He tells the story of his vacation in a
long, improbable splurge between a Berlin techno track and a
Swedish grindcore band. It begins with the fistful of tranquillis-
ers that he needed to swallow to get on the aeroplane (he hadn't
flown in eight years) and ends with him coming home on the *QE2*
with the film critic Barry Norman, the TV chef Delia Smith and
the football pundit Alan Hansen. What elevated company these
OBEs keep! The *QE2* voyage was 'a cruise for *Radio Times* readers',
Peel adds cryptically, leaving us to wonder if his presence on board
was some kind of competition prize. The celebrity group in which
he and Sheila found themselves proved to be most convivial shipmates. 'A good time was had by all. We ate and drank prodigiously.'
Presumably Delia had plenty to say about the food.

The wining and dining with the rich and famous doesn't end
there. Next month Peel will be invited to the *Kerrang!* Awards at the
Hammersmith Palais, where he's placed on the same table as Britt
Ekland and Dave Hill of Slade. The conversation is not without its
surprises: Peel reveals on air the following night that Ekland claims

to be a regular listener to the show. ('I was tempted to say: "Name one record that I've played in the past ten years."') But the evening is a painful one. Rising to present an award, Ekland slips on a piece of grapefruit and breaks her ankle.

'I was thinking about going and picking her up,' says Peel, who notes that the broken ankle has made the tabloids, 'and carrying her onto the stage. But then I thought, was I capable of carrying her? She's not a big woman, but was I capable of carrying her up the steps? I thought my children didn't deserve to see newspaper head-lines that said "Veteran DJ Dies Underneath Britt Ekland". I thought they deserved more than that.'

To cheer the actress up, he dedicates a song to her – a drill 'n' bass track on the Warp label, full of psychotic edits and chopped-up breakbeats – just in case she's listening in hospital and coming round from her anaesthetic. Her agonising mishap isn't even the ceremony's most reported incident. Slipknot, who won three awards, stole the headlines by punching each other in the face to celebrate and setting their table on fire.

John Peel Show
Radio 1
19 September 2000

Le Shok – Prince Jazzbo – Cinerama – Pluto Monkey – Benümb – The Aislers Set – Flying Saucer Attack – Dave Clarke – Eska – Red Prysock – Radiohead – Torul – Bidgood's Good Boys – Yabby You

Fears of further fuel protests have caused panic-buying at petrol stations across Britain, forcing many to close. Roadblocks by farmers and truck drivers have severely hit the flow of fuel in recent weeks, amid complaints that Britain's prices are the highest in Europe.

Today's scare is later revealed to be a false alarm started by a radio station in Cardiff.

Radiohead, a band whose music Peel dabbled in at one time but hasn't cared about for years, have sent him a copy of their new album, *Kid A*, the long-awaited follow-up to the multimillion-selling *OK Computer*. 'When bands are extraordinarily popular and I don't fully understand why,' he says, 'I always suspect that there's a kind of sinister cartel of interests that are promoting them. I'm an avid conspiracy theorist.'

Kid A, however, is wantonly uncommercial. As Radiohead endeavour to extricate themselves from a stadium-rock narrative that they want no part of, they've made an album as dissimilar to *OK Computer* as David Bowie's *Low* was to *Hunky Dory*. It's low-key and womb-like (as well as being shockingly shorn of guitars), and parts of it should be right up Peel's street. He put it on, expecting nothing much.

'I didn't initially pay a great deal of attention to it,' he admits. 'As it sort of drivelled on at home, I thought, "Actually, if I didn't know it was Radiohead . . . if it was a demo or something like that, I'd be playing this on the radio." So, because I like to be consistent, I'm playing it on the radio.'

He selects 'In Limbo', one of the more intangible songs on an album that takes Radiohead a long way from 'No Surprises' and 'Karma Police'. Later in the week Peel will play *Kid A*'s title track, a sparse four minutes of ambient electronica that barely sounds like Radiohead at all. It's ironic that he's finally getting into their music, because he unwittingly played an important part in the way that *Kid A* was conceived.

'I thought we had missed the point,' Thom Yorke tells *Q* magazine this month, recalling the world tour for *OK Computer* that turned Radiohead into reluctant superstars. 'The first thing I did after the tour was buy the whole Warp back catalogue. I started listening to

John Peel and ordering records off the net. It was refreshing because the music was all structures and had no human voices in it. But I felt just as emotional about it as I'd ever felt about guitar music.'

Peel might get a faintly warm glow from reading those words. He and Yorke clearly share a belief in the educational power of radio; Peel once said on a Radio 3 talk show, *Private Passions*, that much of his knowledge of classical music, for instance, comes from listening to the radio while driving. He'd be the first to understand that in Radiohead's new doctrine, there are no right answers, only ever-multiplying questions. Like Yorke, the more music Peel hears, the more he realises he hasn't heard enough.

'I like the idea of being cast in the role of expert,' he said in that same edition of *Private Passions*, 'and regularly shown to be wrong.'

John Peel Show
Radio 1
6 March 2001

Captain Beefheart and His Magic Band – Matmos – Barcelona – The White Stripes – Universal Project – Seedling – Gag – Sascha Funke – Beans – Suicide Milkshake – Joshua Ryan – I Am Kloot

Pop star Michael Jackson is the guest speaker at the Oxford Union debating society. Making his first public speech in over a decade, Jackson, forty-two, tells the audience of five hundred people that he feels robbed of a childhood and accuses Western society of producing a generation of neglected children predisposed towards materialism.

Peel sees music as a clock that can only go forwards, but there are times when even a nostalgiaphobe like him can't help looking back and being reminded of the distance his programmes have travelled.

He ended the millennium, as did everyone else, in a list-making mood, giving the listeners the go-ahead to vote for their first all-time Festive 50 since 1982. It was won by Joy Division's 'Atmosphere', a chilling flashback to a time in history when many young people in Britain feared the world was heading for nuclear destruction. At the other end of the Festive 50 were Bob Dylan and the Beatles, filling the heads of 1966 music fans with poetry, empowerment and hope. Peel sounded crushingly bored of the chart almost as soon as it began.

But if that was an unwelcome taste of his life flashing before his eyes, some memories are not so disagreeable. Captain Beefheart's first session for *Top Gear* aired on the same day in February 1968 that Bernie Andrews allowed him to take the reins without a co-presenter for the first time. What an easy, straightforward decision that now looks; what a difficult proposal it must have been for Andrews to get past his dubious BBC superiors. The show was recorded by a listener on reel-to-reel tape, just as hundreds of Peel shows in the late Seventies and Eighties would be recorded on blank cassettes. There's now an online community of Peel fans who write enthusiastically about their favourite shows and share their tapes. It's a good job they do, because the BBC has kept no copies of them.

'Thanks to the unknown benefactor who recorded that from the radio,' says Peel after repeating the Beefheart session in full at the start of tonight's show. His listeners of today may have noticed that one or two of the tracks began and ended abruptly. 'In case there were any sharp edits in that,' Peel explains, 'it was to remove my whining 1968 voice from the music. So in case anybody illegally recorded that, they'd be able to enjoy it to the full.'

So that was the reason for the editing, then. Not because Peel was embarrassed to let the listeners hear what a well-spoken, earnest young man he used to be. Not because his voice would have betrayed all the hope he felt at that time in the Sixties, before his revolution nosedived, crashed and burned. Some memories, even now, are a bit too close to the bone.

John Peel Show
Radio 1
30 May 2001

Greenskeepers – Locust – Ronnie Ronalde – The Detroit Cobras – Bolz Bolz – The Icarus Line – Stakka and Skynet – The White Stripes – Bushman – Inigo Kennedy – Lift to Experience – Lee Perry

The trial begins of Jeffrey Archer, the novelist and former deputy chairman of the Conservative Party, who is charged with perjury and perverting the course of justice. Archer won a libel case in 1987 against the Daily Star *over allegations that he paid for sex with a prostitute, but evidence has now come to light suggesting he lied under oath.*

The White Stripes have made a further two albums since Peel bought their first one in Groningen. *De Stijl* emerged in the middle of last year, whereupon Peel began promoting it with all guns blazing for an intensive period that finally ended about a month ago. Their new one, *White Blood Cells*, doesn't officially come out until July, but Peel has a copy of it already and is playing tracks from it every night. He's already identified a key song in 'Hotel Yorba', a jaunty country number with an infectious chorus. Tonight he goes for 'Fell in Love with a Girl', a two-minute punk romance that might have been the result if Black Francis had wrested control of the Buzzcocks from Pete Shelley. Peel's on target; these will be the two big songs all right.

John Peel Show
Radio 1
20 June 2001

Jeff Mills – Meanwhile, Back in Communist Russia – Rechenzentrum – Leo Garcia – KaitO – Pram – DJ Amadeus – Panoptica – Pascal Comelade – The Shins – Prefuse 73 – Mull Historical Society

A public inquiry opens into the crimes of Harold Shipman, the Greater Manchester doctor convicted last year of killing his patients with lethal injections. Shipman, currently serving fifteen concurrent life sentences at HM Prison Wakefield, is suspected of committing as many as 250 murders before his arrest in 1998.

If any paparazzi have been following Peel these last twelve months, they'll have accumulated a surreal portfolio. When he's not attending heavy-metal parties with Swedish actresses and ex-members of Slade, he's dining on luxury ocean liners with TV cooks and former Liverpool FC central defenders. Then, just last week, he was spotted in conversation with Jeff Mills, the Detroit techno maestro, and Carl Cox, the consummate party DJ, the Shoom first-nighter, the three-deck wizard of the UK rave scene.

The venue was Barcelona, where Peel had been invited to the annual Sónar dance-music festival. The three men, all leaders in their own field, must have made a curious picture. Cox: large, dapper and gap-toothed, his spectacles and permanent smile lending him the appearance of a genial boxing promoter. Mills: slim, sci-fi obsessed, cultivating an otherworldly aura to match his extraterrestrial music. Peel: a chubby figure in shorts inquiring of the two black men if they'd heard any good happy hardcore lately.

But Mills and Cox might just as easily have put a question to Peel. For although his DJ set at Sónar won't have been the weekend's must-see attraction for the hip Spanish kids and the clued-in industry types, Peel won't have been out of his depth by any means. Indietronica, folktronica, laptoptronica: these are some of the melodic new developments that his programmes have been keeping tabs on. Kieran Hebden (Fridge and Four Tet), Lali Puna, Múm – a few of the big names in these hybrid genres – have appeared in his programmes for over a year. Labels like Morr Music and Nonplace (in Berlin), Output (Milton Keynes) and the Leaf Label (Yorkshire) are increasingly starting to influence his running orders. It's only a matter of time before he'll have to learn to spell names such as Dntel, Tunng, Fennesz and Murcof.

So the question to Peel might be: 'Are your Radio 1 shows the beginning of hipsterism as people will one day know it?'

John Peel Show
Radio 1
27 June 2001

The Briefs – The White Stripes – The Strokes – Morgan Heritage – Gnac – Anthony Atcherley – New Order – Klute – The Tennessee Twin – Kettel – Jahmali and Jahmel – Nação Zumbi – 100 Pets

The jury in the Jeffrey Archer perjury trial is told that he will not be going into the witness box to defend himself. Over the past few weeks the jury has heard that Archer concocted a false alibi and forged diary entries prior to his libel trial in 1987.

Last month a listener emailed Peel to ask if he'd be getting Sonic Youth to record a session – it would have been their fourth – when their European tour reached London. No, Peel replied curtly. 'The last time we tried to book them to do a session, their record company decided that it was the Lamacq programme or nothing. You get so fed up with big record company stuff like that. We get it all the time, you know, so we just don't bother. Life's too short.'

Tonight, Peel is worried that the Strokes – a much-hyped band from New York who have done their first session for him – are becoming so popular that their management might stand in the way of any future visits to Maida Vale. This is becoming a major source of irritation for him. As much as Clive Selwood's *Peel Sessions* albums on Strange Fruit have made the vast archive accessible and navigable for the everyday punter, it's the sessions of the future that matter to Peel, not the sessions of the past. There was a time when he would have made a dry comment about David Jensen or Janice Long getting first dibs on a new single by a successful band that he'd first discovered three years earlier. These days he doesn't sound quite so amused. He even threatened in May to name and shame the bands whose record labels have chosen Lamacq's show over his own.

'It's disappointing when bands get too big for the programme, as they sometimes do,' Peel will say when he repeats the Strokes' session in August. 'Not usually the bands' fault, we find, but management people, record-company people interfere and say, "Don't bother doing that Peel thing, it really doesn't matter, nobody cares."'

By then, the Strokes' debut album, *Is This It*, will have entered the UK charts at number 2, well on its way to racking up gold discs in most of the major territories. Next year it will start going platinum. And sure enough, when it does, the Strokes won't bother doing that Peel thing again.

John Peel Show

Radio 1

25 July 2001

The Detroit Cobras – Elena – Gorky's Zygotic Mynci – The White
Stripes – King Tubby – The Colt Brothers – Piano Slim and his Rockin'
Four – Rechenzentrum – Octave One

*A Times/MORI poll makes the former chancellor Kenneth Clarke a
clear favourite to succeed William Hague as leader of the Conservative
Party, following the elimination of Michael Portillo in last week's
ballot. But Clarke's rival, the little-known Iain Duncan Smith, appears
to be gaining support among grass-roots Tories.*

Peel isn't a man who speaks in blues clichés, but if he were, he
might say that 2001 is the year when he's brought it all back home.
Each time he tries to express his excitement for the White Stripes,
he ends up talking about someone like Jimi Hendrix, Lightnin'
Hopkins or Howlin' Wolf. He really believes they're that special.
Hendrix is not a name to drop lightly, but actually it's Hopkins, a
prolific country-blues artist of the Fifties and Sixties, who may be
the more flattering comparison in Peel's mind. He claims to have
shaken Hopkins's hand as a young man, after jumping onstage at
a club in Dallas, and has spent a lifetime buying most of the vinyl
that Hopkins ever released: possibly as many as a hundred albums.
Peel rarely lets a year go by without raving about Hopkins to his
young listeners. He played a song called 'Rollin' Woman Blues'
(which Sheila owns in her collection of 78s) as recently as a fortnight ago.

It was Hopkins, in 1961, who indirectly inspired Peel to begin his
career in radio. When Peel walked into the studios of WRR-AM
in Dallas armed with some of his blues records, wondering if Jim

Lowe and Bill 'Hoss' Carroll, the presenters of the R&B show *Kat's Karavan*, would care to play one or two of them on air, the sight of Hopkins's *The Rooster Crowed in England* – an album sold in a limited edition of two hundred by Dobell's Record Shop in Charing Cross Road – made their eyes light up. Hopkins had had a number 1 hit in Dallas the year before ('Mojo Hand'), so a young Englishman turning up with one of his super-rare records had their immediate respect. 'And then Hoss Carroll said: "Let's talk to the man who has loaned them to us,"' Peel later recalled. 'So they put me on the radio.'

Jack White – like Peel a blues devotee – loves hearing stories like these. Earlier this evening the two men had dinner in a Thai restaurant in London, where they talked about Captain Beefheart, Gene Vincent and Son House. One of Peel's favourite songs by the White Stripes is 'Death Letter' on *De Stijl*, originally recorded by Son House in the mid-Sixties. The venerable Delta bluesman later performed it in the session he recorded for *Top Gear* in 1970. White's mouth falls open. Peel *knew* Son House? Well, not 'knew' him exactly, Peel explains, but was fortunate enough to broadcast a session by him when he was on a blues tour in Europe. White's brain does the mathematics. He's eating Thai food with a disc jockey whose career intersects with the life and times of Edward James 'Son' House, a man born in 1902. This is not possible! But it *is* possible, and it happened, and Peel agrees it would be a great idea to rebroadcast the Son House session next week, so that a new generation can hear it.

A few hours later and Peel is now at Maida Vale, where the White Stripes will shortly play a concert live on air in front of a small audience. There's been more interest in this performance along the corridors of Radio 1, Peel has noticed, than in any previous session or concert he's ever presented. This pleases him. For once it's the *John Peel Show* that can offer the coolest American stars, not the *Evening*

Session or *Lamacq Live*. And the announcements are Peel at his best: not remotely promotional, not lording it over his colleagues, not prepared to jive up the occasion by using anyone's language but his own. 'Very impressed with the red trousers there, Jack,' he calls across to White as he and Meg get ready to start. 'Very similar to the ones that I wore for the Liverpool–Real Madrid final in Paris all those years ago.' Ten seconds later, White is pumping away at his guitar and letting out his first whoop of abandon.

The concert, instantly bootleggable, is presented in three parts. The first gets under way with 'Let's Shake Hands' (their 1998 debut single) and concludes with a ravaged version of Dolly Parton's 'Jolene', with White squawking in a desperate falsetto. A pause of uncertainty follows before the audience begins clapping. 'These are not people who believe in holding back,' Peel deadpans. The listener will have to picture the record-company and media liggers packed into the balcony. Peel plays some King Tubby while they digest the airy admonishment.

The second bite of the White Stripes, by which time everyone sounds warmed up with a drink, begins with 'Death Letter', the version that Peel likes so much. It becomes a tidal wave of slide guitar from Jack and an apotheosis of sledgehammer up-and-down drumming from Meg. It's frustrating not to be able to see them, because the soulful looks they sometimes exchange while playing – they've now been revealed to be ex-husband and ex-wife, not brother and sister – are incomparable. The next section, in which they finally get around to promoting the new album, sees Jack really cut loose. For song after song, the lusty young firebrand takes leave of his senses, while his ex-wife's simple whomp of a beat monitors him as mechanically as a baby alarm. To Peel's delight, they encore with a song that was discussed earlier over dinner: Gene Vincent's 'Baby Blue'.

'Anyone who ends their set with a Gene Vincent song wins the unstinting approval of this programme,' says Peel at the end, at last giving in to salesmanship. 'The White Stripes – thanks very much. People will go away from here and their lives will never be quite the same again.'

Five days later, he receives the news that John Walters has died.

2002–3: THE NIGHT MANAGER

'There are a million other pressing issues, but it's one step at a time. This issue needs to be resolved before any of the other vast, ever-expanding tier of problems.' DAMON ALBARN, Stop the War campaign, February 2003

John Peel Show
Radio 1
25 April 2002

Tennessee Twin – Speedy J – Count Lasher and Charlie Binger's Six – Low – Jack Payne, Leslie Sarony and Tommy Handley – Rascal and Klone – Stylus – Wire – Smog – Rachel's – Dianogah – Ciccone

After a fifty-five-day trial at the Old Bailey, two sixteen-year-old twin brothers are cleared by a jury of the murder of Damilola Taylor, a ten-year-old Nigerian boy who was stabbed to death in Peckham in November 2000. Ken Livingstone, the mayor of London, calls for an inquiry into the police handling of the case.

Peel has never been a man to shy away from giving his listeners the gory details of his latest medical conditions. On his first afternoon sitting in for Jakki Brambles in 1993, he announced on air that he had 'some kind of disgusting respiratory disease' that had turned him into 'a snot generator' – just at the precise moment when most people would have been sitting down to their lunch. More seriously, in May that year, he told his listeners one Saturday night that he'd been coughing up blood in the studio.

In September 2001, after being hospitalised and missing a week of programmes, he returned with the following news: 'I went away from you a regular guy and I come back to you a diabetic.' The diagnosis was something of a relief. 'I've been developing all these rather disagreeable symptoms, and getting frightened about them and thinking that any one of them could take me to the next world at any moment.' At least the doctors now knew what was causing the symptoms.

In addition to diabetes he has high blood pressure, for which he takes medication. He suffers dizzy spells on hot days. Mysterious lurgies come and go, sometimes knocking him for six. 'I have to tell you, avid consumers,' he says early in tonight's show, 'I've been feeling terrible all day. I'm relying on the next couple of hours to perk me up.' He and Sheila took a long holiday together last month (now that he has conquered his aversion to flying), visiting first India and then New Zealand. But even then he couldn't completely take his foot off the gas: he told a radio interviewer in Auckland that he was doing some work for the British consulate. Whatever ailment he's since come down with, it'll force him to miss the second weekend of the All Tomorrow's Parties festival at Camber Sands, which starts tomorrow. He's meant to be DJing between the acts, but by the end of his two-hour show tonight he talks of feeling 'amazingly disorientated'.

Curated by Steve Albini and his band Shellac, All Tomorrow's Parties has given itself a fairly wide remit this year, with a line-up stretching from the Fall to Cheap Trick. Peel would have enjoyed himself. Quite apart from the DJing and the chance to catch up with Albini, there were at least twenty bands on the bill who would have liked to buy him a drink. Tonight he plays about an hour of music recorded during the first leg of the festival last weekend – most of it from the haunting Minnesota trio Low – and holds a competition to win a four-berth chalet and free tickets for the second weekend. The Internet, of course, can provide instant answers to questions ('After which planet did Shellac name a 1993 single?') that once would have sent listeners scurrying to the specialist magazine racks of their local record shops. The winner of the tickets, a young man studying at the University of Sussex, has his name read out by Peel less than an hour after emailing his reply to the final question.

Email is the only way, now, to contact Peel in mid-programme, since the phone number of Peel Acres is not known to most of the British population. 'I know you don't do requests,' emails Dave in Grimsby, 'but can we have some deep and dirty drum 'n' bass? If not, sod you.'

Others, however, prefer to approach Peel in the time-honoured way: by sending him records in the post. Noel Hawks, who runs the mail-order business of the London reggae shop Dub Vendor, has been keeping Peel abreast of the latest Jamaican singles, albums and pre-releases for over twenty years. After Peel plays a track from a compilation of calypso tunes that Hawks has sent him (*Boogu Yagga Gal: Jamaican Mento 1950s*), he thanks Hawks – whom he's never met – for once writing a letter to the *Guardian* about him. The broadsheet, in a moment of madness, had accused Peel of operating a whites-only music policy on his programmes. Hawks pointed out in his letter that several thousand fans of reggae, hip hop, techno, blues and African music might be wondering when exactly the author of the article had last listened to Peel.

John Peel Show
Radio 1
7 November 2002

Venetian Snares – U-Roy – Part Chimp – Element – Lonnie Donegan
– Melys – Alphazone – The Von Bondies – James P. Johnson – Laura
Cantrell – The Hunches – Blind Blake – MIA – The Vaults

*Home secretary David Blunkett issues a warning that al-Qaeda could
unleash a poison-gas attack or a nuclear 'dirty bomb' on Britain. His
words appear in the foreword to a new report on government anti-
terrorism measures. Blunkett later tones down the warning, attributing
his original draft to a 'clerical error'.*

Laura Cantrell is a thirty-five-year-old singer originally from Nashville who moved to New York in the Eighties. She writes and performs in the genre known as alternative (or alt) country. When her
debut album, *Not the Tremblin' Kind*, reached Peel in early 2000, he
proclaimed it the best record he'd heard in ten years. He and Sheila
spent time with Cantrell and her husband Jeremy on their visit to
New York that summer.

Having played songs from *Not the Tremblin' Kind* on his shows
almost every week for the next eighteen months – until a few of
them threatened to dislodge 'Teenage Kicks' from pole position
in his list of all-time favourites – Peel more recently began plugging Cantrell's follow-up, *When the Roses Bloom Again*, which was
released in September. She's also recorded three sessions for him,
the second of which she performed live at Peel Acres and the third
of which was broadcast two nights ago. Cantrell is a DJ with her
own country show on a New Jersey radio station, which makes Peel
like her all the more.

This week Peel has been sent a CD of Cantrell's new single, 'All the Same to You'. A press release is enclosed for the benefit of anyone in TV, radio or print media who hasn't heard Cantrell's name before, or who needs their memory jogging. Pretending to stumble over her surname, Peel reads from it aloud: 'In the UK for December dates including [the festival] Further Beyond Nashville, this excellent New York-based singer-songwriter has been championed by Bob Harris.'

Peel's tone is brisk. 'Well, I think we want to hear her.' There's little point in him playing 'All the Same to You', since his listeners first heard it back in August as an album track on *When the Roses Bloom Again*, so instead he goes for the bonus song on the CD single ('High on a Hill Top'), which will be new to them. His voice adopts a tone of the purest innocence. 'Laura Cantrell,' he says. 'Remember the name, if you can.'

Cantrell won't have written the press release herself (and may be mortified if she ever hears about it), but her UK publicist has picked the wrong night, as it happens, to write Peel out of history. In the past few days, the major label DGC has released a fourteen-track compilation of Nirvana's greatest hits, which starts with an unreleased song, 'You Know You're Right'. Recorded at their final recording session in 1994, the song has been the source of a long-running legal dispute between bassist Krist Novoselic, drummer Dave Grohl and Kurt Cobain's widow Courtney Love. Everyone is intrigued to know whether the song lives up to its advance publicity. But it has yet to be heard on any of Peel's shows. He's now starting to receive emails from listeners asking if there's a problem.

'The truth of the matter is, I haven't got the record,' he says. 'It's an illustration of the extraordinary way that major labels work. Back when Nirvana started – the first LP – I don't think anybody played it on the radio except for this programme. Then of course they did sessions for the programme and so on, but once they get onto a major label, they stop sending us the records. You can be pretty sure that Chris Moyles, Tim Westwood and people like that will have copies. But we don't. We can go and *buy* them like everybody else.'

Peel has begun standing up for himself. It's good to see. He should have been this dogmatic years ago. Sonic Youth sessions? Too much hassle. Go begging to Nirvana's record company? As if I would. Peel's proud little radio programme, which started the wheels spinning that turned an unknown trio into huge stars who ended up in the law courts, is still underrated – to this day; to this very *evening* – by a blasé record company that grew fat on the profits. In the meantime, rather enjoying his display of well-merited petulance about the Cantrell press release, Peel remarks after a noisy track by an unsigned Stowmarket band called the Vaults: 'I think we'll have to see if we can get Bob Harris to get behind them.'

John Peel Show
Radio 1
26 December 2002

The Datsuns – Cove – Lynx and Flow – Antihero – Quinoline Yellow – The Dawn Parade – The D4 – Interpol – Burning Love Jumpsuit – Poet'z – Boom Bip – Ladytron – Nina Nastasia – Saloon

Iain Duncan Smith, the Conservative leader who last month urged his party to 'unite or die', is publicly criticised by his former chief of staff. Jenny Ungless, who resigned earlier this year, accuses Duncan Smith of making a number of poor leadership decisions, including ordering MPs to vote against adoption for gay couples.

Peel has talked a lot about *The Perfumed Garden* this year. After the magazine *MOJO* published a list of them, he began revisiting songs that he'd played in his marathon final show in August 1967. Once unable to say the programme's name without blushing, Peel now accepts – as he should – that it was a groundbreaking, historically important episode in British pop radio. Tonight, counting down the Festive 50 from numbers 50 to 1, he does something he hasn't done since that final *Perfumed Garden*. He presents a five-hour show without a break.

The two Peels, thirty-five years apart, couldn't be more different people. In 1967 he was an unconditional advocate of flower power who talked like George Harrison impersonating Prince Charles. He spent two out of every three weeks on a ship, living the life of a nocturnal psychedelic Pied Piper, while a homesick American teenager waited miserably for him back on shore. Neither of them knew if Peel would have a job in radio at Christmas, or if their marriage had a future.

Now, at sixty-three, Peel is the oldest DJ at Radio 1 and has been married to Sheila for twenty-eight years. He's the winner of countless awards, the forty-third most popular Briton in history (according to a programme on BBC2 in October) and one of the last practitioners of a gentle, erudite style of radio broadcasting that is slowly dying out. In 1967 he was effectively homeless. Tonight he speaks to his listeners from the house he's lived in for half his life; a house where Blur, Supergrass, Belle and Sebastian and the White Stripes have played; a house where four children have grown up.

We join him at the point where the tape recording starts: in the middle of number 23 in the Festive 50 ('The Chelsea Hotel Oral Sex Song' by the anti-folk singer Jeffrey Lewis), with two hours of the show to go. Peel is alone in the house. BBC1 is showing a late-night Boxing Day film, *Airplane II: The Sequel*, with *Steptoe and Son Ride Again* to follow. Peel is trying hard not to tire.

The Festive 50 has some old favourites as well as new ones. At 22 are the Fall, who will record yet another session for Peel in February. He's lost count of how many this will make. The perennially droll

Half Man Half Biscuit are at 14. Cinerama, led by the Wedding Present's David Gedge, are at 13 and 2. The winners are Saloon, a band from Reading, with a song that nobody can remember voting for. 'I've been doing these programmes since the reign of George IV,' Peel says, 'and this is the least expected number 1 of all of them.' Rumours of vote-rigging will cast a sour note on the rest of Saloon's short career.

The last time Peel found himself on the final lap of a five-hour radio show, there was no time to contemplate victory. Tony Benn, the Postmaster General, had shut down the pirate stations – a decision that Benn, who became every bit as much a national treasure as Peel, would always maintain was unavoidable – leaving Peel to counsel and console the bereaved children of *The Perfumed Garden* as dawn broke on a summer morning. He then had almost ten hours to wait until Radio London switched off its transmitter at 3 p.m., at which point he and the other DJs climbed into the tender boat and puttered off towards Harwich, where they would catch the train into Liverpool Street. What did Peel do in the meantime? Did he sleep? Or did he just pass the hours in silence, taking one last look round the ship, wondering what a big city like London held in store for a twenty-seven-year-old well-spoken Jefferson Airplane fan?

This time there's no formal farewell, no journey back to dry land, no take-care-and-we'll-meet-in-the-next-life. Peel has one record left to play. A telephone has been ringing at Peel Acres. There's no one in the house to answer it.

'I apologise for the fact that I started to drift into unconsciousness about an hour ago,' he signs off. 'Coming up next, it'll be the news. While I calm down and relax, Schaffhäuser vs Jacob Fairley, and the Cossack Remix – from a compilation album that I shall feature more in the next few programmes – of "Warenkorb #4".'

Four minutes of German minimal techno play the show out.

John Peel Show
Radio 1
29 January 2003

Devon Irons – Herman Dune – The White Stripes – Fallout Boy – Mos
Eisley – People Like Us – Rankin Taxi – Keaton – M.A.S.S. – Dipps
Bhamrah – Random Inc. – Vehicle Derek – Lil' Sach – Anthony B –
Das Bierbeben – The Avengers – Mira Calix

*The Home Office is considering plans to deport Abu Hamza, the
controversial imam of Finsbury Park mosque, following yesterday's
revelation that his 1980 marriage to a British woman, which entitles
him to remain in the country, was bigamous. It is not clear if Hamza
knew the woman was already married.*

There's an interview with Peel this month in *Muzik*, a monthly magazine for serious fans of electronica and hip hop. The blurb at the
top of the page describes him, magnificently, as 'the original bad
bwoy of Radio 1'. The reason for the interview is that Peel has been
asked to compile a mix CD for Fabric. The Farringdon nightclub,
regularly voted in the top five of the world's best clubs, was won
over by Peel when he played a typically off-the-wall DJ set there
a year ago. The crowd chanted his name, sang along to 'Teenage
Kicks' at the tops of their voices, and mobbed him after his set as if
he'd been Sasha or Danny Tenaglia. He really does generate enormous goodwill everywhere he goes.

 Muzik asks him what Fabric can expect from the mix CD. He says
he'll start with the commentary of Alan Kennedy's winning goal for
Liverpool against Real Madrid in the 1981 European Cup final, and
see where he goes from there. The commentary went down well,
he found, in his set at Sónar in Barcelona, a city where Real Madrid
are detested. But after that, the course of the mix is anyone's guess.

Mogwai, Laura Cantrell, Patricia Routledge and Anal Cunt may all be about to make their *FabricLive* debuts.

There's no doubt what the huge worldwide scoop on tonight's Peel show is, and it has nothing to do with Fabric. Scattered throughout the programme are three new songs by the White Stripes, previewing an album, *Elephant*, that isn't expected to hit the streets until April. Peel doesn't say how he acquired his copy, but bearing in mind how well they've bonded as friends, there's a possibility that Jack White – or someone very close to him – is the one who put it in an envelope and mailed it to Peel Acres.

John Peel Show
Radio 1
5 February 2003

Blues Goblins – The Delgados – Tigerstyle – Crimea – The White Stripes – History at Our Disposal – Bushman – Children's Hour – The Bug vs Rootsman featuring Mexican – Cat Power – Million Dead – Rankin Taxi – Alphabetical Four – The Black Keys

Foreign secretary Jack Straw endorses a seventy-five-minute speech given to the UN Security Council by the American secretary of state, Colin Powell, in which he called for war to be declared on Iraq. Straw describes the satellite images and communications intercepts presented by Powell as a 'most powerful and authoritative case'.

Peel is in trouble with the White Stripes' record company. By playing songs from *Elephant* so far in advance of the release date, he's contravened an embargo. XL Recordings have asked him not to play any more, since his shows are on the Internet and the songs can be downloaded and bootlegged. Already in a bad mood after watching Liverpool lose an FA Cup match on television tonight, Peel's response to XL is withering.

'Unfortunately I'm not allowed to play you any tracks from it,' he tells the listeners after holding up his copy of *Elephant* and slapping it several times, 'because by doing so I interfere with the global marketing strategy. And God knows, you don't want to do that. But just to show that we still love the band . . . what's the matter?'

His producer speaks to him off mic: 'We can play two.'

Peel: 'Yeah, but . . . but I *hate* that, d'you know what I mean? I've got the record here. It's got something like fourteen tracks on it. And I have some record-company twerp saying [*eagerly*], "You can play two of them!" And you think, "No, I won't play any of them." D'you know what I mean? I hate being told what to do. I don't think it's *right*.'

He plays a track from last year's White Stripes EP *Dead Leaves and the Dirty Ground*, adding that he still loves their music, even though he hates their record company 'and everybody connected with it'. Two weeks from now, XL will post him a copy of the band's new single, 'Seven Nation Army', with a little note attached saying that he's allowed to play it on his show. He'll send the single back.

John Peel Show
Radio 1
19 February 2003

H10326 – Celine – Aereogramme – Sharkey, A.M.S. and Robbie Long – Crimea – Tommy McClennan – Melt-Banana – Ceephax Acid Crew – Tom Lehrer – Higher Intelligence Agency – Iron and Wine

Britain's two most senior churchmen, the Archbishops of Canterbury and Westminster, have appealed to Tony Blair to justify the 'moral

legitimacy' of invading Iraq. Their joint statement comes four days after
a million people in London marched against the war as part of a day of
protests in six hundred cities across the world.

Conceived by Grant Wakefield and Miriam Ryle, two filmmakers
who travelled to Iraq four years ago, *The Fire This Time* is a CD featuring music from Orbital, Aphex Twin and other electronica artists,
interspersed with field recordings and narration. Over the course of
seventy-eight minutes, it relates the history of conflict in the Gulf
with the aim of publicising the effects that the 1991 Gulf War and
the sanctions on Iraq have had on the civilian population. 'Terrifying
and timely,' the *Independent on Sunday* wrote in a review of the album
last year. *Uncut* magazine called it 'a shattering protest record'.

Peel – who plays tracks from the album without comment tonight
and tomorrow – has broadcast through wars in Vietnam, Northern
Ireland, the Falklands, the Balkans and the Gulf. Towards the end of
last November, as the Iraqi disarmament crisis appeared to escalate,
he said to the listeners: 'As you will have noticed, it's been quite a
long time since we've had a war. In my quaint, old-fashioned way,
I'm not terrifically keen on having another one.' The next record he
played was June Tabor's 'And the Band Played Waltzing Matilda', a
song written about the slaughter at Gallipoli.

The invasion of Iraq now looks unstoppable. Blur singer Damon
Albarn, who along with Robert Del Naja of Massive Attack has
been working with CND and the Stop the War Coalition to raise
opposition and awareness among musicians, told Sky News this
week: 'Each individual has their own opinions about whether war
is an answer to any problems. I don't feel like we've been given any
choice in the matter. I think if you had a referendum tomorrow,
Tony Blair would have no choice but to call off the war.'

But there'll be no referendum. In 2003, pop stars are as powerless
as archbishops.

John Peel Show
Radio 1
20 March 2003

DJ Damage – Grandmaster Gareth – Mad Cobra – Biffy Clyro –
Autechre – Benny Goodman Sextet – Sons of Cyrus – Cowcube –
Jerry Lee Lewis – Ictus – Stephen Malkmus and the Jicks – Magoo

*Twelve Royal Marines become the first British casualties on day
one of the Iraq War. They are killed when a US Marines Sea Knight
helicopter crashes in Kuwait.*

Peel voted for Blair. But he soon wished he hadn't. As the optimism felt by Labour voters in 1997 started to dissipate by 1998,
Peel was one of the first to announce publicly that he would never
support the party again. Jack Straw had outraged the families of
the ninety-six Hillsborough victims – and angered Liverpool supporters like Peel – by ordering a report that concluded there was
insufficient evidence for a new inquiry into the 1989 disaster.

'The Government,' said Peel in an interview with the *Independent
on Sunday* in April 1998, 'seems to glory in not doing what they said
they were going to do. I was jubilant when they were elected, but
it's turned to despair.' Even at that stage he was dreading a possible
invasion of Iraq, noticing a worrying appetite for war beginning to
develop. 'We bombed them, bombed them again and starved them
for years,' he said. And the irony of it all was, his enthusiasm for
Blair had been mutual.

At some point in the last few years, Blair is reported to have called
Peel 'a radio legend'. Nobody is too sure where or when he said it,
but the quote resurfaced in 1999, when the *Daily Telegraph* wrote,
in a preview of BBC2's *John Peel Night* marking his sixtieth birthday: 'Peel, once described by Tony Blair as "truly a radio legend", is

credited with launching the careers of such bands as the Clash [*sic*], the Smiths and Pulp.'

Mark Radcliffe and his sidekick Marc 'Lard' Riley both remember, in separate accounts, Blair being keen to meet Peel when he dropped in at the annual photo session of Radio 1 DJs in London one year. There's some disagreement about whether Blair and Peel shook hands – Radcliffe says they didn't, Riley says they did – but there's no argument about Peel's feelings towards Blair that day. He felt he had betrayed the Labour Party and he wanted nothing to do with him.

Now it's a Thursday night in March 2003. Earlier today, the tanks rolled into Iraq. Allied troops have been reported as capturing the southern port city of Umm Qasr and bomb blasts have been heard near Basra.

'I feel more and more like a stranger in my own country,' sighed Peel one night in the Eighties, after Margaret Thatcher's Conservatives had sailed into power again. 'I know I shouldn't really say that. We're not supposed to comment on the news.'

But isn't every Peel programme a comment on the news? Isn't that what this has all been about, this life in British radio that began in 1967 with him playing the music of the revolution and condemning those who glorified in the prison sentences of Mick Jagger and Keith Richards? Hasn't Peel's convergence with the news – gradually shortening the distance and blurring the boundaries, until his shows in 1984–5 were a musical continuation of the 10 p.m. headlines about the miners' strike – been the story of Peel's career?

In John le Carré's *The Night Manager*, Richard Onslow Roper, a murderous and guilt-free arms dealer, gathers a group of South American crime lords together in the jungle. Over dinner he asks one of them: 'Know why Bush went to war against Saddam?'

This is the 1990–1 Gulf War. Bush is Bush senior. Someone thinks he knows the answer. 'The oil, for Chrissakes.'

No, says Roper. Guess again.

The money? The Kuwaiti gold?

'For the *experience*,' Roper says. 'Bush wanted the experience.' And when they've had time to think about that, he adds: 'Governments? Worse than we are.'

The hero of *The Night Manager* is the young night auditor of an exclusive Zurich hotel who runs the front desk when the daytime staff have clocked off. He keeps the hotel ticking over and deals with any sophisticated requests that the more importunate guests might send down at ungodly hours of the night. It's not a bad analogy for Peel.

The TV news channels are reporting the war in seconds and minutes. BBC News 24. ITN. Sky. Journalists are embedded with the troops. Such-and-such a town has fallen.

Peel is back in his old familiar time slot of 10 p.m. to midnight, playing two hours of records to end the day. Or to pause it. Or to define it. Contextualising modern life with music. Commenting on the news without commenting on it. Shepherding his listeners safely across the midnight border with the sounds of the most extreme vinyl he can lay his hands on. Reconciling the irreconcilable by making sense of the nonsensical. He's been doing it since 1967.

The night manager cues up a record. It's Jerry Lee Lewis, singing a country ballad called 'Before the Next Teardrop Falls'. The jilted boyfriend wishes the bride all the happiness in the world with the groom. Only the crack in his voice is the giveaway that he's lying.

'Nobody did it better,' says the night manager.

It's 10.47 p.m.

* * *

John Peel died in Peru on 25 October 2004 at the age of sixty-five. His final show on Radio 1, broadcast from Peel Acres eleven days earlier, included a session from Trencher (a band from London whose music had been dubbed 'Casio-grindcore' by the rock press), as well as tracks by Jimmy Reed, Conway Twitty and the Fall.

Andy Parfitt, the controller of Radio 1, described Peel on the day of his death as a man whose influence 'has towered over the development of popular music for nearly four decades'. A spokesman for Tony Blair called him 'an extraordinary and unique personality . . . a genuine one-off and a warm and decent human being too'.

The following January, it was reported that Radio 1 had appointed three DJs – Rob da Bank, Ras Kwame and Huw Stephens – to present programmes in a new strand, One Music, intended to keep the spirit of John Peel alive.

According to recent figures, the combined record sales of David Bowie, Rod Stewart, Elton John, Pink Floyd, Genesis, Queen, Bob Marley, Mike Oldfield, Bryan Ferry and Roxy Music, Joy Division and New Order, UB40, the Cure, Frankie Goes to Hollywood, Morrissey and Nirvana now exceed 1.5 billion.

SOURCES

Many of the news stories that appear in *Good Night and Good Riddance* were sourced from British daily newspapers published between 1967 and 2003. These were then edited and rewritten. In the interests of political balance I tried to even out my story-hunting between the *Guardian*, *The Times*, the *Independent*, the *Observer*, the *Sunday Times* and the *Independent on Sunday*. The Jubilee Library in Brighton until recently made back issues of several of these newspapers available to the public to read on microfilm. In 2014, the Jubilee began putting some of its facilities online. It could not have been a more helpful library during the two and a half years it took me to research and write this book.

Other resources that I consulted regularly for facts and background information include Hansard (www.hansard.millbanksystems.com), the University of Ulster's CAIN history of the Northern Ireland conflict (www.cain.ulst.ac.uk), the *Radio Times'* Genome archive (www.genome.bbc.co.uk/issues), the Radio Rewind website (www.radiorewind.co.uk), the Free Festivals 1967–1990 site (ukrockfestivals.com/free-festivals) and the BBC's Keeping It Peel site (www.bbc.co.uk/radio1/johnpeel).

I also took information and quotes from a number of magazines and books, as well as from various websites, which are listed in the details for each chapter below.

INTRODUCTION: PEEL NATION
1 History of Caversham Park: Brian Rotheray, 'A History of
   Caversham Park', BBC Monitoring, www.cadra.org.uk/pdf/
   cavershamhistory
6 BBC research and Peel's under-sixteen listeners: Peel interviewed
   by Radio B92, 2002

9 History of jungle: Charlie Allenby, 'Ragga Twins on Jungle's Year Zero', *Dazed*, c.April 2014

12 'These programmes may be hateful . . .': Peel on the *John Peel Show*, 23 September 1982

13 'You're listening to the John Peel wing-ding . . .': ibid.

15 'By ensuring that up to ninety per cent . . .': Nick Currie, 'John Peel Died Yesterday', imomus.livejournal.com/57688.html, 27 October 2004

18 'There have been some great broadcasters . . .': Peel on the *John Peel Show*, 14 December 1991

18 'I was a little late in coming to an appreciation . . .': Peel on the *John Peel Show*, 23 December 1982

21 'almost religious devotion to seeking out and broadcasting unconventional rock music': Garth Cartwright, Peel obituary, *Guardian*, 27 October 2004

21 'delight in the new, the unexpected and the good': Peel obituary, *The Economist*, 4 November 2004

21 'ability to broadcast as if he were speaking to just one person': Peel obituary, *Daily Telegraph*, 27 October 2004

23 'a view that should be allowed to be aired': Peel, 'God Save the Queen: What the Papers Say', *Sounds*, 18 June 1977

24 'If it wasn't for John Peel, there would be no Joy Division and no New Order': Bernard Sumner quoted by BBC News, 26 October 2004

24 'We never had anybody like John Peel in the States': Dan Auerbach, onstage at Glastonbury, 25 June 2010

25 'the most important DJ of all time': Jack White interviewed on *John Peel's Record Box*, Channel 4, November 2005

27 'What we need to do is represent the zeitgeist . . .': Ben Cooper interviewed by Ben Cardew, *Guardian*, 3 August 2014

1967: THE GARDEN

31 'There was a feeling of unification . . .': Kevin Ayers interviewed in *A Technicolor Dream*, Eagle Rock Entertainment, dir. Stephen Gammond, 2008

31–44 Information about Radio London and other pirate stations: author's interviews with Tony Blackburn, Keith Skues, Dave Cash

and Johnnie Walker, September and October 2008. Additional
information: K. Skues, *Pop Went the Pirates*, Lamb's Meadow
Publications, 1994

1968: THE LORD'S DAY
45 'We'd all really forgotten about the bells and beads . . .': Mick Farren
interviewed by *The Quietus*, March 2013
47–8 'The pirates were the biggest boot in the arse the BBC ever had':
'Hang the DJ!: The Musicians' Union and the Early Days of Radio 1',
The Musicians' Union: A Social History, University of Glasgow, www.
muhistory.com
51 'a flood of angry and bewildered letters': Peel, *International Times*,
issue 28, 5–18 April 1968

1969: THE HORROR COMICS
62 'Better not laugh too much . . .': Captain Beefheart interviewed by
Meatball Fulton, July 1969, published in *Captain Beefheart: The Man
and His Music* by Colin David Webb, Kawabata Press, 1987
63 '[The BBC] wanted to take it off after programme one . . .':
International Times 93, 3 December 1970
64 Editorial comments in *Melody Maker* about Peel winning best disc
jockey award: *Melody Maker*, 21 September 1968
76 'Saturday's "happening" was a great and epoch-making event . . .':
Richard Gott, 'A Glimpse of Britain in 10 Years', *Guardian*, 7 July 1969
76 'I hope nobody gets hurt': Keith Richards in *The Stones in the Park*,
directed and produced by Leslie Woodhead and Jo Durden-Smith,
Granada, 1969

1970: THE SEVEN CATEGORIES
78 'People talk about the Sixties . . .': Grant Showbiz interviewed
by Otis Gibbs, October 2013, www.soundcloud.com/otisgibbs/
episode-52-grant-showbiz-part
82 Background on Arthur 'Big Boy' Crudup: www.msbluestrail.org/
blues-trail-markers/arthur-crudup, www.organissimo.org/forum
and www.guitartricks.com/forum
85 'was the only person on radio . . .': C. Selwood, *All the Moves (But
None of the Licks)*, Peter Owen, 2003

1971: THE CHARACTER WITNESS

97 'Our strained relationship . . .': Tony Blackburn, *Poptastic! My Life in Radio*, Cassell Illustrated, 2007

98 'Never has such an outstanding rock star . . .': Victor Bockris, *Lou Reed: The Biography*, Hutchinson, 1994

110 'Patched jeans and dirty sweaters . . .': John Sparrow, 'Why Do the Young Look Like This?', *Sunday Times*, 6 September 1970

110 John Mortimer and the glass of water: Index on Censorship, www.indexoncensorship.org/2009/01/sir-john-mortimer-1923-2009

1972: THE ROCK 'N' ROLLERS

113 'John Peel thought we'd sold out . . .': Marc Bolan to Spencer Leigh, 'Ain't No Square with My Corkscrew Hair', February 1976

113 'progressive pop': Ken Garner, *The Peel Sessions*, BBC Books, 2007

119 'I've invented a new category of artist . . .': Michael Watts, 'Oh You Pretty Thing', *Melody Maker*, 22 January 1972

122 'Next day all hell broke loose in the playground': Marc Almond quoted in Peter Doggett, *The Man Who Sold the World: David Bowie and the 1970s*, Vintage, 2012

122 'Get it on? I couldn't wait to get it off': J. Peel and Sheila Ravenscroft, *Margrave of the Marshes*, Corgi, 2005

127 'Nowadays . . .', 'the hideous people', 'busy working on their fifth and sixth LPs': Peel on *Top Gear*, 27 November 1973

1973: THE CONVERSION JOB

128 'It was unplayable as far as DJs were concerned . . .': Tom Newman interviewed by Lenny Kelcic, *The Story of Tubular Bells*, Evolution Garden Media, 2011

132 'I wouldn't say we were striving for perfection': Rod Stewart interviewed by Roy Hollingworth, *Melody Maker*, 21 April 1973

135 'I like the way they dress . . .': Teddy boy interviewed by Chris Tarrant, *ATV Today*, 17 August 1973

137 'It would be very hard to exaggerate . . .': Richard Williams, *Catch a Fire – Classic Albums*, produced by Nick De Grunwald, directed by Jeremy Marre, written by Terence Dackombe, 1999

139 'Ronnie came over to me in the middle of a song . . .': Ian McLagan interviewed by the author for *MOJO* in 1995

144 'When I first started making music . . .' Brian Eno interviewed by
Radio 1 in 2005 for the 'Keeping It Peel' broadcasts

145 'getting a sheet of white paper . . .': Robert Fripp interviewed by
the author for *Uncut* magazine, 2013

1974: THE WHEELCHAIR

146 'I go and see John Peel playing . . .': Hermine Demoriane, *The
Tightrope Walker*, Secker and Warburg, 1989

149 'It never made money . . .': Selwood, *All the Moves (But None of the
Licks)*

152 'Nothing ever sounded so different to me . . .': Julian Cope,
Krautrocksampler, Head Heritage, 1995

157 History of Sterns: www.sternsmusic.com/about.php

159, 163–4 Robert Wyatt's accident and the *Top of the Pops* incident:
Marcus O'Dair, *Different Every Time: The Authorised Biography
of Robert Wyatt*, Serpent's Tail, 2014, and Michael King, *Wrong
Movements: A Robert Wyatt History*, S.A.F., 1994. The Frith quote
comes from the latter

1975: THE UNTOUCHABLES

165 'There's always a pendulum swing, right?': David Bowie
interviewed by Cameron Crowe, 'Ground Control to Davy Jones',
Rolling Stone, February 1976

165 '1974 didn't really happen': Jimmy Page interviewed by Nick Kent,
NME, 7 December 1974

167 'If you listen to "Sick Again" . . .': Robert Plant interviewed by Cameron Crowe, 'The Durable Led Zeppelin', *Rolling Stone*, March 1975

177 'I must have had blinkers on . . .': Rod Stewart interviewed by
Barbara Charone, *Creem*, November 1975

177–8 'What happens is, you get into this sort of elitist . . .': Michael
Des Barres interviewed by the author, 2010

178 'Everything had sort of come our way . . .': David Gilmour,
'Making of Shine On', *In the Studio with Redbeard*, December 1992

1976: FAST TIMES

181 'The Eagles and the Captain and Tennille . . .': Joey Ramone in
Marc Spitz and Brendan Mullen, *We Got the Neutron Bomb: The*

Untold Story of LA Punk, Three Rivers Press, 2001

185 'From then onwards . . .': Alan Warner at www.wizwas.com/index.php/2009/12/03/the-door-to-yesterday-9

193 'A lot of people phoned in . . .': Peel interviewed by Sue Lawley on *Desert Island Discs*, Radio 4, 14 January 1990

194 'It wasn't formed [yet] . . .': Mick Jones, 'The Night That Punk Went Overground: July 4th 1976 – An Oral Account', *Louder Than War*, 4 July 2012

1977: MIGHT TAKE A BIT OF VIOLENCE

199 'I had just been at Mick's flat . . .': Johnny Green, *A Riot of Our Own: Night and Day with the Clash*, Faber and Faber, 1999

207 'unbearably pretentious': Peel interviewed by Radio B92 in 2002, www.b92.net/feedback/misljenja/jp.php

1978: ATOM SPLITTING

219 'I can tell immediately by their expressions . . .': Viv Albertine, *Clothes, Clothes, Clothes. Music, Music, Music. Boys, Boys, Boys*, Faber and Faber, 2014

225 Peel and singles: he remarked on his programme on 9 January 1980 that between twenty and twenty-five new singles arrived in the office every day

230 'raven-tressed tempter': Peel on 11 October 1978

1979: NOW IS THE WINTER

240 'The anguished singer . . .': Des Moines, *Sounds*, 26 October 1979

242 'Get the foreigners out . . .': Eric Clapton onstage at the Birmingham Odeon on 5 August 1976, quoted in John Street, *Rebel Rock: The Politics of Popular Music*, Blackwell, 1986

1980: KITCHEN APPLIANCES

259 'The new wave sold out . . .': Mark E. Smith in *Printed Noises* fanzine, issue 4, 1980

277 'I always think of them in a rather romantic way . . .': Peel talking to John Walters in episode five of *Peeling Back the Years*, Radio 1, 24 October 1987

1981: THINK OF NOTHING

278 'Looking back, it does seem to be a very slack period': John Walters to Ken Garner, *The Peel Sessions*

291 'things are going to get worse before they get better': Peel on 3 April 1980

293 'black shadow that Poland casts across the whole of this Christmas': Michael Foot, Hansard, 22 December 1981

294 'It wasn't until the third record . . .': John O'Neill interviewed by Justin Maurer in 2011 at www.razorcake.org/interviews/interview-with-the-undertones-by-justin-maurer

295 'This is our continent . . .': Tony Benn speaking at Hyde Park in London, 24 October 1981

1982: ECLIPSED AGAIN

302 'Just like a flower when winter begins . . .': translation of lyrics to 'A Little Peace', sung by Nicole Hohloch, written by Ralph Siegel and Bernd Meinunger

1983: THE CORPORATIONS ARE BIGGER THAN ANY NATIONS

318 'When I accidentally meet John Peel over the years . . .': Morrissey, *Autobiography*, Penguin, 2013

327 'When I first heard a demo tape from the Smiths . . .': Peel introducing 'How Soon Is Now?' on Radio 1, 1 October 1997

333 'New Order and "Truth". Average serving . . .': Peel on the *John Peel Show*, 14 May 1981

333 'Hark! I hear the plaintive call . . .': Peel on the *John Peel Show*, 21 December 1982

1984: FEELING DIZZY AND UNWELL

337 'One of the basic tenets . . .': Jim Thirlwell interviewed by Helen FitzGerald, *Melody Maker*, 13 October 1984

344 'For quite a long time we've had all this candyfloss . . .': Morrissey interviewed by Paul Gambaccini and Henry Kelly, *TV-am*, c.Feb–March 1984

350 Background information on the Shockheaded Peters: Paolo Hewitt, *NME*, 27 October 1984

1985: GOD MADE THEM HIGH AND LOWLY

354 'My guitar is totally out of tune': Jim Reid to an interviewer backstage at North London Polytechnic, 15 March 1985, www.youtube.com/watch?v=LlsL5m1nirs

357 'I'm not afraid to say that I think Band Aid was diabolical . . .': Morrissey interviewed by Simon Garfield, *Time Out*, 7–13 March 1985

359 'They were using feedback to the point of excruciating pain': Peter Reichardt in *My Magpie Eyes Are Hungry for the Prize: The Creation Records Story*, Virgin, 2000

369 'It's the little things that drive me up the wall . . .': Nigel Blackwell interviewed by John McCready, *NME*, 14 December 1985

1986: RUCTIONS AT THE TUFTY CLUB

372 'The dawn of independent music . . .': Bobby Gillespie interviewed by Stuart Maconie, *NME*, 5 August 1989

379 'If you'd told us in 1980 or 1981 . . .': Steven Daly interviewed by the author in March 1998. Quote first published in *My Magpie Eyes Are Hungry for the Prize: The Creation Records Story*, Virgin, 2000

1987: ONCE AGAIN WE WRONG-FOOT QUALITY CONTROL

391 'What do your children think . . .': John Walters and John Peel in discussion, episode six of *Peeling Back the Years*, Radio 1, 31 October 1987

392–3 Beastie Boys background: Alex Ogg, *The Men Behind Def Jam: The Radical Rise of Russell Simmons and Rick Rubin*, Omnibus, 2002

393 'Since Live Aid, modern music . . .': Jack Barron, *Guardian*, 23 May 1987

398–9 Haçienda background: Dave Haslam, 'The History of the Hacienda', Pride of Manchester website, www.prideofmanchester.com/music/hacienda.htm, June 2003; and John McCready, 'Working on a Building of Love: The Great Days of the Haçienda', *The Face*, spring 1997

1988: GOODBYE TO ALL THAT

411 'I tend to analyse . . .': Bruno Brookes, *One on One: 21 Years of Radio 1* documentary, 1988

SOURCES

1989: THIS PARTY IS FAR FROM EXTINCT

425 'In New York it's just starting to get cool ...': Mark Arm of
Mudhoney, Manchester University, 20 March 1989, taken from
Mudhoney gigography at www.ocf.berkeley.edu/~ptn/mudhoney/
tourbook/1989.html

428 'Chris [Novoselic, bass] and me are from Aberdeen ...': Kurdt Kobain (Kurt Cobain), interviewed by John Robb, *Sounds*, 21 October 1989

429 'Right around Christmas of '88 ...': Bruce Pavitt interviewed
by Josh Adams, Stereoboard.com, 'The Seattle Miracle: Bruce
Pavitt, Sub Pop And Experiencing Nirvana', 4 March 2014, www.
stereoboard.com/content/view/184387/9

431 'I wouldn't say we were ahead of our time ...': Shaun Ryder
interviewed by Jon Wilde, *Melody Maker*, 12 November 1988

436 'He listened religiously ...': Steve Albini speaking at the Face the
Music conference in Melbourne, November 2014

437 'Unlike most of his colleagues ...' Dave Rimmer, 'John Peel: Two
Decades On', Q, December 1986

1990: LION ROCK IN LYON TRAFFIC

443 'I didn't come up out of trying to be cool ...': Gawtti of the Boo-Yaa
T.R.I.B.E. interviewed by Alex Alonso, Street Gangs, 31 December
2006, www.streetgangs.com/features/gawtti-boo-yaa-tribe

444 'non-armed political movement ...': Gerry Adams, 5 March 1989

445 'It was the beginning of a new era ...': Alex Paterson interviewed
by Howard Shih, *Perfect Sound Forever*, August 1997, www.furious.
com/perfect/orb.html

457–9 Information about the life of Ionel Dumitrascu and his relationship with Peel: author's conversation with Dumitrascu, March 2015

1991: BITS AND PIECES

460 'I don't see Nirvana getting as big as Metallica ...': Kurt Cobain,
'Bleach Bums', June 1991, archived at www.Nirvanaclub.com

471 Background on AIDS in Malawi: Gregory Barz and Judah M.
Cohen (Eds), *The Culture of AIDS in Africa: Hope and Healing
Through Music and the Arts*, Oxford University Press, 2011

472 Background on 'LMG' by Pornography: www.808state.com/
forum/viewtopic.php?t=1939

1992: THIS ENERGY OF WHICH YOU SPEAK

476 'It's touching some nerve somewhere': PJ Harvey interviewed by Richard Cromelin, *LA Times*, 27 December 1992

483 'John was the first person ever to take notice of what I was doing . . .': Harvey quoted by Cam Lindsay, 'Stories from the Queenie', *Exclaim!*, September 2007

1993: THE PRIME EXHIBIT IN THE ZOO

507–8 'I told him . . .': Gary Davies quoted by David Lister, 'Radio 1 DJ Quits and Warns of "Minority Station"', *Independent*, 12 November 1993

1994: THE SUN COME OUT AND STOLE MY FEAR AND GONE

509 'There was resentment that someone . . .': Matthew Wright quoted in Simon Garfield, *The Nation's Favourite: The True Adventures of Radio 1*, Faber and Faber, 1998

509–10 '[He] broke the news to them in much the same manner . . .': Sheila Ravenscroft, *Margrave of the Marshes*

511–12 'It doesn't mark any beginning or end . . .': Peel interviewed by *Interzone* magazine, 1994

514 'More recently . . .': Sheila Ravenscroft, *Margrave of the Marshes*

1995: THE HALL OF FAME

523 'Courtney's first appearance backstage . . .': Peel, 'Hole at Reading', *Guardian*, 30 August 1994

1996–7: THE THOUGHT OF IT ALL GOING WRONG

535 'There are several things going on now . . .': Peel's letter to Matthew Bannister, 25 January 1996

1998–9: THE ORDER OF THE INSTITUTE OF NATIONAL TREASURES

550 'Popular music guru John Peel . . .': 'Critic's Choice; Legend with Lots of a-Peel', *Daily Record*, 28 August 1999

556 'I get baffled by the sheer number of categories . . .': Peel interviewed by Tobias Jones, *Independent on Sunday*, 12 April 1998

559–60 Meltdown review: ARTWWWeb at www.artwwweb.blogspot. co.uk/1988/07/spiritualized-sonic-youth/html

561 'It's an interesting experience . . .': Peel interviewed by Chris Berthoud, *Home Truths*, 26 November 1998

2000–1: THE LONG JOURNEY HOME

570 'I was talking to some friends from New York . . .': Jack White interviewed by Norene Cashen, *Metro Times*, 26 May 1999

570 'There's a worldwide recession in the music industry': Alan McGee, 'This Is the Revolution. There Will Be No Record Companies in Five or Ten Years', *NME*, 13 June 1998

571 'an incredibly exploded music industry . . .': David Turin of People Tree quoted by Edward Helmore, 'Stop Thief!', *Guardian*, 20 November 1998

572 'For the first time ever . . .': Peel, 18 May 2000

574 'I just liked the look of it': Peel interviewed by Radio B92 in 2002

579 'I thought we had missed the point . . .': Thom Yorke interviewed by the author for *Q* magazine, 2000

580 'I like the idea of being cast in the role of expert . . .': Peel interviewed by Michael Berkeley, *Private Passions*, Radio 3, 16 March 1996

587 'And then Hoss Carroll said . . .': Peel speaking on *Radio Radio*, Radio 1, 8 February 1986

2002–3: THE NIGHT MANAGER

590 'There are a million other pressing issues . . .': Damon Albarn interviewed by Emma Warren, *Independent on Sunday*, 9 February 2003

590 'some kind of disgusting respiratory disease': Peel, 5 April 1993

591 coughing up blood: Peel, 29 May 1993

591 'I went away from you a regular guy . . .': Peel, 18 September 2001

591 Peel on blood pressure: interview with Eddy Lawrence, *Muzik*, January 2003

598 'the original bad bwoy of Radio 1': ibid.

601 'Each individual has their own opinions . . .': Damon Albarn interviewed on Sky News, 15 February 2003

602 'The Government . . .': Peel interviewed by Tobias Jones, *Independent on Sunday*, 12 April 1998

602–3 'Peel, once described by . . .': *Daily Telegraph*, 17 August 1999

603 'Know why Bush went to war . . .': John le Carré, *The Night Manager*, Hodder and Stoughton, 1993

BIBLIOGRAPHY

Albertine, Viv, *Clothes, Clothes, Clothes. Music, Music, Music. Boys, Boys, Boys*, Faber and Faber, 2014

Barnes, Mike, *Captain Beefheart*, Quartet, 2000

Bockris, Victor, *Lou Reed: The Biography*, Hutchinson, 1994

Bracewell, Michael, *Roxy: The Band That Invented An Era*, Faber and Faber, 2007

Collin, Matthew, with contributions by John Godfrey, *Altered State: The Story of Ecstasy Culture and Acid House*, Serpent's Tail, 1997

Cope, Julian, *Head-On*, Magog, 1994

–– *Krautrocksampler*, Head Heritage, 1995

Demoriane, Hermine, *The Tightrope Walker*, Secker and Warburg, 1989

Doggett, Peter, *The Man Who Sold the World: David Bowie and the 1970s*, Vintage, 2012

Gambaccini, Paul, Tim Rice and Jonathan Rice, *The Guinness Top 40 Charts*, Guinness, 1996

Garfield, Simon, *The Nation's Favourite: The True Adventures of Radio 1*, Faber and Faber, 1998

Garner, Ken, *The Peel Sessions*, BBC, 2007

Gillett, Charlie and Simon Frith (Eds), *Rock File 3*, Panther, 1975

–– *Rock File 4*, Panther, 1976

–– *Rock File 5*, Panther, 1978

Green, Johnny, Barker, Garry and Lowry, Ray, *A Riot of Our Own: Night and Day with the Clash*, Faber and Faber, 1999

Hall, Stuart and Tony Jefferson (Eds), *Resistance Through Rituals: Youth Subcultures in Post-War Britain*, Routledge, 2006

Kershaw, Andy, *No Off Switch: An Autobiography*, Serpent's Tail, 2011

King, Michael, *Wrong Movements: A Robert Wyatt History*, S.A.F., 1994

Lazell, Barry, *Indie Hits 1980–1989: The Complete UK Independent Charts*, Cherry Red, 1997

[619]

McDonough, Jimmy, *Shakey: Neil Young's Biography*, Vintage, 2003

Morrissey, *Autobiography*, Penguin, 2013

O'Dair, Marcus, *Different Every Time: The Authorised Biography of Robert Wyatt*, Serpent's Tail, 2014

Ogg, Alex, *The Men Behind Def Jam: The Radical Rise of Russell Simmons and Rick Rubin*, Omnibus, 2002

Peel, John and Sheila Ravenscroft, *Margrave of the Marshes*, Corgi, 2005

Radcliffe, Mark, *Thank You for the Days: A Boy's Own Adventures in Radio and Beyond*, Pocket Books, 2010

Rees, Dafydd and Luke Crampton, *The Guinness Book of Rock Stars*, Guinness, 1994

Rogan, Johnny, *Roxy Music: Style with Substance – Roxy's First Ten Years*, Star, 1982

Sandbrook, Dominic, *White Heat: A History of Britain in the Swinging Sixties 1964–1970*, Abacus, 2009

Selwood, Clive, *All the Moves (But None of the Licks)*, Peter Owen, 2003

Skues, Keith, *Pop Went the Pirates*, Lamb's Meadow Publications, 1994

Spitz, Marc and Brendan Mullen, *We Got the Neutron Bomb: The Untold Story of LA Punk*, Three Rivers Press, 2001

Street, John, *Rebel Rock: The Politics of Popular Music*, Blackwell, 1986

Wall, Mick, *John Peel*, Orion, 2004

Weller, Helen (Ed.), *Guinness British Hit Singles*, Guinness, 1997